Chennault

Giving Wings to the Tiger

CHEN

M A R T H A   B Y R D

NAULT

Giving Wings to the Tiger

The University of Alabama Press
Tuscaloosa and London

Frontispiece: Maj. Gen. Claire Lee Chennault. Official U.S. Army Air Forces Photo, courtesy Rosemary Simrall.

Library of Congress Cataloging-in-Publication Data

Byrd, Martha, 1930–
    Chennault : giving wings to the tiger.

    Bibliography: p.
    Includes index.
    1. Chennault, Claire Lee, 1890–1958. 2. Generals—United States—Biography. 3. United States. Army Air Forces—Biography. I. Title.
UG626.2.C48B97 1987   358.4'1332'0924 [B] 86-19238
ISBN 0-8173-1292-7 (pbk: alk. paper)

British Library Cataloguing-in-Publication Data is available.

For J.A.R.

Contents

Illustrations

Preface

To write an individual's life is a joy, a privilege, and a sobering responsibility. An author seeks the essential essence of the subject, striving for factual accuracy yet acknowledging that facts alone are insufficient, that interpretation must be made and judgment, however tentative, must be rendered. To do otherwise is to deprive the reader of the insights gained, to try to live by the fiction that history is distinct from the personalities of those who make it.

Claire Chennault's career fell into three distinct phases, his role in each shaped by a character and personality so full of contradictions that at times there seem to have been two men competing within the same life for the ascendancy of two different value systems. In uncanny ways he was torn between the cultures of East and West, at times personifying the dragon of Western fairytales, warlike, spitting fire and eating people, only at other times to be more the Chinese dragon, kindly and peaceful, a gentle vegetarian eating clouds and spitting mists.

One Claire Chennault cared not a fig for popular opinion or the consensus of the crowd. He went his own way, fearless, strong, little concerned for the perquisites of rank, indifferent to criticism. This was a modest and unassuming man, quick to praise and thank and give credit to others, a man who spoke quiet words of common sense in soft and reasoning tones. A different Claire Chennault exaggerated his achievements, denigrated his opponents, was irascible with his colleagues, and overreacted to slights, real or imagined. He often displayed a touching need for approbation, for bolstering and reassurance.

He was tender with dogs, children, and the helpless or oppressed. His love letters expressed a depth of feeling that brings tears to the eyes. The men under his command saw him as fatherly, protective; his feelings about them were emotional, compassionate. It was hard for him to fire individuals who were incompetent, although he demanded much of those who were capable. His loyalty to his friends became as legendary as his hatred for his enemies.

He was also a hard man, a man who was stern with his sons because he believed they would need to be tough, a man "with a bead nobody could stare down," a man who did not flinch at the harsh realities of a cruel profession.[1] His philosophy of war was cold: kill the bravest first.

The persona he turned to the world was one of dauntless courage, cheer, humor, and optimism. He was quick to tease or quip and unwilling to accept obstacles that stood in the way of goals he believed attainable or desirable. Less often seen were the insecurities, the wide fluctuations in his emotional outlook that plunged him into deep depression. As though driven by an insatiable need to overcome challenge, he tended to hurl himself into a task with tremendous energy and an awesome intensity, even though he exercised great patience and understanding for those working with him. If denied a sense of achievement, however, he sometimes reached the limit of his control, a point when he could no longer cope with stress or frustration or failure. The diligence with which he sought both physical activity and outdoor solitude suggests that he understood his own emotional needs and sought to balance his moods. Exercise, especially competitive games, served to release his pent-up energies, while time spent alone in the natural world put his soul at peace with itself.

He could be earthy and coarse, a physical man of simple, basic drives. He could be gallant and chivalrous with a naturalness that bespoke an aristocratic background which he lacked. He also lacked social experience; in some respects he was a bumpkin and needed others to make simple arrangements for him. Yet without apology, he made himself equally at home in the company of heads of state or airplane mechanics. He seemed to have derived equal pleasure from an elegant lunch with Madame Chiang Kai-shek and from eating catfish on a Louisiana riverbank. He was ambitious but not for money. His homes were modest, comfortable but not fine. His daily life was simple and unpretentious, his tastes plain.

Nor was power for the sake of power the motivating factor in his life. Power was simply another tool—important, like money, to the extent that it was necessary to get things done. Far more important than either power or money were the opportunity to implement his innovative concepts and the personal gratification of being right. Chennault needed achievement in the same way he needed air to breathe.

Chennault was at the cutting edge of the evolution of U.S. policy, first on the use of air power, later on the formulation of a postwar relationship with Asia. Both times he spoke up, loudly and often tactlessly but with conviction and the willingness to take the heat of the opposition. That in itself is the first measure of a productive citizen, for the individual who keeps silent can make little contribution. His was a keen and creative mind, but his formal education was limited. Independent reading kept him abreast in the technical areas of his profession but did not give him the broad intellectual perspective that would have enabled him to function most effectively at the high decision-making levels where his innovative thinking nevertheless placed him. The result was a painful personal frustration that sometimes found expression as touchiness or vanity. In the officer corps of the U.S. Army he never ceased to feel that he was an outsider, handicapped because he lacked the credentials of West Point or a background—the style and class—that would give him equal standing with his peers. This sense made it hard for him to accept professional failure as distinct from personal failure, and instead of working within the system, he flailed against it, antagonizing people who disagreed with his views and smoldering with misdirected anger at those who stood between him and the achievements that he felt could and should be his.

Chennault could lead subordinates more effectively than he could persuade superiors. When he had to please or convince others, he seemed not to have basic interpersonal skills, not to understand the appropriate limits of opposition, not to have sufficient depth to concede that life had tones of gray. In aerial tactics he carried subtlety to a fine art, but when working with words, he invariably relied on bluntness rather than finesse. He could not verbalize abstractions and convey them to others. At times he seethed with the frustration of perceptions that he could not articulate satisfactorily; the reality he saw was often quite different from that perceived by others. This dreadful separation, this curse of personal conviction unaccompanied by persuasive skills, plagued him throughout his career.

In some areas of his profession he was a visionary, a man whose mind scaled the walls of present limitations. Understanding too much too soon, he collided with the barriers of conservative tradition. He was not the first creative and dedicated military officer to find the system unresponsive and slow, but when he violated its rules to involve himself in the politics behind military operations, he turned the system against him to his detriment. The lesson is noteworthy for the potential officer but also for the military services, which often limit their own effectiveness by rigidity and the toleration of mediocrity.

In circumstances where he was accepted and could function with assurance, where he could utilize his strengths without being penalized by his weaknesses, Chennault was a veritable giant, with sure instincts for combat and the leadership of men. He could instill a sense of mission; he could inspire others to astounding levels of performance and exertion. He was happy working in China because the Chinese respected his ability and granted him status that satisfied his own concept of his worth, without condemning him for being as he was. In circumstances where he sensed, correctly or incorrectly, that he himself was being negatively judged, his own more negative qualities came to the fore. He craved power less than respect.

Too talented for oblivion, too strong willed to stay within the confines of the military system, Chennault forged his own way and in so doing fathered the clandestine aerial warfare that was eventually subsumed in the covert action branch of the Central Intelligence Agency. More than any other single individual, Chennault by his life and actions set a popular precedent for clandestine military action in time of peace. It began with the American Volunteer Group, which used secrecy and deception to circumvent the niceties of inconvenient laws. It matured with Civil Air Transport, which became Air America, the first and largest of the CIA's aerial proprietaries.

Chennault was a pragmatic man, a man who believed in doing what needed to be done, a man who could handle the specific morality of his actions if he could identify a higher morality to which he could give his allegiance. This is the essence of the clandestine mentality, the rationale behind all covert action. Chennault kept his own sense of motive clean and clear, freed from conventional restrictions by a romantic idealism. As long as he firmly believed in the rightness of what he was doing, he felt no qualms for his conduct.

It is significant that he was most comfortable when in solitude and in the world of nature, for those who feel fundamentally inadequate seek the constant reassurance of others; aloneness is the greatest enemy of self-deception. Of his personal convictions he was confident and sure. As a child he formed a simple but appealing philosophy—to fight for the right—and he never deviated from it. Born to a world where one had to fight to survive, he fought until his name was synonymous with "fighter." To ease life's internal pain, to make his existence meaningful, he devoted himself to the art of fighting well. He found religious, philosophical, and personal gratification in fighting for what he deemed right; it was to him a worthy thing to do. The concept of freedom that became precious to him as a boy was the single most compelling drive in the man; it contributed to his difficulty in working within the military system; it was the basis for his passionate opposition to communism.

His career took him far from his humble origins, but he remained consistent and true to himself and the childhood that shaped him. He never ceased to be the simple country boy, devoid of pretentions, happily sinking his line into good fishing waters or spinning a yarn over a good drink of whiskey. Yet always, beneath his relaxed camaraderie, he held an inner self apart, seldom sharing his private thoughts. He allowed few people near enough to sense his vulnerability.

In a very real sense there were indeed two men, one abrasive and contentious, seeking always to circumvent his weaknesses, and in the process earning the scathing contempt of his superiors. The other was a gentle man, confident in those abilities and strengths for which he was much loved. Among those who worked for him, whether pilots or secretaries, he aroused a loyalty and respect that went beyond the ordinary dimension of leadership. Those who served him give him a solid, ringing endorsement of admiration and affection, the greatest tribute that can be paid to an individual.

During his life he sought to fashion a world to fit his personal philosophy and abilities. The following pages chronicle that life, delineating the events he helped to shape through his eyes and from his perspective. I have sought accuracy and objectivity to the extent possible while nevertheless guiding the reader toward an understanding of the man, his strengths and his limitations. Where possible I have used Chennault's own words or the words of those who knew him.

Chennault must be viewed primarily through his actions, for despite his swashbuckling exterior, he was a very private individual. Soneone who knew him intimately cautioned me that "casual acquaintances never pierced his facade."[2] The written record he left behind, as well as the impressions he left with those who shared their personal remembrances of him with me, substantiates the comment. He was not a verbal man. His diaries were essentially factual notations, with little elaboration or explanation. Many of his most important papers were ghosted, for after 1940 he often asked others to write for him. Although these professional papers must nevertheless speak for him professionally, I have judged his personal letters as more important indicators of his thoughts and motivations.

My debt to others is immense. The individual members of the Chennault family have been generous in their trust and assistance. Anna Chennault gave me access to her husband's diaries as well as sharing her insights. Friends and fellow officers have granted interviews, answered letters and phone calls, and shared their diaries as well as memories and the general's letters. Archivists and librarians have given courteous help, found elusive documents, double-checked references, and combed distant manuscript collections for relevant material.

The bibliography and notes list most of the contributors and sources. To them, and to others whose contributions were less formal but nevertheless valuable, I extend my deep gratitude. A few individuals merit special thanks. Without the guidance and encouragement of Haywood S. Hansell, Bruce K. Holloway, Donald L. Rodewald, and Sebie B. Smith, a manuscript might never have emerged from a mass of notes. Mary Beaty and the reference staff of the Davidson College Library went beyond the call of duty in assisting my research. Most important, my husband, Jerry A. Roberts, made the endeavor possible by his unwavering support and enthusiastic participation. Mistakes and shortcomings are my own.

MARTHA BYRD

Davidson, North Carolina

Abbreviations

AAF	Army Air Forces
AAFSAT	Army Air Forces School of Applied Tactics
AAFTAC	Army Air Forces Tactical Air Command
ACNL	*Air Corps News Letter*
ACTS	Air Corps Tactical School
AFSHRC	Albert F. Simpson Historical Research Center
AG	Adjutant General
AGFRTS	Air and Ground Forces Resources and Technical Staff
AGO	Adjutant General's Office
AMMISCA	American Military Mission to China
ATC	Air Transport Command
AVG	American Volunteer Group
AWPD	Air War Plans Division
CAC, C/AC	Chief of the Air Corps
CACW	Chinese American Composite Wing
CAF	Chinese Air Force
CAMCO	Central Aircraft Manufacturing Company
CAT	Civil Air Transport
CATC	China Air Transport Company
CATF	China Air Task Force
CATI	Civil Air Transport, Inc.
CBI	China, Burma, India
CIA	Central Intelligence Agency
CID	Criminal Investigation Division
CLC	Claire Lee Chennault
CM-IN	Classified message sent into the Pentagon
CM-OUT	Classified message sent out of the Pentagon

CNAC	China National Aviation Corporation
CNRRA	Chinese National Relief and Rehabilitation Administration
CO	Commanding Officer
CT	China Theater
EBL	Edward B. Lockett
ELOC	Eastern Line of Communications
FAC	Federal Aviation Commission
FDR	Franklin D. Roosevelt
FDRL	Franklin D. Roosevelt Library
FRUS	*Foreign Relations of the United States*
GPO	Government Printing Office
HMSO	Her Majesty's Stationery Office
HQ	Headquarters
MAAG	Military Assistance Advisory Group
NA	National Archives
ONI	Office of Naval Intelligence
OPC	Office of Policy Coordination
OPD	Operations Division, War Department General Staff
OSS	Office of Strategic Services
RAD	Radio or radiogram
RAF	Royal Air Force
RDF	Radio Direction Finding
RG	Record Group
RKC	Robert K. Chennault
SACO	Sino-American Cooperative Organization
SEAC	Southeast Asia Command
SEGAC	Code name for Madame Chiang Kai-shek

SOS	Service of Supply
SPF	Stilwell's Personal File
SPF	*Stilwell's Personal File* (facsimile edition)
SWHA	Southwest Highway Administration
TGC	Thomas G. Corcoran
UNRRA	United Nations Relief and Rehabilitation Administration
USAFA	U.S. Air Force Academy
USF	U.S. Forces
USSBS	U.S. Strategic Bombing Survey
VLR	Very long range
WD	War Department
WDCSA	War Department Central Services Administration

Chennault

Giving Wings to the Tiger

Prologue

On 23 April 1958, Maj. Gen. Claire Lee Chennault testified for the House Un-American Activities Committee of the United States Congress.[1] The Cold War was at its peak. In the eyes of many Americans, China was "lost"; the armistice to a limited war in Korea had been "short of victory." Where French Indochina had once been, there was now Vietnam; a worried United States had begun sending aid to the non-Communists who warred with the Vietminh for its control. From Chennault the Committee sought understanding. For two decades he had fought in Asia, first for the China that was now lost, then for the anti-Communist cause that now gripped the nation.

Like the world he had fought for, the general was dying. The black eyes no longer flashed. In the coarse texture and prominent grooves of his face, the happy lines incised by countless hours of squinting in the sun during open-cockpit flight no longer dominated; the grim furrows plunging down around cheeks and mouth had deepened. His clothes hung on a body that seemed loose, as though a tight spring had begun to lose its tension. Three months later Chennault would be dead.

When the Committee asked him to summarize his career for the

1

record, he did so dispassionately: U.S. Army 1917 to 1937; aviation adviser to Generalissimo Chiang Kai-shek during World War II; postwar partner in Civil Air Transport, a commercial airline founded in China but since 1949 operating from Taiwan under the flag of the Nationalist Chinese.

Only about the airline did he give more than the sketchiest information, as though earlier events no longer mattered. When the Committee requested "just a further word or two" about his war years, he condensed a decade of turmoil into 350 words that carried no hint of the personal confrontations, the quiet conspiracies, the drama and glory and success or the agonizing failures and the bitter personal ending.[2]

The Committee asked him to trace the events in the Far East during and since the war, "with an appraisal of the encroachments made by communism."[3]

In a soft southern drawl, unchanged by twenty years of living in China, Chennault recapitulated in matter-of-fact sequence the clash between Chinese Nationalists and Communists up to 1949, when the Communists gained control of mainland China.

Who won the Korean War? asked the Committee.

"The Communists," he replied bluntly. He saw the United States losing the Cold War and facing a long-range Communist campaign to ruin the United States financially. "I believe the Communists . . . want us to continue pouring aid into those areas, break us, build up a national debt, spend everything that we earn from day to day, month to month, and year to year until our currency is no longer of any value. Then they will be ready to take the United States in turn."[4]

He spoke with the conviction of a man making a deathbed testimonial, a man with business to finish.

"After we arm friendly people and teach them to use what we give them," he explained, "we do not set up the plants necessary to service and maintain equipment and to manufacture on a small scale. . . . We send people along to distribute that aid. . . . We send out some of the dumbest, most ignorant people I have ever encountered. We have to change our whole method of giving aid. We have to get down and contact the people, make friends with the people at all levels."[5]

With these simple words, Claire Chennault perhaps unwittingly expressed the personal philosophy that had guided his two decades of life and work in China: he had made friends with the people at all levels. More than once his career had led him into circumstances of great complexity where there was little precedent to serve as guidance. Invariably the approaches he devised were direct, elemental, simple ones. They had brought him a life of controversy, for sometimes others saw his ideas as simplistic nonsense, outrageous or impracticable or even immoral. To his admirers, however, he had the great gift of being able to cut through to the simple heart of the matter, to "reach in and grab hold of where the pain is."[6]

And although the public knew little about it, many of Chennault's simple, direct approaches were even then being very quietly implemented in the covert action branch of the Central Intelligence Agency. Chennault's airline, imbued with his philosophy of brushing obstacles aside to "grab hold," was playing a major part in the process.

1

The Shaping of the Man

_____

No doubt Claire Lee Chennault entered the world kicking and screaming but with fire in his eyes, for from the day of his birth in Commerce, Texas, the personality traits that marked him seemed intact, his essential nature needing only the refining fire that hard experiences lost no time in providing.

Even his name—Claire Lee—carried the warning that life was a cruel teacher. He would never know the maternal uncle whose name he bore, a man who had died not long before, under circumstances guaranteed to give a growing child cause to think twice about human values. The first Claire Lee, an eighteen-year-old deputy sheriff, while taking a handcuffed prisoner to jail on horseback indulged in a moment of human kindness and offered the arrested man a light for his tobacco. The prisoner took advantage of Lee's proximity, hit him on the chin with handcuffed wrists, and, having knocked him out, proceeded to shoot him with his own gun.[1]

The surname Chennault placed the child in a family of stubborn and fierce and independent pride, a family that worked hard, loved hard, and fought hard, a family that laughed and told yarns and lived life to the fullest but did not flinch when action needed to be taken.

Because of this last trait the boy was born in Texas rather than Louisiana, where his parents had grown up. Claire's father, John Stonewall Jackson Chennault, as accustomed to being in command of himself and his world as had been the fighter whose name he shared, found one day in the early 1890s that he had a slight problem with the law.

Carpetbaggers roamed the South at the time. One of them paid a second visit to Chennault's hometown of Rayville, Louisiana, trying to exploit ignorance by collecting a fancy price for unbroken mustangs which he falsely represented as valuable farm stock. Chennault, deciding that enough was enough, suggested that the carpetbagger leave the parish at once. The man declined. Chennault then, as he told the tale, quite efficiently put a bullet through the brim of his hat without having first invited the unwelcome visitor to remove it from his head. The crooked horse trader set off for friendlier markets with dispatch but not before raising a small ruckus with the authorities. Chennault was known for his good looks and high spirits; he was also a superb shot. When it was suggested that he had attempted murder, he contemptuously replied that, if he had meant to kill the scoundrel, he would not have missed. Nevertheless it was deemed expedient for him to be temporarily "across the line." He found work in Commerce, Texas, where, on 6 September 1893, his young wife Jessie Lee gave birth to their first son.[2]

Claire Lee Chennault grew up in Franklin Parish, for after John and Jessie moved back to Louisiana early in 1894, they chose to live near Jessie's father, Dr. William Wallace Lee. The doctor was a proud and independent man, a graduate of Tulane's first class of medical students. He acknowledged his kinship to General Robert E. Lee with pride and was equally proud of having served as a surgeon in the Army of Virginia. Healthy and shrewd enough to survive being held a prisoner of the Union army, in 1867 he had moved from his native Mississippi to Franklin Parish, where he practiced medicine for the next forty-four years.[3] He had not been enthusiastic about his daughter's marriage to John Chennault. John was a strong-willed and irrepressible man, powerful of build and quick to fight although guided by an unrelenting sense of justice and fairness. These qualities he had sought to put to good use by studying law, a career he abandoned when he was unable to refashion his plainspoken, argumentative nature in the style required to plead a case before a court. Like most men in northeast Louisiana in those years, he put bread on his table by growing cotton.[4] After he lost his first wife in 1891, he won Jessie

Jessie Lee and John S. Chennault, Claire Lee Chennault's parents, in their wedding portrait, 1892. John's waxed mustache was a special point of pride. (Photo courtesy W. S. Chennault)

in a lively courtship. Despite her father's reservations she found him the most exciting man around.[5]

Under Dr. Lee's watchful eye and with his help, John rented and later bought a small farm known as the Talley Place on Deer Creek, near the small town of Gilbert. He was a hardworking man. He gradually increased his holdings of cotton land and employed black tenants on shares. It was not an easy life, nor was it a prosperous time. The Civil War had stripped Louisiana of its economy, its social structure, its means of rebuilding, and even its hope. The sharecropper society that emerged from the war's wreckage was designed as a stopgap measure, but it persisted until well into the 1930s and provided the basic structure of a harsh world in which men floundered on a treadmill of poverty and obligation and debt. Under political leadership that was limited in vision and often corrupt, Louisiana stagnated. There was no money for public education, which was abysmal, nor for roads.[6]

It took strength of will as well as body to do more than survive in such a world, but the Chennault heritage was a strong one. The American Chennaults were descended from French Huguenots who sought relief from religious persecution by immigrating first to England, then to America in 1700. Four Chennaults fought in the American Revolution, including one named Stephen.[7] His will, dated 29 March 1819, left to each of his daughters a featherbed and to his son John thirty dollars plus a share of the debts that were due him. Whether this John collected on the debts is not known, but he moved into what is now Tennessee, became a cabinetmaker, and married Sam Houston's aunt, Hannah Elizabeth Saunders of Kentucky. Their son Stephen pressed on into northeast Louisiana to wrest farmland from the wilderness of the Mississippi floodplains near Rayville. John Stonewall Jackson Chennault, born in 1862, was his son.[8]

Hard work notwithstanding, John's life had its share of tragedy, which left its mark on Claire. In 1895 Jessie bore a second son, but the child died the following year. A third son, William Stephen, was born in 1897 and thrived, but four years later Jessie herself became ill, probably with tuberculosis. She returned to her father's home for care and died there in 1901.[9] Claire was then eight, and even before that time his mother's pregnancies and illness had caused him to live for long periods with either Dr. and Mrs. Lee or his mother's sister, Louise Lee Chase. Aunt Lou, a strong woman who ruled her household with a firm hand and the sure authority of the Bible behind her, now found room in her heart and home for the growing Claire, tucked him in

Claire stands beside his younger brother, William, in 1898. (Photo courtesy W. S. Chennault)

among her own sons, and set before him the example of her own fighting spirit and indomitable will. She was a woman who needed no modern liberating, a woman quite able and willing to do what needed to be done. Claire took it all in and repaid her with lifelong devotion.[10]

When he was ten his twice-widowed father married Lottie Barnes, who had been Claire's teacher—and a much loved one—at the local school.[11] Claire helped his father build the family a new home, a small frame house with a modified bay window, a porch in front, and a touch of gingerbread trim. The site, just outside Gilbert, was called "the hill," for during the wet spring the few feet that it rose above surrounding terrain could keep it dry when surrounding areas were flooded.[12] At this time cash was scarce, and John Chennault carefully recorded the cost of the chimney: $36.60, including $1 for sand, $1.05 for a helping hand, $1.80 for one bushel of lime and $1.75 for another, and $17 for 1,700 bricks.[13] Now on the National Register of Historic Places, the unrestored house (minus its chimney) is shaded in back by a pecan tree that Claire helped his father plant.

John Chennault was stern but kind with his sons. An occasional pat on the head or spank on the rump had to suffice as an expression of affection, but he gave them freedom to roam and to learn and to make mistakes on their own, and he taught them how to handle guns and to do things with their hands. Their world revolved around him, for theirs was a society dominated by men, and men taught their sons the skills and attitudes they needed to be masters of it.[14]

Although there were chores to impart discipline, few restraints and few fears hampered a child's growth in such a world. The area was sparsely settled, with small towns dotting the plain through which the murky Tensas River snaked its way toward the nearby Mississippi. The cypress swamps had a haunting beauty all their own, and the uncleared land was heavily timbered and rich with game. Pecan trees grew wild and enormous; muscadine vines turned forests into tangles. Heat waves shimmered upward from the steaming cotton fields, planted, "chopped," "laid by," and picked with the backbreaking hand labor that made cotton growers old before their years.

Over this world of field and forest and swamp, Claire, William, and their cousins Dave and Ben Chase hunted and fished and played the games of competition and survival that small boys play. They skinny-dipped in the waterholes, waged war, using green walnuts for ammunition, and caught catfish and bream in the lakes and bayous. They shot squirrels, which went into Mulligan stew. They learned how to build a pyramid trap using green strips of cypress wood held together by tension, and in these ingenious devices they caught birds which they fried, making a feast of sorts. Claire trapped and made a little pocket money selling the hides of skunk and 'coon. His contemporaries held him in some awe, for with the dogs Whupsie and Hannah to back him up, he seemed unafraid of man or beast. The boys hunted white-tailed deer on horseback, and Claire, astride his two-gaited bay gelding, was known for skill in penetrating the dense undergrowth.[15]

He was soon known for other traits as well, for during those childhood years he began to show the inner tension that drove him throughout his life. More than the others, he seemed driven to win, compelled to outdo. In part he was trying desperately to please a hard father, a man who could bend a sixpenny nail into a staple with his bare hands and was known to believe that "second place is not worth a damn."[16] Perhaps he was also trying to win the approbation of others to compensate for the unconditional love of a mother that had been taken away. No doubt he was also simply testing himself, seeking to find the limits of his mind and body and personality. He grew up in a rough society in which boys and men fought with bare hands and fists, when shrewdness and quickness meant the difference between being hurt or inflicting hurt upon others. A favorite game was "Bully," a contest that required the winner to "rassle" another boy to the ground and hold him there by any means he was capable of exerting. At this Claire excelled, for he was a strong wrestler with good coordination and reflexes. He let his friends down once, however, giving early evidence of a tendency to overestimate his abilities, for when a newcomer challenged him to a fight, Claire advised his buddies to put their money on the first fall. He won the bout, but only after having taken a few falls himself.[17]

Claire also derived special pleasure from playing the role of fox in "Fox and Hounds," a game of chase the boys often played at night. Easily able to outrun and outwit the others, he relished that moment of personal triumph when he could jump out of hiding and startle his companions at the game's end. Perhaps because at some subconscious level he realized that the victories he felt compelled to achieve caused pain or disappointment to others, and in that respect did not bring the deep personal rewards he sought, he found that winning brought little joy.[18] But he came to realize that he was quick of mind and would rather lead than follow, that he could teach younger boys more happily than he could be dominated by older ones. He found that he could control fear more effectively than most. He found that he enjoyed solitude, that he was happiest going his own way.

Personal survival training, among peers or on the resources of the land, was a vital part of his childhood experience. He learned to do without, to improvise, to accept the difficult as merely a more compelling challenge. He learned to find food, to find his way in wild country without benefit of maps or roads. Tales of his wrestling with alligators and fending for himself for weeks at a time in the wilderness may have been exaggerated, but there is no doubt that he early acquired a keen shooting eye as well as the sixth sense that enables the hunter to anticipate the actions of the prey.

Hunting, fishing, and the enjoyment of a physical, outdoor life became a major part of Claire's self, his equalizer and emotional stabilizer, the means by which he restored himself from tension, exhaustion, or despair. The degree to which he was at home in the natural world amazed his friends who came from a less rural background. An army colleague at Maxwell Field during the 1930s was appalled to see Claire plunge into the swamps of the deep South wearing only a pair of swimming trunks and carrying only his fishing rod, for the swamps were infested with water moccasins. Chennault, amused at the man's horror, explained that the snakes did not bother him nor he them.

"You just slap the water," he said. "They will go away, unless of course, it's mating season. Then they get kind of horny."[19]

The organizations that provided both social life and a sense of community in young Claire Chennault's world were the church, the school, and the town baseball team. The latter was in many respects the most important, for it was the embodiment of personal and civic pride, the province of the virile young men. Teenagers had to earn their place by proving their worth. At this Claire competed fiercely, not content to make the team, but striving to be one of its stars. He won a coveted spot as pitcher and second baseman at a younger age than most, and lest he lose it, he worked diligently to make certain he was also one of the team's better hitters. He enjoyed the skills of the game, but even more he enjoyed the gamesmanship, the rows with the umpires, and the contrived suspense and excitement surrounding the contest on the field. To this he contributed in full measure, throwing himself into every game as though his very soul depended on its outcome.[20] Fifty years later he still played with the same gleeful intensity.

School offered much less challenge, much less excitement. Public education was almost nonexistent, in part because Louisiana's more prosperous planters had depended on parochial schools before the war. Not until 1910 did the state begin a serious program of public education. The Gilbert school building which Claire attended was valued at $250; the teacher, if she was paid as much as the 1898 state average, made $240.43 a year. The session was short and the program ungraded;[21] the bright student quickly absorbed all it offered and became bored. Claire caused his share of the trouble that inevitably followed. Either from mischief or a burst of enthusiasm for natural science, he once took a captured skunk to class.

Yet Chennault learned to read well and to enjoy books. Here the church contributed, for the Bible fascinated him, and he read it for the history and stories it offered. He joined Gilbert's Baptist Church, a small congregation housed in a structure more sturdy than beautiful. From its pulpit he doubtless heard the same fundamentalist sermons preached to other rural Baptist congregations of the day, teachings that revolved more around hellfire and damnation than around the gifts of grace and salvation. He accepted and rejected as he chose. Although the faith he acquired was simple but strong, the organized church played so little role in his adult life that, when he attended, the local citizenry quipped that they were prepared for the ground to tremble.[22]

Books other than the Bible gave him various perspectives. He came to understand the role of fantasy when he tried to reenact a fairy tale and cast silver bullets from melted dimes to kill the ghost in the local haunted house. *Huckleberry Finn*, one of his favorites, offered a hero more easily copied. But he also read Dr. Lee's books on military history, and he was enchanted by the drama and color of warfare, by the romance of faraway places with unpronounceable names. He grew up hearing tales of military exploits, of family adventures revolving around the Chennaults and Houstons and Lees, fighters all.[23]

The knack for telling a good yarn was an art shared by most of the members of the Chennault family as well as by their circle of friends. Although tales might get better year by year as historical accuracy blurred around the edges, the essential truth of character and personality remained unchanged. What Claire heard reinforced what he saw. Life was hard on both the just and the unjust. It taught that love could be taken away, that one must be wary whom one trusts, that fierce independence and the ability to take care of oneself are essential. Taking these and other lessons to heart, he learned to keep the part of himself that could be hurt hidden deep within, shielded from the world by an easygoing exterior that exuded confidence and bravado. He learned to fight his own battles, tutored in the art of survival fighting by one of Dr. Lee's black servants. As he matured, his body grew compact and wiry, well coordinated and strong. He had his father's black hair and black eyes, his father's fiery temper, personal reticence, and hard strength. He also inherited his father's tendency to confront life head-on and to derive great pleasure from doing so.

John Chennault wanted his sons to have education beyond what Gilbert offered. For their "tutorship valuation" he allotted ten head of cattle, two mules named Colby and Emma, five shares of bank stock, and the proceeds from part of his land.[24] It was to Lottie Barnes, however, that Claire gave the credit for persuading him to continue his schooling. He had already begun to burst the bonds of the life to which he had been born when she became his mother, mentor, and friend. Perhaps because she also enjoyed an outdoor life and did not dissuade him from the physical pursuits he enjoyed, he considered her his "best companion" and accepted her guidance.[25] On 25 January 1909 he entered Louisiana State University.[26]

"Big Daddy," as John Chennault was often called, accompanied his son to Baton Rouge, paid his expenses, and left him with $17 in cash[27]—a generous sum, inasmuch as room, board, laundry, and fees came to but $126 per year. Tuition was free to Louisiana residents. Higher education had fared better than the state's secondary system, and LSU was a respected institution, housed in the Pentagon Barracks of the U.S. Army post. Its students were governed as cadets under military discipline, and in World War II 16 generals, 42 colonels, and approximately 5,000 other officers were LSU alumni—a total exceeded only by West Point, Virginia Military Institute, and Texas A&M.[28]

LSU had colleges of arts and science, education, engineering, and agriculture. Claire enrolled in the last; it was the only study for which his Gilbert background had qualified him. In addition to shop, breeding, and soils and fertilizer, he studied English, algebra, geometry, and physics. His grades steadily improved and showed that he could be a good student—geometry, his worst subject, went from a 45 to an 85 in the first three months—but his demerits also rose, starting out with a respectable 4 the first month but rising to an alarming 40 by the end of April.[29] His penchant for swimming in hot water began early.

The tales of his college exploits suggest that Claire had to work hard and was probably homesick. He belonged to the Graham Literary Society and was a private in Company A of the Corps of Cadets, where he acquired a reputation for "taking his soldiering seriously."[30] As a boy from the sticks and swamps, with rough edges unsmoothed by the social graces, he experienced his first persecution in the traditional hazing. Unamused, defensive, and angry, he reacted by returning the embarrassment to its perpetrators. Ordered to patrol a doorway and let no one pass, he took the assignment at face value, gritted his teeth at the water "accidentally" spilled on his head from the balcony above, and refused to let the hungry cadets exit for supper until the hoax had formally ended.

On one occasion, however, Cadet Chennault upheld the honor of his school against the U.S. Navy. When the battleship *Mississippi* anchored in the river nearby, its boisterous crew challenged the LSU "soldier boys" to one more round of the old contest between Army and Navy. LSU won several events without difficulty, but the middies then set them up by suggesting a match while intimating that the navy was not very good at boxing. The cadets had no trained boxers, but Chennault was needled into accepting the challenge. At 140 pounds, he was then five feet, seven and one-half inches tall, two inches short of his eventual adult height.[31] Through sheer guts and stubbornness he stayed in the ring for the allotted ten rounds of punishment, after which it came to light that his opponent was the Navy's middleweight champion. The champ, however, declined Chennault's invitation to take off his gloves and settle the fight "like real men."[32] Claire took defeat as personal humiliation, and after he later joined the army he made learning to box one of his first priorities.[33]

On 28 November 1909, just as Claire was completing his second semester, Lottie Barnes Chennault died. "I was alone again," he wrote in his memoirs, "and really never found another companion whom I could so completely admire, respect, and love."[34] She had not only shared his love for the outdoors but had given him sympathetic, loving tutelage, encouragement, and reassurance. Apart from this powerful tribute, he said or wrote little about her, but her death, coupled with that of his own mother, left a void in his life that was never totally filled.

The emotional devastation of losing his second mother possibly played a part in Claire's decision not to return to LSU. Family finances were also strained, for John Chennault had been hurt by the boll weevil epidemic and the financial panic of 1907. Claire explored the possibilities of attending either West Point or Annapolis, but they were not to be his way out, possibly because he had neither a strong academic background nor helpful political connections. He considered taking up farming, but his father discouraged it. His Uncle Nelson, a public schoolteacher, suggested that being an educator was a reasonable way of life within his grasp because Louisiana had just undertaken to extend its high school program throughout the state. Teachers were needed, but certification requirements were still low and primarily consisted of the approval of the superintendents of individual parishes. The State Normal School at Natchitoches offered a strong high school program plus specific teacher-training courses. Its graduates were considered the state's most qualified educators.[35] Claire enrolled, completed a course of study on 30 July 1910,[36] and that fall began to teach in the Louisiana public school system.

According to legend, on the first day of classes under schoolmaster Chennault, an eraser (or was it an inkwell?) was thrown at him as he wrote on the board. When Chennault asked the culprit to identify himself, the largest and toughest of the classroom bullies stood up and showed his fists. Chennault dismissed class, invited the boy outside, and proceeded to give him the beating of his life. Other students reminisced in later years that their young schoolmaster sometimes disciplined by means other than words. Claire himself often laughingly insisted that his most important qualifications for his first job were physical toughness and being a minor—so that he could legally subdue his unruly students by physical means. But in addition to subduing his pupils, he won their grudging respect. He used his genuine enthusiasm for sports as a teaching tool and took part in the state's track rallies in 1910.[37]

That spring Claire attended the high school graduation at Winnsboro, where his Uncle Nelson taught. During the course of the year the state had tightened the requirements for graduation. Of the ten or more students who might have graduated, only one, a petite brunette with steady hazel eyes, met the new standards. Her name was Nell Thompson, and Claire was impressed. They courted throughout the next year, while she taught at the Winnsboro school, and he was also impressed by her independence, her lively curiosity, her quiet strength, and her cheerful spunk. They were married on Christmas Eve 1911.[38]

For several years Claire continued to teach, returning to LSU in the summers of 1912 and 1914 to upgrade his certificate. Perhaps because his own schooling had been deficient, he took the initiative in advocating a consolidated school system, obtaining, in the process, his first taste of political leadership. Going from one farmhouse to another, he promoted a tax of eight mills to provide housing and maintenance for a consolidated school. The tax passed, the building was erected, and Claire Chennault was named its first principal. Pupils were brought to school in covered farm wagons, the local forerunner of school buses.[39]

During those years Claire and Nell gave each other books as gifts and read them aloud to one another as recreation.[40] They had managed to avoid sharecropping, but the cycle of poverty nevertheless threatened to engulf them. In those days before dependable birth

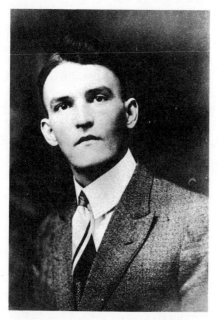

Claire shortly before he married
Nell Thompson in 1911.
(Photo courtesy W. S. Chennault)

control, children arrived regularly, John in 1913, Max in 1914. From his offspring Claire derived deep satisfaction and unabashed pride. He savored their unquestioning love; he found personal gratification in being able to nurture and protect them. When they were tiny he often sang them to sleep in a soft, tuneless monotone. As they grew older they sensed that he expected them to stand alone, to take care of themselves and be as hard as he himself was, but the babies always had a special place in his heart.[41] Through the years his family became increasingly important to him, for it provided an emotional security and warmth that his soul craved.

The need to seek better opportunites for his children gave him one reason for deciding to break away from the rural northeastern Louisiana which had nurtured him and which he loved. For several years he moved restlessly from one city to another, changing jobs often. Unhappy, he wrote a friend that he felt "like a tadpole in a tar bucket."[42] He did some teaching. He took a course in body building, which was then in vogue, and afterward worked as an athletic director in a YMCA. During part of those years his salary was only $12.50 per week, but he managed to save a fourth of it. "It isn't the total amount of salary that really matters," he concluded, "but the difference between income and outgo."[43]

For a short time he lived in New Orleans, finding there an atmosphere and flavor that fixed the city in his heart as his "all-round favorite" place, even though all his experiences there were not pleasant. Tiny Max swallowed an open safety pin and was afterward so ill that the specialists at a baby clinic told the young father to take his child home because he was dying and "they didn't want him to die in the hospital." With a fierce defiance that others were later to encounter in different circumstances, Claire refused to accept official pronouncements. He took his baby son home and "worked on him." Whether from the strength of his father's will or for some other reason—Aunt Lou was convinced it was the cornbread and "pot likker" they fed him—Max survived, and his father suspected that a personal interest, "or maybe a bit of understanding learned from my old Grandfather," had played a role.[44]

Throughout his life Claire remained closest to Max and to his next child, Peggy, whom he delivered himself when the prearranged help could not be roused from a drunken toot.[45] Their lives he had held, literally, in his own hands. Shortly after Peggy's birth, still in search of a better life, he moved to Ohio to work in a Goodyear factory. He was there in April 1917, when the United States entered World War I. Shortly thereafter he joined the U.S. Army.

2

The Lean Years

Claire Chennault and U.S. military aviation grew up together. He was ten years old when the Wright Brothers made the first powered flight in 1903, although it is unlikely he knew of it at the time. In later years his father did not recall Claire's having shown any interest in flight until after the beginning of World War I.[1]

The war saw the first widespread military use of the airplane. After the Allies and the Central Powers had battled to a halt along the Marne in September 1914, reconnaissance planes for both sides began regular patrols over the opposing lines to keep their respective commands informed of the enemy's dispositions. The pilots in their unarmed planes—little more than toys, compared with modern aircraft—often felt more kinship with each other than with their own forces on the ground. It was not unusual for pilots on opposite sides to wave at one another in utmost friendliness as each went about his business.

By the end of 1914 pot shots were being exchanged, however, for commanders quickly realized that they must deny their enemies the privilege of aerial spying. The first experiments with machine guns aloft were unsuccessful because the plane had insufficient lift to handle the extra weight, but the demand created a plane that could meet it; by 1915 the pursuit (fighter) plane had begun to emerge. By that time the machine gun had driven the armies into a network of opposing trenches stretching from Switzerland north to the sea, the area between them a no-man's land where the slightest movement brought a deadly rain of lead. Neither side could move, but because the security of the trenches could be in part neutralized by accurate and overwhelming artillery fire, the airplane became the eyes for the artillery.

As the plane increased in importance, air-to-air combat became more common. Bombers, also emerging during these years, attracted less attention at the time. Clashes between pursuit planes usually took place in full view of those on the ground and had a dramatic impact on morale. The bold, daring "air knights" in their flimsy, brightly decorated planes completely captured the public imagination, for they lived glamorously, savoring every moment of life while fully expecting instant death in dizzying crashes or blinding bursts of flame. The pursuit pilots became Chennault's heroes. He may have thought or dreamed of flight earlier, but his long love affair with the fighter plane began during World War I.[2]

When the United States declared war on the Central Powers on 6 April 1917, it ranked fourteenth among the nations in aviation strength. The entire aviation section of the U.S. Signal Corps numbered a mere 130 officers and 1,100 men, of whom only 26 "could really fly." But when the French asked the United States to send to the front in 1918 a flying corps of 4,500 planes with men and auxiliary services, Congress appropriated $640 million, roughly eight times the total appropriation for U.S. military aviation to that point.[3]

The "flower of America's youth," its imagination captured by the romance of the battle in the skies (the struggle in the trenches offered scant chance of survival), applied for flight training. Of 38,770 applicants between mid-1914 and mid-1918, 18,004—roughly half—were rejected.[4] Chennault was one of them. His first encounter with a plane had fired him with enthusiasm, for flight presented both challenge and excitement, an opportunity for the glory and romance that life had thus far denied. Rejection was a sore disappointment. He was accepted for officer training, however, and was sent to Fort Benjamin Harrison, Indiana, where on 27 November 1917 he was commissioned a first lieutenant in the infantry reserve. Nell's birthday gift that year was a dress sword; as an officer Claire had to have one, but joining the army had solved none of the family's financial problems.[5]

Chennault at Fort Benjamin Harrison, Indiana, November 1917, boxing with unidentified opponent. (Photo courtesy Rosemary Simrall)

Lieutenant Chennault, after transferring to the aviation section
and being assigned to the Ninetieth Division at Fort Travis in San Antonio, looked about for a way to learn to fly. His repeated applications for flight training were meeting with the standard rejection—
"Does not possess necessary qualifications to be an aviator"—but
words had never held him back before. He managed a transfer to
nearby Kelly Field, one of the twenty-five flying schools built in the
United States during the war, and made friends with some of the instructors. The military was a much less security-conscious organization then than it is now, and before long, without benefit of official
sanction, he was experiencing firsthand the joy of flying the miracle
of fabric and dope and wire called Jenny—the Curtiss JN-4, the standard U.S. trainer.

Like Benjamin D. Foulois, an early pilot and later chief of the U.S.
Army Air Corps who had taken his flight lessons by correspondence,
Chennault flew from the beginning as though it were the most natural of all possible endeavors. After he was assigned to an outlying
field with responsibility for checking the planes in and out and keeping records of the time flown in them, the clandestine flying became
easier. When there were no cadets to make use of the planes, Chennault did so himself. With few regulations or restrictions to interfere,
he shortly accumulated eighty hours of bootleg flying time.

In October 1918 came an assignment as nonflying adjutant with the Forty-sixth Pursuit Squadron, then slated to go to France. The squadron was marching toward its port of embarkation when it was ordered to return to Mitchel Field, for the armistice was near; no more units would be shipped overseas. Instead there was a brief tour at Langley Field, Virginia, where Spanish influenza struck. Placed in charge of a hangar converted into an emergency hospital, Chennault himself became so ill that he was mistakenly locked in the morgue. He recovered, he insisted, as the result of consuming a bottle of bourbon given him by a sympathetic friend.[6] Shortly thereafter his application for flight school was accepted, probably because, after the initial rush of volunteers slowed down, the Air Service began taking men from the officer ranks in order to maintain the high quality of its trainees.[7] As the war approached an end in Europe, Chennault went once more to Kelly Field, this time for legitimate flight training.

Flight training, then as now, combined classroom work and flying. Cadets flew dual with an instructor until they were ready to solo, then flew under supervision until they had mastered basic skills. Figuring that he already knew how to fly, Chennault let arrogance and stubbornness almost cost him the coveted military aviator rating. His first instructor, "Pop" Liken, had a habit of jerking the controls out of a student's hands and executing a maneuver himself rather than explaining what a student was doing wrong. The practice infuriated Chennault, who warned Liken he would refuse to take back the controls. The confrontation came. Chennault calmly folded his arms while the plane hurtled toward the ground, and after a shaken Liken had recovered and landed the plane, he recommended that his hotheaded student be washed out of flight training.

The washout rate was about one in eleven,[8] but before the final verdict each student pilot got a second chance. Chennault was turned over to Ernest M. Allison, a kindred soul who allowed Chennault to solo in the "washing machine" because he concluded, "This man can be taught to fly."[9] Allison began teaching him aerobatics. Chennault loved flight—loved the stimulation and challenge and exaltation of defying gravity and balance and perspective. He graduated on 9 April 1919, but the war was over. He received his honorable discharge on 16 April 1920 and was sent home.

He could see no alternative but to settle down in Franklin Parish and be a cotton farmer. His thrice-widowed father had taken a fourth wife in 1910. Chennault's half brothers, Nelson and Joe, were growing up as peers of his own children, who numbered four after Charles

Above, left:
Nell Thompson Chennault poses in Claire's leather
flying coat at Kelly Field in 1918.
(Photo courtesy Max Chennault)

Above, right:
Nell, ca. 1920, with Peggy (left) and Charles.
(Photo courtesy Max Chennault)

Right:
Claire Lee Chennault, first lieutenant,
December 1918.
(Photo courtesy W. S. Chennault)

was born in 1918. Claire found it good to be among family again, but the realities of a summer in the cotton fields were more than he could stomach. The army, for all its faults, looked better.[10] On 1 July 1920 the twenty-seven-year-old father of four applied for a commission in the regular army of the United States. He was accepted in September, even though, as far as the army was concerned, he was then not twenty-seven but thirty years old.

For reasons of his own, Chennault used different birthdates at different times. When he went to LSU in 1909, he gave his birthdate as 2 June 1893; at the normal school he gave it as 1892. When he first joined the army he used the date 6 September 1890, and that date remained on his official record, much to his father's chagrin, for at the time the elder Chennault had still been married to his first wife, and Claire's mother had been a mere fourteen years old. Chennault's U.S. passport bears the date 6 September 1893, the date recorded in the family Bible and confirmed by reconstructed events. Why the inconsistencies? Chennault was sensitive at having married and fathered so many children while still so young, and it embarrassed him that Nell was slightly older than he. Still, the incorrect dates had begun to appear before he married. Considering his mother's early death and the years when he made his home with the Lees or the Chases, it is likely that little notice was paid to birthdays. A member of the family who was close to him felt that he "simply forgot," gave whatever date popped into his head, and allowed the incorrect dates to stay on the records because he never considered them worth correcting.[11] His indifference to such detail later brought him grief.

The airplane had introduced some heady concepts into military thinking, but the conclusions to be drawn from the experience of war were neither obvious nor easy. The Air Service that Chennault had joined in 1920 was at the starting line of two decades of spirited controversy—decades during which the planes and doctrine that carried the United States into World War II were evolved.

From the beginning several trends became apparent. Airmen saw a potential for air power that overshadowed both its past accomplishments and its present capabilities and would make current modes of warfare obsolete. They theorized that, by bombing an enemy's cities and industries, air power could exercise decisive military force independently of ground forces. Air as a force, they claimed, had not only its own distinctive medium and technology but its own function and doctrine as well. Consequently they sought to make the air arm an autonomous branch of the service equal in status to the army and navy, in control of its own budget and promotion list, and under the command of flyers rather than ground officers.

The ground officers would hear none of it. Planes were valuable in support of ground troops; officers wanted undisputed control of them. The airmen, believing those not experienced with air power would not use it wisely, were willing to fight. They understood that the technology had barely been scratched, that air power was a potential military force with sobering implications. As they struggled for autonomy in organization, they began to hammer out the doctrine that would govern its future employment. That concern in turn was tied to the progress in design and technology that would make implementation of the doctrine possible. The airmen had little to work with, for the Army Reorganization Act of 1920 made the Air Service an integral part of the ground organization, and it suffered disproportionately in the postwar budget cuts.[12] It was a time that Henry H. "Hap" Arnold, then a major accepting any command that came open in order to continue flying, called the "lean years," when those in the air arm were "trying to find ourselves."[13]

Between budget cuts and the toll of crashes (330 for the year 1 July 1920–30 June 1921 alone),[14] the Air Service seemed at times in danger of shriveling away. Aviation as a whole was still primitive, with aeronautical engineering only beginning to probe the limits of possibilities. The self-starter had not yet been developed; the pilot or a mechanic cranked the plane's propeller by hand and then bolted out of its way. There was very real reason for flyers to have the image of daredevils, for every flight was a challenge. Flying fields were a luxury; planes put down in a field, in a pasture, or on a road. There were no established air routes or navigation aids, no radio beacons or radar sets. Between 1919 and 1922, when parachutes became regulation equipment, 8 percent of the army's pilots were killed each year.[15]

During those years Chennault was learning. He was assistant supply officer at Gerstner Field; he filled an assortment of posts at Ellington Field. There he also took advanced pursuit training with the First Pursuit Group, whose proud esprit de corps had survived the war. As he began to think about how to fight with planes, he began questioning the way things were being done and developing ideas of his own. Soon he was known as a "go-getter,"[16] a man who pushed both himself and his plane to see just how far each could go. He graduated from the pursuit training at the top of his class, but its commanding officer, Maj. Carl Spaatz, noted on his record that with such a large family he would probably be too timid to fly pursuit.[17] The self-contained, red-headed Spaatz, already showing the dependability that earned him key positions in World War II and the honor of being the first chief of staff of an independent air force afterward, doubtless thought he was doing Chennault a favor. When the First Pursuit Group moved to Selfridge Field in June 1922, a disappointed Chennault was transferred to the Twelfth Observation Squadron at Fort Bliss, near El Paso, Texas. Its major duty was patrolling the border for illegal immigrants. Brig. Gen. William Mitchell, who had headed the Air Service abroad during the war and who then became its assistant chief and most vocal spokesman, noted that the squadron was in "very bad shape."[18]

Chennault had various duties, including that of engineering officer, but he spent much of his time flying and practicing the dizzying aerobatics he had come to love. Airshows, put on primarily by civilian barnstormers, were standard entertainment in those days, and on Washington's birthday 1923 Chennault gave a memorable demonstration of his skill. A sizable crowd had assembled for a show that was routine until the Twelfth Observation Squadron introduced Grandma Morris, a delightful little lady in bonnet and long skirt who had come to El Paso to take her very first plane ride. With a flourish appropriate for the occasion, the pilot helped her into the two-seater and then went to the front to crank the propeller. The crowd gasped as the plane jerked, the pilot fell to one side, and the plane took off crazily down the field, narrowly missing adjacent trees and the hangar. It hurtled into the air and for the next fifteen minutes the crowd held its breath and prayed for Grandma's soul, for the plane looped and rolled, dived to within feet of the ground before roaring off again, and banked in dizzying turns. Grandma ended her flight with a perfect three-point landing and jumped out of the plane to shed her disguise. Tales of Grandma Chennault enlivened many a storytelling session thereafter.[19]

Chennault saw a career beginning to form when he was transferred to the Hawaiian Department in September 1923. With zest for the adventure ahead he piled his family—Pat and David had brought the children up to six—into their Studebaker touring car for the trip to California. Caught by a cloudburst near Gila, Arizona, they charged through a flash flood and emerged drenched but unharmed. The exuberant boys, displaying their father's own tendency to create action if none existed, enjoyed exploring the boat on the way to the islands. After what seemed to be a long trip they were glad to get off—and in

"Grandma" being escorted by Lt. Ployer P. Hill to the DH-4 in which she was to take her first flight, Fort Bliss, 22 February 1923. (Photo courtesy Milt Miller)

later years they reflected that their fellow passengers were doubtless glad to see them go. For Nell it was a hard journey.

Base housing was too small to accommodate the Chennaults comfortably (Robert, the youngest of their six sons, arrived in January 1925). While in Hawaii the family lived on the peninsula in Pearl Harbor in a large, open house. Chennault got pontoon boats for the children and helped the older ones teach the younger how to take care of themselves in the water. Seven-year-old Peggy, just to see if she could do it, swam about half the width of Pearl Harbor with a proud father rowing alongside. Even getting to school was an adventure, for their father rowed the four school-age children to Ford Island, where they transferred to a motor launch that took them to the coal dock at the Navy Yard, where they caught the bus into town.[20]

The years in Hawaii were Chennault's happiest time in the service. It was a time free from personal tension, a time when he could take both pleasure and pride in his work. After filling assorted positions—transportation and radio officer, engineering officer, and acting operations officer and trial judge advocate—he got a "lucky break" and was able to move from observation back into pursuit.[21] There he began carving out his own niche, for he had the "Right Stuff," defined in the more formal terms of the day as "an eagerness for combat" and the "proper combination of reckless disregard for danger and prudence in aerial combat."[22] Temperamentally and physically well suited, with quick reflexes and a competitive nature devoid of fear, he thrived on flight. Increasing deafness, possibly a result of open-cockpit flying, posed little problem; he was granted a waiver.

Within six months he had his first command, the Nineteenth Pursuit Squadron. Training and operations revolved around tactical maneuvers, aerial gunnery, test flights, and cross-country flying. To these Chennault added, with considerable enthusiasm, formation aerobatics. His idea was that combat flying in close formation would be essential for concentrated firepower, which in turn would be essential to combat success. Showing his instinct for leadership, he aroused the professional pride of two of his squadron's oldest and most conservative pilots and soon had them experimenting. The others followed, of course, lest they be outdone. Soon the whole squadron was practicing formation maneuvers to some degree.[23] When seven British ships put into Honolulu in the summer of 1924, they were "much pleased" with their welcome, for the aviators "showed great skill and gave us a most entertaining show."[24] Morale in the squadron was high.

Chennault enjoyed command and set his own style for it: he was on the same side as his men. He argued their cases when they were in trouble and praised them for good work or innovative ideas. He agitated for kitchen improvements—the squadron's range was at times unserviceable—and worked to get them a building for recreational uses, arguing that it would be "conducive to esprit de corps and high morale in the organization" because "the men are housed in tents and have no building or room in the squadron for reading and indoor games."[25] When a major inspection was held in August 1925, the Nineteenth "appeared to be better trained" in close order drill than the other units and was commended for its high standard of aerial training. According to the report, the Nineteenth's results in bombing and machine gun firing "may well be taken as a standard for this department." Already Chennault's priorities were showing, however, for spit and polish in noncombat areas was lacking: "execution of simple movements was ragged, out of step, without uniformity or snap."[26]

With his first command responsibilities came his first frustrations with bureaucracy and his first battle of will—which he lost. The Nineteenth was in the process of acquiring an insignia. One had been submitted to the War Department for approval but had been returned because it was "not suitable . . . the Air Service Wings belong to the entire Air Service and are not distinctive of any one squadron." Chennault took up the challenge and solicited the help of the art department of the *Honolulu Advertiser*.[27]

"In case of War this insignia would be one of the first to greet the enemy," he wrote by way of exhorting the artists to special effort. The resulting insignia bore, in Chennault's words, a "golden winged misericorde which signifies a winged implement of death—the misericorde being used in medieval times to deliver the death stroke to a fallen knight on the field of battle—and chosen for use in this design to designate Pursuit Aviation which is the deathdealing branch of the Air Service." He submitted this earnest work of art to the commanding officer of Luke Field, who in turn sent it to Hawaiian Department headquarters. From there it came back through channels, "for correction . . . makes use of Air Service wings."[28]

Undaunted, the new commanding officer forwarded a new design "in compliance," respectfully calling attention "to the wings of the misericorde which have been changed to fully extended eagle wings and do not resemble any of the Air Service designs of wings." The fate of the misericorde is lost to us at this point. The next recorded correspondence, with the *San Antonio Express*, concerns a fighting gamecock. Presumably this campaign went more smoothly, for the fighting cock became the Nineteenth's insignia.[29]

In more serious vein, Chennault found himself in basic disagreement with the army on the respective roles of the Air Service and the Coast Artillery. The latter insisted that it could shoot down any airplane before it could reach its target. The pilots vigorously disputed the point, for the gunners based their claim on their record of shooting at towed targets moving at a steady speed and altitude; such conditions, the pilots insisted, would not prevail in actuality. Albert F.

Hegenberger, later to serve as Chennault's chief of staff in the Four-teenth Air Force and as commander of the Tenth Air Force, was at that time the operations officer of the Fifth Composite Group, of which the Nineteenth Squadron was a part. He too took exception to the manner in which the joint training with the Coast Artillery took place; he carried on a steady war within channels, with Chennault providing the supporting statements for Hegenberger's official pro-tests. Friendship between the two men was forged in many a session of lively discussion. Both saw the air as limited only to the extent that man's vision was limited. Hegenberger noted that Chennault often came up with original solutions to problems only to find him-self helpless against the opposition of those whose approach was more conventional.[30]

The response to creativity within military organizations has long been a problem, for when a nation's future and the expenditure of large numbers of human lives are at stake, the known approach often seems safer than the untried innovation. Chennault's was a fertile and agile mind when addressed to fighting or flying. His creative in-stincts were at their best in informal bull sessions. When he faced the formal military structure, his approach aroused consternation. Al-though his later memoir contains unfortunate distortions, it suggests that he tried to make his point about antiaircraft fire at a maneuver-ing target by disrupting a practice exercise, buzzing the frightened participants, and using his low-flying plane to chase the outraged commanding colonel down the beach.[31] He was reprimanded and punished, but the basic lesson—that his behavior had been inappro-priate and insensitive—eluded him. As a man he never outgrew the trait that had caused him, as a boy, to delight in startling his buddies after having outsmarted them.

During his years in Hawaii, Chennault concentrated on experi-menting with flight as it would affect warfare. As U.S. relationships with Japan steadily deteriorated, he became sensitive to the possi-bility of U.S.-Pacific conflict. The vulnerability of the islands was ob-vious to him; he responded to the worst of the war scares by putting his squadron on early morning patrol over Oahu, a move that made him the object of some ridicule. He was still "taking his soldiering se-riously," however; he considered it his prime responsibility not to let his men be taken by tactical surprise. After he had begun to regard air power as the major defending element against an attack that would come by air as well as by sea, his mind turned to the question of how the defenders would locate the approaching enemy. During maneuvers he stationed men on top of water tanks to spot, but a more complex alert system was taking shape in his mind.

He concluded his tour in Hawaii at Luke Field's Unit School, where he taught a course on pursuit organization methods and operations and took a course in supply methods and maintenance of airplanes. His fourth log book ended in October 1926 and recorded a total of 1,353 hours and 30 minutes of flying time.[32] He took pride in a well-deserved reputation as a superb pilot, pride that was only momentarily pricked when he let a cross-wind catch him in landing a PW-9. The plane drifted, turned, hit a parked motorcycle, and went up on its nose. The accident report noted that he had also cracked up a DH in New Mexico in 1923, but it nevertheless rated him "above average" as a pilot and stated that the "accident was not thru the fault or neglect of anyone concerned."[33]

While Chennault was in Hawaii, Mitchell turned the struggle for recognition of air power into a public controversy, thereby bringing upon himself the court-martial that precipitated his resignation from the Air Service in February 1926. Shortly afterward Congress passed the Air Corps Act. The change was to some extent one of terminology—"Corps" formally acknowledged a function other than "Service" (which translated into observation) for air power—but it did authorize an expansion program and established the position of assistant secretary of war for air. The primary and advanced training schools, as well as the school of aviation medicine, were consolidated into the Air Corps Training Center at San Antonio. From mid-1926 until August 1930 Chennault was stationed there, first as an instructor, then as operations officer and the director of primary and basic training at Brooks Field.

Chennault used the time to consolidate his strengths and to gain experience in teaching and administration. Those who mastered the fundamentals of flying the PT-1 in primary training went on to basic training in the DH-4MB (a bigger and heavier version of the World War I DH-4) to polish their skills in approaches and landings, simple aerobatics, and a small amount of night and formation flying. Only half of the cadets successfully completed primary training and entered basic. As the senior check pilot and final authority on the wash-out board, Chennault was known by the traditional nickname "Pop" and was viewed by the cadets with some fear and awe, for they saw him as a brusque figure who "spared no words," although admittedly he was "firm and fair." His face had begun to acquire the leathery texture and deep lines of the open-cockpit pilot; with his piercing black eyes and a small, fierce mustache, he could strike fear into the hearts of the insecure.[34]

Laurence Kuter, later one of Chennault's friends and fellow Air Corps generals, progressed in the familiar washout routine until he was sent to Chennault for the final test. As Kuter recalled it, Chennault picked out a farm building and a tree as pylons and set him to flying standard figure eights. These Kuter executed as he had been taught, by kicking the rudder, and the result was a choppy, awkward turn. In a tableau reminiscent of his own washout test in 1919, Chennault seized the controls and flew the plane back to the field at full throttle.

"Those aren't good enough," he stated flatly.

Figuring he had nothing to lose, Kuter spoke up. "No, they're pretty poor."

"So what do you mean?" Chennault snapped. Kuter explained that he was trying to do the eights the way his instructor told him to, even though he did not think it was the best way to handle the plane. Chennault was hooked.

"You think you know more about flying that airplane than your instructor, don't you?"

"Yes, I do," an undaunted Kuter fired back. Chennault softened, and the two piled into the plane for a second check ride. With the pressure off, Kuter convinced Chennault he had the makings of a pilot and won a different instructor with whom to complete his Brooks Field training.[35]

While stationed in San Antonio the Chennaults lived in a partly Mexican district in a house remembered by the children for the swing on the front porch and the big garden where their father grew okra and tomatoes to make his favorite gumbo. The family acquired its first radio, a kit that included earphones, and a piano, on which John began taking lessons. Pat, like John destined to become an air force officer, took his first plane ride in a World War I DH-4 piloted by his father. Rosemary, the youngest of eight children and for some years thereafter Chennault's "Baby," was born in September 1928. There was a bad time when Bob and Pat were struck with a serious illness— for some days Bob lay immobile with a high fever, and they feared he might die—but both boys recovered in time.[36]

Chennault's assistant operations officer during those years was Russell Randall, later a fellow Air Corps general. The younger Randall considered their relationship to be almost that of brothers. The two men worked harmoniously together, for Chennault encouraged

Randall to make his own decisions and develop his own approaches; they shared similar ideas on aerobatics and combat maneuvers.

They differed, however, on fishing. Randall was a saltwater man; Chennault swore that anything other than freshwater catfishing was heresy. Randall kept needling his chief, tempting him with tales of the impressive quantities of red fish, trout, or pompano he could catch on the southern Texas coast near Matagorda and Port O'Connor. Chennault gave in. Insisting that the fishing would be bad, he pointedly took along a flask. On their first day the catch was better than 250 pounds. Chennault ate his words, and the two men downed the flask together. They fried fish on the beach for their supper, slept under the wing of their plane, and flew home the next day with enough fish to make everyone happy. It was an experience they often repeated thereafter. For Chennault there was the very practical aspect of feeding his large family. More important, however, as Randall put it, when they talked fishing, "an inner light would shine from his eyes."[37]

The Air Corps of the late 1920s had its own distinctive atmosphere, freewheeling and a little glamorous, liberally seasoned with swagger and bravado, a small, elite group of only 1,500 officers. "We all knew each other, and we had a hell of a lot of fun."[38] Desk and paperwork were subordinated to flying, in part because very little had been tried and proven. Flyers were still learning by doing. Funding was so limited that at times the number of hours the pilots could fly had to be restricted. Chennault, putting in as much time as he could, had logged 2,318 hours and 30 minutes as a pilot, plus 61 hours as an observer, by August 1930.[39] In July 1929, while piloting a C-9 Ford tripacer with eight passengers, he nosed up on landing in soft ground, but although his decisions were deemed to be questionable in that particular instance, the accident report stated that his "judgment is rated as excellent and his skill is excellent."[40] He flew with confidence and ease. Sometimes on a cross-country flight he would stop at Gilbert, land in the field near his father's home, and visit with family and friends while the school turned out en masse to inspect the plane. Once he nosed up trying to stop short of a ditch and had to wait several days for a new propeller. Since there was always the likelihood of mechanical failure or bad weather, he carried his gun and fishing pole in case of delays en route.[41]

Although the atmosphere of relaxed regulations was one in which he thrived, Chennault's colleagues of those years nevertheless began to see the beginning of the apartness, the distance from his fellow officers that became more marked during the 1930s. In circumstances where "about all we had to do was fly,"[42] he took his work so seriously that other officers sometimes considered him overly conscientious, a man who obviously had ideas of his own, even though he did not force them on others. Known as an intensive and thorough teacher, he was often quiet and withdrawn in social situations.[43] He had begun to sense that he carried two handicaps to his future Air Corps career: he had neither served abroad during World War I nor attended West Point. He sought to overcome both deficiencies by sheer dedication to his profession.[44] Understanding that American military aviation was still in its infancy, he gave free rein to his penchant for pushing the limits and let it lead him into various explorations.

Between 1927 and 1929 he was part of a small group at Brooks Field that did the pioneering U.S. work with paratroops. The impetus came from Mitchell, who during the war had drawn up a plan for taking Metz with troops and guns dropped by parachute. The plan was never implemented, but shortly after it had been published in May 1926 in the *New York American*, various experiments with paratroops began. Chennault and Benjamin Chidlaw (later general) took part, but the primary figure was Erwin H. Nichols, a master sergeant in the parachute department. During the summer of 1928 Nichols supervised a steady succession of jumps with an acceptable low casualty rate—only two cracked legs in ninety-three jumps—and in October, when the American Legion held its tenth annual convention in San Antonio, the experimenters staged a demonstration. Planes flew over the field and dropped a six-man machine gun crew. Their gun, with its own chute, followed from a Martin bomber. Within three minutes the crew was organized and ready to fight.

It was an impressive display, unflawed except that one man landed in a patch of cactus. The observers included the army's chief of staff, Maj. Gen. Charles P. Summerall, who was quoted as being "highly pleased with the exhibition," while an official War Department news release stated that "the airplane has made possible new elements of surprise in warfare."

Nichols, Chennault, and Chidlaw continued their experimentation into 1929 and refined the maneuver until the men could be ready to fight within one minute of reaching the ground. A report from the chief of the Air Corps stated that the technique of landing men and guns by parachute was constantly being improved.[45]

Yet for some reason the efforts were halted. Chennault later remembered that Summerall called their work "more of this damned aviation nonsense" and that the War Department ordered the experiments ended "before somebody is hurt."[46] For whatever reason, the project was stopped. The United States conducted no further paratroop development until 1940. During those intervening years the significant work on paratroop tactics was done by the Germans and the Russians. The latter sent an aviation mission to the U.S. in February 1930 under the auspices of Amtorg, a New York trading corporation that represented Russia's trade and industrial organizations. The Brooks Field paratroop demonstration was staged for the mission's benefit. Identifying in Chennault a creative approach and innovative skill, the Amtorg party quietly approached him afterward with the offer of a job in Russia helping to build a paratroop arm.

He was tempted. It was gratifying to be sought by a foreign power, especially since advancement in the peacetime Army between the wars was slow. He had been in the regular army for nine years, and not until April 1929 was he made captain. He was thirty-seven years old with a large family to support, and here was the offer of financial reward and recognition, as well as that enticing lure of adventure, that hint of romance associated with unknown, faraway places. According to his memoirs, the Russians offered to let him write his own terms and did not flinch when he made them high for the times—a five-year contract at $1,000 a month plus expenses and the equivalent of the rank of colonel.

Chennault eventually rejected the Russian offer, although mail and exotic gifts arrived at his home for some months. The pursuit plane was his primary interest, paratroops only an exciting excursion into the emerging areas of his profession. Nor did he want to risk losing his U.S. citizenship, for he took his patriotism as seriously as his flying. His love for his country and his respect for the services charged with her defense went deep into his nature. His response was emotional, seldom voiced yet expressed in subtle ways. He was indifferent to his civilian clothes, which were often rumpled, his pants as likely to be held up with a length of binder's twine as with a belt. His uniform, in contrast, was treated with unwavering respect.[47]

His decision to stay with the Air Corps was no longer in doubt after he was selected as one of thirty-nine officers to attend the Air Corps Tactical School for the year 1930–31. The assignment opened the door to further promotion and the possibility of more responsible command in the U.S. Army Air Corps. The idea of spreading his wings abroad had been planted and would later reemerge, but in the summer of 1930 he put aside its temptations and began preparing for the year at Langley Field. Nell and the children would stay in San Antonio; it would be a year of some deprivation but considerable opportunity. He approached it with high expectations and great seriousness. To this point his skills had grown in logical sequence, and he was ready.

3

Growth, Conflict, Controversy

A rising army officer with the potential of general rank usually attends his service school, then the Command and General Staff School at Leavenworth, and finally the Army War College in Washington. In 1920 the Air Corps Tactical School was established at Langley Field as an Air Service school comparable to the army's Infantry School, but from the beginning there were two subtle differences.[1]

First, advancing aviation technology was pushing the potential for the military application of air power into areas of possibility requiring theoretical analysis, and this in turn had to be structured into tactical approaches. Whereas armies and navies had existed for centuries and had their philosophies well defined by such great men as Karl von Clausewitz and Alfred T. Mahan, air was a mere upstart. ACTS of necessity had to evolve the doctrine it taught, for at that time no body of doctrine existed.

Second, after the passage of the Air Corps Act in 1926, airmen soon realized that the number of their officers being assigned to Leavenworth—the key to advancement—was not increasing in proportion to the size of the Air Corps itself. They accordingly developed their school around the assumption that their top officers might not go to

Leavenworth, hence ACTS must meet most of their professional
training needs.

From the beginning the school acknowledged two distinct functions for air: *service*, which usually meant observation for the ground
forces, and *force*, which was the "true arm" or combat application of
air power. The basis was the World War I experience, not merely the
colorful, romantic dogfights of the Red Baron and the Sopwith Camel
but also the first, exploratory efforts to use bombardment directly
against the heart of the enemy's strength. The Germans had tried it
first, with Zeppelin raids on London in 1917, to which the British
promptly responded by creating an independent air force for direct
action against the German industrial system. The United States had
also developed a bombing arm. Its largest mission was in October
1918, when Mitchell used 200 bombers escorted by 110 pursuits to attack, with success, the German reserves gathering for battle. Both
American and British efforts had been small and inconclusive (the
British dropped 550 tons of explosives, the Americans 138 tons), but
some, including Mitchell, were convinced that this was how air
force, or power, would most effectively be applied in the future.

Official army doctrine, however, gave the supreme role in warfare
to the infantry, while the mission of an air service was to support the
ground forces by reconnaissance, by denying reconnaissance to the
enemy, and by obstructing the enemy's concentration and movement of troops and supplies. Since an air service could accomplish
this mission only if it had air superiority (or supremacy or control),
and since pursuit was the element within the air arm that attained
and held control of the air, pursuit was "the most vital element of the
air service."[2]

A questioning atmosphere prevailed at ACTS. Its most important
course, called "The Air Force," integrated the teachings of the four
other branches of the curriculum (pursuit, attack, observation and
bombardment), and at the end of each year its text traditionally
went into the wastebasket, to be rewritten in light of the newest
thinking. In this climate of change the concept gained strength that
air force had a broader mission than supporting surface forces. As airmen saw it, gaining air superiority might be the mission of pursuit,
and obtaining information might be the mission of observation, but
was not the mission of the air force as a whole to eliminate the enemy's ability to make war? And could not this broader mission be carried out most effectively by bombardment to destroy the enemy's
vital centers?

By introducing the capability of striking directly at vital centers, air power posed a challenge to the long-accepted doctrine that the ultimate objective of battle was the destruction of the enemy's military forces. A 1926 ACTS text presented the idea that the enemy's capital, industry, and other resources—his vital centers—had not previously been considered military objectives because no means existed for striking at them; armies were positioned in front of these vital centers to protect them, and consequently armies had come to be viewed as the objective. Now, with air power, the vital centers could be the objective, and costly battles of attrition such as Europe had recently undergone could be eliminated. The text suggested that the aim of any national war policy was to destroy the enemy's will to resist; the mission of air was to further the national policy. One means of doing so might be to attack the enemy interior directly by bombardment, "a method of imposing will by terrorizing the whole population of a belligerent country while conserving life and property to the greatest extent."[3]

The individual most closely associated with the emerging doctrine of strategic bombardment was an Italian, Giulio Douhet. During the 1920s he conceived future conflict as total war characterized by a massive aerial offensive against which he saw no defense. He visualized such a war as ending quickly, for civilian morale would speedily collapse in the face of devastating bombardment. Denied public support and the output of its destroyed industries, a nation would have to surrender. Although U.S. thought departed from that of Douhet in some particulars, the Italian's influence showed.

Because the bombardment arm of the Air Corps offered the only means of implementing this new concept of warfare, bombardment rather than pursuit began to be viewed as the most important element in an air force. The change was reinforced by the results of Air Corps maneuvers during which pursuit had trouble finding and intercepting bombardment. With the endorsement of Lt. Kenneth Walker and Capt. Robert Olds, leaders of ACTS bombardment thinking at the time, the 1930 revision of the text for the air force course included the statement, "a defensive formation of bombardment airplanes properly flown, can accomplish its mission unsupported by friendly pursuit . . . when opposed by no more than their own number of hostile pursuit."[4]

When Chennault went to ACTS in August 1930, the doctrinal debate was on the verge of its most dynamic and productive period. The fundamental concepts of strategic bombardment as eventually implemented by the U.S. Army Air Forces between 1942 and 1945 had been isolated and were being examined. Bombardment had been identified as the most important element of the air force. Control of the air was deemed essential, but the view was gaining favor that it could best be achieved by a determined bomber offensive to destroy enemy air power on the ground.

Chennault was unconvinced. As though realizing that this would be the first real challenge of his career, as well as his first opportunity to make a substantive contribution to the growing military air arm, he waded into the heady atmosphere of Langley Field with all the eagerness, conviction, and blatant self-assurance of another Mitchell. Flying fighters had become a compelling facet of his very being, the way he integrated mind and body and soul into a whole. "Nobody ought to train to be a pilot unless he just can't be satisfied to do anything else," he once wrote Max.[5] His entire psyche was interwoven, not just with flight, but with pursuit, its capabilities and potential. Nothing he encountered during his year as a student at ACTS made him change his mind. When he graduated on 27 June 1931, his conviction and professional qualifications were recognized by his assignment to be the school's pursuit instructor.

Over the summer of 1931, ACTS moved to Maxwell Field at Montgomery, Alabama. Pleased to have his family reunited, pleased to have had recognition and now to have challenges and opportunity, Chennault threw himself into his work with singular dedication. The ongoing debate on air doctrine dominated the scene, sweeping through the classrooms and offices of Austin Hall like a tornado, sucking everyone into its vortex. It required a new perspective on warfare, a searching look at the relationship of military forces to national policy and the nature of conflict. Morality was one disturbing issue; the bombardment of cities would bring loss of life by civilians as well as the armed forces. Grappling with this fact, airmen began to make a firm distinction between civilian and military targets, a concept strengthened after Maj. Donald Wilson suggested identifying key segments of an economy—steel, transport, electric power—as critical links which, if destroyed, could cause an imbalance in an industrial nation's ability to wage war.[6]

The participants in this decade of debate were far from unanimous. Between 1931 and 1935, the loudest part of the controversy concerned the relative strengths and roles of bombardment versus pursuit. Walker, Olds, Wilson, and Capt. Harold George were among the more articulate of the bomber advocates. Chennault led those who saw undeniable roles for pursuit. He was not alone—Captains George Kenney and Hoyt Vandenberg were two of his supporters—but he was unique in his ardor. The pursuit enthusiasts were also outnumbered, and Chennault alone was willing to put his future on the line and take the lead for the minority in an internal power struggle.

That a power struggle as well as doctrinal debate was involved could not be doubted. In the future the Air Corps would be led by those individuals who emerged on the winning side of the doctrinal decision. A questioning mind and free speech might be part of the ACTS structure, but individuals would inevitably become identified with the views they championed. Organizations simply do not reward their gadflies, and Mitchell, even after retirement the undeniable leader of Air Corps thinking, led firmly in the direction of strategic bombardment.[7] The air officers followed. The position gradually emerged that pursuit would be ineffective against the more powerful bomber, which could attain air superiority by destroying the enemy's planes and facilities on the ground. Pursuit seemed to be of steadily diminishing importance.

Many pursuit advocates, reading the handwriting on the wall, switched to bombardment. Not Chennault. Convinced he was right and not one to shirk a fight, he championed pursuit with a vehemence one observer described as "just rabid." All that was required to open debate was "to get Claire and Ken and George and 'Skim' Welshmer [an instructor in antiaircraft artillery] in the same room and make one statement, and they were off. They would argue all the rest of the afternoon." Arguments were discreetly described as taking place in loud tones with occasional profanity, but one officer observed, "If they had had tomahawks, they would have scalped one another." The bomber advocates insisted the bombers could go through anything and would shoot down the attacking fighters; Chennault, a "zealot for fighters," vowed that defensive pursuit could shoot down any bomber they had.[8]

Chennault was "not much of a smiling man," and he approached these sessions with the fervor of the evangelist as he sought to save bombardment from itself. His eyes flashed fire one minute and narrowed the next, while the thin line of his mouth and the square set of his jaw became steadily more pronounced, as though a succession of confrontations during which his teeth were tightly clenched was altering even his physical appearance. In these sessions he often chain-smoked, punctuating his arguments with brusque little snorts (a habit the students effectively imitated in year-end skits). Those who lacked enthusiasm for this no-holds-barred verbal "rassling" learned to support the one who had the floor. Students at the school would pray for rain so the aerial demonstrations might be called off, for they were so intense, one officer found, that "they gave me ulcers of the stomach."[9]

Chennault was in his element. He relished a good fight, but he also understood that the successful fighter must have more going for him than conviction alone. Realizing that pursuit design and tactics lagged behind bombardment, he reasoned that here he could make a worthwhile contribution. Those who recorded the events of those years were fascinated more by his vociferous arguments than by his less dramatic lectures and writings, but passions have cooled over the years, while the hard lessons of a major war have been analyzed, and Chennault's contributions to military theory and pursuit tactics now appear substantial. Most of them remain valid today.

On the principle that any offense should—and would—have an effective defense, he concentrated on improving existing tactics. He started work on a new pursuit manual, preparing his classroom lectures in meticulous detail as his concepts developed.[10] With a sure instinct for balancing historical precedent with present capabilities and future potential, he began by studying the use of air power in World War I. He found much that impressed him. He called attention to those principles which had been tried and proven in combat. He noted that Boelcke, who first realized the significance of two planes fighting as a team, was the real father of fighter tactics. He also noted weaknesses in the early approaches, and as he went deeper and deeper into specifics, he often deemed it necessary to find flying partners, go aloft, and test theoretical approaches in the air.

An idea began to germinate. The navy had a trio of acrobatic pilots who stunted in formation at air shows and patriotic events. Chennault convinced the ACTS commandant, Lt. Col. John F. Curry, that if the Air Corps had such a team it could represent the Air Corps at public functions, serve as a test unit for developing tactics, and demonstrate tactics for the ACTS students. Delighted when asked to form and lead the group, Chennault chose his partners by the simple expedient of challenging any comer to stay on his wing through half an hour of head-spinning aerobatics. Three succeeded: red-headed, freckle-faced John H. "Luke" Williamson; calm, chubby William C. "Billy" McDonald; and Haywood S. Hansell, who sported the startling nickname "Possum"—probably, he said, because he looked like one. Hansell was a lieutenant—he and Chennault had started flying

mock combat with one another while at Langley Field—but even
though both Williamson and McDonald held reserve commissions,
they were serving in the Air Corps as enlisted men in order to keep
flying.[11]

This lively foursome formed their trio, McDonald flying alternate,
and before they disbanded in early 1936 they had become famous as
"The Three Men on a Flying Trapeze," a speed and precision flying
act at airport openings and air shows, billed by the press as "dare-dev-
ils who laugh at death," "exhibitionists par excellence" who "held
the crowds spellbound" and flew with a "perfection that seemed as if
the three planes were activated by one mind."[12] Their plane was the
P-12E, the sportiest little biplane of the day, with a top speed of 189
m.p.h. at 7,000 feet.

The precision flying that so impressed observers resulted from
hours of practice. The public saw a polished product, but the formation maneuvers had first to be devised by trial and error, and the Trapeze put on practice performances at Maxwell two or three times a

The Men on the Flying Trapeze, taken at Maxwell Field, Alabama, ca. 1933–34. From
left: William C. "Billy" McDonald, alternate; Haywood S. "Possum" Hansell, left
wing man; Chennault, leader; John H. "Luke" Williamson, right wing man. (Photo
courtesy Haywood Hansell)

week for about three years in addition to the twenty or more public appearances. Everything in the program was a legitimate aerobatic maneuver except the closing review, when the pilots flew a V, banked at about 60 degrees for the length of the field. Sometimes, when they flew over Montgomery, school would be let out to watch.

Usually they decided how to execute a certain maneuver while still on the ground, discussed it, then went up and worked out the details. Sometimes, however, they made interesting discoveries by accident. One weekend they were invited to put on a show near Chennault's home in Louisiana, where considerable trouble had been taken to prepare a field for their use. When the flyers arrived, they noted with sinking hearts that clouds were moving in and the visibility was getting low. They needed a ceiling of about 1,500 feet for their act, but hundreds of people had assembled from miles around, and hating to disappoint them, they began to perform nonetheless. Chennault signaled for an Immelmann. In a few moments they were in dense cloud and could see nothing, not even each other. Hansell did some quick thinking and decided to roll and come down. He did so, startled to emerge beneath the clouds and find the three of them still together and still in formation, but Hansell and Williams now on opposite sides of Chennault, who flew point. In writing his pursuit text, Chennault noted that "experience proves" that properly trained individuals who have flown together "need not follow an inflexible rule as to relative positions in formation in order to get effective results."[13]

The forerunner of today's Thunderbirds, the Trapeze was a good show, enjoyed by spectators and participants alike. At one time the flyers experimented with tying the tips of their wings together with lengths of rope about ten feet long, but it hampered flexibility, and Hansell insists, "It wasn't really much of an accomplishment—we normally flew much closer than that."[14] There were remarkably few accidents, although Chennault and Hansell once tangled tails and Chennault made a memorable landing with immovable stabilizers and elevators.

In part because its participants obviously derived much delight from what they did, many did not perceive that the Trapeze played a serious role in the evolution of combat tactics. Chennault himself could hardly distinguish between the two functions, for they held no conflict for him; flight was serious business but also a glorious and thrilling spectacle to be enjoyed. More of his thought and energy went into the fighting aspects of formation flying, however, than to its demonstration value. Perhaps the most important thing to come from their experience was the realization that a three-plane element was too difficult to maintain, too rigid and cumbersome for combat utility. When they tried mock combat with three planes, they found it too unwieldy, whereas with two planes flying together the second could always position itself to take advantage of the enemy's turn.[15]

The tactics Chennault developed for effective pursuit employment made up a sizable portion of his text, which was approved by the chief of the Air Corps and published in 1933. Having carefully studied the aerial combat of the war in Europe, he remembered those concepts that had worked and built upon them. To the recognized advantages of surprise and of maintaining the offensive, he added as further fundamentals the need to get into close range, to concentrate fire on the vital portions of the enemy's craft, to maintain altitude and speed for control, and to approach from the optimum direction to minimize the enemy's ability to return fire. He identified effective range, persistence, and cooperation as the factors that would determine the success of combat; he stressed that maintaining high morale was vital.

He made teamwork the basis of his entire concept of pursuit action. Teamwork afforded more protection for each pilot and enabled pursuit to mass sufficient firepower to destroy the plane under attack. Two planes working together more than doubled their strength because they not only doubled their number of guns but reduced their own chances of getting hit. They must be flexible. A formation must be workable under a variety of specific situations; no definite type or size could be adhered to blindly. In almost all circumstances pursuit would operate in mass, but in isolated cases individual action might be appropriate. Always, he wrote, the most efficient results would be obtained when individual pilots were "thoroughly proficient" in the tactics of individual combat, for decisive action would necessitate coming to close grips with the enemy.

With a realism that was one of his enduring contributions, he pointed out the practical necessities, acknowledging human limitations. No pilot should have to watch more than one other plane in order to stay in position. The leader must be visible so he can be followed. Maneuvers must be kept simple enough for the formation to stay together with minimum concentration. Flexibility was the key, so that there might be maximum maneuverability in combat while taking into consideration all other factors—visibility, ground fire, the number of the enemy. When outnumbered, he advocated "dive and run" tactics, relying on one or two bursts of effective fire, well-aimed, to destroy the enemy while using speed in the dive to get out of range.

Forces should be concentrated to gain the advantage of mass. He used the organization that had become standard during the 1920s, starting with the element of two or three planes and moving up to the flight (two or three elements), the squadron (two or three flights), the group (two or three squadrons), and the wing (two or three groups). When large enough, a formation would be divided into three echelons, assault (to lead), support (to protect), and reserve (to assault, protect, exploit).[16]

Specific tactics for different formations and combat situations were developed in detail, but apparent throughout *Pursuit Aviation*, whether when broad principles or specific employment was discussed, is Chennault's distinctive and powerful touch: an amalgam of common sense, a direct approach to the heart of the problem, and aggressive, unflinching action. This is the Chennault stamp, his unmistakable legacy.

Meanwhile the bomber-pursuit debate proceeded. Could pursuit, operating in defense of a target, destroy bombers at a rate high enough to make a bombing offensive impracticable? The answer depended on technology, on the relative speed, range, maneuverability, and firepower of bombers and pursuit planes at any given time. An effective pursuit plane had to have adequate range to intercept the bomber, high maneuverability and rate of climb to close up to it, firepower sufficient to destroy it, and a substantial margin of speed so that the bomber could not escape. Range and firepower added weight that worked against speed and maneuverability, posing technical problems in design that seemed insurmountable. In contrast, under existing technological conditions, it seemed quite within the realm of possibility to increase the speed and range of the bomber.

Taking the practical approach of working within existing technology, Chennault focused on interception as the key problem. Radar had not yet been invented, but when the bomber advocates claimed that their weapon was limited only by its radius of action, he was quick to counter that it was also limited by whatever defense would be pitted against it. A warning system, he doggedly insisted, could—and would—make reliable interception possible. He conceded that a constant airborne alert would be impossible to maintain, but he visualized an observation network that would provide defending pursuit with advance warning of the approach of enemy bombers. With knowledge of an approaching enemy's course and position in time for defending pursuit to climb to the necessary altitude, interception became a straightforward military problem.[17] He saw it as backwoods common sense, the fundamental law of the hunter versus the hunted.

The effectiveness of pursuit, he told his classes, depended upon equipment, training, tactics, cooperation with other branches, and organization (his term for all agencies engaged in collecting information). Pursuit had been ineffective in the previous war because it lacked intelligence, he said, and "in the future, an organization must be provided so that pursuit can operate upon accurate information against definite targets."[18] In developing his ideas for interception, he enlisted the help of radio operators at other bases, who would report to him when bombers took off from their respective fields. Chennault would then make mock interceptions, much to the consternation of many a startled bomber pilot.[19]

In May 1933, with Franklin Roosevelt newly inaugurated as president of the United States and Adolf Hitler beginning his fourth month as chancellor of Germany, joint Antiaircraft–Air Corps exercises were held at Fort Knox, Kentucky. One question the maneuvers were designed to answer was whether a warning net could detect enemy bombers and provide enough information quickly enough to enable defending pursuit to intercept oncoming bombers before they reached their target. The test net was set up in three concentric arcs, with observation/listening posts six miles apart radiating from Fort Knox. The area was radially divided into twelve sectors for clarity in reporting. Each of the sixty-nine posts, which together covered some 16,000 square miles, was equipped with a telephone; these were supplemented by three radio posts. The Signal Corps staffed the posts and reported to the pursuit group's operations office. When hostile bombers were spotted by posts in the outer arc, the alerted pursuit planes took off. As subsequent reports confirmed the enemy's course, the fighters deployed for interception.

The net functioned "very satisfactorily and efficiently," according to the commanding officer's final report. Despite inexperienced personnel, limited equipment, and restrictions imposed to enable other defensive measures to be tested, the majority of the enemy bombers were intercepted.[20]

Chennault, who served on the staff of the defense commander during the exercise, thought the conclusion was obvious: bombardment was vulnerable to pursuit when the latter had intelligence, and the ground net concept should be improved and developed as a part of defensive pursuit operations.[21] The Air Corps high command, however, saw matters differently. After exercises on the West Coast in May, it reported that an effective air defense was based on the ability to attack and destroy hostile aviation on the ground before it took to the air. The Air Corps was consequently thinking in terms of two types of aircraft, one for patrol/observation and one for offensive bombing missions with sufficient machine gun firepower to protect itself.[22]

Chennault's tactical development, dedicated instruction, and spirited defense of the preceding two years notwithstanding, pursuit had reached rock bottom.

4

"I always thought
the air was unlimited."

In the months following the Fort Knox exercises of 1933, Chennault made his first attempt to influence Air Corps thought outside the structure of ACTS. He was more at home in a cockpit or classroom than at a desk, but he wrote three lengthy articles, cumulatively entitled "The Role of Defensive Pursuit." *The Coast Artillery Journal* published them; ACTS printed them in pamphlet form, although without the school's official endorsement.[1]

In the first part, called "The Next Great War," his thesis was that the aerial weapon would play a prominent role in any future conflict. Consequently, while still at peace, the nation should develop not only a striking force but also a defense capability that could destroy hostile bombardment forces before they reached their target. He noted that Germany, Italy, France, and Great Britain were planning defenses based on pursuit planes and warning nets plus antiaircraft guns and searchlights.

In part 2, "Interceptions," he set forth the core of his argument, the basis on which he believed pursuit would continue to be a vital element in an air force. After identifying three phases of successful air defense—detection and reporting, interception by pursuit, and destruction or repulse of the enemy—he elaborated on interception. Its essential ingredient was "timely information of the approach,"[2] and the distance from which it must originate could be calculated mathematically using such information as the altitude and speed of the enemy, the rate of climb and speed of the defending pursuit, and so forth. Using values for known planes and circumstances, he demonstrated that advance information on the enemy made interception and defense feasible.

Carefully noting that the mere collection of information was not enough but that it must be properly transmitted, evaluated, and acted upon, he then turned to aerial observation and the ground intelligence net, analyzing their limitations, requirements, and advantages. His years in Hawaii had made him sensitive to the islands' vulnerability to attack, and he predicted, with painful accuracy, that because of existing aircraft ranges, a hostile aerial attack would have to be launched from "a floating airdrome" or a captured land base.[3] Consequently the warning net for an island or a coastal point must have observation/listening posts equipped with radios and far enough out to sea to satisfy the mathematical space-time factor. Otherwise such areas as Oahu could not be defended. He considered the United States too vast for a total warning net such as later became possible with radar and satellites, but he advocated a mobile intelligence system, equipped, trained, and operated by an "Air Defense Information Group" that could be set up rapidly in a threatened area. Today the argument seems unassailable, but at a time when very few observers anticipated that two great oceans would cease to provide protection from hostile attack, it was leading thought.

Part 3 of "The Role of Defensive Pursuit" was a detailed analysis of the Fort Knox exercises and their results. Although this first net had not functioned as a complete intelligence system, he concluded that it was a "necessary step in the preparation of any defense against the invasion of hostile bombardment."[4] Five years later, in China, he would demonstrate what he meant by broadening the net concept into a total intelligence system, with observation posts deep within enemy territory.

Not until 1940–41 did Britain's Royal Air Force, with its string of radar towers providing the advance information that enabled it to win the Battle of Britain, establish without doubt the validity of Chennault's basic concepts. In 1933 U.S. citizens were more concerned with unemployment and bread lines and the dust bowl that was turning the Midwest into a desert. The danger of aerial assault seemed slim. Not until 1940 was the U.S. Air Defense Command established. A warning net was under construction but was not yet fully operational when Japanese carrier-based planes—hostile pursuit launched from a floating airdrome—struck Pearl Harbor on 7 December 1941.

In his second major written work, his revised pursuit text, Chennault positioned pursuit firmly within a balanced air force with the mission "to destroy hostile aircraft," thus contributing to air supremacy. "No new aeronautical development or invention" since World War I, he wrote, had altered the basic principle that attaining and maintaining air supremacy depended on pursuit. In a thinly veiled slap at the Air Corps leadership, he wrote, "New theories and methods should be warmly welcomed but should not be accepted in lieu of proven principles until the new has conclusively demonstrated its superiority over the old."[5] This was perhaps his most significant contribution to subsequent thought, for when, a decade later, American bombers were shot out of the skies over Europe, the bitter lesson that the bomber was indeed vulnerable to defensive pursuit came back to haunt.

Sometimes Chennault's ideas were dismissed as being motivated by his own preference for flying fighters. It is also obvious that others reacted negatively to his personality, that in many cases individuals let personal prejudices color their conclusions. His abrasiveness in argument worked against him, frequently leading to misinterpretations. Just as the glamor of the Trapeze overshadowed its serious role, Chennault's ardor for pursuit pressed him into a characterization that was incomplete. He was considered one sided, someone who believed that the pursuit class alone mattered. To the contrary he believed—and so wrote—that although the action of pursuit was essential it was "decisive only when exploited by other forces." Once pursuit had established air supremacy, then "the air force will concentrate upon the destruction of such strategical objectives as industrial centers, rail and marine transportation facilities, and munitions and fuel production plants." Far from writing bombardment out of the picture, he stated clearly that "bombardment missions will be of paramount importance and pursuit will cooperate to the limit of its range in executing these missions."[6]

By 1934 the bombardment doctrine evolving at ACTS called for long-range penetration into hostile territory regardless of enemy opposition. The issue of offensive escort—of pursuit forces accompanying bombers to protect them from defensive pursuit—was a part of the debate. Some insisted that the heavy, armed, fast bombers could protect themselves; others doubted.[7] Here also the matter was largely technological—a question of range and speed and aircraft design—for no existing pursuit plane was suitable for the escort role. Much attention was given to the design of a multiseater pursuit plane for "Special Support." In *U.S. Air Services*, Chennault argued that "the weight of experience and of logic" was against it. The special support plane as then conceived, he insisted, would be as vulnerable to enemy pursuit as the bombers themselves.[8]

Seeing pursuit as a flexible, powerful force if allowed to operate freely and to capitalize on its potential strengths, Chennault fought any effort to restrict pursuit to close escort. He firmly believed that, with offensive action not tied to close escort, pursuit could seek out and destroy the enemy air force and in this way could more effectively provide the protection required. Close protection, he argued, caused pursuit to lose the initiative and hence the combat; only if pursuit were allowed to operate offensively did it bring its winning characteristics into play.

On this issue his most vigorous clashes with the bomber advocates took place. Some of them, seeing escort only in terms of close escort, shut their minds completely to Chennault's arguments. He had no doubt that the high-speed, highly maneuverable fighter plane, coupled with an intelligence system to provide timely warning, would continue to be a major factor in the defense any nation put forth against hostile air attack, important far out of proportion to the numbers involved because of its potential to defeat an enemy's aerial spearhead, to destroy the enemy before a lodgement could be gained. The obvious corollary was that an offensive bomber strike needed the protection of friendly pursuit. Chennault reasoned that, if offensive bombardment had pursuit escort, the defenders would simply need more pursuits. He thought that the fighter plane would become more, not less, important.[9]

He made little headway as he battled to shape a role for the fighter within emerging concepts. His approach was to seek solutions to the technological problems then limiting the pursuit class. Most important, as he saw it, was "a single-seater with a real working margin of speed over any other type."[10]

He did what he could to obtain such a plane. He served for a time on the Air Corps Board, then on the Pursuit Development Board, where he constantly agitated for extended range, greater speed and more firepower—all essential for fulfilling escort and offensive roles. Pursuit range, he insisted, was limited only by pilot stamina and fuel capacity.

During 1935 and 1936 the Air Corps held a series of design competitions that produced the all-metal, low-wing monoplane fighter with enclosed cockpit and retractable gear. Chennault took a little teasing about the closed cockpit, for he initially opposed it on the grounds that its comforts could bring carelessness. He saw the open cockpit as a safety factor that kept the pilot more acutely aware of the element in which he functioned. In lieu of the open cockpit, he drawled, he would settle for carpet tacks scattered through the suits of his fighter pilots to keep them alert.[11]

The main thing Chennault wanted, however, was a fighter with speed. At Wright Field for tests in October 1935, he listened as aircraft designer Alexander P. de Seversky insisted that he could build a plane capable of flying 500 miles an hour but that nobody in the Air Corps could fly it.

"By golly, if you make it, *I'll* fly it," Chennault retorted. The pursuits he flew that fall of 1935, Seversky's P-35 and Curtiss's P-36, attained little more than half that speed but were substantial improvements over existing models. Chennault preferred the P-35, the first of the Thunderbolt line, and the Air Corps ordered seventy-seven of them. In the light of the tests and Chennault's criticisms, Curtiss revamped the P-36, which was retested and ordered by the Air Corps in April 1936. Subsequent changes led to the P-40, the war horse of World War II.[12]

Meanwhile agitation for a multiplace fighter continued. The idea appealed to the War Department, which hoped to reduce the number of plane types required and thereby achieve greater economy. In November 1935, against the recommendation of the Air Corps Board, the department approved an experimental design for an all-purpose interceptor, bomber, observation, and attack plane. Chennault was scathing in his denunciations of the concept, which took form as the XFM-1 (Bell Aircuda) and was a dismal failure. He regretted that some of the scarce Air Corps money had gone into its development; he claimed the engineers were so fascinated by the challenge of constructing it that they failed to recognize its uselessness for combat.[13]

The Air Corps eventually decided to develop the heavy bomber at the expense of other classes. The result was that the United States entered World War II with a useful bomber, the B-17, but without either planes or developed doctrine for other purposes. The belief that the bomber did not need protective escort may have been a matter of necessity rather than choice. Neither the pursuit experts nor the technologists thought it feasible to design a plane with the speed and maneuverability of pursuit and the range and firepower of bombardment, and there were not sufficient funds to test the concepts. Chennault's was one of the few voices continuing to insist that defensive pursuit would be effective against offensive bombardment, but the trend of thought in the 1930s moved inexorably toward the invincibility of the bomber, the essential weapon of strategic bombardment.

In June 1934 the Federal Aviation Commission was created to recommend to Congress a "broad policy concerning all phases of aviation and the relations of the United States thereto."[14] It was a bear of a task. Military aviation was embroiled in a controversy that was almost a feud, for although the War Department favored a General Headquarters Air Force, firmly under the control of the General Staff, airmen believed the air arm must have a separate organization and a unified structure. Between 1926 and 1935 no fewer than twenty-nine bills advocating either a department of aeronautics or a single department of defense were presented in Congress. None passed.[15]

Considering the tension involved in keeping the rebellious airmen in line, Army Chief of Staff Gen. Douglas MacArthur was not enthusiastic when Clark Howell, the respected editor of the *Atlanta Constitution* and head of the new commission, promised to probe the role of military aviation with an open mind. The War Department prepared an eighty-six-page position paper; any Air Corps officer called to testify before the commission was to read this document and refrain from volunteering information contrary to the official policy stated therein.[16] MacArthur could be eloquent on the subject of freedom, but he did not see it as applying within his army.

Late in November the Howell Commission called six of the outstanding voices of ACTS to testify: Chennault, George, Olds, Walker, Wilson, and Capt. Robert Webster. Their names had been furnished by Congressman J. Mark Wilcox, who believed that these men would concentrate on basic issues. The War Department "authorized" the airmen to testify but refused to cover their expenses. When asked to designate them witnesses and to issue orders for them to attend, the department insisted that their appearance was "entirely voluntary"; they could give their personal views if they were requested to do so, but if those differed from approved policy, the men must make the distinction clear.[17] After such a beginning, the six could hardly deceive themselves that their careers were not on the line. Wilson, Olds, and Walker were then at the Command and General Staff School in Leavenworth, but the group met at Louisville en route to discuss their strategy. It is possible Chennault was not present at their planning session, but it is apparent he agreed with their decision: to express their views as honestly and clearly as possible, even when their opinions ran counter to official War Department policy.[18]

This they did while secretaries transcribed their words and the War Department's liaison, Maj. Gen. C. E. Kilbourne, sat in the back of the room. George, Olds, Wilson, Walker, and Webster spoke in turn. The object of war, they said, was overcoming the enemy's will to resist; air power was not a weapon to be compared to a rifle but a new method of waging war. They insisted that our industrial areas were vulnerable to air attack, that a coalition could wage effective war against us, that we must depend on air force for our immediate defense, and that air force could not be developed unless it was independent and "free from the Army incubus." Creation of a separate, independent air force was the "rational, simple and inevitable solution."[19] The cumulative effect of their presentations was powerful.

Chennault spoke last. He began by saying that he fully supported the evidence given by his colleagues; he felt it needed no repetition. Instead, he said, he would try to illustrate the difference between the thinking of ground and air officers by analyzing maneuvers that had recently been held at Raritan Arsenal. It was a loaded subject, for the conduct of the maneuvers had infuriated airmen, and the individual in command had been none other than General Kilbourne, now sitting in the hearing room. An undaunted Chennault, after declaring no intent to be critical or antagonistic to the War Department, methodically reconstructed the exercise, in which Kilbourne had allowed a theoretical enemy an uncontested landing and refused to let the air force strike the invading force offshore. Chennault noted that the air force was kept out of the picture until it was too late. He then said he would "like to play that game just once more, giving the airman's idea of the employment of an air force" and illustrating what might happen "if we had an independent air force, organized according to the recommendations made here today."[20]

He presented a scenario including advance intelligence that located the approaching enemy, plus a defending air force that used the information to destroy the enemy before it could land. Vice Chairman Edward P. Warner posed a question about whether the enemy landing in the Raritan maneuvers had been intended as a complete surprise, to which Chennault replied that there had been eight to ten days' warning. Here Kilbourne interjected, "You are in error." He requested permission to speak because the officers "have been under a severe misconception or misunderstanding." Chennault was allowed to finish, after which Kilbourne insisted that "the General Staff does understand air power, as expressed by these officers," although he admitted that theirs was "the first constructive presentation by a group of air officers as to how to use it." At that point the official transcript ended; "informal discussion" followed.[21]

Chennault and Kilbourne doubtless pursued the matter more fully off the record. Chennault's memoirs suggest a heated exchange during which Kilbourne pounded the table and justified his conduct of the maneuvers as the best way to bring the opposing forces into contact, to which Chennault replied, "General, if that is the best you can do in the way of planning for future wars, perhaps it is time for the Air Corps to take over."[22]

Chennault's memoirs were written between 1945 and 1949, when he regarded his U.S. Army Air Corps career with bitterness and saw the political alignments of the Cold War as a matter of compelling urgency. There are regrettable inaccuracies and omissions in his account of the years before 1941, for he had little interest in reconstructing them. His memoirs also consistently evince a belligerence and hostility that the records for his early career do not always substantiate. Although direct and frequently tactless in his utterances, Chennault was correct in his professional relationships. The transcript of the Howell Commission hearings suggests that he took great care to make his points without offense.

His memoirs imply, however, that his outspoken testimony before the commission was the reason his name was permanently removed from the list of officers scheduled to go to the Command and General Staff School at Leavenworth. War Department records confirm that he was on the list in 1935 but was removed in 1936. Others were removed as well, however, apparently because too many had been proposed.[23] While it is true that officers were sometimes "disciplined" by such measures, a more likely explanation is that by advocating pursuit against the increasingly bomber-oriented main thrust of Air Corps thought, Chennault had reduced his chances for advancement.

He had also reached the point where his limited background began to have a negative effect on his career, for the contrast between his presentation and that of his peers to the commission is startling.

Where the others were unemotional, well prepared, and almost pro-
fessorial in their intellectual and reasoned approach, he spoke ex-
temporaneously on a charged topic, admittedly demonstrating
mastery of the military situation but arousing antagonism in the process. The pattern of opposition and negative reaction had nevertheless been shaped. Not perceiving that it was destroying his chances of
influencing policy, Chennault plunged on, his approach unchanged.

Not long after the Howell Commission hearings, he found himself
at cross-purposes with Arnold, then a lieutenant colonel at March
Field, California, and one of the leading officers of the Air Corps. Arnold conducted extensive maneuvers designed to settle the continuing argument of bombardment versus pursuit. The results and
conclusions were circulated. Chennault, in the belief that several vital factors had been overemphasized while others were ignored,
wrote a nine-page critique challenging the technical and tactical for-
mat of the maneuvers as well as each of Arnold's conclusions. Where
Arnold had decided that fighters would rarely intercept bombers,
that single-seat pursuits might not even remain in the picture, and
that an entirely new type of multiseat fighter should be developed
"without delay," Chennault insisted pursuit would be required in
any front-line situation to maintain aerial supremacy and to operate
offensively. His own conclusions were that a superior single-seat interceptor should be developed, an effective aircraft warning service
should be constructed, and all pursuit units should be given intensive
training in all phases of interception and attack.[24]

Time was to prove Arnold wrong, Chennault right. Chennault had
not stopped fighting, but by this time he had lost the battle. Doubtless he sensed it, for one observer at ACTS saw him as increasingly
contentious, "like a man with an inferiority complex, lashing out."[25]
His manner became ever more defensive, even though those who
knew him well felt that he retained supreme confidence in both himself and his ideas. Hansell saw in Chennault an egoism that rose
above vanity—"he simply believed in himself"—and considered it
one of his greatest strengths, because only those who believe in themselves fully can fight vigorously for a cause.[26]

That Chennault fought vigorously cannot be denied. He would
have been more successful had he been more tactful and gracious,
less aggressive and certain he was right. The certainty, however, was
there, and he lacked the ability to be diplomatic. An officer who
served under him observed, "He'd never try to shade any colors. He
spoke his mind."[27] Dedicated to his profession, inclined to strong re-

actions and plain language, intolerant of dissent, he found it hard to understand why others did not see as he saw or work as hard as he worked. He refused to play politics. To do so would have been contrary to his principles, for he wanted desperately to believe that a man would be judged on the basis of what he knew and could do, not on standards that were not directly related to his achievements. Yet army custom more often rewards the individual who "goes along" than the one who rocks the boat.

Inevitably Chennault began to sense alienation, a separation from the main currents of Air Corps decision making and power. He responded with a defiant pride in being a "mustang," an officer who had not been to West Point. Sometimes, when fishing with his brother Joe, he would grumble and mutter that West Pointers were less desirable than "ROTC types"; still, "polo players," people too occupied with their social life to take their professional life as seriously as he felt they should, were the worst. For them he had a particular aversion, a scathing contempt because they used some means other than performance and hard work to further their careers.[28] The lesson that it worked, however, was not lost.

In contrast, Chennault's relationships with enlisted men were warm, relaxed, and informal. He had the reputation among them as being "easy to talk to," a man approachable without all the fuss and restraints of rank and military discipline. A young recruit named Sebie Smith helped him move his belongings into his Montgomery house but had no contact with him thereafter until 1933, when Smith was trying to find some way to get back into flying school after having washed out. He sought help from Chennault, who explained that, while he could not change the rules, Smith had his sympathy, for "anybody who likes to fly is a man after my own heart." Smith went away feeling he had made a friend; later, when he needed a loan, Chennault signed his note.[29] Throughout his Air Corps career Chennault was known as an enlisted man's officer, an officer who would give a man a fair shake but chew him out when he needed it. Although the mental and verbal demands of teaching at ACTS represented a challenge he enjoyed and took on eagerly, fundamentally he was a man of physical action, better equipped to command and to fight than to persuade.

During their five years at Maxwell Field the Chennaults took little part in the busy, ritualistic social life typical of the peacetime military base. It appealed to neither of them. They attended only those functions he deemed necessary, but their lack of participation fur-

ther isolated them from the main current. In his spare time Claire enjoyed golf, tennis, horseback riding, or bridge, although if someone
dared inquire, "Whose deal is it?" he would rudely comment that
anyone who could not remember had no business playing. Nell was
involved with her children, her home, her church. At first Claire
urged her to have a drink when they went to the parties, but she
chose not to. He nagged her about it until one evening when she took
a drink and apparently then another and another, for a conspiring
friend kept spiriting away her full glass and replacing it with an
empty one. Claire was sufficiently alarmed to warn, "Be careful—the
stuff packs quite a wallop!" No one betrayed the joke. After that evening he said no more.[30]

The family lived five miles from the airfield in a columned, ante-
bellum house that had not burned during the Civil War only because
its eight huge rooms, each twenty feet square, had served both sides
as a hospital. A cannon ball was still embedded in one of the eigh-
teen-inch-thick walls. The house sat in a large field, and during the
years he lived there, Chennault farmed on a small scale. Sometimes
he sold his surplus vegetables, and he was angered at being told to
stop because it was unbecoming for an officer to do so. A captain's
pay did not go very far in supporting a family of ten, and at times he
had taken on odd jobs at night to supplement his income.[31] He was
almost obsessed with the desire to give his children a good education,
to prepare them so that they might avoid the professional limits he
was experiencing. He would have sacrificed anything to give them
the opportunity. He did not allow them to fritter away their time. He
was pleased when first John, then Max, entered Auburn.

The Chennault home was informal and lively, a male province in
which there was much impassioned talk of flying. The assistant commandant of ACTS recalled that the family "functioned with the least
friction that I ever saw," for each child had been trained to take care
of the one below him.[32] Rosemary was the family pet; her father "always picked her up first," and when the boys wanted the car, they
sent her to ask. Nell was known to use a hairbrush and Claire a Sam
Browne belt as disciplinary aids, but the boys were unruly and later
wondered how their mother survived. She was understanding when
they dismantled airplane fuselages in the upstairs bedroom. When
she insisted they be home by midnight, the older ones named the
huge double back doors into the house "eleven" and "twelve." Sometimes the family played softball, with Claire as pitcher. He enjoyed
watching his sons play high school football. He taught them to play

bridge. When they did something stupid, he muttered that they would "probably grow up to be bomber pilots."

Hunting and fishing, long his favorite pastimes, served as his emotional release, his way of coping with a career that was posing increasing personal frustration. Most of his children hunted with him at one time or another, and shortly after moving to Montgomery he met James A. (Jimmy) Noe, a Louisiana businessman who was elected state senator in 1932 and elevated to lieutenant governor in 1934. The casual hunting partners gradually became firm and lasting friends, for they shared similar backgrounds and common experiences. Both were men of individual pride and honor, shaped by poverty and hard work, motivated by a simple value system that "held no truck with liars or phonies."[33] They hunted together and drank together, and they could sit on a log in the swamps and talk without restraint.

"We should be building airplanes and training soldiers instead of cutting grass and planting flowers with our young men," Chennault told Noe one day, and some ten years later Noe wrote him speculating that they would not then be embroiled in war had the nation built the 100,000 airplanes that his friend had insisted they should have.[34]

The Flying Trapeze gave Chennault an important physical and emotional outlet. The group appeared at events all over the South and East. Chennault enjoyed the trips thoroughly—the camaraderie with flying men, the temporary escape from the intensity of ACTS, the involvement in the frenzied air shows that offered spectators thrills and drama and fear. They performed at the Cleveland Air Races in 1934 and 1935 and at the Miami races in January and December 1935. Everywhere they went they were a major attraction. The roars of approval from the crowds, as large as 100,000, were balm to the ego. For all his rough combativeness, Chennault had a childlike need for approval, and the Trapeze brought recognition and admiration, with newspaper pictures and trophies and fans asking autographs. When the Air Corps forbade the team to engage in "stunt flying," he countered that the definition of "stunt" was vague; instead he requested authorization "to engage in all maneuvers for which it is properly trained." The request was granted, although another—that the team be allowed to perform on Sundays—was denied.[35]

Hansell left the Trapeze in 1934 and McDonald took his place. Both Williamson and McDonald applied for regular commissions when their enlistments expired, but these were denied. Angered, Chennault took their rejection personally. He waited until he had left the Air Corps, but then he spoke out with characteristic lack of restraint. His newspaper article implied that professional jealousy played a role in the decision. Other nations rewarded accomplishment with promotion and recognition, he pointed out, not by turning its experienced men away.[36]

The trio gave its final performance at the Miami All-American Air Races in December 1935. Their "section roll" (planes revolved around the leader while all three planes retained their relative positions) brought cheers from the crowd and won them the trophy for group acrobatic flying. More significant, after the performance the trio was invited by international businessman William D. Pawley to come aboard his yacht for some serious discussion about their future.[37]

Pawley had been involved in aviation for some years. In 1935 he was Curtiss-Wright's sales agent in China as well as president of the Central Aircraft Manufacturing Company, an aircraft assembly plant in Shanghai. With him on this occasion were several members of China's Commission on Aeronautical Affairs. The Chinese were seeking American advisers to help them build a Chinese air force. Was Chennault interested in heading such a mission? Years later Chennault told a friend his immediate response was "yes," because the prospect seemed new and exciting, while Air Corps life had begun to pale.[38]

Although he had been given the temporary rank of major, his pursuit course was under attack; the bomber advocates had suggested eliminating it from the ACTS curriculum as early as 1933. Only Chennault's reminders of pursuit's valuable role in support of ground forces had saved it thus far. For the school year 1935–36 Chennault was a post officer also assigned as an instructor, while Maj. Byron Gates headed the pursuit section at ACTS. Chennault continued his professional efforts. During the year he published three articles urging defense, for he saw impending danger in the Italian invasion of Ethiopia, the Spanish Civil War, and Japan's increasing encroachment in China.[39] But he realized that his Air Corps career had peaked. He was convinced he was as capable as any of his fellow officers if not more so, yet the system meant he would always be taking orders from those who knew less than he. It galled and hurt and angered him; he began planning to retire in 1937, when he would have completed twenty years of service.[40]

As his physical and emotional health began to show the effects of tension and overwork, he depended ever more heavily on the escape he found in hunting and fishing. The family vacations had always been for him times of great relaxation and fun, even though the children sometimes complained about the steady diet of fish. At Cooter's Point on the Tensas, where the "cooters" (snapping turtles) abounded, he once caught and prepared turtle meat so often that they rebelled, and when he began calling it by a different name each time it was served, the little ones, undeceived, would burst into tears when turtle appeared once more for dinner. The houseboat on which they sometimes spent these summer leaves was named "Who Cares," and two months soaking in this philosophy while fishing the Tensas River in the summer of 1935 revitalized him enough to keep going a while longer. Gradually, however, his spirit seemed to break. He was depressed, burdened by a sense of personal failure, feeling that he had outlived his usefulness to the Air Corps. At home he spoke to Nell of his frustrations at being consistently thwarted in implementing his ideas. He was listless and tired; his blood pressure was low. As a flyer he was grounded, and at night he would sit in bed chain-smoking and brooding, searching for a direction that would give meaning to his life.[41]

Flu, bronchitis, and low blood pressure plagued him throughout the winter. By the summer of 1936, when he took another two-month leave on Lake St. John, his mind had focused on the offer from China. The ties to Franklin Parish were strong, but life there offered him little but a future grubbing cotton, and he wanted much more. Ambition burned in him even more fiercely now than during his youth. He wanted to fly; he wanted to fight; he wanted opportunity to implement his ideas and the possibility of achievement. He wanted enough money to take care of his family and educate his children. And yes, he wanted adventure.

During the months following their first meeting, he quietly negotiated with the Chinese. On 20 July 1936 the Commission on Aeronautical Affairs cabled him that the Chinese government desired his services and accepted his terms. He would have full control of advanced pursuit training with a two-year renewable contract at a salary of $12,000 per year. He would have a determining voice in the selection of any pursuit planes the Chinese purchased; he would draw up the training manuals, textbooks and tactical directives; he would have the cooperation of the Chinese government in organizing an aircraft warning system. The Chinese would pay his transportation to China and back to the United States at the end of his contract. In the event of his death his family would receive insurance in the amount of one year's salary.[42] Convinced that the opportunity would lead to better things, Chennault decided for China. Acceptance had to be conditional on his retirement from the Air Corps, but he notified the Chinese that he thought he could be there by the first of the year 1937.[43]

Even before his final acceptance, Chennault had recruited a nucleus of personnel for the China mission. Williamson and McDonald, at loose ends since the denial of their requests for regular commissions, were his first choices. Others included Sebie Smith and John Holland as mechanics, Rolfe Watson as an armament expert, Sterling Tatum as an instructor. Each man had his own need to make a change, to "get out from under." The salary China would pay ($350 per month plus quarters for mechanics, $550 for instructors) was fantastic compared with what they were earning. All except Chennault were free to leave by mid-1936, and in the late spring they were flown to Washington to conclude negotiations and sign contracts at the Chinese Embassy. The advance group, in expectation that Chennault would come later, sailed in July on *The Empress of Russia*.[44]

Chennault kept his intentions to himself. In July 1936 he was reassigned to the Twentieth Pursuit Group at Barksdale Field in Shreveport. Shortly after reporting there in September he was sent to the General Hospital at Hot Springs. He was in and out of the hospital the remainder of the winter, and when the retirement board met on 25 February 1937, it found him "guilty of most of the ailments common to men of my age and experience." It recommended retirement, which he accepted. Noting that "events of the past six months have not been of such nature as to inspire writing about," he addressed a long letter to his brother William. Perhaps he had been reluctant to convey to others the depth of his own despair, for now he explained a long silence with the words, "The news of the day never seems to coincide with the expectations of the morrow so that, in baffled bewilderment, I delay each writing until, perchance, the high tide of hope may fill to the brim the gauge of desire." "Within the past two years," he wrote, "both the Army and the Air Corps have unmistakably indicated that they each, jointly and severally, could muddle along without my advice and services. While I sincerely believe that the time may come when they will regret our separation, I feel that both pride and honor urge me to cooperate fully in assuring that separation at present."[45]

When news of his retirement began to spread, he was offered, but turned down, other job possibilities, including one with Curtiss-Wright as a demonstration pilot and salesman. He opted for China against the advice of nearly all his friends and acquaintances.[46] To William he explained, "The job may amount to very little except a good paying position but it *may* amount to a great deal, depending upon the course of events in the next few years." He explained that the option was open for a three-month trial before a more definite commitment. If it looked good, he realized that, even "if I live to be a million, I'd never have such an opportunity in this country. Neither would I ever have such a likelihood of trying out [my ideas] in the heat of war."

Chennault's need to achieve, his need to accomplish and prove his worth, stand out in this personal outpouring to his brother as facets of his personality which he acknowledged and understood. Another reason for his decision also stands out, and this he perceived less clearly: China offered a means to assuage the personal frustration with which his Air Corps career was ending. It offered an escape from a sense of failure and inadequacy that he only partially confronted in his own introspections.

"I have given the very best of my thought and effort to my profession," he wrote, and this was true. "Nothing that I have advocated or recommended has been attained," he went on. He took his failure very personally, but he felt a need to place the blame elsewhere, seeing a conspiratorial "they" who were responsible for the fact that "every move I've made has been fought bitterly, and my future career as an officer has been thoroughly blocked."[47] Emotionally blinded by a nagging fear of his own shortcomings, he could not perceive that much of his failure was not personal but rather had resulted from larger circumstances of long-term finance or policy outside his power to influence. There was an element of running away in his decision to go to China, a desire to escape from personal realities he could not, or would not, change. China offered a fresh start. "I felt a compulsion to go," he said twenty years later, "that I couldn't resist."[48]

Admitting that he would miss his Air Corps friends, he nevertheless felt few pangs over leaving the service and awaited the final severance with a sense of relief; it would be "the single act" of the War Department for which he would feel "any sense of obligation."[49]

Nell was strongly opposed, but in this, as in everything else, she supported him without protest or complaint.[50] She was concerned for the children. John was in the Air Corps, Peggy had married, Max was in his third year at Auburn, Charles was graduating from high school and was planning to enter Louisiana Tech. The four youngest children were still at home. Their education was of all-consuming importance to Claire; his concern over how to send all of them through college was one of the primary forces pulling him toward China.

It was not practical, however, for the family to accompany him. Nell chose a house on Lake St. John, near Waterproof and their family and friends in Gilbert. They bought it and Claire moved the family into it in mid-April. Annie Dorty, a black servant who had been with the family for some years, moved with them. It was a modest but comfortable house with a large sleeping porch, and the lake, with cypress trees presiding around the edges, offered good fishing. Claire arranged for the family to receive his retirement pay, and Nell, who was frugal and had a reputation of wanting the value from her dollar, would stretch it by growing a garden and keeping chickens. He made arrangements through the Chinese Embassy and the Chase Manhattan Bank in New York to send her additional money from China.[51]

His retirement orders were issued late in March 1937. When he sent Max his April check ($33) for his expenses at Auburn, he told him that "the day following retirement, I will leave for San Francisco and other points west—but that must still be a secret." On 2 April he received another cable from China asking him to leave "at his earliest date."[52]

On 30 April 1937 Claire Lee Chennault was retired from the U.S. Air Corps "incapacitated for active service on account of disability."[53]

"Time moves on," he wrote William, "cycle upon cycle, and life must find its justification in accomplishment. When an old, well known road is blocked, a new path must be opened. Obedient to the universal law, I am now surveying the outlines of a new life—a life which will have little in common with anything I've known before."[54]

5

The Great Adventure

"Sailed on the Great Adventure at 2:00 P.M. aboard Pres. Garfield."[1]

Writing these words on 8 May 1937, Chennault began a diary which he kept until 23 November 1941. When his work went well, his brief entries were regular, documenting the difficulties and setbacks as well as the progress but imparting an overall tone of confidence and satisfaction. Sometimes frustrations overwhelmed him and he let the diary lapse. He recorded his winnings (and a few losses) at poker, cribbage, or mahjongg. He noted his bank balance, his frequent bouts with colds and bronchitis, his mail from home, important anniversaries. After the newness of his adventure wore off, his entries began to reflect the preoccupation of a lonely man with his social life; they faithfully record the names of people with whom he ate or played cards or spent the evening. His diary was a matter-of-fact record of the external events of his life, punctuated by occasional reflections.

"At last I am in China," he wrote on 31 May, "where I hope to be of service to a people who are struggling to attain national unity and new life." He too was searching for new life, and during the succeeding months China seemed to liberate him, to knock the chip off his shoulder and release the patient, compassionate side of his nature long hidden behind brusque pugnaciousness.

The China he encountered was a vast land in a state of political, economic, and social flux.[2] After the Manchu dynasty was over-thrown in 1911, the various regions withdrew into their particular identities, each led by a warlord who wielded control through a com-bination of military power, a small governing aristocracy, and severe taxation that kept the bulk of the people tied to the land in chronic poverty. Combating this sectionalism, the Kuomintang (National-ists) and Communists each sought national political power; for a de-cade they had warred with bitterness and mutual cruelty.

By 1937 it appeared that unity had almost been achieved by Gen-eralissimo Chiang Kai-shek and the Kuomintang, for only a few war-lords still held out, and the Communists had been driven into a remote area of northern China around Shensi. The unity, however, was tenuous and fragile, a complex structure of compromises, and Chiang Kai-shek knew it. Skilled at political manipulation, he could control the warlords. Mao Tse-tung's Communists, however, were an ideological threat and consequently more serious. Believing that a strong government could not be achieved until the Communists had been destroyed, Chiang saw these "bandits" as his greatest enemies. Therefore when Japan began encroaching on northern China in 1931, Chiang's response had been to surrender Manchuria and to concen-trate on building internal strength.

Japan was not the only foreign power exploiting China's weakness, although most other nations used economic rather than military means. China's coastal cities each had its foreign settlement and its Westernized Bund, the visible symbols of economic control, while gunboats flying the flags of other nations patrolled the mouths of China's rivers. Beneath the unfailing courtesy and unflinching labor of its 450 million citizens, China seethed with a revolution that was only beginning to take form.

Chiang Kai-shek had enlisted the advice of a succession of foreign-ers as he tried to build a modern state on China's ancient foundation. One of the most important for this narrative was an Australian, W. H. Donald, who had lived in China for many years and advised a succession of warlords before joining Chiang in 1934. Believing that China would eventually have to fight for her life against Japan, and realizing that China lacked the industrial base and economy to sus-tain a large modern army, Donald advised Chiang to invest his lim-ited resources in a modern military air force.[3]

The first steps toward a Chinese Air Force had already been made. Early CAF officers studied aviation in Russia or Japan; in 1933 they obtained the guidance of an American mission led by Chennault's Air Corps associate retired colonel John Jouett. The Americans built the Central Aviation School and airbase at Hangchow, but for complex reasons they lost favor and were replaced by an Italian mission in 1935. Some cynical observers concluded that the Italians (and others) were more interested in exploiting China than in helping, since China had no aircraft industry and was a plump market for foreign industry.[4] An international assortment of aircraft company agents flocked to China in pursuit of the sizable sums of money that might be made. The Chinese were often exploited in the resulting competition, while the time-honored Chinese custom of "squeeze" compounded the problem. Before long the Commission on Aeronautical Affairs was suspected of corruption, the air force had divided into warring factions, and all progress had ceased.

At that point Donald had made two recommendations. For the sake of consistency in philosophy and organization, he urged hiring American instructors and advisers; the result was the solicitation of Chennault and his group. To combat internal corruption, Donald persuaded Chiang Kai-shek to appoint Madame Chiang to the newly created post of Secretary General on the CAF's commission.[5]

By birth Madame was Mei-ling Soong, a daughter of Charlie Soong, whose westernized and influential family dominated a generation of China's destiny.[6] Intelligent and capable, with a finely tuned instinct for politics and power, Madame took advantage of her Methodist training and American education both to identify China's weaknesses in comparison with the West and to exploit the West for China's benefit. With Donald as her constant companion and coach, drafting her speeches and letters and guiding her public moves, she assumed leadership of the CAF early in 1937 and began a penetrating investigation of the corruption and malpractice which had hampered it.

Chennault probably knew most of the complex circumstances surrounding the CAF before he arrived in China, for Jouett was a friend with whom he would have talked, as were other members of the first American mission. Little in his past had prepared him, however, for his first meeting with Madame. She was not only quite a few rungs above his accustomed social level, but the women in his experience had tended their hearths rather than making waves in a male-dominated society. On this occasion he was well served by his ingrained indifference to rank or status, a stubborn self-assurance that made him surprisingly at ease across the broad spectrum of society. Madame did not intimidate him. She did impress him, however, and she offered him not only a satisfying job but gratification for the vague, romantic yearnings he had formed as a child. Something deep within him had always been stirred by glory and formality, moved by high moral causes. Madame and China's struggle touched him at a vulnerable point.

She "will hereafter be 'The Princess' to me," he wrote after this first audience with her, as though she had given him a tangible focus for an internalized idealism, much as the princess in the tower had done for the medieval knight. At no time, then or later, did he ever make a secret of his admiration for China's first lady.

Nor was it an entirely one-sided relationship. Eventually the two established an almost intimate rapport, for Madame and her new aviation adviser responded to one another as kindred souls. Perhaps they sensed that they were both fighters, individuals who could be hard in the pursuit of a goal, but there were other factors as well. Madame was beautiful and capable of great charm, although it was her style to command rather than to appeal. Chennault, for his part, derived great pleasure from the company of women, who in turn found him attractive, a man with "vibes," a strong masculine figure who exuded virility yet was capable of great gallantry. The friendship that developed between them was relaxed and easy, marked by mutual personal pleasure as well as professional loyalty and trust.[7] During the next hectic months Chennault spent a few evenings playing cards with Madame and Donald. Sometimes he joined them for tiffin or tea. These occasions he noted in his diary with comments such as "Enjoyed it very much," but not until the summer of 1939 was he sufficiently comfortable with her that he could record, with obvious satisfaction, "Won from Madame at cribbage."

The story is told that at the end of that first meeting, he gave her his eye-flashing grin and drawled, "I reckon you and I will get along all right in building up your air force." Her response, also drawled, was, "I reckon so, Colonel."[8]

The title "colonel" came about because Madame was concerned about his prestige vis-à-vis the Chinese officers. Chennault had retired as a captain, but his work in China required him to deal as an equal with generals. Madame inquired whether he could assume a more prestigious title. It was his first encounter with "face," but he proposed an easy solution. His good friend Jimmy Noe had recently filled out an unexpired term as governor of Louisiana. As a former governor, Noe could appoint him a colonel, a title which, like "judge," was a common honorific in the South. It was as simple as that. From then on he was the Colonel.[9]

In late June Chennault began a three-week, 4,500-mile flying tour to survey and evaluate the Chinese Air Force. He had three companions—McDonald, Smith, and P. Y. Shu, a captain in the CAF assigned to serve as his interpreter. Shu had earned a degree at the University of Michigan. Unlike many of the English-speaking Chinese, he had no difficulty with Chennault's Southern accent. Shu would remain with Chennault for the next twenty years; in part because of his poor hearing, in part because the subtleties of the language posed sobering opportunities for misunderstanding, Chennault made no pretense at learning more than rudimentary Chinese.[10] He may have been influenced by Donald, who believed that foreigners could more effectively guide the sensitive Chinese if they did not speak Chinese, for the Chinese could then maintain privacy and dignity in their presence.[11]

Tingling with excitement, Chennault approached the tour with anticipation. He expected to "get to see lots of new, strange places and people,"[12] he wrote Rosemary, and he was not disappointed. He found the land beautiful, with its wide expanses of green fields and its dramatic rivers and gorges. The farmer in him responded to the beautiful vegetables and fruits. He was impressed by the use of human waste for fertilizer and by the intense cultivation that used every inch of the scarce arable land. He enjoyed being back at the controls of a plane, but he quickly realized that flying in China posed special problems. Not only was the weather subject to violent and sudden changes, but there were few roads, railroads, or recognizable landmarks to facilitate navigation. From the air the picturesque villages and their neatly terraced rice paddies all looked alike. Maps were rare, and his friends noted that he became uncommonly interested in studying the stars.[13]

At the bases he mingled easily with the Chinese officers and their wives, deriving genuine pleasure from the social as well as business gatherings. At Canton he found the primary flying school "laboring under great difficulties but doing good work;" at Hankow the squadron had "practically no equipment." Everywhere facilities were so poor as to be "worthless in war."

War, however, caught up with them at Loyang, where Chennault

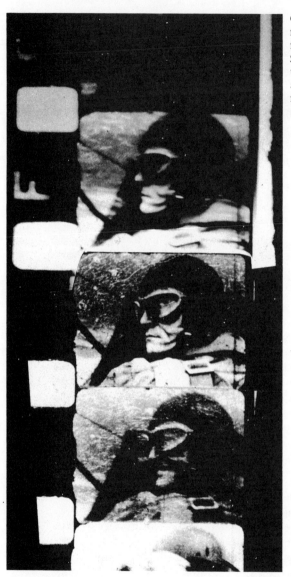

Chennault in open-cockpit
flight, China, 1937. Reproduced
from an 8 mm movie made by
Sebie Smith, who stood up in
the rear cockpit of the
accompanying Douglas BT-2, in
full prop wash, to take the film.
(Photo courtesy Sebie Smith)

Chennault with his interpreter,
P. Y. Shu, China, ca. 1937.
(Photo courtesy Sebie Smith)

and his companions spent the morning of 9 July inspecting the basic flying school run by the Italians. That afternoon they drove out to the Dragon Gate to see the ancient statues of Buddha in the caves; in the evening they attended a Chinese opera. During those hours the Japanese were turning a confrontation at the Marco Polo Bridge into the Sino-Japanese "incident." Upon hearing of the crisis, Chennault conferred with Smith and McDonald and then wired Madame, "offering services in present emergency at Peiping. Rec'd reply thanking us for offer." The commission shortly directed Chennault to report to General Mao P'ang-chu, commanding officer at Nanchang, where Chennault was assigned as adviser and tactical instructor for the bulk of the combat units of the CAF.

This was the opportunity Chennault had hoped for. An observer noted that he was "fired with enthusiasm"[14] as he plunged into China's war and tried to persuade other Americans to join the nucleus that he had already formed. For the next six weeks he worked frantically, giving lectures, critiques, demonstrations. "I'll do what I can to help," he wrote in his diary, but all the negative impressions he had received thus far were daily confirmed as he watched the painful performance of the fledgling air force. In the three fighter groups supposedly ready for combat, only a few pilots had even the minimum flying skills. The Italian mission had graduated everyone, regardless of skill, because this policy kept the face-conscious Chinese happy.

With astounding good humor and a dismaying lack of concern for their own lives, the Chinese pilots ran up an accident and fatality rate that made Chennault shake his head in wonder. Solutions were far from obvious. The cadets were the sons of the upper class. Their classical philosophical education did little to help them become competent airmen; it even compounded the problem by giving them a feeling of superiority to their mechanically oriented American instructors. The cadets had almost no background in mechanics, no experience with nor love for machinery and the operation of it. Practice to gain proficiency was not part of their culture; not only did the admission that they were not perfect involve loss of face, but they saw practice as wasteful. Planes were precious. Why risk crashing one in practice?

Gunnery was agony. Chennault had been leading a bird with a gun for as long as he could remember, but his Chinese gunners had never hunted birds in flight and could not accept the notion of firing ahead of the target. Bombing lessons were fraught with peril, for metal was scarce and the frugal Chinese would run onto the bombing range during practice to collect the exploding fragments. Eagerness to learn did not compensate for their total inexperience with such things as radios, bomb sights, or engineering principles. It was a situation Westerners had to see to understand, if indeed they came to understand at all.

While fuming at the difficulties, Chennault was touched by the Chinese spirit. He had shown intolerance approaching contempt for shortcomings among his American professional associates, yet now he seemed able to accept Chinese limitations with understanding. He refused to be defeated. When he realized that his lectures were not holding his students' interest, he abandoned them for different approaches. He soon had McDonald and Williamson teaching the best of the pilots the fundamentals of fighting in a unit of three planes— one to strike from above, one from below, and one to finish the attack.[15] He himself began what was to be one of his most important contributions to China's cause: refining the aircraft warning net, barely in place by mid-1937, to serve the critical triangle formed by Shanghai, Hangchow, and Nanking.[16] Of necessity China's net was crude, utilizing the existing crank-type telephones and a few radios.

In the weeks immediately following the incident at the Marco Polo Bridge, China and Japan sparred, for both feared Russia's intent and neither wanted a full-scale war with the other. Thus far Chiang had tolerated Japan's encroachments, preferring to use his limited military strength against the Communists. Not all Chinese agreed with his approach: in December of 1936 he had been "kidnapped" and held prisoner until he agreed to form a United Front against Japanese aggression. He had moved slowly in doing so, however, and now the pressure became insistent. Forced to consolidate his internal alignments and to make some critical military decisions, Chiang held a dramatic series of conferences during which Communists and warlords alike pledged their loyalty to his central government for the duration of the struggle against Japan. Armed with this assurance, Chiang now agreed to fight.

Chennault witnessed some of the political process and was deeply moved.[17] On 22 July, Madame summoned him to Nanking, the capital, for two days of meetings. He returned to Nanchang in good spirits, "greatly encouraged by conference with Madame. China cannot be defeated while she leads." He spent the next day in conference with General Mao on war plans and strategy, noting "We are in perfect agreement on both. China has a chance for victory if she doesn't wait too long."

A week later, the last day of July, Chennault's diary records that he and Mao were inspecting the planes of the line when a courier arrived "with secret orders from Nanking. It is War! Units began moving out in P.M."

The entry is significant in terms of the accusations each side made against the other when hostilities actually erupted two weeks later. Also significant are Chennault's moves during those weeks, although his diary gives us only a tantalizing outline. Chiang, forced into a war for which China was ill prepared, had decided that, rather than send his central government armies to reinforce the local troops at Peking, he would force the Japanese to fight him farther south, at Shanghai.[18] The U.S. assistant naval attaché in China, Capt. James M. McHugh, who was an intimate of the Chiang household, later wrote that he and Donald were the only two foreigners who knew that Chiang instigated an incident to precipitate the fighting in Shanghai.[19] The evidence suggests, however, that Chennault was much more than a casual observer.

On 6 August he was in Nanking, where the plan for the initial employment of the CAF was decided upon. The next day CAF units began moving into position to protect Nanking. Chennault noted that he hated to see them go: "Regret interruption of training. These pilots know so little."

On 9 August Madame summoned him to Kukiang, the "City of Nine Rivers" at the base of the mountains that rise some 3,000 feet above the steaming Yangtze valley. In the relative cool at the summit was Kuling, the resort where Chiang had his summer capital. At Kukiang, Chennault, Madame, and Donald had a long conference, after which Madame went on to Kuling but Chennault and Smith stayed overnight in the Chiang's suite on the top floor of the bank. It was Chennault's first encounter with European plumbing, and when Smith enlightened him on the function of a bidet, his reaction was a dumbfounded, "Well I'll be damned."[20]

The morning of 10 August, after Chennault had been joined by General Mao, eight coolies carried the two men up the formidable trail to Kuling in a sedan chair. It was a two-hour trip, followed by "lunch with family" and a meeting with the Generalissimo, who quizzed Mao with crisp abruptness about the combat readiness of the CAF. A sweating Mao answered; Madame translated for Chennault. Mao had received a good aviation background in Russia, and during the preceding weeks at Nanchang he and Chennault had established a comfortable relationship based on their respect for each other as airmen. When Mao informed Chiang that only 87 planes were ready for first-line combat and only 120 in second-line reserve, the Generalissimo exploded, and Mao, threatened with the loss of his head, paled.

Chiang turned to Chennault, who verified Mao's report and went on to elaborate on the unpleasant truths. The policies of the commission had been to keep all planes on the active roster, even though they might have been totally demolished. The planes that actually existed were a hodgepodge of types from half a dozen countries. Despite the efforts and expenditures of the past six years, the Chinese Air Force was small and ill equipped. Its men were untrained for combat; it was not prepared to wage war.[21]

Chiang listened silently. He was a complex man, rooted in Oriental traditions but fascinated by Western nations and envious of their power. In many respects he reflected the tensions of his country, for although he had adopted Western culture in superficial ways, he had never relinquished an intense Chinese pride. Behind a passive and emotionless facade, he could be sharp, quick, cruel, ruthless, stubborn, unstable, and treacherous. He inspired little love, but he had strengths that impressed his countrymen, and he loved China and could rise to heights of greatness in her behalf.[22] Later his weaknesses would seem more obvious, his strengths less important, but Chennault met him at the peak of his popularity and effectiveness as a leader.

Exactly what took place between Chiang and Chennault on this day has not been revealed, but Chennault later told a good friend that, at the end of the discussions, their eyes met for a long, searching look when it seemed to Chennault that Chiang examined every element of his soul. When at last the Generalissimo looked away, a bond of mutual trust had been forged between them. For better or worse, Chennault had committed himself to the Chiangs and their cause.[23]

Emotionally charged, Chennault returned to Kukiang that evening, appearing to Smith "a little excited and afraid the war might be very serious soon."[24] At Madame's request he set off at once for Shanghai, where he arrived at 7:00 A.M. on 11 August. He had been sent to warn the International Settlement that war was imminent, but according to his diary "no one believes it." He met "no welcome" at the fourth Marine Post. He talked to some pilots from China's American-built commercial airline, China National Aviation Corporation, hoping to persuade them to join the CAF. No one was interested. That night as he tried to return to Nanking, his train was commandeered to transport Chinese troops toward the coast.

Since 1932 there had been an uneasy truce and a demilitarized zone
around Shanghai, but now tensions were mounting and the truce was
breaking down. Chinese troops were concentrating near Shanghai.
Since the sixth, when they heard rumors that Nanking had decided
to wage full-scale war, the Japanese had been intensifying their diplomatic efforts to keep the conflict localized in the north. Then, on 9
August, Chinese guards at Shanghai's Hungjao airfield shot a Japanese officer, Omaya, who had driven to the field and, according to
Chinese accounts, tried to force his way in.

Chennault's role in the incident is like a shadow, vague and elusive but inescapable. Three weeks earlier, on 20 July, the chief of staff
of the Japanese Marines stationed at Shanghai had demanded that
the Chinese cease all air force activities over the city. Chennault was
in position to know this. He was in position to know Chiang's wish
to force the Japanese to fight him at Shanghai. He also had the know-
how to implement Chiang's intent behind logical cover. On the
sixth, the day rumor reached the Japanese that China would fight, he
was in Nanking for conferences. He returned to Nanchang that night,
and the following morning instructor Sterling Tatum flew from Nanchang to Shanghai, where his wife was expecting their first child. Accompanied by John Holland, whose wife was also in Shanghai, Tatum flew a Chinese military training plane and landed at Hungjao,
where he was told that he should not have used the field because it
had been closed to military traffic. The damage was done; the men
went on to see about their wives.[25]

On the morning of 9 August, before he left for the conference with
Chiang at Kuling—a conference in which very definite allegiance
was forged—Chennault received a telegram from Tatum saying that
he had a new son.[26] It may have said more, for that was the morning
on which Omaya was shot.

There is a two-day lapse between the landing of Tatum's plane and
the incident itself, but the plane was at the airfield, the Japanese understandably would have felt the need to check it out, and one American remembers hearing Tatum holding his new son and saying, "Just
look what you and I have caused." Holland seems to have been an
innocent participant; he heard nothing of the speculation linking
their flight and the Omaya incident until after he returned to the
United States some weeks later.[27]

One thing we know: on 30 August, two weeks after the fighting at
Shanghai erupted, Chennault received a gift of $10,000 from Chiang
"as appreciation of my services." His diary offers no elaboration

other than "Feel that I haven't earned it due to lack of equipment."
It was quite a large bonus if it was merely for guidance to the CAF
during its first two weeks of war.

In any event, Japan's diplomatic efforts to prevent escalation came
to an abrupt end. The Japanese Navy, more eager to fight than the
army and charged with the defense of Japanese interests at Shanghai,
called for reinforcements. Chiang Kai-shek rebuffed efforts to negotiate the mounting crisis. He had made his decision to resist by the
end of July, as Chennault's diary reveals. His troops were in position.
Following sporadic fighting on 13 August, during which some Japanese shells fell on Shanghai, the Generalissimo ordered the Chinese
Air Force to retaliate by attacking the Japanese at Shanghai the following morning.

With war upon them, the CAF confronted a horrendous void in
personnel. There were no officers with combat experience; responsibility fell on Chennault by default. Although he had been brought to
China as a pursuit expert, he was now propelled into a far broader
role. He was not surprised. Before leaving the States he had written William he was "confident that they are hiring me to prepare
them to whip H—— out of Japan in a couple of years," and consequently "it is even possible that my 'feeble' efforts may influence history for some few hundreds of years."[28] He had anticipated much
more time to build a fighting force, however, and now he knew he
had almost nothing with which to work. Nevertheless he plunged in.
He and McDonald drew up plans for the next day's mission, which
his diary noted as "very poor." The Chinese pilots had been given a
plan too difficult for them to execute, and their bombs, intended for
the Japanese headquarters ship *Idzuma*, fell short and dropped in the
International Settlement, causing considerable loss of life and property. Despite their blunder, 14 August became Chinese Air Force Day
in recognition of the CAF's first real combat mission.

The following day, a Sunday, the Japanese bombed Nanking. Only
in Spain had extensive aerial bombardment of cities been used in
warfare, and to some observers it was still inconceivable. After the
air raids became more common, Chennault frequently stayed in the
open during them to study the Japanese planes and tactics. Although
he admitted privately that this was the only thing that ever made
him fearful, he defied the danger for the sake of learning. [29] At this
first personal experience of bombardment, however, he ran for shelter along with the others. Smith, running behind him with his movie
camera grinding away, captured a rare moment on film.

Those first days of war set the pattern for subsequent weeks. The crowded Chinese cities, with their highly flammable construction, were a primary target for the Japanese Air Force. During the 1930s the advocates of bombardment had theorized that civilian morale could not withstand bombardment, hence wars utilizing it would end quickly. The Chinese proved them wrong. As the raids intensified, they suffered and endured, burying their casualties and learning to live in the rubble and to seek shelter when the dreaded planes came. The Americans who shared their ordeal sensed that the Chinese became morally stronger and more united under the Japanese onslaught. It was as though they surmounted their tragedy by spiritual endurance and a stoic patience that seemed to lie at the very heart of the Chinese character. The Chinese might die, but the life of China would go on.

Chennault conferred with the Chiangs nightly once war had begun, and on 1 September Chiang gave him responsibility for all training and operations of the Chinese Air Force.[30] The next day he drew up training programs for pursuit pilots at Nanking and Anking, for bomber crews at Hankow, and for gunners at Ichang. The following day he initiated night flying and dive-bombing practice. With Madame's backing, he worked to have the turf airfields hard surfaced—a time-consuming, back-breaking task performed by thousands of coolies by hand—so that all aerial operations would not be stopped by the mud when it rained. He also looked beyond the fall of Nanking and set in motion the construction of dozens of airfields in China's interior. During succeeding weeks he sometimes called a halt in operations until more training could be accomplished, noting that the Chinese pilots "lack the proper background" and are "very inconsistent."

Nevertheless he soon began to pierce Japanese invincibility. The "Jap bombers use very poor tactics," he observed. "Come over in small units, ragged formation." Using one-on-one instruction, Chennault began teaching the Chinese pilots to regard the Japanese bombers as "easy meat for pursuit." He himself served as the control officer in Nanking's aerial defense. He and Henry C. Y. Lee, a CAF officer serving as interpreter and liaison, managed to put one radio in every third Chinese fighter. All available information from the steadily expanding warning net came into a central control room, where it was plotted on a map with concentric circles. Studying the information, Chennault radioed his instructions to Lee, stationed atop a nearby mountain, and Lee relayed them in Chinese to the pilots.[31]

Chennault saw the warning net as crucial and kept working on it. He stressed the importance of regular reporting and complete information so that the CAF could "obtain, evaluate and act upon intelligence in such time limits as to prevent the enemy from reaching his objective." He and General Wang Chen-chou, in charge of antiaircraft defenses, cooperated in arranging a grid of searchlights to blind the Japanese pilots bombing by night at the same time that it spotlighted the bombers for Chinese fighters waiting at lower altitudes.[32]

Japanese losses began to mount. By mid-September Japan found it necessary to send fighters on the bombing missions to take care of the Chinese defense. Chennault recorded that their first escorted bombing mission cost the Chinese "5 Hawks, 2 Boeings, and 2 Fiats—over 50% of our pursuit," but the next night "Chinese pursuit, acting under my instructions, avoided combat with pursuit and shot down 3 light bombers."

Chennault could not resist the temptation to write an exaggerated "I told you so" to some of his Air Corps friends, and in later years he seems to have convinced himself that his exaggerations were true. In mid-September 1937 he wrote Hansell that the CAF had been so effective that since 26 August the Japanese "haven't been near Nanking with any kind of plane, day or night."[33] Although this statement is essentially substantiated by his own diary as well as by Smith's, Chennault later enlarged upon it to claim that the Japanese did not bomb Nanking for the six weeks prior to mid-October. The larger assertion was not accurate. Between 19 September and 15 October Smith's diary recorded nine Japanese raids over Nanking, and Chennault's diary also recorded damaging raids.[34] On 16 October he even wrote, in despair, "Am greatly discouraged over my inability to hit the Japs. Every plan is upset by lack of training, indifference or stupidity of Ch. pilots and mechanics."

If this were the only episode involving a story that became better with the telling, it would be both inconsequential and easily understood. Unfortunately there were to be others, cases in which numbers grew, in which interpretations were contrary to prevailing opinion. Sometimes he succumbed to the temptation to inflate his successes. At other times he was simply careless about figures and allowed emotional memories to soften the less favorable reality. The tendency hurt him, for he lost credibility with individuals who could have advanced his cause and might have helped him achieve the success he sought.

Chennault later reflected that the air fighting per se was not very important in this first stage of China's war but the lessons in doctrine were very important indeed.[35] In the skies over China, he watched the combat answer to many of the bitter arguments that had been held at ACTS: offensive bombers did need fighter protection; with warning, defensive pursuit could offer effective opposition; bombardment did not bring an immediate end to resistance. Convinced that the United States would eventually have to fight Japan and that this information would be helpful, Chennault began compiling serious and thoughtful reports for Washington and helping Naval Attaché McHugh to do the same.

The U.S. government's primary concern in 1937, however, was to stay out of the growing war. Partly for their own safety, partly to avoid precipitating an international incident, it wanted its citizens out of China. There were approximately 8,000 Americans in China in fall 1937, most of them missionaries or businessmen but a sizable number directly or indirectly involved with China's military effort. Cordell Hull's State Department had never approved of Americans' taking part in China's military affairs; periodically it made official statements saying so. Yet starting with the Jouett mission and continuing through the group associated with Chennault, the department had issued the men passports and allowed them to proceed, because the Commerce and War departments were eager to have them go. A growing Chinese Air Force meant more sales for the U.S. aircraft industry, and during the depression foreign sales were needed to keep the industry healthy. The situation embodied typical ambiguities in the U.S. relationship toward China, for behind the somewhat emotional illusion that America was China's champion and protector, U.S. foreign policy pursued its own self-interest, essentially unchanged since the turn of the century, when Theodore Roosevelt had acknowledged that Japan's interests in China were vital, while those of the United States were not. China's integrity was desired, but it was not sufficiently critical to justify war in her defense. U.S. policy toward the Far East consequently sought a subtle balance—discourage Japanese aggression and encourage Chinese resistance, but do neither to the point of war.

Confronted with the rising tension of 1937, the State Department first decided that future passports should be stamped "not valid for travel to or in any foreign state in connection with entrance into or service in foreign military or naval forces." Later, after Consul General Clarence Gauss inquired specifically about the role of the American aviation instructors already in China, Hull responded that such activities did "reasonably come within the purview" of U.S. statutes. Foreign Office officials began urging Americans to leave, and those who elected to stay after being offered evacuation were warned that they did so at their own risk. Williamson and several other members of Chennault's group terminated their contracts and went home.[36]

Chennault elected to stay. He kept quiet and tried to be inconspicuous. Telling companions that he had already had enough trouble, he would cross the street to avoid meeting State Department officials. To other Westerners in China his manner appeared courtly and gracious, but they also noted that he was guarded and close-mouthed, that he kept to himself, was seldom seen in foreign circles, and had few close friends. On the rare occasions when he talked, others listened intently, as though compelled by some strange dignity in his bearing. He seemed to live within himself. Agnes Smedley, a writer who met him during this time, shared a pleasant tearoom lunch with him but found herself irritated that she could not "get at him," could not fathom what went on behind his "grave, appealing exterior."[37] He continued to receive warnings.

It was well known that he was trying to recruit additional Americans to come to China to help the CAF. The State Department went to great lengths to prevent them from entering China. Madame protested that this itself was "unneutral," but the department held its ground. Chennault's diary makes no mention of the issue until 21 September, when he made the cryptic entry, "All Am. ordered to evacuate. Guess I am Chinese."

He continued to be discreet but in no way apologized for his actions. He kept up with home news through a subscription to the *Montgomery Advertiser*, and when it reported that he was fighting for China under an assumed name, he responded with his old vociferousness. "China is now fighting the war of all the Pacific nations," he wrote the paper. He had "no apologies to offer" for his prior service to the United States or his present service to China.[38] The heat of his reaction suggests he was not as doubt free as he wanted others to believe.

Chennault sensed his growing entanglement with China, was concerned about it, and on several occasions tried to extricate himself. On 16 August he wrote Madame the first of many letters of resignation, a practice that may have reflected moments of deep discouragement or possibly was a strategem learned from Donald, who tutored Chennault in ways to manage the Chinese and on at least one occasion advised him to resign to force a decision.[39] In this first formal resignation, Chennault wrote, "Because of conditions which make it impossible for me to work efficiently and effectively, I feel it to be my duty to request my dismissal from service with the Central Government." He told her the CAF had able leaders, its pilots had "demonstrated their courage and ability in unmistakable and glorious manner," and he himself had proven his loyalty. He requested permission to return to his native country.[40]

Madame persuaded him to stay, apparently by promising to effect some changes. What did he need? He supplied a list, and a few days later she sent him the plans and budget which she was presenting to the commission for the motor transport, airfields, and equipment he had specified.[41] She also took steps to improve his living conditions, for the Americans had been staying at Nanking's Metropole Hotel, where constant bedlam was conducive to neither work nor rest. She arranged for them to move temporarily into the home of her brother-in-law, H. H. Kung, who was China's Minister of Finance and at that time in the United States. Donald also had a room there, and the Chiang house was only a quarter of a mile away. Chennault found the house "beautiful & cool," but because it was white it showed up well at night and made a good target for Japanese bombers. After a near miss the Chinese camouflaged it with black splotches.[42]

The fighting during those first months of the war was intense and cruel, the bloodiest of the long war. Chiang committed his best German-trained armies at Shanghai, and they fought well. For several weeks they were able to hold the Japanese at bay, but the Japanese had heavy gun support from their ships in the Whangpoo River as well as control of the air. The casualties mounted. The Chinese held their ground. Not until November, when Japanese reinforcements landed to outflank them, did the Chinese lines collapse. Withdrawal was not ordered early enough to save the troops; their retreat under fire was bitter and costly; the elite core of China's army sustained enormous losses and was decimated as an effective body.

Any portion of China's wealth that could be uprooted began a mass exodus away from the coastal areas in search of safety in the distant, isolated interior. Universities packed up and headed toward remote Szechwan or Yunnan, students and professors alike on foot, carrying their belongings on poles over their shoulders or pushing them in a wheelbarrow. Factories were dismantled, their machinery packed into railway cars or onto river barges for the long trip up the Yangtze. Railroads, roads, rivers, and trails came alive with refugees as millions of Chinese fled the guns and the bombs in the largest mass exodus the world had yet seen.

As China's essential self withdrew out of harm's way, Chinese soldiers prepared to defend Nanking. Sensing that they were being lured a further 200 miles into this intractable land, the Japanese felt a growing sense of desperation to complete their conquest. While the Japanese armies moved upriver toward Nanking, their air forces pounded every Chinese city within their reach. "Canton is being massacred piecemeal,"[43] Donald wrote Chennault, but there was little the latter could do. His diary reflects a growing frustration and sense of helplessness.

"I seem to be only aviator desirous of operating against Japs," he wrote in despair. Interpreter Shu quickly learned the telltale signs of anger, for when Chennault pursed his lips and worked his jaw as though chewing, it was best to keep out of his way. But he "never got angry on the outside, only on the inside,"[44] and after Chinese pilots bombed the U.S. Dollar Line's *President Hoover* in a galling fiasco, he was able to persuade Chiang not to execute the commander. Already he had come to accept the reality that China imposed her own imperatives on foreign institutions, but in this small way he was able to start a slow reversal of the Chinese custom of rewarding failure with execution, a tradition which had kept the ranks of experienced officers small and, naturally enough, had discouraged initiative.

Early in September Chennault and his assistants moved from Kung's house to a cottage on Purple Mountain above the Nanking Country Club. The cottage became their informal headquarters, with staff meetings held over the breakfast table. When the evenings were quiet, they relaxed with Ping-Pong or cards. His companions quickly realized that he could not hear approaching shells and needed cues from them if they needed to take cover. From their front porch they could watch the Japanese raids over the city and airport below them, and sometimes Chiang Kai-shek and Madame sat with them. Madame had endeared herself to the Americans in China by her spunk, her ability to put them at ease in her presence, and her hard work on behalf of the air force. They observed that, while she sometimes wept as they watched their capital being torn to bits, Chiang did not flinch. His face remained devoid of readable expression.[45]

It was early November when the Chinese evacuated Shanghai. Shortly afterward it became apparent that Nanking would also fall, for precious little stood between the Japanese bombers and China's capital. At one point Chennault noted, "We are down to 5 Hawks and 2 Boeing P-26s." Chiang Kai-shek began moving the capital to Chungking, an ancient, walled city perched on a cliff at the conflu-

ence of the Yangtze and Chialing rivers in Szechwan. As far back as
the thirteenth century Szechwan had been the center for China's resistance to foreign enemies—at that time the Mongols—and when
Chiang had surveyed his country in 1935 to formulate his long-term
plans for victory, he had concluded that, if China could retain Szechwan, Kweichow, and Yunnan, it could eventually defeat its enemies
and complete its revolution.[46] Larger than France, a rural province
where harvests were plentiful but modern conveniences rare, Szechwan was separated from the coastal provinces by high mountains and
the formidable gorges of the Yangtze. Surely there, where the winter
clouds and fog were so pervasive that the dogs were said to bark in
fright if the sun shone, China's government could find protection
from the Japanese bombers.

But Chiang would defend Nanking to destruction before he left.
Chennault disagreed with his decision, for he saw little to be gained.
He may have tried to dissuade the Generalissimo. If so he got nowhere. "Japs are getting close but the Leader insists on staying here,"
was his wry diary entry on 29 November. Chennault himself left
Nanking on 5 December, just before the conquering Japanese Army
began the three-week rampage of murder, torture, and pillage that
made it barbaric in the eyes of the rest of the world.

During the Rape of Nanking, Chennault was busy between Nanchang and the new military headquarters at Hankow, regrouping the
pitiful remnants of the CAF and laying plans for Hankow's defense.
The prospects were grim. China had now lost nearly all of its important centers of commerce and industry, culture and political power.
Cut off from the coast, the nation would also be cut off from the rest
of the world; little remained with which to fight. Chennault reported
to the United States that Japanese pursuit was superior, that the Japanese I-97 "climbs like a sky rocket and maneuvers like a squirrel,"
while the Japanese pilots "I see in combat are *good*."[47]

Frustrated at lacking the means to fight, Chennault found his spirits tumbling when the weather turned cold and rainy at the end of
December. He took a cold that worsened into pleurisy, and he spent
a "lonely X-mas eve." On Christmas day he gave the CAF staff a box
of cigars. The men reciprocated with a box of sweet oranges. His
pleurisy lingered. Chennault stayed in his hotel room until the boredom became unbearable. By the thirty-first he felt better, and as he
reflected on the preceding months, he concluded that the year "has
been good to me in many ways. Perhaps next year will bring us victory and peace. New Year's Eve very quiet in this dark, near deserted

city. I feel for the poor Chinese who have been the victims of this war." On New Year's Day 1938 he moved to Hankow, had lunch with Madame and Donald, and with rising spirits once more plunged into the seemingly hopeless struggle.

Hankow was the largest of the Wuhan cities, the chief river port and commercial center for the Yangtze valley. Its atmosphere in early 1938 was exhilarating. Chiang and Madame were there and had become symbols of resistance and courage that *Time* magazine acknowledged by naming them man and woman of the year 1937. The wide paved streets bustled with parades, marching soldiers, and patriotic citizens; banners, slogans, bugles, and shouting filled the air; the river was full of traffic. Later, as the battle of Hankow progressed and destruction mounted, an American missionary found his first impression of a "horrible, miserable city" reinforced, for the administration gradually deteriorated, the Yangtze flooded, a cholera epidemic raged, the great flow of refugees grew ever more pitiful, and the suffering army, poorly led and improperly cared for, gradually lost its will to fight. But early in 1938 there was still hope, still a spirit of patriotic resistance, and to the missionary the atmosphere "wasn't just martial; it was giddy."[48]

The accounts of China's struggle (not always objective or accurate) aroused tremendous emotional support for the Chinese, but the Western nations remained neutral. In his quarantine speech on 5 October 1937, President Roosevelt deplored "world lawlessness" and stated that there "must be positive endeavors to preserve peace," but no positive endeavors seemed to follow. Even when the Japanese bombed and sank the U.S. gunboat *Panay*, killing two and wounding thirty, the United States was content to protest and insist on reparations.

Only the U.S.S.R., deeming support of China to be enlightened self-interest, intervened militarily on China's behalf. Starting in August 1937 with a Sino-Soviet non-aggression pact, Russia extended China substantial financial credits, made every effort to supply planes and other military equipment, sent a military mission headed by Generals Georgi Zhukov and Vassili Chuikov (later heroes of Berlin and Stalingrad) to help China develop her army, and dispatched entire units of the Soviet Air Force into China to fight alongside the CAF.

Russian squadrons fought over Shanghai and Nanking in the fall of 1937; by early 1938 Russia had in China seven squadrons of fighters plus five squadrons of light bombers. Under the command of General Asanov, they flew independent missions against the Japanese. The

Russian airmen maintained a low profile and iron discipline. Tough looking, serious-minded individuals, often with shaved heads, they said little to anyone and scrupulously avoided the bars and night spots. Chennault recognized that they were formidable fighters, but he thought they displayed little individual initiative, and he sometimes lost patience with them. "Russians have quit fighting and gone to dodging," he recorded in his diary in disgust just before the fall of Nanking. Nevertheless, after the first few months of the war little of the Chinese Air Force remained. Aerial resistance from early 1938 on lay almost entirely in Russia's hands.[49]

China tried to build a mercenary air force by recruiting and hiring foreign aviators. As the motley collection of airmen began to drift into Hankow, it became obvious that very few of them had military training or experience. A few had fought as mercenaries in Spain. Others were cow pasture barnstormers who flew by the seat of their pants and knew little of combat discipline. Some could hardly fly at all. One was a "crackerjack pilot, but a screwball and a fool."[50] Most of them were misfits. Hankow's Dump Street, a gaudy night district of dance clubs, prostitutes, dope peddlers, cheap whiskey, and foreign spies, quickly became unofficial headquarters for these aviators.

Trying to figure out how to use them to China's advantage, Chennault recommended that those with the best backgrounds be sent to the training centers as instructors. Others he channeled to the Fourteenth International Squadron, taking shape in Hankow under an American named Vincent Schmidt, "an excitable kind of a guy"[51] who had fought in Mexico, Spain, and Ethiopia and who after a year in China would go on to fight for Finland. The Fourteenth Squadron was equipped with thirty Vultee V-11 bombers that William Pawley had been able to get for China. During the winter and early spring of 1937–38 Chennault supervised its training and missions. The men were paid a bonus of $1,000 gold for every Japanese plane they shot down, but their loyalties were not to China, and their independence made them difficult to handle. They continued to spend much time on Dump Street, and Madame Chiang Kai-shek, displaying either a touching naivete or a highly refined sense of humor, made it a habit to visit them to deliver an uplifting sermon and pep talk on Sunday mornings, when hangovers tended to be worse.[52]

Eventually the Chinese airmen rebelled at working with the foreigners, and the foreigners themselves began objecting to their assignments. After an attempt to "straighten them out," Chennault indulged in a terse "Darn them all" and concluded that both commission and foreigners had "everything balled up for fair." On 7 March the commission formally announced that the squadron had been disbanded "in the interest of homogeneity"; the group had failed to meet expectations because of "loose discipline, carelessness regarding military secrets and lack of experience of some members."[53] A few remained to serve as instructors or private pilots, but most of them left China.

Sometime during the first months of the Sino-Japanese War, Chennault, in the center of the crisis and alone in the sense that he, more than anyone else, had the skills China so desperately needed, began very quietly to fight the Japanese as a combat pilot rather than merely an adviser. Much of the world had responded with indignation and horror to the aerial assaults on defenseless Chinese civilians, shuddering as it read of mutilated bodies in the rivers, of bloody streets strewn with torsos and arms and legs, or of Japanese soldiers who burned cigars into the foreheads of their prisoners. Chennault was closer to it than most. During one Nanking raid a Japanese bomber crashed into a Chinese house, and when Chennault reached the scene he found the man weeping beside the bodies of his dead wife and children, unable to understand how it could have happened "with all the doors and windows locked."[54] The innocence and helplessness of this man and countless others who endured terrible misfortunes with dignity outraged him. The children in particular touched him; he contributed regularly and generously to the relief funds for their care. He was infuriated that the Japanese bombed undefended towns and railways, "using Ch. insignia sometimes." His ingrained sense of a simple and harsh morality—an eye for an eye and a tooth for a tooth—was stirred by China's suffering. This was why men fight, and he was trained to fight.

The story can be only partially reconstructed. In July 1937 Madame obtained for his use a Curtiss Hawk 75 Special, an early demonstrator model of the later P-36. It was his personal plane, although it was also flown by McDonald and a few others. Initially Chennault used it for reconnaissance, to watch Japanese movements and dispositions. After returning to base one day with bullet holes in the plane, he made it clear he wanted guns installed and kept in good working order.[55]

He also used the Hawk as a teaching aide. When the Chinese pilots went up to practice, he sometimes flew with them to demonstrate. When they began flying combat missions, he flew above or behind them, in position to observe and thus better to instruct them in combat tactics. He flew alone, and China's skies are vast. There was some speculation about a mysterious single plane sometimes seen in critical places, but who could know the pilot's identity? On one occasion during the battle of Nanking, Chennault broke up a large formation of Japanese bombers in full view of the city, later telling Naval Attaché McHugh, with whom he worked in close confidence, that he had shot down several on his way home.[56]

He said little to anyone, then or later, of his actions, and many who knew him well are convinced he never flew in combat, although rumors of his doings reached his Air Corps friends back home. Flyers are a distinctive brotherhood; they stick together and when necessary keep silent. There were extremely practical reasons to keep any combat activity quiet: the United States was trying valiantly to maintain its neutrality, and as a violation of U.S. statutes and War Department regulations, combat would render its practitioners liable to prosecution, possibly including loss of retired officer status and pay.

McDonald, about whose combat flying there was more open speculation and joking, was one of the few people whom Chennault took into his confidence. The two made a pact never to talk with anyone else about what happened in combat, and to his death McDonald honored the agreement. He admitted to some close associates, however, that "he understood" Chennault had "made a few claims and collected on them."[57]

Chennault also promised Madame not to divulge his unofficial activities, and it was part of his code that a gentleman kept a promise given to a lady.[58] He avoided discussion of the subject except among his most intimate friends. He was urged to divulge the details when writing his memoirs, but he refused, although the veiled allusions are numerous. When close associate Joseph Alsop wrote in *The Saturday Evening Post* in 1950 that Chennault's score stood above forty Japanese aircraft knocked down in combat but he had "always been exceedingly secretive about his doings as a soldier of fortune," the writer received a long letter from Chennault expressing extreme irritation and enumerating the very practical reasons for secrecy. "I shall continue to deny any connection with combat activities throughout my retired service in China," he wrote.[59] He was as good as his word. In taped interviews made shortly before his death, he stubbornly refused to be tricked into a definite statement, although he came close. "They paid me what they said it was worth—and I didn't talk about it," he acknowledged, adding, "I didn't teach any-

thing [to the later Flying Tigers] that I didn't know."[60] But in none of
his writings or public utterances did he ever claim to have shot down
an enemy plane.

Part of the reason, of course, was that he was indeed sensitive to
the "soldier of fortune" image. The stereotype of the mercenary is
that of an international adventurer who exploits the trouble of others for personal profit, and Chennault placed his efforts in China on
a much higher plane. He once told his brother Joe, "They can call me
a mercenary if they want to," reflecting that far from feeling apolo-
getic for his actions, he was incredulous that so few people seemed to
understand or to be alert to the creeping danger in Japan's aggression.[61] Believing in the rightness of what he was doing, convinced the
cause was just, he could accept pay without personal compunction.
The absence of guilt, however, could not quite compensate for pride
that was pricked by a negative image. It was better to keep quiet and
let people speculate.

6

China Crossroads

Chennault's diary for the first half of 1938 is spotty, with no entries for weeks at a time. Plagued by an acute shortage of planes—at one time the Chinese were reduced to three bombers—he could neither train nor fight, and the onset of the rainy season further hindered activity. "We bomb Japs on Tuesdays and Fridays and they bomb us on Mondays and Thursdays," he noted dryly. Nevertheless what he called the first victory for Chinese pursuit took place on 18 February, when the Chinese challenged an escorted Japanese raid and held their own losses to eight while downing nine of the Japanese.[1]

Scheming and plotting brought a few dramatic successes. Speculating that the Japanese would conduct a large raid on Emperor Hirohito's birthday, he persuaded the Russians and the Chinese to fly a combined mission, which he planned with great care. By assembling almost all the planes in China, he was able to form a respectable Chinese force of sixty-five fighters. His hunch about Japanese intentions proved correct; they attacked on 29 April with fifteen bombers escorted by twenty-four pursuits (at a press conference in 1945, shortly before he left China, Chennault nearly doubled the Japanese force to twenty-seven bombers and forty fighters, but fifteen and

89

twenty-four is what he recorded in his diary at the time).[2] The warning net worked perfectly; it provided the needed margin of time to get the defending forces into position.

The Chinese engaged the Japanese over Hankow and forced them to expend fuel reserves in maneuver. When the Japanese turned back, they were ambushed by the larger force of Russians, poised to intercept. With insufficient fuel to maneuver or escape, the Japanese lost heavily: twenty-one planes were shot down in the area. According to intelligence reports, only six of the Japanese returned safely to their base. Chennault's report to Washington, which carefully refrained from implying that he had any direct involvement with CAF operations, called this "the most decisive defeat of the Japanese to date." He warned, however, that "the war isn't won yet by any means . . . [the Chinese] become over-confident and careless after a little success. They simply refuse to follow up an advantage, preferring to wait for the enemy to come to them." He also noted "the ineptitude of the Chinese pilots and their failure to assimilate instruction," factors that resulted in high plane losses from accidents.[3]

The training problem was much on his mind, for late in February he was asked to take charge of the CAF training schools. These had been relocated to the remote southwestern provinces of Kwangsi and Yunnan, out of Japanese reach; the primary and basic schools were at Liuchow, the advanced school at Kunming. Chennault was reluctant to accept, for several reasons. Training fields and facilities were marginal, while there were too few planes and an acute shortage of qualified instructors. In addition, Chiang Kai-shek, desperate for military strength and not understanding that time was required to produce skilled pilots, had ordered a thousand pilots to be turned out at the earliest possible date and had specified that no more than 10 percent of any class might be washed out.

The main thing Chennault could not stomach, however, was the corruption and political climate in the Commission on Aeronautical Affairs and the CAF high command. More serious than salesmen slipping money into the right hands as a privilege for doing business—a custom that had been accepted in China for years—was inept CAF leadership, a problem Chiang could not—or would not—correct.[4] When Chennault urged him to take drastic measures against incompetence and corruption, the Generalissimo replied that the Chinese were the only people he had to work with, and if he got rid of all those who were at fault, who would be left?[5] Against the advice of Chennault, Donald, and Madame, he kept his loyal supporter General Chou Chih-jou as head of a commission torn apart by internal rivalry.

In February Madame resigned as secretary general, ostensibly on the grounds of ill health but in reality because of an impasse over the investigation of corruption she and Donald had undertaken with such enthusiasm the preceding year.[6] Although it had aroused untold anger and resentment and had sent one figure in the drama to jail, the evidence in general was inconclusive and brought no marked improvement. When Madame resigned, Chiang gave her brother, T. V. Soong, complete charge of the troubled Chinese Air Force. Soong was an able man—so able, in fact, that he eventually amassed one of the most impressive personal fortunes in the world. He had neither liking nor respect for his brother-in-law, however, and Chiang, though needing Soong's talents, seemed afraid to let him stay in positions of responsibility for very long at a time. Nevertheless Soong accepted the challenge of the CAF, reorganized the commission, abolished the position of chief, and named General Chien Ta-chun, an army officer with no aviation experience, as director. Chennault thought this accomplished little. The muddle grew when Chiang intervened over Soong's head to appoint his loyal friend Chou as head of the training schools. An angry Soong dumped the problems back in Chiang's lap and left for an extended trip to Hong Kong.[7]

Chennault had little patience with politics, which seemed to him only to stand in the way of doing what needed to be done. He wanted no part in the training program until the internal feud had been settled. He stayed in Hankow and tried to work through the commission to correct the deficiencies and eliminate the stumbling blocks encountered by McDonald, who went to Kunming to work with the schools. Chou insisted, for instance, that the Chinese use a complicated phonetic code instead of the simpler Morse code signals in their radio exchanges. Even if the poor pilot were able to learn the phonetic code, he had no time to use it if a crisis arose. As a result the radios in the planes were essentially useless.[8]

The evidence began to mount, however, that the commission resented Chennault's control of the CAF and wanted to oust him. Talk became common that Chennault knew little about bombardment or about an air force as a whole. Any effectiveness he might have had was negated by evasion, indirection, or misunderstanding or simply by actions that conflicted with his advice. Power within the commission increasingly went to General Mao, who spoke Russian and was the liaison officer between China and the U.S.S.R. Mao's idea was to eliminate all foreign advisers as well as political interference by interposing the air force command between Chiang and the Russians, who continued to be China's primary source of military support.[9]

Donald had warned Chennault that Mao would pursue his own ends, but Chennault had naively retained his respect for his fellow aviator. Now, however, he concluded that the CAF was not making progress and he himself was no longer of any value to the Chinese cause. Disgusted, he decided it was time to go home. He wrote Donald, enclosing his monthly contribution to the children's refugee program, and explained his conclusions. Donald talked it over with Madame and responded in agreement, saying, "You can get no mental or moral comfort from hanging on just to draw pay."[10] On 6 June Chennault sent Soong his resignation.

Soong's initial reaction was to accept it, but before answering Chennault he carefully investigated the situation in the training schools. After the observers he sent to Kunming and Liuchow had spoken in support of Chennault, Soong asked him to stay.[11]

Physically ill as well as disheartened, Chennault wrestled with his decision. The Japanese were advancing rapidly. The battle for Hankow had begun, its outcome never in doubt. The Chinese Army was no match for the Japanese on the ground, and he estimated that the Japanese had more than 1,000 planes active in China, opposed by no more than 125. Chinese pilots had improved but still "lack aggressiveness." Airfields had been prepared in the interior for use after Hankow fell, but he knew—and warned Washington—that their effectiveness would be limited because communications deep in China "are slow and unreliable."[12]

When Smith and Watson visited to tell him they were going back to the States, they found him depressed and uncertain what he was going to do. There was some vague talk about his serving as an aviation adviser in Egypt.[13] He had written the War Department offering to return to active duty, for he felt he had learned a great deal that would be useful to the U.S. Air Corps. The answer was no.

Resentments and painful memories were rekindled. He sought to push them into the background by going to the American celebration at Hankow's International Club on 4 July. Vice-Consul John Davies introduced him to Paul Frillmann, a Lutheran missionary, who saw him as playing a role, wearing the traditional aviator's leather jacket with long white scarf and surrounded by an admiring group of "international hangers-on," the misfits and adventurers inevitably found in any foreign community. Chennault pitched one inning in the traditional softball game, although he was running a fever. Frillmann played left field. He was amused to see that, despite the "flourishes, wind-ups, spitting on leather, and all the rest," the opposition hit him. When Frillmann missed a fly and Chennault sent a dark glare his way, the missionary concluded that his fellow American was a "lousy pitcher, and a vain one." Chennault's own diary entry was a terse, "No runs."[14]

Sometime during those weeks Soong told the commission he would tolerate no further interference with Chennault in the exercise of his duties, and Chennault agreed to stay.[15] He moved to Kunming in early July. He flew by way of Hong Kong and took time there to fill a long shopping list that included malarial drugs, aspirin, laxatives, toothpaste, shaving cream, film, socks, ties, handkerchiefs and six cartons of Camel cigarettes, his favorites.[16]

"Kunming is way down in southwest China," he wrote Rosemary on 24 August, "about 6,000 feet above sea level with higher mountains all around—about ten miles away. It is near a very large lake on which thousands of people live all their lives in sampans and small junks. Boys and girls are born and grow up to live and die on these boats, never having any other home. They have no school and they never go more than ten miles from their lake. They have no radios and they can't read so they know nothing about the world except such rumors as they hear."[17]

Yunnan province had been China's Siberia, a place of exile for undesirables. Most of its citizens were primitive and backward; their isolation, here at the edge of the Himalayas, was extreme. Yet Kunming (the old name, Yunnan-fu, "South of the Clouds") lay in a beautiful area, rich and fertile, laced with a network of aqueducts contained between wide parallel embankments where the spruce trees grew in stately rows. Ancient temples and huge moss-covered trees dotted the surrounding hills, for the town dated from the Ming dynasty of the fourteenth century. In many respects it had changed little in intervening years.

Kunming's natural beauty was marred, Chennault wrote, because "nearly all the natives smoke opium and opium smokers are always lazy and dirty." The city was built in old Chinese style, which meant a wall with gates, houses of plastered mud bricks and mud tile roofs, and "narrow, dirty and rough" streets. The war was bringing Kunming into the mainstream of Chinese life, however, for some indus-

been moved there, and the National University, which left in 1937, opened in Kunming in early 1938. A few newer homes now being built of "stone, wood and real bricks." He lived in which was "real comfortable. I have a bath tub and a toilet—.y rare conveniences in Kunming." He found the condition of the .aining schools grim, with "All classes behind badly. Only three flying days here in July due to rains and poor field." In a small, orange-backed pocket notebook, he noted they needed "facilities, fields, planes." On another page he wrote, "No floodlight. Get radio officer. No ammunition. Need cook utensils. No spare parts." He busied himself drafting plans. "Require full authority over all matters pertaining to Primary, Basic & Pursuit. Control of Amer. instr. Transfer, assign duties, recommend disch. reemploy. Emp. add. Americans."[18]

When Soong came to Kunming in August, he "approved my plans and recommendations. Am in charge of flying training." With business matters resolved, the two had lunch with Yunnan's Governor Lung Yun, a formidable figure with only one eye and a reputation as a powerful warlord who was not at all enthusiastic about the leadership of Chiang Kai-shek.

In succeeding weeks Chennault worked from dawn until dark but felt he accomplished little. August, like July, was wet. The airfield was not hard surfaced. "Only four flying days in Aug. due to rains and mud. Terrible." His emphasis therefore fell on ground instruction, and the cadets he had inherited, not being pleased with the changes he initiated, were hard to handle. The instructors included Americans and Chinese with varied backgrounds; it was hard to maintain a single philosophy of training and/or operations.

The command structure was complex. The Chinese could not gracefully accept a recommendation from a foreigner, nor the commission from the commandant. Recommendations and instructions were changed so that they were no longer the ideas of "inferiors," hence what was done was not what had been suggested. The procedure thereafter was for the instructor or adviser to protest or resign; the Generalissimo or Madame would hold a conference and would issue the original orders in their names. The orders could then be carried out, since they came from above and could be followed without loss of face.

Obtaining supplies was also a cumbersome process with predetermined formalities. Chennault submitted his requests; the commission made up its separate requests. Both advised Kung, minister of finance, who then weighed the independent recommendations of two of his personal officers and also of Pawley, with whom Kung worked closely. Kung let the contracts for what he decided upon through a purchasing bank in Hong Kong. The whole business was usually repeated, with different advisers and different purchasing banks acting on behalf of T. V. Soong.[19]

It was the Chinese way. Chennault never came to understand the Chinese, whom he found complex and difficult, but he admired their loyalty, their generosity, and their friendliness.[20] He did not condemn, and he had gradually won the respect and goodwill of the rank and file of the air force. He seemed to respond to Chinese courtesy and grace with the same qualities, even though his basic forthrightness was unchanged. He moved among the Chinese with pleasure and confidence, neither patronizing nor exploiting. With the exception of those who saw him as a threat to their own power, he had become a "ding hao," an "all right man." Even General Chou, with whom Chennault had to work closely to effect any change in the training schools, gradually came to be a quiet but firm supporter. When Chinese pilots rebelled at being checked by American instructors, Chou settled the mutiny quickly and efficiently.

But even with Chou behind him, Chennault faced serious obstacles. There were always too few planes. At one time McDonald observed that, with existing planes and conditions, it would take two years to give one class the seventy hours of flight training that had been specified as the goal. Soong was trying to put together more international squadrons, and French pilots and planes began arriving in midsummer. Chennault organized them into a self-contained unit in which the squadron commander, Labitte, was responsible for training and tactics and had full disciplinary power. The French squadron experienced the same handicaps as the others; at one time they had thirteen planes, but four had no propellers and four had no guns.[21]

Always, interminably, there was opposition, delay. Madame warned Chennault that passive resistance would be his greatest problem.[22] Even with her help he could not always surmount the hurdles. After a trip to outlying fields, he returned to Kunming and found "training affairs in terrible snarl." He and Chou had a "heated discussion relative to authority of Ams." Then the weather turned cold and wet. There was no heat in his quarters. He shopped without success for an overcoat. A cold turned into flu and kept him in bed for some days and left him "feeling rotten" for the remainder of the win-

ter. Early in December one of the American instructors led his formation through that of another, and two cadets collided. Chennault
was "greatly discouraged. . . . All Chinese super critical and out for
blood." He took a Sunday off to go hunting and revive his spirits.
"Very tired," he wrote afterward, "but wonderful day outdoors."

Behind the surface frustrations Chennault encountered was an
ugly situation about which he could do little but which embroiled
him in one of the most prolonged controversies of his career. China
during the 1930s afforded a tempting market for the world's aircraft
manufacturing companies; when it began developing an air force
China was invaded by a number of aircraft agents. The competition
was fierce, for there was a lot of money to be made. The situation
soon became ugly, involving not only questionable business practices but also complex political undertones within the Chinese government. As minister of finance, T. V. Soong had tried to deal with
the agents in an open and direct manner, but in 1933 he fell out of
favor with Chiang and was replaced as minister of finance by H. H.
Kung. Most of the agents soon encountered obstacles and had trouble
getting contracts negotiated. The exception was William Pawley.[23]

A skillful and aggressive businessman with a reputation for playing
for big stakes and usually winning, Pawley at that time represented
Curtiss-Wright and Douglas. Assessing the business opportunities in
China, he made two decisions: whenever possible he would do business only with Kung direct, and he would build an aircraft factory
that would make it both easier and more profitable for the Chinese to
do business with him.

A hardworking man with an air of crispness and a gentlemanly,
pleasant, and flamboyant figure, Pawley did nothing on a small
scale. Because he was a high-pressure salesman who employed enterprise and imagination to get China's business, he was an obvious target for cries of foul play from the competing aircraft agents. His ties
to Kung were suspect; Kung's own reputation was far from clean.
Pawley was a major focus of the Madame-Donald investigation into
the prevailing corruption, but no specific proof of malpractice was
unearthed.[24]

Widely entertained by the various agents when he first arrived in
Shanghai in 1937, Chennault had noted in his diary, "Conditions are
very bad regarding business methods out here." He determined that
his best course of action would be to show impartiality to all and fa-
vors to none.[25] Through the succeeding months he held to it, basing
his decisions and recommendations solely on China's needs. One of

the conditions in his contract with China was that he have "a deter-
mining voice" in the selection of all pursuit craft, and in August 1937
Madame asked him to recommend planes for her to purchase. He
listed five: Curtiss-Wright's Hawk III and 75, Seversky's P-35, Chance
Vought's dive bomber, and North American trainers. Madame accepted his advice and sent the purchase request to Kung, who ordered
the North American trainers and the Curtiss-Wright planes (which
he could get through Pawley) but not the others.[26]

Part of the problem was credit, as China did not have cash. Buying
where he could, Kung secured Bellancas in the United States, Glad-
iators in Britain, Dewoitines in France, and Henshel bombers in Germany. Most of them proved worthless to the CAF. Although he was
partial to the Seversky fighter, Chennault also liked the Hawk III and
the 75. McHugh, who followed events carefully and also tried to
maintain impartiality, noted that Chennault worked patiently and
tactfully under conditions that would have driven most men to dis-
traction. He held his tongue, refrained from blaming the equipment
for his difficulties, and earned McHugh's admiration for being both
patient and fair. But the planes ordered from Pawley did not arrive.[27]

Part of the problem was trouble with Pawley's factory, Central Aircraft Manufacturing Company. It had been built along imaginative
lines: the aircraft companies advanced China the money for its construction, the loan to be repaid from the money China would save by
buying planes partially built and completing the assembly in China.
CAMCO proved extremely useful and beneficial to China, both for
the purchase of new planes and for repair and service.[28] Originally in
Hangchow, it moved to Hankow in early 1938. As the Japanese continued to advance, in June CAMCO began moving to Loiwing, near
the Burma border in Yunnan. The machinery was shipped by rail to
Hong Kong, then by boat to Haiphong, then by rail to Kunming. It
took time. The Hawk IIIs that CAMCO was scheduled to assemble
during the summer were delayed.

There were also delays in delivery of the Hawk 75s, which began
dribbling into Hong Kong in June. When they were test flown, their
speed (255 m.p.h.) failed to match that of the demonstrator (275
m.p.h.), and their critical altitude was only 8,500 feet, whereas the
contract specified 10,500 feet. In such condition, they had no tactical
advantage over the newest model Japanese fighters, the I-96 (Mitsu-
bishi A5M4, or Claude) and I-97 (Nakajima Ki-27, or Nate). The
problem was identified; Pawley ordered parts to correct it.[29]

There were more delays in getting the parts. Canton fell in October

1938; French Indochina closed traffic on the Haiphong-Kunming railway. Meanwhile China's shortage of planes was acute. The 75s, though operational, were vulnerable. Tempers flared and rumors flew, among them that the trouble with the Hawk 75s was caused by changes which Chennault had demanded, that Chennault had tried to have the contract for 75s canceled and only Pawley's direct appeal to Kung had saved it, and that Chennault considered the Seversky unbeatable and opposed purchase of any other plane. These and other charges he stoutly denied, in calm but clear letters to the commission and to Burdette Wright, but he also stated that he felt much of the trouble was caused by Pawley's business practices. Pawley was angered by the accusations, and the feud between the aircraft agents, with Chennault squarely in the middle, grew steadily more intense.[30]

On the last day of the year Chennault had the sad duty of notifying the wife of an American instructor that her husband had crashed and died. That night it was "dinner with Reynolds at G. Hotel du Lac. Met Col. Stilwell, mil. attache. No New Year celebration, bed at 10:30."[31] It had been a difficult and discouraging year, and in view of their later relationship, it was appropriate that he first met Stilwell at the end of it, when he was ill, troubled, and at odds with his fellow Americans.

Early in 1939 the commission prepared to order more planes. A. L. Patterson, agent for the Air Motive Company, arranged a credit of U.S. $12 million and tried to get the contract. His primary competition came from Pawley; the negotiations grew ugly as each accused the other of foul play. Chennault spent a great deal of time in Chungking at Kung's request, sharing quarters and working on the contracts with Dr. Arthur N. Young, the American economist who served as financial adviser to China from 1929 to 1947.[32]

The damp chill that pervaded Chungking in the winter usually made Chennault sick, but he would have endured whatever was necessary to get planes. He particularly wanted the fifty-four P-35s specified in the Patterson contract, for he believed the P-35 to be "the only single seater with sufficient speed, range and fire power which could possibly attack the Japs on their bases at Hankow, Canton and even Shanghai." He intended to use it as a long-range bomber capable of reaching the Japanese yet with sufficient speed to give the Chinese pilots confidence in being able to escape Japanese aerial competition.[33]

Patterson's proposal was finally accepted, but the contract was complex and its complicated provisions could not be met. Evidence mounted that Patterson's prices were much too high, as Pawley had charged. The Seversky P-35 came under attack, and so did Chennault for having recommended it. Fanned by Pawley, who impressed McHugh as being rabid in his hostility to Chennault, the rumor spread that Chennault himself received a commission on all planes sold in China. When the fulfillment of the contract stalled, the U.S. State Department entered the fray by expressing its interest in seeing a contract, once negotiated, carried through. Since Kung and the Chinese had fulfilled their end of the bargain, they were justly angry, and when the chargé d'affaires called on Kung, the latter implied that Chennault's judgment might have deteriorated because of his long absence from America. Chennault's status with the commission was at its lowest ebb. The commission tried to prevent him from attending a special meeting, but the Generalissimo ordered that he be included.[34]

McHugh's long and detailed reports to Washington make it clear that the fracas was greatly affected by the rivalry between Soong and Kung, who not only hated one another but fought bitterly for control of the Bank of China. While Soong supported Chennault, Kung worked with Pawley and the commission in an effort to eliminate Chennault as well as the competing aircraft agents. One reason Kung accepted the Patterson contract at all was that he needed to give an order to the "other side" to counter accusations from Madame and Donald about his exclusivity in dealing with Pawley. Chennault had no doubt that Pawley's animosity and "malicious falsehoods" concerning him were "actuated by the fact that I will not limit my recommendations to airplanes which he sells. This I cannot conscientiously do."[35]

Chennault stuck to his conscience, and he alone emerged from the long and ugly episode with his reputation intact. Even so there were scars. He perceived that he had been "used rather obviously to attain objectives which I never planned," and the realization put him in what McHugh called "a fighting mood."[36] Most distressing, however, was that he never obtained the planes he needed, and his disappointment was bitter. Had the Chinese had the P-35 when it was first requested in the fall of 1937, he felt the Japanese drive up the Yangtze might have been stopped. From his perspective, China had been denied the optimal weapons of defense by unscrupulous businessmen. For Pawley he now felt nothing but contempt, and like the rampaging elephant with blood in his eye, he never forgot it.[37]

After a long and tedious stay in Chungking, during which he shared with the Chinese the first of many bombings on their hapless capital, he went back to Kunming. His diary shows that he "got plenty tight," "got tight again," and finally, in desperation, "got drunk."

"Twice we've gotten the defending pursuit on an effective basis but it soon relapsed because of the jealousy of Chinese officers, the shortage of first class pilots and the lack of offensive spirit of all Chinese personnel," he wrote a friend in the summer of 1939, a time for reassessment. He had come to China with a two-year stay in mind. He had hoped to direct the Chinese Air Force in combat with sufficient success to defeat the Japanese. In this he had failed. He had "fought bitterly for more than a year to get our system [of training] in operation and have to be on the alert constantly to prevent sabotage."[38] He was discouraged. The adventure had begun to wear off, the romance to pale.

On the plus side, he had learned much about aerial combat and much about the Chinese way. "Take warning by the cart ahead," Madame had advised him once, and perhaps she helped him to understand the pride that prevented the Chinese from accepting foreign advice even when it was sought. Chiang at times offered him more powerful positions, but he declined them, realizing that the power was empty. In his capacity as adviser he would not force; he would not, as McHugh thought he should, "crack the whip."[39] Yet the slow progress discouraged him, and his fighting instincts rebelled at the strategy of waiting. Chiang Kai-shek's policy after the fall of Hankow was to continue to retreat, to scorch the earth, to continue defying the enemy. He believed help would eventually come; he believed China would survive.

Chennault found it hard to take. Sitting with Chiang and watching the unopposed Japanese planes pound Chungking into rubble, he protested, "I'm going home. We're not getting anywhere. We're not beating the Japs." The Generalissimo's reply was a calm, "Now look, we're holding our own pretty well. Don't you get impatient." As Madame interpreted, the Generalissimo said, "We're going to win this war if it takes a hundred years." "I don't think we're going to live a hundred years to win the war," Chennault protested, but Chiang merely laughed, and his approach remained the same.[40]

From the beginning of the war, Chennault had done what he could, through McHugh, other American intelligence officers, and in his own name, to keep his government informed of Russian assistance and policies, of Japanese and Chinese aerial tactics, and of the increasing sophistication of Japan's planes and equipment. By the spring of 1939 he was personally convinced that "another World War is inevitable," and he began giving serious consideration to his own role should the United States become involved. Although he wrote Max, "Had just as soon fight out here where I know the people as fight in Europe where I'd be a stranger," he felt that his greatest contribution might be in helping to prepare the U.S. Air Corps for the type of fighting they might encounter.[41]

"I've seen many illustrations of the tactical problems which we write about in our text books," he wrote his friend Millard Harmon at ACTS on 28 July. It "has often occurred to me that my experiences and observations would be of some value to our Air Corps officers." His rejection by the War Department the preceding year rankled. He asked Harmon if he thought it advisable to offer his services again.[42] Harmon apparently encouraged him, for Chennault applied once more for active duty. Offered a position instructing Coast Guard antiaircraft but not work with pursuit, he retreated further into his wounded pride.

On 23 August 1939 Germany and Russia signed a nonaggression pact; on 1 September Germany invaded Poland. Chennault spent much of the subsequent month in Chungking. His diary records a number of long conferences with the Generalissimo, Madame, and General Chou, who had once more been named head of the commission when the unfortunate General Chien was jailed for wastage of funds. The diary does not include the topics under discussion. In early October, however, Chennault's "leave and trip to U.S. was approved," and in company with Colonel Chiang of the CAF, he began the long flight to the States on 19 October.

Chennault had been away from his family and his home for two and one-half years. His mood en route was excitement and anticipation. He flew the Pacific on the new Pan-American Clipper, carefully logging the takeoff times and the number of miles in each hop, doubtless marveling at the progress of aviation and speculating on its future possibilities. In Louisiana he spent time with his family, teasing Rosemary about having measles when he had come so far to see her and taking pride in watching David and Bob play football at Waterproof High School. It was an unusually cold Christmas, with the mercury hovering below zero. Lake St. John froze over. When Chennault left home on 27 January, he crossed the Mississippi by ferry among ice floes.[43]

His business on this trip is not clear, but one purpose, possibly secondary, was to help the Chinese secure additional Air Corps personnel to serve as instructors and trainers. In December the Chinese Embassy made a formal request to the State Department for several senior aviators to serve as instructors for an advanced CAF tactical school similar to ACTS. The department replied, however, that it would prefer not to receive the request and would have to say no if it did. But rather than turn the Chinese away without hope, the State Department volunteered that Chennault was in the country and might be able to help them; the activities of non-service personnel were a private matter.[44] It is the first suggestion on record that the department had begun to look upon Chennault as a vehicle through which to accomplish goals that neutrality laws or public opinion prevented the government from pursuing openly. Chiang Kai-shek apparently recognized the subtle gesture and later exploited it.

Chennault may or may not have known that he had the State Department's private blessing, but he visited a number of Air Corps bases and aircraft companies. In Washington he gave a classified talk at the War Department, privately noting that the department was preoccupied with the mounting crisis in Europe and did not have a current map of Asia available. He also gave a talk at ACTS and showed movies on China. According to one transcribed interview, he believed that the Chinese had the Japanese worn down and the war would be over in two more years. If he warned of danger to the United States in Asia or expressed his belief that the Sino-Japanese war would spread, he did so in off-the-record meetings. He was openly candid, however, about the deficiencies in the Chinese Air Force, where he characterized supply and communications as "poor" and averred that the duration of training was "controlled largely by Buddha."[45]

By the end of February, his spirits depressed, Chennault was back in China. There he faced the formidable challenge of extending the warning net into Yunnan, for during his absence the Japanese, in hopes of destroying the training schools and crippling the CAF before it could get into the air, had begun bombing raids on Kunming. Chennault gave the responsibility for the net to John M. Williams, a communications man who shared his ability to innovate, improvise, and scrounge. Williams had to do plenty of each in Yunnan as he took charge of the net, for the distances were vast, the transportation was primitive, and there was no telephone or telegraph system.[46]

Radios were smuggled in from Hong Kong to provide the communication links. An imaginary clock face (or sundial) indicated direction; six taps, or six o'clock, meant planes coming from the south.

Special codes were devised for altitude, type, and number of planes when this information was known. Some of the listening stations were so isolated they could be reached only by mule trails, while a few were inaccessible even by trail and had to be supplied by air. Most of the observers were Chinese Air Force personnel who were trained to operate and maintain their transceivers.

The system was crude, but it worked. When an incoming raid was reported, colored paper lanterns were hoisted to the top of signal poles, and Kunming's citizens ran for shelter in the cemetery outside town. The time could be predicted quite accurately, and once when a warning came during a soup-to-nuts dinner for visitors, Chennault took his own good time over the special meal, apparently oblivious to the uneasiness of his guests, who hesitated to run for the cemetery while their host sat calmly savoring his Yunnan ham.[47] During the summer, however, after sweating out a particularly bad raid in a ditch, Chennault challenged Williams to refine the net to the point where it could supply continuous information and could enable the defenders to intercept the approaching enemy. His own manual on interceptions had been translated into Chinese; he saw to it that training in interception intensified.[48]

Williams devised a Morse code to accommodate Chinese characters and solve the phonetic code problem. Then, using means fair and foul, he gradually acquired enough equipment for the main air-ground units to have a power unit, two-channel transmitter, and two receivers; they listened to all reports and relayed the information to pilots or line crews as indicated. The six available units were set up so that they could be moved from one base to another. In the main headquarters at Kunming, each listening post was indicated on a large map so that the path of oncoming planes could be followed visually.

There were amusing problems of interpretation, because the Chinese tended to report a sighting time earlier than was actually the case—each wanted to be the one who first picked up the enemy. Copper wire tended to disappear and gasoline seemed to "evaporate," but the thefts stopped after Williams and Governor Lung Yun discussed the matter over tea. Yunnan's warning net was peculiarly Chinese, but it filled a critical place at a critical time, and the events of the next few years convinced a proud Chennault that, given the circumstances, the "communications and air-ground control net" that his men built in China had no precedent and no superior.[49]

7

Birth of an Idea

Although he had one eye on building Yunnan's warning net and the other on training the CAF, during the summer of 1940 Chennault wrestled internally with personal frustration. He had wanted to stay in the States. He felt he was accomplishing little in China, where working conditions often disgusted him. When he was rejected for a return to active duty, however, he reasoned that his life now lay in China, where at least he was financially rewarded for his work. If he was going to live there, he wanted a home and his family with him, but Nell was reluctant to join him, for she was tied to her children, and she did not see China as the place to rear them. Shortly after returning to Kunming, Chennault received papers from home that upset him. Depressed and unwell, he buried himself in work by day but over a period of several months spent his evenings in the company of Kunming's lowest elements, often drinking heavily and seeking female company. His dissipation brought him little pleasure. He slept poorly. Heart palpitations worried him.

His family was much on his mind. When Max became the father of a daughter, the proud grandfather wrote a gently teasing letter, "What was all that talk I heard some months back about twins? And

all that came of it was a little girl who weighed less than 7 pounds!"
But he assured his son that, "after all, a little girl is mighty sweet."
Max was then considering a career change, and his father mused,
"While we all desire and strive for security in our lives, there is really
very little security anywhere in the world."[1]

Certainly there was no security in China that summer of 1940, for
the Japanese blockade was almost total, and Chungking lay helpless
under its second summer of daily bombardment. In August, when the
Japanese began using their new Zero fighter, the remaining units of
the CAF were wiped out in a matter of days. China could no longer
mount even a token defense. Thousands died; fires raged; the bombers kept coming. When the colored paper lanterns went dancing up
the signal poles, Chungking's citizens ran out of town or sought shelter in the caves tunneled into the rock cliffs on which the city stood.
When a raid was over, the survivors salvaged what they could from
the ashes and resumed their lives.

Watching, a participant and yet a detached observer, Chennault
was convinced that a broader war was imminent, that China should
be helped, that the United States should prepare to fight a German-
Japanese coalition. He saw Japan as a greater enemy to the United
States than Germany; in a letter home he railed against U.S. policies
of selling war materials to Japan.[2]

Although the Chinese heroism he witnessed moved him, he began
to realize that Chiang Kai-shek was floundering in the sheer magnitude of China's problems. Grieved and shaken by the remorseless aerial attacks, the Generalissimo turned on the hapless officers of the
CAF to vent his fury. On one occasion Chennault spent six days in
Chungking waiting, without success, to see him. Those around
Chiang feared his temper and told him only what they thought he
wanted to hear. The result was a dangerous isolation from reality
that grew steadily worse. The information released by the government became ever more distorted. One American reporter concluded
that Chiang's only war strategy at this time was to convince America
that its best interests lay parallel to those of China, so that it would
come to China's aid.[3]

Chiang definitely wanted help. In June he sent T. V. Soong to the
United States to seek it. Soong was welcomed in Washington, for
Americans were deeply moved by China's suffering. There was more
than an emotional concern, however, for Washington feared Japan's
intent and saw selfish reasons why China should not go under. The
problem was to find acceptable ways to extend help. Isolationist sen-

timent was still strong; neutrality laws were still in effect. Military equipment that might be purchased under the prevailing "cash and carry" policy was in critically short supply; everything that could be spared from building up the U.S. services was being sent to the British. Nor did China have funds with which to make purchases or even the required security for loans. Secretary of the Treasury Henry Morgenthau had arranged small loans to China in 1938 and 1939, but the money could not be used to buy arms. What China wanted, more than anything else, was a 500-plane air force for defense against Japanese attacks. An unsuccessful effort had been made to get the planes from Russia. Now, negotiating gingerly with a cautious United States, Soong and financial adviser Arthur Young worked on China's requests and prepared tables of equipment for 300 pursuits and 200 bombers.

"It would assist in convincing authorities here," Soong cabled Chiang, "if program transmitted were supported by Colonel Chennault."[4] Chiang summoned Chennault. Sick with bronchitis but relieved to be jolted out of a rut, Chennault pulled himself together and on 12 October flew to Chungking. Chiang Kai-shek made it clear that he wanted American planes and American pilots. He wanted Chennault to help him get them. The result was to be the American Volunteer Group, the first U.S. experiment with a clandestine air force, a military unit financed and equipped and staffed by the neutral United States but fighting Japan under the Chinese flag.

The idea was not new to the moment. During the battles over Nanking in 1937, Chennault had sometimes speculated aloud on what a well-trained, well-equipped, well-led group of American pilots could accomplish in China. During 1938 he and Pawley had worked together in attempting to form one. In December 1938, when he received a job inquiry from one of the better pilots of the disbanded Fourteenth International Squadron, Chennault replied that there was a "project under discussion." Should it materialize, he wrote, "you will like it." He planned to be in military control, for he said, "I'll count you in the outfit." Shortly afterward he followed up with a note on a Christmas card; the pilot should write Pawley "for job as a pilot in a special squadron."[5] That winter had passed, however, without seeing such a squadron become reality.

In the late spring of 1939, following the debacle over the Pawley and Patterson plane contracts, Kung asked Pawley to do what he could to get American planes and men for China. According to Pawley's later account, he promised to "do everything possible to put

China's problem before various men of influence in the United States."[6] CAMCO's vice president was Bruce Leighton, a retired U.S. Navy officer. Both Pawley and Leighton lobbied in Washington to pave the way for Chinese requests for aid, and in January 1940 Leighton discussed it with navy authorities. Pointedly suggesting that it was in America's interest to prevent Japan's gaining control of China, he said this could be done by an effective air force in China. Although Leighton visualized CAMCO handling such a force under commercial contract with China, without the U.S. government participating directly, it was obvious that official cooperation would be necessary in securing loans, additional planes (CAMCO could manufacture some in China), and a nucleus of American pilots.[7] When Chennault was asked, in a postwar interview, whether he knew anything about Chinese requests for aid submitted to the Navy Department in January 1940, his reply was that he knew nothing. But he was in the States during this time, and his diary records at least one meeting with Pawley. He and Pawley may have conceived a mutual dislike, but each had reasons to want an effective air unit formed. Chennault's primary business on his 1939–40 leave may have been to advance it. No doubt he was quietly and discreetly feeling out the prospects when mingling among Air Corps personnel or visiting aircraft companies.[8]

The special squadron project had seemed less and less likely to be realized as the months went by, however, and when he was called to Chungking in October 1940, Chennault told Chiang it was not possible. He cited the U.S. neutrality laws, the backlog in the aircraft factories, the commitment to Britain, and the push within the U.S. armed services to prepare. Chiang would not be dissuaded.[9] On 21 October, according to Chennault's diary, he and General Mao were "ordered back to US for duty with Dr. T. V. Soong."

Chennault and Soong would be working in carefully prepared ground, for on 18 October Chiang Kai-shek held a long and serious talk with the U.S. Ambassador to China, Nelson T. Johnson. With some eloquence Chiang presented China's plight. The coast was blockaded; the sole remaining access to the outside world was via the Burma Road, 2,100 miles of primitive thoroughfare that snaked over 10,000-foot mountains and into mile-deep gorges to link Chungking with Rangoon. Both the road and its key junction and trans-shipping center at Kunming were now under Japanese aerial assault. Unless help came soon, Chiang said, China might collapse. The Russians were withdrawing their aid; Chinese morale was low; the economy was on the verge of collapse; the Chinese Communists were exploiting the internal crises. China needed a stabilization loan and she needed 500 to 1,000 airplanes, with American pilots to fly them, for the immediate defense of the Burma Road and China's cities.

Johnson forwarded Chiang Kai-shek's message to Roosevelt with his own endorsement that the United States should send help at once, on a large scale. Roosevelt tended to agree. By the time Chennault reached Washington in mid-November, a number of officials were scurrying around with some sense of urgency to see what could be done.[10]

Chennault, Mao, Soong, and Young went to work on the aviation proposals. They frequently met in Young's apartment to guard the secrecy of their business, but an amused Mrs. Young, banished to another room, nevertheless heard everything that was said because the group had to speak loudly to counteract Chennault's deafness.[11] As finally submitted on 25 November, the proposal listed 350 fighters and 150 bombers with pilots and crews, 150 basic trainers, 10 transports, 20 percent spare parts, material to build 14 major fields and 122 landing strips, plus ammunition and ordnance for one year.[12]

The Chinese request forced the United States to make fundamental decisions on a number of complex issues. By this time the Axis held most of Western Europe; the aerial Battle of Britain was uncertain in outcome. The Tripartite Pact between Germany, Italy, and Japan had been signed, clearly warning that any war the United States entered would be a global one. Intelligence indicated that Japan would soon move against British and Dutch possessions in the Pacific. Britain's survival was undeniably vital to U.S. security; all possible aid must be extended, and including help in defending Pacific possessions.

Immediately after his November reelection to an unprecedented third term, Roosevelt had introduced the concept of lend-lease. It was to revolutionize U.S. procedures for giving assistance and made possible help for China as well as for Britain, but the bill faced weeks of debate in Congress, and haste seemed to be needed. From all sides came the message that China might fall without immediate succor. The emerging China lobby, composed of vocal and influential Americans as well as Chinese, was pressing China's cause in ways subtle and blatant; the American press, fed by Chiang's controlled Ministry of Information, painted vivid scenes of valiant battles and heroic struggle. The emotional impact was undeniable. But what could be spared? And how could it be provided?

Chennault had ideas on both counts. During the long flight back to the United States he had toyed with possible strategies for a fighting group of American airmen, a group of volunteers who would spearhead a rejuvenated CAF and would serve their own country as well as China by acquiring combat experience and testing American planes and tactics. Both Germany and Russia had similarly tested themselves in the Spanish Civil War; Russia had done more of the same in China. China had the airfields and the warning net; all that was required to strike a telling blow at Japan—their common enemy—was the air force.[13]

With Chennault handling the military and technical expertise and Soong providing the diplomatic, political, and moral persuasion, the two set out to convince Washington that U.S. self-interest would be served by providing China with planes and men. They made quite a pair, Soong the urbane diplomat and banker, with Harvard's finishing touches superimposed on Chinese graciousness, Chennault the assertive fighter whose rough edges were never fully polished. Each kept his own counsel behind an enigmatic face, Soong's smiling, Chennault's grim. Each, in his own way, knew how to be devious and crafty.

Two of their initial targets were Morgenthau and Secretary of the Navy Frank Knox, both of whom were sympathetic to China and sensitive to U.S. vulnerability in the Pacific. Morgenthau was captivated by the exciting possibilities that existed in using U.S. planes, operating under the CAF, to bomb Japan. He began to explore the idea, encouraged by Chiang, who said "the battle-ships of the Japanese Navy could be wiped out within a few months," and by Johnson, who pointed out that Japan could be bombed from excellent fields in Chekiang, and such efforts now might make a U.S.-Japanese war in the future unnecessary.[14]

Morgenthau was well primed by 30 November, when Soong gave him a four-page memo prepared by Chennault, although it did not bear his name. It was an argument for a 500-plane air force, staffed with personnel from the American and British training centers, to operate either in conjunction with the Chinese army, or independently if desired. The "advisability of carrying the air war into Japan proper" could be decided "according to the political strategic necessities of the war in Asia and Europe."[15]

The more Morgenthau thought about it, the more excited he became. On 8 December, as he and Soong were returning from lunch with Roosevelt, he suggested that the 500-plane air force was probably impossible—as remote as 500 stars—but how would Soong react if the United States furnished a few long-range bombers with crews to bomb Japan? Soong wired Chiang, who wired back that they could "effectively bomb all the vital centers of Japan, and harass their fleet and transports."[16]

Morgenthau paid an early morning call on Hull, to whom Soong had also given Chennault's memo. He was delighted to find the conservative secretary of state so enthusiastic over the possibility of bombing Japan that he talked on "with his mouth full of breakfast." The idea was presented to Roosevelt on 19 December, when Morgenthau found the president "just as thrilled as I am." Roosevelt told his secretaries to work out a program. Morgenthau, for one, approached the task with gusto.[17]

Chennault was without doubt the author of the proposals. How much influence he exerted in persuading Washington to accept them is another teasing question that remains unanswered. In a meeting with Soong and Young on 20 December, Morgenthau asked, "This Colonel Chennault, where is he?" The wording suggests that Morgenthau had not spoken with Chennault prior to this time. Chennault, Mao, and Soong attended a meeting on the "special air unit" the following evening at Morgenthau's home, however, and minutes have been preserved. Morgenthau began by explaining that, as a result of Dr. Soong's memo, the president was "seriously considering trying to make some four-engine bombers available to the Chinese in order that they might bomb Japan."[18]

Chennault was asked his opinion on the type of bombers to be preferred. He suggested either the Lockheed Hudson or the B-17 and stressed that it would be necessary for pursuit ships to accompany them. The bombing would have to be done at night, because the pursuits did not have sufficient range to defend the bombers by day. China should also have about 130 pursuits to defend the bomber bases, he explained, and Mao added that a further 100 would be necessary to keep the supply line open through the Burma Road. When personnel was discussed, Chennault said he could find Chinese gunners and radio operators, but American pilots and mechanics would be necessary.

Was it a pipe dream, Morgenthau asked, to think of putting bombers on these scattered Chinese fields and hiding them from the Japanese? It was not sound tactically, Chennault said simply, but it could be done. Could incendiary bombs be used, Morgenthau inquired? Chennault replied that a lot of damage could be done with them, and in his opinion this tactic would be well justified even if the Chinese lost some of the bombers.[19]

The inscrutable Chennault talked with Knox on 19 November, very shortly after reaching Washington, and possibly at other times. A full month earlier, before Chennault reached the States, Knox had written a memo to Hull suggesting a possible way to enable volunteer U.S. airmen to go to China. This idea may have been a carryover from the earlier efforts of Leighton or Pawley. Knox talked with Pawley in December, and although Pawley and Chennault each later claimed to have been the one who won Knox to their cause, neither was solely responsible. The secretary was well informed and acutely aware that the Navy would bear the burden of a Pacific war. He weighed the issues and concluded that air support for China was wise.[20]

Twice Chennault conferred with Gen. George C. Marshall, the army's new chief of staff. A man of severe reserve and cold logic, Marshall faced the staggering task of preparing a long-neglected army for a global war. Apparently he saw little in Chennault or his ideas that impressed him favorably, although he listened carefully when Chennault briefed him on the combat performance of the new Japanese Zero. In a conference the day after the two men talked, Marshall spoke grimly of a "new fast pursuit plane which has just appeared in the hands of Japan and has grounded all the Chinese Air Force." Although Chennault grumbled to Young that the army officers with whom he talked seemed not to believe him nor to be interested in learning what they could from him, the slight may have been more apparent than real. Marshall, for one, had perceived the threat.[21]

Secretary of War Henry L. Stimson was far from enthusiastic about either the Chinese requests or the mounting enthusiasm among the cabinet for dropping some bombs on Japan. Fearing that the plan for aiding China was getting out of hand, "rather half-baked," more the product of Chinese than of American strategy and in need of some "mature brains," he invited Morgenthau, Knox, and Marshall to his home on 22 December. The four spent an hour of a "beautiful fine day, like a new Indian summer," in serious discussion and concluded that Marshall should "make up a new survey of it."[22]

The key decisions were made in a meeting in Hull's office the following morning at 9:30. The dominating fact was a critical shortage of planes. Marshall thought the few available bombers would be better used in Britain. Some pursuit planes, however, could be obtained for China. Curtiss-Wright had indicated in mid-December that they could produce 300 P-40s above existing orders if the orders were placed at once. (Chennault had "found" the planes when he visited the Curtiss plant in Buffalo; he and his friend Burdette Wright had worked out a plan whereby Curtiss could add another assembly line.) These planes could be available in June, July, and August 1941. After extended discussion, it was decided that the orders should be placed by Britain, with the understanding that Britain would release 100 planes in January, February, and March to go at once to China but would take delivery on 200 in the late summer. The British would thus receive 200 planes of a later model in exchange for 100 P-40Bs given up now. The British agreed, after being assured that it was a matter of some urgency and that Roosevelt definitely wanted China to get something right away.[23]

When Chennault attended another meeting at Morgenthau's home on New Year's Day 1941, the discussion centered on protecting the Burma Road, not on bombing Japan. Only 100 pursuit planes, one portion of the special air unit Chennault and the Chinese had visualized, had survived the first decision process. For the time being the remainder lay in the background, a fire that had not been quenched.

The New Year's meeting concluded on a comic note, for Morgenthau had become concerned about a leak regarding the Chinese requests—a leak so accurate that he felt either Soong or Mao must be responsible. He made his point by joking that their meeting this day had never taken place, and if the word got out, "I never saw you." Soong was disturbed at the hinted reprimand and began berating Mao, who got the nervous giggles, much to Morgenthau's amusement. Lingering behind as the Chinese left, Chennault told the delighted secretary that, after the leak, Soong had given Mao a pistol with instructions that he was a soldier and should now go to his hotel room and shoot himself. In recounting the tale later with some relish, Morgenthau admitted that he drew slightly on his imagination, but according to his version, Chennault had averted the tragedy by protesting, "You mustn't do that, Soong. Think of the bad press that you will get." Shortly thereafter Chennault and Mao went to Buffalo to the Curtiss plant to see the planes demonstrated and to negotiate particulars for their purchase. With that business concluded, Mao returned to China, his oft-threatened head still intact.[24]

Roosevelt continued to wrestle with the overall problem of how much, and how, to assist China. After challenging Morgenthau to find a way to arrange a $100 million loan to China at once, he approved a trip to China by his administrative assistant, economist

Lauchlin Currie, who had been asked by Chiang to advise on economic matters. Currie returned with firsthand information on China's situation and submitted a sobering report. He perceived a dangerous Chinese economic situation that was spawning grave social and political conditions. He noted that censorship and repression were prevalent, while Chiang seemed to exhibit a paternalistic attitude toward the great masses of citizenry and to have no feeling for democratic processes. Disaffection among the liberal and progressive elements of the country was growing. The United Front had come to a bloody end under complex circumstances that held little hope for future cooperation between the Kuomintang and Communists. Currie thought that conflict between them would be suppressed during the war, but there was "dubious prospect of maintaining political stability" afterward.[25]

Currie's concluding recommendations, which come close to being the China policy Roosevelt pursued over the succeeding five years, were that Chiang be steered toward democratic reforms through American advisers, economic and military aid, and a policy of treating China with the respect accorded a great power. By using this leverage, Chiang might be influenced to lead China along paths that would avert civil war and a Communist victory.[26]

Currie's report coincided with the 11 March passage of the lend-lease bill, which gave the president a powerful weapon to employ in the undeclared war. When Japan and Russia shortly afterward announced that they had concluded a nonaggression pact, suggesting to the wary that Japan was securing its flanks in preparation for an advance into the Pacific, Roosevelt declared that China's defense was vital to that of the United States. China thus became eligible to receive lend-lease aid; Currie was asked to supervise it.

Thomas Corcoran, another presidential assistant, was asked to hold some private conversations with congressional leaders to gauge how they felt about de facto military aid to China. Having concluded that there would be no opposition, Corcoran was then released from his White House assignment to begin helping Soong set up China Defense Supplies, a unique corporation intended to serve as China's purchasing agent. Since its funds came from U.S. lend-lease and its sole customer was China, it was in effect a discreet means of converting economic support into military aid.

Corcoran was given another task as well, for Roosevelt needed someone to evaluate Chennault and to make a judgment on the aerial warfare propositions under consideration. The two men met, one fresh from Harvard Law School and immersed in the heady experience of being one of Roosevelt's controversial—and sometimes powerful—assistants, the other a fighting pragmatist who saw military strategy from the bottom up. Corcoran later recalled feeling amazement as he listened to Chennault presenting the daring concept of aerial guerrilla warfare, using American-flown fighters operating behind Japanese lines to destroy Japanese bombers and shipping. He was tempted to write Chennault off as a fanatic. Yet he was fascinated as the older man talked on, describing the airfields already built by Chinese hand labor, the warning net, the thin Japanese occupation and the loyalty of the Chinese citizens, the advantages of interior lines, the poor roads, and the unique mobility of air power. Corcoran concluded he was "dealing with something original, whether it was genius or madness; something so original that politically it would either be lost so completely we could always explain ourselves out of it or would succeed so magnificently that it could never be challenged."

When Corcoran reported to Roosevelt, he too was piqued by Chennault's unorthodox approaches. As Corcoran reconstructed their conversation, Roosevelt asked if the plan were dangerous, and his reply was yes, but less dangerous than doing nothing and losing China. Was Chennault difficult? Corcoran judged he was "original brass" and had "strong opinions," but then so did Stonewall Jackson and Hannibal. Was he manageable? Corcoran deemed yes, although "you will have to let him run the show and you run him." Roosevelt told Corcoran to "keep talking. . . . don't let him quit . . . and get him around to people who won't talk."[27]

Chennault was about to be initiated into the fine art and inestimable value of politics, an avenue of advancement he had disdained in the more naive days of his Air Corps career. It is not surprising that his notions underwent a transformation, for between Soong and Corcoran, he received his introduction to political lobbying from masters of the art.

Perhaps in part because he represented a world that was strong and virile, a he-man world of adventure and action in contrast to the restraint and tedium of government, Chennault won the support of a number of influential individuals who were frustrated by America's neutrality amid world crisis. Once he had an audience, Corcoran noted, "he was irresistible."[28] Among his new allies was the journalist Joseph Alsop, who actively assisted Soong and the Chinese efforts. It hurt nothing that Alsop also enjoyed personal access to the White

House through kinship to the Roosevelts. The framework, still shad-
owy, began to form.

Chennault began working on the complex specifics of the First
American Volunteer Group, the AVG, in early January 1941. Shortages meant that compromises became necessary. In vain he pleaded
for procurement "based upon a logical program covering a reasonable period of time." In vain he warned that "effective military operations depend upon a regular sustained flow of materials and supplies. Sporadic procurement may make possible occasional surprise
attacks, but cannot support the sustained offensive which is necessary for success." But little was available, and the Chinese were so
delighted to get anything at all that enthusiasm threatened to outrun
sound thinking. They accepted the first planes without armament or
spare parts in the interests of haste, and the resulting headaches were
severe.[29]

Personnel was an even more critical issue, starting with Chennault
himself. The preceding July the War Department had informed all its
retired officers that the Constitution (Article 1, Section 9, Clause 8)
forbade their accepting employment as civilian instructors of foreign
military personnel. Upon receipt of his notice, Chennault talked
with McHugh, who wired Washington. The reply was that persons so
engaged must have the consent of Congress; Chennault might therefore have to give up his post or be liable to court martial. There was
doubt Chennault could pass the physical for the coast artillery position that the War Department continued to offer him, but since "it
is gathered that the War Department would be reluctant for him to
discontinue his services to China," a way might be found. Washington obviously wanted Chennault in China, and if necessary would
compromise to make it possible. It was quietly arranged that he
would be employed by a private organization, the Bank of China,
rather than by the Chinese government.[30]

There remained the matter of the pilots and ground crews. The
laws seemed to forbid American citizens from serving in the armed
services of a foreign belligerent; those doing so might be subject to
fine, imprisonment, or loss of citizenship. For some time, however,
authorities had turned their official backs while men who wanted to
fight for Britain quietly crossed into Canada and enlisted in the Royal
Air Force. Knox thought it might be possible to adopt much the same
idea for those wanting to go to China, but Chennault and Young
sought to avoid difficulty by using the term "instructors" who must
"be prepared to defend the school property and personnel" and hence

would have combat duties. The State Department indicated it might issue passports to American citizens to serve as "aviation instructors."[31]

Other approaches were considered, but the ruse finally adopted for the AVG was that applied to Chennault's own position: let the men be employed by a civilian agency rather than by the government itself. On 15 February Marshall reported that a man had been found—Pawley—who was willing to take a chance on the recruiting despite the neutrality laws. CAMCO, as a private concern already operating in China, provided a believable front. Chennault favored organizing a new company especially for the purpose, but Soong preferred CAMCO. Although the Chinese government owned a majority of the stock, Pawley's New York holding company, Intercontinent, owned the remainder and was the logical administrative force.[32]

Neither Pawley nor Chennault was enthusiastic about working with the other. Pawley told Knox it might be better for him to drop out entirely, as his differences with Chennault were of long standing and it would be next to impossible to work with him. Mutual friends, including Young and McHugh, persuaded the two to set aside their personal animosity so that Pawley could handle administration while Chennault took charge of military matters. Chennault agreed to work harmoniously with Pawley and initially did so. After close contact with both on many details, Young testified that "the greatest good will is met in all quarters."[33]

Getting the men was yet another problem. Marshall opposed the idea of making U.S. servicemen into mercenaries; Roosevelt also had reservations about taking part in a "guns for hire" scheme and continued to mull over the issue. After Pawley consulted legal counsel and was advised that recruiting the men would be in violation of the neutrality laws, there was some consideration of trying to get the neutrality laws amended to make the AVG legal. That plan was abandoned as likely to take too long. Corcoran always thought Roosevelt was swayed by A. E. Housman's poem "Epitaph on an Army of Mercenaries," with its telling lines that depicted the mercenary as the one giving his life to save a situation others refused to face.

Eventually Pawley agreed to take the chance; Roosevelt agreed to clear the way. Although it is generally accepted (and stated by Chennault in his own memoir) that Roosevelt signed an unpublished executive order giving authority for American reserve officers and active duty enlisted men to withdraw from the U.S. service and join the AVG, no such order was signed by the president. His consent was verbal; specifics were handled by Currie, Marshall, and Knox, and Knox gave Pawley the clearance to proceed.[34]

Currie was instrumental in persuading the services to turn their men loose. After initial hesitation, Knox gave Chennault and Leighton letters of entry to the naval air stations and made it clear that navy flyers could resign without prejudice and return to the navy after their volunteer contract was finished. Acting Deputy Chief of Staff George Brett did the same for the War Department, although it was reluctant to release its men. As early as 21 December, Morgenthau had assured Chennault that the army would release enough men from active duty "to help the Chinese with the ships." The chief of the Air Corps, however, Maj. Gen. "Hap" Arnold, saw building up the air forces of the United States itself as his first duty. He thought Chennault was a crackpot and he was not about to accept the concept of the AVG as the forerunner of the U.S. air forces in Asia. A member of the AVG later recalled hearing Chennault say that he asked Arnold for 100 pilots with 500 hours of experience, but Arnold exploded that he could not supply them without folding up his whole pursuit section. Chennault retorted that, if Arnold could not spare so many, then he had no pursuit section to begin with. Unfortunately, that was exactly Arnold's concern.[35]

Pawley had spoken to some groups of servicemen about fighting for China as early as December 1940, but serious recruitment for the AVG did not begin until late March. CAMCO hired a recruiting staff, but recruitment dragged. The salaries offered were high—$600 per month for a wingman, $750 for a squadron commander, $350–400 for mechanics. On 2 April Chennault received approval from Soong to offer a $500 bonus to pilots for each Japanese plane shot down, but even with this added inducement the rosters were slow to fill. By the end of May only fifty-five pilots had been accepted. At one point Young suggested they might try to enlist 250 French aviators then at loose ends in French Indochina.[36]

Chennault requested experienced P-40 pilots, but most of those who signed up were bomber pilots and few had ever flown the P-40. He wanted men who could learn quickly and men who could get along with others under pressure, but in some instances officers who helped with the recruiting channeled toward the AVG those who did not have good chances for advancement in the U.S. service. There were potential troublemakers and misfits among them.

Nor were the recruiters always welcomed at the bases: Chennault later said that at Hamilton Field he was told to get off the field before he was locked in the guardhouse. Many an applicant for the AVG met disbelief that approached hostility when requesting that he be allowed to "resign" from the U.S. armed forces. Incredulous commanders were given a Washington number to call; the way was quietly cleared. The volunteers were discharged from the service "for the convenience of the government," although when the press revealed what was going on, the State, War, and Navy departments denied it.[37]

Putting together a competent staff proved a problem. In a later argument, Pawley claimed that he suggested hiring administrative staff people but that Chennault had vetoed the suggestion because he did not want anyone except flying personnel on his staff. Chennault denied the allegation, but he may have done the group unnecessary harm through such misunderstandings with Pawley. The Air Corps was not willing to release experienced staff personnel, however, and substitutes had to be found. Chennault began searching for adaptable individuals with useful talents. He tried to corral his brother Joe, but the latter wanted to finish college first. He wrote P. Y. Shu to start assembling good stenographers, typists and translators in China.[38]

Learning from John Davies that missionary Paul Frillmann was in the States and restless, Chennault sent for him. At their interview Frillmann concluded that Chennault did not remember him from their Hankow ball game, and he signed on with the AVG as chaplain and recreation officer, little dreaming that in the line of duty he would catch many more high flies. He was startled when Chennault gave him his first task: to list the food that would be required for 300 Americans in China for a year. When a chuckling Davies told him, "You'll never be the same man again," Frillmann began to wonder whether his family had been right to call him a fool for going off with "a bunch of harum-scarum adventurers."[39]

Chennault struggled, unsuccessfully, to keep the project out of the "harum-scarum" category. "It is desired to emphasize," he wrote in his somewhat formal style, "that a group of American pilots cannot operate efficiently and successfully in China unless supported by American technical and clerical personnel and supplied with adequate operating equipment and facilities." His efforts to procure both personnel and equipment often met with failure, but he was able to arrange for some of his newly recruited ground crewmen to attend an

intensive training course at the Allison engine factory to prepare
them to service the P-40's liquid-cooled engine.[40]

The working relationship between Chennault and Pawley deteriorated as business negotiations proceeded. Pawley's contract as the
exclusive agent for Curtiss-Wright in China entitled him to a commission on Curtiss-Wright planes sold to China, and he considered
this case no exception. The United States, which would actually be
paying for the planes through a loan to China, took the stance that
Intercontinent should not receive any selling commission because
the government had arranged the transaction. Since CAMCO's Loiwing plant in China was the only adequate facility at which the planes
could be assembled and maintained, Pawley was in a strong bargain-
ing position. When it was suggested that he waive his contract with
Curtiss-Wright and deal separately with the Chinese government for
actual services rendered in China, he refused. He would waive the
"selling commission," but he insisted upon a flat 10 percent fee for
future services in China. Tempers flared. Someone suggested that perhaps neither Curtiss nor Intercontinent should take any profit, since
the transaction had been made possible by the U.S. government, but
obviously something had to be settled with Pawley or the whole plan
would fall through. The problem was not resolved until a stormy conference in April, during which Morgenthau used forceful persuasion
and effected a compromise.[41]

The contract between the Chinese government and CAMCO was
signed 15 April 1941. A gem of ambiguous wording, it specified three
"advanced instruction and training units" (squadrons), each
equipped with eighteen American "active trainers" (fighters) and
under the "immediate direction of an American supervisor" (commander). CAMCO would recruit the employees and would pay them
from a special revolving fund set up in the Bank of China, receiving
no commission on their pay. As requested by the "supervisor,"
CAMCO would furnish "technical assistance in the maintenance,
overhauling and repair" of the craft and would handle the receiving,
transportation, unboxing, assembly, and storage of new planes and
parts. For this service Intercontinent would be paid $250,000 rather
than the $440,000 originally claimed as commission. CAMCO would
be reimbursed for expenses, but the contract was on a nonprofit
basis.[42]

Although Pawley's supporters believed he had made a personal sacrifice for the AVG, Chennault's interpretation was that he had put

his business interests ahead of China's need. Chennault's opinion of Pawley was low, as illustrated by an incident that took place when the two made a trip in Pawley's plane. Bad weather developed over the mountains of California; it looked as though they would crash. At such times men tend to clean their slates, and Pawley turned to the stubborn airman to say, "Well, Claire, it looks like this might be it." With a cold, unemotional finality that chilled the others present, Chennault looked him straight in the eye and said his only regret was that their bodies would be found in the same wreckage.[43]

The final hurdle was a snag over location. The original plans were to train and base the group at Kunming, but as the winter months gave way to spring, Chennault shuddered, remembering the wet summers that turned Kunming's grass airfield into a quagmire. China and Burma had been cautiously cooperating toward joint defense for some months, however, and in April the British agreed to send material to China to prepare all-weather airfields around Kunming, in return for which the Chinese agreed to send troops and part of the AVG to Burma should the need arise. The Kunming preparations, however, did not get completed in time. The British commander in chief in the Far East, Air Chief Marshal Sir Robert Brooke-Popham, was keenly aware of Burma's danger and was eager to have the American group there. When approached by CAMCO personnel, he obtained permission from the British War Office to make available a hard-surfaced RAF airfield and minimum base facilities at Toungoo, an isolated field in Burma's jungle north of Rangoon. The AVG would be allowed to use the facilities for training but not as a base from which to attack Japan.[44]

Chennault completed his U.S. preparations during June. By that time sentiment in Washington had begun to polarize. On the one hand there were those who had little patience with the Chinese and the build-up-China policy, and on the other there were those who identified sympathetically with the Chinese, their culture, and their need. For this latter group, Chennault was becoming the individual around whom to rally. China Defense Supplies was providing the nucleus of support for China and was gathering an ever more influential roster of officers: Roosevelt's cousin Frederick T. Delano at its head; William Brennan as congressional liaison; a marine intelligence officer and Harvard lawyer, Quinn Shaughnessy; William Youngman, released from the Federal Power Commission at Roosevelt's suggestion to be general counsel and courier to Chiang; Whiting Willauer, a Princeton and Harvard man with a reserve commission in naval intelligence and known to be crazy about flying, slated to be the liaison man in China.

The framework was in place: Pawley and CAMCO would take care of the planes and business arrangements; Chennault would work with Chiang Kai-shek and would handle the fighting; Chennault's "Washington Squadron," the men of China Defense Supplies, would smooth the way in the United States and would keep the supplies moving to him.

In the background, seldom discussed but diligently pursued by both Currie and Chennault, plans proceeded for putting together the larger air force the Chinese had requested. The limitation of only 100 pursuits of only one type, as contrasted with the initial request for 350 pursuits of two types, Chennault wrote, "must necessarily result in failure to attain the original tactical objectives, and possibly may result in the eventual consumption of the equipment without obtaining suitable results." The "suitable results" Chennault had in mind were smashing the impending Japanese offensive before it could be launched, something he was confident an air offensive from China could do if begun in time and delivered with sufficient weight.[45]

Although war had not been declared and peaceful solutions were still being sought—Hull and the Japanese diplomat Nomura were holding almost daily talks—the major barrier to the expanded AVG was the shortage of planes, for by mid-1941 official Washington was waging de facto war. In July Roosevelt approved a proposal that the United States equip and maintain the 500-plane force to operate in China; goals included the bombing of Japan by November. Aid to China was deemed justified because the "continuation of active military operations by the Chinese is highly desirable as a deterrent to the extension of Japanese military and naval operations to the South." CAMCO was authorized to recruit for this second force, and as in the earlier case, arrangements were handled orally, with no file records maintained. The first contingent of men was at sea, en route to China, when war began on 7 December. The Second American Volunteer Group, as conceived, never materialized.[46]

In early July Chennault paid a brief visit to Louisiana and then returned to China. His blood raced with anticipation, for he knew war was coming soon. He looked forward to the opportunity to test his concepts; he felt keen excitement over the First AVG and optimism that the Second would follow. "For the first time in my battle against the Japanese," his memoir recalls his thoughts, he believed he would have "everything I needed to defeat them."[47] His confidence approached arrogance, an attitude which his commanding officers later resented, but it was as though his entire twenty years in the service, followed by his four years in China, were reaching their culmination at this moment.

His 1941 passport listed his occupation as "executive,"[48] but he considered himself a soldier. In that frame of mind, he made the 17,000-mile journey back to Burma and the opening of another distinctive chapter in his career.

8

Flying Tigers

The men never regarded themselves as "Flying Tigers" until later, when they could survey their brief AVG experiences and remember only the exciting and the glamorous. They were "the AVG," and they were proud of it. They ranged in age from kids with fuzz on their chins to sedate middle-aged men. They came from thirty-nine of the forty-eight states, from the army, navy, and marines. After shake-downs, there were about 300 of them, of whom fewer than 100 were pilots. A few had ties to China through missionary parents and were seeking a way to help a country with which they felt a special bond. Some were in debt and in trouble and had signed up for the money. More were attracted by the promise of something new and different. Nearly all of them wanted to make a break with their lives up to this point and turn things around, start over. All of them loved flying and airplanes, and some saw the war coming and were eager to start fight-ing. As a group their common denominator was a generous dash of adventurousness, a willingness to tackle the unknown and to give it all they had. They seemed to realize that they might make history, for like the men who journeyed to Quebec with Benedict Arnold in 1775, a large number of them kept journals.[1]

From recruitment to disbandment they were involved in controversy. Clandestine operations were not as common then as now; the AVG was a barb on a leading arrow. Roosevelt and the chief of naval operations, Admiral Harold Stark, authorized U.S. naval escort for the *Jagersfontaine*, a Dutch freighter sailing in July with more than 100 AVG personnel aboard. It was all very hush-hush, but little escaped Japan's knowledge. Japanese military leaders cited the AVG as one more evidence of a military coalition between the United States and China; Japanese diplomats asked that American aid to China be reduced. Washington had made its decision, however, and the AVG got under way with official blessing, even though very few people knew what was taking place. When Washington columnist Drew Pearson began asking questions, a call from the White House quieted him.[2]

The men of the AVG knew little or nothing of the politics behind their existence. From the time they signed their contracts as "employees" for "an aircraft manufacturing, operating and repair business in China" until their discharge a year later,[3] their world was circumscribed by the planes they flew or maintained, the strange land in which they lived and over which they fought, and the bonds of friendship and loyalty they developed with one another and with Chennault.

He met some of them at the Rangoon docks. With mosquito boots on his feet, tropical shorts and shirt on his lean body, and a beat-up Air Corps cap on his head, he set the tone. His was a natural magnetism and charisma peculiarly suited to these unique circumstances, for he exuded a rough, masculine courage and strength together with other virtues that young men admire. With black eyes flashing in his weathered face, he left no doubt as to who would be in charge. A fighter pilot, he sometimes told them, needs to have complete belief in himself and in his ability to handle anything that walks, swims, flies, or wears skirts. With this kind of man, the men of the AVG could identify, and from the time they first met him, he "had them all in his pocket."[4]

The group had no identity, no structure, until Chennault provided the focus. He welded them into a fighting unit by his decisive authority and quiet but unswerving determination, by his unorthodox informality and individualistic approaches, by his skill as a teacher and fighter and by his unwavering determination to defeat the enemy. He earned their respect for his ability and their affection for his leadership, for from the beginning they were "his boys" and they knew they could trust him.

Much of August was consumed by conferences with the Chinese and the British, who let Pawley use the Mingaladon airfield in Rangoon to assemble the AVG's P-40s. Mechanics were brought from CAMCO's Loiwing plant to supervise Chinese laborers in the task. Facilities had to be improvised and some scrounging was necessary, for there were no forklifts or similar aids. It took three weeks to assemble the first plane; it was not delivered to Toungoo until 3 August. Chennault's relations with CAMCO grew tense, for planes, men, and supplies were arriving in dribbles. Feeling that he could delay training no longer, he flew to Toungoo on 21 August, where he found "conditions very unsatisfactory," with only thirteen planes and thirty-seven pilots and the men rebelling against military discipline, poor food, and primitive living conditions.[5]

He threw himself into shaping the group. A sense of unity and purpose must come first, and he began immediately with a long and informal talk with the men. He "told us exactly what we would run into in a couple of months from now, and I might say it looks pretty exciting, with the Japs probably giving us a warm reception," wrote one.[6] He explained the significance of the Burma Road as China's only supply line to the outside world. He explained the men's peculiar status as foreign volunteers fighting for China. The AVG had been officially constituted for service with the Chinese Air Force on 1 August by order of the Generalissimo, and each of them must sign up as a volunteer for the CAF to give them the protection of international law governing captured belligerents. He created an immediate atmosphere of accessibility and common endeavor by meeting individually and in small groups with those who were making trouble or who had legitimate complaints. He began the troublesome business of trying to provide a mess that would keep the men healthy and content within the limitations of the food China offered and could afford. Most important, he got a training program under way, and the atmosphere began to freshen.[7]

Chennault approached the work at Toungoo with enthusiasm, enjoying the tremendous opportunity to train a group of fighting men with complete freedom of action. He felt certain these would be the first American airmen to meet the Japanese; their lives were in his hands, and he would largely determine how well they met the experienced Japanese flyers. The textbooks were Royal Air Force, U.S., and Japanese flying and staff manuals, the latter captured, translated, and analyzed so that the AVG could learn as much about Japanese tactics as the Japanese pilot himself. Chennault supplemented the manuals with his own accumulated observations and conclusions. He handed out mimeographed sheets detailing the specifications and performance of the various Japanese planes, against which were juxtaposed corresponding data on the P-40. Blackboard exercises identified the vulnerable areas of the Japanese planes until the pilots were drawn to them instinctively.

Chennault kept things simple and direct in an effort to instill the basics so firmly that a man flew and fought almost by reflex action. He drilled them on the assets of the P-40. The Zero had speed and maneuverability, but the P-40 had diving speed and firepower, and the pilots became convinced that "If we used those, we could get by with them. . . . if we tried to develop something out of the P-40 it didn't have, we were gone. . . . He told us: Never stay in and fight; never try to turn; never try to mix with them. . . . get altitude and dive on them and keep going—hit and run tactics; never lose speed . . . or take for granted that the planes you could see were all there were because we would always be outnumbered."[8]

He stressed that the Japanese were superb pilots who must not be underestimated, but they flew precise formations and utilized set tactics rather than taking individual initiative. They could be defeated by tactics that would break up their formations and force them to fight on AVG terms.

Early morning classroom sessions were followed by practice sessions in the air. The technique was the simulated dogfight, with Chennault watching through field glasses from the bamboo control tower. He gave them running commentary on their flying by radio, as well as dictating detailed notes to his secretary so that he could later go over them individually with the men. He advocated the two-ship element with a lead plane to attack while a wingman provided cover. The British had begun to use the same tactic, and they in turn had taken it from the German rotte formation. It eventually became standard, but it was not then in use in the American services and was new to the men. Excitement began to permeate the group. The fighting formation was three pairs with one weaver—"tail-end Charley"—behind for the first pass, after which the planes would fight in pairs. Chennault stressed accuracy and economy and practice at gunnery; nobody *ever* gets too good at gunnery, he insisted. To stay in a fight to the finish, you cannot afford to throw away your ammunition.

Chennault's tactics were not revolutionary, but they went directly to the heart of combat. They were based on the principle of the hunt, of creating favorable conditions for a kill. Their essence was common sense and self-preservation, for Chennault integrated everything he knew about planes and flying and handling men with all he could learn of the area and the enemy.[9]

The training did not always go well. The shortage of planes meant they had to stagger the sessions, and the planes received heavy wear. The pilots who came from the navy had no experience with liquid-cooled engines. Those who had never flown fighters before (more than half of them) had trouble putting the P-40 on the ground, for the taildragger tended to groundloop, and its landing speed was 100 m.p.h., at that time considered "hot." On one day Chennault watched six in a row crash upon landing. While he was indulging in a few choice expletives, a seventh plane fell victim to a mechanic on a bicycle, the mechanic so fascinated watching wreck number six that he plowed into plane number seven and tore off a piece of aileron. "It sure is depressing," wrote a member of the overworked ground crew.[10]

The shortage of personnel hindered progress. Pilots continued to arrive, a few at a time, until late November. Chennault could not work individually with them all. He selected his best pilots, made them squadron leaders with full responsibility for their men, and entrusted the training of late arrivals to them. As soon as they had enough planes he initiated squadron practice for attacks on bombers and ground targets. He shuffled personnel to find those best able to serve in staff positions. Some worked out well—Thomas Trumble became his secretary, and the two worked together in mutual trust for some years thereafter—but others caused recurring problems.

Of necessity he enlisted the help of some "tropical tramps," the adventuring opportunists. One was Boatner Carney, a former Air Corps captain and troublemaker who had been in Kunming as a CAF instructor since 1938. Another was Harvey Greenlaw, a former instructor in the Jouett mission who had stayed in China. Despite his West Point background, he was inadequate to the task of operations officer and earned the judgment of "one of the lousiest executive officers the general was ever cursed with." His wife's presence caused tension, for she quickly earned the favor of some of the men and the contempt of others. Chennault gave her a job keeping a group diary and putting out a newsletter, but she did neither with sufficient dedication to avoid causing trouble. She was one of the very few ever to be aware of the violence of Chennault's temper; he controlled it with an effort so intense that he sometimes became physically ill.[11]

Controversial in an entirely different way was Joseph Alsop, the suave Washington journalist who had become a lieutenant in the navy. He renewed his acquaintance with Chennault while on a mission to the Orient as a naval observer. Deciding that Chennault offered work "to greater advantage for the common cause," he asked to be released from the navy to join the AVG. The Navy Department was willing; it wrote McHugh, who wrote Chou, who asked Chennault, who said he could use Alsop in administrative work and press relations. Secretary Knox, Currie, and even Madame Chiang Kai-shek were involved in the correspondence relative to Alsop's new status, Madame writing that he "seems to be a nice boy, and if he is qualified for the position I surely hope he will obtain it."[12]

Obtain it he did, joining the AVG in October and providing Knox and Roosevelt with an inside contact who could report on what went on in Burma. There he was soon immersed in paperwork, for the AVG had an enormous burden of correspondence—with Chungking, Kunming, Loiwing, Rangoon, Singapore, Washington. At this Alsop was valuable, but he seemed somewhat a misfit in the AVG's rough-and-tumble atmosphere; he always seemed to be trailing Chennault with papers to be signed.[13]

As the summer wore into fall, the men of the AVG developed a distinctive group personality and morale. Theirs was a military organization that somehow was not military, and the men themselves were puzzled by it. One pilot despaired of discipline and was astounded at the constant griping, although "strangely enough we do get things done and in the last analysis it's the fight that counts."[14] They wore what they chose and sometimes did not shave; there was no marching or military procedure; saluting was not required, although most of them saluted Chennault by choice. He made it clear that each member was considered a specialist capable of performing his work well under difficult circumstances and without close supervision. To be treated with respect was, for some of them, a heady experience. Orders sometimes went through a chain of command but sometimes reflected a personal approach: "Son, can you do it?" or "We have a problem for you and your group. Can you get ready in 24 hours?" Chennault's style was to tell his leaders what he wanted done and let them do it their own way. "Individuality is given freedom," wrote one, and "never have I seen a better spirit of group solidarity than here."[15]

Observers were less enthusiastic, and those wedded to conventional approaches were appalled. Others concluded that Chennault required more discipline than many conventional leaders, although his methods necessarily differed. The AVG was formed in a sweltering, insect-infested jungle in Burma, where the teakwood barracks had no screens and snakes were sometimes encountered on the path to the latrines out back. They were in some respects outcasts of their own government, doing a job their government wanted done but was not willing to do publicly.

They had little equipment and few of the trappings of a conventional organization. In their place Chennault instilled the realization that there was a task to be done, and he inspired each man to do his best. "Real ability is the first measurement of a man's worth here,"[16] wrote one, and most of those who could not hold the respect of their colleagues were eased out. In their free time they applied themselves with equal dedication to the pursuit of pleasures. A group image as hell-raisers began to form in the streets and bars of Toungoo and Rangoon.

The men gave their squadrons distinctive names—Adam and Eve (a painful pun, in terms of pursuit), Hell's Angels, and Panda Bears. They painted their squadron emblems on their planes, and they turned the sharply pointed spinners into the noses of tiger sharks by adding a sinister eye and rows of large white teeth around the open cowling. They borrowed the idea from P-40 pilots in the Royal Air Force in Africa, but they made it their own. They began to exhibit a fierce pride not unlike that of Chennault himself.

Chennault's performance had another side, one his men seldom saw. As administrative problems began to take an increasing amount of his time, he displayed not only impatience and carelessness with details and long-term planning, weaknesses which might be excused on the grounds that staff and facilities were limited, but also an inability to admit that any difficulties were in any way his own responsibility. He was soon at loggerheads with Pawley and other CAMCO personnel regarding the services that CAMCO would provide. The last P-40 was not delivered until the end of November, and by then crack-ups and wear meant that the ones delivered earlier needed major repairs and overhaul. The manager of CAMCO's Loiwing factory assured Chennault that he would "offer our facilities for the good of the cause," but he declined to give an operating schedule until Chennault provided detailed projections of what would need to be done.[17]

Chennault was hard to deal with in these circumstances. Frequently obstinate, at times he was either intentionally obtuse or painfully lacking in interpersonal communication skills. His hearing cannot be blamed, as much of the business was transacted on paper. The relationship between him and Pawley, never good, deteriorated. Participants took sides; later their recollections of what had taken place differed sharply. Because many records were lost in later Japanese bombing raids on the CAMCO facility at Loiwing, neither side had verification. Chennault's version of affairs was that Loiwing was manufacturing a substantial number of trainers for sale to the Chinese; he interpreted their reluctance to work on AVG planes as another case in which Pawley had chosen the course that offered the greatest personal profit. A CAMCO manager, however, remembered that the trainers had been completed and the first P-40 assembled as of 28 May, that shortages of planes did not slow up the AVG as much as Chennault's own delays in beginning their training. The first shipment of planes did not reach Rangoon until 23 May, however, and two CAMCO men who worked on their assembly confirmed that the first plane was not finished until early August.[18]

One thing is clear: in 1941 and to a more marked degree later, Chennault was unwilling to give Pawley and CAMCO any credit for any part of the AVG. He did not easily share power, and as the letters and radiograms went back and forth between Toungoo, Loiwing, and Rangoon, where Pawley's Intercontinent office handled finances and purchasing, tempers rose.

Minor frictions began to escalate, each assuming disproportionate importance because of the major problem of aircraft overhaul and repair. When the volunteers were not paid on time and complained, Chennault found some 20 percent of their accounts to be in error and wrote, with flat finality, that any office staff should be able to do better. But Intercontinent's staff in New York gave Pawley its side—that delays in cables caused some delay, but most of the trouble was the result of an "endless morass of delayed, conflicting and erroneous information" sent them by the AVG headquarters.[19]

Then there were problems with the pilots. A high percentage of those hired in the later stages of recruitment did not have the optimum qualifications. Some quickly resigned; the lack of pursuit experience shown by others contributed to the high accident rate. A protesting Chennault said he was losing men who claimed that they had been told they would only be asked to fly defensive missions against unprotected bombers; he urged the recruiters to stop misrepresenting the AVG to the prospects and to "explain fully and frankly . . . the precise realistic probabilities of service in the Group." The recruiting staff fired back that Chennault himself had hired pilots with less pursuit experience than the ones he complained about. (Records show that Chennault hired two individuals in the States.) Further-more, in defense of their realism in recruitment, the staff quoted one returned pilot who assured everyone that he had not gone to Burma expecting to knit sweaters.[20]

The difficulties even went as far as groceries, for Pawley had shipped a load of AVG foodstuffs to Loiwing for CAMCO employees. Chennault insisted on an accounting, a halt to the practice, and reimbursement for AVG funds spent.

Always, in the background, was the problem of planes. AVG me-chanics and armorers performed a substantial amount of the assem-bly and could manage a number of field repairs if they had spare parts, but there were almost none. The AVG's Procurement Commit-tee suggested that the British might be able to provide parts; Chen-nault sent Alsop on a supply mission to Singapore. The British were willing but had no parts. Alsop was ordered on to Manila to see Gen. Douglas MacArthur, who had recently been called back into U.S. ser-vice and was working at a frantic pace to prepare the Philippines against possible Japanese assault. On his own initiative, Pawley made the trip to Manila and obtained seventy-two spare tires and some parts. Chennault was furious that Pawley had acted for the AVG; he ordered Alsop to proceed to Manila for further negotiations.[21]

By mid-November, with the war only three weeks away, twenty-six planes were grounded for lack of tires and sixteen more for need of some minor assembly. Another sixteen needed major assembly or rebuilding. It was actually a Chinese responsibility to provide parts, but Chennault had not previously taken the prudent steps to ensure that they were obtained. Now, sensing that time was running out, he began pulling out all the stops. A cable to Currie hit Washington "as a bombshell," for officials there had no inkling of any crisis in supply. Currie quickly raised some dust and sent off a shipment of parts by Pan-American Clipper.

"Everybody has cooperated splendidly," he wrote Chennault. Some were "pulled right out of the operation bases," for the air com-mand in Washington had extended "more or less formal adoption" to the AVG. There was even a vague promise that a supply officer would be provided. "Your standing with the air corps is higher than ever be-fore," Currie assured Chennault, "and there is general praise for the way you have conducted yourself throughout."[22]

Washington was tense during the months when the AVG was tak-ing shape. Germany had extended its conquest through the Balkans,

Greece, and Crete; the British were on the defensive in North Africa and seemed to be losing the battle of the Atlantic to the German U-boats. Germany had unleashed the Wehrmacht on the U.S.S.R. in late June; it was moving with frightening speed toward Leningrad and Moscow. The United States knew that Japan intended to take advantage of the European crisis to establish its "Greater East Asia Co-prosperity Sphere." If Britain lost its far eastern empire, it might collapse. The United States itself would be hard-pressed to maintain war production if Japan cut off access to Malayan rubber.

Washington sparred with Japan, hastened war preparations, made tentative plans for cooperation with Britain, and began seeking ways to be of more positive support to China. Plans for the Second AVG were approved in July, as noted above. The British also got behind the AVG, and Brooke-Popham offered Chennault a volunteer pursuit squadron and possibly a squadron of bombers. They, like the Second AVG, were engulfed when the war began.[23]

Concerned that the Chinese seemed unprepared to make effective use of lend-lease assistance, the War Department sent to China a military mission, AMMISCA, headed by Brig. Gen. John Magruder. Chennault resented that Washington supplied AMMISCA with a generous number of staff officers whom he felt he could have put to better use; he feared the mission would hamper more than help. Nobody quite knew how the AVG, the War Department, and AMMISCA fitted together. The War Department was reluctant to assume responsibility for AVG supply, but a crisis arose over ammunition. When the planes were first designated for the Chinese, the Americans had decided ammunition should come from the British, but there was no official agreement, and misunderstandings resulted. When it became apparent that the British could not supply ammunition, Currie and China Defense Supplies took the stance that the United States must fill the need. Stimson agreed, and ammunition was shipped.

As war came nearer, both Marshall and Stark recommended the maximum practical aid to the AVG. Marshall and Arnold wanted the United States to exercise some control over the AVG command in return for supply, but the State Department disagreed. The relationship of the AVG to the War Department was never clarified. Despite obvious ties to both the United States and Britain, the AVG remained a Chinese organization, independent within the CAF.[24]

Chennault's status as group commander was technically advisory and carried authority to define the missions of the Chinese aircraft. Ultimate authority rested with the Generalissimo, and in the past Chennault had usually communicated with Chiang Kai-shek through Madame. In June 1939, when Chou had been reappointed head of the Commission on Aeronautical Affairs, Chennault had agreed to stay on only if Madame would continue to use her influence to make certain that his views on aviation matters reached Chiang. At that time Madame had agreed to support him fully from the background, although she had refused to resume her former position with the commission. Well aware of the factionalism within Chiang's government, Chennault was consequently upset when, on 20 November, Madame sent him word that, since he now worked with Soong and she was no longer needed, he should now communicate directly with the Generalissimo.

Not wanting to lose her help at this critical juncture, Chennault responded vigorously. "I am greatly disturbed," he wrote, reminding her that he relied on her, for when she did not serve as his liaison, "interested persons take the opportunity to persuade the Generalissimo to issue unacceptable orders and otherwise make it very difficult for me to work for you and China as I would wish." He sent her copies of his correspondence with Soong over the past two months. He promised to keep her posted in the future. Placated, she responded on 1 December, "You may communicate direct with me as heretofore."[25]

During the final weeks before the war began, Chennault seemed both confident and uncertain. He made it clear to his men that he expected hostilities quite soon; when necessary he ordered them to buckle down. When the group's readiness was questioned in September, he had told Soong it should be prepared to operate at full strength prior to 1 November, but almost simultaneously he wrote Currie that the situation was serious and their only hope was for superior planes. He feared the War Department might jeopardize the whole expenditure by "pinching in small things."[26]

As late as 2 December he had only eighty-two pilots and sixty-two planes in commission, while another seventeen planes were out of commission and no satisfactory plan for repair and overhaul had been arranged. Yet he continued to be contentious and petty with Pawley; a meeting on 3 December about the purchase of parts was so heated that the secretary was unable to record all the proceedings. Later in the month Pawley decided it would be best for all concerned if he personally withdrew from all AVG matters. The breakdown between him and Chennault, he told Soong, was the result of Chennault's "continuous stream of telegrams and letters comdemning me and CAMCO for everything that appeared to be going wrong."[27]

Chennault's letters home reflect both his certainty that war was coming and his expectation of being in Louisiana for Christmas 1942. Perhaps he thought the Japanese would be defeated by then, or perhaps he felt he would need to retire by then, for his chronic bronchitis had become so bad he had given up flying—a desperate measure for a man whose very life had revolved around the controls of a plane. He reflected that he had no regrets about having come to China, and when he received a raise in pay he sent Nell a ruby and gave her some detailed advice on purchasing stock and land. He also requested more information about Waterproof's football games. "Nothing but this war could have kept me from seeing my boys play this year and I hope that I'll see them play in college yet."[28]

He was touched when his son Pat named a new son Claire Lee II. "Looks like I was unnecessarily modest in refusing to name a Jr.," he wrote. He had given one of his sons his father's name, but he had not named one for himself. The gesture possibly reflected his fundamental need to attain some sense of worth through achievement, for now he reflected, "My kids think more of me than I did of myself." He looked forward to teaching his new grandson to hunt and fish "and spoiling him possibly."[29]

On Sunday, 23 November, he took time off to go jungle fowl hunting, but he "missed only bird I saw." It was the last entry in his diary.

The news of Pearl Harbor first reached the AVG via a Japanese-controlled radio station in China; it was shortly confirmed by KGEI from San Francisco. Some of the men were elated, others sobered. One of them thought he detected a note of satisfaction on Chennault's face, as if to say, "Well, I'm glad this sham is over. Now we can turn to with real effort and get this business over with."[30] The only immediate action at Toungoo was further precautions against surprise attack.

Chennault immediately cabled Madame, suggesting the group move into Yunnan at once, as "we are not prepared for combat operations here." Their mission of protecting the Burma Road could more efficiently be accomplished from Kunming, he said, where there were more complete base facilities plus a warning net. On 9 December he received permission to move, as well as confirmation that his chief duty was to protect the Yunnan-Burma Road. Two days later, however, he received new orders from Chiang: "Keep the AVG at Toungoo for time being and cooperate closely with British." He responded at once that he would do so, but he warned that their position was "very dangerous due to lack of warning net." Toungoo was close to the border of Thailand, from which Japanese planes would doubtless come, and to Chou Chennault expressed reservations because the "British promise great deal but have no facilities or materials to cooperate." He sent the Third Squadron to Rangoon's Mingaladon field, because it offered better security than Toungoo.[31]

Chiang's resolve to cooperate with the British in the defense of Burma soon began to weaken. He did not want the AVG to be destroyed on the ground, as U.S. forces in Hawaii and the Philippines had been during the first days of war. On 15 December he ordered Chennault to keep one squadron at Rangoon but move the others to Kunming. The British military attaché protested that Chennault had been spoiled by the good warning net in China and should not expect the same in Burma, but Chiang held firm. He would not risk basing the entire AVG in Burma.[32]

The pattern set for the AVG during that first week of war held through most of the turbulent months to follow. One squadron stayed in Rangoon to fight alongside the RAF until that city fell in March 1942. The three squadrons rotated the duty, each in turn fighting until the pilots were exhausted and the planes so badly in need of repair that further operations were not feasible. At Kunming the remainder of the group defended the base and worked frantically to keep enough planes and men in flying condition so that the mission could go on. The AVG fought its first air action on 20 December against ten Japanese bombers over Kunming and destroyed six of the ten without losing any of its own men. Although he was pleased, Chennault knew the test had only begun.

Three days later the Third Squadron in Rangoon fought its first action against formidable odds: fifteen AVG to fifty-four Japanese bombers escorted by twenty pursuits, including eight of the new Zeros. Two AVG pilots were killed. Another parachuted out of his burning plane and was strafed by the Japanese as he descended. It served to make the AVG fighting mad, to make the men vow that the odds might be against them, but they had shot down six planes that day and had just begun to fight.

On Christmas Day, when the Japanese sent sixty bombers with eighteen pursuits, the AVG sent up twelve. The fighting lasted an hour and a half. Afterward the squadron leader wired Chennault that all his pilots had returned safely and had accounted for thirteen Japanese planes. "Like shooting ducks," he said.[33]

Neither the British nor the Americans had anticipated the speed and scope of the initial Japanese offensive. Not until the Battle of Midway in June 1942 were the Allies able to strike back effectively. Until then the war in the Pacific was an unmitigated humiliation

A cracked-up AVG P-40, Kunming, 1942. (Photo courtesy Richard Rossi)

and disaster, relieved only by the victories of the AVG. Needing something to shore up morale, the press embraced the men and shark-nosed planes of the Flying Tigers. The result was a degree of publicity far out of proportion to the group's small size and limited, though admirable, achievements. The flyers made, however, "good copy." Chennault and his adventuresome mercenaries, a little group formed in such secrecy and with such official reservation, were suddenly heroes.

The name by which the AVG became famous originated in the offices of China Defense Supplies in Washington, where Youngman, Willauer, and Shaughnessy decided that the AVG should have a distinctive emblem. Somebody suggested the Chinese dragon, but Soong rejected it as outdated. The eagle was rejected as too American. Soong suggested a tiger, but Willauer was a Princeton man and the others gave him (and the Princeton tiger) a hard time, saying that the animal was tied to the mundane earth. Soong then invoked the Chinese saying "Giving wings to the tiger." He reminded them that the tiger was the most formidable animal alive, but when endowed with wings its prowess was "super-colossal." Why not flying tigers? It was an apt term, invoking the legend that if one ate the heart of the saber-toothed tiger, one inherited its courage and strength.[34] The men of the AVG, for the most part unaware of the glamorous image beginning to grow around them, were going to need all the courage and strength they could summon.

9

The Inevitable End

The United States government had never been comfortable with the idea of the AVG—Americans fighting for pay in the employ of another country to circumvent neutrality laws and public opinion. Once war had been declared, Washington moved immediately to bring the AVG back under the American flag. "We have in this volunteer air group the nucleus of an American task force in Burma," Currie wrote Roosevelt the day following Pearl Harbor. He suggested converting the group into a regular U.S. Army task force by offering to give the men back their commissions and ratings, then rushing supplies and personnel to Burma to put the group at regulation strength.[1]

After the president and the State and War departments had agreed, AMMISCA was instructed to induct the AVG if the Chinese approved. There was also the matter of Chennault himself, and on 12 December Magruder broached the question with him, pointing out that, if he were commissioned and the group incorporated, other military channels could offer reinforcement, and the command of the AVG would be made more efficient.[2]

Chennault's reaction was negative. He had offered his services to the army and had been refused. He had put the AVG together against all odds, and now that it was ready to fight and the army was not, he jolly well wanted the opportunity to go ahead and fight without Washington's calling the shots. He visualized the "swamping of my very limited administrative personnel with such a mass of regulations, reports and other paper work that I will have very little time to devote to tactics and operations."[3] If the purpose was to defeat Japan, why not do it the most effective and expeditious way? He hated to give up the AVG's relative freedom to move quickly and take advantage of tactical opportunity, a freedom to which he later attributed the AVG's high combat success.

Chennault also doubted that the War Department had any intention of replacing the AVG with a first-class pursuit group. Even if it did, he believed that his small, streamlined unit, economical and flexible, could operate in China to far better advantage than a full-strength regular unit. Replacing the support provided by the Chinese—fuel, transportation, communications, mess, laundry, labor, quarters, repair services, and ammunition—with American services would require large numbers of men and the transport of substantial amounts of machinery and equipment. He correctly surmised that Washington did not comprehend the limitations of China's transportation system.

Chennault admitted that there was a need for U.S. supply. He estimated he would need six planes per week and ten pilots per month in replacements, but he thought the best interests of all concerned would be served if the group was supplied by the army but was allowed to remain independent. It was a well-trained group of men, combative and eager to fight but independent by nature and motivated by unusual freedom of operation as well as by the handsome bonus paid each man for his efforts. He anticipated that the men would resign rather than be inducted, the group would dissolve, the War Department would be unable to replace it with a unit of comparable effectiveness, and the poor Chinese would once more be defenseless against the Japanese bombs. It was, after all, at Chinese initiative that the group existed at all.[4]

The War Department had already considered—and rejected—the idea of reinforcing the AVG with U.S. Army units, for Washington could not maintain government and volunteer forces side by side. The volunteers were not covered by the articles of war, they could resign or refuse to fight, they did not have to conform to military discipline, and they received far more pay than they would have in the regular services. The contrast would have been devastating to morale in regular army units. If Chennault understood this point, he did not admit it. Having made sacrifices for his freedom, his chance, he was not going to give it up without a struggle.

The men of the AVG responded with dismay and resentment when word of induction began to leak out early in January. The unit faced a crisis in morale just as the fighting over Rangoon became most critical. Assuring the men that he opposed induction and would fight it, Chennault made every effort to salvage the AVG as originally conceived.[5]

He also tried desperately to salvage the Second AVG. "If furnished with a very small number of aircraft of proper types and models and a few more men immediately," he wrote shortly after the group's first battles, "we are confident that in cooperation with the Chinese we can so damage and demoralize the Japanese air force that it will cease to be a factor in the China-Burma-Malaya theater of war." He emphasized that any action taken must be immediate and must have the full support of the allied powers. An all-out air offensive "should be wholly adopted or wholly rejected, as half measures will not accomplish the full objective."[6]

It became Chennault's litany that a small but effective air force, free to strike at the most advantageous time and place, could produce results far out of proportion to its strength. He saw the opportunity. He raged inwardly at not being able to exploit it. At the end of January he wired Currie that he could begin attacks on Japan's industries at once if the air force could be provided, "to operate under my command and control of Generalissimo only." McHugh supported him, writing Currie that "the time element is of the essence," for after the Japanese took Singapore and could turn their entire effort toward Burma, a small force would be insufficient.[7]

They might as well have recommended the Yangtze change course. During the first critical weeks of the war, when Washington established its priorities for waging coalition global war with limited resources, the China-Burma-India theater ended up at the very bottom of the heap. Far from an immediate push to destroy Japan's war-making potential with air power, Japan would wait. Germany was the primary enemy; the Allies would concentrate on Europe until Germany was defeated. They would limit Pacific action to what was necessary for securing Australia and China as bases for future offensives.

It was U.S. policy to support China, and for 1942 "support" meant maintaining communications, delivering lend-lease supplies, and providing help in improving China's combat effectiveness. A unified command under (British) Gen. Archibald Wavell was set up to encompass the American-British-Dutch-Australian responsibility, but Chiang Kai-shek was named supreme commander of a separate China theater. A high-ranking U.S. officer would serve as the American representative in China, supervising lend-lease, controlling the Burma Road, commanding all U.S. forces in China, and, at Chiang's request, serving as his chief of staff.[8]

At the end of January, Lt. Gen. Joseph Stilwell was named U.S. commander in China. It was a choice pregnant with trouble, promising to rekindle all the old antagonisms between ground and air officers, for even though the primary support for China would be through air power, Stilwell was an infantryman. Stilwell was also a fighter, not a diplomat, yet his job would be primarily diplomatic—guiding, encouraging, persuading, and keeping China in the war until the Allies could defeat Germany and then come to China's aid. In Stilwell's favor were his knowledge of the language and his love for the country, for he had been stationed in China and had enjoyed it. He had earned Marshall's respect and trust. He was also a dedicated soldier who would do his duty, and the job promised abundant frustration but little glory. Stilwell's own reaction was, "I'll go where I'm sent."[9]

The selection of Stilwell's staff became entangled with relationships between Washington and Chungking, particularly those involving Chennault's status and the induction of the AVG. For a time the conviction had been growing in some circles that Chennault should be commissioned and named the senior American air officer in China, under the Generalissimo's command. Magruder made the suggestion to Chiang on 1 December; both Chiang and Madame agreed. When the China theater was created, Chiang asked that Stilwell's mission include an air officer of high rank. It was apparent that Chennault would have been acceptable to the Chinese, and the War Department, appreciative of Chennault's efforts with the AVG, could at that time have supported the appointment. On 8 December Currie observed that Chennault was "highly regarded" by Arnold.[10]

When Magruder began negotiating with Chiang and Chennault about the induction of the AVG, however, political undertow threatened to engulf the entire structure. Chiang can hardly be blamed for his reluctance to give up control of China's only effective defense force, especially in the wake of the devastating defeats Japan had

dealt the Allied air forces in the opening days of the war. He bar-
gained and vascillated, trying to use the AVG to get advantages such
as increased lend-lease or Chinese command of U.S. units in China.
The United States in turn tried to use supply of the AVG as a tool
against Chiang. Chennault supported Chiang, but was in some respects a pawn. In disgust he watched the AVG being torn apart by official wrangling.

On 20 January Chennault wrote both Magruder and Madame, suggesting that the impasse could be circumvented by letting him be
commissioned and appointed by the Generalissimo as the air officer
commanding in China while Washington was asked to continue supplying the AVG. The War Department would thus have a general officer in China, but the combat effectiveness of the AVG would not be
disrupted, as it surely would be if it were inducted. Chennault obviously wanted the command, but he also wanted the AVG to remain
independent of the War Department. He was frank with Magruder,
who evaluated his motivations as a combination of loyalty to the
Generalissimo and personal ambition. Chennault was especially
worried that he might be superseded by an officer who was inexperienced in China. Because of his own peculiar position as someone
knowledgeable about China who had an intimate working relationship with its leaders, he believed he could do what needed to be done
more expeditiously than anyone else. Magruder's assessment was
much the same: he advised Washington that Chennault was "probably the only man with qualifications and experience who can effectively take operational command of both American and Chinese Air
Forces."[11]

Madame joined Magruder in recommending to Washington that
Chennault be the ranking air officer in China. He noted that Chennault held the respect and confidence of the Chinese; his record there
was superb. Soong wrote to Stimson. The War Department assured
Chiang that Chennault would be promoted to brigadier general and
would be the highest ranking American air officer in China. Although the AVG would not remain independent, it would become
the U.S. Twenty-third Pursuit Group and would be maintained at full
strength. Madame was satisfied. She told Chennault to prepare the
AVG to be inducted.[12]

In Washington, however, negotiations hit a snag, possibly precipitated by reports that the AVG displayed poor discipline or none and
that the men were not eager to accept a reduction in pay. (The latter
assumption may have been unfair; some of the men later protested

that they had never been asked how they felt about pay and heartily resented the slur on their patriotism.) Stilwell decided that Chennault was playing "politics and petticoats." Chennault was not named the ranking U.S. air officer in China. Instead Col. Clayton L. Bissell was made the air officer on Stilwell's staff. He would be Chennault's superior if the latter were recommissioned.[13]

Now Chennault was dismayed. He had known Bissell since 1930, when Chennault was a student at ACTS and Bissell taught the pursuit course. They had disagreed drastically on tactics. Bissell had not supported the concept of a warning net for interception, and Bissell was a rule-book officer, inclined toward stern attention to the details that Chennault found least important.[14] He believed that Bissell would be an absolute disaster in China and protested, precipitating some lively discussions in Washington. Stilwell fumed that the whole situation put Chennault in the position of saying who could and could not be on his staff.[15]

Currie wired Chennault that he believed it to be in China's interest for him to accept command of the fighting forces and let Bissell be over all, for even though "attitude toward you in Army is excellent," Bissell would be better able to secure army cooperation for "really large scale effort."[16]

Chennault responded that "China's interest is of paramount importance" but went on to note Bissell's lack of knowledge of conditions in China. He feared he could not "handle situation out here. He is very headstrong and has always differed with me in regard to pursuit tactics." If the training and employment of the AVG were deficient, let them select an officer with whom he as a subordinate could work harmoniously—Lawrence Hickey, M. F. Harmon, or G. C. Brant, for instance. He was also willing to retire, for his health was precarious; bronchitis had kept him bedridden for much of December and January.[17]

Chennault's attitude impressed Washington as petty and unprofessional. Arnold "hit the ceiling." The War Department was growing alarmed at the degree to which Chinese politics dictated its own decisions, and Chennault's closeness to Chiang made him suspect. Chennault's reputation—he was considered hard to get along with and out of the mainstream of Air Corps thought—may have influenced decisions, and a tinge of professional jealousy may have entered the picture also, for already Chennault and the Flying Tigers were making headlines as the only Allied unit in the Pacific that had not been caught by surprise. In any event, Stilwell supported Bissell and insisted that the latter rank Chennault, even though Chennault had been ahead of Bissell on the promotion lists before he retired. Arnold ordered it to be done, and Currie wired Madame, asking her help in easing "this difficult situation."[18]

Madame had little success. After a long talk with him late in February, she wired Currie that Chennault felt he had fulfilled his pledge to acquire and train a competent air group for China. He was now willing to withdraw and let Bissell or any other army appointee take over. "He firmly believes," Madame wrote, "that neither he nor Chinese officers can work harmoniously under Bissell because of latter's high-handed methods and ways of accomplishing objectives." Chennault would welcome Bissell as his adviser, however, if doing so would help him get equipment for an independent AVG.[19]

"This Chennault mess is a nuisance," Stilwell wrote in his pocket diary as he got ready to fly to China. "Stick to Bissell," he decided.[20] Stilwell's opinion of Chennault had dropped, Chennault's resentment of the army command had grown, the Chiangs felt they had been misled, and Bissell took up his China duties in full realization that the one successful air unit in the entire theater was opposed to his command. The China-Burma-India time bomb was fused before the theater even became operational.

The political decisions about China were made against a backdrop of sobering Allied defeat. Within weeks the Japanese enjoyed overwhelming success at Pearl Harbor, Midway, Guam, Wake Island, the Philippines, Hong Kong, Thailand, Malaya, Burma, and the Netherlands East Indies. Scrambling to keep up, Allied planners focused on two immediate necessities: MacArthur's forces in the Philippines must hold out as long as possible to buy time to reinforce Australia, while in Burma the defense forces must try to stem the Japanese advance before all contact with China was broken. The AVG, with its mission to defend the Burma Road and its Rangoon terminus, was suddenly on center stage. The Burmese defense forces included one squadron of RAF Buffalo fighters plus a squadron of bombers, and in January Air Vice Marshal D. F. Stevenson became the Royal Air Force group commander at Rangoon.

While at Mingaladon the AVG was under Stevenson's operational control. RAF and AVG fought together, sharing an operations room and common intelligence, although they had two separate radio transmitters on different frequencies for control of the air battles. The general principles of fighting were agreed upon in conferences by Stevenson, the RAF wing leader and the AVG squadron leader, and although the RAF did not direct combat actions of the AVG, all worked together on common information. The AVG flew some support and strafing missions for the British and also tried to defend Rangoon. The RAF was responsible for the AVG's food, housing, and transportation, and because the airfield was a favorite Japanese target for night bombing, the men were billeted in the homes of Rangoon's English families and were assigned vehicles to take them to and from the field. As the military situation worsened, the men slept where they could, sometimes in trucks or camped out beside the field.

There was some friction. When the RAF credited the AVG with only three Japanese planes on 23 December, Chennault requested an investigation, saying he would pull his men back to Kunming for target practice if they could not do better than that. Both sides then agreed on the system of confirmation approved by the RAF. The warning system was poor—a few members of the Burma observer corps linked by telephone and one portable RDF set—and accurate intelligence was hard to get because the native population was not enthusiastic about supporting the British. The Brewster Buffaloes (and later a few Hurricanes) were no match for the Japanese planes, and the RAF did not enjoy the high success ratio of the AVG. The American pilots sometimes disparaged "the blooming Limeys" as lacking eagerness to fight.[21]

The Japanese launched a major air assault on Rangoon at the end of January. In five days of almost continuous air fighting, the Japanese lost more than fifty planes and pilots; the AVG lost two pilots and the RAF ten. The Japanese temporarily abandoned daylight raids but continued to pound Rangoon by night. Singapore fell in mid-February; the Japanese Fifteenth Army was soon advancing on Rangoon. The high command tried to hold the city as long as possible, for the docks were piled high with lend-lease goods that were being pushed up the Burma Road as fast as the chaos allowed.

AVG operations took on a tinge of desperation as gasoline and oxygen supplies dropped and the Japanese attacks intensified. The civil government and social structure of Rangoon collapsed; looting and arson became rampant; the jails, insane asylums, and zoos were opened by fleeing guards, and their former inmates roamed the streets. All possible AVG ground personnel were sent back to Kunming, heading up the Burma Road in motley convoys of assorted vehicles, some supplied by CAMCO, some "appropriated" from Rangoon's disintegration. Chennault left it up to squadron leader Robert Neale to remain in action at Mingaladon as long as possible.

The night of 26 February, when Stevenson told Neale they would have to remove the RDF warning system that night, the remaining planes of the AVG pulled out.[22] The last two days had been busy: on 25 February the AVG accounted for twenty-two Japanese fighters and one bomber; on 26 February, eleven more fighters. Thanks to AVG efforts, the evacuation of Rangoon was free from Japanese air attack. The grateful British openly acknowledged that the AVG had carried the brunt of the Rangoon fighting and accounted for the bulk of the Japanese losses.[23]

Chennault was in Kunming—much of the time confined to bed—during the weeks the AVG was giving battle over Rangoon. He gave them little specific combat direction, although he followed events closely by radio and sometimes sent his squadron leaders advice. Worried about the lack of adequate advance warning and the steady depletion of the planes, he discouraged offensive missions against the Japanese air concentrations in Thailand. Although he privately believed the AVG had no choice but to continue to defend Rangoon, he asked the British to replace it with an RAF squadron because the Chinese were running out of planes. Stevenson was so alarmed that he appealed to Churchill, who wrote to Roosevelt, who brought the matter up with the Combined Chiefs of Staff, who asked Chiang to keep the AVG in Rangoon. The Generalissimo consented.[24]

There was a lull in the fighting in Burma after Rangoon fell. Stilwell arrived and began grappling with the complexities of his mission. He met Chennault briefly in Burma on 3 March, flew on to Kunming, and spent the night in Chennault's house (gratefully noting that it was cool). The following morning the two had a talk at the Kunming airfield, when Stilwell felt he "calmed down" Chennault. Chennault told Stilwell he would be glad to serve under him, and Stilwell, relieved, noted, "He'll be okay." Stilwell thought the AVG pilots "look damn good." He was encouraged as he flew on to Chungking.[25]

There Madame expressed her concern about Chennault's status (she warned him that Chennault resigned regularly); he reassured her. With Chiang he began to work out the details of his duties and the extent to which he was to command the Chinese armies, but he met the same kind of obstructions Chennault had long ago encountered. It was mid-March before he returned to Burma and the staggering task of halting the Japanese conquest.

The battle for Burma went from bad to worse, a debacle of unpreparedness and political vulnerability heightened by complex command relationships between British, Burmese, Chinese, and U.S. forces. The major responsibility lay with the British, but Japanese ground forces rendered them ineffective with a new wrinkle in warfare—soldiers fully armed, disciplined, and trained like European regular armies yet employing the mobility, individual initiative, and unorthodox tactics of guerrillas.

Chennault responded with guerrilla tactics of his own. After Rangoon fell, the AVG moved to Magwe, then Loiwing. They had few planes left, but they made every one count by avoiding major aerial battles and conducting surprise raids, often quite effective, to destroy Japanese planes on the ground. They evaded danger to themselves by moving frequently from one landing field to another.

The question of the AVG's future was settled in early April. Chennault had continued to insist stubbornly that he would resign, but obviously he was loath to give up the AVG. Stilwell, believing that Chennault was playing personal politics, was resentful, and the two had an inconclusive and unsatisfactory talk on 21 March. Through Madame, Chennault appealed once more to Currie, lamenting that the group was becoming ineffective because equipment and personnel had been exhausted, yet there was "great opportunity." Could not men and planes be assigned to the AVG rather than to the U.S. Tenth Air Force, which was taking shape in India? It would be three months before the Tenth could become effective; the AVG was effective now. He posed the anguished question, "Is induction [of the] AVG still desired even if destruction of group results?" Currie responded that Arnold was still adamant, but the Generalissimo's wishes would probably be the controlling ones. The indecision, he warned, was hurting China.[26]

Chennault went to Chungking and checked into the Air Force Rest House on 1 April. John Davies, at Currie's request, went to see him there and sought to persuade him to "play ball" with Arnold because the latter had tremendous influence. Chennault expressed some of his objections to the plans for induction while continuing to protest that the AVG could do with 150 men what would take the army a thousand. He talked with Madame before making his final decision. When all parties met that afternoon, as Stilwell put it, to "finish off the damn AVG thing," Chiang gave his approval for induction and Chennault concurred. The AVG would come to an end on 4 July, to be replaced with a complete U.S. fighter group. In the meantime every effort would be made to maintain the efficiency of the unit. "Thank Heavens," Madame wired Currie in relief.[27]

April was the turning point for the AVG. The adventure was gone. The fight had been well fought, but now the men faced depreciating equipment, mounting casualties, and Japanese conquest in Burma. Morale began dropping; some men resigned, others became difficult to manage. Their diary entries began to reflect resentment of the constant hazard even while noting accomplishments with pride. "It is always like this," wrote one. "Outnumbered every time we are engaged in the air or intercept the enemy, but still for all that the enemy losses are enormous." When Chennault joined them at Loiwing early in April, they sensed in him a mounting aggressiveness. "The demands made on him and the AVG are so great as to be absolutely impossible, except that Chennault will never admit impossibility," wrote another. Some of the missions seemed to ask the men to do more than seemed reasonable, given the equipment and training.[28]

A few official words of appreciation would have helped, but these were not forthcoming. Resentment led to a tense confrontation precipitated by a request for volunteers for a specific mission. The men refused to step forward. In AVG fashion, Chennault called a meeting to talk it through. All parties aired their grievances, with frank and sometimes heated language. Chennault appealed to the men's pride, saying they could show the white feather and get out, and the phrase angered the pilots. They learned that he had accepted a commission and had to obey orders, but they wanted an end to low-level ground-support missions, and they wanted more planes and supplies so that they would have some reasonable expectation of success and survival. Some drew up their resignations, but Chennault refused to accept them, and the men did not want to desert. Several pilots volunteered for the disputed mission, which was called off for other reasons. The crisis simmered down.[29]

Chennault tried to eliminate the problems. He suggested that both Chiang and Roosevelt send the AVG some words of praise and appeal to them to stay in the fight, and this was speedily done. Two more significant suggestions were not met: the early transfer of the Twenty-third Pursuit Group so the AVG could be promptly reconstituted under that name, and the immediate transfer of pilots and crewmen from India as reinforcements. The long-term gap between Chennault and the War Department, partially closed by his recommissioning, soon began to seem wider than ever, for Chennault had finally agreed to "play ball" in order to get support for his group, and the support was slow in coming.[30]

Supply and reinforcement—the albatross that came to curse all

U.S. operations in China—was the most vulnerable area from the beginning. As it became clear that Burma would be lost and the Burma Road closed, planners began work on air transport into China over the Himalayas from India, the effort that became famous as "The Hump," but initially there were few planes and few facilities to implement it.

In hope of shortening delivery time, AVG replacement planes were sent by ship to Africa and were then ferried by air the last 7,000 miles. The pilots who went to get them were out of action for some weeks, and the planes needed repair and maintenance when they arrived, so the effort was only partially successful. Attempts to send Chennault bombers were even more disappointing failures. The famous Tokyo Raid, led by Lt. Col. James H. Doolittle, was planned in January as a boost to Allied morale, but its sixteen B-25s were expected to land in China and reinforce the AVG after bombing Tokyo. On 18 April they bombed Japan and escaped from the home islands without trouble, making the mission a dramatic success as a morale booster. Unfortunately all the planes crashed or were abandoned as night overtook them, and the crews, lacking adequate maps or navigational aids, tried unsuccessfully to find landing fields in China. The raid had been planned in great secrecy (even Chiang Kai-shek had only the barest information), and if Chennault was briefed at all, he was told little. According to Doolittle, Washington did not want Chennault to know about the raid in advance because his closeness to the Chinese made a leak seem inevitable. Afterward Chennault was bitter, for had advance planning allowed him time to set up a homing beacon and a ground-to-air communications system, he thought he might have gotten the men and planes safely down in China.[31]

The first six B-25s for Chennault's Eleventh Bombardment Squadron reached India in early June, but they were ordered to conduct a bombing mission in Burma en route to Kunming. The mission stretched their range and four were lost, a fiasco that the AVG blamed on Bissell. Two other groups of bombers slated for China never arrived because they were diverted to the Middle East, where Rommel and his Afrika Korps were playing hob with the British. In June even the few planes thus far assembled in India for the Tenth Air Force were transferred to the North Africa battles.[32]

The men of the AVG knew only that they received precious little to work with, that the demands put on them were great, and that, although their success in combat was outstanding, their government seemed unappreciative. They resented the buildup of the Tenth Air

Force in India while they starved for equipment. Once the army began the preliminary steps toward induction, resentment became anger. When an army colonel implied that they could not really fight and claimed that he could lick the AVG's best pilot in a dogfight, $5,000 appeared on the table within seconds as the men demanded to know when he would like to start.[33]

The AVG had limited contact with Stilwell, and the little they had was not good. During evacuation after the fall of Rangoon, a group of AVG ground personnel reported to Stilwell in Lashio and requested a billet and food, but they were given a tongue-lashing and were refused help because they were dirty and disorganized and one of the men was drunk. They thought it was inhumane not to take care of those who had been fighting on your side, even if they were not spit and polish; they interpreted the incident as complete lack of appreciation for the AVG's defense of Rangoon.[34]

Most of the AVG's resentment, however, focused on Bissell, who impressed them as being cold, opinionated, didactic, and arrogant. The more they had to do with him, the less they liked him. When recruitment got under way, Bissell spoke to the group in a way that the men perceived as insulting; if they did not sign up now, he indicated, they would be inducted soon as they hit the States. One man interpreted Bissell's threats as "you're not going to get home if you're not in the Army." Some of the men took it upon themselves to teach the Chinese the phrase "Piss on Bissell," and the smiling coolies, who thought it was a salutation, greeted all incoming planes with smiles and bows and a chorus of "Piss on Bissell."[35]

Chennault himself, once the decisions were final, initially tried to work well with his fellow officer. The early correspondence between them was courteous and free from tension, and Bissell for his part made every effort to be helpful. When Chennault was ordered into regular service as a colonel on 9 April, he had no eagles and asked Bissell if he could provide a set. This Bissell did, but at the end of April both men were promoted to brigadier, Bissell one day ahead of Chennault so that he would be the ranking officer. Chennault kept his hurt and anger to himself and wrote Bissell the correct letter of congratulation, but when Doolittle came through Kunming shortly afterward, he found Chennault still wearing eagles. Doolittle had been promoted on the same list and gave Chennault his stars while being considerate enough not to tell him that he had received them from Bissell only hours before.[36]

By the end of April the battle in Burma was disintegrating into a rout. British forces started over the jungle-clad hills to India in the longest retreat in their history. While some of the Chinese troops moved north and east toward the China border, Stilwell directed others toward India, where he hoped to retrain them for a campaign to reconquer Burma. His experiences in Burma had begun to sour him, and in his personal writing, where he vented his spleen, he wrote, "Somebody has to control the mess and I am the goat."[37] Feeling a sense of responsibility for his command, he declined evacuation by plane and successfully led a party of 114 soldiers, staff, nurses, and refugees out of Burma on foot. The dramatic gesture did not raise his stature in the eyes of airmen, who thought it was a strange choice for a commanding officer and interpreted it as a slap at the air forces.

The AVG fought desperately as Japanese forces pursued the retreating Chinese troops toward Yunnan. On one raid thirteen Japanese fighters were destroyed at a cost of one damaged AVG plane, but most battles went less well, and the evacuation toward Kunming was chaotic. The Burma Road was a narrow, twisting, unimproved road with hairpin curves so sharp trucks might have to back up as many as six times to get around, with grades so steep that failed brakes meant certain disaster. After crossing Burma's mountain crests and entering China, it dropped into the mile-deep Salween Gorge, snaking its way for some twenty miles down precipitous cliffs to cross a suspension bridge over the swift and angry Salween, then winding its tortuous way up the equally forbidding cliffs on the other side. The Salween Gorge reminded Americans of the Grand Canyon, but to the Chinese it meant the last obstacle between them and the advancing Japanese Army.

On 7 May the AVG daily intelligence report noted, "Hostile ground forces are advancing along the Lungling-Paoshan road." Chennault ordered a mission to "destroy and block the road." The flight leader's report said their four planes "aimed to destroy the Burma Road by blowing it up at a point where a landslide would result or repairs of the road would be difficult." The Chinese were by then retreating in panic; they blew up the Salween bridge, even though some Chinese forces were still on the west side.[38]

On 8 May the AVG intelligence report noted, "Hostile forces are attempting to build a bridge across the Salween River." Again Chennault ordered bombing and strafing missions as well as pursuit support for a small force of Chinese bombers. The Japanese offered a vulnerable target, for the narrow road had few turnoffs and was jammed with traffic. The AVG pilots approached the task with their

customary verve. By 10 May intelligence reported the Japanese retreating back into Burma, and Chennault urged Madame to have
Chinese troops hasten to take advantage of the reversal.[39]

"Believe AVG inflicted heavy losses Jap vehicles and some personnel in six bomb and gun attacks on this column," he reported. "I believe these attacks definitely convinced the Japanese that a
mechanized column could not operate along the Burma Road when
opposed by a determined air force." Six years later the Japanese denied that they intended to invade Yunnan, although it seems strange
for them to have started a bridge over the Salween if they did not.
Chennault and the AVG believed, with good reason, that they had
halted the Japanese invasion of China. Their forces were almost exhausted, and they welcomed the summer rains that brought temporary respite from battle.[40]

The Burma battles over, the AVG could now concentrate on protecting Chungking from Japanese bombardment. Chennault and part
of the men moved to Peishiyi, a field some eight miles from Chungking. When the dozen planes flew over the city for the first time, coming up the river in formation and banking steeply before breaking to
wheel and dip and cavort over the city "like a school of happy flying
fish," Chungking's citizens ran outdoors to gasp in disbelief. It was
the first time they had seen their Flying Tigers, China's heroes, and
for the half hour that the pilots put on their show, the elated Chinese
sent their roars of gratitude and joy skyward with a common voice.[41]

The AVG's end, however, was near. In mid-June the official induction board made the rounds of the AVG bases. Only forty-one men,
six of them pilots, signed up. One who did not noted that they had
been out of step with their complacent, isolationist country when
they signed up the year before; now they were out of step once more,
for they were tired and wanted to go home and see their families before starting to fight again. Many of them had come from the navy
originally and wanted to return to it rather than join the army. Some
were bitter over the way the army had treated them during their fight
in Burma. Others resented the government's approach, which they
considered high-handed. They hated to see the group broken up, for
theirs had been a unique experience, and they knew that something
was going out of their lives that could never happen again. For Chennault, the agony was even more intense. His spirit drained away; his
jokes became mechanical, his manner perfunctory; the hard lines
around the eyes seemed to deepen.[42]

Regret that the AVG was ending was balanced by pride in its

record. The men had destroyed 297 enemy aircraft and had lost only 14 of their own planes in combat. They had defended Rangoon and had made its orderly evacuation possible. They had played an important role in stopping the Japanese advance at the Salween. Other achievements were less easily measured. They had fostered hope and promised victory, inspiring both Chinese and American pride at a time of utter despair. The cost in men was four prisoners and twenty-two dead (four in combat, five on strafing raids, three by bombers, ten in crashes). The cost in money was $3 million to recruit and operate, $8 million for planes. Fifty-four surviving planes were purchased by the U.S. Army for a credit against lend-lease of $3.5 million. When the books were cleared, Chennault turned over to Madame a remainder of $7,990 to apply to war charity. Across the bottom of his record of discharge, she wrote in her own hand, "He performed the impossible."[43]

It seems somehow consistent with their strange history that the men of the AVG in Chungking spent the last night of their official existence playing musical chairs with Madame at the home of China's aged and almost unknown president. The group's legacy was more far reaching than the men could know. The advantages of having an aggressive and effective military unit independent of War Department control and shielded from public scrutiny had not been lost on others who, like Chennault, believed in fighting the most expeditious way. Five years later, when political tensions gave birth to the U.S. Central Intelligence Agency, it began evolving a special division to conduct clandestine operations. To Chennault's quiet satisfaction, it even eventually acquired an air force of its own, shaped by Chennault himself and not too unlike his original Flying Tigers.

10

The China Air Task Force

The China Air Task Force (CATF) which replaced the AVG was a gamble. It was isolated and surrounded, sandwiched between the Japanese in Burma/Thailand and occupied China, vulnerable to action by Japanese ground forces. Unconnected by land or sea with the outside, it depended on aerial supply. It was substantially outnumbered. On paper its strength was the Twenty-third Fighter Group of four squadrons (Seventy-fourth, Seventy-fifth, Seventy-sixth, and Sixteenth) plus the Eleventh Bombardment Squadron, but planes and men were slow to arrive, replacements ran behind schedules, the limited repairs that could be made in China were slow, and when the CATF could put thirty fighters and half a dozen bombers aloft, it felt powerful. Shortages were as severe as, if not worse than, during the days of the AVG.[1]

Always one to look for an alternative solution if the optimum was not on hand, Chennault divided his small command with unabashed aggressiveness, rotating his squadrons among Lingling, Kweilin, Hengyang, Chenyi, Yunnanyi, Kunming, Peishiyi, and other small fields, so that the force seemed to be much larger than it was, taking advantage of being able to move quickly and to keep the enemy off guard. One squadron guarded the vital Hump air route and struck at targets of opportunity in Burma. Another concentrated on the Hankow-Canton railway and the inland waterways of the southeast. From Kweilin the planes swarmed over the northern part of Indochina; from Lingling they attacked the Japanese at Hong Kong and along the coast of the South China Sea, where Chennault saw tremendous opportunity to sever Japan's line of communications to the troops in Burma.[2]

The fighters (in May 1942 the United States officially changed pursuit designations to "fighter") also supported the Chinese armies in Chekiang, where the Japanese launched a harsh campaign in retaliation for the Tokyo Raid. Their results were so positive and the Japanese targets so lucrative that Col. Caleb V. Haynes, commanding the CATF bombardment, reported "an imperative need" for more bombers, stating "it must be obvious" that fifty or a hundred bombers could provide the balance of power to force the Japanese to withdraw from eastern China.[3] Even with their small force, the CATF record for July was twenty-four Japanese fighters and twelve bombers destroyed at a cost of five P-40s and one B-25, a ratio of 6:1 when 4:1 was average for U.S. forces. If we had 500 planes, one pilot wrote his father, "it would take more than all the planes Japan possesses to prevent us from driving them completely off the Chinese continent in 4 months."[4]

Chennault ached for more with which to fight. "The opportunities here are too many and too productive of results to neglect," he wrote Stilwell on 16 July. He asked for more planes, for replacements for losses, for newer models of fighters so that he could maintain an edge over the Japanese in combat. If he had 100 P-51s and thirty B-25s by mid-October, he said, he would employ them so as to destroy Japanese aircraft at a favorable ratio, encourage Chinese resistance, disrupt Japanese shipping in China and off the coast, damage Japanese installations within his range, and "break the morale of the Japanese air force while destroying a considerable percentage of Japanese aircraft production."[5]

The claims were optimistic but not unreasonable. With the AVG and CATF he had begun developing a unique operational approach, selecting aggressive, innovative men who were eager to fight, training them well, then turning them loose by eliminating most of the restraints under which a conventional Western military force operates. Chennault himself was an instinctive fighter who saw battle at its most primitive level; he was much in harmony with the fifth-cen-

tury Chinese military theorist Sun Tzu, who set high value on deception and cunning. Seeing tremendous potential for such fighting
within the peculiar circumstances China afforded, he yearned for the
opportunity to implement it. And with his usual lack of tact or patience for those who did not see things the same way, he tended to
view the more conventional approach as pointless, even stupid.

His 16 July letter was the formal opening round in what became the
great China-Burma-India debate: should the limited resources that
could be allotted to China be used aggressively and immediately by
the air forces, as Chennault advocated? Or should they be used to
build up the Chinese ground forces for a struggle yet to come? Chennault identified accessible and vulnerable targets, with significant
rewards to be gained from an immediate offensive while Japan was
committed elsewhere.

Chennault's argument reflected not only his personal eagerness to
fight and his conviction that this was the most effective way to damage the enemy, but also the viewpoint of China and her ruling structure. His loyalty to the United States was strong and undeniable, but
he was also tied to China in very personal ways, not only seeing but
identifying with China's needs. The tie caused his own higher command to be suspicious of him: Bissell insisted on receiving copies of
his communications to Chiang and eventually ordered him to move
his headquarters from Peishiyi back to Kunming, presumably to put
a distance between him and the Chinese governing officials. Chennault protested on the grounds that Kunming was already over-
crowded with the Hump terminus traffic and accommodations were
scarce, but Bissell was firm, and eventually Chennault had to comply, moving into a dark, cold, mud and bamboo structure with a dirt
floor because it was the best space he could find. It did not improve
his disposition.[6]

By mid-1942 China's economy was constricting from the blockade.
Morale was drooping as a result of hunger, deprivation, and the at-
tendant suffering of a long war that showed no signs of ending.
Against this backdrop of China's needs and Chennault's ideas for
what might be done to alleviate them, Chiang Kai-shek sent Washington three demands. In plain terms he insisted that the United
States (1) send three American divisions to India to join the Chinese
in reopening the lines of communication through Burma, (2) provide
an air force of 500 planes to operate continuously at the front in
China, and (3) supply 5,000 tons of supplies per month, an amount
roughly fifty times the Hump's capacity at that time. He pointedly

suggested that he might have to surrender unless these demands were met within three months. Washington, hard-pressed, resented the threat. Resources were few, and at that time every theater was critical—the British were retreating in North Africa, the Germans were pressing on Stalingrad, and control of both Atlantic and Pacific oceans was still in dispute—but Roosevelt sent Currie back to China to seek some solution.[7]

In the meantime Stilwell, having summarized the first six months of war with the words "We got a hell of a beating," had dusted off the boots that walked out of Burma, crammed his World War I campaign hat upon his head, and planned a campaign to recoup losses. He asked Washington for one or more U.S. divisions, which he proposed to use alongside Chinese troops to retake Burma and drive the Japanese from Thailand. With ground supply routes reestablished, the next step would be to recapture the Hanoi-Hainan-Canton area as a foothold from which to strike Japanese sea and air routes with air power. The only way to avoid a major commitment of U.S. forces (which was not likely to be made) was to persuade the British and the Chinese to cooperate in a Burma campaign, and the success of such a campaign would hinge in large measure on China's fighting effectiveness. Vital to Stilwell's plans, therefore, was a major program of reorganization and reform for the Chinese Army.[8]

The Chinese Army reflected one of China's harsh realities: human life was the country's most abundant resource, to be sacrificed as necessary so that the life of the nation might go on. Not only was the army's upper hierarchy a complex political web with appalling examples of corruption and ineptitude woven in, but its 300-odd divisions were ill equipped, undernourished, and poorly trained and led. Their recruitment and medical care were inhumane by Western standards. Thousands died of neglect or abuse.[9] Acting as Chiang's chief of staff, Stilwell drew up plans for reducing the army to thirty divisions, a force that could be properly fed, equipped, and trained. He planned to retrain in India those Chinese troops, designated X-force, which had fought in Burma. Burma would then be retaken by a joint pincer action: X-force with American and British help advancing from India while part of the thirty reformed Chinese divisions (Y-force) advanced from Yunnan.

The second element of the great CBI debate was now in place. Both Stilwell and Chennault acknowledged that there would be limited resources. Chennault wanted to use them to conduct aggressive aerial warfare from China at once, supplying the forces by air. Skeptical of "reform" after his own agonizing experiences with the CAF, he envisioned defeat of Japan by air before Burma could be recaptured. He believed that aggressive aerial fighting, backed by a good warning system and interior lines that afforded mobility, would enable him to protect his bases. Above all he was quite confident that aerial transport could provide the necessary supply for a small but potent air force. Chiang's demand for 500 planes and 5,000 tons monthly came from Chennault, who believed a force of this size could conduct effective minimum operations and yet be adequately supplied by the Hump airlift.[10]

In contrast, Stilwell was skeptical of aerial supply and strongly felt the need for a secure base. He very firmly believed that the reform of the army, the recapture of Burma, and the establishment of a ground line of communications were vital preliminaries to any air offensive against Japan. Marshall shared Stilwell's views.[11] Chiang had not yet taken sides; his July demands included both air forces and U.S. divisions to take part in retaking Burma.

Critical to the success of either strategy was the Hump, the first attempt at using air transport as a primary means of supply. There were no precedents. It began as a desperate, high-priority measure to maintain contact with a blockaded China. This became both more important and more difficult after the loss of Burma, for the route stretched from Assam Province in northeastern India across Burma to Kunming. To avoid Japanese fighters, the transports had to take a northerly course, over the plunging gorges of the Irrawaddy, Salween, and Mekong rivers and the ice-covered peaks of the towering mountain ranges that separated them.

During 1942 the Hump fell far short of expectations and minimum needs, not reaching 1,000 tons until December. Bissell had opposed the effort from its beginning, proposing in its stead a 4,000-mile leapfrogging route from New Delhi, but as the commander of the Tenth Air Force after August, he was responsible for the route. Officers sent from Washington to assess its shortcomings concluded that 10,000 tons monthly was feasible, the physical problems being large but not insurmountable. They concluded that the defeatist attitude of Stilwell and Bissell seemed to be limiting performance.[12]

Chennault agreed, confident that it could be done. His belief was based in part on observations of CNAC, China's national commercial airline, which had pioneered the route and quietly but consistently outperformed the U.S. air transport forces in using it. Chennault had been close to CNAC's operations and personnel since 1937. Many of its pilots were good friends of his; some from the AVG had joined its ranks in July 1942. Their experience, their flying skill, and their determination to get the job done complemented a no-nonsense management.[13] At heart believing that anything was possible if one tried hard enough, Chennault found the poor performance of the Hump painful. During the eight months of its existence, the CATF received an average of only 800 tons of supplies a month.[14]

There is no arguing that the CATF operated under appalling conditions, and it is a measure of Chennault's leadership that it was able to maintain morale, compensating for shortages by aggressiveness and improvisation, superb discipline in the air, and an exuberant, defensive camaraderie, including the Flying Tiger name and much of the soldier-of-fortune atmosphere of the AVG. Men new to China were initially dismayed at the lack of amenities and the absence of modern facilities to sustain combat; it took time to reconcile the incongruities involved in waging aerial warfare in a country still dependent on the wheelbarrow. Aviation fuel arrived in barrels manhandled onto barges or water buffalo carts or simply rolled over the trails; it could take seventy-five days to roll enough barrels from Kunming to Kweilin to support one day's operations. Planes were fueled and bombs loaded by hand; airfields were built or repaired by thousands of laborers who carried stones in baskets, cracking them with hammers and placing them by hand.

They got few PX supplies. They wore whatever clothing was available, and they did not always shave. They were jostled out of bed for air raids by Chinese who ran up and down the halls of their hostels beating on little tin cans with chopsticks and calling in broken English, "Get up please, air raid, get up please." They fell prey to insidious intestinal disorders, and although feeding them posed a severe drain on the Chinese economy, most of the Americans found the Chinese mess unappealing.[15]

"I'm getting hungry as hell," one pilot wrote home. "Please send me some things to eat."[16] It was generally believed that the cooks took a little "squeeze" from their positions; at Lingling the men once suffered a severe bout of food poisoning from food prepared with tung oil. Yet they overcame difficulties, they fought superbly—one lieutenant was awarded the Distinguished Flying Cross after he single-handedly engaged thirty-nine Japanese planes and broke up their attack[17]—and their esprit de corps was based on solid pride even while marked by loud complaints over shortages or hardships.

The complaints, which sometimes reached the press, caused concern at higher echelons. Bissell, who had a hard time maintaining morale in the Tenth Air Force, sent Chennault a little reprimand that suggested jealousy. He pointed out that Chennault's men had excellent esprit de corps as members of the China Air Task Force, but "their feeling of kinship with the rest of the Tenth Air Force was very close to nil"; a number of them seemed to believe that the Tenth Air Force existed for the sole purpose of denying them equipment and sabotaging their plans. With admirable restraint, Chennault acknowledged feelings of detachment and isolation, which he considered normal griping, and noted that both officers and men consistently gave creditable or outstanding performances.[18]

That their performance was outstanding could not be denied. A poignant episode serves to illustrate the spirit of the command. When a pilot crashed in the Yangtze near Changsha, John Alison, his commanding officer, received a wire reading, "American pilot, landed in river, hit in stomach, guts hanging out, send doctor quick." The downed pilot was 200 miles away and it was already late afternoon, but Flight Surgeon Dr. Raymond Spritzler prepared to go. It meant cramming himself into the baggage compartment of a P-43 reconnaissance plane and planning to bail out, for there was no airfield at Changsha. Alison started to forbid the doctor to go but realized that he would go if their positions were reversed, so he allowed the rescue mission to depart. Shortly afterward he received word that the crashed pilot had died; a little later he realized that the plane carrying Spritzler was lost. He spent a bad night agonizing because he had lost three men, but the next morning Spritzler and his pilot returned safely. They had indeed been lost in a stormy night, but the Chinese warning net had heard them overhead and had set a field on fire to guide them to an airfield where they could land.[19]

Chennault endeared himself to his ragtag command by the zest and uncanny wisdom with which he directed the guerrilla-style warfare. Over and over he coached the men on how to fight and survive: always look around, stay together, hit and get out so you can recover speed and come back, withdraw erratically so the enemy cannot anticipate your vulnerable moments. Concentrate your force where the enemy is weakest; do not let him use his strength against you and make the most of every advantage you have. Use your wits; know your ship and your enemy.

Above all he insisted, "Don't do anything stupid just to be brave," and his commanders loved him for it. They also loved the freedom he gave them to fight and command to the best of their ability, free from unnecessary restrictions. They thrived on the opportunity to exercise initiative and resourcefulness. Bruce Holloway, a squadron and then group commander who later wore four air force stars, considered his experiences in China probably the most valuable part of his career, not only a learning experience under a master coach, but also sheer delightful adventure, a time when aerial fighting still entailed romance.[20]

A New York newspaper elected Chennault to the Society of Red Tape Cutters in humorous recognition that his was a refreshing approach, for when he found a man who could fight, Chennault gave him the means and got out of his way. When a squabble developed between fighter and bomber crews, he devised a "squirrel cage" of fighters, close and literally surrounding the bombers for maximum protection, and it came to be a tremendous morale booster as well as an effective fighting tactic.[21]

Most of the missions were small, but on several occasions a sizable force was mustered to keep the Japanese off balance. Once, when he had thirty-two planes available, Chennault heard a Tokyo broadcast speculating that the CATF had about 300 ships, and he decided "we're doing all right."[22] On 25 October, in celebration of Chiang Kai-shek's birthday, Hong Kong was surprised by twelve B-25s and seven P-40s from Kweilin; at the cost of one B-25, the CATF virtually annihilated the defending force of twenty-one interceptors and did undetermined damage to the docks and harbor crowded with convoys en route to the Southwest Pacific. Chennault wanted to follow through. He seethed when Bissell insisted that instead he send his available forces to raid Japanese airfields in Burma.[23]

Again at the end of November, Chennault gathered strength for a major raid. To make certain that the Japanese were caught off guard, he employed in reverse the practice of the International Squadron in Hankow: word was "leaked" through the bars that the CATF would bomb Hankow, and the next day the largest mission to date, ten bombers and twenty-five fighters, started toward Hankow, stayed on course long enough to convince the Japanese of their target, then abruptly turned back and struck Canton's harbor and airfields. The CATF had no losses; Japanese losses were approximately twenty-two. One of the pilots, met by Chennault when he landed after the raid, observed that he had never seen their commander in a happier mood. The *New York Herald Tribune*, editorializing that Chennault and company were "consistently outplaying and outfighting" the Japanese, called this "as satisfactory a victory" as those won by the AVG.[24]

The successes required careful planning and a little creativity, a shrewd appraisal of the enemy, a great deal of dedication and a "can do" attitude that became Chennault's trademark. "Success attends those attacks which are carried out with determination, daring, and persistence," he had written in *Pursuit Aviation*,[25] and as a commanding officer he had the gift of instilling this philosophy at the level of sheer moxie and machisimo. Sometimes taken aback by the scope of his expectations, his men were nevertheless pushed to a level of performance they had not believed possible simply because he so matter-of-factly expected it from them.[26]

The casual style and unorthodox approaches of these Flying Tigers was emphasized by the correspondents, always in search of colorful material. They included, with relish, the fact that sometimes the airmen's zest for fighting outran their authority, although few knew that Chennault himself had secretly had a special B-25 bomber converted in India for his own use. The top gunner's position, with bubble canopy, was made into a comfortable spot where he could have a 360-degree view, but in case they were needed, there were eight fifty-caliber machine guns in the wings, two thirty-caliber scatter guns in the tail, and a seventy-five-millimeter cannon in the nose. When his intention of using it became known, he was required to turn it over to the bomb squadron.[27]

But even without secret acquisitions of bombers, the correspondents had plenty of material. Colonels Haynes and Robert Scott, the first commander of the Twenty-third Fighter Group, were portrayed as "hell on wheels"—as romantic, individualistic fighters who, like Chennault himself, would "go ahead as they please and damn the consequences" if orders from above were likely to hamstring operations against the Japanese.[28]

"We sit around the staff office," correspondent Theodore White wrote, "and the bomber chief says to the fighter chief, 'Let's go down next week and tear hell out of Hanoi.' And the fighter chief says 'Can you give me four or five days till I get a few more ships in condition?' Then they get down and they really do knock the guts out of Hanoi."[29]

A favorite scuttlebutt tale concerned an enlisted man who was fired with zeal and wanted to test some theories about the Japanese air defenses, for which purpose he suborned a pilot. The two then borrowed an unarmed cargo plane which they loaded with bombs. They flew to Hanoi and pushed their first bomb out the cargo door to set a huge fire. By its light they carefully chose and bombed their objectives. No one within the CATF knew of it until the Japanese announcement of a heavy raid. Chennault reportedly laughed, more pleased at their initiative than disturbed by their acting without orders.[30]

Such an organization aroused consternation among traditionalists, and when the press began reporting outspoken complaints about the CATF's shortages in planes, equipment, and trained personnel, Stilwell sent Chennault a sharp reprimand that members of his command were trying to exert pressure through the press to obtain equipment, and this must be stopped at once. Correspondents' privileges with the CATF were temporarily suspended.[31]

Not long afterward Bissell sent Brig. Gen. Francis M. Brady to Kunming to inspect. Brady spent a good bit of time with Col. Clinton "Casey" Vincent, whom Bissell had sent to China to serve on Chennault's staff. Vincent liked and respected Chennault but had nevertheless concluded that any similarity between the CATF and a military organization was purely accidental. Marveling that Chennault had been able to do as much as he had with his existing staff, Vincent had assessed administrative procedures as "poor—the Group just runs by itself."[32]

Brady came to the same conclusion, and on 22 December he wrote Bissell that the CATF was continuing as a "one-man show" and was not operating "according to our ideas of a military air force organization." He attributed the shortcomings to the influence of the AVG and the lack of a proper staff and called Chennault "somewhat rusty on air force and army procedures and customs due to his long separation from our service and close association with the Chinese forces." He noted a number of specific shortcomings, including the absence of uniformity in clothing. He suggested that the men shave and bathe regularly.[33]

Considering most of the bad marks either undeserved or ridiculous, Chennault compiled an item-by-item response carefully restrained in tone yet conceding nothing. "My methods here are deliberately planned because of the situation in China and I believe that the results attained in Burma and China since December 7, 1941, fully justify my methods," he wrote, the set of his jaw almost visible behind the words. He considered himself "perfectly capable of operating air force units in regular army style" and noted that most successful military operations were a one-man show. He reminded Bissell that he had repeatedly requested an adequate number of staff officers; he cited cramped, dark, and inadequate quarters and constant shortages. Practice flights could not be held regularly because of the shortage of fuel; servicing of airplanes was slow because of a shortage of hand pumps; pilot ready rooms were too small for conducting the extensive studies suggested while the pilots were on alert duty. Trucks were worn out from hard service; the spare parts he had repeatedly requisitioned for their repair had not been sent. The water furnished for bathing "is odorous and often dirty"; strict uniformity in dress was not required because of wide variations in temperature between day and night, although dress was more uniform now that adequate winter clothing had been received. This was a particularly sore point, for his men had suffered from the cold while the delivery of winter clothing over the Hump—a Tenth Air Force responsibility— had been delayed. As for saluting, Chennault stated without apology that strict adherence to military customs was not required.[34]

· Obviously he felt the Tenth Air Force simply did not understand the prevailing conditions in China. Bissell's continuing letters, spelling out the CATF's administrative shortcomings and expressing eagerness to help them learn how to manage their affairs, set those telltale muscles in his jaw to twitching.[35]

During Chennault's months as commander of the CATF, his life changed little from its previous pattern. He lived in his tile-roofed adobe house near the airfield at Kunming, sharing his quarters with some of his commanders and staff. Flight surgeon Col. Thomas Gentry, who had been with the AVG and who, in his capacity as Chennault's personal physician, was constantly urging him to quit smoking, had one room. The other two were occupied by Colonels Haynes, Vincent, Holloway, and Scott. The house impressed one visitor as simple and austere, with a few chairs, some books, Chinese scrolls and mottoes on the walls, and an oil portrait of Chennault hanging beside the Frigidaire in the dining room. Here the men lived much as would a small family, sharing their meals and relaxation and creating their recreation. They were cared for by two Chinese houseboys, a chauffeur, and a cook. Chennault tended a small garden, grew his favorite hot peppers, and taught the cook how to make Louisiana gumbo.[36]

In their free evenings, games offered recreation and a source of exercise. Chennault always took part, seeming to need the physical activity as a release from personal tensions. His spirited competition posed a problem for the younger men, for he no longer had their stamina but was loath to admit it. After pitching several innings in their softball games, his arm would be tired, but he was unwilling to leave the game, and his side invariably lost. Disappointed, he would "sort of sulk off," then suggest badminton or Ping-Pong, at which any of the younger men could beat him. If they did, "he got lower and lower."[37]

He played not just for fun but with an almost desperate competitive need to win. One of his secretaries was Doreen Davis, who had made her way into war-torn China to marry a member of the AVG. Chennault had given her away at her improvised wedding (she wore a black suit, the only one she had), and she stayed with him as a civilian secretary after the AVG disbanded. She was willing to fly with him so that he could work while en route, and when work was finished they would pass the time with cribbage. She was always careful not to win, for she knew how much winning meant to him.[38] The men were less likely to forfeit a victory. When Chennault wanted to wrestle, as he sometimes did, he invariably challenged the largest and strongest of the group. The man selected would avoid the contest if he could, but Chennault was hard to turn aside. There were times when he ended up being thrown into the corner.

The easy informality of his relationships with his men masked personal feelings of isolation, resentment, and loneliness. Even his competitiveness bespoke his frustrations, suggesting that he was continuing the search for tangible evidence of his own worth, either to himself or to others. He missed his U.S. friends and was delighted when Noe spearheaded a collection among Louisiana citizens and raised $15,109.36 to buy him a bomber. It was not enough for a plane, so he suggested that the money be given to China's war-orphaned children.[39]

He missed his family and was at times saddened by his lack of closeness to them. His father died in August, but he mentioned the loss to almost no one. His sons were either in the service or in related war work, and his pride was tempered by concern and disappointment that the war had possibly ended their college careers. "After this war is over, it's really going to be tough for an uneducated man to get a job," he wrote them. He urged the younger ones to stay in school because the family was already doing enough for the cause. When they did not heed his advice, he was hurt. "I can manage millions of Chinese and a few hundreds of Americans well enough to make the headlines but can't even influence my sons," he wrote, concluding that he was "not so hot."[40]

He needed affection, tenderness, warmth. He was given a black dachshund pup that he named Joe, made a member of the household, and trained with gentleness and pleasure. At night Joe slept on a pad in the house; by day he tagged along behind Chennault at airfield or

office, where he soon developed a talent for keeping the rat population under control. When visitors came in, Chennault would intro-
duce him by saying, "This is my dog, Joe." Joe would step forward
and wag his tail unless, with canine perceptiveness, he sniffed out a
caller critical of his master, in which case he withheld the greeting.
Joe Dash was soon an unofficial mascot, even scrambling up the near
vertical ladder on the side of a C-47 by backing up to get a running
start, then flowing up like a snake, stubby little legs moving so fast
nobody could see quite how he did it.[41]

The days at the Kunming office followed a comfortable routine.
Chennault and Joe Dash were driven there each morning in a bat-
tered old Buick that Frillmann had driven up the Burma Road when
the AVG evacuated Rangoon. The mornings filled with staff meetings, paper work, or a conference in the operations shack, where
Chennault would explain to his pilots what he wanted done and let
them figure out how to accomplish it. After lunch interpreter Shu
took a nap and Chennault settled into his chair, smoked a Camel,
then let his head sink down on his chest. With secretary Trumble
holding Joe Dash to keep him quiet, for twenty minutes or so all
would be still. Then Chennault would raise his head, give a little
waking-up snort, shake himself, light another Camel, and get the
afternoon's work under way.

Trumble stayed with Chennault as a civilian after the AVG disbanded. Their working relationship was strengthened by the intangible bond created by their shared viewpoint regarding China and the
Chinese; both could accept the notion that China had a right to do
things in the Chinese way and could see behind surface poverty and
filth and corruption a self-respecting, achieving people who despised
the foreigners who patronized or exploited them.

When the afternoons were quiet, Chennault might say, "Tom, let's
go hunting," and the two would drive into the countryside. These
were his restorative hours, when he dismissed the war from his mind
and renewed his relationships with the earth. He inspected the crops
and savored the peacefulness and beauty of the land, sometimes
painted yellow from the bloom of mustard plants much like those he
had seen as a boy. Game was plentiful, and in pursuit of it he moved
with his old vigor. The younger Trumble, astounded, sometimes had
to struggle to keep up. Trumble had never hunted, but Chennault
taught him how to shoot. He preferred a pump shotgun, he explained, because an automatic made it tempting to keep shooting
after the game was too far away.[42]

When their ducks fell into the water, Joe Dash was pressed into service as a retriever. The water in Kunming's ponds was icy cold, and when ordered to retrieve, Joe would dip in his paw to test the temperature, then draw back to howl and yowl as though pleading for mercy. But Chennault would sound stern as he repeated, "Joe, go get that duck," and Joe would plunge in. Back on shore with the prey, he would be dried off with a waiting towel and praised for his achievement. If the bird put up a fight, Joe could not bring it back but would not turn it loose, and someone had to jump in to retrieve both duck and dog.[43]

Hunting was not only one of the very few ways the men could spend their time off; in addition the game was an important part of their mess, and marksmanship became a point of pride, a vital element in maintaining their morale. Chennault held the unchallenged title: when he was shooting pigeons in the pine groves, he would wait until two birds crossed in flight and bring down both with one shot. The shotgun ammunition came from Chennault's friends in Louisiana, and he meted it out to the others of his household on the basis of what they had turned in the week before.

Holloway and Vincent, on their way home about dark after one unsuccessful hunt, thought they spotted teal on a pond. Holloway shot the birds and braved the chilling water to retrieve them, only to find they were coots. Coots are not good eating, but the two men decided to take them home rather than have nothing to show for their spent ammunition. Eyes twinkling, Chennault responded to their comment "See how hard we tried?" with: "I'll teach you to waste my ammunition on coots!" During supper they were aware of a horrible odor coming from the kitchen. When the plates were cleared Chennault announced that the cooks had prepared a special dish for Holloway. The coot was brought out with a flourish, the conspirators struggling not to laugh. Not long afterward, when Holloway was hunting alone and got lost in the bewildering maze of rice paddies while chasing a sandhill crane, Chennault himself led the midnight search party that found him.[44]

Through these small personal touches, even more than by his zeal for the fight, Chennault endeared himself to the men of his command. With them he was never the cold, aloof commander sheltered behind the formality of rank. He and they were fellow human beings with a job to do, cemented together by common hardships, skills, and goals, by mutual dependence and trust. In a burst of gratitude, the men decided their "Old Man" deserved the Medal of Honor. Without his knowledge they drew up a petition and collected 262 signatures.

They tried to send it to Roosevelt outside channels, but Bissell seized it and sent it to Stilwell with the terse observation that the procedure was "entirely irregular." Stilwell reacted with equal distaste. Even though the petition made clear that it was prepared without Chennault's knowledge, Stilwell charged him with responsibility for it. Doreen Davis later recalled that this was the only time in her long years of working with Chennault that he ever bawled her out, for he was embarrassed and felt that she should have told him. She defended herself, saying she could not have betrayed the men and he should be proud that they loved him enough to want this honor for him.[45]

His men might love him, but the Chennault some saw was a stubborn, defiant, fierce, unsmiling loner, an image compounded by his increasing deafness. A fellow general described him as sitting in conferences like a cigar-store Indian, deaf as a post. He could hear the lower ranges but not the higher, although by intense concentration he could follow a conversation when facing those who spoke. He made few concessions to the problem. One of the few times he openly acknowledged being hard of hearing was when a missionary asked him if he was ready to meet his God. Shaking his head and grimacing, he turned to his companion to ask, "What did he say?"[46]

For the most part the public saw a man of open simplicity, disarming frankness, a penchant for scrapping, and a childish need to win. Seldom perceived, shielded by personal reserve and the informal style of his relationships, was his gnawing sense of failure. He had debated the wisdom of being recommissioned when the idea was first proposed; many times thereafter he regretted having accepted it, for being a general had brought a renewal of the old tensions and conflicts he had gone to China to escape. Once more part of the army team, he not only lost the individual freedom that was important to him, but he was daily confronted with his own inability to influence the Air Corps to follow the course he believed best.[47]

If he had been outside the mainstream of Air Corps policymaking during the 1930s, he was even more so now. While he had been creating the unconventional AVG, four of his former colleagues—Harold George, Kenneth Walker, Laurence Kuter, and Haywood Hansell—had been in the Air War Plans Division drafting AWPD-1, the basic plan under which air power was initially employed when the Second World War began. AWPD-1 gave strategic bombardment a major role; it was adopted in January 1942, and shortly thereafter the U.S. Army Air Forces became coequal with the army's ground and service forces. The long fight for autonomy was culminating but without Chennault's participation. Instead of staying with the team, he had pursued his own way, and the success and recognition this brought him served only to alienate him further from the leading U.S. Air officers. Their route had been the dedicated, unglamorous struggle, their battles fought behind conference room doors, their rewards the personal satisfaction of duty well done but little glory or public recognition. Chennault, on the other hand, had attracted excited public attention by operating outside the organization. Even when his fellow officers denounced Chennault's position, they sometimes privately envied him his courage to move against the current and were jealous of his independence and fame.[48]

More a maverick than ever before, Chennault sometimes said he wished he did not have to be a general, but he could see no other way to continue the fight he had begun. He had exercised more power before he wore his stars, and he could never admit that he enjoyed any of the superficial privileges and status of rank, although in very human ways he did. He saw them, however, as poor compensation for the freedom to act.[49] With the AVG he had found the niche in which he functioned best, working with strong and independent men of action, free from administrative impediments, in an environment that encouraged creativity and expressed appreciation. All those things were important to him. When he reflected on the personal satisfaction the AVG had given him, he observed that few individuals ever have the opportunity to do the things they want and to be of service at the same time.

He had feared that, in incorporating the AVG, the War Department would hinder rather than help China's efforts. During his first months in command of the CATF, he often felt this to be the case. He saw pilots and equipment sacrificed through what he judged to be mistakes and failures; he saw the United States begin to lose the confidence and admiration of the Chinese that he had worked to develop. The army's failures became personal failures to which he reacted with hurt and anger, and he chafed at having to fight the system, at being unable to do what he felt should be done.

His frustration vented itself in his relationship with Bissell. With all lesser problems compounded by inadequate supply—a condition for which he held Bissell and the Tenth Air Force responsible—his initial determination to go along with the system soon degenerated into a snarling confrontation with his immediate superior. Bissell's reprimands were sometimes justified, as were some of Chennault's complaints, but Bissell's approach bespoke a patronizing condescension that brought out Chennault's contentiousness. He had a defensive tendency to sense slights where none were intended, but more than one observer of their feud concluded that Bissell was "gunning for" Chennault.[50] Bissell became ever more critical, Chennault ever more irascible, the messages darting back and forth ever more barbed in tone. Cumbersome communications compounded misunderstandings, for the chain of command went from Chennault (Kunming) to Bissell (New Delhi) to Stilwell (Chungking) to Bissell (New Delhi) and finally back to Chennault, who could not even negotiate with the Chinese who ran his mess and took care of his base without going through the tedious channels. Matters that could have been settled in hours took weeks.

Their disagreements were often petty, running the gamut from major to individually trivial. The sum total was ugly. Chennault had no respect for Bissell as a combat airman, for although he had been a World War I ace, in Chennault's opinion he had not changed his tactical concepts since. Bissell had no respect for Chennault as an administrator. When Bissell pounced on a "flagrant breach of discipline" at Hengyang, where smuggling was suspected, Chennault bristled at his holier-than-thou stance. The contraband goods were coming into China from India, and he tossed the responsibility back into Bissell's lap by asking him to take more effective measures to prevent the illegal traffic from his end.[51]

When Chennault inquired why the CATF received no post exchange supplies, Bissell insisted that Stilwell had even released all the PX supplies consigned to his own headquarters for the CATF. But on this one Bissell stumbled, for Chennault knew that a shipment of whiskey intended for the aborted Second AVG had been held in India on Stilwell's orders and later found its way into the Karachi Officers' Club and Stilwell's own headquarters in Chungking. There, in a moment of intended camaraderie, Stilwell offered Chennault a drink and pulled out one of the telltale bottles of Old Taylor, whereupon Chennault thundered in righteous indignation, "Goddammit Stilwell, that's MY whiskey you're drinking!"[52]

The most heated exchanges concerned Chennault's staff, a sore point with him ever since he had been denied trained staff personnel for the AVG. Forced to use the men available in China, he had then been criticized for being a poor judge of men and doing poor staff work. His reaction was an unflinching loyalty to those individuals who were willing to serve him, whatever their shortcomings. An ugly incident took place in April 1942, when Boatner Carney, one of his makeshift AVG staff men, killed an army man in a drunken brawl. Theater headquarters conducted intensive investigations; the incident was in large measure responsible for Bissell's close scrutiny. Carney had a reputation for being mean and nasty when drunk, but Chennault stood by him, made him promise to leave liquor alone, and kept him under house arrest until the trial, at which Chennault testified on his behalf. Carney got two years and was shipped back to his native Louisiana, where his senator petitioned for a pardon. Again Chennault spoke up for Carney, but after the pardon was granted he asked his friend Noe to keep an eye on him and make him stay straight, since "I put my neck out far enough in his case."[53]

Chennault would stand up for his friends, but this kind of trouble he could do without. He needed competent staff, and shortly after Bissell was named to head the Tenth Air Force, Chennault requested a qualified personnel and administration officer who was thoroughly familiar with army procedure, reports, and records. Bissell complied but then began to choose Chennault's other officers as well.

Chennault bristled when he was ordered to replace his chief of staff, Col. Merian C. Cooper. Cooper was an incurable romantic, a pilot in World War I who in 1920 organized the Polish Kosciuszko Squadron to fight the Russians. In 1942 he had been detained in Chungking while en route to the Soviet Maritime Province on an intelligence mission connected with the Tokyo Raid. Captivated by the AVG, he accepted Chennault's invitation to serve as his executive with delight. He was magnanimous in spirit and enthusiasm and good humor, even though absentminded (he might find his lost pipe under his hat when his head got warm) and prone to digress inconsequentially. He and Chennault got along well, and for the particular type of unconventional warfare waged by the CATF, he was valuable.[54]

Chennault considered it important not only that his staff understand his "complex China operational conditions" but also that they be men with whom he could work in harmony and confidence. He resented Bissell's interference. When Bissell began to name his commanders also, he protested with fury. Acknowledging that they had mutual problems, Bissell finally suggested, "You give me the same confidence that I repose in you." Unfortunately Chennault saw no evidence that Bissell reposed any confidence in him whatsoever, and he simply did not believe Bissell's assurance that the CATF "has always been given first priority on everything."[55]

He may have been unfair in his judgment, but the judgment was made: Chennault believed Bissell and the Tenth Air Force were depriving him of the opportunity to fight. The CATF was choking to death from shortages. Years later Chennault acknowledged that the Hump "had terrific problems: didn't have suitable airplanes, and we had bad weather, high-altitude flying but no radar aids." But as he saw it, "Equipment was available in the States. It was all available—just a question of bringing it in and utilizing it."[56]

Chennault could live with Bissell's inspections and nitpicking and reprimands. He could even acknowledge that he felt a grudging admiration for Bissell's administrative skills. He once called him either the biggest little man or the littlest big man he had ever met.

What Chennault could not tolerate was not having the means and the freedom to fight. He still considered the air unlimited. He regarded Bissell as an "old" airman who lacked the vision to reach out toward air's potential.[57] He began pulling out all the stops to gain independence of command.

11

A Clash of Purpose

Wendell L. Willkie challenged Roosevelt at the polls in 1940, was defeated, and afterward became a leading, vocal advocate of international cooperation. He figures in this narrative as the vehicle through which Chennault propelled himself and his ideas outside the CBI command. In October 1942 Willkie visited China. He especially wanted to meet Chennault, who had emerged in the news media during the past year as a colorful, strong, determined, and prescient figure; Chennault's lined and unsmiling face, jaw stuck out in defiance, had adorned the front of *Life*, which portrayed him as one of fighting America's heroes. Although a little miffed at Willkie's request—"I'm just small fry, & he's interested only in Big Personalities"—Stilwell took the visitor to Chennault's headquarters at Peishiyi and left the two alone "to whisper together" for about two hours.[1]

Willkie found Peishiyi "one of the busiest and most exciting bases I have ever seen." Chennault himself spoke "quietly but with great conviction" of the potential he saw in China for a small, effective air force; he expressed "a sense of bafflement" at the failure of others to see what to him was so clear. Willkie thought him "a hard man to forget." He regarded Chennault as tall (even though he was of average height), "swarthy, lean, and rangy, and there is something hard about his jaw and his eyes." His men "swore by him and performed miracles for him." Willkie was convinced that Chennault's air force had accomplished "some minor miracles with wholly inadequate forces."[2]

With Stilwell Willkie was less impressed, for the crusty soldier discouraged conversation. Stilwell himself noted that Willkie "hardly spoke to me. Utterly indifferent. Never asked me about anything."[3] What Willkie heard from others was "unanimity in thinking that General Chennault should be given a command independent of control from British India," and he requested a written report from Chennault so that he could take his ideas directly to Roosevelt.[4] The request may have been prompted by McHugh, Willauer, Soong, and other members of China Defense Supplies. It is certain they were responsible for Chennault's compliance with it; Willauer later considered one of the major accomplishments of China Defense Supplies to have been that "we made Chennault reduce his plans to paper for the first time."[5]

Chennault's plan was presented in a letter to Willkie dated 8 October 1942. It was a startling restatement of the idea he had introduced in Washington in December 1940 and had repeatedly advocated since: with a very small air force in China he could inflict significant damage on Japan's war-making capability. What was different about this version was an overweening arrogance and a deceptive simplicity. He asked to be assigned 105 fighters of the newest design plus thirty medium bombers and twelve heavy bombers (with replacements to keep the force at that strength). With such a force and full authority as the American military commander in China, he felt he could bring about the downfall of Japan and make the Chinese lasting friends with the United States.

By striking at the Japanese supply lines, Chennault proposed to destroy the Japanese Air Force by forcing it to fight him in eastern China over friendly territory, where his own forces were protected by the warning net and could destroy the Japanese at a favorable ratio. Other U.S. forces could then advance more rapidly across the Pacific, while the air forces destroyed the industrial centers of Japan and cut Japan's waterborne supply routes. To do these things, he said he needed full, real authority as the American military commander in China, reporting only to Chiang Kai-shek (three months earlier he had been willing to serve under Stilwell and had requested independence only from Bissell). He also needed supplies totaling 1,200 tons monthly at first and increasing as the fighting increased, and an aerial supply line between India and China. He would use interior lines and mobility to protect the terminus of the supply route and the eastern Chinese airfields.[6]

This letter is the most often quoted of Chennault's wartime arguments for his aerial strategy, and although the basic ideas were his, Cooper's hand is obvious in their presentation. The points were made with short, emphatic punch lines, unlike Chennault's own tendency toward long sentences. Cooper had made movies in Hollywood between the wars, and his flair for the dramatic evoked from this bit of strategy the contrived plot and cumulative excitement of a script: "Japan can be defeated in China. It can be defeated by an Air Force so small that in other theaters it would be c...led ridiculous. I am confident that, given real authority in command of such an Air Force, I can cause the collapse of Japan." The script even had a star. Most letters are written in the first-person singular, but in the Chennault-Willkie letter the personal pronoun dominated to a startling degree. He disclaimed egotism by elaborating upon the record of the AVG and the CATF.[7]

No hint of doubt crept through. "My entire above plan is simple," Chennault wrote. "It has been long thought out. I have spent five years developing an air warning net and radio command service to fight this way. I have no doubt of my success."[8]

Chennault's earlier proposals had expressed confidence but recognized uncertainties and limitations. His July letter to Stilwell had been much less sweeping in its claims. A letter to Arnold written only two weeks before the Willkie letter expressed confidence that "the Jap air force could be destroyed as an effective fighting force within less than six months by a very modest American air force equipped with modern airplanes," but it also included the disclaimer, "Assuredly, we could destroy a large number of his airplanes and pilots and thus prevent both from being employed in other theaters of war." In a report to the Office of Naval Intelligence dated only three days earlier than Chennault's letter to Willkie, McHugh—not known for understatement and ardent in his support of China and of Chennault—said Chennault believed he could put the Japanese on the defensive, greatly weaken their effort in the Pacific theater, and ultimately drive them out of China—claims appreciably more modest than causing the collapse of Japan.[9] The conclusion is inescapable that, in his zeal, the enthusiastic Cooper overstated Chennault's own argument.

The Willkie letter also suggested insubordination, for it criticized the Stilwell-Bissell stance as that "of the standard orthodox, rigid military mind." Up to this point Chennault had grumbled in private but had been professionally correct, even when arguing, in his procedures. This was his first foray into politics, however, and while his experiences in Washington had opened to his vista the tremendous power to be gained from getting the right word to the right ear, he had not learned the attending arts of discretion that are critical to political survival. He was, as McHugh concluded, "frustrated and desperate."[10]

It is also possible that he did not read the finished document carefully, for it contains an important typographical error—105 fighters rather than 150, the number he had reported to McHugh and others and which he later substituted.[11] Chennault could be too trusting of others, too easily used or led, and in this instance he allowed words to be put in his mouth. More than one of his working associates had found, however, that "he backed you when you worked for him, even when you were wrong," and if he later felt any reproach concerning the wording of this important document, he kept it to himself. Unsuccessful in getting a decoration for Cooper, he later wrote his friend and former associate that "all of your assignments were well done" and a decoration was "a very small thing compared to that sense of satisfaction."[12]

The fateful letter was not finished before Willkie left China, and Chennault gave it to McHugh, who was delighted. He usually found the airman "a very taciturn man." He had "never dreamed that Chennault would 'take down his hair' as frankly as he did." McHugh hastily dispatched the letter to Knox with an outspoken report of his own in which he "shot the works" because he was "fed up with this confusion out here." Fearing the U.S. would never win the war "by pussyfooting," McHugh reported that Stilwell and Bissell did not even visualize the use of air power as Chennault proposed it. In his opinion the war in China would be materially aided by the removal of them and their huge staffs.[13] McHugh also pointed out one unavoidable and unfortunate fact: that neither Stilwell nor Bissell had the confidence of the Chinese, while Chennault did.

Through McHugh, Chennault's letter reached Knox, who passed it on to Stimson, who gave it to Marshall. Eventually it reached Stilwell, whose reaction was, "The rattlesnakes are striking." He protested to Marshall, who protested to Admiral Ernest King, chief of naval operations, about McHugh's open criticism of the War Department. McHugh had been equally outspoken in presenting his views to the British in India, an indiscretion that Marshall thought did irreparable harm to the military effort in CBI. At Marshall's insistence King ordered McHugh banned from service in China.[14]

McHugh protested on the grounds that his report was made as an official, secret document, prepared in accordance with standing instructions from Knox and sent to him with appropriate security. Because he was on close and friendly terms with the Chiangs and others in China's ruling circles, McHugh had been given unique duties in addition to the traditional ones of naval attaché. Since November 1940 he had reported directly to Knox (at the latter's request), while through Currie (also by request) he served as a special out-of-channels messenger between Chiang Kai-shek and Washington.[15] The tendency in CBI to utilize unorthodox channels of communication, bypassing ambassadors or theater commanders or the War Department itself, was beginning to cause problems that promised to worsen.

Reactions to Chennault's letter varied. Roosevelt seems to have identified with Chennault's scrappy spirit and found it refreshing to have a commander who was confident and eager to fight. Stimson read it "with great interest," although he sided with Marshall, who considered it "just nonsense; not bad strategy, just nonsense." To Stilwell it was a "jackass proposition."[16]

It was an unabashedly ambitious claim, especially in view of the small size of the force proposed. Air power was yet unproved, and there were few guidelines as to what it could accomplish, but when first presenting his ideas in 1940-41, Chennault had called for a 500-plane force, and he had accepted the 100-plane AVG as a temporary compromise to accomplish a quite limited goal. From the beginning he had stressed that his plan should be "wholly adopted or wholly rejected" because half measures would not yield decisive results. Again in August 1942 he had appealed to Stilwell for 500 planes, apparently considering that figure the minimum.[17] Why now the downward shift?

The answer lay in his relationship to the Chinese and the Chinese Air Force. Several times Chiang had asked Washington to send him a high-ranking air officer to revamp his entire air force. This had not been done, nor had efforts to improve the CAF, including training Chinese pilots at U.S. bases, brought noticeable improvement. But Chiang had included a 500-plane air force in his three demands, and a revitalized CAF might even yet become an effective weapon if it had proper command. Soong and Chiang negotiated with Chennault.

Chennault well understood—and reported to his superiors—the CAF's ingrained opposition to control by a foreigner. He had had his own hands tied more than once, and after warning Madame that conditions in the Chinese flying schools were deteriorating badly, he resigned as chief adviser for flying training because the training had not reached standards he could endorse. He was willing to consider command of the CAF only if he received specific guarantees that would make it possible for him to do a good job. Full authority with the Commission on Aeronautical Affairs was one. Another was separation from control of Bissell and the Tenth Air Force, for otherwise he felt the Chinese would not have a fair chance. As he explained the issue to those in China Defense Supplies, he thought he understood what it took to make the Chinese perform, and Bissell did not.

Chennault had in mind the same approach he had planned to implement with the Second AVG. He visualized an integrated air force in which complete air units of the U.S. Army Air Forces would be organized, with both Chinese and American personnel working side by side. This arrangement would make it possible to work as equals, eliminating some of the problems of face. By close association with U.S. personnel, the Chinese could overcome their lack of mechanical experience and learn more at a faster rate. He had confidence that the Chinese could field an air force as well as Americans could, once certain barriers had been overcome. When training was complete, the composite units would be turned over to CAF operational control.

Not until December did Soong decide "to put the whole damn thing" under Chennault, but in requesting the 150-plane U.S. force, Chennault counted on having the 500-plane CAF under his operational command and planned to use the Americans as an elite striking force to spearhead it.[18]

Meanwhile Washington had prepared its reply to Chiang's three demands. Currie's visit had smoothed the way for compromise, and Roosevelt promised Chiang his 500-plane air force, plus 100 transports by early 1943 on the Hump airlift. There would be no U.S. combat troops in the near future, but the U.S. would continue to provide 3,500 tons of lend-lease monthly for the Chinese. Roosevelt urged Chiang to work with Stilwell in recapturing Burma to reopen a land route for supply. A pacified Chiang told Stilwell to begin preparing for the Burma campaign to begin in the spring.[19]

In Washington, however, agitation in favor of Chennault's plan became more insistent. Members of the State Department, concerned with the political implications of aid to China, pointed out that

Chennault's small force had made an "amazingly effective show-ing." If Chennault could carry on operations that would make a pos-itive contribution toward defeating the Japanese, his efforts would affect political factors such as China's continuing to be pro-United States in sentiment after the war. Gauss expressed fear that Stilwell's plan could not be realized within the near future; he advocated in-creasing the combat air force and the Hump airlift as the most sub-stantial contribution the United States could make to China at that time. The British agreed, although they refrained from entering the debate.[20]

There were others. Officials of China Defense Supplies and the Chinese embassy were faithful lobbyists. Madame Chiang visited in Washington from late November until early spring, charmed and captivated a large segment of the American public, and impressed upon Harry Hopkins, Roosevelt's closest and most trusted adviser, that the Chinese greatly admired Chennault but did not like Stilwell, who, as she put it, did not understand them. The Office of Naval In-telligence, influenced in large measure by McHugh, continued to ar-gue the case for Chennault. Spokesmen for the new Sino-American Cooperative Organization endorsed Chennault as agreeable and helpful (while Stilwell was not); they speculated that if he "were given control and some planes he could clean the place out."[21] After his summer trip to China, Currie supported Stilwell's projects but rec-ommended that Stilwell himself be transferred because of a basic mis-understanding between him and Chiang. On this point Roosevelt was inclined to agree, but Marshall and Stimson felt that no one could be found to replace him.[22]

Roosevelt respected Marshall and Stimson and their judgment. He seldom went counter to their advice, but when conflicts had to be re-solved, his approach was to support the effort that promised results most quickly and with the least cost. He had begun to fear that the situation in China was unsatisfactory at a basic level. His goal was to support China, to bolster its internal strength and its status among the world powers so that there would be a pro-U.S. power in Asia upon which to base postwar reconstruction. The War Department approach was militarily sound: ensure the lines of supply and the strength of the ground forces before launching an aerial offensive. In the meantime, however, China's friendship might be lost. Roosevelt was leaning toward Chennault's argument for an immediate small-scale aerial offensive and was inclined to give him a free hand, but before making a decision he arranged through Hopkins for Joseph Alsop to go to China, ostensibly as a lend-lease representative but primarily to report to him directly about Chennault's plans and circumstances.

It was not unusual for Roosevelt to seek information from unofficial channels. He essentially conducted his own foreign policy, often without even advising the State Department of his thoughts. He had a variety of correspondents; he made great use of personal emissaries. It seems to have been one way in which he compensated for his physical limitations and the confinements of the presidency; he obviously derived great pleasure from his unorthodox relationships and sources of information. "I wish I could go with you to Chennault," he wrote Alsop before the latter's departure for China. "I am suggesting as an alternative that he be told to return here for a short visit if he thinks it advisable."[23]

Alsop had been captured by the Japanese in Hong Kong in December 1941 while on a supply mission for the AVG but had been repatriated in June. Now he returned to China with enthusiasm. Hopkins was soon receiving reports of a "grossly dishonoring" situation in which Chennault was being subjected to endless petty persecution and was "constantly though obscurely hindered in the application of his superb tactical imagination and even in the execution of his plain duty." Stilwell and Bissell, Alsop reported, were bungling the prosecution of the war effort. Acknowledging that Stilwell was brave and able, Alsop said he lacked understanding of what could be done in the air, and his harassment (through Bissell) of Chennault reflected "conventional suspicion of an unconventional man." Furthermore, although Stilwell was "reasonably decent," most of his officers held a low opinion of the Chinese; their attitudes were known and were causing serious political damage. Stilwell dubbed the Generalissimo "Peanut," a small but tactless gesture that caused untold trouble.[24]

Over subsequent months Alsop became Chennault's most ardent advocate. His long and emotional letters to Hopkins (even Alsop realized that he must sound "almost hysterical") bewailed the lost opportunities in China, painted a dismal picture of existing conditions within CBI, and portrayed Stilwell and Bissell as plodding groundlings who lacked understanding for the potential of air power. Alsop saw Chennault, however, as a man of remarkable ability, "that rarest of all types of men, a really powerful military leader with a truly original mind," who was being thwarted in his efforts to defeat the Japanese.[25] His letters played an undeniable role in the decisions which followed, for they persuaded Hopkins, who got the word to Roosevelt.

At the end of the year Roosevelt suggested to Marshall that Chennault be separated from Stilwell's command and be given 100 planes with which to strike the Japanese north of the Yangtze. Marshall's reply was forceful, clear, and negative. As he saw the problem, the limited capacity of the Hump airlift would determine the size of the air force that could be operated from China until a land route could be opened through Burma. The Burma campaign was necessary, but its success would be jeopardized if Chennault's force was withdrawn from its support. Chennault was the one "to command our all-out air effort against Japan from China when the supply of the necessary force can be assured," Marshall stated (an opinion he later reversed), but at present Chennault "appears to disregard the actualities of the logistical problem" which Stilwell was struggling to master. Roosevelt was not convinced. An independent air force for Chennault should be kept in mind, he said, but for the present he bowed to Marshall's judgment.[26]

Early in January 1943 Chiang Kai-shek made a formal request for United States help in the reorganization, training, and future planning for a Chinese Air Force which would be bolstered by U.S. airmen and under Chennault's control. A few days later he endorsed Chennault's strategy for an immediate aerial offensive and withdrew his commitment for Y-force to participate in the upcoming Burma campaign.[27] Apparently realizing that they would not receive everything they wanted, Chiang and Soong had decided to back Chennault and a reformed CAF rather than Stilwell and a reformed army.

For some years Chiang had believed that air power would be the most effective military force for China to use against Japan—a belief Chennault endorsed. There is no doubt that Chiang also had China's best interests in mind, just as each of the Allies pursued its own political goals within the coalition, the British seeking to preserve their colonial power, the Russians determined to gain security in eastern Europe, the Americans eager to get the military business over with quickly but nevertheless hoping to advance their own concepts of world order. Chiang had one eye on China's unfinished revolution. Although Stilwell reasoned that a reformed Chinese army would strengthen Chiang's position after the war, Chiang believed an air force, developed under Kuomintang control, with no prior loyalties either to the Chinese Communists or to independent provincial leaders, would be a more secure asset. To some extent he was afraid of his own army, torn by conflicting loyalties and power struggles and bound into a precarious alliance. Chiang was unwilling and possibly unable to institute the reforms Stilwell advocated, loath to risk the loss of those divisions whose loyalty he could trust.[28]

The weighting factor, however, may well have been the confidence Chiang reposed in Chennault himself. During the five and one-half years of his service in China thus far, the farm boy from Louisiana had demonstrated that he could be frank without being rude, critical without being condemnatory, and accepting without being condescending. He had been willing to serve China while remaining loyal to his own country. He had attained a personal prestige rarely if ever accorded by the Chinese to a foreigner.[29] From this point on, Chiang was squarely behind him in any questions of strategy or supply that arose between the United States and China. Believing that the shift toward an aerial strategy would be disastrous, a disgusted Stilwell wrote, "Chennault's blatting has put us in a spot. He's talked so much about what he can do that now they're going to let him do it."[30]

There matters stood when Roosevelt, Churchill, and the Combined Chiefs of Staff assembled at Casablanca on 14 January for the second great wartime conference, best remembered for a stiff handshake between Generals DeGaulle and Giraud and the surprising policy announcement that the Allies would demand unconditional surrender from the Axis powers. Casablanca's decisions reflected the fact that the European war was still foremost; top priority went to the battle against the German submarines in the Atlantic. The Americans were more concerned with China and the war against Japan than were the British, but at the insistence of Marshall and King, it was decided that the initiative gained thus far in the Pacific would be maintained. Since China might be needed later as a base from which to strike Japan, the conference approved a limited campaign to begin in November 1943, to retake northern Burma and build a road—the Ledo Road, later renamed the Stilwell Road—from India across Burma into China. Since Roosevelt, here supported by Marshall and Arnold, wanted to give Chennault the means to bomb Japan "for psychological reasons," Casablanca also endorsed additional aircraft for the Hump and the buildup of air power in China "to the maximum extent that logistical limitations and other important claims will permit."[31]

Immediately after Casablanca Arnold flew on to China to discuss plans for the Burma campaign and encourage Chiang Kai-shek to take part. The flight over the Hump prompted him to muse that "we all take our flying too much as a matter of course," for a fifty-mile-an-hour tailwind upset navigational calculations and for some hours the plane was lost, its uneasy passengers grimly speculating as to which shoes might be best for hiking out of the jungle below them.

They eventually landed safely at Kunming, but Chennault was amused to learn that Bissell's own pilot had been aboard and was one of the culprits.[32]

The visit to Kunming gave Arnold the opportunity to evaluate Chennault for himself. During the preceding months Stilwell had insisted that Chennault was well supported by Bissell and was being given wide latitude and every possible consideration; the problem with the CATF, according to Stilwell, was that Chennault had decided limitations. A skeptical Arnold had polled his staff, noting that officers returning from China all gave the impression that Chennault had a minimum of assistance from the Tenth Air Force, yet "when we ask Stilwell for a report this is the reply we get."[33]

Arnold's staff had supported Chennault, noting that he might not be a good administrator, but "his unit was sent to China to fight and not to administer. It has fought well." Chennault was considered to have proven himself a leader, and with respect to his current claim that he could obtain air supremacy in China, "evidence to date indicates that Chennault can do it if anyone can." Before the trip to China, Arnold had concluded that a separate air force for Chennault should be set up once the supply problem could be overcome. He had recommended this expedient to Marshall.[34]

In Kunming, Arnold began to have doubts. He shared the admiration of others for the Flying Tigers' aggressive spirit; he sensed in Chennault a clear grasp of tactics and the air situation in China. But he also thought Chennault "was not realistic" about the logistics of his operations. Like most others who saw CBI operations firsthand, he was appalled at the difficulties. In a message to Marshall he listed long distances with no servicing facilities, the absence of satisfactory weather stations and service, and the delay in receiving supplies as three reasons why air operations in China were "so dependent upon the supply service in India that complete independence is *impossible*." He "urgently" recommended that Chennault's units continue to be part of the Tenth Air Force, for "Stilwell states and my inspection confirms that Chennault does not exercise the necessary administrative and executive control of his present units to warrant independence."[35]

Chennault flew with Arnold to Chungking on 5 February for conferences with the Generalissimo. It was snowing, and Chiang's house was cold. A shivering Arnold sipped hot tea and tried to cope. He found Chiang difficult, not a "big man" nor one with an orderly mind. He wondered whether Madame had all the brains, for Chiang seemed to cast logic aside and to believe his will could accomplish the impossible. Arnold had been charged by Roosevelt with working out ways to augment the air effort, but Chiang clearly explained that he wanted Bissell removed and Chennault given complete control of operations in China. In this new version of his three demands, he insisted on 500 airplanes by November, either for Chennault or for the Chinese Air Force, and 10,000 tons monthly over the Hump. This was exactly double the 5,000 tons demanded the preceding June and appreciably more than the 4,000 tons by April that Arnold had felt he could promise. It was obvious to Arnold that Chennault was held in very high regard by the Chinese, something that very few Americans could boast; that the Chinese disliked Bissell, calling him an "old woman" for his obsession with detail; that Stilwell had little use for Chennault. Here he suspected a bit of jealousy.[36]

One immutable fact colored all Arnold's conclusions: the supply of aviation gasoline determined all aerial operations in China, and while Bissell might be an "old woman," he was an efficient detail man and the supply problem required one. Both Chiang and Chennault professed lack of knowledge or understanding about supply or transport; to Arnold they seemed to gloss over such issues with a wave of their hands. Arnold decided that Chennault utterly failed to appreciate the problems of supply and administration of his task force, that he saw only how the Tenth Air Force hindered his operations and not how it helped him.

Realizing that more than an ordinary command decision was involved, Arnold returned to Washington feeling disturbed. He carried a letter from Chiang to Roosevelt in which the Generalissimo voiced his newest demands and described Chennault as a man of genius who enjoyed the confidence of the Chinese Army and Air Force and of Chiang himself. Only with Chennault, Chiang wrote, was it possible to work with the necessary unquestioning cooperation.[37]

Roosevelt soon made up his mind. He did not answer Chiang for some weeks thereafter, but on 19 February Marshall wrote Stilwell that matters had "come to a head." The president had decided to activate the Fourteenth Air Force, under Chennault and independent of Bissell, at once. The Fourteenth would still be under Stilwell as commanding general, CBI; the promotion of Bissell and Chennault to major general would be sent to the Senate at once, and at Stilwell's request there would be one day's interval to ensure that Bissell remained senior in rank.[38]

Chennault knew little of the decisions being made, even though they pivoted around him. Trumble, who was then working in Chungking as his liaison with the CAF and the Commission on Aeronautical Affairs, sent him excerpts of Chiang's letter to Roosevelt. He found therein "a lot of startling information." I feel, he wrote his friend, "just a little like a fellow who said he wanted an elephant and then got one. I suppose that I can figure out how to handle it as time goes on."[39]

12

A Clash of Personality

The 15 February 1943 issue of *Time* magazine released the mounting tensions in Kunming like the bursting of a levee. In a plain-spoken article about the "bitter, burning conflict" among Chennault, Stilwell, and Bissell, it portrayed Chennault as a brilliant, unorthodox genius and miracle worker, Bissell as a bemedaled autocrat, Stilwell as an infantryman who had only an air force and told Chennault, "It's the man in the trenches that will win the war," while Chennault shouted back, "Goddammit, Stilwell, there aren't any men in the trenches." *Time* concluded that the friction was as dangerous as a bare nail in a shoe.[1]

Indeed it was. Stilwell arrived in Kunming that morning, Bissell that afternoon. When the smoke cleared, Chennault assumed that he would be removed from the theater. He would be glad to leave the problems in the hands of others, he mused, but "I hate to be turned out." He wrote Stilwell a letter of apology, saying the truth had been distorted and that Stilwell was the "only Regular Army General I know of who has long observed the Chinese, served with the Chinese Army, and in whom the Chinese have had sufficient confidence to entrust the command of their forces."[2]

185

Until this time the relationship between the two generals was workable though far from ideal. Both men were of strong and independent temperament, blunt and outspoken, with scant skill in diplomacy; neither was inclined to tolerance. But Chennault's obvious strengths were assets Stilwell appreciated; he was not antiair, although he saw limitations to what air power could accomplish. Nor was he anti-Chennault, although there was no warmth between them. Ironically, the two could have made a powerful team, for Stilwell's grasp of total operations was more balanced than the single-minded, skyward focus of Chennault, with his unwavering belief in air power's potential. A superb tactician and fighter, Chennault was weak in precisely those areas of planning and preparation where Stilwell was strong.

Chennault's inability to work within constraints sabotaged the partnership before it could be realized. Unquestioning obedience to orders is the foundation of the military system; by violating it and going out of channels to seek change, Chennault forfeited, in Stilwell's view, the right to any personal consideration. Chennault's decline on Stilwell's scale of values started with his objections to Bissell's appointment, was reinforced by his reluctance to bring the AVG into the Air Corps, mounted with his bickering with Bissell, and culminated with his letter to Willkie. Although Chennault had intended that his Willkie letter reach the War Department, by sending it through McHugh he had committed a second sin on top of the first: he had bypassed his theater commander while advocating a strategy contrary to that which his commander recommended.[3]

At this point the two men declared a personal war. Differences between them escalated as each sought enough supplies to implement his own plans. The odds appeared to be with Stilwell; he had the War Department's backing, and he controlled the allocation of supplies. But in one of the most bizarre situations ever to arise in American military affairs, Chennault was to have two heads of state—Roosevelt and Chiang Kai-shek—on his side.

Chennault agonized about gasoline. He never had enough. In January he received less than half what he had gotten in December. Depressed and ready to quit, he was gripped by the specter of persecution, convinced that Stilwell and Bissell were after him. In February he predicted a Japanese offensive in eastern China and requested planes and supplies so that the CATF could help the Chinese armies repel it. Angered by the *Time* article and deflated by word that Chennault was to have the separate Fourteenth Air Force, Stilwell curtly replied that his primary mission was to protect the Hump airline, and he would get supplies as circumstances permitted.[4]

In Washington, where the specific decisions about the Fourteenth Air Force were being made, Roosevelt was under steady pressure from Chiang, Soong, the Chinese embassy, and China Defense Supplies. Alsop expressed his opinion that the War Department was not planning to assign Chennault enough planes or supplies to enable him to implement his plan.[5] Stilwell hurt his own cause by writing Marshall that Chiang Kai-shek had been "very irritable and hard to handle" and should be "talked to in sterner tones." Feeling that Chiang should be accorded the same respect that he himself demanded as a head of state, Roosevelt scolded. The Chinese had the right to different methods, he said, and Chiang had the right to be treated with respect. "Hopeful" for the Burma operation but convinced that the aerial strategy offered the political results he wanted, Roosevelt decided the United States should move as rapidly as possible to give Chennault 500 planes and enough supplies to enable him to see what he could do.

Told that it was essential for Chennault to get his share of the supplies, Marshall assured his commander-in-chief that Stilwell would assist Chennault to the maximum. He warned, however, that "as soon as our air effort hurts the Japs, they will move in on us, not only in the air but also on the ground," which Chennault's fighters could not defend.[6]

Marshall's reservations notwithstanding, Roosevelt answered Chiang's letter and granted most of his demands. Chennault was promoted to major general on 3 March; on 11 March the Fourteenth Air Force was activated. It was the only air force created during the war for political rather than military reasons. The need was there, but its foundation had not been laid. An uneasy Arnold cautioned Chennault that his position was one of "extreme complexity" and warned him not to "bite off more than you can chew."[7]

Already Chennault had asked for more than Arnold could supply, but all other factors paled before the dismal performance of the Hump during the early months of 1943. In December it had been put under the control of the Air Transport Command. With strength increased to 137 transports, including twelve of the larger C-87s, its commander thought he could lift 4,000 tons a month. In April, however, the total was only 1,910 tons.[8] A complex misunderstanding increased Chennault's frustration, for Arnold sent him a new chief of staff, Brig. Gen. Edgar E. Glenn, who arrived with verbal instructions that Chennault should be given complete control of the Hump. When an indignant Stilwell sought confirmation, Marshall said it was all a mistake—there was to be no change in status for the Hump. Knowing little of decisions at the higher levels, Chennault assumed that Stilwell was deliberately trying to thwart him, and the bile of suspected persecution flowed.[9]

The 308th Heavy Bombardment Group for the Fourteenth began reaching China in March. When it proved impracticable for its B-24s to ferry their own supplies into China as planned, Roosevelt asked Marshall to assign thirty more transports to the Hump, even though they would have to be taken from the forthcoming invasion of Sicily. Stilwell was told to give Chennault a firm allocation of 1,500 tons per month and give him a chance to see what he could do, but in March Chennault received only 615 tons and in the first two weeks of April only 48. Some of the supplies were channeled to Y-force, but the primary problem was the Hump itself. With the advent of the rainy monsoon, the heavy transports literally bogged down in the mud of Assam's inadequate airfields.[10]

Chiang had little understanding of the problems involved, even less patience with delay. He had expected immediate and substantial improvement once the Fourteenth Air Force was named, but little seemed to have changed. On 10 April he wrote Roosevelt, asking that Chennault be called back to Washington so that he could report to him personally on the plan they had been discussing. Just what plan, Marshall inquired of Stilwell, was Chiang talking about?[11] An angry Stilwell descended upon Chennault. "HE HAS NO NEW PLAN," was his startled conclusion. "Peanut is just talking about Ch.'s '6-months-to-drive-the-Japs-out-of-China' plan."[12]

"What a day!" Vincent wrote in his diary. "Uncle Joe arrived today with orders for General Chennault to 'pack his bag.' The two of them are leaving tomorrow for Washington." Roosevelt, possibly curious to meet the controversial Chennault, had agreed to call him home, but at Marshall's request Stilwell was ordered home also.[13]

Chennault was given time to fly to Chungking and confer with Chiang before the two generals boarded a C-87 for the four-day flight. The atmosphere in the plane was tense though civil; Stilwell sat in one end, Chennault in the other. Using his briefcase as a desk, Chennault wrote down the plan he was supposed to present. Even as he did so, Soong was reassuring Hopkins that the Chinese forces could stop an attempt by the Japanese to take the eastern China airbases, while Chiang was asking Roosevelt to allot the entire resources of the

Chennault with Nelson, his half brother, in Washington, March 1943. (Photo courtesy E. Nelson Chennault)

Hump for the next three months to stockpile reserves for the air offensive.[14] Chennault and the Chinese had obviously closed ranks.

The plan Chennault committed to paper while en route to Washington differed in emphasis and tone from Cooper's version of the preceding October. The handwritten original, showing very few words
crossed out as he recorded his thoughts, began by methodically noting the extent of the Japanese occupation in China and the uses Japan made of each specific area. It was an enormously profitable
occupation, entirely dependent on shipping. Japan did not want to
fight in China; Japanese forces there were minimal, and Japan was
heavily committed to the defense of its outer perimeter in the Pacific.
That outer defense would have to be weakened before Japan could
fight more vigorously in China. Chennault concluded: "Since Japan
does not desire to fight in the air over China, every effort should be
exerted to make her fight there."[15]

Then Chennault reiterated his litany. Since the vital Japanese
shipping and supply lines were within easy operating range of U.S.
air units in China, "the Japanese air force can be rendered ineffective
by the action of an extremely small air force in China." Success
would depend on prompt delivery of supplies and equipment; mini-
mums could not be reduced without spoiling the major part, if not
all, of the offensive. His own estimate was 4,790 tons monthly at first,
increasing to 7,128.[16]

Chennault's restatement of how air power might be used from
China coincided with a long-range plan made by Washington staff in
which China figured as the base for an eventual aerial offensive or a
possible invasion. Chennault's plan dovetailed with this scheme but
raised the possibility of significant action from China immediately
and with a relatively small force. The big qualifier was the need for
minimum supply, as Chennault repeatedly stressed. When he and
Stilwell presented their views to Marshall on 30 April, Chennault
said there was no point "in putting in aircraft, even individual
planes, unless we have supplies to operate." He reminded all concerned that operations in China were wholly determined by the
amount of supplies that it would be possible to bring in by air.[17]

He nevertheless believed that "we can destroy a considerable part
of the Japanese air force and at the same time we can destroy a great
deal of their shipping," for the Japanese supply lines in China were
heavily dependent on river boats that were vulnerable to planes. He
acknowledged danger: Japanese reaction might "take the form of a
powerful land offensive designed to occupy the central China prov-

inces where our airdromes are located." To address this problem he
deferred to Stilwell, who said he thought the Chinese might be able
to hold the eastern airfields against existing Japanese forces, although he doubted whether they could hold against a major effort,
and if they chose to do so, the Japanese could throw in a million
men.[18] This was the War Department's major reservation, but Chiang
personally assured Roosevelt that ground action against the air bases
could "be halted by the existing Chinese forces." Chiang also twisted
the knife, noting that Chennault's air offensive had been approved
some time ago, and since "no obstacle to prompt action now appears
to remain," he hoped it might start soon.[19]

Facing a complex tangle, Roosevelt summoned Chennault to the
White House. We have only Chennault's memoir to tell us about that
meeting (and possibly two others during subsequent weeks), but
Roosevelt probably talked at some length about his own views of
China, using the time to evaluate his guest and his ideas. A Chinese-
American integrated air force, conceived with the idea of building a
CAF that could stand alone after the war, coincided with Roosevelt's
goals and received enthusiastic support. So did Chennault's belief
that merchant shipping was Japan's Achilles' heel. The memoir credits Roosevelt with asking Chennault whether he could sink a million
tons of Japanese shipping a year, to which he replied that if he had
10,000 tons of supplies a month he could do that and more. Chennault could compensate with conviction for what he lacked in depth
or sophistication, and reportedly the President "banged his fist on the
desk and chortled, 'If you can sink a million tons, we'll break their
back.' "[20]

There is no evidence that Roosevelt and Chennault were in anything other than complete harmony of thought, although Chennault's personal convictions were not pro-Roosevelt. Before the war
he had been highly critical of the New Deal, and because he saw the
conflict between the Kuomintang and the Chinese Communists as an
ideological battle closely tied up with the Soviet Communist issue,
he was skeptical of Roosevelt's efforts to accommodate the Soviet
Union. In private he expressed fears that America would later pay
for these "misguided policies" with blood and gold.[21] Apparently
Roosevelt convinced Chennault that he, the president, was solidly
behind Chiang and the Nationalists, however, and of course Chennault wanted the president's support for his fight. It behooved him to
get along.

It is also likely that Alsop advised Chennault on how to put his best foot forward with the president, for before leaving China, Chennault had wired Alsop, then in Washington, to "meet and advise."[22] The journalist played a subtle role in this long-term drama. He had the political and social skills to balance Chennault's fire-from-the-hip simplicity, as Chennault realized. Alsop in turn perceived Chennault's strengths: his genius in tactics and his amazing ability to create such things as an effective warning net from little more than chewing gum and wire. He also realized that Chennault needed him, that by working for him he could make a real contribution to the war effort. Accordingly Alsop had applied for a commission in the army, and Chennault had asked to have him assigned as his aide—a move that caused Stilwell to sputter that "Chennault has swelled up like a poisoned pup."[23] Roosevelt, however, showed an uncommon interest in having Alsop work with Chennault; he assured each of them that he would see what he could do. Alsop solved the immediate problem by affiliating with China Defense Supplies, and in that capacity he returned to China after the Washington conferences, his travel cleared by the White House as high priority.[24]

Roosevelt also consulted privately with Stilwell, who felt that he had been shabbily treated by the president and was at a disadvantage in trying to argue his case. When he warned that the Japanese would react to Chennault's offensive with ground action, Roosevelt told him, "In a *political fight* [Stilwell's emphasis] it's not good tactics to refrain from doing something because of something your opponent may do in return."[25]

Stimson took the lead in resolving the impasse. He thought Stilwell's "much the safer plan," but he invited Chennault to state his views at a private meeting in his home on a Sunday morning. In one-on-one situations where he was treated with courtesy, Chennault was poised and effective. He spoke of the limited capacity of the old Burma Road and the difficult terrain its proposed replacement would have to cross. He expressed belief that both he and Stilwell could operate effectively with what the air route could deliver into China. Stimson was surprised to learn from him that planes could operate over the Hump during the monsoon by flying on instruments. CNAC was already using them, but few of the army transports were equipped.

"He made a very good impression on me," Stimson recorded. "He was modest and frank." Although still skeptical, he began seeking a way to satisfy both Chennault and Stilwell, both Roosevelt and the War Department. The vital issue, he concluded, was getting enough supplies into China for both ground and air forces. He told the president he thought it could probably be done.[26]

CBI might be a minor theater, but it was emotionally charged, and its options were major topics when the TRIDENT conference opened in Washington on 14 May. Roosevelt showed concern for China's stability and Chiang's prestige, at one point giving a little lecture that he would not tolerate an attitude of "it can't be done." The British did not share his concern for China, but they endorsed Chennault's strategy; they had little enthusiasm for a Burma campaign, which promised miserable stewing around in the jungle with no ultimate advantage to the British position in either India or Burma.[27]

Roosevelt had his own notions on the shape of a postwar Asia, and for the moment he could see no alternative but to support Chiang Kai-shek. China seemed near the point of disintegration. Alsop observed he had often seen the Chinese cry wolf, but this time they seemed "really frightened," and some of them were "downright terrified." At least three provinces were gripped in a famine that was especially bad in Honan, where millions were dying and the living were eating clay and bark. Throughout the vast land, despair and disillusionment had replaced the buoyant defiance of the early war years; occasional armed uprisings foreshadowed mounting unrest against the Kuomintang, its oppressive conscription and taxation, its corruption and the unrelieved suffering it allowed. Inflation had reached 6,000 percent of prewar levels; blockaded and with her richest provinces occupied, China was financing the war with meaningless banknotes printed in the United States and flown into China over the seriously overtaxed Hump.[28] Madame, still in Washington and staying at the White House, where her quick temper and imperial manner aroused the consternation of the staff and made Roosevelt himself uneasy, had Soong's help in making certain that Roosevelt knew the full extent of China's desperation. The only solution, they said, was to grant the Generalissimo's requests at once.[29]

Truth versus reality had long been a problem in assessing China's situation, for China's advocates were influential. The Chinese were not as noble, innocent, brave, and capable as most Americans had been led to believe, nor was the aerial war in China accomplishing as much of significance as journalistic accounts suggested. Some feared that Roosevelt accepted the myth, but Roosevelt steered his China policy through a maze of ugly choices with unpredictable international consequences. At that time he was privy to a Federal Bureau of Investigation report that foreshadowed much of the later agony of U.S.-China relations. The report asserted that Madame and the Soong family were "money mad" and had a "death grip" on China, that Madame's visit to the United States was for the express purpose of assisting in a conspiracy to defraud the United States of lend-lease funds for the Soong family's personal benefit, and that after the war the Chinese Communists intended to overthrow Chiang unless he got rid of his wife and the attending corruption.[30]

On 17 May Soong told the Combined Chiefs of Staff that China would make a separate peace with Japan unless China's allies at once met their commitments and came to her relief. Roosevelt made his decisions. Starting 1 July, Chennault was to have the first 4,700 tons of supplies per month over the Hump, which was to be expanded to a capacity of 10,000 tons monthly by 1 September. The War Department was doubtful that air supply could do the job; it obtained agreement on a modified Burma campaign so that the Ledo Road could be built. Three offensive actions against Japan would proceed concurrently in 1943: MacArthur would clear the Bismarck Archipelago and New Guinea, the U.S. Navy would seize the Marshalls and Carolines to start a drive across the Central Pacific, and in China Chennault would start hitting the Japanese as soon as his supplies were in hand. Roosevelt assured Chiang that relief was on the way.[31]

Stimson considered that "the thing had been pretty well gummed up."[32] So did Marshall, who not only disapproved of the China strategy but resented the ways in which Chennault and the other China supporters influenced the president. Marshall neither liked nor trusted Chennault. His staff suggested that he confer privately with the independent-minded airman and stress some hard facts: that the Fourteenth Air Force was an integral part of the U.S. Army and under Stilwell, no matter how undesirable that might seem to Chennault; that it was unacceptable to deal directly with the Chinese authorities and all matters, including complaints, must be handled through Stilwell; that should Chiang and Stilwell disagree, the War Department would support Stilwell "to the utmost."[33]

Chennault's stay in the States afforded him little relaxation or pleasure. When he went to Lake St. John for a brief respite, Nell thought "he looked fine though tired." In Washington he played a few rounds of golf with his brother Joe. Noe gave a dinner for him and the Louisiana congressmen at the Mayflower, a happy evening during which a picture caught him in a hearty, unrestrained laugh. But most of the time he was subdued, almost sad. When he talked with the father of one of his young commanders who had recently been killed, the bereaved man was impressed by his "wonderfully sober and thoughtful face" and "tremendous force" yet found him so "quiet moving and so quiet spoken that he is almost difficult to hear with others about."[34]

Chennault had much on his mind. Wartime Washington, a bustling madhouse, made him realize that the problems he faced in his operations cave, gouged out of the mountainside above Kweilin and often penetrated by Japanese bomb fragments, could never be fully understood by those who fought the war from the planning perspective, nor could he himself understand or be understood by them. He felt out of place in a world of diplomats and cocktail parties—what a dumb way to drink—and he realized that his gaunt and war-worn appearance contrasted painfully with the sharp uniforms, brisk aides, and bustling efficiency of the staff officers. It was hard for him to hear the proceedings during the conferences, hence awkward to take part. He sat through them wearing his inscrutable cigar-store Indian expression. Afterward the story circulated that Churchill, upon learning who he was, observed that he was "glad that man is on our side."[35]

Chennault sensed that the gap between Washington and China was a matter less of distance and supplies than of culture and values; he realized that in his own way he bridged it. In his first days in China in 1937, he had walked along the crowded waterfront in Canton, absorbing the sights and sounds and smells of China at its most impoverished level. Families lived on junks so close together that a person could step from one to another. They used the river for drinking and cooking and washing and waste disposal, mothers holding their babies while cooking on charcoal over an open fire, a flimsy roof overhead and a straw mat for a bed. There was no prospect that their lives could ever be better. "And life goes on," had been his only comment.[36] Like the Chinese, he had struggled against poverty and despair, and in his gut he accepted that the perfect world with which we want to deal does not exist. In a memo to Marshall he tried to say as much, observing that even though he did not believe the risk of a Japanese offensive against the eastern Chinese fields was great, the greater risk was in continued inaction. "The proposed China air offensive may be expected to meet the requirements of the situation as well as it is possible to do with limited military expenditures."[37]

Realizing that he did not have the confidence or trust of his high command, he felt personal pain and isolation, the price he must pay for his conviction and ambition and commitment to China. He also felt a sobering weight of responsibility. He felt an obligation to air power, which he passionately believed was capable of great things that he wanted to demonstrate; to the men under his command, who trusted and depended upon him; to Chiang, whom he had promised to help; and to Roosevelt, who seemed to see China and her need much as he did and who consequently had overruled the War Department in his favor. Theirs was a strange alliance, and at their last private meeting Roosevelt invited Chennault to write to him directly, outside military channels, giving him an unprecedented status but increasing his weight of personal accountability.[38]

He had his elephant, but time was of the essence—the best flying months in east China were August through November—and he turned down an invitation from Churchill to return via London. Writing Arnold, who had suffered a heart attack and was recuperating, that he would "endeavor to employ every man and every weapon furnished me in such manner as will meet with your approval and be a credit to the U.S. Air Force,"[39] he hurried back to Kunming, buoyed up by having won his way and yet, as during his boyhood, finding no joy in the winning.

As he began preparations for his offensive, Chennault carried the added burden of alienation from his theater headquarters. On 19 May, Bissell signed a negative efficiency report stating that Chennault "does not render generous and willing support to plans of his superiors regardless of personal views" and that his earlier separation from the service prevented his gaining experience in field grades and the opportunity "to know and understand administrative and logistical requirements of larger forces." As far as Chennault was concerned, it was Bissell who did not render generous support, and ignoring the broader issue of his efforts to advocate his own strategy, he protested that he had rendered most willing support of the only directive he had received.[40]

It was true that the directive given to Chennault when he took over the CATF in 1942 granted him "widest latitude"[41] in carrying out his operations, but it was also true that Chennault's attitude toward his higher command often bespoke lack of confidence and respect, his tone defiant, his pleas for planes and men reflecting supreme confidence in his own ability to drive the Japanese out of China even while deprecating the efforts of others. Passionately convinced that opportunity was being lost, singlemindedly dedicated to the fight at hand, he could see nothing else. Compromise was not in his soul, and his manner did not ingratiate him with his superior officers, some of whom assessed him as egocentric and imperious.

News conference, Chennault's headquarters, Kunming, China, 1943. From left: Harold Isaacs, *Newsweek*, with Joe Dash at his feet; Annalee Jacoby, *Time*; Albert Ravenholt, United Press; Clyde A. Farnsworth, Associated Press; Brig. Gen. Edgar E. Glenn, Fourteenth Air Force chief of staff, standing; Chennault; Theodore White, *Time/Life*. (Official U.S. Army Air Forces photo, courtesy John Williams)

But the crowning blow, as far as Stilwell was concerned, was an institution that went into his diary as the K.M.H. of P.: the Kunming House of Prostitution. The control of venereal disease among the Americans in China was a formidable problem. Prostitutes were available on almost any street corner. Each town had its Slit Alley or Dump Street, and there were few recreational facilities to occupy the men in their free time. The venereal disease rate was high among the native population; it skyrocketed among the visiting servicemen. Some strains endemic to China were especially debilitating to Westerners and posed serious long-term problems. While it was common practice for the armies of some nations to have established houses that were controlled for disease, Americans had only begun to acknowledge the problem. Lectures on morality sought to discourage sexual contacts, movies sought to distract the men, and prophylactic kits sought to prevent trouble if all else failed.[42]

It was not enough. At one point the sickness reports coming across Chennault's desk showed the number of days lost to venereal disease increasing by a factor of more than 200 percent a month. Chennault was horrified: he was losing more men to disease than to combat injuries. The health of his men was his responsibility, and he had to deal with it, but he knew a nonfraternization order would be disobeyed. The medical staff made a proposal. The Chinese agreed to standards of inspection and supervision. A U.S. captain, assisted by a Chinese woman, flew to Kweilin to recruit some Hong Kong refugee girls to staff a restricted house.[43]

Stilwell heard of it and was outraged. "Officers pimping. Hauling whores in our planes. Sent for Chennault. He *knew*." There was suspicion that the house was also a front for a smuggling operation. "It looks messy," Stilwell wrote. Disgusted, he summoned the inspector general and wired Marshall. There was no doubt in his mind that Chennault had authorized the venture and had lied to him about it. He was disappointed when Chennault was cleared: "No hope on whore-house matter. Can't get him."[44]

Similar episodes occurred at other bases. The conditions at one became so bad that the colonel in charge felt he had to do something to keep his entire base from being on sick call. He took it upon himself to set up a clean house and tried to hide it from the higher command. When word reached the top, Chennault stood by his officer, for he saw the brothels as a practical necessity. Correspondent Eric Sevareid, pondering the problem as he toured China in the fall of 1943, observed that the few females sent abroad by the United States were "good girls," the wholesome Red Cross nurses, but a more intelligent procedure (although admittedly one that the U.S. public was not prepared to accept) would have been to keep the Red Cross girls at home and send to the war areas large numbers of young and carefully regulated prostitutes.[45]

The episode of the "K.M.H. of P." was important because it put another barrier between the two generals charged with implementing U.S. policy in China. An officer sent from Washington to soothe the command tension found himself speechless when the high-spirited generals involved Madame in a heated argument over the whorehouse, but he concluded that Stilwell and Chennault really got along "beautifully" on operational matters.[46] Their areas of agreement, however, did not compensate for basic differences. Stilwell had no respect for Chennault as a man and considered his attitude to be "definitely hostile and prejudicial to military discipline."[47] Increasingly the problems between them can be attributed to conflicts in character and personality, to starkly different value systems and approaches to the solution of problems.

Stilwell was an ascetic and an idealist; he set high personal standards for himself and others, perhaps higher than could reasonably be met. Chennault had his own bent toward the romantic ideal, but never did he deny the wilder and strictly physical aspects of human relationships, for himself or for others. He was comfortable among the Chinese social customs that accepted concubines and mistresses; he saw brothels as a way of protecting China's "good" women. His soul may have longed for the unattainable perfection, but in practice he was an undeniable realist, a believer in the practicable, seeking always to sweep obstacles aside in order to get on with the business at hand.

Realism and idealism sometimes struggled with one another, but were usually at peace within his own private life. His officers, sometimes surprised when he took their side in disciplinary matters, concluded, "He would forgive you damn near anything so long as you were willing to fight."[48] When he realized the Chinese employees of the AVG were stealing, he asked Madame to raise their wages, as their low pay invited theft. When he learned that Chinese ground crews were "politely robbing" the Fourteenth of gasoline, he devised a way to stop the practice while preventing the Chinese from losing face, for he was "not convinced there is any real crookedness."[49] But even though his understanding of human frailty endeared him to his men and to the Chinese, it contributed to rumors of scandals surrounding him and his headquarters, for when he did not react to transgressions with moral indignation, some concluded that he condoned them.

Chennault's very special relationship with China and the Chinese was an additional factor contributing to the growing chasm between him and his headquarters. Stilwell, repeatedly thwarted in his efforts to carry out the military aspects of his mission, became increasingly antagonistic toward Chiang and his regime, seeing only its corruption, its ineptness, its petty manipulations to gain its own ends. Chennault, in contrast, took the political aspects of helping China quite comfortably in stride. "He has made it his particular business to get on well with the Chinese," a correspondent observed. Within his command he made a conscious effort to minimize racial friction. He tolerated no verbal or physical abuse of individual Chinese; he made it a point never to say anything derogatory or critical about the

Chinese as a society; he did not openly criticize China's leaders, nor did he allow others to do so in his presence. As an ambassador in a theater charged with political ramifications, he was more effective than Stilwell, as some officers who worked with both men noted.[50]

Living and working in the Chinese society, Chennault did not judge: he accepted with a natural ease that acknowledged the bad along with the good. Perhaps at an unconscious level he was groping back to an ancient heritage, for a Chinese scribe once told him that centuries ago the name "Chennault" had been "Shinado," meaning "high tree," but that Genghis Khan had chased the original Shinados from China into Europe, where they settled in France and became Occidentals.[51]

Chennault was not free of racism: he looked down on black Americans, and he once wrote in a personal letter that Japan was a greater enemy to the United States than was Germany, because the differences were racial. But his good relationships with the Chinese were a sincere manifestation of his feelings, not an expression of superficial expediency. He might not understand the Chinese, but he liked them. He moved among them comfortably and with pleasure, easily adapting to their traditional courtesies and customs. His acceptance of Chinese culture spanned the social strata from Chiang and Madame to the coolies who worked for him and to whom he was unswervingly loyal; when he came back to China after the war, he hired ridiculous numbers of them to tend his house rather than turn them away.[52]

Nowhere was Chennault's acceptance of Chinese customs and limitations more obvious than with the CAF, which was a maddening organization, inept and corrupt and riddled with politics. He had to contend with the worst of it, but even though he went through cycles of optimism and exasperation, he never swerved from his commitment to the Chinese, never ceased to have faith in their abilities.

He once gave Holloway a challenge in cross-cultural communication. When the CAF got their first P-43s, the Chinese ground crews tended to fill the gasoline tanks so full that on takeoff they would overflow and ignite, causing the plane to explode. Holloway's task was to explain to them how this could be prevented. Understanding that the Chinese lost face if they did not do things "full bore," or if they showed ignorance by asking questions, yet also realizing that they lacked the technical background to understand why they must leave expansion space in the top of the tanks, Holloway planned his strategy thoughtfully. When the mission was completed, he was confident he "had them straightened out." The problem continued. A dejected Holloway reported to Chennault, who assured him he had done a good job, "but we'll just have to think of some other way to get it across to them." They could not be changed, on their own ground, overnight.[53]

"It requires patience and persistence in sticking to the point," he wrote Trumble in Chungking. "I can even understand their view point. . . . they are often as afraid as I am that the thing won't work. . . . One thing to remember is never to lose your temper or to display a great amount of impatience. . . . After it is all over, they appreciate your self control and give you full credit for it."[54]

It was soon evident that the decisions made at TRIDENT created more problems than they solved for CBI. Stilwell had to persuade a reluctant Chiang to cooperate in an altered Burma campaign and prepare the forces to conduct it. The India-China wing of the ATC had to expand for greatly increased transport over the Hump. Chennault had to organize the Fourteenth Air Force and begin the aerial offensive he had proposed. Nobody had enough of anything to work with; Chiang could see no progress on any front. When Roosevelt mentioned plans to send Maj. Gen. George E. Stratemeyer to CBI to coordinate aerial matters, he requested instead that Chennault be made the chief of staff of the CAF (which Chiang said he wanted to put under Chennault's full command) and that someone be put at the head of the Tenth Air Force "who can work harmoniously with Gen. Chennault."[55]

Beginning to lose patience with what he considered the "awful mess" in CBI, Roosevelt figured that Stilwell hated the Chinese and that the Chinese knew it and returned the sentiment. He was ready to recall Stilwell and give Chennault an independent command, but Marshall insisted that Stilwell's American point of view was needed. Chennault, he feared, was unduly influenced by the Generalissimo.

Roosevelt yielded on Stilwell, but Bissell was replaced by Brig. Gen. Howard C. Davidson, and Chennault was named chief of staff for the CAF, so that he had access to the Chinese without having to go through his theater command. Stratemeyer, an able officer of calm demeanor and mature judgment, was put in charge of all U.S. aviation matters in Burma and India. Although he was not in command over Chennault, his responsibilities included making certain that personnel, supplies, and materials reached him.[56]

Chennault was now in the unusual position of having direct access to both Chiang Kai-shek and Roosevelt. His relationships with Stilwell were strained, but Bissell, his thorn in the flesh, was gone. He and Stratemeyer respected one another and could work together. It remained to be seen whether the Hump could deliver the allotted supplies and whether the Fourteenth Air Force could accomplish its military goals as well as political goals.

The key to Chennault's offensive plan was a network of airfields in eastern China from which Japanese shipping could be attacked. Some new fields were under construction, but Lingling, Hengyang, and Kweilin were already in use, even though they were crude and marginal in their facilities. For some months the Seventy-fifth Squadron at Lingling had only five-gallon cans for refueling its planes. They had no cars, no trucks, no typewriter. Only when atmospheric conditions were favorable could they communicate with their nerve center in Kunming, 600 miles away, by means of a hand-cranked, low-power, high-frequency radio.

At each base the men were isolated and exposed, facing a numerically superior enemy with only their wits and their "gung-ho" spirit to sustain them. Eager pilots competed for the planes—there were sometimes not enough to go around—and ground crews worked around the clock. Their planes were often the low-priority models, lacking equipment that was standard in other theaters. Their hostels were reasonably comfortable, but they received little in the way of PX merchandise. There was no beer ration in China, no bright lights to which one could escape. At only one base could they get ice cream that had been approved by the U.S. medics for American consumption. Their assets: the warning net provided a measure of protection; the other landing fields scattered around the countryside gave them maneuverability when their own bases came under attack; the friendly local population protected them when they were downed in combat.[57]

Vincent, the real life version of Col. Vince Casey of Milton Caniff's comic strip, "Terry and the Pirates," commanded this forward echelon from headquarters in Kweilin. Early in July Chennault told him to "go after shipping." They did not yet have the supplies and equipment that would be required, but with an almost childlike faith, Chennault was confident that these would come. Had not the president ordered it?[58]

The monsoon was not quite over, but when the men could see to fly, Vincent's plucky little command began attacking river shipping in the Yangtze, key railhead-port complexes, and targets of opportunity that offered good return. The Fourteenth claimed 41,000 tons sunk in July. The Japanese were stung; they retaliated against the air bases in strength and with cunning. In their attacks the Japanese lost heavily, but the Fourteenth lost also and had fewer to lose. By the end of the month the Fourteenth had only thirty-three P-40s left in eastern China, another thirty-one in Yunnan. Replacement planes were not forthcoming, and the advantage could not be pursued.

Chennault asked the Tenth Air Force for reinforcements and wrote Arnold urging that supplies and aircraft be expedited. Stilwell, learning that Chennault was "screaming for help," thought it was "funny as hell," because "six months ago he was going to run [the Japanese] out of China." He told Marshall that Chennault was receiving his allotted aircraft (in actuality almost none had yet reached him) and that no harm would be done if the operations from the eastern airfields were stopped. The War Department was inclined to agree, for Chennault had said he would force the Japanese to fight him so that he could destroy them, and if he could not handle their retaliation, then his offensive strategy would not work.[59] At this point Chennault did not consider the planned aerial offensive yet under way; its minimal strength had not yet been assembled. Stilwell, however, considered that it had already taken place and had ended in failure. Chennault's eagerness had boomeranged.

Two weeks of bad weather afforded a reprieve for the repair of planes and fields, but when flying weather came again in mid-August, the Japanese employed some of Chennault's own tactics against the forward echelon. Flying new fighters which could operate at an altitude far above the P-40's ceiling, they would seize an opportune moment to make one deadly pass and would immediately climb back to safety. By this time the Fourteenth had received a few P-38s, but most of its fighters were still P-40s, and they were outclassed. Chennault began offensive missions with his bombers to take the defensive pressure off the fighters, but the August missions were plagued by bad weather and bad luck as well as by determined Japanese opposition. On an unescorted raid on Hankow, two B-24s were lost and ten badly damaged; a second raid by escorted bombers was met by forty enemy fighters and lost four more of the Liberators in a forty-five-minute battle. Another fell victim to an accident, and within two weeks the squadron of heavy bombers had been put out of action until reinforcements could arrive.[60]

There were successes—some missions were flown without loss, and total damage to the Japanese was estimated to be high—but Chennault was particularly distressed at the loss of seven P-40s that fell victim to China's navigational challenges rather than enemy action. The supply albatross was the heaviest. The Fourteenth had been given a priority on 4,700 tons monthly for July, August, and September, but the total amount lifted by ATC in July was only 2,916 net tons. Even though far short of the need, it was the best performance by ATC to date, and Chennault sent its men a message of congratulations and appreciation.[61]

Disappointed by results, realizing that he would not receive the requested supplies and reinforcements and that his opportunity to damage Japan significantly would be lost, Chennault plunged into another of his periodic depressions. He wrote Roosevelt that only one of the six agreed-upon measures of supply and reinforcement had been met. The tentative operations possible during July and August had "brought us little nearer to crippling the enemy air power or weakening his sea communications," and he had concluded "the effort must be on a considerably larger scale." Although he could not promise "full success," if Roosevelt still wanted to pursue the aerial offensive he was confident the objectives were still "largely attainable." But two points were crucial. He urged haste in providing the promised personnel and equipment, so that this season's flying weather might not be lost, and he requested a renewal of his priority on Hump supplies. To Hopkins he added that he was ready to pledge his reputation, "such as it is, that the return on the investment will be crippling the enemy's total air power and weakening the sea communications on which his whole system of conquest depends."[62]

The fervent Alsop, a civilian and free to speak with less restraint, bewailed the "obstruction here and bumbling in the Pentagon" which had already wasted a great opportunity. He pleaded with Hopkins to "raise Hell to give the General his chance."[63]

Chennault's depression deepened. "I have lost a great deal of enthusiasm which I felt when I left Washington," he wrote Noe. When Willauer stopped by with bolstering gifts of rum and Scotch, he found him irritably preparing for a meeting with Stilwell and Stratemeyer. "I could do with less meetings of generals and more planes," he muttered.[64] With little confidence that he would receive the tools in time, he realized that the 1943 offensive as he had planned it would simply never materialize. Since 1940 he had been convinced that a small offensive air force operating from China could make a significant impact, but three things were crucial to its success—highly trained and motivated men, a steady flow of supplies and replacements, and freedom to fight—and he had never been able to obtain all three at once.

Failure brought pain that was hard to face, and much like the child running away from home even while hoping mother will stop him and make everything all right again, Chennault wrote Chiang, resigning as his chief of air staff. He then drafted a telegram to the War Department requesting transfer to home duty, for he had concluded that his usefulness to China during 1943 was over. A concerned Alsop hastened to intervene. Dr. Gentry, Chennault's physician, confirmed that the discouraged fighter was physically healthy but under a severe strain from overwork; he thought the problem could be largely solved by subordinate commanders on whom Chennault could place responsibility.

Alsop persuaded Chennault to burn his messages and "take no further action for the present." Warning Soong to hold his message in strict confidence because Chennault did not know it was being sent, Alsop asked whether the circumstances did not justify a plea to Hopkins or Roosevelt for intervention. Soong agreed and communicated with Hopkins, who prepared a memo for the president detailing five specifics that might be done to salvage the China situation for Chennault. Chiang added his complaint that the TRIDENT commitment was not being honored. A complex power struggle was taking place within the Chinese government, and through Soong, Chiang had renewed pressure on Washington to remove Stilwell.[65]

Having backed Chennault's strategy because it promised positive action at once, even if on a small scale, Roosevelt was thoroughly disgusted. Everything seemed to be going wrong. "We are falling down on our promises every single time," he complained. "We have not fulfilled one of them."[66]

Chennault's optimistic cheer returned with the fall. In September the Fourteenth received another fighter squadron; for the first time it had enough planes and fuel to conduct offensive missions while simultaneously defending its bases. In late October the long-awaited squadrons of medium bombers reached China. (Without explaining his actions to either Chennault or Chiang, Stratemeyer had held them in India until the supply level reached a point where they could be used to advantage.)[67] A squadron of P-51s raised morale as well as operating effectiveness. The Chinese Air Force began to show marked improvement. Suichwan and other forward fields were completed; improved communications equipment heightened the effectiveness of the warning net. Ranging over an area so wide that the Japanese could not effectively mass their defenses to retaliate, the Fourteenth and the CAF increasingly used intelligence gathered from behind

Japanese lines and coordinated their strikes with guerrilla activity. Their efforts began to tell. The Americans and Chinese were not only achieving air supremacy, but enemy shipping had almost disappeared from the Yangtze between Hankow and Kukiang.

On Thanksgiving Day the Fourteenth demonstrated its growing potential with a meticulously planned and flawlessly executed raid against a major Japanese base on Formosa. Those who conducted it had their Thanksgiving dinner the evening before, expecting that some would not return, but there were no losses in the precise twelve-minute attack which caught the base by surprise and claimed the destruction of forty-two enemy planes. Spirits soared.[68]

Vigorous efforts to improve the India-China ATC began showing results in October, when the goal set for July was achieved. In December the 10,000-ton goal set for September was exceeded.[69] By then, however, Chennault's priority on supplies had expired and the good flying weather was gone.

"I am hacking away at the Japs as often as opportunity offers," Chennault wrote a friend in Washington. He regretted the delays that had kept him from launching his proposed offensive, for he believed "the war in the Orient could have been changed considerably if the plan which I took to Washington had been followed."[70]

13

"It looks like one
hell of a mess"

The year 1943 had been a dreadful one, for China and for the Americans who fought there. With the benefit of hindsight, it seems unfortunate that Stilwell was not promptly removed; his admirable abilities could have been better used elsewhere, for both his own good and that of his country. Roosevelt's goal to provide moral support to China could have been more effectively met by giving Chennault command in China, eliminating the friction interjected by conflicting strategies, and allowing Chiang and Chennault to determine together what they would do with the supplies the ATC could transport. Chennault's aerial offensive would not have defeated Japan, but without fractionated effort it would have made a more significant contribution. Certainly such a course would have made it easier for the Chinese to continue functioning with dignity, and much of the bitterness and hostility that developed between the two nations could have been prevented.

Those plotting the future course of the war, however, believed that Americans would eventually need to operate from bases in China to defeat Japan. One possibility—strategic bombardment—was presented by Arnold late in 1943. The first truly long-range bomber, the

207

B-29, was beginning to come off the assembly line. The plan for its debut specified ten groups of twenty-eight planes each to be operating from China by the fall of 1944; they would increase to twenty groups, supplied by up to 4,000 C-87s from Calcutta. Compared to the air effort then in China, an effort that had barely been manageable, the numbers boggle the mind.[1]

Considering the plan "bold but entirely feasible," Roosevelt quickly relegated Chennault's plan to second place. Churchill, sharing Roosevelt's penchant for the daring and innovative, was equally enthusiastic. Chiang approved. Construction began at once on the huge airfields that would be required. Because vastly increased quantities of supplies would be necessary, the campaign to retake Burma and restore a land supply route to China was reinstated and was scheduled for February 1944. Army Service Forces were confident supply needs could be met with the help of pipelines paralleling the trace of the Ledo Road.[2]

CBI had suddenly become much more complicated. It was even given a more complicated structure designed to accommodate its strained politics. Vice Adm. Lord Louis Mountbatten became supreme commander of the Southeast Asia Command, a unified British and American command that did not include China.

Chennault did some cold thinking about the B-29s. It was hard not to choke on the contrast between their projected supply support and his own. It was also hard to see how strategic bombardment alone could do the job. He reasoned that the B-29s were not suitable for striking at shipping or for forcing the enemy to expend his air power or for supporting the Chinese ground forces. Concluding that there was still a need for a balanced air force, he drafted a plan for a three-phased offensive to be conducted by the Fourteenth: attain air supremacy, assault Japanese shipping, then bomb Japan.[3]

Stilwell, facing a difficult Burma campaign and fed up with the emphasis on aerial operations, paid Chennault's plan little attention. An officer of the Fourteenth Air Force, handing Stilwell a report from Chennault at about this time, was startled when the message was ignored and a curt Stilwell snapped, "What can the air force do to the Japs?"[4] But Chennault's plan made an impression on both Stratemeyer and Maj. Gen. Albert C. Wedemeyer, who evaluated it for SEAC. Nevertheless they turned it down: available supplies would be needed by the B-29 program. Chennault pressed his case. He argued that the Japanese military structure was held together by shipping and air, hence the Fourteenth's campaign would contribute

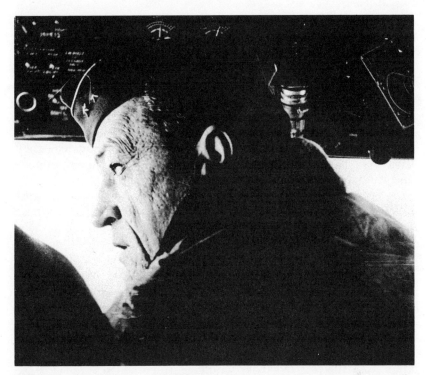

Major General Chennault, in right seat of cockpit, ca. 1943–44. (Photo courtesy Milt Miller)

to the success of other Pacific operations and would possibly increase the strain on Japan to the breaking point. He made his point. He was given the go-ahead, although without the minimum supply levels he specified. It was 1943 all over again: do what you can, but do it with less than you need.[5]

There was a break when both Chennault and Stilwell accompanied Chiang Kai-shek to Cairo, where the Combined Chiefs of Staff met in December. This extended session, first at Cairo and then at Teheran for the first meeting with Stalin, marked a turning point in China's relative position among the Allies. Up to this point China had seemed essential, but the U.S. Navy, with new fast aircraft carriers, might capture the Marianas in 1944, and from them the B-29s could reach Japan. China had begun to seem like a vast sinkhole for military supplies and energies, and Chiang was difficult. His current demand was that the Burma campaign be supported by a British naval operation on such a large scale that it would weaken the invasion of Europe (OVERLORD) scheduled for the upcoming June. As negotiations seesawed, he frequently changed his mind and pushed the patience of all to the breaking point. Churchill, never enthusiastic about the "support China" policy, grumbled that the Chinese ought to go look at the pyramids while everyone else conducted their business. An obliging Chennault took the Generalissimo and Madame sightseeing. By the time Roosevelt and Churchill left for Teheran to continue their conference with Stalin, all parties had agreed—they thought—on a Burma campaign that included a British amphibious operation and participation of the Chinese Y-force.[6]

At Teheran, Stalin confirmed that he would enter the war against Japan as soon as Germany had been defeated (something the Chinese did not learn for some time), but the Russian army had faced the German Army in Europe alone since 1941. Stalin wanted the pressure taken off by a second front in Europe at once. Roosevelt and Churchill conferred. Churchill wanted to cancel the amphibious operation in Burma and use its landing craft to strengthen OVERLORD. Even though Russia's participation against Japan made China's help less vital, at first Roosevelt and the Americans insisted they must keep their commitment to Chiang. When it became obvious that the British would not give in, Roosevelt yielded. Burma's amphibious operation was called off; OVERLORD would be strengthened at the expense of CBI.[7]

Chiang had some justification for feeling he had been betrayed. He reacted to the news with the familiar cry that China could not hold out much longer. To prevent its collapse, he would have to have a billion dollar gold loan, 20,000 tons monthly over the Hump, and double the reinforcements agreed upon for the Fourteenth Air Force and the CAF.[8] This time Washington did not tremble. Not only were there now alternative sites for a military base apart from China, but objective reporting had begun to raise questions about the Kuomintang's worthiness for support. While Chiang was in Cairo, there was a small coup in China—an attempt to oust several officials who were most responsible for government corruption and inefficiency. The coup was quickly squelched, but it was significant that it had taken place. Roosevelt bluntly told Chiang that his government was not as democratic as it should be.[9]

Confronted with Chiang's newest demands, the president replied courteously but firmly: the loan would be considered, but the best the United States could do for China was to help in opening up a land route through Burma. Roosevelt hoped Chiang would do his part.[10] Chiang's fortunes had crested. For purposes of the peace, China would be given every opportunity to function as a Big Power— Chiang became officially one of the "Big Four" at Cairo by signing the Cairo Declaration on Allied war aims—but China's potential military importance for the winning of the war had begun to diminish. Plans were confirmed at Cairo, however, for the B-29 Superfortresses to be put into action as soon as possible from India and China bases in a plan called MATTERHORN.

The specific planning for MATTERHORN was complex. Chennault's command was boosted by two groups of fighters to defend the B-29 bases at Chengtu, deep within Szechwan. Chennault questioned the wisdom of staging the B-29s through Chengtu rather than more eastern airfields, for the heavily loaded bombers would have to fly at low altitudes across a wide belt of occupied China, vulnerable to Japanese fighters as well as providing plenty of advance warning to Japan. If the bases were in the east and their defending fighters could maintain an aggressive rather than passive defense, Japanese strikes could more readily be stopped, while the range and bomb load of the B-29s could be increased. He made little headway. Washington agreed with Stilwell that defending eastern bases would require fifty ground divisions—divisions then neither trained nor equipped.[11]

Several possible command arrangements for MATTERHORN were rejected before the War Department assigned the B-29s to the specially created Twentieth Air Force. Its headquarters were in Washington; Arnold was its commanding officer, Hansell his chief of staff. All major decisions on deployment, missions, and target selection for the B-29s would be made by the Joint Chiefs of Staff and executed through Arnold.[12] While the command was being discussed, Chennault spoke up against divided control of the Fourteenth Air Force and MATTERHORN. They "should be regarded as a boxer's right and left," he wrote, otherwise "neither will achieve maximum effectiveness. Timing will be wrong. The blows of one will not prepare for and increase the force of the blows of the other. The fullest protection against enemy counter-operations will not be afforded."[13]

In a letter to Roosevelt dated 26 January 1944, Chennault raised basic questions of military policy. Summarizing the benefits to be derived from obtaining air supremacy, attacking Japanese shipping, striking the Japanese homeland with B-29s, and pulverizing Japanese staging areas within China and elsewhere, he relegated the B-29 plan to third place. His reasoning was that it would take a long time to produce decisive results, whereas attacks on shipping and air power could be immediately decisive. He not only stated his opinion that dividing command between the Fourteenth and MATTERHORN was "militarily unsound" but attached a copy of a letter to Arnold "listing the defects in the MATTERHORN Project" as well as restating his own plan of operations. Roosevelt responded on 15 March that, when the B-29s were assigned to the Chinese area, their operational command would be his. "Good luck to you and them!" wrote the president encouragingly.[14]

The War Department made its decisions, however, and Chennault had no part in MATTERHORN's command. Some of his supporters thought it unjust that he was not given command of this new aerial effort in China. Chennault probably agreed. Certainly he stated his feelings clearly and forcefully, writing Hopkins that he felt it was his duty "to place the facts as I see them squarely before [Roosevelt] and before you." When Brig. Gen. Kenneth B. Wolfe was named commanding general of the new XX Bomber Command in China, Chennault expressed full confidence in him, but he continued to urge a less cumbersome authority. After Arnold had carefully explained the complex command problem, however, Chennault thanked him and assured him that he would cooperate fully. This he did. Stratemeyer reported good mutual understanding and "entirely satisfactory" relationships. Perhaps, as Alsop thought, Chennault "expected no better," but bombers had never been his passion, and he was eager to pursue his own aerial offensive.[15]

Although trying to get along, Chennault was fundamentally worried that the emphasis on MATTERHORN would undermine the aerial offensive he had long championed. He continued to believe that the campaign against Japanese air power and shipping was both necessary and potentially decisive; he fought for it with bulldog tenacity. "When convinced he was right," one of his staff officers observed, "he could be stubborn to the point of obstinacy." The correspondents who covered him sensed at this time a "great singleness of purpose," an unswerving faith in the potential Chinese Air Force, and "very clear and positive ideas against Japan." They were impressed by his relentless dedication to the task at hand. "Nothing," wrote one, "destroys his faith in the validity of what he is doing."[16]

During those latter months of 1943 and early 1944, when MATTERHORN was being planned, Chennault was waging his antishipping campaign with vigor and a mounting sense of significant accomplishment. In his view, during November and December his men were acquiring the know-how, and in January they passed beyond the experimental stage. His primary striking force was two squadrons of B-25s. They worked in pairs, the lead plane using machine guns and cannon against antiaircraft while the second concentrated on bombing. Then they reversed positions and flew a second pass. B-24s flew sea sweeps; fighters strafed and bombed. They struck at ships, at harbor installations, at railroads, at depots and bases.

When Chennault requested permission to extend his radius to Kyushu, Arnold praised his aggressiveness but decreed that attacks on the home islands were to wait for MATTERHORN. When pilots in P51Bs confronted the Zeke 52, a newer model Zero that was faster and had greater diving speed, they reported, "We just can't beat these guys in the air." Chennault told them to "get 'em on the ground, and you won't have to fight 'em in the air." When weather in the east prevented flying, the Fourteenth concentrated on Indochina, the Gulf of Tonkin, the Formosa Straits, and the south China coast. By early 1944 the planes had almost nullified Indochina's value to Japan; shipping in the area was paralyzed and the natives were rebelling. His men were exuberant at success against odds, and Chennault himself could see the Japanese waterways teeming with shipping that the Fourteenth could sink if it only had more planes and more supplies.[17]

"I hanker to get at it," he wrote Hopkins. He thought that if he had the supplies, he could sink at least 200,000 tons of shipping per month. His estimates were overly optimistic, for he was misled by the Fourteenth's claims regarding ocean shipping sunk. Japanese data examined after the war indicate that the actual sinkings of ships over 500 tons were only 52 percent of claims.[18] Chennault was convinced, however, that Japan's weakest point was shipping, and that destruction of it was the key to breaking up the Japanese empire. He thought the B-29 campaign against Japan's steel industry would be significant but not decisive by itself, but if used in conjunction with the Fourteenth Air Force offensive against shipping, B-29 operations had "great possibilities of a decisive nature."[19]

He watched the great possibilities begin to slip away as the supply noose tightened. MATTERHORN was planned to be self-supporting; it had its own transports, and the B-29s were to fly their own supplies over the Hump. As early as January, however, the Fourteenth's supply allotment was cut because of MATTERHORN's needs. Chennault gritted his teeth. He could see the Fourteenth becoming a "glorified Fighter Wing to protect the Matterhorn operations," but his pleas altered nothing. When his annual bout with bronchitis and flu put him to bed, his spirits plummeted. Convinced he was right, hurt and angry at not being able to prevail, he wrote Hopkins that his position meant little to him if he was not allowed to do the job he was there to do. In his January letter to Roosevelt, he wrote, "If you accept my recommendations, but feel my job may be better done by another man, I shall come home with some relief and with great gratitude to you for your faith in my judgment." A worried Alsop noted that the general was physically drained, "almost too tired to fight," and set out to do what he could to help.[20]

At Alsop's urging, Chennault presented his ideas to the SEAC officers in India. There he found an ally in Wedemeyer, who wrote Arnold to question the use of the B-29s from China and to urge that all the Hump tonnage go to the Fourteenth Air Force.[21] Arnold, who nurtured behind his perennial smile a firm faith in the efficacy of strategic bombardment and an unwavering determination to carry the war to Japan, was totally unconvinced.

Arnold was also becoming fed up with Chennault. Like Marshall, he resented Chennault's direct access to the political power structure. Furious that Chennault had written directly to Roosevelt advocating the Fourteenth's operations and expressing his own evaluation of MATTERHORN's weaknesses, he demanded an explanation. Chennault begged him to consider the proposal on its merits. He insisted that his intent was not to be individualistic, as Arnold accused, but to make the maximum contribution. The president had asked him to write; he had sent a copy to Arnold because he firmly believed that by combining the capabilities of MATTERHORN and the Fourteenth the aerial offensive could be immediately decisive.[22]

Arnold was unmoved. He was also angry about Alsop (the actual author of Chennault's letter to Roosevelt) and the strings that were being pulled on his behalf. Chennault had learned that Alsop's commission had been blocked primarily because Stilwell did not want him serving in the theater. At Alsop's request, Chennault and several other officers interceded with Stilwell, who withdrew his objection. Chennault then asked Arnold to commission Alsop, but Arnold replied that he could not, nor did he approve. Chennault turned to Roosevelt with a request for a presidential commission. At the same time he wrote Arnold to request his cooperation; the president, he explained, had expressed "a strong personal interest" in the case. Arnold saw this as another end run. Willauer, then in Washington, warned Alsop that his application was "deader than a smelt." But Willauer suggested that Alsop's mother pay a social call on the president. She did, and the matter was settled. Lieutenant Alsop became Chennault's aide and wrote Roosevelt an emotional letter of thanks.[23]

Neither Chennault's pleas nor the Fourteenth's successes during late 1943 and early 1944 altered the decisions regarding MATTERHORN. It remained in the plans as the primary Allied effort in China for 1944. Starting in June, it was to be a strategic air campaign against Japan's coke ovens, for Japan's steel industry was estimated to be operating at full capacity and vital to its war economy.

The MATTERHORN planners had no way of knowing that their target selection was wrong. It was raw material, not processing capacity, that was the weak link in Japanese steel. Japan's steel production in 1943 was only one-third its capacity because Japan was critically short of ore. *And the ore was not reaching Japan because of the Fourteenth Air Force's steady campaign against river and coastal shipping.*[24] Chennault was more right than he knew.

Japan had to import almost all of its raw materials: oil from the Indies, rubber and tin from Malaya, bauxite from Indochina, tungsten from China, iron ore from Hainan. Everything had to come by ship, and the ships were being sunk by submarines, by carrier-based aircraft, by land-based aircraft, and by mines. Even when the war began, Japanese shipping was tight, and the steady attrition had an impact. The supply of iron ore was especially critical. Japan began the war with a stockpile but had to expend nearly half of it during 1942. As shipping became shorter, Japan began to rely more heavily on ore from China; in 1943 Chinese ore was 88 percent of the total imported. It traveled down the Yangtze on the lowly river boats, and against these the Fourteenth Air Force was deadly. First the Fourteenth had stopped the daylight movement of the larger ships above Nanking. When bigger targets disappeared, the pilots went after the smaller ones and laid mines to catch the stragglers. From April 1943 onward, Japan's iron ore imports declined. The total for the first half of 1944 (1,150,000 tons) was just about half that of the first half of 1943 (2,200,000 tons). By December 1944, monthly imports were down to 37,000 tons. The B-29 attacks on Japan's steel plants, first from China and later from the Marianas, were to have little effect on Japan's supply of steel, for by the time they were in full swing, the Fourteenth Air Force had already strangled Japan's steel industry.[25]

War is often waged blind, and this war was no exception. Even Chennault did not fully perceive that the Fourteenth's effectiveness lay in its steady attrition of the many barges, sampans, and small powered craft that plied the rivers, and Chennault was less blind than many. His hunting instincts had long ago convinced him that intelligence was vitally important. Like the near-sighted bear who must rely on his ears and his nose, he had compensated for being unable to see an approaching enemy by using a warning net. Early in 1942 he had realized he needed to know much more than the net could tell him; like the bear, he must add the cunning that comes with a deep, broad-based knowledge. When a young Baptist missionary escorted Doolittle to Kunming in April, hiding him from the enemy en route, Chennault quickly realized that the young man's understanding of China could be valuable. His name was John Birch.

Birch was an intense and dedicated man with strange habits—he could gorge himself with a tremendous quantity of food and then go without eating for days on end. Where some saw him as "the nearest thing to Christ in person I have ever known," others were wary of a fiery temper. For a short time Birch served the AVG as an assistant chaplain. When a close relationship began to develop between him and Chennault, he joined the CATF as an intelligence officer. Birch and Chennault shared a trait that was fundamental to each: like wolves on the trail of a wounded prey, they would pursue their goals relentlessly, never wavering in determination, never deterred by obstacles, never distracted. Chennault came to feel toward the young man much the same closeness a father feels toward a son. Birch, for his part, developed a near-fanatical admiration for Chennault, perhaps in part because he was philosophically in harmony with Chennault's approach of demanding all a man could give up to safe limits, yet sparing nothing to help or protect him.[26]

Chennault's intelligence network grew slowly and quietly. More missionaries were recruited. Chaplain Frillmann from the AVG rejoined him, after having had intelligence training in the States, and Chennault teased him a little, saying he could have put him into intelligence without delay, back in 1942, had he known that was what he wanted. Soon Chennault's agents were dispersed throughout occupied China, along the coast and around Hankow, serving as liaison between the Chinese armies and Chennault's airmen, passing on information on subjects ranging from Japanese ship movements and troop activity to the black market and subversive cliques. They used hand-cranked radios to communicate with Kunming, and since the field sets would not carry to their maximum distances, a relay intelligence center was set up at Kweilin. Much of the CATF's and Fourteenth's effectiveness—and their reputation for prescience—

stemmed from specific information about the enemy, for in addition to his own network, Chennault received and welcomed intelligence from Ultra, the highly secretive code-breaking program developed by the Poles and the British.[27]

Top priority, as far as Chennault was concerned, was the rescue of his men who had to come down in enemy territory. His agents helped set up an elaborate underground railroad of loyal Chinese to rescue them, and when an agent in the Office of War Information advised Chennault that the "pirates" around Lungtien peninsula would help rescue his men if the Fourteenth stopped sinking their junks in the channel, the pirates' junks were spared.[28]

The United States was also beginning to realize the need for comprehensive intelligence on a much broader scale than it had ever had before, and William J. Donovan was developing the necessary organization and modus operandi. As early as 1940 Donovan recommended a central intelligence agency, but the idea was ahead of its time. After Pearl Harbor, when it began to be realized that the disaster might have been avoided had enemy intelligence been properly collected, analyzed, and disseminated, Donovan commanded more attention. By June of 1942 the Office of Strategic Services was taking shape. It was technically under the Joint Chiefs of Staff, but Donovan was a man of boundless energy and creativity who tended to work outside channels and in secret. He saw three distinct needs which became the three branches of OSS: research and analysis, special operations outside the conventional military organization, and a psychological warfare of propaganda and subversive activities.[29]

Donovan's agents were in China seeking ways for the OSS to operate as early as October 1942. They met little enthusiasm from Stilwell but much more from Chennault, who figured the more information he had, the better. He was already cooperating with Milton E. Miles, a navy officer whose special task was to do whatever he could to prepare the China coast for eventual U.S. landings. Miles and his Naval Group China in turn worked closely with Tai Li, the head of China's intelligence organization. For some months in 1943 the OSS, Miles, and Tai Li all worked together as SACO, the Sino-American Special Technical Cooperation Organization. Tai Li's methods were little better than those of the Nazi Gestapo, however, and for a number of reasons SACO worked poorly. Donovan decided OSS must be separate. Late in 1943 he went to China to make it so.[30]

Donovan and Chennault were kindred souls, each impulsive and more inclined to be governed by inspiration and innovation than by bureaucracy. In the summer of 1942 OSS had developed a plan for an extensive intelligence operation in occupied China using business operations as cover. Stilwell had rejected it; Chennault had complained about Stilwell's overcaution. After that initial meeting of the minds and SACO's failure, it became apparent that the Fourteenth Air Force provided the best cover for OSS operations in China. Once Donovan and Chennault got together, it was quickly arranged. A highly secret network in Japanese-occupied territory was soon functioning; it used a Canadian communications network. More pertinent to Chennault's specific operations was the 5329th Air and Ground Forces Resources and Technical Staff (AGFRTS, quickly corrupted to "Ag-farts"). It was staffed by OSS research and analysis personnel who were trained in target identification and selection. By May of 1944, both OSS and Naval Group China had functioning offices within Chennault's headquarters. Chennault was confident that "results will begin to justify the organization within a short time."[31]

The various antennae linking Chennault with the broader battleground accounted for many of his astute tactical decisions, but other factors also came to bear. Most of his men realized that he studied the Japanese assiduously and worked constantly at outwitting them, going to such lengths as "opening things up" so they could bomb an airfield at night while he watched and studied their technique with an eye on refining his defenses. Few realized, however, that he also depended on a sense of guidance that had its roots in his deep religious belief.

Frillmann perceived it more than most, for the two discussed religious matters in some depth when Chennault first asked him to serve as AVG chaplain. Chennault sought to give his military mission a philosophical completeness that only religion could provide. As they talked the issue through, and later as they came to know one another better, Frillman was impressed that Chennault seemed to be free of denominational bias, while his own faith was quietly secure. Chennault knew the Bible surprisingly well. He tried to live by its teachings and by the simple but just moral code he had acquired as a boy. He worshiped the God who had created a natural world full of wonderful and beautiful things.[32]

But part of Chennault's leadership strength, his image and public personality, was unvarnished machismo. Unlike Gen. George Patton, who could weep openly and did not hesitate to pray on his knees or to beseech the Almighty for clear weather so his men could have air support, Chennault kept his religion a very private part of his nature, a facet of his life he almost never discussed. To the men of his command he felt he must show no weakness, no vulnerability, for more than anything else he must inspire their unquestioning confidence. Only if they had supreme confidence in him could they perform at their peak potential. He even feared to show emotion in the face of death, lest it be interpreted by some as weakness. The loss of one of his men distressed him deeply, but outwardly his reaction would be to push the command harder, to stress sound tactics or preach his familiar doctrine, "If you know your airplane and you know yourself, you needn't have accidents." Not until years later could he quietly acknowledge that "every time one of my boys died, I died a little too."[33]

Chennault was asked once, when he was near his own death, whether he had felt he was in China as an instrument of Providence. At first he would not talk about it, but when pressed, he replied, "I believed somehow that I had been picked to do that job. . . . You don't know how many nights I had to pray to find out what to do. I'd go to sleep, sleep soundly until four o'clock in the morning, wake up with an answer—I knew what to do. Call my staff together at six o'clock in the morning and tell them what to do, right away. They all thought it was me. That I'd figured all that out."[34]

During these months of the winter 1943–44, as the Americans planned action to defeat Japan, the Japanese planned how they might thwart it. They too had intelligence organizations. The buildup in India told them a big offensive would be launched in Burma; they began planning an invasion of India to prevent it from succeeding.[35]

Their growing shortage of shipping was a separate but more serious threat. To meet it, the chief of Japan's general staff told his commander in China in November that the Allied air force in China had to be neutralized or destroyed because it was hurting the seaborne supply lines. Shortly afterward the Fourteenth conducted its Thanksgiving Day attack on Formosa, a slap at Japanese pride that also presaged even greater shipping losses to come. The Fourteenth's "extremely effective" attacks were making it hard for Japan to supply its army around Hankow, while river shipping on the Yangtze had become "extremely unsafe."[36] Having been unable to stop the Fourteenth Air Force in the air, the Japanese began staff studies on the feasibility of destroying the eastern China airfields and reopening the railroad from Canton to Hankow as alternative transportation.

When the end of the year brought the threat of B-29 assault from China, they decided this course of action must be pursued. Japan's eastern China offensive would be code named ICHIGO; it would be led by Gen. Shunroku Hata as head of the China Expeditionary Army.[37]

As far back as September, Stilwell had tried to forestall a possible Japanese drive against the eastern airfields by suggesting that Chiang order Nationalist and Communist troops in the north—troops that did little except keep wary eyes on each other—to attack the Japanese on a broad front. This was the first time it had been suggested that the Communist troops be utilized and supplied and brought under the central government umbrella. Chiang responded with icy silence. Nothing was done.[38]

Concluding that he could accomplish little at his headquarters in Chungking, Stilwell had then gone to the Assam front, determined to lead the X-force across the rugged northern reaches of Burma to Myitkyina and open the Ledo Road to China, whether or not the British helped by launching their amphibious assault, whether or not the Chinese joined in with the Y-force. Their campaign turned out to be one of the war's dramatic sagas of endurance and hardship and innovation. X-force was assisted by experimental long range penetration groups that were airlifted deep into Burma to cut the Japanese supply lines and strike their flanks. Both the Chinese armies and the penetration groups were supplied by air, and the best in Yankee ingenuity surfaced as the supply forces learned to package live poultry and pigs—and even eggs—so that they survived an air drop. It worked amazingly well, and by February Stilwell and the Chinese armies were deep into Burma.[39]

At that point the Japanese opened their offensive against India. The British forces were soon fighting for their lives and for the vital India air bases and lines of communication that fed Stilwell's drive.

Hard-pressed and overextended, CBI was already tense with worry when, in mid-April, at the eastern extreme of the vast China-Burma-India theater, Hata's armies opened Operation ICHIGO by beginning to advance south, from Kaifeng on the Yellow River along the railroad toward Hankow.

14

"The situation here in China is appalling"

ICHIGO did not surprise Chennault. Monitoring reports of the ominous Japanese troop increases, he saw the offensive building, saw its shape emerging, felt the ominous constriction of the vise should the Japanese attack from both north and south simultaneously. Ever the hunter trying to outguess his prey, he imagined himself in his enemy's circumstances and reasoned that Japan was feeling the mounting pressure on its outer perimeter in the Pacific and wanted to prepare a last line of defense by eliminating the threat from China.

In April he wrote Roosevelt of these fears. Japan's first move, he said, would likely be south from the Yellow River to seize the section of the Peking-Hankow railroad that was then held by the Chinese. If this first step succeeded, the Japanese would be in position to drive across the Szechwan plain to take Chengtu and Chungking. He thought it more likely, however, that they would move southward to seize Changsha. Not only was it the center of the rice-rich Hunan province, but from there the Hankow-Canton railway pointed south, and the eastern air bases were within reach.[1]

Stilwell and the War Department in opposing Chennault's strategy had of course argued that just such an offensive was possible. When the issue was extensively debated in Washington in the spring of 1943, Chiang had assured the Americans that the Chinese armies could handle the ground portion of a Japanese threat against the air bases. Chennault and Chiang had undoubtedly agreed on this point before Chennault left China, and in Washington Chennault had supported the argument, although with an important qualifier: the Chinese armies could stop a Japanese offensive if—and it was a big if—the Chinese had vigorous air support and the Japanese were not reinforced.[2]

His conviction had evolved slowly. When he first used it as an argument in support of an aerial strategy, he confined it to the protection of Kunming and Chungking, each deep in the remote, largely roadless interior, protected by deep river gorges where aerial defense could be effective. The battle of the Salween gorge in 1942 seemed to support his thesis, as did a Japanese offensive up the Yangtze toward Chungking in early 1943. On this later occasion, Chiang had raised all sorts of alarms about the outcome, but the drive was stopped. Later the Japanese appeared to have begun withdrawing once they had achieved their immediate goals—the seizure of rice and river boats. At the time, however, Chennault wrote Roosevelt that the Japanese had been dealt a "decisive defeat" by the "unexpectedly strong resistance" of the Chinese ground forces, augmented by air support. As he told the president, the battle reinforced his view that the Japanese could not advance more than 100 miles into the interior if they could not supply their drives by water.[3]

In a cover letter to Hopkins, written two weeks later, Chennault said the Japanese had not been "signally defeated," but "they must, and I believe they can," be driven back. China's desperate economic plight made for urgency, and Chennault's concern for the Chinese had a bearing on his interpretation of events. "The morale of the people can be improved and the inflation at least temporarily checked," he wrote, "if the Japanese are conspicuously beaten on Chinese soil."[4]

Chennault's confidence that the Chinese could defend his eastern air bases received another boost when the Fourteenth Air Force helped the Chinese contain a Japanese offensive around Chang-te late in 1943. Before it opened, he had begun building a working relationship with Marshal Hsueh Yueh, who commanded the Chinese armies in the threatened area. During the fighting Chennault's intelligence teams mingled with the Chinese armies to radio target information to the Fourteenth's supporting aircraft. Excited by the technique he was evolving for tactical support of ground troops, Chennault wrote Hopkins in December that the Chang-te fighting had proved his theory that "existing Chinese forces with adequate air support can stop any Japanese advance which is not so great as to weaken their defense elsewhere."[5]

It is possible that here Chennault looked upon Chinese efforts with a positive rather than negative filter, for his assessment of the damage they inflicted upon the Japanese at Chang-te was higher than that made by most Americans, although some agreed with him that the Chinese had fought hard and well. Wanting the Chinese to be able to support him, Chennault seems to have accepted into his consciousness those things that reinforced his predispositions. He did not accept, then or later, the War Department's view that the Chang-te offensive had been limited in scope, designed only as a rice raid. He believed the Japanese would have kept on advancing and taken his airfields in December if they had not been stopped; he believed the Chinese armies, with air support, had stopped them.[6]

Now, four months later, the Fourteenth faced ICHIGO. It was a reinforced effort. It was not in a defensible gorge but along the coast where the Japanese could take advantage of China's limited roads and railroads. The role of the Chinese armies would be relatively more important; the existing forces in the east would need reinforcements. The armies that Stilwell had strengthened and prepared for battle, however—the Y-force—were now poised in Yunnan to take part in the Burma campaign. Stilwell had started building a Z-force of Chinese divisions to protect the east China airfields, but very little had yet been done.

The strategic conflict between Stilwell and Chennault was building to a climax, and Chennault was more apprehensive than confident of the outcome. He thought the effort in Burma was misdirected. He saw imminent danger in the east. "We will have lost a great deal of ground," he wrote Kuter, "even if we reconquer all of Burma, if we lose eastern China."[7] He was both angry and disturbed by continued short supply. In early February he wrote Stilwell that a determined Japanese offensive was expected in March or early April; he warned it might well succeed unless the Fourteenth was supplied. His plans for 1944 had included accumulating a stockpile of gasoline during late winter and early spring so there would be enough on hand for the good flying weather of summer. In January and February he received 7,601 and 7,017 tons of Hump supplies, but for March his tonnage was cut to 4,379; a bite of 3,603 was taken out by MATTERHORN.[8]

In early April, with his supply stocks at 40 percent of the levels he deemed necessary, he sent Stilwell a clear warning and requested an increased allotment to make up the deficit.

Stilwell, however, had problems of his own. Between his own drive across Burma with X-force and the Japanese offensive against India, some transports had even been taken off the Hump route to handle the emergency there. His answer was hard advice: "You will simply have to cut down on activity to the point where you can be sure of reasonable reserves for an emergency."[9]

Chennault was sitting on a message from Vincent warning that, if the forward units did not use "another gallon of gas between now and June, we still will not have enough for the summer." Angered by Stilwell's tone and seeing no way he could follow Stilwell's advice, on 8 April he sat down to write his theater commander a long, very specific letter. In brief, he was "convinced that the actual security of China as a base for future military operations against Japan is probably now at stake."[10]

It was not the first time Chennault (or the Generalissimo) had sounded the alarm for a Japanese offensive that threatened China's security. Chennault may have realized that his credibility had begun to erode, for he told Stilwell that the Japanese "must now mean business," since they no longer had the men to spare for rice raids or training exercises. "The air threat is the most serious in my experience in this theater," he wrote, and the "disposition of the enemy's ground forces in China is also more threatening than has been the case since Pearl Harbor." He outlined the offensives he anticipated. He appealed for enough supplies to give the air forces "a reasonable chance of success." As it was, facing multiple demands with inadequate supplies, "The plain fact is that . . . [they] cannot conceivably meet such demands." He thought "the security of China itself is now in jeopardy," but the danger could be averted by placing the air forces on a sound footing.[11]

"I earnestly trust that you will take measures to this end," he concluded. He received no reply for some weeks. Stilwell, immersed in Burma, did not receive his letter until after the Japanese offensive had begun.[12]

Meanwhile Chennault received a letter from Roosevelt encouraging him with his antishipping campaign. "You are the Doctor and I approve your treatment," were the president's jaunty words. Feeling appreciably less jaunty, Chennault responded by stressing the anticipated Japanese offensives, which he expected "to be both serious and determined in character. . . . I wish I could tell you I had no fear of the outcome. I expect the Chinese forces to make the strongest resistance they can. . . . But owing to the present concentration of our resources on the fighting in Burma, little has been done to strengthen the Chinese Armies in the interior, and for the same reason the 14th and Chinese Air Forces are still operating on a shoe string. If we were even a little stronger, I should not be worried. Since men, equipment, supplies and transportation are all still very short, I can only say to you that we shall fight hard."[13]

His assignment of blame for eventual failure to Stilwell's strategy was plain. Nor was the plea for supply relief very subtle. He concluded with the promise that the Fourteenth would do its best to make its shoestring stretch to cover any eventuality.

Since January 1944 Chennault had been getting, on the average, more than half of the total Hump tonnage each month. The problem was not solely supplies but also transport. The eastern line of communications to the Fourteenth's forward airfields stretched more than 800 miles from Kunming eastward. After ATC planes unloaded at Kunming, supplies began their tedious journey east by rail as far as Kutsing, thence to Tushan by road—500 miles of a stone and clay road that negotiated a rugged mountain range by precipitous grades and as many as twenty-two consecutive hairpin turns, a road perilously slick during the rains and subject to landslides on its numerous deep cuts and fills. Trucks using the road wore out in a matter of weeks. Beyond Tushan materials moved again by rail to Liuchow, then by road, barge, sampan, or coolie-drawn cart for the last stages of their journey. The Fourteenth needed at least 3,200 tons monthly moved as far as Kweilin, with 1,000 tons of that moved farther east. In April 1944 the ELOC was moving much less than that amount.[14]

Getting the supplies forward was the responsibility of the Army's Service of Supply, which hired Chinese agencies. Because this activity occurred within China, it was basically a Chinese responsibility under Chiang as the theater's supreme commander. Stilwell as his chief of staff suggested that improving the eastern supply lines was one thing that should be done, but he did not push the matter, no doubt thinking there were enough demands on the Hump tonnage without adding more. During 1943 the out-of-channels lobbyists tried to fill the void. L. K. Taylor, an American who served as adviser to China's Southwest Highway Administration, thought SWHA could handle the job if it could get more trucks and enough spare parts to keep them running. Alsop (then working for lend-lease) kept Hopkins informed of the need, and China Defense Supplies assigned Willauer to the problem.[15]

Chennault had been working on improving the ELOC for more than a year. His knowledge of China's limited internal transport system not only predated that of most Americans in China but was personal and intimate. Since 1937 he had coped with agonizing delays in moving men and goods from one spot to another, with vehicles that constantly broke down because neither the knowledge nor the facilities for their maintenance were available, with roads that were little better than tracks. Making an extended automobile trip from Kunming through the eastern provinces in 1938, on one day he recorded in his diary with some surprise, "Nice drive, good road." Then he had trouble getting gasoline. "Lost temper but will find it somewhere on road, no doubt." But the road got rougher. A spring broke. He radioed McDonald to come get him by plane, making the terse notation, "Haven't found temper yet."[16]

He knew the ELOC had to be made better. His plan for 1944 operations included a plan—and a plea—for its improvement.[17] All through 1943 he worked behind the scenes to move matters along. He warned Hopkins that China's internal transport system must be "greatly strengthened." There were too few trucks; he persuaded Madame to issue an order making it possible for SWHA to commandeer. There were insufficient funds to operate the road, a result of escalating inflation plus a feud between Soong and Kung, who froze allocations to the Ministry of Communications because he wanted to eliminate its head. There was endless haggling over whether the trucks would be paid for return cargo. Theft and squeeze and the lure of the black market meant that supplies dwindled en route. By September 1943, again on the verge of losing his temper, Chennault warned Madame that he would withdraw U.S. planes from the advanced airfields unless the road improved in a hurry.[18]

He also asked Willauer to make a detailed study of the ELOC and advise him what should be done. Armed with this analysis, he began trying to convince CBI headquarters that the U.S. Army should immediately provide help. In January 1944, with ICHIGO looming, Chennault added an intensive letter-writing campaign. The problem was acknowledged; the SOS was given a new head; plans were drafted. SOS requested 1,200 trucks and quartermaster services for maintaining road and vehicles. At Chennault's request, Chiang granted additional funding for SWHA and permission for SOS to pay the expenses of the trucks returning empty. Orders were issued to remove nonessential traffic from the road.[19] But it had taken a year to reach this point, and by April, when the need became urgent, the problem was far from solved.

Chennault's critics have been quick to note his shortcomings in logistical planning and have been less generous in acknowledging that he, like many others in China, was often unable to accomplish the goals that he perceived. From the beginning he believed that the limited transport system in China would restrict the Allied involvement, and as early as May 1942 he had told the Magruder Mission, "we should concentrate more on preparing satisfactory communication facilities and transport service [than on building airfields]."[20]

The supply and transport problem was one reason why Chennault believed in limiting the warfare in China to aerial involvement, why his plans consistently incorporated very small forces and sought to offset their smallness by timing and superior tactics, by operational freedom and reduced bureaucracy. He was only partially successful in persuading the War Department of his views. The shape of the war in CBI outgrew his concepts, put conflicting demands on the limited supplies, and fractionated the total effort. His forces and supplies came after the advantage of good timing had been lost; operational freedom was curtailed by short supplies, if not by specific orders. By the spring of 1944 he had the 500-plane air force he had hoped to employ against enemy air and shipping during 1943, but it was no longer able to concentrate on its intended mission: it could conduct offensive operations only if resources remained after the defense of the B-29 bases, support of the Y-force offensive in Burma, defense of the Hump, and support of the Chinese armies against a major Japanese offensive in the east.

To these missions was now added another, for during early 1944 the Pacific strategy that had been evolving over the past year was agreed upon in Washington: Nimitz would assault Saipan in June; MacArthur would invade Mindanao in November. Whether the next move was to Luzon or to Formosa, the Fourteenth Air Force would be needed to provide aerial cover over the South China Sea. CBI was ordered to begin stockpiling supplies immediately for this new Pacific aid mission.[21]

Chennault choked. Orders to stockpile supplies for the coming summer when he did not have enough gasoline to meet the crisis of the immediate spring made no sense. Were people not listening? There were days when his planes could not fly because there was so little fuel. His opinion of staff officers and rear headquarters, never high, sank lower still.

About this time his friend Kuter visited the theater, and as was customary he radioed ahead to ask its commander's permission to enter. He had a number of officers with him, and Chennault testily replied that he already had enough generals and could not imagine why he should accept a navy captain, but come ahead. Reflecting that Claire was still his fiery old self, Kuter was startled to see Chennault meet their plane carrying a swagger stick, an affectation painfully out of character. He was soon reassured that Chennault was unchanged: after a brusque greeting he climbed on the wing of the C-54, used his stick to measure the gasoline remaining in its tanks, and had the plane drained of all but enough to take them back. Kuter and party were given a small plane for the remainder of their eye-opening tour of China.[22]

Back in Washington, where a skeptical Marshall expressed fears that the United States was paying a terrible price for the results it was getting from the Fourteenth Air Force, Kuter reported that Chennault was employing his small air force just as effectively with the tools he had as any other air force commander. Kuter favored support for the Fourteenth as opposed to the Burma campaign at this point, but he made little headway against the rising tide of opposition to Chennault in the War Department. Stimson, who resented Chennault's support of Chiang rather than the War Department, considered him "not very loyal when it comes to a pinch."[23]

Marshall was also at the end of his endurance. It was his habit to hold his tongue during meetings of the Joint Chiefs of Staff but to speak plainly in the car afterward, and after one JCS meeting in which Kuter dared observe that Chennault's airmen were doing the Japanese considerably more damage than were Stilwell's soldiers, he found himself well "chewed out" by an angry Marshall, who said Chennault was "disloyal" to his commanding officer. Kuter tried to make the point that this was an Allied war, that Chiang as well as Stilwell was Chennault's commanding officer, but Marshall would hear none of it. Kuter concluded that the very name Chennault was anathema to the chief of staff, who "could see no good in him at all."[24]

The spring of 1944 in CBI was a cruel and heart-wrenching time. Political tensions increased, for Roosevelt began exerting firmer pressure on Chiang. The Americans wanted to send a team of military observers to the Chinese Communist forces in north China, a request Chiang parried by saying that observers were welcome in any area controlled by his central government. When Chiang kept delaying putting Y-force into action in Burma, Roosevelt became more and

Generalissimo Chiang Kai-shek with Chennault, Kunming, China, 1944. (Official U.S. Army Air Forces photo, courtesy Wayne Johnson)

more insistent. Eventually it was made quite clear: unless the Chinese attacked across the Salween, lend-lease would be ended.

The B-29s began to arrive at Chengtu, and problems began to accumulate. Washington and Chungking clashed over the price of the huge runways (Chiang insisted on being paid at twenty to one when the black market rate between Chinese currency and American dollars was 240 to one). Instead of the P-51s he requested for Chengtu's defense, Chennault received P-47s, which used more gasoline. MATTERHORN proved to be far from self-sufficient; after February it competed with the Fourteenth Air Force and the Chinese ground forces for Hump tonnage. MATTERHORN also meant that total tonnage brought into Calcutta had to be increased, and as Calcutta became more congested, a shortage of gasoline developed in Assam.

There were too many competing needs—MATTERHORN, the Ledo Road and the drive toward Myitkyina, buildup of the Chinese armies, the meeting of the Japanese offensives in India and possibly in east China, and the mandate to stockpile supplies to aid the Pacific drive in the summer. "Everybody is frantically scrambling to do everything," Stilwell wrote Arnold. He started groping for priorities, for clarification of his mission.[25]

Chennault, with every fiber of his being tightened in single-minded determination, concentrated on getting ready to fight. He felt deserted and misunderstood by his commanders, as indeed he partly was. His 8 April letter to Stilwell went up the command channels and aroused genuine concern in Washington, but the main interest lay in the safety of MATTERHORN, not eastern China. Japanese forces had already begun to move south across the Yellow River when Stratemeyer asked Chennault to come to India to talk about defending Chengtu. Chennault wrote back, assuring Stratemeyer that he could defend the Chengtu base; his 8 April warning regarding Chengtu had been "to point out the increased danger of hostile air attack if Peking-Hankow Railroad is held by Japs." With their perception possibly influenced by the magnitude of MATTERHORN, both the theater and Washington commands began to focus on Chennault's words about a Japanese aerial offensive and to ignore what he said about danger on the ground. Chennault should be able to meet an air offensive, Stilwell reasoned, so he paid little attention to what was happening in China and spent most of his time in Burma, where early in May he ordered his already exhausted command to take Myitkyina.[26]

On 14 April Chiang bowed to American pressure and agreed to open an offensive across the Salween with Y-force; the next day Chennault gave the Generalissimo a report that he had requested on the status of the air forces. He was blunt and clear in warning about the danger, for Chiang had done little or nothing to prepare for the Japanese onslaught. Chennault urged immediate and drastic measures to give the combined air forces adequate strength and supplies, because without them they "may not be able to withstand the expected Japanese air offensive and will certainly be unable to afford air support to the Chinese ground forces over the areas and on the scale desired." He pointed out that Y-force had received all the U.S. equipment and had been strengthened at the expense of the armies in the east; he implied that it would make more sense to attack in the east—toward Ichang or Hankow—than along the Salween.[27] The report, dated 15 April, was to have unexpected repercussions.

Chennault had divided the Fourteenth Air Force into the Sixty-eighth and Sixty-ninth Wings, the latter stationed around Kunming to defend the Hump and support Y-force, while the Sixty-eighth, under Vincent, would meet the Japanese threat in the east. On the gamble that Japan's initial moves would be from the Yellow River toward

Hankow, Chennault planned to leave the south exposed and to send one medium bombardment and four lighter squadrons to join two CAF fighter squadrons at CAF bases around Sian. The necessary airfields there were incomplete; he pushed Chiang to make them ready.[28]

The squadrons he would send north were those of the Chinese American Composite Wing, the organization through which he was slowly but surely building a new CAF. Since activation in July 1943, the CACW training center in Karachi had been taking partly trained Chinese airmen and preparing them for combat. The American instructors became each squadron's combat leaders when instruction was completed. The composite squadrons had begun moving into China late in 1943. Administratively part of the CAF, for operations they were part of the Fourteenth Air Force and were assigned to the Sixty-eighth Wing.[29]

The airfields in the northeast were not ready, and the CACW was not in position when the Japanese began moving across the Yellow River on 17 April, two weeks earlier than Chennault had expected. It was a costly failure of intelligence, for the Japanese were able to get under way unhampered by direct air attacks. By early May, however, the CACW was operating from the northern bases and was fighting well. It attained local air superiority and slowed the Japanese down, but the Chinese ground forces simply did not resist. Chennault reported that the Japanese columns moved virtually at will, while the Chinese "have shown slight evidence of plan, or of capability to hamper Japanese movement."[30] A critical factor was lack of support from the people of Honan, who had been drained of all strength by the famine and drained of all hope by the government's unrelenting taxation, conscription, and mismanagement of their needs. In some instances they turned against the Kuomintang armies; Chiang began to fear an internal revolt.[31] It was soon apparent that Chennault and his airmen must carry the burden of defense almost alone.

At this point Chennault received a double-barreled message from Stilwell. It warned him that Stratemeyer had authority to limit fighter operations in the theater—a restriction that would make it almost impossible for the Fourteenth Air Force to respond effectively to an emergency. The second barrel was even more devastating: the defense of the B-29 fields at Chengtu was to be Chennault's primary mission, even at the expense of support of the Chinese armies. Stilwell had drafted the order ten days earlier, basing his decisions on

Chennault's 8 April letter warning of an aerial offensive against Chengtu.[32] In the context of events, Chennault could not see any sense in the order at all.

He asked that the order be reconsidered. He tried to refocus concern by explaining that, since Chengtu received two hours of warning from the net and there were 200 fighters for its protection, its defense "gives me no concern." At present he was "busily engaged in attempting to stem the Jap repeat Jap invasion in the Yellow River Area and preparing to support [Y-force] operations. The defense of the Chengtu area is child's play in comparison to the more difficult problems that confront us." He asked for clarification of Stratemeyer's authority over fighter operations and expressed hopes that his hands would not be tied. "In times like this I need your support and most of all your confidence. I trust that I will be so honored."[33]

Stilwell was unmoved. On a memo pad he worked out his thoughts, noting Chennault's ambitious claims but not the problems preventing their realization. He figured Chiang "has been assured by experts that air power can do the trick, and now he craves to see it done." Deriving grim pleasure from watching Chennault and Chiang get their comeuppance, Stilwell concluded, "Leave them their pittance."[34]

He sent Chennault a caustic reply. "I am glad to hear that the defense of Chengtu is child's play. I had gathered from your letter of April eight that the security of China as a base for MATTERHORN and other military operations against Japan might be in doubt. It is a relief to know that we have no problem at Chengtu." He did not declare an emergency, which would have enabled him to divert supplies from MATTERHORN to the Fourteenth as Chennault had requested, but insisted, "There is no intention of limiting the scope of your operations in any way."[35] Chennault was free to fight but with only part of his forces and with limited supplies.

Even as the American effort in China faced its most severe challenge, the hostility between Stilwell and Chennault reached its height. Chennault's April message warning of the Japanese danger had reached Stilwell when he was trying to persuade Chiang to commit Y-force to the fight in Burma. The last thing Stilwell needed in those circumstances was for the Generalissimo to become alarmed. He therefore wired Chennault on the twelfth, "If you had in mind any communication for the Geemo on this subject, make sure that it goes through theater headquarters." Following instructions, when Chennault prepared to deliver to Chiang the 15 April report, he went by CBI headquarters in Chungking to show it to Maj. Gen. Thomas G. Hearn, Stilwell's chief of staff. The latter was ill and unavailable. Chennault went on to his appointment with Chiang and delivered the report. The next day he returned to Stilwell's headquarters, found Hearn still unavailable, and left a copy of the report for Stilwell.[36]

Stilwell was in Burma promoting X-force and did not see Chennault's report for several weeks, but at his headquarters it received angry attention. The intelligence staff claimed that Chinese intelligence organizations did not see any indications of a Japanese offensive and were unconcerned. (Chennault claimed throughout that his intelligence was better than that of theater headquarters, and in this instance he was right.) The operations staff bristled at the statement that strengthening Y-force had meant weakening the armies in the east. Did Chennault mean that China would fall because the ground forces were employed in the wrong place? (This was exactly what he meant; he thought the Burma campaign was a mistake.) When Stilwell saw the report, he interpreted it as intentional defiance of orders and demanded a written explanation.[37]

By then ICHIGO was well under way. An alarmed Chiang urged Stilwell to release planes and gasoline from MATTERHORN to stop the Japanese. Stilwell refused. He reasoned that, since Chennault had been given a larger air force and more supplies than he had originally requested, he was now "trying to prepare an out for himself by claiming that with a little more, which we won't give him, he can still do it."[38]

Stilwell was experiencing the very human gratification of having his own predictions vindicated by events when he received Chennault's explanation about the 15 April report: Chiang had requested it; he had tried to see Hearn before delivering it but could not; he had left a copy for Stilwell's information; he had considered it a potential source of embarrassment to all parties if he did not produce the document at the scheduled appointment. Chennault felt there was no violation of policy, since it was a "purely factual" report from which he had eliminated any recommendations. There were obvious difficulties in his dual role as commander of the Fourteenth Air Force and chief of staff to Chiang, he noted, but since both Roosevelt and Stilwell had approved the arrangement, he deemed it "reasonable to assume" that Chiang could "call upon me for advice on air matters at anytime without reference to your headquarters. This is my understanding of my status in this regard and I acted accordingly."[39]

Stilwell concluded that "Chennault will obey the orders of the theater commander only when it suits him to do so." He considered Chennault to be interfering in policies foreign to his responsibilities and knowledge, making back-door submissions and attempting to discredit and criticize his superiors. He forwarded copies of the pertinent documents to Marshall with the formal request that Chennault, "guilty of direct disobedience of my orders," be relieved. Since Chennault "discusses the difficulties" of his dual capacity and since the duties "prove to be conflicting to the point of non-cooperation and disobedience of my orders, I desire that he be relieved of 14th Air Force responsibility and devote his full time to the supervision of combat and training of the Chinese Air Force." Stilwell would already have taken this step, he wrote, had he not recognized that there "might be political repercussions."[40]

In mid-May Stilwell's exhausted force of Chinese and commandos took the Myitkyina airfield. The Japanese hurriedly reinforced the town; Stilwell's men were soon fighting an ugly battle for survival. From across China Chennault tried to attract his commanding officer's attention with a letter asking that a directive be issued "prescribing the mission of the Fourteenth Air Force in meeting the threatened loss of our operating bases in eastern China." He asked that headquarters let him know what was being done, that he be given enough supplies to fight with, that he be told just what would constitute an emergency in which MATTERHORN's resources could be tapped.[41] He wrote Arnold, expressing concern but also confidence that the Japanese could be held if the Chinese were given intensive air support. Arnold dared to suggest that Chennault could not do everything expected of him on less than 8,000 tons a month, and if that could not be supplied, the United States should pull out of China.[42] By this time, however, CBI was a no-win affair: the United States could not pull out, yet there seemed to be no way to guarantee Chennault 8,000 tons a month and still meet other commitments.

There was growing concern—and some bitterness—among officers in CBI that Stilwell was "playing regimental commander instead of running his theater." One observer bluntly suggested that, if Stilwell insisted on leading the Burma campaign in person, Stratemeyer should be named theater commander. Chennault held his tongue, but he felt certain that Stilwell did not comprehend the magnitude of the east China crisis. Stilwell refused the Generalissimo's request that he come to Chungking to confer; unmoved by a plea from Chiang that the last two weeks of May would be critical, he refused

to declare an emergency and to release any of MATTERHORN's resources to stop the Japanese.[43]

Alsop and Willauer, the driving force behind Chennault's political
entanglements, decided he must communicate the seriousness of the
situation to Roosevelt. At first Chennault refused. He insisted there
was no use trying any more, for the president would only refer his letter to the War Department, and this "would cause a commotion
without doing good." In his opinion, his recommendations were usually disregarded until it was too late. When Willauer went to Kunming to pick up the letter, he found not only that it had not been
written but also that Alsop as well as Chennault was "in the complete dumps." Willauer "did a bit of table pounding." The letter was
written—probably by all three men—and on 26 May was sent on its
way. It described the Japanese threat, expressed confidence that a
major air effort could stop it, and asked for "something very like carte
blanche" to draw on the resources of the theater. The second phase
of the Japanese offensive, it warned, might start at once.[44]

The prediction was right. The next day the Japanese drive renewed
its move southward in six lines of attack, bypassing prepared Chinese
positions and heading toward Changsha. Chinese resistance here had
been anticipated to be strong, but it crumbled. Chennault, not knowing that two days earlier Stilwell had requested his recall, sent his
commanding officer an urgent radio followed by a letter. He thought
the Japanese would attain their objectives unless the Chinese armies
were powerfully assisted. He was "confident we can do the job if you
will give us your fullest backing but believe the job cannot be done
on the basis of continuing to make the best with what we have."[45]

Stilwell doodled on Chennault's follow-up letter, penciling a firm
NO over each request. To his wife he poured out his feelings of regret
and resentment: he had predicted the Japanese offensive would come
and tried to get Chiang to go along with him in building up the
Chinese army to meet it, but Chiang and Roosevelt "knew better."[46]

But the circumstances in CBI were changing, and Stilwell was beginning to see matters in a different light. Washington planners had
decided that, if possible, Japan would be defeated without a major
campaign on the mainland of Asia. Stilwell had just been informed
that CBI's mission henceforth was support of Pacific operations; he
was ordered to give first priority to the security and expansion of the
Hump with the goal of "maximum effectiveness of the Fourteenth
Air Force." Stilwell had hoped for more—for American ground
troops, eventually for an expanded air force. But now a member of

his staff believed the only thing they could do to stop the holocaust in east China was to "throw Chennault at the advancing Japs."[47] Perhaps Stilwell recalled that Roosevelt had called CBI a political front, for even though his manner continued to be brusque, he summoned his energies to support Chennault and the Chinese in the crisis in east China.

What did Chennault mean, Stilwell inquired, by "we can do the job"? Chennault replied, "I believe we can defeat Japanese offensive if we receive 10,000 tons. I am certain we cannot with only 60 percent of our minimum supply requirement." Stilwell discussed the matter with Mountbatten and decided to take off the clamps. On 4 June, when he received a message from one of his staff officers urging diversion of supplies to Chennault, he penciled on it, "Tell him not to worry. We are taking suitable measures."[48]

Stilwell then went to Chungking to confer with Chiang, their first such meeting in six months, and on to Kunming to talk with Chennault and the Fourteenth Air Force staff. The latter was startled by his "very hostile" attitude, his abrupt and condescending manner, and his expressed contempt for the Chinese forces in east China as not being worth saving. At first he snapped that he could spare only thirty minutes for their meeting. Apparently he began to sense the degree of their concern, however, for he relaxed somewhat and the meeting became helpful. Although Stilwell insisted that there was "nothing to stop" the Japanese, Chennault said he felt confident that, with the help of the B-29s to destroy the Japanese air force at Hankow, he could do it. Stilwell was willing to consider it. He diverted 1,500 tons from MATTERHORN and increased Chennault's allotment to give him almost the 10,000 tons he requested. Then he wired Washington asking permission to use the B-29 stocks in east China as an "ace in the hole."[49]

When Marshall and Arnold refused to release the B-29 stocks on the grounds that the early bombing of Japan would be better than the benefits gained by delay, Stilwell responded that the instructions were "exactly what I had hoped for." He informed Chennault they could not touch the MATTERHORN stocks and ordered him to concentrate on defensive operations, counter air operations, and close support of Chinese ground arms. Disappointed, Chennault responded that he had been doing so and would continue. He thanked Stilwell for his efforts.[50] He had expected nothing, but he too had hoped for much more.

On 6 June Allied forces began fighting their way ashore on the Normandy beaches. The long-awaited second front was a reality; the end of the enormous struggle could be foreseen, a matter of time. On 9 June Stilwell received his answer from Washington about relieving Chennault of command. It came from the deputy chief of staff, because Marshall and Arnold were in Europe. "In view of the current situation in China and the political aspects of this case, it is not believed wise to take positive action at this time." If east China were lost, "as might well be possible," the message read, "the responsibility would inevitably be charged against you repeat you."[51]

15

"We are holding the sack"

The summer of 1944 saw CBI at its peak of military action. Heroism and sacrifice were requested and given, and it is ironic that in the long term it made little difference in the final outcome of the defeat of Japan. From beginning to end, CBI was out of sync. By this third summer of American effort in China, the tension of unfulfilled strategies and clashing personalities was building toward an explosion of sobering scope.

The Burma campaign wrote its own singular history of skill and endurance. Fighting in the jungle proved every bit as ghastly as Churchill had predicted it would be, while the Ledo Road that followed the painful advance was an engineering marvel. Not until July did the British have the Japanese India offensive controlled so that they could support the drive into Burma.

Meanwhile Stilwell's personal exertions pulled and pushed the Ledo force through the steaming valleys and over the interminable hills. He demanded so much of his American commando unit, Merrill's Marauders, that morale became a serious problem. Most gratifying to Stilwell was that the American-trained Chinese armies fought well, although it took his presence at the front to keep them moving. He tried valiantly to persuade Chiang Kai-shek to coordinate the action of Y-force, moving west, with that of X-force, moving east. Each would have taken pressure off the other, but Chiang refused to move before May, by which time the Ledo force was almost to Myitkyina. Possibly Chiang had waited until a speedy end to the campaign seemed likely, but if so he was foiled, for the long siege at Myitkyina dominated the summer, the sick and war-worn soldiers clinging to the airfield in sheer desperation until the Japanese forces there were defeated in August.

At that point Stilwell judged that his men must have a rest and ordered a halt until mid-October. This infuriated Chiang, for Y-force was by then committed, the gorge and the bridgeless, raging Salween at their backs, heavily fortified Japanese positions in front. The Chinese generals rejected American advice to infiltrate the thin Japanese lines and bypass the strongholds; they insisted upon head-on assault, and each attack required intense air support from the Sixty-ninth Wing.[1]

But the Burma campaign took the hump out of the Hump by making it safe for the ATC planes to take a more southerly route over the Himalayas. Tonnage began to rise. By fall it reached tantalizing totals—almost 25,000 tons in October and 35,000 in November[2] — but the effort exacted its price. During those months, with both Y-force and the Sixty-ninth Wing of the Fourteenth Air Force stalemated on the Salween, ICHIGO swept through east China. Changsha fell in mid-June. A few weeks later Japanese forces began driving north from Canton to meet those coming south. Hengyang fell in August, Lingling in September, and Kweilin and Liuchow in November.

These events seem almost lost within the larger context of the global war. In June the V-bombs began to fall on England; the U.S.S.R. opened a massive drive against Germany's eastern front that would not halt until Russian soldiers entered Berlin. Paris was liberated, and the Western Allies swept across France, generals Patton and Montgomery fighting tooth and toenail for supplies, in the best Stilwell-Chennault tradition. Marines seized Saipan, then Guam and Tinian and Peleliu; MacArthur's forces landed on Leyte; the U.S. Navy mauled Japan in the battles of the Philippine Sea and Leyte Gulf. The fall of Myitkyina coincided with the Warsaw Uprising, the fall of Kweilin with Roosevelt's election to a fourth term.

Even within CBI the military operations were eclipsed by the undercurrents of policy and power struggles that raged in the background. China was like a mighty war wagon with no driver, in imminent danger of being pulled to pieces as the stallions in the traces, nipping at each other's backs, raced for stables in widely divergent locations. To a military man such as Vincent, newly appointed brigadier general at the unprecedented age of twenty-nine, the scenario was incomprehensible.

"This present war as it is being fought out here makes less sense to me than any I have ever studied," he wrote Chennault in June. "The Chinese divisions pushing west and the Japanese taking Eastern China. Have the powers-that-be completely washed their hands of this affair and given up?" He wondered why they did not turn the B-29s loose on Hankow and wipe out the main Japanese concentrations that were killing his men. He felt certain that Hsueh Yueh underestimated Japanese capabilities and expected greater support from the Fourteenth than it could give. In the first month of the offensive, the Sixty-eighth Wing had fought valiantly, had suffered unbelievable deprivations, and had maintained an astonishing esprit de corps and combat record, but Vincent realized there was no way it could stop the Japanese drive alone.[3]

He was concerned for the record. "I know you realize that we are holding the sack inasmuch as we are on record as stating that the Japs can be stopped on the ground with good air support," he wrote Chennault. "We are also on record as stating what we must have in the way of airplanes and supplies in order to furnish this effective air support—AND WHICH WE HAVE NOT RECEIVED." Vincent insisted he would "fight to the last ditch" and "the fullest extent of our ability," but he rebelled against policies from higher headquarters that ensured his defeat.[4]

Chennault agreed. He realized that Hsueh's preparations had not been realistic, that the Chinese had been nonchalant, that Hsueh would likely be defeated. The only way he could see to salvage the situation was for the air forces to destroy most of the Japanese supplies and personnel moving up to the front.[5] He set his mind. It had to be done. Without help his men would have to fight well and hard. Neither then nor later did he express any anger toward Chiang, any resentment toward Hsueh or the other commanders. He understood the depth of China's desperation, the complexity of its problems. This was no time to withdraw the support he had freely given, no time to turn his back. "Stubborn as hell," some called him. He stuck to his goals, even though friends observed that "sometimes it got to be embarrassing because he stuck to it so hard."[6]

For the men of the Sixty-eighth Wing, the summer was one sortie

after another—5,287 of them between 26 May and 1 August—in pursuit of Japanese ships, barges, rail cars, and trucks. At times the fighting was intense. During the first two weeks of June the fighters
averaged three or four sorties per plane per day, a pace that wore out
both planes and pilots. Maintenance crews put in frantic hours but
managed to keep about 150 fighters operational.[7]

As the Japanese moved down the river valley toward Hengyang,
the Chinese prepared for a major stand. Between 17 and 25 June the
Twenty-third Fighter Group (the bombers were little used because of
the shortage of gasoline) threw itself into the battle at such a pace
that it earned a Distinguished Unit Citation. On all but three days
the weather was bad. The pilots flew their missions through a low
"tunnel" under clouds that arched over the river and rested on the
mountains paralleling the river valley. AGFRTS air-ground liaison
teams operated with Hsueh's troops to coordinate the air effort with
the armies. The close support worked well and gave Chennault quiet
satisfaction, but the Chinese resistance he had expected and hoped
for did not develop. The Twenty-third, in the words of its citation,
waged a "lone, gallant stand" against 70,000 enemy troops.[8]

There had been times when the men of the Twenty-third reveled in
challenging odds. Of six planes against seventy-five, one had said,
"Easy, because every place you turned you had a target."[9] But men
tire more rapidly when they are suffering defeats. Squadron commanders worried about their men and resented not getting replacement pilots. Little was known about what is now called combat
fatigue, but they realized that after flying about a hundred missions
the pilots would start "doping off," and their casualties would rise as
much as 50 percent. The command was already exhausted from two
weeks of constant effort when Chennault wrote Vincent on 26 June,
"You must be prepared to redouble your effort, or even better than
that if the Japs are to be stopped north of Kweilin."[10]

Why were his men willing to maintain such a killing pace? Unlike
him, they had no personal ties to China, no obligations to Chiang, no
strategic stances to vindicate, no professional reputation to enhance.
Most of them were vital young Americans who would much have
preferred to be home. Yet one of them who met Chennault during
these months concluded it was no wonder that he was a "living legend to the Chinese" or that the Fourteenth Air Force "loved him to a
man." Theirs was a simple encounter. The soldier had been serving
behind Japanese lines, working with the Chinese guerrillas in rescuing downed pilots. One way to save the pilots was to offer higher re-

wards than the Japanese did, and he sometimes ran out of money. On his own initiative he asked General Li Tsung-jen for a loan, assuring him he would be reimbursed for this expense as well as his others in helping to care for the rescued Americans. Now with some trepidation the soldier faced the commanding general to explain what he had done and to ask for the money. "How much did you promise him, son?" was the only question. He was given a voucher for the amount.[11]

Chennault's leadership was genuine because he himself was a fighter, and he understood the fighting man. "We were the first cadre," remembered one, "and he come out to greet us. . . . No more like him. They broke the mold. . . . you talk to anyone of the 75th men and they'd take the shirt off their back for him."[12] Walking along to inspect a newly arrived group of pilots, with Joe Dash trotting along behind him, he would ask a young man where he was from. Cold sweat running down his back, one lieutenant replied he was from a farm in Minnesota. "Farm boys make damn good pilots," the general declared. "I was one, you know, from a farm in Louisiana." He told the new pilot his commander was one of the best and admonished him to "pay attention to what he says. We got a job to do but I want my boys back safe."[13]

So it would go, down the line. Chennault sensed when they needed reassurance, when they needed to test themselves. A young lieutenant stationed near Chengtu, where there was little action, ferried a plane to Kweilin and persuaded squadron commander Tex Hill (an AVG ace now back in China) to let him fly combat while he waited for transport back to base. In his zeal he broke formation to shoot down his first Japanese plane, but Chennault sent him a personal message of congratulations, leaving it to Hill to ground him (rightly) for violating combat discipline. Years later, retired as an air force colonel, the pilot called Chennault the one general under whom he had served to whom he would most willingly give his loyalty.[14]

"He played it straight, and he expected you to do the same," another explained, while yet another described dangerous solo reconnaissance missions over Japanese airfields when his task was to lure the Japanese into the air so that he could bring back information on how many planes they had and how quickly they could get aloft. The pilot knew his flights were risky and dangerous, but he knew that Chennault realized it also, and he was touched that the general "was mindful of my rest." Chennault's efforts to take care of his men spared nothing. He believed that his principal job was "to solve problems and to keep the combat units in the best possible condition for fighting."[15] To his men he was father and hero and more, the embodiment of all their vague notions about why they were there and why they must do their best.

"I resisted every attempt that was made to restrict these pilots, to pressure them with excessive discipline," he later explained. "I felt they needed a lot of flexibility, and I gave them all the leeway I could manage, regarding them in all operations as individuals. It paid off. They were very good."[16] They might not have the best equipment, or enough supplies, or help from the Chinese, but the enemy was there, and Chennault gave it all he had. Because he would not give up, and because he put his trust in his men, they would not give up either.

A second question is raised by the summer's campaign. Why were the Chinese armies unable—or unwilling—to hold? Why was there more and more talk, well supported with evidence, that they were simply not fighting, not trying? At Changsha, Chinese soldiers insisted they evacuated the city only because the Japanese used gas, but American liaison men there reported no evidence either of gas or of serious resistance.[17]

"China is in a mess," wrote John S. Service, a Foreign Service officer assigned to Stilwell's staff, and "China is still Chiang Kai-shek. . . . for the sorry situation as a whole, Chiang, and only Chiang, is responsible."[18] Many others agreed, for as China's crisis deepened, Chiang and the Kuomintang seemed powerless to govern, gripped in some ghastly paralysis that rendered them unable to comprehend the magnitude of their problem or to relinquish a stubborn faith that, if they just held on, the war would end and then they could carry on as before. Madame appeared to abandon her concern and her efforts for China after she returned from the United States in 1943. The extent to which the Nationalist government had lost popular support was evidenced across the board, from open revolt and talk of assassination or overthrow, to widespread talk about Chiang and Madame, gossip about pregnant mistresses and domestic squabbling, temper tantrums and thrown teacups, and economic scandal and personal extravagance and profiteering amid China's economic disaster.

The corpse of a dying Kuomintang China was beginning to stink. As the Chinese themselves lost respect for their government, Chiang clung to power by exploiting the weaknesses of others, becoming ever more authoritarian, more arbitrary, more locked into a policy of "active noncooperation" with the Americans.[19] Chennault, who viewed the mounting debacle from the perspective of one who admired

Chiang for his strengths and understood the peculiarly Chinese nature of his problems, regarded the Generalissimo as worn down by a
multiple burden: the power struggle with the Communists, factionalism within his government, the seven-year war with Japan, the
lack of harmony in thought and purpose with Stilwell. He realized
that Chiang's prestige had declined seriously, that his regime was tottering. But where most Americans put the blame on Chiang himself,
Chennault perceived subtle but cruel American practices that undermined the Generalissimo and contributed to China's demoralization. He saw the problem as one of two disparate cultures, "each
with its own deeply ingrained and sometimes mutually incompatible
superiorities and deficiencies." He sensed that a double standard was
being applied to Chinese and American efforts. He was aware of the
American tendency to patronize, to denigrate, to make decisions
without consultation or consideration of Chinese needs, to interpret
China's defeats as ineptitude while those of the Americans were
called gallant resistance. He felt much could have been done to help
China—and thereby the U.S. cause—by mutual understanding, help-
fulness, and respect, but he saw little of those qualities among the
American leadership in China.[20]

At the end of June Chennault wrote Roosevelt a bitter and outspoken letter. The loss of east China then in process had been totally unnecessary, he said, caused by policies that withheld supplies from
him until it was too late. The political effects on China, coming as a
shock wave against a foundation already weakened, might well be
disastrous. He believed that Chiang needed encouragement and support, that there should be close coordination of Chinese and American activities to halt the progressive demoralization of people and
government. He outlined a possible military strategy to recoup the
damage: use the Fourteenth from interior airfields against Japanese
supply lines, simultaneously helping the Chinese in the newly occupied areas to organize guerrilla warfare "greater in scale, better
planned and better supplied" than any yet attempted.[21]

To make this strategy possible, however, Chennault told Roosevelt, the American forces needed leadership "of most unusual quality, combining the utmost political astuteness with the maximum of
military imagination and readiness to experiment and improvise."
At first impression this seems an obvious hint that he be put in overall
command. Perhaps it was. But at this time his imagination had become captivated by something else: the concepts and potential of
guerrilla warfare. Of necessity he had evolved a guerrilla approach

for the AVG and CATF; it had come naturally to him, for it rang true to all his instincts of the fight. During this summer of 1944 he prepared proposals for an extensive guerrilla campaign in east China, and from their wording it is clear that he was thinking of directing this kind of endeavor under a sympathetic theater commander. In any event, he was convinced that China could not be helped "in an atmosphere of mutual suspicion and contempt."[22]

Roosevelt, by this summer of 1944, was tired. He had been in the White House for eleven years, and he desperately wanted to see it through, to see the war ended and an organization established to maintain world peace. Chiang's active noncooperation wore on the nerves. Roosevelt began to stiffen, to think China needed to help itself. Although Chiang had finally set Y-force in motion, his best armies were still idle in the north. While they watched the bandits, eastern China and the bases built for the aerial offensive against Japan were in peril. There was growing fear in Washington that Chiang's actions vis-à-vis the Communists might jeopardize worldwide relations with the Soviet Union.

A worried Roosevelt sent Vice President Henry A. Wallace to China in June to see whether the United Front might not be patched back together to strengthen China. Wallace had some success: he obtained Chiang's agreement that a military mission, subsequently called the Dixie Mission, might go to Yenan. Chiang made it clear, however, that he considered the Chinese Communists dangerous, men of bad faith, internationalists rather than true Chinese, "more communistic" than the Russian Communists.[23]

He also made it clear, although as a very incidental part of the conversations, that Stilwell's uncooperative attitude impeded operations. He had no confidence in Stilwell's judgment. He did not request Stilwell's recall, but since Stilwell "has no understanding of political matters," he requested that Roosevelt appoint a personal representative who could serve as a direct liaison between them for both military and political affairs.[24]

Like most Americans who visited China, Wallace was numbed by the complexity of its problems and concerned about what he saw. He did not find himself in sympathy with Chiang, for the signs of China's internal distress were abundant. But Chiang was China's leader, and Wallace was "deeply moved by the cry of a man in great trouble."[25] Stilwell was deep in the Burma jungle; his staff felt that it was being given the runaround by Chennault's staff and was not being allowed to present Stilwell's point of view.[26] Wallace visited Kunming and was impressed by Chennault's "simple outline" of the threat in east China. His conclusion was that the military crisis was not hopeless, that it might even provide the incentive for reform and action. But he believed a change in command was essential. The complex gears of CBI needed more lubrication than Stilwell's brusque nature could provide.[27]

It would be best, Wallace thought at first, if Chennault replaced Stilwell, for Chiang had told him he found Chennault "most cooperative." Alsop, usually Chennault's most enthusiastic champion, dissuaded him, arguing that, not only would the War Department never agree, but Chennault could not leave the campaign he was then directing. Although Chennault was "very far from pleased" when Alsop afterward told him how he had advised the vice president, he nevertheless understood and agreed with Alsop's explanation of his reasons. Wallace recommended to Roosevelt that Chennault be kept in "his present effective military position" and that another general officer (he mentioned Wedemeyer as having impressed Chiang favorably) be appointed to command U.S. forces in China.[28]

Marshall, considering Wallace's recommendation for Stilwell's recall to be more of Alsop's "usual poison," asked Stilwell if he could accomplish any good by taking an active part in the military operations in China. Stilwell was not enthusiastic. He would not even attempt it without complete authority, he replied, and even so he could see scant hope of recovering the situation. He thought the Communists should take part. There was a "faint chance" of salvaging something, but it would have to be put before Chiang "in the strongest terms," and one commander must have full powers.[29]

Marshall agreed. Convinced that Chennault's air offensive and the huge airlift created to support it were not yielding any dividends in China but were nevertheless hobbling the war in Europe, he threw his formidable weight more firmly than ever behind Stilwell. The resulting memo, drafted by the Joint Chiefs of Staff, condemned Chennault and tweaked the president for having backed an ineffectual strategy. It reported that the Chinese ground forces were "impotent," the situation in China "deteriorating at an alarming rate." Had Stilwell's advice been followed earlier, the land route to Burma would already be open and the armies in China better prepared to resist the Japanese offensive. The memo concluded that "Chennault's air can do little more than slightly delay the Japanese advances." The time had come for the "military power and resources remaining to China" to be entrusted to someone "capable of directing that effort in a fruitful way."[30]

Roosevelt accepted Marshall's recommendation. On 6 July he wrote Chiang that he should take immediate action to prevent disaster to the U.S. effort in China. Specifically, he must delegate to Stilwell "the power to coordinate all the Allied military resources in China, including the Communist forces."[31] This was far from what Chennault had in mind when he wrote Roosevelt urging leadership that would give Chiang "encouragement and support."[32]

It was obvious to all that, if Stilwell had command of the Chinese armies, he would employ against the Japanese in east China the central government troops now positioned against the Chinese Communists. He would probably supply and use the Communist armies as well. It was also obvious that Chiang opposed both measures. From the beginning he had consistently favored Chennault's strategy over Stilwell's. He had repeatedly sought Stilwell's recall, the two had never established a mutual respect or effective working relationship, and the tension between them had mounted in the spring of 1944 when Stilwell refused to divert gasoline to the Fourteenth Air Force. It is hard to believe that either Roosevelt or Marshall expected Chiang to comply.

Marshall, having decided to force the issue in Stilwell's behalf, did tell Stilwell that he must make an effort to get along with Chiang. Stilwell accepted the rebuke in good grace, but it was too late; Chiang's subsequent actions suggest that he very early decided not to comply. Chennault seems to have learned about the confrontation from the Chinese rather than the Americans. He "very carefully" stayed out of it. He knew Chiang and China's internal situation well enough to be quite certain that Stilwell would not be given direct command of the Chinese forces.[33] Chiang, in the Chinese way, agreed in principle but insisted that some matters must be settled first. For the next three months Roosevelt encouraged, Marshall and Stilwell planned, and Chiang did nothing while the Japanese steadily closed the gap between Hankow and Canton and Chennault tried to stop them.

After the Chinese surrender of Changsha in mid-June, the Japanese moved swiftly on Hengyang, site of a major base of the Fourteenth Air Force and an important transportation junction where the Chinese railroad branched, one line going southwest through Liuchow to Indochina, the other southeast to Canton. The Japanese took the airfield on 26 June and then turned on the walled city. At Hengyang, Hsueh Yueh had a capable and determined commander, General Fong Hsien-chien, and under his leadership the Chinese put up a stubborn and effective defense. The first Japanese attack failed. So did the second.

Here, with an army willing to fight, was the test of Chennault's belief that the Chinese could hold if they had air support. The air-ground partnership was so effective that during the first week in July it looked as though the Japanese would have to withdraw. The planes operated directly against the Japanese forces, guided to their targets by the radios of the AGFRTS men moving among the Chinese soldiers. Japanese supply lines were severed. From Hankow south the railway was destroyed; steady attacks by the fighter-bombers precluded its repair. Trucks on the road and barges on the parallel Hsiang River were attacked so vigorously that the Japanese began limiting transport to hours of darkness. The pilots then began night-time attacks, even though they had little specialized equipment. With no food brought up, the Japanese soldiers had to live off the land; with no ammunition delivered, they could not fight.

There was a lull the first week of July; the Sixty-eighth Wing and the Chinese prematurely celebrated victory. Chennault's spirits soared. He and Vincent even dared to hope that the Chinese would rally and reverse their earlier losses. But the Sixty-eighth Wing had now exhausted its slender reserves of gasoline. During the second week of July it received absolutely no supplies over the ELOC: fuel for the alcohol-burning trucks had been diverted for the use of Y-force. Given a reprieve in the air, the Japanese accumulated supplies and renewed their attack. The Fourteenth's pilots, making every drop of fuel count, kept the Japanese in their trenches by day, halted many of the enemy supply vehicles, and air-dropped ammunition (from the Sixty-eighth's own stores) into the besieged city. The Japanese, already "embarrassed" by their supply difficulties, now found their situation "confused" and their operation not progressing "according to plan."[34]

Between 17 and 24 July, with the Sixty-eighth Wing almost grounded for lack of fuel, Chinese internal politics began to shape the military decisions. Early in the war Chiang had adopted two policies: he gave preferential treatment to central government troops and stationed them near the regional armies to retain some control. When these regional forces lost men and equipment, they were not replenished; instead the remnants might even be broken up and reassigned to units under command of officers loyal to the central government.[35]

Hsueh Yueh was not one of Chiang's favored generals, for the "Tiger of Changsha"—a sobriquet earned for a well-fought campaign in Hunan in 1941—was a general who cut off heads if his orders were not obeyed, a man capable of exerting strong and positive leadership. Stilwell considered the fighting Cantonese to be "the only tough guy in the army." In 1943 it had been suggested that he had been one of those involved in the quickly suppressed coup while Chiang was in Cairo. As a member of the progressive faction of the Kuomintang, Hsueh was detested by the reactionary war minister, Ho Ying-chin, but in the wake of the 1943 power struggle, the latter was firmly in control in Chungking. The forces Hsueh commanded in Hunan numbered about 150,000 men, but they had little equipment and had not been part of Stilwell's program of army rebuilding. Some of them belonged to the central government; others owed their loyalty to Hsueh as the provincial leader.[36]

The Americans knew little about Hsueh, his army, or his intentions. Early in the summer Stilwell's headquarters requested permission to send observers into his IX War Area. Hsueh agreed reluctantly and received them coolly, but the observers reported he badly needed arms and ammunition, and a train load was sent. The amount was relatively small, but Hsueh became more cordial. Chiang's officers assigned to the American Kweilin headquarters, however, protested that the shipments to Hsueh might fall into the wrong hands and might be used against the central government. The Americans had been suspicious of the government's policy toward the eastern armies, but this was their first clear indication that Chiang was withholding supplies and equipment from them.[37]

On 20 July Chennault asked Stilwell to assign a troop carrier flight to China and to supply the Chinese at Hengyang by air. At the same time General Pai Chung-hsi appealed to Stilwell for arms and equipment such as had been provided for Y-force; he wanted to arm two armies—his own, not central government troops—for the defense of Kwangsi. Pai's sympathies were well known: he had agreed to join the United Front to meet the Japanese threat in 1937, but the alliance was shaky.[38]

Stilwell was at his headquarters in the jungle in Burma, and the Myitkyina battle was foremost in his mind when he received Chennault's request, Pai's request, and a third request from Hsueh Yueh himself. Through U.S. Brig. Gen. Malcolm Lindsey, who was training Chinese troops for Z-force at Kweilin, Hsueh requested American help in getting Chinese Army equipment that was stored in Kweilin transferred to his troops. He could not make the request of the National Military Council, he explained, for it would be refused. Lindsey concluded that Chiang was afraid of a separatist movement in which Hsueh might be included.[39]

Stilwell found himself in a vise. The Generalissimo had told him on 5 June that "the situation was one to be solved by air attack" and requested that he give the Fourteenth Air Force the MATTERHORN supplies and all the resources of the Hump. Obviously Chiang wanted to pry resources away from the B-29s and the Burma campaign to apply to the crisis in east China, but Stilwell also understood that no supplies were to be given to the Chinese ground forces in east China—that only the air effort would be supported.[40]

Stilwell neither reported this embargo to Washington nor mentioned it in his diary, omissions that raise questions as yet unanswered. It is impossible to ignore the fact that his subsequent actions were influenced by the very human reaction of "I told you so" or that his decisions seemed dictated more by his long-term conflict with Chennault than by the Generalissimo's wishes. The memo written in response to the requests received from Chennault, Pai, and Hsueh shows his attitude clearly:

> Here is my slant. QUADRANT and SEXTANT [Allied conferences] turned down help for ground forces and accepted Chennault's plan for beating Japs with air alone. Generalissimo was sold on this plan and has insisted on full tonnage for air force. Chennault has stated that with ten thousand tons he could stop the Japs. He had twelve thousand last month. If he now realizes he cannot do it, he should so inform the Gissimo, who can then make any proposition he sees fit. . . . I do not see how we can move until a certain big decision [whether to give Stilwell command of the Chinese armies] is made. You can tell the Chinese we are doing our best to carry out the plan the Gissimo insisted on.[41]

This message was reworded by Stilwell's staff and sent to Chennault, but the version he received did not tell him to consult Chiang himself about a change of policy. It merely stated that the Generalissimo had decreed that all tonnage should go to the Fourteenth Air Force and that no tonnage could be given to the ground forces.[42]

Now Chennault was in a vise. His "greatest fear" was that Hsueh would run out of weapons and ammunition. On the twenty-fourth

Vincent reported Hsueh still in the fight and confident. Hsueh had massed considerable forces, in front of Hengyang as well as along the Japanese flanks all the way back to the Yangtze. They were putting up a good fight. One attack briefly retook Changsha but was thrown back; another got within five miles of Hengyang. It was to no avail. Hengyang fell on 8 August.[43]

The next day the drama intensified when a Chinese gave the American consulate in Kweilin a message from Marshal Li Chi-shen saying that a provisional government would be established in the near future, which the provinces of Kwangtung, Kwangsi, Hunan, Fukien, Anhwei, Szechwan, Yunnan, and Sikang would support and in which they would participate. Its aims would be to replace the dictatorial Kuomintang government with a democratic one. It would seek national unity and cooperate with the Allies in crushing the Japanese. This provisional government would be headed by Marshal Li, president of the Military Advisory Council, and Chiang would be asked to resign. "It is expected that this can be obtained without armed conflict."[44]

"Hooray for crime!" was Stilwell's gut reaction to the news, but the official actions were discreet beyond reproach. Both Stilwell and Ambassador Gauss ordered their staffs to stay out of China's politics, make no commitments, express no opinions and deal only with local authorities strictly as local authorities.[45] The coup, however, had trouble getting under way.

In the midst of this drama, on 17 August, Chennault radioed Stilwell that he "would be willing to contribute one thousand tons my tonnage for bringing light machine guns, grenades, demolitions and so forth as would contribute to the effectiveness of General Hsueh Yueh's army." Chennault was aware that there were political complexities, for he told Stilwell, "I would not be interested in turning this over to the Minister of War because the chances are great that it would never reach Hsueh Yueh."[46]

A few weeks later, when the Japanese advance was renewed toward Kweilin, Chennault repeated his request with an urgent wire to Stilwell saying the one thing that could be done to save Kweilin would be to cut red tape and arrange to send small arms, rifles, hand grenades, and ammunition to Hsueh without regard to Chinese political channels. Hsueh "may not have the closest political ties with the Chungking government," Chennault wrote, "but he is actually fighting repeat fighting."[47] From his AGFRTS field representatives, Chennault knew that Hsueh had 16,000 soldiers and only 2,000 worn-out rifles. Nevertheless the defiant Hsueh, a fighter who was steadily rising in Chennault's estimation, was even then berating the War Ministry in Chungking for its inactivity, insisting that the Chinese should fight rather than put up such a heroic defense in the enemy's rear.[48]

Chennault had a long and trusted relationship with the Generalissimo, and there is no evidence that it was strained by his open support of Hsueh. Chennault knew that Hsueh and Chungking were in constant communication. He knew that Ho Ying-chin was irked that Hsueh was outspoken in criticism of fumbling by Chungking generals; the antagonism and competition between the two went back a long way. Chennault also knew more than most Americans about China's internal circumstances, for he held mutually trusting relationships with the Chinese. More than one American observed that he was "greatly beloved and respected" by them, and during that summer of 1944, they begged him to get ammunition for them so they could fight.[49] Chennault was moved by their spirit. And he, like Stilwell, responded to his personal human needs—to fight, to justify his stand and prove his point that air power could effectively strengthen ground troops and the airfields could be held.

Whatever its motives, Chennault's offer to give up tonnage in favor of Hsueh was a hot potato that Stilwell was not about to touch. His chief of staff suggested it was a start they could make, but Stilwell regarded the time for halfway measures as past, and "any more free gifts" would only "play into the hands of the gang." As far as he was concerned, the cards had been put on the table but no answer had been given (to the question of his own command of the Chinese forces); "Until it is, let them stew."[50]

Stilwell's headquarters drafted the answer to Chennault, explaining that Stilwell was "working on a proposition that will give this spot a real face lifting and is loath to commit himself to any definite line of action right now. Consequently we must hold off making any offers of help to ground troops until things precipitate a bit more." Sent by radio, when transcribed the words "face lifting" became "face lossing." Such errors were easily made and not unusual, but in this particular case results were painful. The message was read as it stood and was taken to mean that Stilwell was seeking to humiliate the Chinese armies. It is a measure of the bitterness within the theater that this interpretation was believed. A shocked Alsop made inquiries at theater headquarters in Chungking and was told that Stilwell felt he would be more likely to get the overall command if the Generalissimo were weakened by defeat.[51]

However the series of decisions and actions is interpreted, their result was the same: the Americans would not help Hsueh's armies, even though they were defending the bases that supported the American effort against Japan.

The tensions and failures of the summer of 1944 took their toll on Chennault's physical health and emotional endurance. Since AVG days he had been renowned among those who worked with him for his even temper, his patience, his quiet voice, and his ability to put failures behind him and go on. "You are the most patient and reasonable man I have ever known," a colonel who had returned to the States wrote, but underneath the calm exterior, behind the front of quiet confidence, Chennault's anger was building. His plan for operations in 1944 had included the statements that "adequate Chinese ground forces must of course be maintained in the airbase areas" and that, if the Japanese attacked, the Chinese should be given "certain key items of equipment" which they lacked.[52] Deep down, he was angry that this had not been done. The temper surfaced more often. Hill had some "rocky roads" with his chief, some tense arguments and confrontations. Vincent had even more trouble, and the night after the fall of Hengyang "we both got a little mad" as Vincent angrily insisted he was not getting proper support and Chennault in turn insisted he was doing all he could for the Sixty-eighth Wing. After the fall of Kweilin the tension mounted. Vincent thought "my people have done more than can be expected—without support, without supplies, and without replacements." He resented Chennault's "Sunday morning quarterbacking" and his stubborn refusal to admit that the Chinese had quit or that the air force by itself could not hold back the Japanese drive.[53]

By late September Vincent's anger was turning into concern for the "Old Man" and his increasing irritability. By November he felt the flight surgeons were shirking their duty in not recommending that the Fourteenth Air Force chief be rotated on the grounds of war weariness. Frillmann watched Chennault through those months and thought it tragic that the same traits that had seemed heroic two years earlier—aggressiveness, willfulness, and the refusal to admit that anything was impossible—seemed now to bring the fighting leader dangerously close to personal failure.[54]

No individual finds it easy to accept failure, and Chennault was no exception. The outcome of any endeavor in which he took part seemed to become tangled with his concept of himself, with his own personal performance. Behind his bravado there was a painful striving for success, for achievement, for visible proof to reinforce the intangible concept of worth that seemed, deep down, to elude him. He frequently sought a scapegoat, another back on which to load the burden. Often his failures stemmed from differences in the way he and others perceived the same situation, and he found these particularly hard to stomach. Why could not others see? Much of his irritability during the summer of 1944 stemmed from the frustration of getting his supplies too late. His messages to Stilwell often noted the time lapse between allocation and delivery, but the significance seemed lost on those not at the front. The additional tonnage allotted to the Fourteenth in June did not begin reaching the forward echelon until after Hengyang had fallen.

All through the summer, supply was the most critical issue. The ELOC was the major culprit, for the ATC was further expanded in July to accommodate increasing demands, and Brig. Gen. William H. Tunner (soon dubbed "Willie the Whip") took over the India-China wing in September with the attitude that any necessary amount could be taken over the Hump. Under his drive, the aerial transport system that later enabled the U.S. Air Force to fly the Berlin airlift came of age.[55]

Within China, however, supply improved but little. Chennault aggravated the problem by a prolonged disagreement with Tunner, who believed in air transport as passionately as Chennault believed in fighters. Tunner wanted to establish within China a fleet of C-46s and C-47s with their own crews and organization to handle the intra-China transport. Chennault "screamed bloody murder," contending that his own troop carrier transports could do the job better, that any additional planes in China should be his, and that ATC personnel and equipment would cut into the Fourteenth's Hump allotment. Yet when emergencies arose, the Fourteenth called on ATC planes and in so doing interfered with Tunner's regular scheduling.

After one such emergency, Tunner went to talk with Chennault and found him in the doctor's office getting a rubdown, his face drawn, his eyes without their usual glint. Realizing that Chennault was ill and sorry for having come, Tunner tried to leave but was told to "get it off your chest." Chennault listened to his argument with eyes closed, then agreed. Tunner quietly put his aerial transport plan into effect, and by the time Chennault realized what he had done, it was working well. Chennault ended the long argument with a simple, "Oh, all right," and afterward he gave Tunner and the ATC generous praise for their share of the Fourteenth's successes.[56]

During those trying months Chennault lost two of his closest and most trusted employees, for both Tom Trumble and Doreen Davis Lonberg were ill and tired and felt they must go home. Doreen had been an efficient and understanding secretary as well as an agreeable companion who added cheer and warmth to his often bleak life. His emotion at losing her came out as anger, and when he refused to see her off, she felt that he was "mad at me for leaving a job he would not leave."[57]

Very few people, however, saw his tension or realized how the pressure was hurting him internally, for Chennault was private to the point of shyness. Although friendly and understanding, with a disarming informality in his relationships, he was close to very few individuals. The press corps perceived a man who was indifferent to the superficial aspects of discipline yet endowed with a natural dignity and confidence sufficiently secure to allow him to participate in spit-on-the-palms ball games with his men. For he kept up the badminton and softball games; newcomers saw him as the "real McCoy," or a "tough looking hombre." There were times when he relaxed with a drink and a good Chinese dinner, and on these social occasions his fellow officers found him "a lot of fun to know."[58]

Sometimes nostalgia welled up and made him reflective. He wrote Max requesting canned oysters and okra, for he missed his favorite gumbo as well as the good fishing he had known in the States. When his cousin Ben Chase wrote to ask whether he would consider running for either senator or governor once the war was over, he replied, with sincerity as well as humor, that he would rather be a game warden. The Louisiana Department of Conservation promptly mailed him a commission and a badge.[59]

The November evacuation of Kweilin was hectic as well as personally disheartening, but amid the confusion Chennault went out of his way to be helpful and spent a few relaxed minutes with Msgr. John Romaniello, a civilian who had served the base as chaplain and in whose home he had often visited. For those who would help, those who were on his side, he felt a deep and genuine gratitude and loyalty.[60]

At no time during the Japanese conquest of eastern China did Chennault give up, even though he felt frustration and discouragement and sometimes anger. His letters pleading for supplies portrayed the consequences of Japanese success as dire indeed, and obviously the loss of the forward bases would hurt. But if he lost the eastern bases, he told the War Department, he would operate from the inner arc of fields. "The campaign will not be lost by any means."

With supplies he felt certain the Fourteenth could push the Japanese back.[61]

He demonstrated what he meant. One of the easternmost bases, Suichwan, was evacuated in the early stages of the Japanese offensive, but the Japanese bypassed it. Chennault then moved a skeleton operation back into Suichwan and nearby Kanchow, isolated in the corridor between the Japanese and the sea. He kept both fields supplied by air from Chihkiang. Each two gallons of gas delivered cost three gallons in intra-China fuel, but between 8 November and 31 January planes from these two forward bases claimed 80,000 tons of Japanese shipping.[62]

Despite the summer's defeats and failures, Chennault believed that the Fourteenth's efforts against ICHIGO proved his theories of aerial strategy in China. His views were supported when the Japanese, after the war, admitted that they could not move the necessary supplies for their campaign, so effectively had the Fourteenth interdicted their supply lines.[63] Had the Chinese armies held out, ICHIGO might have been recorded as another "rice raid." Rather than placing the blame on the Chinese or on Chiang himself, however, Chennault attributed the failure to Stilwell's policies and the American strategy.

Chiang did the same. At the end of this bitter summer he blamed China's defeats on Stilwell for withholding support from the forces in east China.[64] Was he merely trying to escape blame, to put the failure on other shoulders? Doubtless that was a factor, for Chiang was a master at political power plays. But it also seems possible that Stilwell misunderstood Chiang's full intent about the distribution of supplies. Proud of his command of the Chinese language, Stilwell did not use an interpreter in talking with Chiang. The latter was hard to understand, even for many Chinese, for he spoke the Chekiang dialect rather than the more widely used Mandarin. The words "hao hao," for instance, to Chiang meant "I see," although in Mandarin they meant "good." The potential for misinterpretation certainly existed.[65]

Stilwell left nothing in his own words about the embargo that withheld supplies from Hsueh Yueh. It is hard to understand why, if he did not privately desire to see the Japanese succeed in east China, he made no effort to have the embargo lifted, why he did not notify the War Department that Chiang himself was making a major contribution to an American defeat.

The U.S. Army's historians concluded that Chiang withheld sup-

port from his eastern commanders because he perceived that his own
vital centers—Kunming and Chungking—were not threatened, and
consequently there was little reason to weaken his regime by sending
aid to commanders of questionable loyalty. Chennault concurred in
their assessment,[66] but until the day he died he believed not only that
eastern China need not have fallen but also that the 1944 defeats undermined Chiang's regime and made the eventual Communist victory in China possible. For this he held Stilwell responsible. More
important in Chennault's thinking than withholding supplies from
the Chinese armies in the summer of 1944 was Stilwell's long-term insistence on the campaign in Burma, a strategy that divided the limited supply effort and prevented the Fourteenth Air Force from
having sufficient stockpiles, internal lines of communication, reinforcements, and continuing supply at the level necessary for effective
operations. He would always believe that with a little more fuel and
a few more aircraft, he and the aerial strategy he favored could have
prevailed.[67]

16

"It is going to work out all right"

The military tragedy of the late summer of 1944 was played out against the more lasting tragedy of deteriorating Sino-American relations. Roosevelt tried an emergency patch by sending Chiang a personal representative, Brig. Gen. Patrick Hurley. He was a large, expansive man given to war whoops and an unrestrained informality. The Chinese were more discomfited than reassured, despite Hurley's obvious sincerity and patience. Little changed.

Stilwell continued to fight in Burma. Chennault continued to fight in China. Each believed the other's effort was pointless. Each blamed the other for the shortages that made his own fight harder. Both were victims of the disagreement between Roosevelt and the War Department, which denied either general the unequivocal support of his government. Roosevelt had backed Chennault; the War Department had backed Stilwell. Neither had ever fully prevailed. China was the victim.

Washington must be assigned the primary blame for the CBI debacle, for it was there that authority lay. Roosevelt was the civilian commander in chief of the armed forces; his was the ultimate responsibility for the nation's foreign policy, for making certain that the po-

258

litical goals of the war matched the military goals for which the armed forces fought. The War Department's responsibility was military, to determine and then direct the military strategies that would bring the military victory at the least cost to the nation. America had little experience with international war or politics; she tended to separate the two, to think in terms of winning the war as the first priority, as though once the bad guys had been eliminated, everything would be all right. U.S. military personnel were indoctrinated with the separation of political and military responsibilities, a set of mind that partly explains why unconditional surrender became policy, why Eisenhower let the Russians claim Berlin, why the Russians were encouraged to enter the Pacific war.

In CBI the military and political goals were a seesaw. When one rose, the other hit the ground. Washington could have stopped it. Chennault could have been removed to ensure unquestioning support for the War Department's approach. Or Stilwell could have been replaced with a general more sensitive to the political need, more able to assist Chiang without friction. Allowing both to remain merely ensured that the seesaw continued to bump up and down.

But if Washington is blamed, Chennault must be blamed also. He loosed the gremlins; he had the gall to violate the chain of command and advocate an alternative to the War Department's military strategy. He saw the political ramifications of the war in China, although more at a personal and intuitive level than with an intellectual, philosophical detachment. His actions were prompted by several factors, for he tried to serve three masters: China, his own country, and himself.

China to him was Nationalist China, the China Chiang and Madame had been building when he first identified with their struggle. His alignment was in part emotional, for his years of working alongside the Chinese had cemented friendships that enabled him to view China from the inside out, to understand in an elementary sense the political and cultural patterns that determined its actions. But he also saw Nationalist China as the opponent of communism, which he perceived as a long-term enemy for political and individual freedom. He was sincere in his allegiance to both China and the United States. His loyalty to both was genuine. He saw their interests as the same: Japan must be defeated, but Nationalist China must be preserved. He sought to implement his own concepts of how both goals could be met.

Chennault cannot be credited with greatness for his lack of ethnocentrism, for he was not selfless in his actions. He listened to the nagging voice of pride, which told him he knew more about China and how to fight Japan from China than the desk generals in Washington did. He listened to his wounded ego, which told him the ideas he had evolved for aerial warfare were worthy of more consideration than they had received. He listened to the demons who had driven him since childhood to achieve, to lead, to win. He elected to defy the military traditions that hold an officer to silence when he disagrees with his high command, traditions that demand unquestioning obedience to orders. He was pushed and pulled and used by others, but it was he who violated the structure. Convinced he was right and his superiors wrong, he acted on his own.

His independent cussedness enraged both Stilwell and Washington. Their reprimands did not change him. Twice in the late summer of 1944 he set his teeth against the bridle like an ornery horse and ran, but the first episode had its comic as well as disturbing aspects. One mission of the Fourteenth was to help U.S. submarines locate and destroy Japanese shipping, a goal to which Chennault was wholeheartedly committed. The Fourteenth's major contribution was reconnaissance, but on 13 August Stilwell learned that MacArthur was "in a sweat over Chennault trying to bomb Manila."[1] MacArthur even wired Chennault directly, saying that word had just reached him that he intended to strike the Manila docks and "under no circumstance" must he do so.

"I invite your attention," wrote the general noted for his prose, "to the complete lack of authority for such an operation in the Southwest Pacific Area and your failure to communicate with me with reference to your desires to operate within the scope of my theater boundaries."[2]

Personally observing that the Southwest Pacific commander seemed "just a bit touchy about possible trespass on his kingdom,"[3] Stilwell reassured MacArthur. He then looked into the matter, however, and investigation revealed that on 11 August a wire over Chennault's name had gone to Admiral Christie, commander of the submarines operating from west Australia, that "Lucky Fellows will attack Manila Docks on Monday." Further details of time and radio frequency were given, with the expressed hope that "units Jap fleet in Manila Bay may be flushed. Good hunting."[4] Stilwell asked Chennault what was going on.

The message had actually been sent by the naval officer in charge of naval support missions. This organization had moved into Chennault's headquarters along with the OSS personnel, and Chennault had welcomed both as a means of expanding the Fourteenth's activities. "We are all working together as a team," he wrote of the new arrangement—and indeed the U.S. Navy was so pleased with the Fourteenth's spirited help that Chennault was later awarded the navy's Distinguished Service Medal.[5] In this particular case there is some indication that Chennault had proposed a target-of-opportunity mission and the message was not cleared with him before sending. When Stilwell asked for explanation, Chennault first replied that the message was "for sole purpose of establishing line of surface rescue vessels" and Manila Docks was one end of the line. Stilwell could not reconcile this with the 11 August radio and asked for further explanation.[6]

After another conference with the commander involved, Chennault wired back, "Lucky Fellows was a code word for 308th Bomb Group. Use of phrase Manila Docks was in error. Mention of possibility of flushing units of Jap fleet was included to warn our submarines to be on the alert as there was possibility that our submarines had been to sea for several weeks and that our information was much later than any that they could have." The message had been intended for Christie only, Chennault said. Its "contents were for use of the rescue vessels" and he hoped this would clarify the situation "to satisfaction of all."[7] Stilwell was justifiably skeptical. He questioned the commander involved and afterward wrote in his diary, "Attack *was* to be on docks & harbor." Convinced that Chennault had given him a false official statement, Stilwell turned the matter over to the theater inspector general.[8]

There was an investigation. The inspector general made note of Stilwell's accusation but refrained from any additional official comment. Chennault was admonished that "the initiation of missions extending into another theater should take place only after coordination with, and the concurrence of, the other theater commander concerned."[9]

No additional explanation from Chennault is on record. The men who served under him invariably said, "He backed you if you worked for him,"[10] and in this case he may have been covering for an officer who overstepped his bounds. On the other hand, that Chennault would have taken great delight in bombing Manila is one safe assumption, and that he would not have been unduly upset about trespassing on MacArthur's kingdom is another. He tended to lose the fine points of protocol and military procedures when he had the op-

portunity to hit the enemy a telling blow, and he may well have mis-
represented the facts in this episode because of a conviction that the
protocol was not important. Had he felt any guilt, it would have been
more in character for him to be defiant in the face of the rebuke, and
indeed that was how he responded to the second problem.

This time the issue was gasoline. Although Chennault was "convinced the time is not appropriate," starting in August his monthly
allotment was held at 10,000 tons so that gasoline could be stockpiled
for later missions in support of forthcoming Pacific operations. "The
incongruity of the present situation is incomprehensible," he insisted, warning that reducing the air effort now would mean losing
bases needed for Pacific support later, and it would take more to dis-
lodge the Japanese later than to prevent them from taking east China
now. Since the Fourteenth Air Force was providing the only direct
U.S. help to the Chinese in meeting the Japanese offensive in east
China, reducing that effort, especially without advance consultation
with the Chinese armies, seemed tantamount to betrayal. "It appears that a compromise must be weighed," he wired the War
Department.[11]

The order was not changed. Stilwell, however, could draw upon
the stockpile in an emergency, and he authorized Chennault to use
1,000 tons of it at the end of September. The monthly inventory
showed that the Fourteenth Air Force overdrew the account by 2,400
tons. With restrained tact, theater headquarters advised Chennault,
"It seems as if you have misunderstood the nature and scope of Stilwell's approval." The 2,400 tons was then deducted from his October
allotment to reimburse the stockpile.[12]

Chennault protested, trying to make Stilwell see it his way. He had
consumed almost all his operational reserves; the situation in the
east was critical, and to cut his gasoline supply would reduce his operations 25 percent and take away the only real advantage the
Chinese had. Since Stratemeyer had authority to divert 3,500 tons,
Chennault had based his hopes on this amount and "fought with all
I had and without regrets." He urged "serious weighing of this matter" and was startled when he then received another administrative
admonition saying that the drain on the stockpile had hindered CBI
in carrying out its commitments. When he requested clarification,
Stilwell curtly replied that surely he must understand that it was not
a subject for discussion.[13]

An angry Chennault wanted an opportunity to defend his actions,
but by this time Stilwell was on his way back to the United States. In

response to ever more insistent demands that Stilwell be given command of the Chinese forces, Chiang had decreed he must leave. A reluctant War Department finally consented. Stilwell left China bitter and depressed, convinced that the disaster in eastern China had come about because his advice was not followed. As he saw it, the real issue had been whether or not China itself would make an effort in the war.[14]

It was October 1944 when Stilwell was recalled. By then Washington knew that China's military contribution in the war would be small. U.S. involvement in China was political. In that context there were reasons why Chennault, despite obvious professional shortcomings, should be given command of the U.S. effort in China. The State Department held him in high regard.[15] Chiang had expressed confidence in him. Chennault's Fourteenth Air Force and the CACW he was building were the only military forces in China that commanded the confidence of the Chinese people. Roosevelt must have considered the matter, for on 2 October he wrote Chennault a brief letter urging him to "keep up the spirit because it is going to work out all right." On 4 October Kung, then in Washington, cabled Chiang that Roosevelt had just told him of his intention to recommend Chennault as Chiang's chief of staff. A facsimile edition of wartime documents shows that someone wrote the words "not true" on the message. Kung may have misinterpreted Roosevelt's intent, or the War Department may have changed his mind.[16]

For neither Stimson nor Marshall had any notion of naming Chennault to replace Stilwell. The War Department thought Chennault's strategy had failed abjectly, even though tremendous quantities of supplies had been sent him at the expense of operations in other theaters. They did not think he had demonstrated those qualities of administrative ability and team play necessary for high command; they questioned his close ties to the Chinese government; they discerned a one-sidedness in his tactical approaches. To his professional limitations they added their personal dislike, which on Marshall's part had grown to bitter hatred. There was ugly suspicion that Chennault was involved in unethical financial manipulations that involved taking pay from China and evading his U.S. income tax. Marshall's remarks about Chennault were cutting, prompting Wallace, who considered both Stilwell and Chennault splendid generals, to observe that it was hard to understand what Marshall hoped to gain by completely alienating the Generalissimo and losing east China. Perceiving the intensity of the War Department's opposition, Hopkins may not have backed Chennault at this time, even though he continued to find Chennault one of the most remarkable men he had ever met.[17]

In any event, Chennault was not given the command. He was sorely disappointed. He felt that his demonstrated leadership plus his knowledge of China and the particular problems of fighting there made him the logical choice, and he believed that the Chinese concurred. Since the Washington conferences of 1943, he had sensed that Marshall and Arnold were not in sympathy with him or his views, and their decision now confirmed his fears. For much of this he thought he was the victim of circumstance; for much more he thought he was the victim of unfair treatment, especially by Stilwell and the theater staff. He believed they had worked against him rather than with him, that there had been intentional misinterpretation and obstruction to prevent his strategy from working, and that Stilwell had done China great harm by his contempt for Chiang and his government. Hopkins also assigned a burden of guilt to army policies, telling Davies that although the War Department disliked Chennault, they dared not purge him because after the war Chennault could be expected to leave the army and "speak frankly and publicly."[18]

At this time Chennault kept his hurt to himself. Stilwell left CBI. China was separated from Burma and India and became a separate theater of war, and Roosevelt named Maj. Gen. Albert C. Wedemeyer to serve as Chiang's chief of staff and commander of U.S. forces in China.

As he prepared for his new assignment, Wedemeyer observed that he felt much like the "captain of the Chinese junk whose hull is full of holes, in stormy weather, and on an uncharted course. If I leave the navigator's room to caulk up the holes, the junk will end on the reef and if I remain in the navigator's seat, the junk will sink."[19]

Airmen were pleased at Wedemeyer's appointment to China. He was an air-minded officer, thoroughly versed in air's potential and supportive of an aerial strategy. Perhaps more important, he was known for flexibility and a conciliatory approach as opposed to confrontation. There was hope that he could ease some of the bitterness that had come to dominate CBI relationships. Writing Roosevelt that he "could have chosen no better man," Chennault suppressed his personal disappointment and welcomed the change in command.[20] He was tired.

Before he reached China, Wedemeyer had been skeptical about Chennault. He wrote Marshall that, if Chennault's health were failing, as he had heard, advantage should be taken of it to remove him from the theater without damage to his splendid combat record. When the two men first met on 30 October, however, Wedemeyer found that Chennault's objectivity "contrasted strongly with my memory of Stilwell's diatribes against him." Chennault's deafness made his achievements seem the more remarkable.[21]

Over succeeding weeks, with Washington watching closely, Wedemeyer evaluated Chennault as cooperative and loyal, a doer who was intensely popular with his men and the Chinese: in short, "an intrepid leader, inspiring and enthusiastic."[22] After examining headquarters correspondence, he personally concluded that Stilwell and his staff had been hypercritical. He appointed a liaison officer between his own headquarters and Chennault's to improve coordination, which he found to be almost nil. Accepting Chennault's weak areas, he sought to help rather than aggravate. Deeming many of the staff personnel both in Chungking and Kunming painfully inadequate, he began replacing them. He intended to give Chennault broad objectives with complete latitude in execution, he explained, but he must have better coordination than seemed to have existed in the theater previously.[23]

Treated with respect, Chennault responded in kind. Within weeks an observer was reporting grand cooperation between the two, with "a fine spirit" evident in Kunming. To that point Chennault had known little of theater plans—not even of Stilwell's basic plan to rebuild thirty Chinese divisions. "I wasn't on the inside of things," Chennault said simply, and in retrospect it seems that many of the misunderstandings between him and Stilwell could have been avoided by less reserve and more communication on Stilwell's part. In any event, what might have been a disastrous command relationship between Wedemeyer and Chennault became one of openness and mutual support.[24]

The year ended with a gesture that was gratifying even though it had its ironic aspects. MATTERHORN operations had been a disappointment, and by the end of the year XX Bomber Command was being readied to move to Saipan. For six months Chennault had been advocating that the B-29s be used against the major Japanese base at Hankow. Although the request was consistently denied, he recommended in August that the target objectives for the Superforts be shifted from steel to counter-air force or that the planes be withdrawn from the theater.

Stratemeyer and Arnold suspected that Chennault wanted the raid on Hankow primarily because there was no other way he could make use of the MATTERHORN supplies, but it could not be denied that so far MATTERHORN had been a drain on the Fourteenth and had given it little help. Chennault had predicted that the cost of its operation from Chengtu would be prohibitive for the results obtained, and he was right. Now Wedemeyer asked that the B-29s be sent against Hankow, and Arnold consented. It was a choice target, for the Fourteenth had so thoroughly torn up Japanese transportation that Hankow was gorged with stalled supplies. MATTERHORN commander Maj. Gen. Curtis E. LeMay and Chennault planned a major coordinated effort, and when dubious staff officers began seeking excuses and expressing doubts that they could execute it, Chennault broke up a tense meeting with an impatient, "Oh, hell! Of course we can." The 18 December raid, one of the first with incendiary bombs, was a major success, even though some of the planes missed their elaborately timed bombing sequence.[25] Had it been conducted earlier, the outcome of ICHIGO would have been quite different.

Wedemeyer, adopting Chennault's own approach of being frank but courteous with Chiang, quickly brought into the open the business of supplying Hsueh Yueh. Both Chennault and Wedemeyer wanted to help Hsueh, for his armies were keeping the Japanese away from the eastern corridor containing Suichwan and Kanchow, where elements of the Fourteenth were still operating. When Hsueh requested guns and ammunition through Chennault, Wedemeyer consulted Chiang, who said Hsueh should go through channels. Chennault pursued the matter; Wedemeyer again discussed it with Chiang. When the Generalissimo insisted that no arms should go to Hsueh, Wedemeyer felt he had done all he could and suggested that Chennault tell Hsueh to appeal directly to Chiang. Hsueh was apparently reluctant to do so, for in January he made another request for arms through Chennault and someone in Chungking approved it.[26]

"Trying to conduct this show in a straightforward manner," Wedemeyer was afraid Chennault's efforts to supply Hsueh would cause trouble. U.S. policy was to support the existing government of China, he insisted, and this precluded going against the Generalissimo's wishes, whether or not they seemed wise. Eventually Hsueh, assisted by Chennault and his AGFRTS men, made his peace with the Generalissimo and thanked Chennault for his help. By the end of February the supplies were flowing, but it was too late. The Japanese had already forced the Fourteenth Air Force to evacuate Suichwan and Kanchow.[27]

The fronts began to stabilize in December. The Japanese held the railroad from Peking to Canton, but it had been badly torn up by the Fourteenth's planes and was of limited use. When they tried to establish aerial operations from Hengyang, an observer noted the Fourteenth "was on them like hounds on a fox." They abandoned aerial operations in the area after a classic battle in which Chennault sent the Twenty-third's fighters to lure the Japanese into aerial battle, then dealt the coup de grace with a devastating low-level strike by the CACW after the initial forces broke off to refuel. Chennault would have been pleased had he lived to see the U.S. Air Force create the Lt. Gen. Claire Lee Chennault Award for "the outstanding practitioner of the art of aerial warfare." He would have been doubly pleased to see it go in 1985 to a major who had stressed the development of tactical deception as a study within his command.[28]

On 28 January 1945 Chennault flew to Wanting to take part in the official ribbon cutting that opened the last lap of the Ledo Road. He had believed that the sky and the sea would break the blockade of China in less time and at less cost than the ground campaign to build the road, and his faith in aerial transport was vindicated by the ever-increasing tonnages that came over the Hump. It reached its peak performance of 46,545 tons in March. Because CBI was so dependent on supplies brought from outside, supply figures largely in the history of the theater. To keep matters in perspective, the tonnage reaching the Fourteenth Air Force in December 1944 (14,688 tons) was slightly more than that required by one infantry division in action, and the total amount of tonnage delivered to China throughout the war could have been transported in but seventy Liberty ships had a port been available.[29]

There was no time, however, for regrets. By the spring of 1945 the Fourteenth Air Force, including the CACW, had thirty-six combat squadrons and was freed from the need to protect MATTERHORN and support the Chinese armies. With planes, supplies, and a commanding general under whom he could work without rancor, Chennault approached the remaining months of the war with anticipation. If all went well, the Chinese and Americans would be on the offensive to regain eastern China by summer, and in the meantime he had the means to pursue his mission against Japanese shipping, which he still saw as "the most vulnerable part of the Japanese military organization."[30]

In the remaining months of the war, the antishipping campaign conducted by all U.S. Pacific naval and air forces reduced the Japanese military machine to helplessness. U.S. submarines played the major role. The Fourteenth flew sea searches from western China bases, and these were supplemented by planes from the Philippines, which MacArthur reclaimed. U.S. forces took Iwo Jima and then Okinawa, moving aircraft carriers and land-based planes ever farther into Japanese waters. Within China the Fourteenth's campaign against river shipping continued, the planes now flying from Chih-kiang, Laohokow, Ankang, and other bases at the eastern edges of unoccupied China.

Convinced that a determined campaign against Japanese supply lines and bases would "cut the Japanese down to Chinese size,"[31] Chennault focused on all Japanese transportation. It became harder and harder for Japanese forces in China to move men or supplies. When they attempted an offensive in April, the Chinese, well supported by the Fourteenth, halted it in a few weeks. In assessing their position, the Japanese concluded that, although their ICHIGO operations had captured the Allied air bases, "we checked the enemy's action only temporarily and were unable to strike a fatal blow."[32] By May they had begun to pull back from their forward positions in China.

With the beginning of 1945, the United States was entering its fourth full year of war; China was well into its eighth. China had paid a ghastly price in terms of human suffering and had proportionately lost status as a national entity. The unresolved civil wars, temporarily suspended to accommodate the danger from outside, were threatening to break out as Japan's defeat neared and conditions within China worsened. The Chinese had not been economically, industrially, politically, or psychologically prepared to play the role of a modern state waging modern warfare. When Wedemeyer first personally assessed their condition, he found them apathetic and confounded. Their major need, he concluded, was food.[33]

Thus far the United States had invested appreciable sums of money and no small effort in CBI as insurance against future needs: China's manpower to bear arms, its land mass as a base, its political allegiance as a Pacific ally. By 1945 the military reasons for supporting China seemed less essential: the loss of the eastern airfields meant that planes from China could not provide close support for the Pacific operations, which in any event were moving along rapidly without it. Just what, Wedemeyer asked Washington, was U.S. policy in China?

A White House staff paper prepared at about this time clearly shows that Roosevelt continued to base his China policy on strong support for Chiang Kai-shek, believing that "no other Chinese figure appeared to have so many of the elements of leadership or to offer so good a chance for cooperation with us." The most effective way to strengthen China was "to settle the disputes of her quarreling, fighting factions," and therefore the president determined to resolve the differences between Nationalists and Communists. Civil war was to be avoided.[34]

The answer given to Wedemeyer for guidance indicated that the United States' short-term objective was to unify all of China's resources for the war against Japan. The long-term goal was to help build a united, democratically progressive China cooperative to U.S. interests. U.S. military resources were to be applied against Japan, not in the suppression of civil war within China.[35]

Uniting China meant bringing Kuomintang and Communists together; a democratically progressive China meant governmental and social and economic reforms. The story of the United States and China from this point forward is primarily political. During 1945 Chennault played little part in it; he was still focused on inflicting military defeat upon Japan. He was aware, however, of the political problem and its awesome dimension; he had no doubts that for China the most important part of the struggle would begin after Japan's surrender. He was profoundly disturbed by the events of the summer of 1944, for as he saw them, "in China a situation was created in which attainment of the grand objective of American policy in the Far East—a strong, friendly and united China—had become all but impossible. The Generalissimo's government was undermined, militarily and politically." He personally believed that Stilwell had pursued this goal consciously, "for while the Generalissimo's government was vilified and left unaided in its hour of peril, theater staff carried on a sort of public love affair with the government at Yenan."[36]

Chennault was strongly anti-Russian and opposed to Communism as advocated by Moscow. Neither then nor later was his political philosophy sophisticated or complex. All his experience, however, gave him a gut conviction that communism was wrong—that it was an ideology based upon regimentation, that it was antiindividualism and anti-God. His relationships with the Russian air force during 1938 had impressed him with its iron discipline and the cold efficiency of its enlightened self-interest.[37] His thinking was further developed by Willauer, for the two became trusting friends, drawn together by their concern for China's future. While working on subversive activities in the Criminal Division of the Department of Justice in 1940,

Willauer had acquired "a keen awareness of the depth and ramifications of the Communist conspiracy" that greatly affected the way he interpreted the situation in China.[38]

Another glimpse into Chennault's thinking comes from Witold Urbanowicz, a Polish ace whom he met in Washington in 1943 and who subsequently spent some months (without pay or official status) flying with the Fourteenth Air Force. He and Chennault spent long hours in talk during the evenings. The tortured history of Poland and Russia was a frequent topic, and Chennault especially enjoyed hearing a tale about Tsarist times, when Jews were not allowed to live in Moscow without permission. As Urbanowicz told the story, one day a gendarme spotted two Jews on a street corner. The Jews saw him too. One of them had a permit to live in the city; the other did not. The one with the permit started to run away. The policeman followed, caught up with him, and asked for his permit. The man showed it. In the meantime the other Jew got away.

"Why were you running away when you have a permit?" demanded the gendarme.

"I am running for my health," the Jew replied.

"Why didn't you stop when I called you?" pursued the gendarme.

"Because I thought that you have the same doctor, and he prescribed running for you also."

The story appealed to Chennault's sense of humor, and he sometimes asked Urbanowicz to tell it to others, but in private he and his Polish friend dwelled on the topic of persecution and of Russia's past and present policies. Chennault had no illusions about Communist Russia's benevolence, to Jews or to anyone else.[39]

His feelings toward the Chinese Communists are less clear. His loyalty to Chiang was unwavering, and he had been with Chiang at some of the emotionally charged conferences at Nanking in 1937 when Chiang agreed to fight Japan provided the Chinese Communists would support the central government for the duration. The promise was given. Chennault seems to have accepted that the internal struggle was thus put on ice; he turned his attention to defeating Japan. Since the Chinese Communists held areas behind Japanese lines, their cooperation was important in gathering intelligence for air force targets and in rescuing downed pilots. Throughout the war, with Chiang's consent, Chennault worked with the Chinese Communists in rescue and intelligence, dealing with them in good faith, seeming to accept without difficulty that they were, at least temporarily, on the same side. He did not accept the opinions of some that the Communists were waging effective guerrilla warfare against the Japanese, however, and in his memoir he is scathing as he points out that during ICHIGO they stood by and watched, not even sabotaging the Japanese troop trains that moved through their territory. Chennault assessed them as more pro-Communist than pro-China.[40]

For some time there had been considerable speculation among Westerners as to what Chinese communism meant; both Moscow and Yenan denied an alliance between them. A subtle alignment had taken place which put the anti-Kuomintang and pro-Stilwell individuals in a faction that was supportive of the Chinese Communists, while the pro-Chiang, pro-Chennault believers saw Yenan as a threat. The more upset one was by the inadequacies and lack of democratic reform within the Kuomintang, the more likely one was to see the Communists in a positive light in contrast. In Washington in 1943, Stilwell had described the Chinese Communist as "a man who would like to see taxes reduced to where they are bearable and the legal rate of interest reduced to about 10 percent a month."[41] After correspondents were permitted to go to Yenan in early 1944, their positive reactions were reflected in the press, and the divisions became more pronounced.

At Fourteenth Air Force headquarters, the Chinese Communist issue was not a major consideration, but the portrayal of the Chinese Communists as "agrarian reformers" was considered nonsense; they were viewed as true Communists and ultimately a menace.[42] Chennault held that view more firmly than many, and it colored the way he reacted to Stilwell's decisions. He perceived that China's internal situation "is extraordinarily sensitive, at all times, to external pressures," and he saw many of Stilwell's actions as detrimental to Chiang's regime. Had "the more liberal and modern-minded Chinese" been encouraged to a position of predominance during the time when Yenan was still weak and Chungking was still strong, "the stage would have been set for a reconciliation." He firmly believed that Stilwell withheld support from the Chinese armies during the summer of 1944 in order to exert pressure on Chiang to give him command of all the Chinese military forces, including the Communist troops, and that this was a fatal blow to Chiang's regime.[43]

Twice in 1944 Chennault voiced his political concerns to Roosevelt, although he refrained from directly accusing Stilwell. In April, when Chinese-Russian tension flared up along the Sinkiang border, Chennault wrote that Soong and other influential Chinese (and by implication himself also) privately believed the episode was probably the first move in a "campaign to assert Russian influence in Asia—a campaign which would eventually take the form of a Russian attack on the Japanese in Manchuria, junction between the Russians and Chinese Communists in North China, and ultimate establishment of a Chinese Communist state or states in North China, Manchuria and perhaps Sinkiang. If this is indeed the Russian plan, the Chungking regime can hardly defeat it, and will have difficulty in surviving it, as the Chungking leaders well know."[44]

At the time that the letter was written, the Teheran conference and its spirit of U.S.-Russian cooperation prevailed in Washington. By the time Chennault again broached the subject to Roosevelt in September, serious reservations about Russia's postwar intentions had become more prevalent. Chennault himself was extremely discouraged about his own failure to halt the Japanese. While acknowledging with pain that the United States no longer controlled an area of China from which to strike the heart of Japan, he was more distressed over the damage done to China. Its military power, "never great," was nullified, the supplies now flowing were "too late," and he dwelled at length on the political implications. Widespread discontent was evident within that part of China controlled by Chungking, but "what is even more important, Chungking's loss of strength constitutes an equivalent gain for the regime at Yenan. Yenan will not only benefit by the change in the balance of power within China, but also by the penetration of East China by the Communist guerrillas based around Hankow, Shanghai and Canton." Chennault's own recommendations that the defeated Chinese forces be organized into guerrilla bands to counter the influence of the Communist guerrillas in the occupied areas made little headway, with the exception of limited activity by the OSS.[45]

Chennault's September letter went on to draw dire conclusions for the future. "At the worst, the Russians may choose to support Yenan, involving us in a contest in which, as the supporters of Chungking, we shall find ourselves at a decided disadvantage. Even if we refuse to become involved in such a contest, there is obviously grave danger of civil war in China. Furthermore, if there is civil war in China, the Yenan regime has an excellent chance of emerging victorious, with or without Russian aid."[46]

Chennault thought it was "too much to expect the Russians to resist the temptation to aid Yenan" in a civil war, and the establishment of a Chinese government closely tied to Moscow would upset the balance of power in the Pacific. The only way out, as he saw it, was "to sponsor thorough political reconstruction at Chungking, followed by true unification between Chungking and Yenan."[47]

Unification, or a coalition between Nationalists and Communists, had been advocated by Davies since 1943 as "mutually more beneficial" to all.[48] Chiang also desired peaceful unification between Kuomintang and Communists, although he was not prepared to give up control of the government to achieve it. Chiang too very definitely wanted peace between China and Russia. He was dependent on American help; he was willing to accept American guidance and encouraged Roosevelt to use his good offices. Roosevelt charged Hurley (who was named ambassador in October) with the appalling task of reconciling the differences between Chungking and Yenan, and in November Hurley journeyed to Sian.[49] Chennault saw this as a mistake, an act that would be interpreted as recognition of the Communists as a legal force within China. Recognition, he feared, would encourage them to hold out in expectation of stronger aid and consequently to reject "the spirit of practical compromise."[50]

Here Chennault's position took leave of that of Davies and the growing number of others who advocated unification. They believed that Chiang's government was beyond help and that the Communists should therefore be actively supported, to facilitate the war against Japan or to provide a viable government for China or as a means of making the best of the inevitable. That is, the Communists, the unificationists believed, would become the strongest group in China, and U.S. help now would align them with the West rather than with Russia.

Chennault was realistic about Kuomintang China, but he did not see the situation as beyond repair. In his September letter to Roosevelt, he stated in plain language what he saw to be the best approach. Basing his conclusions on his "long and close acquaintance with the Generalissimo and his subordinates," Chennault warned that reconstruction and unification "will have to be done through the Chinese themselves. It can *only* be done by the persuasion and pressure of American representatives whom the Chinese leaders respect and trust, and it *cannot* be done by any attempt to reduce the Chinese to a condition of military or political tutelage." He saw it as a difficult task that would require absolute priority if it were to succeed.[51]

The negotiations between the Chinese Nationalists and Communists, with Hurley trying valiantly to believe in the good faith of all, were still going on when Roosevelt met Stalin at Yalta in February

1945. Chiang had not been invited; the European war, then winding down, was the major topic. Almost as a sidelight, Roosevelt and Stalin made agreements of import for the future of Sino-Soviet relationships. These were held secret at the time, but whatever Roosevelt's intentions may have been with regard to further personal influence, they came to an end with his death on 12 April. Well before then he had become gravely worried over the evolving shape of Russian-Western relationships, for the war was ending with little assurance that the peace would be secure.

Roosevelt's death hurt Chennault deeply. "My sense of loss was especially keen," he wrote Mrs. Roosevelt, "since he had shown me rare kindness and understanding."[52]

"My husband had a very special regard for you," she responded, "and we often spoke of you and your remarkable work."[53]

17

"Nobody can hurt you
except you yourself "

Germany's defeat was near as 1945 opened, but Allied planners could not yet see the end of the war against Japan. To the contrary, Japan's tenacious resistance at every point fed fears that it might resist to the last man, both in China and in its home islands. The intensive strategic bombardment by the B-29s, having gotten off to a slow start, was only beginning; its effects could not be foretold. The atomic bomb was still a secret known to very few, and even those few had no assurance it would work. There was no reliable way to assess the economic strangulation being caused by the campaign against merchant shipping. Plans had to be made to meet all possible contingencies. At the same time, the military forces in Europe could now gradually be transferred to the Pacific. Given these conditions, Wedemeyer and Stratemeyer drafted plans for the China theater.

They outlined a campaign that would start with the recapture of the Luichow area, would open Canton and Hong Kong, and would prepare the China coast for an Allied landing in case one was needed. It was the basic plan that Chennault had urged upon Wedemeyer, with one important addition. The Tenth Air Force, no longer needed in Burma, would be transferred to China to operate as the tactical air force. The Fourteenth would become a strategic force. Command of the combined Tenth and Fourteenth would be given to Stratemeyer.[1]

Once more Chennault was being ignored as a candidate for ranking air officer in China. He resented the personal slap, but he was even more upset over the basic plan of putting two air forces in China. The logistical foundation in China barely supported one air force, he insisted. Bringing in a second was neither justified nor necessary. When Wedemeyer went to Washington in March to work out details, he took along a colonel from Chennault's staff to present his views, but they were countered by assurances from the War Department that the Hump would be augmented by additional C-54s from Europe. A subtle power struggle between the air forces and the army was taking place in the background, for the airmen wanted to make certain that they retained a sizable proportion of postwar army appropriations. It would not do to disband any aerial units before the Pacific war was ended. The plan was approved.[2]

Back in China, Wedemeyer discussed the Washington decisions "frankly and completely" with Chennault. Their conversation was long and thoughtful. For the first time, many of the barriers that had come to exist between Chennault and the War Department were brought into the open and discussed. Although Chennault felt he was being eased out and said so, he assured Wedemeyer he held no personal resentment; he would carry on in any assigned role as long as his health permitted. Wedemeyer sensed no bitterness as Chennault reflected on the many problems he had encountered in working with his higher command. Most of them, Chennault believed, stemmed from his sincere efforts to get on with the war. Looking back on his relationships with Stilwell, Bissell, and their staffs, he concluded that the trouble was probably caused by their lack of appreciation of the complex problems in China which he could more easily perceive.[3]

Chennault expressed surprise that his behavior had been considered disloyal; the thought had never occurred to him that it might be so interpreted. He had not intended to circumvent Stilwell by writing directly to Roosevelt; he had been asked to write, and he simply complied. When Wedemeyer said he would have urged him to go through Marshall to correspond with the president, Chennault agreed that it would doubtless have been wiser to do so. As for Alsop, whose presence and actions had been deeply resented by the War Department, Chennault regarded him as a patriotic American doing what he thought best for his country. Alsop's personal letters to Hopkins, which had so angered Marshall, had ended when Alsop was commissioned and was no longer a civilian. Chennault insisted that neither he nor Alsop had ever indulged in the intrigue with the Chiangs against Stilwell of which the War Department had suspected them. [4]

Wedemeyer quietly defended Chennault when he wrote Marshall about their conversation. He expressed confidence that Alsop and Chennault were not intriguing against him, confidence that Chennault was not disloyal to him in any way. On the contrary, he sensed "full cooperation and coordination" between their headquarters; Chennault resisted openly when he disagreed with a matter, but once Wedemeyer made a decision, it was obeyed without question. During his absence for the Washington trip, Chennault had carried on the theater policies "loyally and effectively. . . . I cannot in fairness fail to register my complete satisfaction with his fine work."[5] Marshall was unmoved. He wanted Stratemeyer to command in China.

The change did not take place smoothly. The War Department was unable to assign the extra C-54s for the Hump, and when Wedemeyer's staffs reassessed the logistical problems in China, they agreed with Chennault's view, earlier voiced, that another complete air force could not be supported at that time. Wedemeyer asked Stratemeyer if he were willing to come to China to command a smaller force than originally contemplated. Stratemeyer said no. Instead he suggested that the obvious personnel problems might be solved by sending all three of the "old men"—himself, Chennault, and Davidson (commanding the Tenth Air Force)—back to the United States. Wedemeyer was reluctant to take so drastic a step. He told Washington the whole plan was being restudied; he told Chennault that the Fourteenth would be augmented and he would command the expanded force.[6]

During these months Chennault was once again plagued with accusations that reflected on his personal character. Toward the end of 1944, news of the persistent and pervasive smuggling taking place in CBI broke in the press. There were reports of a smuggling ring that had taken $4 million since 1942; 87 major cases and 213 minor ones were under investigation. A wide range of persons was implicated—American servicemen, CNAC and Red Cross civilians, former AVG.[7] About the same time a squadron of Chinese pilots was sent to Karachi to ferry some planes back to China. Before the planes left Karachi, an inspector found contraband stuffed in the plane's nose; upon further inspection, the space under the floor proved to be filled as well. The planes were detained and were stripped of some $300,000 worth of drugs, gold, and valuables. Among those retained for questioning was a man who had worked with Chennault in Kunming in

1938–39 teaching radio communications to the CAF cadets; he was on this mission as the radio man. The Criminal Investigation Division suspected him of being a key figure in the smuggling syndicate; his wife was "known" to be the fence. Chennault was notified.[8]

Chennault had already started trying to clear the AVG's name. "We had some rough characters in the AVG," he wrote Lt. Gen. Daniel Sultan, who had become commanding general of the India-Burma theater upon Stilwell's recall, "but I am proud of the group's record and see no reason why its reputation should be unnecessarily blackened." Now he did what he could to help the accused man and his family, for bonds of friendship and loyalty had been forged by mutual endeavor during those days before the United States began openly to support China.[9]

The accused soon reported that during the interrogations about his own involvement, the investigating officers not only insinuated that Chennault's conduct with the accused's wife had been improper, but that Chennault himself was the leader of the smuggling ring. The implications were ugly, and Chennault was furious. The behind-the-hand talk was more damaging than any open accusation, and he wanted it stopped. One of Wedemeyer's staff officers recalled that the only time Wedemeyer and Chennault exchanged heated words was over this episode, for Chennault wanted to be court-martialed, to be tried openly so he could establish his innocence.[10]

Wedemeyer refused. He assured Chennault that as the commanding general he would not hesitate to act, even against his own brother, if evidence warranted it, but he firmly believed that no evidence would be found against Chennault to justify a court of inquiry. He had found that the complaints about prostitutes and other illegal activities in the theater were often gross exaggerations. In May Lt. Gen. Ira C. Eaker, then deputy commander, U.S. Army Air Forces, visited China and spent a few days with Chennault in Kunming. Afterward he wrote Wedemeyer a personal letter suggesting that Chennault was tired and would happily return to the States if he were officially cleared of the intimations of misconduct. Nevertheless Wedemeyer continued to feel that it would be unwise to make the matter public. His advice to Chennault was to forget it.[11]

It was not the last time that Chennault would be plagued with veiled accusations and insinuations of wrongdoing. Willauer interpreted it as the groundwork for a campaign of character assassination conducted by the Communists. He noted that, while an extensive investigation revealed "not a shred of evidence," the very fact of investigation was later used to substantiate the accusations.[12] His point of view gains credence when considered alongside testimony given at congressional hearings in 1951, when others confirmed that during 1944–45 the Chinese Communists wanted Chennault out of the picture in China. Not only was his opposition to communism well known to be "violent and emphatic," but he was an important figure in the relationships between the United States and Nationalist China.[13]

Wedemeyer was in an unenviable position. He respected Chennault as a fighter and leader of men; their relationship had been one of openness and trust. Stratemeyer would make a more appropriate theater air commander, but Wedemeyer felt that, if Chennault was to be asked to leave China, the request must come from Washington. He was not inclined to be the hatchet man.[14]

In June, Arnold made a trip to the Pacific. He conferred with Stratemeyer in Manila, afterward writing a letter to Wedemeyer which Stratemeyer delivered. Arnold's letter made it clear that Chennault must be replaced. Wedemeyer was asked, pointedly, to reevaluate his situation and "create conditions" that would permit the air force in India to move into China. As Arnold put it, the war in China was changing to "a modern type of striking, offensive air power" rather than the defensive guerrilla air war which Chennault had waged with minimum resources. There was now a need for "a senior, experienced air officer, in whom both you and I have confidence." He thought Stratemeyer was best qualified to lead this new war of movement. "I firmly believe that the quickest and most effective way to change air warfare in your Theater, employing modern offensive thought, tactics and techniques, is to change commanders. I would appreciate your concurrence in General Chennault's early withdrawal from the China Theater. He should take advantage of the retirement privileges now available to physically disqualified officers."[15]

At the same time Marshall wrote Wedemeyer asking why the change had not yet been made. Wedemeyer answered both men by saying he concurred fully with Arnold's recommendations and would organize the China air forces with Stratemeyer as commanding general, Chennault head of the strategic forces, and Davidson head of the tactical forces. This was not exactly what Arnold had requested.[16]

When Chennault was notified, he found it hard to believe. He wired Wedemeyer repeating his opinion that it would be impossible to support additional air units in China before 1946. As he saw it, the plan called for the establishment of three air headquarters to do the work of one and "is not sound from an operational standpoint." He said he was "not clear whether this is in accord with your desires." When Wedemeyer's staff replied that they were sure Wedemeyer understood the implications, Chennault could no longer avoid the painful conclusion: neither Marshall nor Arnold had confidence in him.[17]

He expressed his feelings in a very long letter dated 6 July. It was drafted by Alsop and was addressed to Wedemeyer.

> There is no military reason for the establishment of additional air headquarters in China. We cannot now support the air units we have. We cannot support additional air units for a very long time to come. When this was demonstrated some weeks ago, you decided to abandon previous plans and leave our air command structure unchanged. The fact that General Marshall and General Arnold now desire changes, can only be taken as reflecting personally upon me. I was retired from the Army for physical disability eight years ago. I accepted active duty in China because of a desire to contribute my services in this war. This is still my thought, but I shall not be useful at Chengtu, where I shall merely supersede one of my own Wing Commanders who is performing his duties in a conspicuously satisfactory manner. It has been indicated that my present job can be better done by another man. I therefore propose to request retirement a second time as soon as the transition to the new organization has been accomplished.[18]

Having stated his intent, Chennault went on to address "certain things which must be recorded." Wedemeyer accepted Chennault's request for retirement and asked him to stay on the job through the transition to a new commander. His letter, however, he considered to be full of "bitter denunciations and vitriolic statements." He advised Chennault not to submit it. Chennault took the letter back and reconsidered. Alsop advised him to send it on, in part because by pointing out serious areas of mismanagement within the theater that the War Department would be loath to have publicized, it would make them more likely to drop the relatively minor charges against Chennault.[19]

Chennault accepted his advice and gave the letter to Wedemeyer again, this time with the addition of enclosures. He had carefully documented his statements, and he asked that the letter and supporting documentation be accepted. He adamantly opposed Wedemeyer's repeated advice that the correspondence not be sent on. He wanted the record clarified. He felt that he had not been treated fairly until Wedemeyer's arrival in the China theater; he acknowledged that he had not gotten along with Stilwell and his officers, but he believed those officers were also disliked by everyone else in China. He felt he had been dealt a crooked deal.[20]

Chennault expressed his hope that a complete record would one day be compiled, that a final judgment would be reached after a thorough testing of all the evidence. He said the suspicions about his personal probity were founded in untruth and nurtured by malice; he would endeavor to disprove them. He said he felt he was being blamed for Stilwell's failure as a theater commander and emissary to Chiang Kai-shek, but he could not assist someone by whom he was ignored, and Stilwell's own arrogance, self-righteousness, and open contempt for the Chinese leaders played a role. He thought Bissell must be held responsible for many of the early failures of the Hump airlift and that theater staff placed obstacles in the way of the ELOC and choked the forces in eastern China during the summer of 1944. He thought the strategy of a Burma campaign to restore ground communications with China, and the priority Stilwell gave to it, meant failure for the aerial strategy Roosevelt had charged him to implement. He thought careful study would have disclosed that the road could not conceivably pay adequate returns for the enormous investment it required.[21]

He defended Chiang Kai-shek, saying his "position with respect to the Burma campaign has always seemed to me unexceptionable. He argued that, if there were no landing to sever the Japanese Lines of Communication in South Burma, the campaign would prove both long and costly; and that he could not jeopardize China's internal defense by committing his slender resources to a campaign of this type. . . . It is difficult for me to understand the charges of bad faith which were so freely hurled at the Generalissimo. He never wavered from the same position, which General Stilwell must surely have understood."[22]

Chennault also expressed his belief that Stilwell's policies had undermined Chiang's government, with frightening implications for the future: "we may now be confronted with a choice between total abandonment of the American interests in the Far East or a naked contest for influence in this area between the United States and the Soviet Union. If that choice is forced upon us, it will hardly matter which of the two evils we select; either will probably mean that all the titanic efforts and enormous expenditures of this war have not been enough to assure a lasting peace."[23]

The month that elapsed between Chennault's request for retirement and his departure from China was a hard one. He was angry to have been pushed out, but as Alsop put it, "he didn't go in much for being bitter." Chennault had sometimes told Trumble, "Nobody in the world can hurt you except you yourself."[24] He must have believed this, must have realized in the final analysis that he had made free choices, that it was to some extent his own actions, his own independence and outspokenness and political maneuvering that had brought the ruin of his Air Corps career. He had trouble, however, in making the admission, even to himself. Now, more than ever before, he saw failure as not of his making but rather the result of intentional misunderstanding, of forces he did not want to accept that operated against him. He wrestled internally to accept what was happening to him. He continued to struggle, to protest, especially at the War Department's choice of a general inexperienced in China to replace him.[25] The pictures taken during these weeks show a tight and haunted look on his face, although his public utterances betrayed neither bitterness nor anger.

The official reason given for his request to retire was his health. Under direct questioning by correspondents, Chennault implied that he was leaving because his mission of defeating the Japanese Air Force in China was completed. There was considerable speculation in the press as to what was going on behind the scenes. Noting that Chennault himself loved China and felt deep regret at leaving, a Chinese newspaper suggested that "he is not leaving China completely out of his own accord" but rather was using a traditional and well understood Chinese excuse.[26] The United States suspected high-level army politics. One senator said he had been given a "raw deal" and had been discriminated against because he was not a West Point graduate; others speculated that he had been eased out in response to pressure from the Chinese Communists. Louisiana Senator Allen Ellender called for an investigation by the U.S. Senate Military Affairs Committee, which was assured by the War Department that only purely military considerations were involved. Chennault himself told newsmen he did not seek "any investigation or row."[27]

In China there were banquets and tributes, gifts, and an emotional outpouring of appreciation. The airfield at Kunming was renamed in his honor; the head of China's Ministry of War wrote a poem. From all sides came assurances that "the security you have given our cities in the southwest and the support you have given our armies in the field" would be remembered; the Chinese people were "wordless in their grief to see you go."[28]

In Chungking Chiang bestowed the Blue Sky and White Sun award on Chennault; Wedemeyer pinned a second oak leaf cluster to his Distinguished Service Cross. When he left the city the crowds so completely engulfed his car that the driver turned off its motor, allowing the people to push him to the airport in an emotional tribute he never forgot.[29]

There were letters: a short handwritten note from Field Marshal Wavell in gratitude for "the magnificent effort your pilots made to save Rangoon" and admiration "for all you have done . . . in these last four years"; a long and emotional letter from Chou reflecting on their relationship and promising to continue the work they had begun to build a Chinese Air Force.[30]

He climbed aboard *Six Bits*, the Gooney Bird in which his old friend Luke Williamson had piloted him around China during the last few years, and toured his outlying bases to say goodbye. At Kiangsi he gave his sword belt to Hsueh Yueh. The two generals had not met before, but their lives had been interwoven in ways that only fighting men understand, and as they walked toward each other the emotions of their long struggles and disappointments welled up in each. The "Little Tiger" and the "Big Tiger" embraced with wet eyes, for they shared an unspoken understanding of something the Chinese describe as "eating bitterness."[31]

"The time has come when I must request relief as Your Excellency's Chief of Air Staff," he wrote to Chiang Kai-shek. "Mine has been an active and sometimes a fruitful career, yet there is nothing I have done, no honor that has been accorded me, of which I am more proud than Your Excellency's selection of me as one fitted for responsibility." He reflected on their eight years of memorable association, through good times and bad. "It is with heartfelt regret, therefore, that I lay down my duties and say farewell to China. I shall never lose my love of China and the Chinese people, or my recollection of Your Excellency's great leadership. We have fought a good fight together, and I am only sorry that we cannot be together in victory." Chiang accepted his resignation "with much pathos."[32]

Chennault's orders relieved him from assignment in China effective 1 August 1945. He was en route home, via the Middle East and Europe, when the atomic bombs fell and Japan surrendered. "I wanted to see it through," he wrote one of his fellow China hands, "but not on the terms offered me."[33]

18

CAT and the Civil War

There was little doubt in Claire Chennault's mind but that he would go back to China. Chinese acceptance of his worth seemed doubly valuable when juxtaposed against rejection by his own country, although gradually he was coming to terms with the latter. "You can never turn back the pages of time and correct anything that was done the year before," he said some years later. A situation lost could not be salvaged; a man had "to do something new, something constructive in the present day."[1]

There were other reasons too. He was not yet through; his ambition was not quenched. He wanted to be part of what was happening, to enjoy the power of implementing his own ideas. Such opportunity was unlikely in the United States, much more likely in China, a vast land on the threshold of modern development, a land where he knew both the people and the circumstances, a receptive land that had accorded him honor and recognition, where he could integrate his abilities with his emotional needs. The idealistic yearning was still present; the instincts of the warrior who serves a noble cause still surged within him and demanded a means of expression. In confi-

dence he told some of his Chinese friends he hoped to come back and
devote the rest of his life to serving China.[2]

It was obvious, late in 1945, that China needed a friend. In 1937
Chiang had been held in unrealistic esteem; now scathing criticism
rained down upon him and his regime. Loyal, undaunted, ever willing to put his weight with the minority and in disagreement with the
condemnation, Chennault insisted at a news conference, "The
Chinese government and Chinese armies are no more faultless than
any other government or armies." He enumerated the difficulties the
Chinese had confronted, possessing almost none of the resources of
modern warfare yet called upon to stave off the exhaustion of a long,
cruel fight. Where others saw failure, he saw courage, patience, and
resistance under conditions that would have caused most peoples to
lose heart. He reminded others that China had been in the war first,
its richest territory occupied, its wealth expropriated, its people
starved and oppressed by the enemy and the blockade.[3]

He did not place the blame for China's present plight on Chiang's
shortcomings; instead he acknowledged "deep admiration" for the
Generalissimo's "unwavering courage, wise foresight, and loyalty to
the cause for which we all fight." It was time that "Americans ceased
to be so concerned by the mote in our neighbor's eye" and remembered the immense debt we owed to China, he said.[4]

His mind was in a turmoil as he tried to assimilate meaning from
the events of his nine years in China, his alliances with Roosevelt
and Chiang, his confrontations with the War Department, his associations with his men, and the fights they had waged together. In
some respects he had been used, betrayed, and exploited as a willing
pawn to achieve the ends of others, even though in his eagerness to
fight and to be part of the power structure he had been more than
willing to play his various roles. But with the AVG he had assumed
leadership of an undercover military activity in violation of neutrality laws, only to have it taken away once the need for secrecy had
passed. With the aerial offensives he had put his neck on the block to
achieve ends Roosevelt sought, only to be denied the means to
achieve success as measured by his profession. Chiang as well as the
War Department had deserted him during the summer of 1944, but at
least Chiang had understandable reasons. His own country had
turned him out once it was no longer necessary to scrounge and improvise and create success from one's own determination.

During a stop in Palestine en route home, Chennault had found himself comparing the oppression of the Jews with that of the Chinese. Freedom was what it was all about—freedom to live and believe and love and fight and fulfill the hungers that drove a man. As he pondered freedom's importance, to peoples as well as to individuals, he focused ever more intently on advancing communism and the threat he perceived therein for a free way of life. By September he was convinced "it is my duty to continue the fight."[5] Just what way he could find to do this was the main thing on his mind during the closing months of 1945, quiet months of public appearances and private negotiations.

He was reunited with most of his family in his favorite city of New Orleans, which gave him a gratifying reception: a parade with an umbrella of B-25s and P-51s overhead, followed by a banquet at the Roosevelt Hotel. It pleased him that events were supervised by Vincent, who had earned his rank of general under Chennault's tutelage. Afterward Chennault went to Lake St. John, but he did not tarry. By the end of September he was in Washington, settled into a room at the Statler and working on plans for his future. Louisiana politicians wanted him; he briefly considered running for the Senate as the Huey Long organization's candidate, but he found politics "more of a puzzle to me than Japanese tactics," and he turned the offer down, content to support Noe in fighting such a battle. To friends he made his goals clear: he wanted to work with something in which he could exercise control and make some money, something that offered a stable future but most of all something that would benefit China.[6]

China was in trouble. Japan's August surrender found Chiang Kaishek's regime tottering amid internal decay and economic collapse. Civil war seemed inevitable, and determined not to be drawn into it, the United States sought a postwar China policy that would avoid military involvement but would at the same time make it possible to maintain an American presence in China and influence events in favor of the Nationalists. Lend-lease aid continued under various guises; the wartime army training program was replaced by a military advisory group. The tentative beginnings of the new relationship flipped upside down in November, when Ambassador Hurley, who had made scant progress in getting Kuomintang and Communists into a coalition government, resigned and raised an enormous ruckus, asserting that part of the problem was State Department personnel who supported the Chinese Communists at Kuomintang expense. An amused Chennault, who had long thought that neither army nor State Department personnel in China gave Chiang's government the moral or tangible support it deserved, was glad to see the issue out in the open.[7]

But the Chennault the public saw and heard during these months was less the outspoken warrior and more the quiet, reflective figure. When he shared the podium in Carnegie Hall with Chiang and President Harry S. Truman on the Double Tenth, the thirty-fourth anniversary of the Chinese revolution, his handwritten speech revealed the high-minded idealism behind his more usual pugnaciousness. "Throughout all the ages recorded by history, men have fought and died so that other men could be free. . . . Freedom is not a word, but an ideal and a faith, in English or Chinese or any other language. Freedom is a light which beckons men upward and onward from the degradation of slavery to the heights which rightfully belong to beings created in the image of God." He went on to trace the story of China's revolution, and especially the years of war with Japan, with some sense of the drama of Chinese history, concluding that it was fitting to honor a nation and people "who have preserved their freedom at the cost of unbelievable suffering and the blood of millions of citizens."[8]

On another occasion he gave a somewhat dry but informative lecture about the language and geography and culture of China. He prefaced his talk with the statement that there was a lot of misinformation about China and concluded with a pregnant promise: "The China of tomorrow will be different."[9]

The date of his official retirement from the U.S. Army was 31 October, and to mark it New York's Mayor Fiorello LaGuardia held a little ceremony on the steps of city hall. This was arranged with Corcoran's help. Having played an important role in thrusting Chennault into the unique position he had held during the war, Corcoran now thought the airman had been shabbily used by the administration; he reacted by becoming even more staunchly supportive than before.[10] Corcoran may have suggested that Chennault try his hand, during his first two months as a civilian, at lecturing. In return for stipends that ranged from $600 (a recreation and wildlife club) to $2,500 (the Long Island Zionist Region), he traveled across the country and told the story of the AVG. The idea had been with Madame and the Generalissimo for some years, he said. He made no sweeping claims, for himself or the group, but he did point out that, at a time when the Japanese were everywhere else successful, the AVG alone was undefeated. It overcame its obstacles, he said, by "ingenuity, courage and plain hard work."[11]

His public utterances might be calm, but deep inside Claire Chennault was downright mad. He thought the United States was bungling its relations with China; he felt he personally had been wronged. There were some things he had to get off his chest. He asked Robert Hotz, who had been the Fourteenth Air Force's historical officer, to help him write his memoirs. He was taken aback to realize the complexity of the task; he had thought they could do it quickly and be done with it. They spent some time on a houseboat on a Louisiana river, relaxed with fishing poles and friends, and got the project under way.[12]

Behind the scenes a commercial airline in China was emerging. The Cold War rivalry between Communist and non-Communist nations had begun to shape world politics, and it was obvious to all that improved transport would be essential to any modernization or recovery of postwar China. The two facts complemented one another. Wedemeyer pointedly advised the War Department that China desperately needed help in developing both military and commercial aviation. If the United States did not fill the role, he warned, others would. There was considerable speculation that Chennault would head Chiang's postwar CAF. Indeed, in his July letter to Chennault, Chiang had requested that he "continue to give me assistance from time to time in the expansion of the Chinese Air Force," but there is no evidence in Chennault's papers of additional negotiation on the matter.[13]

Before leaving Kunming, however, Chennault had talked with Governor Lung Yun and some Chinese businessmen who wanted him to set up a Yunnan-based airline. Yunnan's greatest resource for modern development was tin. By hauling Yunnan tin to ports in Indochina and returning with tourists and general merchandise, an airline would link the isolated province to the outside world and would bring it a measure of prosperity as well as independence from Chiang's central government—something important to Lung Yun, who had begun to lose patience with Chiang and advocated a China united under a constitution guaranteeing home rule to local governments. Chennault drafted tentative plans before he left China, but the project died aborning when the feud between Lung Yun and Chiang reached a rude climax. Central government forces took control in Yunnan; Lung lost all power.[14]

Chennault had not been alone, however, in envisioning airlines in China. Whiting Willauer, who had enjoyed his wartime experiences there, was also looking for something to do, something that offered adventure, a sense of accomplishment, and the possibility of making enough money that he could later afford to work in government, doing "important international things." He and three of his former associates in China Defense Supplies, Thomas and David Corcoran and William Youngman, formed Rio Cathay, S.A., a company for creating business ventures in South America and China. Willauer was especially interested in a commercial airline in China, and after Rio Cathay contracted with Pennsylvania Central Airlines for him to make a preliminary study of the feasibility, he asked Chennault to join Rio Cathay and take part. Chennault agreed, and Pennsylvania Central put up enough money to cover the initial efforts of both men.[15]

"I don't know whether Gen. Chennault or I got the idea first," Willauer stated later. "I think we really got it simultaneously." They had become "fast friends and fellow workers" through their earlier work in China, and "it seemed a natural thing for us, with our mutual love for China, to return to China together to try to help in the reconstruction of that vast country."[16]

Chennault returned to China early in January 1946. It is possible that he had some form of official blessing. As had been the case at times in the past, there were shadows in the corners that are hard to define, among them meetings with OSS personnel who provided film and filters and pointedly wished him success with his future plans. His departure from San Francisco was classed "secret" by the Air Transport command. He himself asked that no statements be given out, and two weeks later the papers noted that he had slipped into Chungking as a private citizen, quietly, unobtrusively, almost unobserved. Writer John Hersey observed that Chennault, still wearing his uniform and "beloved by the Chinese people, is in their country on an unannounced mission."[17]

Willauer had preceded Chennault to China and set up headquarters at the Cathay Hotel in Shanghai. Together they began a survey trip, Chennault's special relationships with the Chinese helping to open doors and obtain the information they needed. They managed to do some of their thinking and talking while hunting in the hills around Chungking and Kunming. Willauer, thirteen years Chennault's junior, found the general "a tough old bird" who thought nothing of tramping over the mountains at 8,000 feet for five hours at a clip and was still a good shot—he bagged twenty-five teal and six doves to Willauer's four and six. The stalking, Willauer wrote his wife, was the most exciting part. "You crawl on your stomach for a distance which varies from a hundred yards to half a mile. Some exercise."[18]

A man hunts with only his closest friends, and during those weeks the two men—so different, yet so alike—forged a firm partnership based on trust, mutual understanding, and a genuine liking and respect for one another. Their talents supplemented and complemented rather than conflicted: Chennault the down-to-earth, fire-from-the-hip fighter, at his best leading strong men in challenging action; Willauer the Ivy League, sophisticated organizer and administrator, with a broad picture of the economic and political situation of the entire Orient. Both men had low boredom thresholds. Both thrived on overcoming obstacles and were not above doing so by questionable means if circumstances warranted. Both were able to accept the Chinese way. Most important, both men saw advancing communism as a very real threat, a danger to be fought.

Their survey confirmed what they already knew: China was in desperate need of transport. Food was scarce. The little that was available was not moving into the cities, where people were starving. Famine was spreading in Hunan; there was imminent threat of plague. The area freed from Japanese occupation was comparable in size to Axis-occupied Europe, but the population was larger (approximately 260 million) and the occupation had been longer. The six-year blockade had ended when Japan surrendered, but although supplies sent by the United Nations Relief and Rehabilitation Administration were pouring into Shanghai by November, cargo soon piled up on the docks because there was no way to move it inland. The few rail lines that remained operable were jammed with displaced persons—an estimated five to ten million of them—trying to return home. The limited aerial transport was unreliable and was squeezing—heavily; at Kunming 50,000 were on the passenger waiting list. River transport, China's mainstay, was scarce because of the shortage of boats.[19]

The same problems had been perceived by Ralph Olmstead, who studied China's situation in the fall of 1945 and returned to China in February as UNRRA's director of operations. His task was to get the supplies moving. The largest single item on China's request for UNRRA aid had been equipment and materials for improving transport, and Olmstead recommended that transport—air, water, and highways—be given top UNRRA priority. On 6 February he asked Chennault and Willauer to draft a proposal for a relief airline.[20]

With only twenty-four hours in which to devise a plan, the two men worked feverishly to design an unusual airline. Their proposal called for UNRRA to advance to its Chinese agency CNRRA (Chinese National Relief and Rehabilitation Administration) the funds to purchase surplus war transport planes and form CNRRA Air Transport (quickly shortened to CAT). CNRRA would pay freight on the hauling of relief goods, although at a lower rate than existing commercial lines; CAT planes returning from the interior could haul refugees, raw materials, or commercial cargo if the space was not needed by CNRRA. Chennault and Willauer would provide operating capital and run the airline; they would have to absorb any loss the airline might sustain, but they would hold an option to purchase the planes at cost plus 10 percent.[21]

Olmstead recommended that the proposal be adopted, but what Chennault and Willauer had conceived in a day Chinese and American bureaucracy took eight months to accept. The "relief" airline posed competition for the small, government-operated air carriers already in China: CNAC and CATC (China Air Transport Company, part of the CAF). Pan American Airways, which owned a 20 percent interest in CNAC, insisted that no additional aerial transport was needed and fought with no holds barred. UNRRA officials also hesitated, seeking ways to bypass CNRRA because the Chinese were diluting its humanitarian goals by exploiting it as a vast source of political patronage.[22]

In the meantime Willauer worked on forming a Far East Company to handle the export problems and business in the States, while Chennault and some Chinese business associates began forming Sino-American Company, which would find cargo in China's interior for transport to Shanghai or Canton and eventual export. New to the business world, Chennault learned the hard way. Hoping to make some money to apply to the airline, he joined some Chinese investors to purchase a Canadian corvette, the *Frontenac*, which was loaded with cargo needed in China and began the voyage to Shanghai. The ill-fated venture highlighted not only his lack of business expertise but also his sometimes misplaced confidence in friends, for the individual put in charge of the venture, the same prewar buddy who had been investigated on smuggling charges in 1945, proved inadequate for the challenge. The ship, in poor condition after war service and being laid up afterward, suffered successive breakdowns. Almost none of the original investment was recovered when both ship and cargo were sold for salvage before they ever reached Shanghai. With SINAMCO also Chennault had problems: one of the Chinese participants turned out to be a crook and manipulator who exploited Chennault's name for his own advancement.[23]

During the weeks that Chennault and Willauer waited for an UNRRA decision, China's situation continued to worsen. At one time shipments of relief supplies had to be halted until ports could be cleared. It was apparent the CNRRA airline was needed. New York's Mayor LaGuardia was head of UNRRA and also a supporter of China, a friend of Corcoran, and an admirer of Chennault. Initially opposed to the CAT plan, he yielded to Corcoran's skillful pressure and said UNRRA would agree if the Chinese requested it. Chennault and Willauer had lunch with Madame, who promised her full cooperation. They obtained the backing of Soong and Chou (still head of the Commission on Aeronautical Affairs) and other important government officials. Still others were opposed. China was not only sensitive to potential foreign exploitation—abolition of the unequal treaties of extraterritoriality had been one of the few positive benefits she had gained from the war—but there was money to be made, legitimately as well as through patronage and graft and misuse of the CNRRA funds, practices that were unfortunately an established part of Chinese business patterns.[24]

The political maneuvering was complex and fast-paced. With skill and not a little boldness, Willauer negotiated with a certainty he did not always feel; confidential communications with Corcoran in Washington were slow, and the status of their financial backing was uncertain. Chennault's special status as a trusted friend of China was a key factor in wearing down the Chinese opposition, but he did not enjoy the process. Business and politics were not his forte. Willauer thought the general "dropped the ball badly" on two occasions during the infighting, and Chennault himself began to fret at the talking and indecision. He craved action. The general was seeing Chinese politics at its worst, Willauer noted, and obviously he did not enjoy the dirty side of commercialism. When the stress began to take its toll on his health as well as on his disposition, Willauer found himself assuming the role earlier played by Alsop: he had to keep the general from throwing in the sponge.[25] Their cause was helped in the press by a young newspaperwoman named Anna Chan, who had covered Chennault and the Fourteenth Air Force for the China News Agency during the latter years of the war and took a personal as well as professional interest in the general's plans.

In April, after Chennault had had a personal talk with Chiang, the CAT partners reached a tentative agreement with the Chinese government. Pennsylvania Central Airlines had by then decided not to participate in the venture; in May Chennault returned to the States to raise money. He found businessmen skeptical, understandably reluctant to invest in a high-risk enterprise in an undeveloped country whose inept government faced civil war. He was able to work out a deal with Robert Prescott, a former AVG member who was forming the Flying Tiger cargo-carrying airline, but after Prescott's brother was accidentally killed while en route to China, the Flying Tiger line withdrew its commitment. Although Corcoran raised some money among his associates, it began to seem that the venture would fail for want of initial investment.[26]

Seeing no other choice, Willauer arranged for the bulk of the financing in China. Through a syndicate of Chinese bankers headed by the Kincheng Bank and coordinated by Wang Wen-san and L. K. Taylor (of SWHA), CAT was loaned $250,000 Chinese on an eighteen-month basis at high interest in return for a 42 percent interest in the equity of the airline. It was a hard bargain—Prescott had initially agreed to the same investment for a 24 percent equity—but CAT had few friends and even fewer believers. Corcoran considered pulling out, but by this time Willauer and Chennault were shoulder to shoulder, defiant, and determined to make their brainchild a success.[27]

While in the States seeking capital for CAT and his other business ventures, Chennault took care of two troubling personal matters. Since 1937 he and Nell had drifted ever further apart; letters had become fewer as the years went by. Now, more certain than ever that his life lay in China, he urged her to go back with him. Nell's life, however, was in Waterproof. Divorce was the most honest solution. She had been a more understanding wife than most women would have been, and neither then nor later did he express resentment or regret.[28]

As distressing to him as his defunct marriage were the continuing implications that he was guilty of financial wrongdoing, and here too he sought some relief. Upon his return to China he had been puzzled by what he perceived to be a change in attitude toward him by Chiang Kai-shek, and he soon learned of talk that he had been involved with Madame in a wartime smuggling ring. He was incensed. He probably exaggerated the extent and effects of the gossip, but he felt he had to have a showdown or else go back to the Louisiana swamps.

"I want to stop, definitely and permanently, the dirty, insidious, damaging lies which have hurt me so much during the last four years," he wrote Alsop. He requested his help in gathering the evidence necessary for a defamation of character suit. Alsop responded that he would do his best, but he doubted that it would help.[29]

Chennault then enlisted the help of his brother Joe, an accountant working in Washington, and put him to work on his income tax returns, deferred during the war years. Chennault knew that the War Department believed he had a large sum of money, given him by China, and that he was suspected of having evaded paying income tax on it and of keeping it in a metal strongbox in Louisiana. It is a strange tale, like most suspicions having some basis in truth but assuming disproportionate extremes. The money involved was that which he had received as bonuses for his prewar activities in China. Most of it he had used to repay debts and to invest in the stock market and oil leases in the States. The late 1930s and early 1940s were a propitious time to put money into stocks; his investments were yielding good returns. Even so, the sum was far short of the amount he was suspected of having. Because of his business commitments in China and his divorce settlement, he had to borrow money to return to China.[30]

The story of the strongbox probably derives from a sheet metal filebox in which Trumble kept the AVG papers in Toungoo. Trumble turned the locked box over to Chennault upon leaving China in 1944; Chennault brought it home with him in 1945.[31]

Chennault had stated in his long and bitter letter to Wedemeyer in July 1945 that he would try to disprove the suspicions concerning his personal probity. Now he instructed Joe to report every penny of his Chinese earnings and claim the legal exemption for money earned abroad.

If he thought this would end the speculation about his financial wrongdoing or his motives or his mercenary background, however, he was wrong, for back in China in the fall of 1946, he found himself still in the eye of a storm. There were accusations that CAT was masquerading as a relief airline and was using unfair procedures for personal gain. There were rumors that he intended to participate in China's civil war, that the planned airline would be employed to aid the government against the Communists.[32]

Public buffeting, especially insinuations that his motives were mercenary, was hard to swallow. "It is my earnest desire to *aid* the Chinese people," he protested to a news conference. As for their civil war, he reminded them that during the war he had cooperated with all political parties in defeating the Japanese and rescuing his airmen; now he wanted to cooperate with all groups to repair the war damage. He expressed grief that "some Chinese people are in open armed rebellion against their government—thereby delaying the rehabilitation of their country and diminishing its prestige as a world power." He did not, however, "feel it is my duty to participate in this needless, bitter conflict. My desire is to aid all Chinese."[33]

Chennault was sincere in wanting to help China. He himself, through the Fourteenth Air Force, had wreaked much of the destruction; he felt a moral need to replace. He wanted to see China a strong and unified country, but he was also passionately convinced that a united China must be under Nationalist rather than Communist control. No doubt he was willing to fight if necessary to ensure it. He was becoming more intensely anti-Communist during this time, and in private he expressed himself vehemently on the subject. After some of his public comments raised a storm, however, he tried to keep his views to himself. He wrote, tongue in cheek, to Alsop: "I am a man of peace—a simple soul who sees no evil, hears no evil and speaks no evil (rarely, at least)." But in support of his "deep seated peaceful intentions," he admitted he was "always prepared to fight."[34]

He was uneasy, however, with the political turmoil in which he was now involved. "I am greatly worried about the political aspect which my friends are forcing my planned projects into," he wrote Trumble. "I had—and have—no idea or desire to engage in partisan politics." This he could have done more easily in Louisiana, he reflected, on better-known ground. "It was my desire to do something to restore China's business, trade and transport—not to engage in politics."[35]

The official papers that created CNRRA Air Transport were signed in Shanghai on 25 October 1946. From that point onward, Chennault threw himself into the shaping of an airline that came to bear his unmistakable, unconventional "can-do" stamp. He recruited personnel primarily from those with whom he had worked before. There was no room for those who disliked the Chinese or were unwilling to work side by side in mutual respect or harmony with them, for CAT would be a genuine Chinese-American enterprise. There was no room for the faint-hearted or obstructionist, for the job would be done even though there seemed no way to do it. The flying would be demanding, the creature comforts minimal, the hardships sobering, the dangers real. He looked for men who were independent, circumspect, and confident, those able to cope with the unexpected, to handle their lives as well as their planes with assurance. He looked for men

Chennault (seated), watches Director General Ho Pao-hsu of CNRRA sign the agreement that brought CAT into being, 25 October 1946. Standing, from left: William Green, director of the Agricultural Department of CNRRA; Whiting Willauer; and C. M. Li, Ho's deputy. (Photo courtesy Ted Matsis)

who thrived on challenge and on flying, men who could be hard when hard decisions had to be made. As in putting together the AVG, he wanted no one with any reservations. He may have wished he could be one of them, for in one interview with a newly promoted major he made the wistful remark that he would gladly exchange his stars for oak leaves if he could have the years back.[36]

"CAT comes pretty close to spelling Tiger," Willauer noted, and indeed the personnel roster began to take on a familiar look. Doreen [Davis] Lonberg became CAT's Washington secretary, P. Y. Shu its interpreter. John Williams set up the radio network; Tom Gentry became the flight surgeon. Former AVG pilots included Rosbert and Shilling; others came from the Fourteenth Air Force or the marines who had served in China. Clyde Farnsworth, who had covered the Fourteenth Air Force as a correspondent, signed on as public relations officer. Chinese employees were in a majority; most of them had worked with the CACW or the CAF. The first official CAT flight left Hungjao airfield in Shanghai on 31 January 1947 carrying relief supplies, a jeep, and the quietly pleased Chennault, accompanied by Anna Chan.[37]

During 1947 CAT flew medicine, food, seeds, and breeding stock to the interior of China. On return flights it brought out the raw materials China exported to build up its foreign credits: hog bristles, hides, tobacco, wolfram, and tin. An informal airline more concerned with performance than appearance, it offered few amenities for the occasional human passengers. Planes flew from abandoned wartime airfields or simple dirt strips. Hangars and maintenance facilities were not always available; the pilots sometimes performed the minimum service for their planes. Weather equipment might be as basic as a pole with a revolving wooden rooster on the end, held out the window to gauge wind direction and velocity.

Pilots and crewmen sometimes wore their old uniforms minus insignia and with sleeves or legs cut off, or gaudy tropical shirts, or maybe an Oriental robe. The postwar Orient was a study in contrasts, for items usually considered basic necessities, such as housing and plain food, were so scarce and expensive as to seem almost unobtainable, while luxuries—alcohol and servants and jewels and fine silks and women—were plentiful and cheap. A man could win a troupe of Russian dancing girls in a poker game, and according to the tales one CAT pilot did so. The men relished the luxuries and savored the adventure, and the life-styles they adopted seemed wild and wonderful. Their traditions began to form around flamboyant personalities and places which they made peculiarly their own. James B. McGovern, a superb pilot and lovable man with a tremendous girth and a heart to match, was called "Earthquake" after Earthquake McGoon of the comics. At Pop Gingle's restaurant in Hong Kong, Pop—another kind-hearted man of enormous bulk—gave CAT men unofficial ownership of the back room and kept them happy on cold beer and hot chili. Some of them lived for a while at the blue Oriental villa called the "Opium Den"; they were short on furniture but enjoyed the servants and the pool and the exotic bar with gold and blue stripes.[38]

But behind the pleasures there was great seriousness. Most of the men were eager for a career as commercial flyers, and business more than adventure held them in China. Air freight lines—the concept pioneered by the Hump—had no civilian precedent, no backlog of expertise and experience that might provide guidelines on how to make

One service CAT performed in 1947 was to fly new breeding stock into remote provinces of China, where many animals had been slaughtered for food during the blockaded war years. (Photo courtesy Ted Matsis)

a profit. Some 2,700 such lines were started immediately after the war, but many did not survive.[39] Yet CAT grew and thrived, its growth in part a measure of China's desperate need, in part the result of creative management.

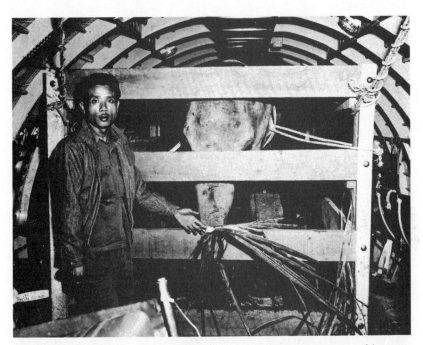

CAT's "can do" attitude was tested when it was called upon to transport this young elephant, who could significantly alter the plane's balance by shifting his feet. (Photo courtesy Ted Matsis)

By May 1947 CAT had more than 300 employees; by December, more than 1,000. They shared in their own growing success with a bonus fund and savings plans. Wages were as high as CAT could manage; pilots were paid ten dollars more per hour for every hour over eighty in a month, and there was no limit on how many they could fly.[40] The lure of the money was important, but it was not all. The same esprit de corps that had marked the AVG and the CATF began to permeate CAT. Behind a rough life of demanding work under adverse conditions, CAT employees were forging a quiet conviction that what they were doing was meaningful, important, and useful.[41]

By midsummer 1947, with his business life beginning to stabilize, Chennault had decided to remarry. A man who had always believed in living life to the fullest, he had never hidden the obvious pleasure he derived from the company of women. He was a ladies' man. Interest in women was a vital part of his nature. He had always sought to be discreet and fair in his relationships, and Nell had accepted them, although doubtless with some personal pain. But Chennault himself looked upon marriage and family as something entirely distinct, as a relationship on a totally different plane from casual personal interactions. In China his casual relationships came easily, but he needed and wanted the affection, respect, and love that he associated with marriage. He wanted company. He wanted the warmth and security of a home. He wanted someone to take care of him. He sought a partner.[42]

From the time of his return to China in 1946, his social life had been lively, visible, the topic of much gossip, and at times a source of consternation or embarrassment to his business associates. Some of the women to whom he was attracted elicited the dismay of his friends, who watched his romantic drama anxiously, not only apprehensive for the business ramifications, but in fear that this man—whom they considered a lovable fool where women were concerned—would be hurt or exploited. Some of the Chinese Nationalists were eager to cement his ties to them and their cause by his marriage to a Chinese, and even though Chennault saw no reasons why he should not marry a Chinese, CAT's Washington backers worried. Willauer reassured them that a cross-cultural marriage would not harm Chennault's position in China, where he was *rara avis*. Americans might think it absurd when they heard how much esteem the Chinese felt for him, Willauer explained, but in China it was a very real sentiment.[43]

Willauer himself could not resist some discreet matchmaking behind the scenes and tried to persuade Doreen to take the initiative and patch up a tiff between herself and the general, for they had obvious ties of affection. The general and his secretary were also two equally proud, independent, and stubborn individuals, however, and Willauer's efforts as marriage broker ended in failure.[44]

Chennault became more and more receptive to the unabashed admiration of Anna Chan. She was the daughter of Y. W. Chan, whom he had first met in San Francisco in 1941; Chan was the Chinese consul who helped arrange transport for the AVG. After the war erupted, Chan had asked Chennault to watch out for his daughters, who were still in China; Anna's sister Cynthia served as a nurse with the Fourteenth Air Force in Kunming. Chennault and Anna courted for some time, often spending the evening at dinner and cards with CAT pilot Joe Rosbert and his future wife, Lil. When they were ready to announce their engagement, they paid a formal call on the Generalissimo and Madame, who gave their blessing.[45]

Chennault hoped the wedding might be performed by Paul Frillmann, who was then serving in the U.S. consulate in Shanghai. He invited Frillmann and his wife to dinner, with Anna and Gentry as the other guests, and afterward Gentry asked Frillmann whether he would conduct the ceremony. Frillmann could not, as he was no longer authorized by his church to do so. Claire and Anna were married by the Rev. Ralph Mortensen in a Lutheran ceremony held at Chennault's Shanghai home on 21 December. The twenty-four-year-old bride was beautiful in a white gown and veil; the fifty-four-year-old groom beamed in his Air Corps dress uniform and cut the cake with a Samurai sword, a gift from Hsueh Yueh. Afterward there was quite a celebration—one of the more memorable wedding gifts was a full-length cape lined with golden monkey skin—but following a Sunday wedding the pair went back to work on Monday. "It was a busy time in the development of the organization," Chennault explained later. The new Mrs. Chennault applied her writing skills to CAT's monthly newsletter, for her husband was happily immersed in the growing CAT.[46]

Chennault and Willauer personified and nurtured CAT's growing sense of identity and pride by involving themselves in every aspect of their company. Willauer served as an overall general manager, spending about half his time troubleshooting at the airports and the other half with legal, financial, and organizational matters. Chennault took charge of operations, working with the pilots and constantly teaching safe ways to cope with China's adverse flying conditions.

A story widely circulated and probably true although distorted in detail by frequent telling illustrated his style as well as the unorthodox nature of the airline. It seems that when a pilot reported for an early morning flight obviously suffering from a bad hangover, the operations manager questioned him closely about his ability to fly. The pilot growled back that if he could climb the ladder to get in the plane, he could fly the damn thing. The skeptical manager decided to call Chennault. The latter was accessible at all hours if he was needed, and on this occasion, wakened from sleep, he listened to the problem and asked, "What does [the pilot] say?" The operations manager repeated the pilot's claim. "Well," Chennault advised as he hung up the phone, "see if he can climb the ladder!"[47]

This kind of confidence and respect for his men was important to them, but the more thoughtful realized that, when it came to flying or to the motivations that bound them to CAT, Chennault's trust was carefully placed in men on whom he knew he could depend.

Chennault confers with Joe Rosbert, left, and unidentified pilot, right. (Photo courtesy Ted Matsis)

Some of them also realized that despite his casual approach he was a hard-nosed driver who stirred them to maximum performance and managed them better than they realized. Chief pilot Robert Rousse-lot, who had much of the youthful zeal that Chennault himself had displayed at his age, assessed his boss as "a pretty shrewd old man. If you didn't watch it, he'd turn your throttle down."[48]

Chennault's approach, as ever, was simple and direct. Two after-noons a week both he and Willauer made themselves accessible to anyone—pilots, clerical help, maintenance personnel, or cleanup crews—anyone who had an idea, or a gripe, or simply wanted to meet the bosses. They knew their employees by name. They took a per-sonal interest in them and their lives, somehow managing to walk that fine line that stopped short of unwelcome intrusion.[49]

"I like to mix with my people," Chennault said once in answer to a question about why affection was so generously bestowed upon him. His only guide and policy, he said, was to mix with his people but insist they "know which one I am." In every organization he led, his approach was to mingle and work with his people, know their

Chennault reads a statement at an official CAT function. This is one of the rare pictures of him wearing his glasses. (Photo courtesy Ted Matsis)

troubles and listen to them, "sympathize with them, do all you can for them, but you always know which one you are."[50] In CAT, as in previous groups, Chennault maintained a separateness and dignity, keeping his personal thoughts and feelings very private. His countenance often appeared stern to people who did not know him. One new secretary, initially terrified at the idea of working for him, soon realized that the grim face hid a patient and understanding man with a warm heart, a sympathetic ear, and the tendency to give a person the benefit of the doubt.[51]

As business and social life merged, peculiarly American institutions evolved. Chennault lost little time in forming a CAT softball team, and work assumed a healthy perspective when his batting average (at one time an enviable .706), or a series of games when they were "robbed by the umpires," could be cause for the boss's "serious concern." On holidays he might host a party for all CAT employees; on his birthday in 1948 they reciprocated with a surprise party, gathering around a huge cake to sing "Happy Birthday" and his favorite,

"You Are My Sunshine." CAT became a family, an endeavor that went deeper than running an airline. Gradually, perhaps inevitably, perhaps intentionally, it became a powerful political-military weapon.[52]

The Chinese Civil War, to some extent suppressed between 1937 and 1945, surfaced in 1946 as the major political/military crisis in Asia. In November 1945, after Hurley had resigned as ambassador, President Truman sent Marshall to China as head of a special mission to bring the two rival armed governments into a coalition, to piece together a framework within which China could begin to shape its political future without bloodshed. Early in 1946 there appeared to be hope, for all parties seemed genuinely desirous of the goal. Chiang moved toward making his government more responsive and representative; both sides agreed to a truce. Marshall flew back to the United States to secure a commitment on economic aid to help a united China begin to rebuild.

While he was away the Russian troops began pulling out of Manchuria, the Chinese Communists moved into the vacuum, and the Kuomintang armies moved to oust them. When his campaign began to stall, Chiang consented to another truce; he ended it to pursue a favorable opportunity for military success. Communist leader Mao Tse-tung, who had maintained good relations with the United States up to this point, then launched a major anti-American campaign on the grounds the United States was aiding the Nationalists while seeking a settlement. His argument carried some weight, and in July Marshall asked for an embargo on U.S. aid to the Nationalists on the grounds that it was ruining the chances of a peaceful settlement.[53]

Chennault followed the events with pain. The menace of communism, which had begun to trouble him in 1945, now impressed itself strongly upon him as a world danger. Following Marshall's efforts, he became personally convinced that the Chinese Communists must be militarily defeated. He saw the embargo on aid as criminal, a move that would pull the props from under the Nationalists at a critical time. He was disturbed that Chiang had failed "to take decisive action"; his own interpretation of the reason was that Chiang sought to place the burden on the Marshall mission. He anticipated that, when the Marshall mission stopped trying to prevent the war which all could see was nevertheless taking place, Chiang had "both the desire and the power to clear the situation rapidly."[54]

Chennault's confidence in Chiang's military capabilities was misplaced. Nationalist forces continued to move deeper into Manchuria, even though U.S. military advisers warned Chiang that he was not strong enough to prevail. The Nationalist armies were soon overextended; the Communists fought back with vigor. With both sides bent on a military solution, Marshall returned to Washington in January 1947 to become secretary of state. A troubled U.S. government, having failed in this last effort to shape China's future, now sought to wash its hands and declared that it would not be directly involved in any conflict between the rival Chinese governments.[55]

Six months later the Chinese Communists launched a vigorous counteroffensive; within a month they were advancing into central China. The CAF, CNAC, and CATC could not provide the degree of support for which the Nationalist commanders in the field were calling. CAT filled the gap as the air transport arm for the Nationalist forces. The pattern began at Mukden and Weihsien, where the Communists took advantage of their control of the countryside and blockaded the cities. The desperate scene was repeated again and again as the war progressed. The Nationalists insisted on positional warfare, often concentrating inside the city walls, and the Communists simply closed in to contain them within their blockaded islands of resistance. CAT flew food and supplies into the doomed cities as long as they could hold out. When they began to crumble, it evacuated as many as possible of the citizens. The missions were dangerous. Sometimes CAT's unarmed planes flew into makeshift dirt airstrips under fire. It was hardly the kind of work commercial airlines expect, but pilots and crews neither flinched nor defected.[56]

"I've never yet had a bad outfit," Chennault said with quiet satisfaction. He credited this success to "the fine quality of the men and the women that I managed to get around me, people who were willing to do anything, sacrifice, work overtime, risk their lives, often, just to do the job."[57]

When CAT personnel were in trouble, others went to heroic lengths to protect or rescue them. They were on the blacklist of those who would be executed as enemies of the People's Republic, but this status became a source of pride: Chennault and Willauer were supposedly at the top of the list. One of the partners often flew as copilot on the more hazardous flights, and on the grounds that he was more expendable to the future of the airline than was Chennault, Willauer took more than his share of this duty. By the winter of 1947 CAT itself had begun a series of retreats and evacuations, for it was necessary to move field offices and maintenance depots as the areas changed hands.[58]

UNRRA and CNRRA expired at the end of 1947. Helped by the sale of a part interest, plus inflation and a fluctuating foreign exchange market, CAT was able to exercise its option to purchase the airline's planes. It had also proved its value to China, and after lengthy negotiations CAT became Civil Air Transport, a private partnership authorized to operate directly under the Ministry of Communications of the Nationalist government, which made it clear that CAT was expected to assist the military effort by hauling food and personnel.[59]

When the new CAT held open house at its new facility at Shanghai's Hungjao airfield, Chennault was at ease in telling newsmen that CAT was at the service of Chinese civil and military authorities, that it transported the items deemed most critical in restoring the country's economic prosperity and in waging war against the rebels.[60] Neither he nor Willauer showed any hesitation or reluctance at the scope of their commitment. During their year of operating CNRRA Air Transport, they had seen the Cold War assuming a shape in Asia that erased any possible doubts about the dangers of advancing communism.

19

Cold Warrior

"The time fuse of World War III is burning now in Manchuria."
These words, with slight variation, became the new litany of a new
Claire Chennault, cold warrior. He launched his anti-Communist
crusade in the pages of the *Washington Daily News* in February 1948
with a hard-hitting article arguing that communism was a deadly enemy that could not survive without continued growth and would not
stop at international frontiers unless opposed. He reasoned that
"Russia will not take the big plunge in the west until she is secure in
the east." He saw the struggle between Nationalist and Communist
in China as Russia's attempt to gain this security, hence he reasoned
that a free and independent China was the only hope for avoiding a
major conflict with Russia. China needed help; it lacked the ability
to train, arm, and supply its manpower. Time was short and the need
was great, but "to prevent consolidation of that eastern bulwark of
communism is the cheapest and easiest insurance we can have
against World War III."[1]

A full year before publishing the article quoted above, Chennault
had made his first significant lobbying effort by writing to Sen. Arthur H. Vandenberg, a Michigan Republican who was then head of

the Senate Foreign Relations Committee. Written just as Marshall's mission to China was ending, Chennault's letter criticized U.S. policy in China and asserted that the effort to create a coalition government had not only failed but had actually aided the Communists. He urged the United States to abandon negotiations and give Chiang immediate and full support. Some members of the State Department would have much the same point of view by August 1948, but in this case, as during the early days of World War II, Chennault was reacting ahead of official policy.[2]

Chennault's argument struck Vandenberg, however, as "entirely invincible." He wrote back that Chennault's "thoroughly splendid" letter had been of "incalculable value." Would Chennault mind if he made it public? Chennault did mind, very much. He responded with a firm no, stating simply that his own views of past and present policy toward China were "unfortunately" in conflict with Marshall's. He feared that controversy was being stirred up deliberately in order to delay implementation of a "firm, sound, friendly policy" toward China, and under the circumstances publication of his views would accomplish no "real good."[3] Vandenberg honored Chennault's wishes but continued to express his conviction that it might be time for the United States to alter its policy of nonintervention in China and actively to encourage the side it favored while discouraging the other. He became a calm but persistent advocate of a reasonable amount of aid to Nationalist China.[4]

As leader of his party—which controlled the Congress—Vandenberg was an important figure in the conduct of a bipartisan postwar foreign policy. The administration needed his continued support. Although convinced that further aid to Nationalist China was futile, Marshall (by then the secretary of state) deferred to Vandenberg's views during 1947, first by lifting the embargo on arms to China and then sending Wedemeyer to China to reassess the Nationalists' problem. Wedemeyer's subsequent report advocated massive aid contingent on sweeping reforms as well as suggesting a United Nations trusteeship for Manchuria. Since Washington could see no way to implement the recommendations, the report was not published and accomplished little except to arouse controversy.[5]

Unfortunately China's turmoil was only one facet of the postwar scramble for new geopolitical alignments around the globe. Most Americans were far more concerned about Europe, where the Russian sphere of influence was moving steadily westward: Greece in the fall of 1946, then Bulgaria, Rumania, Poland, and Hungary. During

1947 the United States, alarmed, began to fight back. In proclaiming the Truman Doctrine, the United States made clear that it would support European governments that sought to resist Communist aggression. The new programs that took shape in subsequent months—the Marshall Plan, the European Recovery Act, and the North Atlantic Treaty Organization—did not encompass the Far East.

Not everyone agreed with this basic division of priorities. Pro-China sentiment in the United States, still strong, soon began to interject a valid question: why it should be important to stop the spread of communism in Europe but not in Asia? Official Washington never satisfactorily answered that question for the public, perhaps because it was far from certain what should be done. In practical terms, however, there was a limit to U.S. resources, and the resources that might reasonably be spared would stretch farther when spent in Europe, where relatively stable governments operated on basic premises that were in harmony with those of the United States.[6]

In contrast, Chiang's Nationalist regime had become thoroughly discredited in Washington's eyes. There was widespread condemnation of the way it managed the UNRRA aid, much of which was wasted, sold on the black market, or diverted to private use. Less than 5 percent of it reached the Communist-held areas, which included about half the people, although the aid had been intended for all Chinese who were in need. The situation boded ill for any genuine reconciliation between Kuomintang and Communist. The Kuomintang itself seemed unable to function according to Western notions of what a democratic government should do. Despite the formalities of elections, a constitutional assembly, and the election of reform-minded Li Tsung-jen as vice president, Chiang and his supporters remained in firm control of a government plagued with corruption and narrow in its outlook. The lot of the ordinary Chinese citizen continued bleak; meaningful programs to alleviate it did not materialize.[7]

Nor did postwar Nationalist China appear to have the moral strength necessary to prevail against the Chinese Communist challenge. Dissension within the Kuomintang continued, efficient government seemed impossible, and dismay combined with disgust when U.S. observers watched some of Chiang's armies, supplied with U.S. equipment, surrender to the Chinese Communists after only token effort.

Yet there was no other power block in China worthy of support—the Kuomintang and the Chinese Communist party were the givens.

Convinced that U.S. aid would accomplish more good for the long-term best interests of the country if expended in Europe, the administration took refuge in a policy of nonintervention in China's internal civil war and stayed uncomfortably aloof from China's problems.

The "do nothing" China policy made the administration vulnerable, and by the latter half of 1947 it was being loudly bewailed in the conservative press, with Henry Luce's powerful *Time/Life/Fortune* complex leading the way and clamoring for aid to Chiang. In Congress, a pro-China faction within Republican ranks became identifiable and increasingly vocal. Vandenberg continued to favor modest aid if it could be effectively used, but he avoided the more controversial and emotional issues by yielding leadership of the pro-China Republicans to William Knowland and Styles Bridges in the Senate and to John Vorys and Walter Judd in the House.

Judd was a fiery and persuasive man who had served for many years as a medical missionary in Shansi and sincerely identified with the Chinese people in their continuing agony. The motives of the China supporters as a group, however, were mixed. They tended to be conservative anti-Communists skeptical of the State Department in its conduct of foreign policy and eager to drive a wedge into Democratic ranks. China was becoming an emotional and partisan issue at the same time that the question of Communists in government, first raised in 1945, was becoming steadily uglier.[8] It is easy, looking back, to see the stage being set for the coming era of McCarthyism and bitter recriminations over the "loss" of China.

Chennault did not become visible and vocal about China policy until early 1948. During 1947 not only was he busy getting CAT under way, but he told Vandenberg he did not want "to be injected into the diplomatic or political squabbles" raging over China policy.[9] His hesitation was not solely a reluctance to become embroiled in controversy; he had endured controversy before and could take it again if necessary. He knew, however, that his restless, physical nature called for action, not words; he had neither the talents nor the tools for political leadership. His natural inclination was to jump in and do something, not to debate or to persuade. As long as he agreed with the policy, he preferred to leave the making of it to others.

By 1948, however, the hard reality was a China rapidly being taken over by the Chinese Communists while the United States watched. Chennault thought it was all wrong. He felt "a deep sympathy" for the Chinese, who had been "friendly and loyal" to him, had "many sound qualities and who suffered so much in the late war." He was willing to enter the fray, he told Vandenberg, if what he did could be "used constructively to assist the Chinese Government in establishing a strong united China, friendly with the United States."[10]

Willauer and Corcoran, both very much at home in the political arena where Chennault floundered, nudged him toward a public role. Their political convictions were strong, as were Chennault's, and they could see positive benefits radiating from Chennault's well-known name and his propensity to draw headlines. There was also an undeniable commercial motive, for each of the three wanted to see CAT become a financial success.

Had their political convictions not been more important to them than their bank accounts, however, CAT's founders could have aligned themselves with the emerging People's Republic of China, which needed aerial transport fully as much as a China under the Kuomintang. The Chinese Communists made clear overtures to CAT during 1949, but neither Willauer nor Chennault was interested. Both men saw their airline as not just a commercial enterprise but a force working for the free world.[11]

"Haven't made any money above expenses," Chennault happily wrote Max late in 1947, "but sure am having a good, busy time." Two years later, when it looked as though they would lose all, Willauer reflected that he cared about the money only to the extent that it would "be used by others as an index of my running things." His personal gratification, he reflected, would come from doing what could be done "to keep up whatever service we can render."[12]

As the Communists advanced, CAT planned and carried out successive evacuations. Indeed, Willauer dreamed up the ultimate in airline mobility: CAT's repair and maintenance facility was housed aboard a World War II LST (landing ship, tank). When CAT personnel needed quarters in refugee-crowded Hong Kong, CAT purchased a ship and converted it into a floating hotel. When queried later about his commercial motives in advocating aid to Nationalist China, Chennault said the airline would not be lost if the Communists took over the mainland, for plans had already been worked out to move it if necessary.[13]

Late in 1947, when the Truman administration introduced a China Aid Act and the debate on its passage began, Chennault was persuaded that the time had come to plunge in. He feared that the amount of aid proposed would make little difference in China, but he believed that the moral support it expressed was important. He also thought China would fare better under a Republican administration, and Truman would be seeking election in the fall. In rueful recognition that he was not at ease in his new role as lobbyist, he wrote his children, "During the war my enemies wore uniforms but now they wear civies and smile."[14]

Chennault's February article, quoted in the opening paragraph of this chapter, was read into the *Congressional Record* by Judd. In March Chennault was "respectfully invited" to appear before the U.S. House Committee on Foreign Affairs to present his views on the importance of maintaining "a free and independent China friendly to the United States" and the measures he thought best for doing so.[15]

In this his first congressional appearance, Chennault told the representatives essentially what he had earlier told the newspapers. He plugged the China Aid Act by pointing out that the United States had actually done very little to build a strong, independent China. During 1937–41, he reminded his audience, China was given sympathy while Japan was sold iron, yet when England was threatened by external aggression the response was quick and significant.

"We have made a lot of mistakes in our dealing with China," he concluded. He saw "no profit in going over them" and believed the United States still enjoyed the "friendship and trust of a great majority of the anti-Communist Chinese."[16]

With this trip to the States, Chennault began a pattern that he followed the remaining ten years of his life—dividing his time and his labor between China and the United States. He went to Louisiana to visit family and friends. Perhaps because his old friend Noe lived in Monroe, he tended to make that small city his base of operations. Later he bought a small house on Cole Avenue to be his home in the United States. On this 1948 visit he was there for Army Day, when he led Monroe's parade and gave a radio talk in which he presented the world's choices as communization and enslavement on the one hand or freedom on the other. Afterward he went fishing with outdoorsman and guide John Elmendorf, caught 150 pounds of fish on one trip and 200 pounds on another, and with much pleasure turned 90 pounds of trout and bream into a fish fry for Louisiana friends old and new. By early May he was back in China.[17]

One facet of the cold warrior campaign Chennault waged during 1948–49 was a personal vendetta closely entangled with partisan politics and the whole issue of aid to China. Once he decided to "speak out," as Hopkins had predicted he would, he spoke with a vehemence and bitterness that startled his friends and diminished his stature. Concerned about the present and still rankling over perceived injustice in the past, he hurled into the arena the whole question of the administration's China policy, past and present. He had never shown discretion or tact in handling differences with his fellow countrymen, and he did not do so now. He began by writing that the United States had a moral obligation to China, partly because the Yalta agreement had encouraged Russia to enter Manchuria in the first place, and partly because the 1946 truce, "sadly calculated to bring about coalition between a constituted government and rebels against it," had prevented the victory over the Communists which China "conceivably" could have won.[18]

One reason Marshall's 1946 mission had sought coalition was that most estimates of Chiang's military capability indicated that he would be defeated if he pursued a military solution. Coalition seemed to offer the only remaining chance to salvage Chiang's regime. In his letter to Roosevelt in late 1945, Chennault had also been forceful in advocating "true unification" between Chungking and Yenan. He saw a great difference, however, between a coalition government and combined military forces. He also thought that during the postwar months the Chinese Communists had more clearly declared an ultimate intent for totalitarian control, an intent that clearly identified the problem as one that would have to be resolved by force. In his opinion, now stated openly, Marshall had not only failed to negotiate with Chiang as a respected equal but had not understood the implications for the Chinese of the enforced compromises.[19]

Chennault was not alone in thinking that the 1946 truce had worked in the Communists' favor. U.S. China policy could have profited from some intense scrutiny. Unfortunately Chennault did not keep his criticisms at the level of issues, where they could have served a constructive purpose. Instead he seemed to be accusing Marshall— probably the most highly respected individual in American public life at that time—of incompetent blundering.

The antagonism that had developed between Chennault and Marshall during 1941–45 was intense and mutual. Marshall blamed Chennault for undermining Stilwell and the War Department's strategy in CBI; Chennault blamed Marshall for War Department policies, especially shortages in supplies, that had prevented his own campaigns from being successful. The more subtle and complex clashes of personal character also stood between the two men, Marshall reacting with contempt and distrust over the implications of Chennault's personal wrongdoing, Chennault bristling with resentment and fury over an accusation and persecution that he perceived to be unjust. Chennault felt he was in the right on a succession of issues about which an aura of scandal had formed. He had accepted pay and had fought for another country but under circumstances that benefited his own country as well. He felt his personal finances had been handled legally and ethically; he resented being suspected of dishonesty. He had allowed controlled prostitution to protect the health of his men; he felt that those who opposed such a policy were unrealistic about human nature. He had been loyal to friends who had been loyal to him, even when their personal conduct was despicable; he felt no apology for his conduct. He had fought as hard as he and his men could fight to defeat the Japanese and help the Chinese; he felt justified in every action he had taken toward that goal. He once said, joking but with a dagger of truth, that the Japanese gave him a little trouble occasionally, but he had to fight the War Department all the time. About the lack of support and understanding, about the withholding of top command, he felt deep resentment.[20]

And now, as though his perspective had been skewed by his personal experiences, Chennault seemed to focus on communism as the root of all evil, the subtle influence that lay behind all earlier failures of effort or policy. "I do not believe that Geo. C. [Marshall] is a communist," he wrote in a personal letter in 1946, "but I do know that he gave Stilwell his full support during a period when S___ was urging the overthrow of the established government (and the Gissimo) and withholding military support of the Nationalist armies in China." About Marshall's and Stilwell's relationships with both China and with himself, Chennault was bitter.[21]

His vendetta intensified with a series of articles in March in the Scripps-Howard newspapers. They composed an abbreviated memoir, by Chennault "as told to" Farnsworth. His thesis was that the Americans in Chungking during the war years had thoroughly denigrated the Chinese Nationalists while conducting a "public love affair" with the Communists, thus effectively stabbing Chiang in the back. He recited much of the sad tale of CBI, its personality clashes, its culture gaps, and its conflicting and competing strategies.[22]

Part of what he wrote was pertinent to a United States still uneasy in its role of world leadership, for Chennault deplored the lack of "friendly dignity and frankness" in U.S. relationships with China. "Wise and friendly help" might have set China upon the path toward stability and self-improvement, he wrote. "While helping China to fight, we could have used our good offices to promote governmental self-improvement." But for that to take place, he considered it an essential prerequisite "that our dealings be on a basis of equality and mutual trust. Americans could gain no influence if they treated their Chinese opposite numbers with suspicion or condescension."[23]

Unfortunately Chennault's remedies for the problem of "the ugly American" were drowned in a flood of accusations, primarily against Stilwell. There was an undeniable need for an open and probing examination of what had happened in CBI, especially in view of the need to formulate a sound postwar China policy. Many false impressions had been formed on the basis of incomplete information; some readjustments were in order. But Stilwell had died in October 1946. He could neither present his point of view nor defend himself against accusation; there could be no give-and-take, no mutual explanations or apologies. Under the circumstances, Chennault's attack seemed tasteless and self-serving, if not cruel, the action of a little man who could not accept his own failures and had to place the blame on others.

Critics said as much, but the stubborn Chennault plowed ahead. His memoir, *Way of a Fighter*, was published early in 1949 and was more in the same vein. His desire for the full story to be told is understandable, and he doubtless feared his side would not be officially given; before the war ended he had written a friend in the War Department urging that any history of the theater be written by those who knew from experience. "First impressions are abiding impressions with the American people," he had said. "If they are inaccurate or unjust, it makes little difference. They survive."[24]

Ironically enough, his own memoir worked against him, ensuring that his treatment in history was harsher and more emotional than might otherwise have been the case. Because his presentation of issues was often shallow, and because he either did not catch or did not care about a number of errors, the book's value as a historical source was diminished. One reviewer observed that it made one suspect Chennault's judgment on other matters as well. Another suggested its title might well have been "Grrr-r-r-r," for it exuded hostility.[25] He fully expected to be sued, for it contained open criticisms of individuals and portrayed a disturbing lack of respect for "the brass."[26] It was the expression of an angry man, a man who felt wronged.

Both Willauer and Corcoran discouraged its publication, feeling that it could only create waves of antagonism and would accomplish no constructive good. Chennault overruled them; he would abandon this fight no more than any he had waged before. Publicizing his side of the story had become part of his anti-Communist crusade, and in this he had become emotionally, passionately involved. He saw the problem in China at a time when the eyes of the United States seemed focused exclusively on Europe. The debate on NATO was beginning, the Berlin airlift to demonstrate American resolve against Russian power plays was in full swing, and the nation's best-seller lists included Eisenhower's *Crusade in Europe*, Sherwood's *Roosevelt and Hopkins*, and Churchill's *The Gathering Storm*. In this atmosphere Chennault considered his book's foreword to be extremely important, for it was a plea for a current policy of aid to China, a contemporary political persuasion which he distributed widely as a separately bound pamphlet. Copies went to congressmen, with accompanying letters reiterating that U.S. policy was unbalanced if only the European anti-Communist peoples were supported.[27]

Reviewers tore *Way of a Fighter* to shreds, agreeing that Chennault seemed determined to destroy his rightful place as one of America's fighting heroes by a vain and bitter chronicle that portrayed him as "spiteful, vindictive, incredibly self-satisfied and insufferably arrogant." China scholar John K. Fairbank, noting that Chennault portrayed the attitude of a fighting man who saw no solution to the world's ills but more and better fighting, deplored Chennault's apparent failure to recognize the social, economic, political, or cultural forces working in Asia.[28] The criticism was not totally justified, for during 1948 Chennault's stand was that Chinese resistance required "well balanced coordination of military and economic aid. Neither alone will be successful."[29]

It was a loss both to Chennault personally and to his country that he was unable to present himself and his beliefs in a manner conducive to thoughtful receptivity. Just as the heat of his arguments had resulted in his being inaccurately accused of championing pursuit to the exclusion of a balanced air force during the 1930s, now he was being stereotyped as a military man who understood little apart from military affairs. The criticism came close enough to sting. "I appreciate my limitations," he said in his own defense before a congressional committee. He tried to make his point by reminding the congressmen that those who criticized him also had limitations, that there was a need for the military approach as well as the political and economic. "No conqueror 'on the make' from Ghengis Khan to Napoleon to Hitler ever just burned out or stuck in a morass or was stopped by ideas alone," he insisted. "In addition to the imponderable operation of the forces of what we call truth, somebody just had to kill him."[30]

It was Chennault's gift—or his curse—that fighting was the skill he had acquired, the career through which he had chosen to make his statement and right the wrongs he encountered. He realized, more fully than many who knew China in less personal ways, the sobering dimension of the U.S.-China problem. He made his contribution to its resolution in the only way that he knew: by extending his unconditional friendship and help to the Chinese people and by applying the expertise he had acquired. He knew flying; he knew fighting. CAT involved both, but it could not alter the course of events in China unaided. Convinced that much more was needed and justified, by 1949 Chennault the fighter had two startling new proposals for Washington to consider, each of them a desperate military effort to salvage a non-Communist China from the debacle of China's civil war.

Chennault's plans for helping China evolved from the specifics of China's civil war, which reached its turning point during 1948. After Weishien fell in April, Chiang insisted on a positional defense of Tsian, even though American military advisers warned him it was doomed to fall. CAT flew supplies—sometimes including ammunition and military goods—and evacuated the wounded, but Tsian fell in September. Mukden, supplied by air since January, fell in October and put Manchuria firmly in Communist hands. The tempo accelerated as the fighting moved closer to the Nationalist capital at Nanking. The Nationalist armies, beginning to disintegrate internally, fought poorly and increasingly deserted en masse to the Communist side.[31]

In Shansi province, however, a doughty warrior named Yen Hsishan, an inscrutable war lord who combined modern reforms with ancient repressions, began to attract attention by his dogged efforts to hold out against the Communist flood. Yen had ruled Shansi for forty years; he had survived other enemies and had no intention of surrendering to the Chinese Communists. He even hired Japanese to help him fight, and because MacArthur was in control of an occupied Japan, one suspects Yen had MacArthur's moral, if not actual, support. As the Communists converged on his central stronghold of Taiyuan, a Chinese Pittsburgh, Yen surrounded the ancient capital with some 9,000 stone pillboxes and 700 artillery pieces and kept the factories operating, little islands of defiant productivity made possible by the supply efforts of CAT and China's other airlines, which flew in food and raw materials.[32]

This was the kind of man Chennault could identify with, and after his visit to Washington he sent translated summaries of Yen's book to some congressmen with the observation that Yen had organized and trained his people to resist at the grass roots, and his example might well be followed. Yen seems to have returned Chennault's esteem; he kept an autographed picture of Chennault prominently displayed on his desk (alongside a smaller one of Marshall).[33]

In November, *Time* magazine interviewed Marshal Yen, who vowed he would never surrender to the Communists and displayed the vials of poison he held ready for the worst eventuality. To stop the Communists, he suggested that the United States fund a dual effort: an army of 100,000 Japanese mercenaries and a 200-plane air force under Chennault.[34] This proposal brought into the open something Chennault had been talking about in private for several years—a volunteer mercenary air force in China. As early as 1945, while en route to the States, he had spoken with some Portuguese volunteers who were willing to go to China as mercenaries to help the anti-Communist resistance. Chennault had written General Pai Chung-hsi about them, but Pai wrote back, thanking him and saying they did not need such men yet.[35]

But when China's situation worsened during the summer of 1948, a Chinese Nationalist general approached Chennault about a revitalized AVG. After some discussions another general urged Chiang to ask Chennault to form such a group. By the end of November it was so much a topic of open discussion that the Communists protested, via radio, "Notorious American aggressor against China, Chennault, dares plan organization volunteer air force to fight the Chinese people." The broadcast accused CAT of fighting alongside the Kuomintang and said it was "clear that American imperialist government is just tolerating these actions of slaughtering Chinese people."[36]

The U.S. State Department had reacted with concern when CAT first became involved in China's war; there had been discussion at the time of lifting passports. When rumors surfaced that Chennault was planning a new AVG with U.S. support, the department was quick to deny any involvement. Chennault publicly denied the plan as well, saying that his recommendations were for an expansion of the U.S. advisory/aid groups and more training for the Chinese, along with greater financial support for China.[37] Despite continued U.S. efforts since the war, however, the CAF had accomplished little of worth, and Chennault knew it. Privately he talked with other leaders as well as Yen; the consensus was that they would welcome the support a mercenary air force could provide.

Chennault started mobilizing private opinion through his friends in the United States. He wrote the newly formed association of the Fourteenth Air Force, and one of his former officers enlisted the support of the earlier founders of the Committee for Defending America by Aiding the Allies and formed a new committee to "Defend America by Aiding Anti-Communist China." They began a small lobbying effort to move official Washington toward implementation of Chennault's ideas.[38]

American concern about the Communist threat was mounting, for the U.S.S.R. had precipitated the Berlin crisis at the same time that it became apparent the Chinese Communists were going to gain control of all China unless drastic measures were taken. At this point the United States began to seek ways to support the Nationalist government so that as large a part of China as possible might be kept free from Communist control. After Marshal Yen brought up the topic of a mercenary air force, Secretary of Defense James Forrestal suggested to the State Department that perhaps it should consider a reactivated AVG.[39] Chennault sounded much like his old self as he told the consul general that with such a force he could stop the Communist drive in two weeks. After due consideration, the State Department concluded that such an organization would be viewed by the rest of the world as direct intervention in the Chinese Civil War, carrying all the disadvantages of intervention yet promising little toward halting the Communist conquest. In other words, the idea was dumped like hot coals, for the vision of the U.S.S.R. organizing a Soviet Volunteer Group in response, with the prospect of armed conflict between the two nationalities, was sobering to contemplate.[40]

Meanwhile the stubborn Marshal Yen fought on. By the end of 1948, Taiyuan was his only remaining stronghold. The city had to have 200 tons of food every day, and this was supplied by CAT in one of the largest and most hazardous airlifts on record. After Tientsin and Peking fell to the Communists, CAT flew from Tsingtao, meaning that each of the fifty flights required each day was over enemy territory for six hours. They flew around the clock, coping with severe cold as well as exhaustion. Almost every flight was fired upon. Yen kept building new airfields, each closer to the city than the preceding as the Communists closed in. Pilots would approach one landing strip to draw fire, then duck into another to land. Theirs was a more difficult and hazardous undertaking than the more widely publicized Berlin airlift, which took place during the same months.[41]

By early 1949 CAT was no longer being paid for the Taiyuan airlift and its other services on behalf of the Nationalists; Chiang's govern-

A grinning Chennault, flanked by Doug Smith (left) and Frank Hughes, in the door of a CAT plane, ca. 1949. (Photo courtesy Ted Matsis)

ment had succumbed to economic chaos. Willauer, "worried sick," was frantically juggling finances to keep the airline alive. "I suppose we will finally bail something out of this affair," he wrote Chennault, "but I swear I would have told them all off if it had not been for [Marshal Yen]."[42]

Chennault made one final desperate effort to help. In talking with *Time*, Yen had raised the possibility that a few planes dropping napalm bombs could wipe out the Communist forces around Taiyuan. Chennault and Willauer conferred with the CAF and other government officials about implementing such a strike. Chennault was probably the one who had put the idea in Yen's head in the first place, and it was he who planned a possible mission to be conducted by CAT volunteers temporarily employed by the CAF. Before launching it, CAT's leaders consulted the U.S. consul general in Shanghai. Exactly what transpired is hazy, but the mission was quietly but firmly abandoned.[43]

Taiyuan fell in April 1949. Marshal Yen was in Shanghai, where he was trying to trade the province's gold (which he had with him) for food and arms. He was persuaded not to use his vial of poison. Later he joined forces with the more progressive arm of the Kuomintang on Taiwan and for a while served as Nationalist China's premier.[44]

Nanking and Shanghai were also taken by the Chinese Communists in April. Nationalist China was once again reduced to the isolated provinces it had retained during the Japanese occupation of 1938–45; on them lay both the responsibility and the hope for the survival of a non-Communist China.

As the Communists advanced, Chennault suggested it was time to liquidate CAT.[45] Earlier he had sold a portion of his interest to buy a Shanghai home, a comfortable residence in the Hungjao compound, surrounded by rice paddies where he anticipated there would be good pheasant hunting after the autumn harvest. His move had astounded his friends. Why was he buying a home when everyone else was selling? Chennault's answer, redolent of his perennial optimism, had been that Shanghai might need to be evacuated for a while, but he was certain the government would eventually prevail. "We have not yet been driven into the Arctic," he quipped.[46]

Chennault's surface optimism was misplaced—he lost his personal Shanghai assets—and it was shared by very few. Willauer believed, however, that he could keep CAT going for as much as another year by expanding into Ningsia, Kansu, and Chinghai provinces in China's far north and west. The plan was to revitalize Lanchow, an ancient walled city on the Yellow River that had once served as the point of contact between the Mongol sheepherders of the north and the merchants of the south. With CAT as carrier, Lanchow could become the hub of a network of aerial feeder routes. A fleet of small planes was acquired; a profitable trade in fine Sining wool seemed assured.[47]

Willauer was also quite interested in the armed resistance these provinces were likely to make, and there are some indications that CAT's commercial operations covered some sensitive intelligence gathering in these remote areas along the border of Soviet and Chinese Communist territory.[48] In any event, early in 1949 Chennault and Willauer drew up plans for Chennault to make a trip to the northwest to cement CAT's trade relations and gather "material with which to work in the States." Willauer anticipated that Chennault would "be doing some testifying."[49]

Before he refined and presented what came to be called the Chennault Plan, Chennault once more became a father. Claire Anna was born in Canton on 8 February, "the easiest daughter I ever had,"

Chennault was to say afterward with laughter, for a delicate mis-understanding almost got him in trouble with his young wife. When the hospital called his home with news of the child's arrival about six in the morning, Anna's sister Connie went to Chennault's bedroom door, knocked, told him the news, and heard a mumbled response that she thought meant he had heard her. He had heard but had not understood: he thought she was reminding him to take his morning medicine. The household went on its way, but the new father appeared at breakfast at 7:30 without a word to indicate the special event. Fearing he was disappointed not to have a son, Connie held her tongue. When Chennault was ready to leave, however, obviously headed for his office rather than the hospital, she could stand it no longer and asked, "Aren't you going to see your daughter?" A teasing Chennault replied that Anna had assured him the child would be a boy. It was some time before the confusion cleared.[50]

Anna accompanied Chennault when, early in April, he visited the three provinces north and west of Szechwan: Kansu, Chinghai, and Ningsia. Willauer had provided him with a comprehensive brief that gave some indication of the kind of resistance the provinces might put forth as well as the sort of aid they would need. It was up to Chennault, with his uncanny empathy with the Chinese, to refine upon it. Governor Ma Hung-Kwei of Ningsia gave Chennault the most spectacular welcome, with hundreds of swords flashing in unison and some daring examples of horsemanship by the province's famous Mohammedan warriors. At the end of the four-hour parade, Chennault admitted it was the most impressive review he had seen in all his twelve years in China. When Ma vowed he would never surrender to the Communists, Chennault was inclined to believe him.[51]

Chennault was even more impressed by the burly black-bearded Governor Ma Pu-fang of Chinghai, a former teacher turned high-handed but benevolent ruler. Ma took him on a tour that included a school as well as his pet reforestation project. Understanding that trees meant productive land while the absence of them on the sandy, windswept plains of Tibet meant desert, Ma had used his "power to persuade" and had given his people a quota of trees to plant each year. He also saw to it that they had an irrigation system, good roads, and compulsory education as well as an army so well run that it could depend on volunteers rather than conscripts.[52] Chennault later described Ma's government as the most liberal he knew of, for Ma, like Marshal Yen, was the sort of practical man with whom he could identify. Like many who cherish democracy's freedoms but bewail its

shortcomings, Chennault could see virtues in the benevolent dicta-
torship. " 'We the people' have very little vision and are content to
get the most out of life from day to day," he once wrote.[53]

It was the essence of the Chennault Plan that these strong and vigorous Chinese of the northwest, primarily Moslems and aloof from
the factionalism of the Kuomintang, could stop the encroaching
Communists if encouraged by U.S. policy and supplied with U.S.
arms. As his "Plan for Aid to Non-Communist China" took shape, it
called for military and economic aid, properly supervised by "competent, top-level staff," with four objectives in mind: (1) to enable
non-Communist Chinese to hold the zone not yet controlled by the
Communists; (2) to improve agriculture and industry, raise the standard of living, liberalize the government, and stimulate education to
provide a contrast between Communist and non-Communist ways of
life; (3) to establish military and economic barriers to the spread of
communism; (4) to integrate the economies of the non-Communist
areas with Japan and other non-Communist Pacific countries, to the
mutual strengthening of all.[54]

He flew to the States in late April. There was time for a short visit
with Anna's mother and sisters in San Francisco, but by 28 April he
was in Washington and ready to start what became the busiest and
most intense lobbying portion of his career. Two other plans for "saving" China had recently been considered but had been rejected: Nevada's senator Pat McCarran had suggested a loan of $1.5 billion plus
military help, and John Roots, like Judd the son of China missionaries, suggested that the United States teach a selected group of
Chinese leaders the basis of democratic ideology and train them in
the arts of propagandizing. McCarran's scheme was quickly dismissed as being primarily motivated by the silver interests of Nevada,
while Roots's approach was deemed too idealistic to be practicable.
The Chennault Plan, however, received serious consideration.[55]

Chennault first introduced it to the Joint Committee on Foreign
Economic Cooperation and the Senate Armed Services Committee on
3 May. Speaking informally in executive session and afterward reading a prepared statement to the committee, he linked the security of
China to that of the United States and insisted that the Chinese
did not want communism but had been offered no defendable alternative. He proposed specific aid to help the Chinese create a zone
of resistance around the nine provinces not yet under Communist
control. Geography was in their favor, with deserts, mountain ranges,
rivers, and gorges isolating them from the coastal areas. "The thing

lacking in China is a reasonable hope of defensive victory to give the will to resist," he said. "This we can create if we choose."[56]

He sought to answer in advance some predictable objections. Corruption was prevalent in every country where the conditions permitting it were allowed to flourish, he said. Those conditions must be held in check by adequate supervision, and the "sanitary areas" must "be sufficiently progressive and enlightened both politically and economically that the people of China and of all Asia can have living proof that democracy can meet their material, political, and spiritual aspirations better than can communism." He emphasized the Chinese inability to manage a supply line and stressed the importance of sending "good men" to see that supplies arrived where they were needed. He noted that none of the $125 million earmarked for aid to China during the past year had gotten there in time to be of use in saving Manchuria.[57]

He acknowledged his deep emotional ties to the Chinese people; they had been formed, he said, because he went to China in the hope of serving his own country as well. He acknowledged his economic investment in CAT. "I care more for the future of my country than for the fate of my airline," he said. He hoped that the United States would adopt a positive policy in China and that he could be useful in its execution. If so, he would dispose of his interest in the airline.[58]

When asked about the Communist leaders, he said he had worked with them during the war but had not communicated with them since 1945. When asked if it was true that Chiang Kai-shek had completely ceased to be respected by the Chinese, he said no. When asked if Madame's family was "washed up," he replied, "I am sorry, I do not know anything about that. I have not seen Madame in a long time."[59] (His loyalty to her was undiminished; in writing *Way of a Fighter*, he omitted references to the Soong and Kung family scandals on the grounds of "my personal friendship and because it was not necessary to my story.")[60]

The idea of a revitalized AVG had obviously not been completely squelched, for the committee asked Chennault if it would help. He responded affirmatively, saying it would be a rallying point for the entire population just as it had been in 1941. He also offered the congressmen some of his own perceptions, including his observation that the Chinese "are the most stubborn and the most independent people in the world if you try to drive them, but I have never seen a people who are more tractable if you lead them. You can talk them into doing anything you want."[61]

Chennault was weary. He had been sick with colds and bronchitis since January, and he wanted to go to Louisiana for some genuine rest and some serious catfishing. But Corcoran had arranged what turned out to be a critical conference between Chennault and Rear Admiral Roscoe H. Hillenkoetter, the director of the Central Intelligence Agency, and this was followed on 9 May by a private meeting with CIA representatives. Of these very private conversations, I shall have more to say later.[62]

In somewhat less private meetings on 11 May, Chennault presented his plan to the State Department. Its head was now Dean Acheson, a man of commanding presence whose diplomatic career had strengthened his bent to be strong when strength was needed, honorable when principle was at stake, and persistent in the pursuit of the best interests of his country. He firmly believed that Europe was of vital strategic importance to the United States, while Asia was not; he had no patience with Chiang or the inept Kuomintang. Chiang had withdrawn to Taiwan early in the year, leaving it to Li Tsung-jen as vice president to preside over the collapse on the mainland. When both Nanking and Shanghai were taken by the Communists in April and it became apparent that the Kuomintang was collapsing much more rapidly than had been anticipated, Acheson thought the best course was for the United States to end all aid to Chiang and to make an accommodation with the People's Republic of China, working toward the goal of drawing this new China into the Western orbit rather than pushing it into alliance with the Soviet Union.[63]

Chennault saw the problem from a different perspective, as detailed in an undated document among his papers titled "United States Aid to the National Government of China." Probably prepared during this summer, it began, "Again the time has arrived when we must make a decision as to what constitutes our best interests in China, and having made the decision, formulate a policy to attain our objectives." As he analyzed the situation, a strong, friendly, non-Communist China would be "vitally necessary" should the United States be forced into war with Russia and its satellites. Planes flying from airfields at Sian and Chengtu could be used against the trans-Siberian railroad and the industrialized Ural Mountains. Without China, "we will be forced into a defensive war in Europe and North Africa which we cannot possibly win." In peacetime, he saw a non-Communist China as necessary "to balance our industrial economy and that of the Pacific Islands."[64] The problem was to convince the State Department that a non-Communist China was attainable.

When he talked with James E. Webb (undersecretary), W. Walton

Butterworth (director of the Office of Far Eastern Affairs), and Dean Rusk (deputy undersecretary), Chennault suggested a policy of continuing U.S. communication with China as a means of preventing the spread of communism through Indochina. He saw the short-term aim as the defense of the remaining zone of non-Communist China. But the long-term aim, as he saw it, was to fight the spread of communism. Americans must demonstrate that what the Chinese people wanted and needed—peace, livelihood, and free institutions—was more available under a free system than under communism. He advocated economic aid coordinated with military aid to increase crop production, improve transportation and communication, and develop light industries. He visualized small irrigation projects and improved seeds and commercial fertilizers to increase productivity, and he was emphatic that competent American personnel must accompany aid to see that it was used as intended.[65]

Elaborating on details of his defense scheme, Chennault told the department that he envisioned giving support not to the Nationalist government itself but rather to a military mission that would procure, distribute, train, and plan tactics. The people, he believed, would fight. There would have to be a unifying Chinese leader; he felt Chiang could carry the burden, for he had "learned a lot during the past year" and would be more responsive to guidance than in the past. He made it clear to the department that if it came to a point where the United States openly encouraged armed conflict, he wanted to be in on the fight.[66]

The State Department listened attentively and courteously but was skeptical. Acheson thought he had Congress behind him in his policy of simply letting U.S. support to Chiang come to an end when the present aid package expired in June. Even the ardent China supporters had acquiesced in delaying shipments of aid. There was, however, a nagging worry that "this blood must not be on our hands," that the United States must not simply abandon Chiang precipitously lest it appear that the withdrawal of U.S. support was the cause of his ultimate fall. Acheson had already ordered preparation of a lengthy apologia to explain China's "loss" to the public. Thoughts had turned to possible ways to bring Taiwan (Formosa) into the U.S. orbit without the burden of Chiang and the Kuomintang.[67]

Chennault also talked with members of the Joint Chiefs of Staff in the newly revamped Defense Department. Here he met more interest, for in seeking to create a new defensive posture in the Far East, some of them agreed with Chennault's statement of the "Domino Theory": "Unless the Communists are held they will conquer all China. When all China goes Communist, all Asia will go Communist too. If that happens we have lost everything we fought the war in the Pacific to win. The whole Asiatic continent will be in the control of a single world force that hates us bitterly. Such a situation would threaten the vital security of the United States so seriously that I personally can see no way that World War III could be prevented."[68]

While the Defense Department debated, Chennault talked finances with the Treasury Department. He gave his opinion that if necessary the non-Communist parts of China could be held with an expenditure of $150 million a year, although he suggested an optimum of $500 million annually. He considered Asia cheap at that price.[69]

The pace of the pro-Chiang lobbying accelerated during this summer, for it was clear that time was running out. *Life* magazine published an article under Chennault's name, written by staff writers from his Senate testimony and cleared with him before printing. Essentially the same article, given the more flaming title, "Hold 'Em! Harass 'Em! Hamstring 'Em! The Chennault Plan," appeared shortly afterward in *Reader's Digest*. Chennault provided letters of introduction and "put into motion the Washington machinery" to brief correspondents who were sent to China at his suggestion to write comprehensive stories.[70]

One sees the skilled hand of Corcoran behind the scenes as copies of Chennault's plan were mailed to congressmen. (A young Sen. John F. Kennedy wrote back that he found it "most interesting and informative" and that Chennault himself had "certainly done an excellent job in your country's behalf.") Chennault shared a radio broadcast with Sen. Estes Kefauver of Tennessee; he was honored at lunch on several occasions by groups of congressmen assembled by Senator Knowland and Alabama's Lister Hill.[71]

Chennault was called to testify before the House Committee on Foreign Affairs on 30 June. He reiterated the points he had made before and elaborated on them. The questioning session afterward was lengthy. When congressmen drew him out on his feelings about the Communists, he expressed certainty that the Chinese Communists had Russian advisers. Without hesitation he confirmed the views he had earlier stated in a blunt article published in *America*: "I do not trust any Communist government to honor its agreements." He defended CAT as the only successful demonstration of private enterprise of American capital in China since V-J Day; he hoped it could continue, because China needed it. He was firm in his stance that there was no advantage to diplomatic recognition of the People's Republic as the government of China because it was "a case of trading a good, live horse for a very doubtful, dead mule."[72]

Meanwhile the State Department sought opinions of the Chennault Plan from embassy personnel in China. Ambassador John Leighton Stuart considered it impracticable and of doubtful value to U.S. interests, although he thought it advisable to aid the Moslem resistors economically. Another embassy offical was more blunt, saying Chennault's plan would be profitable to the commercial airlines that would transport the aid but detrimental to U.S. interests.[73]

The State Department continued on its course of letting the Kuomintang die a natural death, without significant U.S. aid. A token $75 million was requested and eventually allocated, and in August the State Department issued its apologia, the controversial *White Paper*, a massive collection of documents that shed much light but little understanding on the whole problem of U.S.-Chinese relations. As far as the public knew, Acheson's policies had prevailed, and the pressure from the pro-Chiang forces during 1949 had gone for naught.

20

Full Circle

Chennault found a home for his convictions at the Office of Policy Coordination within the Central Intelligence Agency. It is ironic that least is known about this aspect of his career, for it is of great pertinence to present and future generations. Chennault's tendency to play his cards close to the chest, to project the likable, "good old boy" facet of his personality while being prudent to the point of secretiveness about his actions, became more marked after he became involved with the CIA. Those who worked with him, well trained in saying little, offer scant help to the biographer. The CIA itself is niggardly about what it reveals to the public, even after a lapse of thirty-five years. The paper trail that can be followed is dim.

The agency itself was relatively new in 1949. Although Donovan had prepared a plan to convert the wartime OSS into a central intelligence agency, complex decisions were involved in making the transition to peacetime intelligence operations. At the war's end, overwhelmed by other problems more demanding of solution, Truman postponed decision by simply abolishing the OSS. The various personnel and functions were parceled out to the War and Navy departments and to the Department of State.

Early in 1946, as growing tension between the United States and the U.S.S.R. brought the need for intelligence into bold relief, Truman set up the Central Intelligence Group, with the secretaries of state, war, and navy serving to coordinate the information gleaned from the various departments. This also proved inadequate for the mounting Cold War tensions. When the National Security Act of September 1947 created the National Military Establishment, with the secretary of defense and executive departments of army, navy and air force, it also established the National Security Council and the Central Intelligence Agency.

Initially the CIA had no authorization or capability for what has come to be called "special operations," although Donovan's OSS had very matter-of-factly combined the gathering of intelligence with covert psychological warfare and small-scale military operations. When Communists took over Czechoslovakia and threatened to do the same in Italy in 1948, the National Security Council revived the option by setting up the Office of Policy Coordination to conduct covert operations—political, psychological, and economic warfare plus paramilitary activities. Its first task was to seek to influence the elections in Italy.

The Office of Policy Coordination was under the CIA for budget purposes, but the director of the CIA originally had no authority over its activities. Its head was appointed by the secretary of state; both State and Defense departments used it to accomplish their goals. It was originally anticipated that OPC would be small and limited in scope. The guidelines were that its operations must be secret and must be plausibly deniable by the government.[1]

The parallel with Roosevelt's thinking as he created the AVG in 1941 is startling. At that time, the president had been convinced that the best interests of the United States would be served by military action, but such action could not be conducted openly, violated existing laws, and could not (possibly would not) be sanctioned by either Congress or the public—obstacles Chennault had offered a way to circumvent. Roosevelt had depended on Corcoran to evaluate Chennault and the proposed clandestine operations, and Corcoran's reaction to Chennault's plan in 1941—"so original that politically it would either be lost so completely we could always explain ourselves out of it or would succeed so magnificently that it could never be challenged"[2]—sounds like a wordy prototype for the "plausibly deniable" restriction on OPC in 1948.

OPC got off to a running start under the leadership of Frank G. Wis-

ner, a lawyer who had gained experience with clandestine operations in the OSS and who could rival Donovan in personal energy and
forcefulness. Far from seeing OPC as limited, Wisner sought like-
minded activists from former OSS operators and began forming a
clandestine force on a worldwide scale, operating, in the words of
one CIA director, "in the atmosphere of an order of Knights Tem-
plars, to save Western freedom from Communist darkness—and from
war."[3]

OPC quickly became a dynamic force within the agency, its potential tremendously enhanced when the CIA Act of 1949 exempted the
CIA from all federal laws that required disclosure of its activities and
personnel while giving the agency authority to spend money without
the usual public accountability. A new kind of organization designed
to cope with a new kind of world and a new kind of war, the CIA by
1949 had begun to acquire tremendous power. It kept an extremely
low profile; the general public was scarcely aware it existed. It was
the perfect shield behind which a variety of clandestine endeavors
could take place. Wisner concentrated first on Europe. By the spring
of 1949 he had begun making plans for anti-Communist work in the
Far East. At that point he met Chennault.[4]

Appropriately enough, it was Corcoran who first brought Chennault and the CIA together. CIA director Roscoe H. Hillenkoetter
was noncommittal after his initial conference with Chennault, but
another official, Paul L. E. Helliwell, saw possibilities. Helliwell had
been the head of the OSS Intelligence Division in Kunming during
the war; he knew Chennault and thought highly of him. Helliwell
suggested to Wisner that Chennault's airline might be useful in
China.[5]

Wisner did not need pictures drawn. He and several associates met
Chennault at the Hotel Washington on 9 May. When Chennault presented his plan, Wisner perceived a kindred soul, a man of forcefulness and strength. CAT was in financial trouble, however, for
Nationalist government contracts had almost ceased; CAT operations in the northwest, as well as an arrangement with Yunnan to
airlift tin to ports in Indochina, were just getting under way. After
their talk, Wisner had a memo drafted for the State Department stating OPC's interest that CAT stay in operation. He hoped to use the
airline to transport supplies to anti-Communist forces in China. Wisner hoped the Economic Cooperation Administration might make a
grant to CAT to ensure its financial stability.

The Economic Cooperation Administration, set up in 1948 to

administer U.S. aid, rejected the idea of assistance to CAT, and members of the State Department, as we have noted, reacted to Chennault's plan with less than enthusiasm. With no help coming from that direction, Wisner assigned Helliwell to the task of finding some way to subsidize CAT and to ensure that it would be available for eventual OPC use in China.

Helliwell first met with Corcoran, who elaborated on CAT's desperate financial status, and then reported to Wisner that the major problem was foreign exchange to enable CAT to pay its American employees and buy gasoline and parts. It would probably cost OPC $1 million a year to keep CAT flying, Helliwell had concluded, but he was sure it would be worth the cost. Not only did CAT provide a "face" behind which OPC could act in secret, but it would take many millions of dollars to duplicate its operation. Helliwell's conclusion strongly urged that "favorable policy decisions be taken promptly and that thereafter the necessary contacts and representations be made looking toward ultimate operational subsidy sufficient to maintain C.A.T. as an American-owned airline with complete facilities in non-Communist China."[6]

A turning point came in June when Mao Tse-tung denounced the United States and made it clear that the People's Republic of China would lean toward the U.S.S.R. The National Security Council at that point identified the Soviet Union as the principal threat to the peace and stability of Asia; it advocated moves by the United States to contain Soviet power and influence in the Far East. Although Acheson continued to advocate recognition of the People's Republic in hopes that it might be aligned with the West, others in the State Department were less certain. Rusk, Davies, George Kennan, and Ambassador-at-Large Philip Jessup proposed that the United States consider a policy of nonrecognition of the People's Republic coupled with continued support for the Kuomintang in the United Nations and assistance to non-Communist China.[7]

Webb then asked the Department of Defense to review the Chennault Plan. Was it militarily feasible? Could the aid advocated be sent in time and in a large enough amount to be effective? In October, Secretary of Defense Louis Johnson replied that the operational and logistical recommendations of Chennault's Plan were "too vague" to analyze, while the resistance assumed by the plan depended on conditions "not observable at present."[8]

Chennault's "sanitary zone" of resistance had indeed begun to disappear. Ma Pu-fang and his noble Mohammedan horsemen inflicted a dramatic defeat on the Communist forces early in the summer only to be roundly defeated themselves in August, partly because other northwestern leaders proved to be less eager to fight than he (Ma Hung-kwei chartered a CAT plane and escaped with his wealth to Hong Kong and later America) but also, according to Willauer, because Ma lacked the kind of aid that the United States might have extended.[9]

Ma was in retreat from Lanchow when Chennault and Richard G. Stilwell (no relation to Vinegar Joe), head of OPC's Far East Division, met to make the final plans about OPC help for CAT. We know little of what transpired, but Willauer, who had been keeping in close touch with Corcoran by trans-Pacific telephone, wrote his wife on 29 August that aid of some sort to China was 90 percent sure. His operational plan covering Japan, China, and Indochina, he said, was "meeting with some favor." In another letter on 18 September he wrote that "it now looks that aid is about agreed on and that somehow CAT is to play a substantial part."[10] The aid was above board— $75 million for China, with the president not being required to specify the nature of the expenditures, as part of the Mutual Defense Assistance Act of 1949.

The role to be played by CAT was not public knowledge. Hillenkoetter discussed it with Acheson, Kennan, and Jessup on 1 September. The State Department's approval, although not its endorsement, of the CIA's intent to subsidize CAT was granted three weeks later in a meeting between Hillenkoetter, Webb, and Butterworth. Kennan was the State Department's representative on the OPC oversight committee; when he sent Wisner a memo on 4 October that neither approved nor disapproved of Wisner's plans for covert assistance to anti-Communist elements in China, Wisner had all he needed. OPC was ready to go to war against the Communists in China, and CAT would be part of the action.[11]

The final papers between CAT and the CIA were signed on 1 November, with Corcoran signing for CAT. The CIA committed up to half a million dollars to finance a CAT base and to underwrite deficits stemming from hazardous flying done on agency business. CAT would give the agency's operations priority. An advance of $200,000 confirmed the mutual commitments.[12]

By the time CAT and the CIA reached agreement, Chennault was back in China. Before leaving Washington he wrote a number of courtesy letters, thanking individuals for their interviews, their understanding, and their help. One went to W. Stuart Symington, secretary of the air force, which had at long last achieved independent status; another went to Louis Johnson at the Defense Department. He thanked Knowland and Judd for their help in Congress. He wrote Supreme Court Chief Justice Fred M. Vinson that he very much appreciated the evening spent with him. Most revealing of his mood was his letter to Butterworth: "I have imposed on you not less than three times, and I appreciate your sympathetic reception of my views. . . . I am sure you know that I am sensible of my own responsibility to you in your direction of Far Eastern affairs for the Department, and that on my way back to China I shall do nothing to embarrass you."[13]

The Chinese Civil War rushed to its conclusion in the closing months of 1949. The Communists took Canton in October, Kweilin and Chungking in November, Kunming in December. Most of the Chinese swam with the Communist flood, but Chennault's friend Hsueh Yueh fought to the end. "We are worry on one hand," he wrote Chennault in November, but "we shall try to dig out more new energy." He asked Chennault's help in getting money for arms, but it was too late.[14] Nationalist China was being driven off the mainland. CAT and its dedicated crews worked day and night, airlifting personnel and supplies, evacuating government assets, preventing panic by offering a way out of the threatened areas. The men often took grave risks. There were amazingly few accidents or losses, even though CAT itself had to move its base of operations some dozen times. Morale remained high. Chennault and Willauer, working around the clock, were proud to see their organization withstand the intense stress.[15]

Their sentiment was shared by Alfred T. Cox, the first of a succession of CIA operatives who lived their cover as officials in the CAT organization. Cox joined CAT in October; his CIA job was to head OPC activities in China. Cox had worked with OSS in Kunming in 1945, organizing paratroop commando units. Now, in late 1949, he did what he could to support Gen. Pai Chung-hsi, who had inherited the thankless task of directing the Nationalists' last defense. By the end of the year Cox's CIA job was over; there was no more Nationalist defense on the mainland to support.[16]

Chennault and Willauer, in contrast, had more to do than ever before. Sending part of their company on to Taiwan, they set up CAT's main operating base on Hong Kong and worked frantically to keep flying, constantly seeking paying contracts that would enable the airline to survive. CNAC and CATC had also taken refuge in Hong Kong, and on 9 November competition became a desperate international issue when the general managers of both CNAC and CATC defected to the People's Republic in Peking, taking twelve of their planes in the process. There was some evidence that they were motivated both by fear and by greed—they anticipated that the airlines would have to move to Taiwan, and they did not want to leave their families behind them—but the Communists courted them with substantial bribes and a hint of blackmail over some crooked bookkeeping. In any event, the two companies left seventy-one transport planes in Hong Kong. The People's Republic promptly declared them its property.[17]

Chennault was appalled. Even so, when Rousselot, Rosbert, and Lewis Burridge suggested that CAT take over the CNAC and CATC planes, his reaction was to shake his head and speculate that to do so would be "inviting all kinds of problems." Willauer, younger and "a more wild-spirited stallion," was more quickly convinced. He flew at once to Taiwan, found (as he and Chennault had anticipated) the Nationalist officials in a quandary, and quickly drafted a proposal for Chiang. Warning of the danger of invasion plus the negative effects on Nationalist morale, he offered CAT's services as agent for the Nationalist government. Willauer requested authority to take whatever action might be necessary to forestall Communist possession of the transports. Chiang agreed. CAT was given authority to go ahead, with the full resources of the Nationalist government behind it.[18]

"This air force constitutes a balance of power in Asia," Chennault wrote Alsop, "because its possession gives complete mobility to its owners." There was reason to believe the Communists were training paratroops with the capture of Taiwan in mind; given the seventy-one transports, their chances of success would be almost certain. Chennault compared CAT's situation to the British attack on the French fleet during World War II, when the assets of a defeated ally were destroyed to prevent undesirable use of them. "As a matter of national policy," he thought the United States could not afford to "give the Reds in one package more war material than all our economic bans [during the Cold War] have deprived them of."[19]

This was the beginning of the planes case—a prolonged litigation that involved the two governments of China as well as the United States, Great Britain, and Hong Kong before finally being resolved in Britain's Privy Council three years later. At first Chennault and Willauer tried to take custody of the planes by the simple step of having the Nationalist Civil Aeronautics Administration suspend the registration certificates of the craft. Willauer, who thoroughly enjoyed

CNAC and CATC planes, released by the British Privy Council decision in June 1952, on the deck of the light escort carrier USS *Cape Esperance* in Hong Kong harbor. (Photo courtesy Ted Matsis)

the adventures CAT brought his way, personally led a group of CAT personnel in a midnight expedition to let the air out of the planes' tires so there could be no immediate danger of their being flown out.[20]

The unsympathetic Hong Kong authorities were not amused. Sitting in the shadow of the new People's Republic and dependent on its goodwill, the British colony staunchly supported its home government's intention to extend formal recognition to the People's Republic as soon as the capture of the mainland was completed. What Chennault called a legal purchase, Hong Kong officials regarded as collusion. Hong Kong wanted no trouble. Its governor, Sir Alexander Grantham, announced that the planes could not depart until a Sino-British air agreement had been made.

Realizing that they faced a complicated, drawn-out process that would require tremendous resources, Chennault and Willauer asked Cox if OPC could help. Cox felt that it should and would; he sent an "urgent recommendation" to Washington that the government assume the initiative in controlling and underwriting whatever actions might have to be taken to keep the planes out of Communist hands, using Chennault and Willauer as agents. The response was not as far-reaching as the potential agents had hoped. Although it indicated that "every encouragement" should be given to Chennault and Willauer in their actions as private citizens, the U.S. government did not wish to be involved.[21]

Through Corcoran, who knew his way around the private corridors of government, Chennault and Willauer sought to determine just how far "every encouragement" would go. In the State Department, where official sentiment was still firmly against support for the Nationalists, the question of the planes received consideration under the National Security Council's new overall civil aviation policy, which opposed the establishment of airlines that had the potential of becoming instruments of Communist infiltration. Worried officials were watching Southeast Asia with growing concern; they had no desire to see the seventy-one planes of CNAC and CATC in position to assist further expansion by the Chinese Communists. The result of Corcoran's explorations, therefore, was an unofficial green light, for again the government favored a course of action it could not officially pursue. As with the AVG, Chennault would be allowed to do the job. This time, however, the United States would not underwrite the process, although it was deemed to be in the "national interest" that the planes be denied to the People's Republic.[22]

Corcoran moved with astounding speed to incorporate a new company whose stockholders included himself, his brother David, Chennault, Willauer, Youngman, and Brennan—men who had worked together in China Defense Supplies. They would endeavor to recover all the assets of the two defecting airlines; all profit, after expenses were paid, would be divided equally among the stockholders. The new company, CAT, S.A., was incorporated under Panamanian laws, which offered a lenient tax structure and allowed secrecy. CAT, S.A., then gave another new corporation, Civil Air Transport, Inc., authority to act for it in the legal fight to gain control of the planes. CATI was a Delaware corporation, with Chennault chairman of the board and Willauer president; the existence of CAT, S.A., was not disclosed.[23] In the touchy political and legal battles of the next three years, the U.S. government's support of CATI was apparently support of private American citizens and their company.

At first events moved quickly. Chennault and Willauer purchased the planes from the Nationalist government, in the process signing a promissory note for $4.75 million which they did not have. The sale was completed on 12 December.[24] The drama began.

One of the major actors was Donovan. At the end of the war he had resumed his private law practice with a New York firm. Although he was beginning to slow down a little from his feverish activity of the war years, some of his old exuberance returned when Corcoran hired his firm to handle CATI's case. He promptly flew to London, where he and a U.S. State Department representative told the British Foreign Office that Americans had purchased CNAC and CATC, and since the American government had a strong interest in the matter, they hoped the British would move quickly to remove any legal obstacles. The point was made that the planes could be of great strategic value in case of emergency. No doubt the British had already considered the possible necessity of evacuating Hong Kong and appreciated the hint. They promised only an immediate review.[25]

It was imperative that the planes be given U.S. registration before any legal challenges were raised. The State Department consulted the head of the Civil Aeronautics Administration, who expressed willingness to cut any corners necessary to accomplish this end. Pan American still owned 20 percent of CNAC, however, so the next step was for a member of the State Department to talk with William L. Bond, vice president of Pan American with responsibility for CNAC. Bond had known Chennault, strengths and weaknesses, for years. His most recent experience, working with Chennault and Willauer over the initial charter for CAT in China, had convinced him that the two men flirted with the illegal and the unethical. On the other hand, it behooved Pan American not to argue with the State Department, and Bond himself felt that the planes should be denied to the Communists. He may have gritted his teeth as he did so, but he met T. V. Soong the next day, and they arranged the sale of Pan American's interest for $1.25 million. The Civil Aeronautics Administration promptly waived the usual inspection requirements and granted the disputed planes American registration.[26]

Hong Kong authorities were less cooperative. They continued to deny the new owners access to their planes. Donovan flew from London to Hong Kong, accompanied by Richard P. Heppner, a member of his firm and wartime head of OSS in China. Heppner shared Donovan's enthusiasm for the present case. Nevertheless they made scant headway. The first week in January the British granted formal recognition to the People's Republic as the government of China.

Shortly afterward the local Hong Kong courts ruled that the planes were the rightful property of the People's Republic.

Chennault led the subsequent howl of indignant protest, and during February and March the diplomatic pressure rose, eliminating any doubts that CATI had the full backing of the U.S. government. Acheson protested vigorously to London, where almost daily a U.S. diplomat visited the Foreign Office. China bloc members in Congress kept the issue in the forefront and hinted that they might favor cutting appropriations for British aid. The pressure told. On 10 May London issued an order in council instructing Hong Kong officials to hold the planes until the question had been decided "by full processes of the law." The governor of Hong Kong thought it a "sorry business," and Peking formally warned the British that the order gave them reason to doubt British sincerity in extending diplomatic relations. Chennault, Willauer, and their silent partners, however, rejoiced at having won the first round: they would now have the right of appeal to the Privy Council in London. The legal processes could take years, and in the meantime the planes were denied to the Communists.[27]

The planes case gobbled up enormous sums of money for legal fees plus such necessary extras as bribes to guards for the registration numbers on the impounded planes so American registration could be made. CAT had already suffered telling financial loss in its successive moves from one base to another, and its paying business was almost at a standstill. Cox advanced CIA funds to cover successive crises. It was not enough. At the beginning of the year Willauer went to Washington to seek funds. Chennault stayed behind to seek new business and generally to salvage what he could from the confusion of the preceding months. There was also another move to oversee, for CAT was following the Nationalist government to Taiwan.[28]

Willauer's decisions in Washington had far-reaching implications but can quickly be summarized. He and Corcoran kept the question of CAT's future before the State Department, the CIA, and the Economic Cooperation Administration. It was a tense time in international relations, for the new Communist government in China seemed to shift the world's balance of power toward the Communist nations and to strike fear into the hearts of all those who preferred another way. After the Russians exploded their first atomic device in August 1949 and signed a treaty of alliance with the People's Republic the following February, Washington adopted the National Security Council's NSC 64, a key document in the development of domino theory policy. Focusing on Indochina and predicting that a Communist triumph there would put the other nations of Southeast Asia in danger, it concluded that all practicable measures should be taken to prevent further Communist expansion in that part of the world. About Taiwan, which now sheltered what was left of Nationalist China, there was some ambivalence, but since Chiang's government was expected to fall very shortly, no military aid for its defense seemed indicated, and none was recommended.[29]

Yet Washington chafed under a sense of powerlessness to influence events that were deemed to be of great strategic importance. In such a climate covert action thrives; it came to play an ever larger part in official thinking. Willauer capitalized upon it. Telling the CIA that CAT had three alternatives—to sell to the Communists, sell to the United States, or liquidate on the open market—he forced a decision. The discussions were lively but the decision predictable: the CIA decided that continued support of CAT was in the national interest, and the Joint Chiefs of Staff as well as the State and Defense departments agreed. The papers were signed at the end of March. The CIA advanced $350,000 to cover outstanding obligations plus allotting $400,000 to cover deficits until mid-June, when it had an option to buy for $1 million. In the meantime CAT was to make an effort to become self-sufficient.[30]

Chennault had known little of what was taking place in Washington, and when Willauer returned to Taiwan he found his partner's nose "slightly, but not seriously, out of joint" because he had been kept in the dark. He was "mad as hell," however, that $25,000 of his personal funds had been appropriated for CAT's use by its business manager without his consent. Some of Willauer's funds had been absorbed as well, and faced with hard times, both men threw themselves into the challenge of lowering their operating budget and finding enough business to keep the larder stocked.[31] Although basically in harmony with the CIA, Chennault feared it would in time become another huge bureaucracy. Bureaucracies he could do without; he would have preferred to see CAT maintain its independence. He whacked away at already lean budgets and put planes in preservatives. Personnel were offered the choice of leaving or staying at reduced pay. Most of them stayed, in part from personal loyalty to him, in part because CAT's anti-Communist crusade had become, in the words of one, "almost an obsession."[32]

Willauer scoured the Philippines, Indochina, and other areas south of Hong Kong for new business. Chennault concentrated on Korea, Japan, and round-the-island service on Taiwan itself. Neither had much success. Operating deficits mounted. Willauer returned to Washington in June.

By that time the National Security Council was predicting a long-term confrontation between two hostile worlds, one free and one Communist. Among other measures, it advocated greatly increased spending to counter the revolutionary nationalist movements that were surfacing in a third world, the world of the former colonial territories now seeking independence. With a growing fear of a worldwide Communist conspiracy and a resulting vital concern for the status quo, the United States initiated military assistance programs for Southeast Asia.

Again the needs of foreign policy worked in CAT's favor, for not only would the State and Defense departments need transport service for distributing the aid, but OPC considered CAT essential for its own expanded operations. In the State Department there was some discussion of whether the CIA's purchase of the airline would put the government in competition with private enterprise, but no other objections seem to have been raised. The lawyers and bankers did their paperwork, and money changed hands on 25 August. The purchase price was $950,000, of which Chennault received the return of his $25,000 in personal funds plus his ownership percentage (14.46 percent) of the price less the payment of debts.[33]

Chennault wrote Corcoran that he was "quite satisfied." The solution found was "far better than liquidation or pinching down to a size that would satisfy our current operational requirements," and CAT had lacked capital for the third alternative—to purchase the modern transports that would have been necessary to create a competitive airline.[34]

The face of CAT changed little. Few knew the airline had changed hands, and even fewer knew it was owned by the CIA. The explanation offered—and accepted—was that CAT had secured backing from "some bankers" in the United States. Chennault became chairman of the board, Willauer president; Cox resumed his post as vice president. Other CIA personnel slipped into CAT's hierarchy, but few knew the specifics of their work. It was still a spunky, cheeky, can-do outfit, despite the first uniforms and certain other appurtenances of conventionality. Business soon picked up, for CAT flew charter missions in connection with overt aid programs and "detached operations" on a covert basis. Very little was known about the latter. The pilots were selected for reliability and discretion and were told what they needed to know.[35]

Behind the public face, Chennault's relationship with CAT and with Washington changed dramatically. His position posed a problem for the CIA, for it was widely recognized that his distinctive leadership style gave CAT its personality, that vital spark of morale that made it a valuable weapon in the Cold War. This the agency could not afford to lose. The CIA (and no doubt the departments of State and Defense as well) also wanted to capitalize on Chennault's strong ties with the Nationalist Chinese, to use his friendship with Chiang and his unique relationship with the Nationalist power structure to make certain that CAT continued to have a secure haven under the Nationalists' wing. The airline flew, after all, the flag of the Nationalist government. Only Chennault's special relationship with China had overcome opposition to CAT's initial incorporation, which had been granted as a Chennault-Willauer partnership, the only form in which opponents would accept it at all. Chennault was the kingpin on which the whole structure hinged. His presence was considered "vitally necessary on day-to-day basis" to maintain positive relationships with the Chinese.[36]

Chennault could also be depended upon to absorb any criticisms or abuse, to deflect attention away from covert activities yet keep quiet about their source. There were, however, problems. Just as Marshall and others during the war had been convinced Chennault could not separate his loyalty to China from his allegiance to the United States, now the CIA had the same fear. Chennault insisted on complete honesty and openness with Chiang. How far could he be trusted if it came to operations that were anti-Communist but not necessarily pro-Nationalist? The agency tried to evade the problem by calling him back to the United States for consultations at critical times, thus removing him from the scene of the action both for his own sake and for that of the CIA.[37]

As chairman of the board, Chennault had special responsibility for high policy and strategy involving CAT's relationships with the Nationalist government, but he was no longer involved in day-to-day operations. Initially there were fears that he would rebel at not having an active role. After they got into the swing of their new duties, Willauer found to his relief that the general was "in mighty fine form and completely docile about my running things."[38]

In July 1950 Corcoran wrote Chennault that his stock was rising, for the ink was not dry on the CAT-CIA papers before Communist forces in North Korea crossed the thirty-eighth parallel and began driving on Seoul.[39] It seemed that the dominoes had begun to topple.

The Korean War became much more grim much more quickly than anyone anticipated. The United States felt the need to make certain that the aggression did not succeed, for to do otherwise would be backing away from the Communist challenge. Truman and Acheson moved immediately to bring the matter under a United Nations banner; MacArthur was put in command of United Nations (primarily American) troops to get the job done.

A critical shortage in military transport was soon obvious. This was CAT's opportunity to demonstrate that it was worth the price. Planes were rushed out of storage; laid-off pilots and ground crews were called back to work. On 9 September CAT began flying between Japan and Korea under contract with the U.S. Far East Air Material Command. The arrangement was successful and satisfactory to all parties, even though Stratemeyer mildly tweaked Chennault that CAT had "overcommitted itself with a lot of optimistic assertions of what they could do" during the initial weeks. The cooperation continued. CAT flew more than 15,000 missions in connection with the Korean War, although after the first emergency these were primarily flights connecting the Philippines, Okinawa, Taiwan, Guam, Iwo Jima, and Japan.[40]

Chennault and Willauer felt vindicated, for they had seen it coming. In November 1949 Chennault had visited MacArthur in Tokyo and President Syngman Rhee in Seoul. The trip had looked like a lot of fanfare—jet fighter escorts for his plane, "a bunch of Army and Air Force big wigs to meet the Boss" at Okinawa, the Army's finest VIP hospitality in Tokyo, bands and a military review in Seoul.[41] But there was more than fanfare. Chennault and MacArthur had talked around (if not about) the issue of getting aid to the Nationalists, and Chennault reported their discussion to the CIA. In Seoul, Chennault and Rhee had discussed defense, especially aviation. Chennault had recommended his old fishing buddy, Gen. Russell E. Randall, as someone who could survey Korea's need and make a report. The result had been a request to the United States for combat airplanes before the end of 1949, but these had not been provided. After the war erupted, Chennault wrote Knowland accusing the State Department of "glaring deficiencies in military preparedness," for he considered that omissions of planes and tanks from the aid program "were really invitations to the Communists to conquer South Korea by force of arms."[42]

Although the CIA thoughtfully blacked out part of Chennault's report on his first meeting with MacArthur, we can surmise that the two had a major meeting of minds, and each personally confirmed that he was an ardent fan of the other. MacArthur had already gone on record on Chennault's behalf, telling the State Department that, if the United States put 500 fighter planes in the hands of some warhorse like Chennault and gave volunteers the right to join him without penalty, the tide might be turned in Asia. Now Chennault responded in kind, writing Knowland months before the Korean War had begun to urge that Congress appoint MacArthur a supreme commander to take charge in the Far East. Later, when Truman relieved MacArthur from command because he defied the president's orders, Chennault stayed out of the politics but made it plain he supported MacArthur's belief that a military decision should be sought. In fact, an unabashed Chennault told a press conference that MacArthur was "the greatest American we have produced since Abraham Lincoln's day." MacArthur in turn was reported to have described Chennault as a genius. The widely circulated story that MacArthur asked, "Where's Chennault?" when he surveyed the group assembled on the deck of the *Missouri* for the Japanese surrender ceremony, however, is unfounded.[43]

As the Korean War cooled down, the conflict in Vietnam heated up. Chennault had special cause to follow it closely, for he had unwittingly played a small part in its earliest stages. Ho Chi Minh emerged during World War II days as the leader of an Indochina nationalist movement that hoped to take control from the occupying Japanese when the war ended. Because their goal was to prevent the colonial French regime from reassuming power, the French, of course, considered Ho and his followers as enemies. Roosevelt waffled, not wanting to support the French (or the British) in reclaiming the lost colonies, because he believed the prewar colonial structure in Asia would have to give way to a different system. He was nevertheless unwilling to damage U.S. relations with Allies. In the spring of 1945 Wedemeyer had been authorized to do intelligence work in Indochina but had been instructed not to ally his forces with the French.

Chennault had not been made privy to Wedemeyer's instructions, yet when Wedemeyer went to Washington in March 1945, Chennault was left in charge. At that moment the long civil war of Vietnam began. The French forces, poised to launch an attack designed to wipe out Ho and his Vietminh, were instead surprised by a Japanese offensive which defeated them so totally that it effectively marked the end of any French authority in the country. That the way had been cleared for Ho was not immediately apparent.[44]

The shattered French forces cried for help. Chennault consulted Chiang to make certain that the Chinese would allow the fleeing French to come into China. Backed by Chiang's reluctant approval and the authority of a State Department memo that authorized Wedemeyer to be "helpful to the French," Chennault sent intelligence men into Indochina to make contact with the retreating French and to arrange air drops of food, medicine, arms, and ammunition. He was dumbfounded when orders from the War Department directed him to cease providing the French with arms and ammunition, although he was allowed to help them by military action against their Japanese pursuers. Shaking his head over the mysterious ways of military bureaucracy, Chennault complied.[45]

The Japanese offensive had also torn up the Allied intelligence network in Indochina. This the OSS was directed to reestablish as quickly as possible even if doing so meant using resistance groups such as Ho's. Ho was in Kunming—he had gone there to report the buildup of French and Japanese forces—and he and an OSS officer got together and arranged for a series of intelligence listening posts with OSS radios and OSS-trained Vietnamese operators. The business taken care of, Ho asked to meet Chennault. It was a reasonable request, especially as Ho had been instrumental in rescuing a downed American flyer. The meeting took place on 29 March 1945. The conversation was superficial and pleasant, primarily the exchange of thanks. Afterward Ho requested and was given an autographed picture of the general, and later, when the Vietminh sought to establish its primacy among Indochina's nationalist groups, he used it to support his claim to U.S. backing.[46]

It was no secret that Ho Chi Minh and his followers were Communists. Nor was it any secret that Chennault would have worked with the devil himself to keep his flyers out of enemy prison camps. Chennault's sympathies, however, were firmly behind the French as they struggled with Ho for control of Indochina in the postwar years. Chennault saw Indochina as one of Asia's danger points. As early as 1950 he warned of Chinese Communist support for Ho, basing his predictions on troop buildups and road improvements reported by the CAT pilots, plus his own reasoning that Communist China would need the rich resources of southern Asia to balance the poorer provinces of southern China. Behind the steady buildup of Chinese military strength pointed toward Korea, Indochina, and Taiwan, Chennault perceived Russian backing. He advocated increasing U.S. military strength to put teeth in a policy of resisting Communist aggression wherever it occurred.[47]

Despite growing economic and military aid from the United States, by late 1953 the French forces in Indochina were nearly exhausted, while those of Ho and his Vietminh were gaining strength. Desperate for aerial transport to supplement their small air forces, the French asked the United States for the loan of U.S. Air Force C-119s with their crews to fly tanks and heavy equipment into the battle zones. This was a significant step beyond aid, for committing military personnel to combat missions was skirting the precipice.

Once again covert action solved the problem. The secretary of state talked to the director of the CIA, who spoke to Cox in Taipei. CAT was available. From mid-March until its fall in May, CAT pilots—American civilians wearing their gaudy tropical shirts and making no secret of being there both for the cause and for the money—flew supplies to the besieged garrison at Dienbienphu. Two of them, Wallace Buford and James McGovern, CAT's beloved "Earthquake," were killed in active duty.[48]

Much of Chennault's time and emotional energy during 1950–53 went into the settlement of the planes case. He kept the issue alive in the press and in the U.S. Congress through interviews and letters, doggedly arguing for the validity of the purchase, challenging the Hong Kong court decisions, and enumerating the dangers should the planes fall into Communist hands. He was harsh in his judgment of British actions. In one letter addressed to "My Dear Fellow American," he wrote, "The Hong Kong British are protecting their own property in Shanghai and elsewhere in China by paying squeeze to the Chinese Communists out of American property."[49]

The hearings before the Privy Council in London began in June 1952 with Sir Hartley Shawcross handling CATI's case. When the Korean War erupted almost simultaneously, the issue seemed more urgent than before. The final decision rendered on 27 July found for Chennault and Willauer on the grounds that the new government of China acquired the obligations as well as rights of its predecessor. A jubilant Donovan called it the first Cold War victory in the Far East.[50]

Chennault feared that the Communists would physically seize the planes and vowed to prevent it. "If I couldn't do anything else," he wrote Noe, "I would hire a barge and dump them into a deep hole in the ocean." Corcoran did not think such a drastic step was necessary; he went into action to get a U.S. aircraft carrier sent to Hong Kong for them. He argued that the planes were war matériel, the technicality that they were private American property being a matter that could be faced after the planes were safely out of Hong Kong. It was done, and another round of thank-you letters went to congressmen.[51]

Arriving in California for the first AVG reunion, 1952. Foreground, from left: former flight leaders Kenneth Jernstedt and Henry Geselbracht; former squadron leaders Robert H. Neale (shaking hands with Chennault) and David "Tex" Hill (striped tie). Former flight leader Peter Wright in bow tie. (Photo courtesy Richard Rossi)

CATI's troubles, however, were far from over. It now had the problem of reconditioning and selling the planes, in poor condition after having been parked in the open, near salt water. Many parts and accessories were missing, having presumably been stolen. Chennault worked on a scheme with various U.S. investors to purchase the planes and give them to the Nationalist Chinese, but on this project he made little headway.[52]

A more perplexing problem was that the financial settlement with the Nationalist government became entangled with the renewal of CAT's franchise. The two companies were separate—CATI was not part of the CIA purchase—but the Chinese seemed not to make the distinction. Their civil aviation law, passed in July 1952 and similar to that of most nations, specified that the majority of any airline operating under it must be Chinese owned. The CIA, however, had no intention of transferring the assets of CAT to a Chinese company. The Nationalists then demanded payment of the $4.75 million in promissory notes given by CATI in 1949. CATI responded with counterclaims against the Nationalists, expecting a bargaining process to begin. Instead all negotiations reached an impasse.

In June 1953 Willauer lost a son in an accident at the family home on Nantucket. Grief stricken, he hurried home. He did not return to CAT; his duties were taken over by Cox. CAT's franchise was due to expire at the end of 1953; its renewal was one of Cox's more pressing problems, but progress seemed unlikely when Chiang Kai-shek dismissed a member of his cabinet in a fury after learning that CATI had acquired several million dollars from the sale of CNAC assets. CAT was then told that its franchise would not be renewed; if it wished to continue operating on Taiwan, it could use the $4.75 million in CATI promissory notes to form a Chinese-owned company.[53]

Worried CIA and CAT officials did some hard negotiating in the near-panic that followed. Apparently viewing it all with slight detachment, if not amusement, Chennault quietly went to talk with Chiang. He was able to convince his old friend that the information he had been given on the CATI settlement to date was distorted, and Chiang relented. With his opposition removed, the doors of negotiation reopened. When Chennault requested a continuation of the present franchise until a permanent solution could be found, it was granted.[54]

More franchise schemes were devised and submitted; these too were rejected. The process was tedious, and Chennault, who worked diligently toward a solution, observed, "Sometimes I think that laws are made only to interfere with and upset business."[55] Negotiations dragged on into fall 1954, when a new foreign investment law made it possible for CAT to apply for permission to operate two companies. One would be wholly American owned and would hold almost all the airline's assets. The other, Civil Air Transport Company Limited, would operate the routes and would be 60 percent owned by private Chinese investors, who would deposit deeds of trust with the CIA in return for their shares. The agreement was amicable; all parties breathed a sigh of relief.

The CATI dispute was settled the following day, but the last stages had been bitter. At one point the Chinese insisted on an immediate settlement based on an assessment of $5.2 million in assets. Chennault was able to convince Chiang that this figure was much too high, but there agreement hit a snag. Corcoran lost his temper and fired off an outspoken wire to Foreign Minister George Yeh, and the State Department apparently reacted by making it quite plain to both Corcoran and Chennault that an equitable settlement must be made at once. CATI paid the Chinese $1,296,928 in cash and received credit for claims against the government of $1,913,373. Other rights and assets, primarily real estate, with a paper value of $1,539,698 were granted to the Chinese.[56]

Both Chennault and Willauer were glad to have the long dispute settled but were disillusioned by the way the Chinese had treated them. Both men believed their prompt action to buy the planes had probably saved Taiwan from Communist attack; they felt some words of gratitude would have been more in order than haggling over money. They realized very little on their daring project, for expenses had been high and the planes had to be completely rebuilt before they could be sold. The process took years. "I hope this will be a lesson to both you and me," was Chennault's wry observation to Willauer, "never to interfere in the future when we learn that an airline is defecting to the Communists."[57]

Chennault was also more than a little disgruntled by the attitude of George A. Doole, Jr., to whom the CIA had given the task of overseeing the airline. Although Doole seemed quite ready to accept sole credit for having solved the franchise problem, Chennault told Corcoran that Doole "would still be sitting here for a much longer time had it not been for calls made by Al Cox and me on Madame Chiang and my calls alone on the Generalissimo, Premier and the Governor."[58]

The CIA, however, had decided that its airline's management would have to be more closely tuned to Washington than had been the case thus far. The popular Cox was dismissed at the end of the year. The CIA used Chennault to do the dirty work; he announced the change at a meeting in his home, thus making the ugly business more palatable to an organization that had been initially shaped more by personal ties than by cold business practices. Thereafter CAT's personal, informal style, spontaneous and unorthodox, began to give way to a more sterile though doubtless more efficient operation. In delivering a New Year's message to the organization that he had shaped but which was now slipping away from his influence, Chennault looked back on the earlier CAT with pride "and not a little nostalgia for the days that can never be again."[59]

As the new ownership/management style evolved, Chennault remained chairman of the board but was seldom consulted on policy. Although he gradually became a figurehead, the visible personage who symbolized CAT's achievements and spirit, in this capacity his personal influence lingered long after his death. CAT became Air America, the CIA's largest aerial proprietary. But for many of those associated with it, its traditions stretched back to the AVG.

"It all started with the General," mused one, remembering that well into the 1970s Chennault was still talked about, still remembered as the one who "took a bunch of renegades" and imbued them with a potent combination of fervent patriotism and the will to fight. His had been the personal example of pugnacious determination, extreme motivation, and high idealism that identified Flying Tigers. Confronted with hard decisions, those who inherited his gauntlet were likely to ask, "What would Chennault have done?"[60]

21

Reconciliation

Through 1954, Chennault's voice was frequently heard as he relentlessly propounded one theme: the United States should extend all possible help to Asian countries threatened by communism. The existence of an international Communist conspiracy, U.S. foreign policy's haunting fear during the Cold War years, was for him a reality that threatened the very foundation of the free world. He thought Russia was using the Chinese to achieve its own goals, hence Asia was the key area of the world for halting the spread of what he perceived as an evil force.

He never overcame a suspicion of the State Department as Eastern Ivy Leaguers with little understanding of reality. It was a conviction formed with some justification during the early years of the Sino-Japanese War, when more than 80 percent of the State Department personnel in China were in Japanese-occupied territory and had little knowledge of Kuomintang China.[1] His contacts with the department in postwar years did little to reassure him, for he often disagreed with the Truman-Acheson approach to Asia. He supported the Republicans and Thomas Dewey against Truman in 1948—and was disgruntled beyond measure when Truman won, for he was so certain Dewey would triumph that he had arranged a victory party. In 1952 he told the War College he considered postwar policy in the Far East to be "unintelligent or else influenced by bad forces." By then he was an Eisenhower supporter, and after Ike's administration took office he expressed satisfaction that it was "going to reverse the old policy and follow a very realistic program in the Far East." His own opinion, freely given, was that "the most sensibly realistic thing we could do would be to support Chiang in driving the Communists out of China."[2]

Giving "the impression that he had dressed himself carefully and come to the State Department in the general attitude of holy water dealing with the devil," he told the department in 1951 he thought the truce in Korea was a mistake because it would release Chinese Communist forces to threaten Burma, Indochina, or Taiwan. Instead of supporting a truce, he thought the United States should bomb (with conventional weapons, not atomic ones) the Chinese supply base in Mukden plus their lines of supply from there to the Yalu. He could see no prospect for peace in Asia until the Chinese Communists had been decisively defeated and their "Russian puppet" leaders had been replaced by leaders friendly to the United States.[3]

As Chennault saw it, the way to do this with the least cost to the United States was to support Chiang Kai-shek. Give Chiang "equipment, technical training and supervision and a limited air and naval force," he wrote, and make it possible for him to retake the mainland. As he put it in a letter to Noe, "*That* would settle the war in Korea, the war in Indo-China, the civil wars in Malaya and the Philippines and, finally, would stop old Joe from starting a war in Europe. He will *never* go to war in Europe if China is friendly to us."[4]

Washington had little confidence in Chiang or the Nationalists, even though the Taiwan government began making visible progress in democratic government after 1950, when the United States began extending significant aid but insisting on reform in return. Through good times and bad, however, Chennault kept the faith. He privately acknowledged that many of the Kuomintang leaders were unworthy, but even so, "I cannot condemn the entire Kuomintang as unworthy of support and aid." To the end, the non-Communist Chinese granted him unprecedented acceptance and honor, for they saw him as the single figure who stood by them without flinching during their long struggle. "His forgiveness," one newspaper editorialized, "makes him China's best bosom friend."[5]

"The Communist conquest succeeded," Chennault wrote in the

1950s, "not so much because of the superior military strength . . . but because the Reds promised the people a better life: more and better food, higher living standards, and a 'Peoples' Democracy.' " The Chinese had been indifferent, and they allowed themselves to be misled into thinking a better way of life could follow. But the Communists ruled by fear, he said, and now the Chinese on the mainland were "disillusioned, bitter, and anxious to throw off the Communist yoke." He was convinced that an invasion of the mainland by the Nationalists "would be a homecoming." Basing his belief on information gleaned from CAT employees who kept in touch with their families on the mainland, he believed the majority of the Chinese people would welcome and help returning Nationalists.[6]

If he privately entertained any doubts that the Nationalists could do the job, they are not evident in the written record he left behind. To the contrary, he called the fear that the Nationalist would not fight "utter nonsense," insisting that the Chinese Nationalist more than anything else wanted a gun and the opportunity to use it to fight the Communists who had driven him from his homeland. The Chinese Army, Navy, and air forces, he insisted, were eager to fight. They needed only the kind of additional training and equipment that the United States could provide.[7]

Because he believed force, and only force, would keep the Communists from taking all of Asia, he also advocated encouragement of the non-Communist Chinese on the mainland who were a potential guerrilla army. He was convinced the Chinese people would resist invasion by any foreign power, and "If [the Chinese] don't fight you openly, they'll fight you under cover—sabotage."[8] Guerrillas, he said again and again, were an inexpensive yet effective way to fight. In July 1951 he told the State Department he believed it was within practical possibility to organize 1 million guerrillas south of the Yangtze. "We must supply, supervise and actively promote Nationalist military aid" to them, he wrote, giving graphic illustrations of how "a single man with 15 cents' worth of dynamite fuse, moving stealthily in the dark, is just as dangerous to an ammunition dump as a skyful of B-29's."[9]

Although OPC conducted some guerrilla efforts in Asia, little was done openly or on a significant scale. "Old-time campaigners considered this form of internal strife a rag-tag orphan of war," Chennault wrote in 1951, "troublesome until quelled by firm measures. But, though military strategists have been slow to admit it, there are no longer any firm measures that will quell it. Even the torture and mass

murder of civilians may multiply a conqueror's underground enemies. Assuming an outside source of supply, the airplane, the cargo
parachute, and the portable radio, twentieth-century guerrilla warfare can assume maddening dimensions."[10] Americans were to learn,
to their sorrow, the truth of his assessment in Vietnam a decade later.

Neither State nor Defense had any intent of precipitating war in
postwar China by rearming the Nationalists or organizing guerrillas.
At the onset of the Korean War, the U.S. Seventh Fleet was sent to
patrol the waters between Taiwan and the mainland, not only to discourage a Communist attack on Taiwan, but to prevent Chiang's Nationalists from invading the mainland and expanding the war. The
United States was determined to keep the war in Korea as limited as
possible, determined to avoid a bitter clash with either the People's
Republic or Russia that would make reconciliation of differences
more difficult.

On the issue of limiting warfare, time has vindicated Washington's
stance. But on another equally vital issue we might wish Chennault's
views had prevailed. It was a matter on which he was adamant:
Asians should fight their own battles, and the United States should
not send even one soldier to fight there. "We should offer to supply
the sinews of war," he said, but "the threatened country should supply the muscles." He felt even more strongly about this matter as the
confrontation grew.[11]

"Sometimes," he wrote Noe in December 1954, "I feel that the Administration is working around toward my plan for building up the
strength of South Korea and Nationalist China to the point where
eventually they can carry the war to the Communists on the mainland. . . . There is no justification for the employment of United
States soldiers either in the Far East or in Europe. If the people and
the governments in these areas do not wish to fight Communism, we
should let them be communized."[12]

Throughout these years, Chennault was thoroughly absorbed in a
project dear to his heart. When the CIA purchased CAT, Corcoran
handled Chennault's personal interests and made certain the general
attained freedom to pursue "other things," for this was Chennault's
expressed wish. The thing Chennault most wanted was an International Volunteer Group, a modern-day AVG, to fight spreading communism in the Far East. Apparently the idea, far from being dead,
had simply gone underground after it was first broached at the State
Department in 1948, for in July 1950 Corcoran wrote Chennault that
there would be an IVG. If Chennault wanted it, Corcoran would try
to see that it was offered to him as vindication.[13]

Chennault urged that an IVG be formed in almost every letter or article he wrote thereafter. Of what went on behind closed doors, little has come to light. In Washington during the latter part of 1950, Chennault "did some loud talking" and "became rather heavily involved in a very interesting project," according to a birthday letter to his brother William early in 1951. "Being something which I like well, I could not refuse a part in the cast of actors." At that time he anticipated that "the play will be soundly established" during April 1951, but it did not come about.[14]

In the fall of 1952 he and Anna made a six-week tour of Central and South America, ostensibly a vacation and goodwill tour but also to talk with officials about training bases and operating privileges for an IVG. Chennault thoroughly enjoyed the trip, wielding his camera like any tourist and delighting in the warm reception given him by both Chinese and American diplomats as well as the home officials at each stop. But he found little cause for cheer on the IVG's prospects. "I am not at all optimistic about the new airline in South America," he wrote Max. "The big problem down there is the exchange of their money for US dollars which will be necessary to pay American personnel salaries, buy spare parts and engines and other expenses."[15]

In 1954, after the French had met defeat and Indochina had been partitioned into North and South Vietnam, Chennault made another spurt of effort in the press. A well trained IVG, he said, would be far more effective than the combat units then fighting in Indochina. He could organize one in ninety days, he promised. It could slow the Reds down, maybe even discourage them enough so that they would make peace. He saw it as the only way to employ air power and not involve the United States, but he planned for the United States and other Pacific nations to equip and supply it. Bases might be in Australia, Japan, Formosa, Thailand, or Borneo. Given specialized training for support of surface forces and destruction of supply lines, this compact unit, free from the extra personnel, equipment, and red tape of regular units, could move fast. He saw it as an apt answer to the Russian version of an IVG—the Soviet MIGs manned by "volunteers."[16]

The result was stacks of applications from the United States, Canada, Australia, and New Zealand. Applicants were young and old, pilots and nonpilots, military and nonmilitary. A seventeen-year-old wrote that he was a "better than average shot also I have a strong back so if needed I could sure as heck dig a ditch." The aspirants were answered by a Washington secretary who explained that such a group was not being formed at the present time, but "I am sure the General will be very much interested in your comments and your desire to join such a group should one eventually be formed."[17]

Apparently the idea received serious consideration in Washington. At the 6 May 1954 discussion of the National Security Council, Robert Cutler, special assistant to President Eisenhower, briefed the council on a report being made by the Operations Coordinating Board about setting up an IVG for Southeast Asia. The plan included three squadrons equipped with F-86s. Eisenhower's only recorded comment was that the group should include some multitrained pilots so that if the question of using B-29s came up they would not have to call on USAF pilots. When Secretary of State John Foster Dulles asked whether the IVG would be under the ultimate control of the president, Cutler's reply was no, that the group would be like Chennault's Flying Tigers, and the United States would have no responsibility for it.[18]

The IVG was destined never to fly, but in a broader sense Chennault's arguments carried. What he advocated was a fighting force free from the restraints and restrictions of a government with broader responsibilities. To a sobering extent this evolved within the CIA, where clandestine operations became an ever more important tool, a way to cut through the red tape and bypass the public scrutiny and get on with the business, dirty or not. The CIA conducted extensive clandestine operations in China and the other nations of Asia, some of them unsavory, and some of them with CAT's help. It is ironic that, as long as Chennault was around, making no secret of what he thought should be done, his very presence provided the CIA with a blind. When CIA activity in Thailand and Burma prompted the British to make concerned inquiries, the director of the CIA was "very firm" in assuring them that the United States had "no official connection whatsoever." Any Americans involved, he said, were possibly connected with Chennault.[19]

The last decade of Chennault's life was in many respects his happiest. He had found a niche that suited him. His obligations to his own country and to China had fallen into place; he had found a way to serve both. Although he continued to advocate aggressive anti-Communist policies that were not adopted, he had nevertheless earned a status as spokesman that merited respect.

He had come to accept that the nonconformist who succeeds has "a lot of confidence in himself" plus enough experience to make a sound decision and "enough courage to stick to it." He had con-

cluded that part of confidence and courage was having no fear of failure and that the nonconformist would never be liked by his superiors.
"He worries them, makes them think too much. They like to do
things by rule and regulation and they all have a book to follow."[20]
There was always the taste of bitterness, for even with the airline he
had worked so hard to build, he had found himself an outsider in the
end, a man whose strengths might be needed and used but whose
weaknesses would not be tolerated by officialdom. In looking back
over his life, however, he derived private satisfaction from seeing his
own approach to warfare very quietly maturing within the CIA. He
took pride in feeling that the airline he had put together was of value
to his country; he looked back upon his varied careers with a sense of
accomplishment and well-being. There had been times when he was
right, times when he had been able to make positive contributions.[21]

When the pressure of the war years and the initial struggles with
CAT were over, he began expanding his personal activities. While
living in Shanghai in 1948, he devoted happy hours to the organization of a model planes club. One of its patrons was the father of a
CATF pilot who had been killed in 1942. Concerned that his son's
death not be in vain, the father worked with Chennault and the Veterans of Foreign Wars in organizing "Bob Mooney Squadrons" of air-
minded Chinese and American youth. Their hope was that they
might heal some of the wounds of war by bringing Chinese and American youngsters together through an interest in building model
planes. With the same seriousness he had devoted to larger and more
world-shaking aerial affairs, Chennault applied himself to making
arrangements for importing balsa and dope, motors, and blueprints.
The Hungjao airfield, site of much history, was their testing field.[22]

Chennault also took an active interest in Shanghai's American Legion Post, named for Frederick Townsend Ward, an American mercenary who led a corps of volunteers against the Taiping rebels in the
1860s. After he was killed in 1862, Ward was named a "God of War"
by the Manchu dynasty for which he had fought. He was buried in a
temple courtyard in Sungkiang. During the Japanese occupation following 1937, the courtyard was abused and the plaque commemorat-
ing Ward's achievements was confiscated for its metal. Possibly
because he identified with Ward and wanted to protect a fellow mercenary's place in history, Chennault offered to finance restoration of
the courtyard and plaque. The delighted legionnaires promptly suggested the post be renamed Ward-Chennault. Reminding them that
traditionally posts were named after departed comrades, Chennault

laughed with the others as he told them he would have no objection after he "qualified."[23]

He also renewed his activity in the Freemasons, which he had first joined while he was stationed in Texas in 1920. By 1926 he had earned the master mason's degree, but he then let his membership lapse for lack of time. Now he renewed participation, for the lofty morals and dogma of Freemasonry spoke to his needs: enjoy doing good, wage war against vice, protect and instruct the young, avoid insincere friendships, love the friend as a second self, and love your country. There is a parallel between the ideals of Freemasonry and the New Life Movement advocated by the Chiangs in wartime China, for the New Life Movement stressed virtues from China's long heritage: courtesy, service, honesty and respect for the rights of others, and high-mindedness and honor.[24] Perhaps because he identified with the ideal rather than the reality, Chennault felt very much at home in China, for he saw the Chinese as rising above a life that was harsh, cruel, and often bereft of the bare essentials of existence, maintaining their pride as individuals and as a people, meeting the world with a cheer and dignity that overcame the denigration of honey buckets and poverty. He had responded in much the same way to the specifics of his own life, convincing himself that if one worked hard enough and believed sufficiently in his own worth, life could be made better.

After CAT's move to Taiwan, Chennault found more time to hunt and fish, although after 1953 he had to do without Joe Dash, who died quietly in his sleep one night. One of Joe's pups stayed with the family, but it was not quite the same. In the winter months on Taiwan there were ducks on the Tamsui River, and pheasant hunting was good. At one dinner party the Chennaults served five kinds of fowl the general had killed—duck, pheasant, dove, bamboo chicken, and rice birds. Sometimes he served guests his personally prepared oyster and dove pie in wine sauce, a dish privately described as a terrible looking concoction with "all the legs sticking up," but loyally called a famous creation that "just can't be beat" by his Taipei friends.

Chennault and Anna made a good partnership, working well together, understanding each other. "She makes me happy," he told a friend. "She makes a home, she tolerates my Louisiana gumbo." They had a second daughter, Cynthia Louise, in March 1950, and Chennault enjoyed these little girls as he had always enjoyed his little ones. "Cynthia grows sweeter all the time and Claire Anna grows meaner and smarter," he observed. Their nicknames, "Sugar" and "Butterball," suggest that they might have been spoiled. Pictures taken during these years frequently show Chennault holding a child in one arm and its toy in the other, for he took them with him whenever he could. When they were house guests of the Kuters in Tokyo in 1956, when Kuter was head of the Far East Air Forces, Mrs. Kuter, remembering a more forbidding Chennault, found herself marveling at him with his beautiful young wife and the children whom he obviously adored. Kuter found his old friend unchanged, still arguing that he had been right and the "bomber boys" wrong at ACTS in the 1930s.[25]

In Taipei the Chennaults' yellow stucco home was in Wuchang Villa, a walled compound in which some other Westerners lived, but there were as many Chinese as Americans among their friends. Their social life, more important to Anna than to him, was busy and often glamorous. Most of it revolved around CAT, with cocktail parties, banquets, dinners and receptions where the women were elegantly dressed, the dignitaries numerous and the alcohol plentiful. Sometimes he and Anna entertained on the grand scale, as in 1952 when they gave a cocktail party at the hotel. The CAT newsletter described it as "CAT's biggest affair since we settled in Taiwan."[26]

They were more likely to spend their evenings quietly, with a few friends. They played a lot of bridge, and after their visit to the States in 1949, they introduced the new card game Canasta, sometimes arguing happily over the rules. He found time to sit and talk, to whip up a proper enthusiasm over the CAT softball team, to play toss-cards-into-a-hat, a game he insisted was good exercise because you had to bend over to pick up the cards you missed. He was pleased that two of his children, Peggy and David, brought their families and joined him working for CAT, for they gave him an extended family in each country. When Peggy's husband, Bob Lee, stepped on some toes, he advised his son-in-law to do something he himself had never done: try catching his flies with honey rather than vinegar.

He divided his time in the States between business in Washington or New York and relaxation in Monroe. Frillmann lived in New York then, and the two worked together on Aid Refugee Chinese Intellectuals, an organization that helped refugees from the People's Republic to resettle in the United States or Hong Kong. Chennault enlisted the help of Noe and other U.S. friends in finding jobs and homes, and on occasion he made speeches on behalf of the organization.[27]

Sometimes Chennault and Frillmann indulged in some nostalgic reminiscing about their experiences in China. On one such occasion Chennault told Frillmann he had no interest in seeing his own biography written, and he felt quite enough had been said about the Flying Tigers. He wanted two stories told, however. One concerned the combat intelligence system which he and his men had instituted. The other was the story of John Birch's death. Toward the end of the war in China, a late model Zero had been downed in the Communist-held region of northern China, and Chennault had sent Birch to negotiate with the Communists and get the plane. Accompanied by an interpreter who later told Chennault what had happened, Birch made the ten-day journey and met the Communists. Birch had a streak of stubbornness and arrogance as well as a hot temper usually under firm control. On this occasion guards challenged him, and he became overly demanding, reportedly slapping one of the men in the face. In the heat of argument he was shot, unwittingly becoming the first American to fall in the Cold War. Chennault had been emotionally close to Birch; he was hurt by his death, and he confessed to Frillmann having wished that Birch had not acted as he did.[28]

After 1950, when Joseph McCarthy began capitalizing on dissension over U.S. relations with China and made it an issue of disloyalty and domestic subversion, there was some public anxiety regarding the possible existence of a China lobby and sinister designs to undermine the United States on behalf of the Chinese. It took some years to establish that, although there were a few paid lobbyists, the various individuals agitating on the Nationalists' behalf had their personal motivations, whether materialistic or idealistic or both. Although visible and vocal, they actually lacked central direction and accomplished no appreciable changes in U.S. policy. Their interest in China gave them a common focus, however, so the same names tended to show up in many ways. Chennault was one of many military figures (including Marshall) associated with the Committee for One Million against the Admission of Communist China to the United Nations, and he was sometimes mentioned in the press as providing the lobby with its glamor.[29]

Because Chennault also saw Communists in high places and felt that they should be blamed for much that had gone wrong in China and elsewhere, he must share the guilt of a society that allowed McCarthyism, with its technique of character assassination by implication, to dominate government and poison the national scene for four years. Chennault was called to testify before the Senate Subcommittee to Investigate the Administration of the Internal Security Act on 29 May 1952, primarily to elaborate on portions of his memoir that had been read into the proceedings by earlier witnesses. He seemed uncomfortable; he made it clear that he had not requested the opportunity to testify and was there only in answer to a subpoena. The answers he gave under oath, however, corroborated assertions made in his book that both Marshall and Stilwell aided the Communists and harmed the Nationalists by their actions regarding China and their approaches to the Chinese. On this Chennault never softened, never retreated.[30]

Nor did his loyalty to Chiang ever waver. He saw in the Generalissimo the only person who could hold China's diverse forces together, and he believed a united and non-Communist China was essential for the long-term good of the United States. "Whatever else he may have done, good or bad," Chennault wrote in 1957, "the Generalissimo has fought Communism unrelentingly for a much longer period of time than any other world leader has." He and Chiang shared their stubbornness, their pride, their single-minded dedication in pursuit of a fixed goal. Dedication that could not be swayed by compromise was a special kind of integrity to Chennault, and he saw it in Chiang. "He could have compromised with the Communist leaders and remained in China in a position of power," he mused; he was impressed that to his knowledge Chiang had "never compromised with anything which he considered wrong and bad for the people of China."[31]

Described by a friend as "loyal to the point of foolishness" where his friends were concerned, Chennault preserved his own integrity. On one occasion when loyalty posed conflicting demands, he found a way to satisfy both. During the war years in Kunming he had built strong ties with Governor Lung Yun, for it was at Lung's tolerance that the AVG, and later the Fourteenth Air Force, was based in Yunnan. In 1946, when Lung began sounding democratic in his views, Chiang feared he might surrender to the Communists and sent government troops to seize control. Although Lung was given a title in the Nationalist government, he was in reality under house arrest. Two years later, when he appealed to Chennault for help in obtaining his freedom, Chennault quietly arranged for Lung, disguised as an old woman, to be spirited away in a CAT plane. Chiang was reportedly furious, but Chennault had apparently decided that Chiang's vital interests would not be harmed, and possibly Chiang agreed. The incident seems to have caused no lasting hard feelings between them, and Lung, for his part, was grateful—and doubtless generous—in return.[32]

During the months of each year when he lived in Monroe, Chennault puttered in his garden, delighting in his flowers and in growing huge and beautiful vegetables. When a Believe-It-or-Not column reported that someone had grown a nineteen-and-one-half-pound radish, Noe tried unsuccessfully to get seeds for him. Noe remained his closest friend; the two men helped each other in their personal and business ventures. After a three-day visit with the Noes in early 1954, Chennault wrote to tell them his stay was "so enjoyable that I returned to Washington with renewed vision and courage—I hope. There is something about Louisiana which inspires one in either of two directions: do nothing or do a great deal!"[33]

In 1954, after Chennault was no longer actively involved in CAT, Noe suggested that he settle permanently in Monroe and that the two of them go into business together. Chennault considered it. He told his friend, sometimes "I feel that I am not accomplishing much out here and that I should settle down because of the family if for no other reason." He insisted he wanted to "be useful and 'pull my weight.' " They explored some possibilities, but the Orient continued to hold him.[34]

His Monroe days were filled with relaxed visiting, when yarns might be swapped over a bottle of bourbon. Drinking, like hunting and fishing, he shared with only his close friends, and a ritual was involved. The bottle was put in the middle of the table so that each served himself. "Every man knows his own potential," he would sometimes say, and he would pour himself a glass of bourbon, down it, take a deep satisfied breath, then pour a glass of "branch water" to wash it down. Chennault was a controlled drinker, as was Noe, and on one occasion James Noe, Jr., sitting with the older men and listening to their talk, realized they were having a little drinking contest, each waiting for the other to say he had had enough, neither about to concede before the other. One drink followed another over a period of four hours, as the amazed observer listened and watched and marveled that neither showed any evidence of getting tight.[35]

Chennault spent his happiest hours at Cooter's Point, about seventy acres of wilderness on the Tensas River that he had purchased during the war years. He had wanted his sons Bob, David, and Charles to clear it for him, but they had made scant headway with axes and his brother William got them off the hook by urging Claire to buy cleared land if he wanted to farm. Cooter's Point remained a tangle of forest, sheltering wolves and a wealth of other creatures, and when he was there Chennault seemed to be most at peace. He never outgrew his love for the outdoor life that had entered his blood when he was a boy. The sights and sounds of nature seemed to quiet his inner restlessness, and here in his own small piece of wilderness his dream of a retirement home began to take shape. He sometimes regarded it as a memorial to the AVG members who had died; he wanted AVG veterans to come there and feel welcome. He called it his camp, and on a bluff overlooking the Tensas he built a comfortable cabin with a large screened porch. Close to the river he planted a rice field, rigged with a pump so it could be irrigated from the river. The migrating ducks and geese stopped there to feed, and he would sit at breakfast with one ear cocked and grin at every honk.

These birds were not to be shot; he hired guards to patrol the area during hunting season to make sure. Once when Corcoran joined him at Cooter's Point for a hunting trip, Chennault confessed he no longer enjoyed killing the deer but preferred to watch them live. His sentiment did not extend to fish, however, and although he mused that the fishing in the Tensas was not as good as it used to be, because of oil field drainage, still there were "hot spots" where the "big ones" could be taken. Nothing gave him more pleasure than to have friends or family share these joys with him, even though others seemed unable to eat cold fish for breakfast with his own enthusiasm.[36]

His last years were marred by increasingly poor health. By 1953 his pictures show signs that he was aging and tired, and when he had his annual checkup at Walter Reed in the spring he learned that he needed an operation, perhaps two. There was extensive surgery in August 1956. The doctors had warned of cancer, but he was optimistic as ever; the night before surgery he wrote Noe he was convinced it was harmless and had nothing to do with his real problem, his deep bronchial cough that "reminds me of going fishing for bass and catching nothing but grinnell." But surgery confirmed cancer of the lung. He said little to anyone except family and close friends; outwardly his life went on as before.[37]

A gentle mellowing crept into his manner as the months went by. At a celebration in Washington in 1957, when he and thirty-four others were honored at an Air Force Association recognition for those who had made significant contributions to air force history, he went out of his way to tell Tunner, "I've always wanted to tell you that if it hadn't been for you and your convictions and your fine ATC organization, we wouldn't have won the war in China."[38]

There was also a hint of sadness. When business kept him in Taipei later than he had hoped one spring, he expressed poignant regret, writing, "I wanted to get back in time to see my early plants blooming, camellias, azaleas, dogwood, red bud, quince, jade magnolia, crocus, tulips, pear, plum, etc."[39]

He became increasingly concerned with his family. His children by his first marriage were grown and married and had children of their own. He had helped them when he could, gradually healing some of the rifts made by his long absences from home and his later separation from their mother. He stuck by one when he was in trouble and loaned money to several of them to help them buy their homes. Worried when he feared they had assumed too large a financial burden, he advised them to grow gardens to keep down the grocery bills.

He never ceased to regret that all of them had not finished their college careers, and now he sought to make certain that his grandchildren had every possible encouragement to seek an education. At one time he tried setting up a fund to which they could apply for aid, with three of his children serving on a board to administer it. This did not work out, so he arranged in his will to leave stock to help finance their educations.[40]

He was even more concerned with the future of the two daughters Anna had given him. He discussed these things with his brother Joe, often while they fished together, and once when Joe cautioned him that Louisiana did not recognize his marriage to Anna and might not honor a will that included his Eurasian daughters, "he blew up—got so upset I thought he was going to hit me with a paddle." Calmed down, he mused that his little girls would never be fully accepted in either the United States or China, and for them the only answer he could provide was the best possible education, so that any discrimination they encountered over their mixed birth could be overcome by sheer professionalism. He set up trusts for that purpose and gave Joe the task of helping him write a fair will that would take care of both his families. He asked Joe to be an executor afterward. "Keep the lid on," he told him.[41]

In intimate letters to Anna, he wrote, "I shall depend upon you to cherish, guide and teach [our daughters], as best you can, to be proud of their ancestry and to lead upright, honorable lives." Teach them, he urged, "the true principles of life—to be moral, to be honest, loyal, frugal and kind to all who need kindness. Live within your means, envy no one, enjoy both the comforts and the privations of life on this earth. Be humble and work hard at anything you choose for a profession." To Anna herself, he conveyed his gratitude for the love and happiness she had given him. "God has been kind to me in my old age," he wrote, and he encouraged her to "conserve the resources which I shall leave you so that all of you will have the means to live comfortably, enjoy every opportunity that [life] offers for a full, satisfying life and to help others who are in need."[42]

Christmas was the only holiday he observed, and at that season he allowed himself a measure of emotion. "My thoughts and my love are with you very closely," he wrote Rosemary and her family in 1953. He faithfully wrote all his family Christmas letters; he sent gifts which he hoped would bring them "additional joy and happiness." After 1952 his Christmas presents were money that he hoped would enable them to get "something you really want," something they would not have had otherwise. "But of more value than the gifts you receive," he wrote in one Christmas letter, "I wish each one of you happiness and good health."[43]

In 1956, for the first time since 1939, he spent Christmas in the States. He savored being surrounded by children and grandchildren during the season. In December 1957, however, he returned to Taipei for the last time. At a news conference he acknowledged that he had incurable cancer. "I never thought this would happen to me," he reflected to Rosbert, but then he applied himself to enjoying the season. There was a Christmas party at the Rosberts', and on Christmas Eve his friend George Yeh, newly appointed Ambassador to the United States, dropped by to extend good wishes and jokingly said he had come for dinner. A delighted Chennault insisted that he stay, and he did, but after their dinner Anna urged the general to rest. Chennault protested that he felt fine: "My secret prescription is never to believe that you are sick."[44]

On 30 December "The family had tea with Pres. & Mde. Chiang Kai-shek at Shih Liu 17:00–17:45. Children behaved very well." With this entry Chennault began to keep a new diary, a six-by-nine red-backed "Daily Reminder" in which he recorded with stark objectivity the progress of his disease and approaching death. His friends were more emotional. Even the unemotional Chiang seemed moved as he told him, "My brother, I am concerned for your suffering."[45]

He took care of matters in his office. He wrote letters on behalf of individual Chinese whom he was helping to relocate through the Aid Refugee Chinese program. He updated his will and sent it to Joe. When he took leave of his friends in Taipei, he knew he would never be back, but in a loud whisper he told Yeh that, after a checkup in the hospital, he would try to push the matter of the IVG again.[46]

En route home he stopped in Honolulu, where his plane was met by a small group of well-wishers. One of them had been a second lieutenant in the Fourteenth Air Force and remembered the general for a thoughtful gesture. The lieutenant had been called to Chennault's quarters late one night to run the projector for studying the day's combat film. Afterward he started walking back to his hostel, but the general stopped and gave him a ride. And now, thirteen years later, the general remembered his name and the two happily conversed until Anna insisted that the general must rest.[47]

His last months were divided between Walter Reed Hospital and the Oschner Foundation Hospital in New Orleans, with occasional respites in Monroe. During the April trip to Washington discussed in the prologue of this volume, when he presided over business meetings and testified for the House Un-American Activities Committee, he "felt better than usual" but the following day "felt much worse" and returned to Oschner. "Anna very faithful in her attendance upon me—as always," he wrote in his diary in May, but when it became necessary to hire nurses around the clock, he insisted he did not want old or fat ones, so she chose carefully.[48]

He had a "young, personal doc," dedicated and conscientious, who stayed at the hospital day and night to care for him. One night when Chennault seemed to be resting well, the doctor decided to get a night's rest at home and see his family. He left word for the nurses to call him at once if the general asked for him. Chennault summoned. The nurse phoned. The doctor rushed back to the hospital. "What can I do for you, general?" he asked, to which Chennault replied that he felt so much better he wanted to tell the doctor to go home and get a good night's sleep.[49]

Letters poured in, from close friends and from strangers, from cancer patients urging him to keep fighting, from individuals whose lives he had touched. One writer had been the cook in his hostel at Kunming; a woman had accepted his coat when they shared a cold plane ride in 1945; a former sergeant with the Fourteenth Air Force reminisced that "at one time my team beat yours in a soft ball game at Kunming."[50]

There were visitors—Corcoran, the Noes, Robert Scott. Bruce Holloway found him sitting up in his hospital bed, watching a ball game and smoking a corncob pipe, well aware that he was going to die but still outwardly cheerful and undefeated. Madame Chiang came, and each seemed genuinely happy to see the other. When he whispered, "I can't talk very well," her answer was, "You always talked too much anyway, I want to do the talking this time."[51]

For some months his children had talked of a family reunion, some-

Thomas G. Corcoran, center, with Chennault and Anna in Monroe, Louisiana, 1957.
(Photo courtesy Anna Chennault)

thing he seemed to want. "It would certainly be a wonderful thing if
we could get all the children with as many in-laws and grandchildren
as possible together," he had written Max in March. When seventeen
of them gathered in New Orleans to be with him the weekend of 8–10
July, he put up a bold front of bravado and optimism and good cheer.
Those who stayed close to him throughout his last weeks, however,
realized there was also a sadness, a pain that he had not fulfilled himself to the extent he had wanted. He had not finished; he yearned for
more time.[52]

Outwardly he never gave up. During his last years he had derived
great pleasure from attending the annual conventions of both the
AVG and the Fourteenth Air Force associations, and the latter was
planning a reunion in San Francisco for 7–9 August. He planned to
go. It would be great to see "his boys" again. The doctors agreed the
trip would do him good, but he died on 27 July, only days after being
awarded his third star. It came too late, he said.[53] He was buried in
the National Cemetery in Arlington, Virginia.

Notes

Preface

1. Author interview, Holloway.
2. Author interview, Joe Y. Chennault.

Prologue

1. U.S. Congress, House Committee on Un-American Activities, *International Communism, Consultation with Maj. Gen. Claire Lee Chennault,* 85th Cong., 2d sess., 23 April 1958, pp. 3–17.
2. Ibid., p. 4.
3. Ibid., p. 5.
4. Ibid., pp. 9, 14–15.
5. Ibid., p. 16.
6. Author interview, Rousselot.

Chapter 1

1. Two stories are told by members of the Chennault family. The version given here is substantiated by family Bible records on Claire Lee's death, recollections of an elderly Gilbert resident, and an unpublished research paper written by a Gilbert student at Louisiana Tech University in May 1972 and given me by Morgan Peoples. The other, told with eyes twinkling, is that the child was named for his Aunt Claire, the only member of the family with money to leave to a namesake. Unfortunately, the story goes, Aunt Claire lived to be eighty and enjoyed spending every penny of her money. Prodded by interviewers, family members have at times amused themselves by responding with whatever popped into their heads.
2. John S. Chennault, who lived to be eighty years old, frequently told the story of the carpetbagger episode. See Mims, *Chennault,* pp. 49–50. Robert Chennault told me he "always understood" that this was why his father was born in Texas.
3. Peoples, "A Mississippian Moves to Franklin Parish," pp. 154–63.
4. Author interviews, E. Nelson and Joe Y. Chennault.
5. Audrey Tracey, "Maj. Gen. Chennault's Stepmother Reminisces about Him," *Alexandria Daily Town Talk,* 31 October 1976 (copy in Louisiana State Library vertical files).
6. See Joe G. Taylor, *Louisiana.*
7. Rogers, *Descendants of Estienne Chenault*; Quisenberry, *Genealogical Memoranda,* chap. 10.
8. Stephen Chennault's will is among the RKC Papers. The connection to the Houston family was often mentioned in the Chennault home, although sometimes it was said to be through Frances Thomason, wife of Hannah's son

Stephen Chennault; I did not trace the genealogical records. Members of the Chennault family made the family Bible and other records available and granted me many helpful interviews.

9. Chennault family Bible; Chennault family interviews.

10. Telephone interview, Chase.

11. Chennault, *Way*, p. 4; 1903 date confirmed in Chennault family Bible.

12. E. Nelson Chennault and Freeda Chennault; I visited the Chennault house.

13. John S. J. Chennault, *Ledger*, made available through the courtesy of W. S. Chennault.

14. Correspondence and interviews, Joe Y. Chennault.

15. Ibid.; interviews, W. S. Chennault; William Chennault interviews, quoted in Cornelius and Short, *Ding Hao*, pp. 29–31; Lake Charles Air Force Base release, quoting W. L. Thornberry, in Noe Papers.

16. Unpublished research paper written by a Gilbert student at Louisiana Tech University in February 1970, made available by Morgan Peoples; author interview, Joe Y. Chennault (quotation).

17. Lake Charles Air Force Base release, quoting W. L. Thornberry, in Noe Papers.

18. Chennault, *Way*, p. 5.

19. Peabody, oral history, p. 314.

20. Joe Y. Chennault to author, 23 December 1982.

21. Robertson, *Public Education*, pp. 10, 16, 23, 24.

22. Chennault family interviews.

23. Mims, *Chennault*, pp. 58–64; Chennault, *Way*, p. 5.

24. John Chennault, *Ledger*.

25. Chennault, *Way*, p. 4.

26. Richard, Louisiana State University, to author, 30 October 1980.

27. John Chennault, *Ledger*.

28. *LSU Almanac*, 1979–80; Fiser, Louisiana State University, to author, 31 August 1981.

29. John Chennault, *Ledger*.

30. Fiser to author, 31 August 1981; quotation from Ayling, *Old Leatherface*, p. 40.

31. John Chennault, *Ledger*; 1941 passport, RKC Papers.

32. Mims, *Chennault*, pp. 91–94.

33. Author interview, Joe Y. Chennault.

34. Chennault, *Way*, p. 4.

35. Robertson, *Public Education*, pp. 125–26.

36. Telephone interview, Pierce, Northwestern State University (formerly Louisiana State Normal School).

37. "General Chennault Is Disciplinarian," interview with former student L. A. Stout, in unidentified newspaper clipping in Noe Papers.

38. Chennault family interviews; Chennault family Bible; marriage license and certificate, RKC Papers.

39. "Schools Can Buy New Book on Chennault," interview with Franklin Parish school superintendent John L. McDuff, Baton Rouge dateline, 22 July 1943 (unidentified newspaper clipping in Noe Papers).

40. Author interview, Ruth Chennault.

41. Chennault family interviews.

42. Mims, *Chennault*, p. 106.

43. Chennault to Max, 28 November 1941.

44. Chennault to Max, 22 January 1947; author interview, Max Chennault.

45. Author interview, Lee.

Chapter 2

1. In *Way*, and again in a taped interview shortly before his death (Tape No. 6 CLC-EBL, Coronado Cooper Papers), Chennault mentioned seeing a biplane at the state fair in Shreveport in the summer of 1910. The year may be in error, as the state fair in that year was held in November, but at approximately that time he saw a plane at an airshow, talked to the pilot, tried unsuccessfully to get a ride, and decided that, if he ever again had the opportunity, he would fly. See also Mims, *Chennault*, pp. 110–11.

2. Author interview, Hansell.

3. Hennessy, *The United States Army Air Arm*, p. 196.

4. Sweetser, *Air Service*, pp. 98–102.

5. Author interview, Ruth Chennault.

6. Chennault, *Way*, pp. 8–10; Chennault to Max, 28 May 1951.

7. Sweetser, *Air Service*, p. 99.

8. Ibid., p. 113; "Kelly Field during the War," *ACNL* 19 (January 1936):4–6; Project Files, Kelly Field, 352.18, NA; Chennault, *Way*, pp. 8–11; Chennault family interviews and records.

9. Nancy A. Wright, "Yankee on the Yangtze," *Aviation Quarterly* 6, 2 (1980):130–51.

10. Chennault family interviews.

11. Richard to author, 30 October 1980; telephone interview, Pierce; Chennault family Bible; Chennault family interviews and pictures; 1937 passport in possession of Peggy Lee; 1941 passport in RKC Papers. Neither the Texas nor the Louisiana department of vital statistics has a birth record.

12. For between-wars development of the U.S. air arm, see Purtee, *History of the Army Air Service*; Futrell, *Ideas, Concepts, Doctrine*; Greer, *Development of Air Doctrine*.

13. Arnold, *Global Mission*, pp. 91–92.

14. *History of the United States Air Force* (Randolph AFB, Texas: ATC Pamphlet 190-1, 1961), p. 116.

15. *New York Times*, 13 April 1923, p. 1.

16. Flying Tigers, oral history, Jordan interview, p. 4.

17. Tape No. 6 CLC-EBL, Coronado Cooper Papers.

18. Levine, *Mitchell*, p. 282.

19. J. S. Zischang, "Grandma Chennault," *Life*, 3 August 1942, p. 4; Chennault, taped interview with E. Lockett, 4 and 5 February 1958, Coronado Cooper Papers. Details of the Grandma stunt differ in various accounts.

20. Chennault family interviews; Hegenberger, oral history, p. 60.

21. Tape No. 6 CLC-EBL, Coronado Cooper Papers.

22. *Pursuit, Course Text 1924–25*, pp. 24, 34.

23. Chennault, *Way*, pp. 12–16. See also records in Nineteenth Squadron Misc. File, RG 18, 370.2, NA.

24. "Hawaii Entertains British Fleet," *Infantry Journal* 25 (August 1924):205–206.

25. Flying Tigers, oral history, Trumble interview, p. 67; Trumble to Taylor, 3 January 1965, K239.04365, AFSHRC: letters and papers in Organizational History, Nineteenth Fighter Squadron, with enclosures, SQFT-19-HI and SQFT-19(vii)-HI, October 1921–November 1943 (quotation from memo, 26 July 1924), AFSHRC.

26. Organizational History, Nineteenth Fighter Squadron, report, August 1925, in enclosure 9.

27. Ibid., memo dated 11 February 1924 in enclosure 8.

28. Ibid., letter dated 16 April 1924 in enclosure 7, and memo dated 22 June 1925 in enclosure 9.

29. Ibid., letter dated 9 July 1925 in enclosure 8.

30. Hegenberger, oral history, pp. 17ff., 59–60.

31. Chennault, *Way*, p. 14.

32. Certificates dated 20 June 1925 and pilot's log book, RKC Papers. See also H. W. Sheridan, "The Air of Hawaii," *Infantry Journal* 24 (April 1924):457–61; Chennault, *Way*, pp. 15–16.

33. Accident report, 11 May 1926, 200.3912-1, AFSHRC.

34. Flight training is vividly portrayed in the oral histories of Partridge (pp. 38ff.) and Quesada (pp. 14ff.) and in Laurence S. Kuter, manuscript, pp. 59–69, Kuter Papers. Chennault as seen by participants: pictures in *The Flying Cadet*, USAAC, Kelly Field–Brooks Field, 1 (August 1927) and 1 (February 1928); Tunner, *Over the Hump*, p. 116, quoted.

35. Kuter, oral history, p. 51.

36. Chennault family interviews.

37. Russell Randall in *Jing bao Journal*, October–November 1982; Randall to author, February 1984.

38. McConnell, oral history, p. 5.

39. Pilot's log book, RKC Papers.

40. Accident report, 16 July 1929, 200.3912-1, AFSHRC.

41. Chennault family interviews; statement by Mrs. Harry Wafer, Sr., on file in Louisiana State Library.

42. McConnell, oral history, p. 5.

43. Randall to author, February 1984. The Chennaults were seldom mentioned in the social notes of the *ACNL* during those years.

44. Author interview, Joe Y. Chennault.

45. Levine, *Mitchell*, pp. 148–49; Arnold, *Global Mission*, p. 55; Chennault, *Way*, pp. 16–17; pt. 1 of unpublished manuscript, Merian C. Cooper, *Chennault of China*, pp. 77ff., Coronado Cooper Papers; *ACNL* 12 (29 October 1928) and 13 (16 May 1929); *New York Times*, 2 November 1928, p. 1; *ACNL* 13 (17 October 1929).

46. Chennault, *Way*, p. 16.

47. Ibid., p. 17; *ACNL* 14 (5 March 1930); *New York Times*, 28 January 1930, p. 30; Chennault family interviews.

Chapter 3

1. Established in 1920 as the Air Service Field Officers School, renamed the Air Service Tactical School in 1922 and the Air Corps Tactical School in 1926. Of the 320 general officers on duty with the Army Air Forces at the close of World War II, 261 were graduates of ACTS. See R. Finney, *History of the Air Corps Tactical School*; Futrell, *Ideas, Concepts, Doctrine*; Greer, *Development of Air Doctrine*. See also *ACNL* 19 (15 April 1936).

2. Hansell, *Air Plan*, p. 7. Control of the air was defined, in general terms, as the ability to carry out planned operations despite the aerial opposition of the enemy. By 1954 the concept of control had expanded to include denying the enemy the ability to conduct his planned operations.

3. Greer, *Development of Air Doctrine*, p. 41.

4. Futrell, *Ideas, Concepts, Doctrine*, p. 58.

5. Chennault to Max, 25 July 1940.

6. R. Finney, *History of the Air Corps Tactical School*, pp. 31–32.

7. Ibid., p. 27; Hurley, *Billy Mitchell*, pp. 81–82.

8. Davidson, oral history 2, p. 369 (first and third quotations); Peabody, oral history, p. 307 (second quotation); Partridge, oral history, p. 217 (fourth quotation).

9. Author interview, Robert Chennault; Davidson, oral history 2, p. 369.

10. Chennault, *Pursuit Aviation*.

11. Hansell graciously granted me several interviews and answered questions by letter. See also *ACNL* 18 (1 February 1935):34; Hansell, *Air Plan*, pp. 20–21.

12. *Miami Herald*, 11 December 1935; *New York Times*, 11 January 1935; *Cleveland Plain Dealer*, 2 September 1934.

13. Chennault, *Pursuit Aviation*, p. 60.

14. Author interview, Hansell.

15. Ibid.

16. Chennault, *Pursuit Aviation*, pp. 20, 30, 47–48, 53, 59–60.

17. Chennault, "The Role of Defensive Pursuit," pt. 2, "Interceptions," pp. 7–11.

18. Chennault lecture notes, 12 April 1933, 248.2802–11, AFSHRC.

19. Williams, oral history, pp. 23–24.

20. Final Report of the Commanding Officer, Defensive Air Force, RG 18, 353.1B, NA.

21. Chennault, "The Role of Defensive Pursuit," pt. 2, "Interceptions."

22. Futrell, *Ideas, Concepts, Doctrine*, p. 62; Foulois, *From the Wright Brothers to the Astronauts*, p. 229.

Chapter 4

The title of this chapter quotes Chennault interview, 5 April 1948, 105.5-11, AFSHRC.

1. Tape 10 TGC, EBL, CLC, Coronado Cooper Papers. The initials are those of Thomas G. Corcoran and Edward B. Lockett.

2. Chennault, "The Role of Defensive Pursuit," pt. 2, "Interceptions," p. 8.

3. Ibid., p. 11.

4. Chennault, "The Role of Defensive Pursuit," pt. 3, "Pursuit Operations in the Fort Knox Exercises," p. 92.

5. Chennault, *Pursuit Aviation*, pp. 41, 112.

6. Ibid., pp. 39–40, 112–14.

7. Futrell, *Ideas, Concepts, Doctrine*, pp. 62, 75–77; R. Finney, *History of the Air Corps Tactical School*, pp. 30–33; Hansell, *Air Plan*, pp. 12, 18–19; Huie, *The Fight for Air Power*, pp. 89–91.

8. Chennault, "Special Support," pp. 18–21.

9. Ibid.; Hansell, *Air Plan*, pp. 19–20.

10. Chennault, "Special Support," p. 21.

11. Kuter, oral history, p. 183; Hansell, *Air Plan*, p. 21.

12. Smith, oral history, pp. 21–22.

13. Greer, *Development of Air Doctrine*, p. 66; Chennault, *Way*, pp. 29–30.

14. Copp, *A Few Great Captains*, p. 250.

15. Craven and Cate, *Plans*, p. 29.

16. Copp, *A Few Great Captains*, p. 251.

17. Ibid., p. 259; WD to CO ACTS, 15 and 19 November 1934, RG 18, 334.8, NA.

18. Chennault does not mention the meeting in *Way*; Copp, *A Few Great Captains*, p. 259, says Chennault was not part of the gathering. In a letter to the author, 7 January 1983, Copp wrote that he based his statement on a letter from Gen. Harold Lee George, who had specifically listed the others but had not mentioned Chennault.

19. Testimony presented before the Federal Aviation Commission, 248.121-3, AFSHRC, Webster testimony.

20. Chennault's testimony was not included in the printed testimony cited above. It appears in full in reporter's minutes, 27 November 1934, RG 197, NA.

21. Ibid.

22. Chennault, *Way*, p. 19.

23. Memo on Detail to Duty as Students at the Command and General Staff School, 1935–37 Course, 23 November 1934; Memo on Selection of Students for the 1935–36 Course, 12 January 1935; Memo on Students for 1935–36 Course, 17 January 1935; Memo on Detail as Students, 1935–36 Course, 21 January 1935; all in RG 407, AG 210.63 Sec. 2, NA.

24. Arnold to CAC, 26 November 1934, "Employment of Tactical Units Equipped with Modern Pursuit and Bombardment Airplanes," 248.211.65A and 248.211.65C, AFSHRC; Chennault, comments on letter to C/AC, 26 November 1934, sub.: "Employment of Tactical Units Equipped with Modern Pursuit and Bombardment Airplanes," 7 March 1935, 248.282-27, AFSHRC; Greer, *Development of Air Doctrine*, pp. 59, 65.

25. Nalty, *Tigers over Asia*, pp. 13–14; see also Kuter, oral history, p. 111.

26. Hansell, *Air Plan*, p. 20 (quoted); author interview, Hansell.

27. Flying Tigers, oral history, Neale interview, p. 21.

28. Author interview, Joe Y. Chennault.

29. Smith, oral history, p. 18.

30. Chennault family interviews; author interview, Hansell; Ethel Kuter to author, 14 January 1981 and author interview; author visit to the Montgomery house and interview with owner.

31. Author interview, Hill; telephone interview, Noe; Noe to author, 13 August 1984.

32. Peabody, oral history, p. 315.

33. Telephone interview, Noe.

34. Noe to Chennault, 4 May 1944, CLC Papers.

35. Chennault to CAC, 8 May 1935, RG 18, 373, NA.

36. *Montgomery Advertiser*, 29 July 1937, p. 1.

37. *Miami Herald*, 11, 12, 13, 14 December 1935; Peggy McDonald to author, 16 and 20 December 1982. The Miami Air Races were usually held in January, but the race scheduled for January 1936 was moved up and was held in December 1935. The dates are incorrect in Chennault, *Way*, p. 29.

38. Memorial Speech by Ambassador K. C. Yeh, *CAT Bulletin* 11 (August 1958):12.

39. Chennault, "Some Facts about Bombardment Aviation," pp. 387–93; Chennault, "Pursuit in Cooperation with Antiaircraft Artillery," pp. 419–23; Chennault, "Fighting for Observation," pp. 195–99. Another interpretation, that Chennault had lost his fight to preserve an offensive role for pursuit and was trying to find a place for the fighter arm in support of ground forces, is presented in Yoshino, *A Doctrine Destroyed*, pp. 375ff.

40. C. L. Chennault to W. S. Chennault, 15 March 1937; Peggy McDonald to author, 20 December 1982.

41. Jackson to author, 26 December 1984; author interview, Lee.

42. Terms of Agreement between Maj. C. L. Chennault and the Chinese Government, 27 May 1937, Pistole Collection.

43. Ibid.

44. Smith, oral history, pp. 26–35.

45. C. L. Chennault to W. S. Chennault, 15 March 1937.

46. Chennault to McHugh, 4 August 1939, McHugh Papers.

47. C. L. Chennault to W. S. Chennault, 15 March 1937.

48. Taped interview, Chennault with E. Lockett, 4, 5 February 1958, Coronado Cooper Papers.

49. C. L. Chennault to W. S. Chennault, 15 March 1937.

50. Taped interview, Chennault with E. Lockett, 4, 5 February 1958, Coronado Cooper Papers; Chennault family interviews.

51. Chennault family interviews. For reasons beyond anyone's control, Nell was without funds for several months, and there were rumors that Chennault had "deserted" his family.

52. Chennault to Max, 29 March 1937; Terms of Agreement cited in n. 42 above.

53. Retirement papers, RKC Papers.

54. C. L. Chennault to W. S. Chennault, 15 March 1937.

Chapter 5

1. Chennault's personal diary, 1937–41, made available through the courtesy of Anna Chennault, provided the framework for my account of these years; all quoted statements and information not otherwise identified come from it. The diaries of Watson and Smith were valuable for verification and for cross-references. The McHugh Papers are also valuable for this period.

2. Most useful for China during the Chiang years are the works by Lucien Bianco, Hsi-sheng Chi, John K. Fairbank, F. F. Liu, Graham Peck, James E. Sheridan, Paul K. T. Sih, and Theodore White, all listed in the bibliography.

3. Selle, *Donald*, pp. 317–18; report, 20 January 1938, p. 11, McHugh Papers.

4. Ray Wagner, "The Chinese Air Force, 1931–1940," *American Aviation Historical Society Journal* 19 (Fall 1974):162–71; John H. Jouett, "War Planes over China," *Asia* 37 (December 1937):827–30; Leary, *The Dragon's Wings*, pp. 60–68. See also Caidin, *The Ragged, Rugged Warriors*.

5. Report, 10 April 1939, p. 6, McHugh Papers; Carlson to Roosevelt, 29 November 1937, FDR Papers; report, 20 January 1938, p. 11, McHugh Papers.

6. Hahn, *The Soong Sisters*; Seagrave, *The Soong Dynasty*.

7. Chennault, *Way*, pp. 34–35; Donald to Chennault, 4 June 1938, RKC Papers; Trumble to Taylor, 3 January 1965, K239.04365, AFSHRC; author interviews, Joe Y. Chennault, Smith.

8. Hotz, *With General Chennault*, p. 82.

9. Smith, oral history, p. 53; telephone interview, Noe.

10. Author interview, Shu.

11. Selle, *Donald*, p. 38.

12. Chennault to Rosemary, 22 June 1937.

13. Smith, author interview, diary and oral history, pp. 53–58.

14. Diary of Aimee May, entry 19 July 1937, as given in letter to author, 8 February 1983.

15. The Nanchang account based on interviews with Hansell, Smith, and Shu; Smith, oral history, pp. 59–60; Leonard, *I Flew*, pp. 159–60, 181, 265; Smedley, *Battle Hymn*, p. 208; Henry C. Y. Lee, writing in *Jing bao Journal*, February–March 1981; Henry C. Y. Lee, "Ching Pao," in *Chennault's Flying Tigers*, pp. 66–67.

16. Detwiler and Burdick, *War in Asia*, vol. 13, p. 20, establish that the Chinese had begun construction on a warning net before Chennault reached China; Chennault's diary confirms his subsequent work on it.

17. Chennault, Air Warfare in China, 29 August 1952, K239.716252-17, AFSHRC; Chennault interview, 16 April 1948, 105.5-13, AFSHRC; testimony cited in my prologue, n. 1.

18. The controversial question of Chiang's precipitation of fighting at Shanghai is treated in works by the following, each listed in full in the bibliography: Hallett Abend, Hsi-sheng Chi, F. C. Jones, James W. Morley, Li Tsung-jen, David Lu, Dick Wilson; see also *China Weekly Review*, 7 August 1937, p. 377, and 14 August 1937, pp. 410, 412, 415.

19. Introduction to unpublished manuscript, McHugh Papers.

20. Author interview, Smith.

21. Smith, diary and oral history, p. 60; report, 6 May 1938, p. 6, McHugh Papers; Chennault interview, 6 November 1939, 170.2276-1, AFSHRC; Chennault, *Way*, pp. 40–41.

22. Crozier, *The Man Who Lost China*; a penetrating portrait of Chiang is in memo, 26 October 1944, Alsop Papers.

23. Hansell, interview and letter to author, 3 May 1981.

24. Smith, diary, 10 August 1937.

25. Detwiler, *War in Asia*, vol. 13, p. 64; Smith, oral history, pp. 67–68; Smith, interviews and letters to author (dates in Chennault's and Smith's diaries agree).

26. Smith, diary, 9 August 1937.

27. Holland, diary entries for 1937 and letter to author, 27 February 1983; Smith to author, 6 March 1983. See also Chennault, *Way*, p. 44.

28. C. L. Chennault to W. S. Chennault, 15 March 1937.

29. Chennault to Trumble, 2 June 1958, K239.04365, AFSHRC.

30. Chennault's diary says that Chiang put him in command on 1 September; he later told Willauer that he remained in command for a short time only (Willauer Journal, 15 January 1943, Willauer Papers).

31. Chennault, Air Warfare in China, 29 August 1952, K239.716252-17,

AFSHRC; Chennault, The Chinese Situation (undated), 248.211-24, AFSHRC; Smith, diary; articles by Lee cited in n. 15 above.

32. Chennault, Comments on Brief Reflections, 22 August 1937, RKC Papers; William C. McDonald, Jr., "The Chennault I Remember," *Air Power Historian* 6 (April 1959):88–93; Chennault to Alsop, 25 November 1953, Alsop Papers.

33. Chennault to Hansell, 14 September 1937, 248.211-24, AFSHRC.

34. Chennault to Alsop, 25 November 1953, Alsop Papers; Chennault, *Way*, p. 51, uses phrase "nearly six weeks"; Smith, diary.

35. Chennault, Air Warfare in China, 29 August 1952, K239.716252-17, AFSHRC.

36. Cohen, *America's Response*, pp. 68ff.; FDR press conferences, 6 August and 4 September 1937; *FRUS 1934*, IV, pp. 381, 520–30; FDR OF 150C-d, China, FDR Papers; Madame to Chennault, 5 September 1937, RKC Papers; *FRUS 1938*, III, p. 28; *FRUS 1937*, III, pp. 578–79; *FRUS 1937*, IV, pp. 520–21 (quoted); Jack May, diary, August 1937 entries.

37. Trumble to Taylor, 3 January 1965, K239.04365, AFSHRC; report, 10 April 1939, p. 11, McHugh Papers; Smedley, *Battle Hymn*, p. 208 (quoted).

38. *Montgomery Advertiser*, 17 November 1937, p. 1.

39. Donald to Chennault, 4 June 1938, RKC Papers.

40. Chennault to Madame, 16 August 1937, RKC Papers.

41. Madame to Chennault, 6 September 1937, RKC Papers.

42. Smith, oral history, pp. 73–74.

43. Donald to Chennault, 25 September 1937, RKC Papers.

44. Rosholt, *A Tribute*, p. 11.

45. Smith, author interviews plus oral history, pp. 69–82, 85–95.

46. H. Wu, "Total Strategy Used by China and Some Major Engagements in the Sino-Japanese War of 1937–1945," in Sih, *Nationalist China*, pp. 47–48.

47. Chennault, The Chinese Situation (undated), 248.211-24, AFSHRC.

48. Frillmann, oral history, pp. 19 (first quotation), 38–40; Frillmann, *China*, p. 3 (second quotation).

49. Chennault, report to the adjutant general, 1 June 1938, 248.211-24, AFSHRC; report, 6 May 1938, McHugh Papers; Pickler, *United States Aid*, pp. 31ff.; Leonard, *I Flew*, pp. 151–52; Flying Tigers, oral history, Alison interview, p. 24; Clubb, *Twentieth Century China*, pp. 219–20; Davies, *Dragon by the Tail*, p. 193; Liu, *A Military History*, p. 168; *FRUS 1938*, III, pp. 19–20, 384–85.

50. Smith, oral history, p. 119.

51. Ibid., pp. 129, 102–104, 113–15. See also *FRUS 1932*, III, p. 451; Frillmann, *China*, p. 21.

52. Elwyn Gibbon, "Commuting to War," *Collier's*, 12 November 1938, p. 44; Edward L. Leiser, "Memoirs of Pilot Elwyn H. Gibbon, the Mad Irishman," *Journal of the American Aviation Historical Society* 23 (Spring 1978):2–18; Caidin, *The Ragged, Rugged Warriors*, pp. 59–77.

53. *New York Times*, 7 March 1938, p. 14.

54. Leonard, *I Flew*, pp. 129–30.

55. Smith, oral history, pp. 95–96; Chennault, *Way*, p. 46.

56. McHugh, unpublished manuscript, McHugh Papers.

57. *Birmingham News*, 18 February 1965, p. 1; Peggy McDonald to author, 25 October 1980; author interview, Hansell.

58. Telephone interview, Hotz; Chennault to Alsop, 22 February 1950, Alsop Papers.

59. Joseph Alsop, "Why We Lost China," *Saturday Evening Post*, 14 January 1950, pp. 26ff.; Chennault to Alsop, 22 February 1950, Alsop Papers. In a telephone interview with the author, Alsop stated that Chennault had shot down approximately forty-four planes but was extremely secretive about it.

60. Interview with E. Lockett, 4, 5 February 1958, Coronado Cooper Papers.

61. Author interview, Joe Y. Chennault. Claire talked to Joe about sinking Japanese ships, but Joe did not recall that he ever specifically said he shot down a Japanese plane. I weighed the evidence and opinions from a number of sources, not all of whom agree. Some members of the Chennault family "knew" he fought, others did not. Shu insisted he did not; Trumble and Smith felt it extremely doubtful. McDonald, ill and unable to talk with me, indicated "no" through his wife. Yet in a letter to Ivaloo Watson, 16 November 1951, Chennault said her husband, Rolfe, "kept the guns of my personal plane in the finest condition. My guns never failed to fire when I needed them." The introduction to Scott's *Flying Tiger: Chennault of China*, written by George Kenney, said there "is plenty of evidence" that Chennault shot down about thirty planes. Kenney could have had the information from Merian Cooper, who went from Chennault's command to Kenney's in 1943. In a letter to the author, 20 March 1981, Scott said he had the information from reliable sources, but Chennault himself would not confirm it.

Chapter 6

1. Again the primary source is Chennault's diary, 1937–41, from which all information not otherwise documented has been taken.

2. Commanding general's press conference, 14 July 1945, 862.3091, AFSHRC.

3. Chennault, report to the adjutant general, 1 June 1938, 248.211-24, AFSHRC; Chennault, The Chinese Situation, undated, 248.211-24, AFSHRC. The Hankow battles were also described in Ralph Royce, report, 21 July 1939, 248.211-24, AFSHRC, and Report No. 5-38, 6 May 1938, p. 1, McHugh Papers. See also Chennault, *Way*, pp. 64–65, 91.

4. Report No. 5-38, 6 May 1938, pp. 5–6; Report No. 1-39, 10 April 1939, p. 12, McHugh Papers.

5. Davies, *Dragon by the Tail*, p. 242.

6. Report No. 1-39, 10 April 1939, pp. 11–12, McHugh Papers.

7. Confidential report, 20 January 1938; report to ambassador and accompanying memo, 28 February 1938; Report No. 5-38, pp. 5–6, 6 May 1938; Report No. 7-38, 7 June 1938, McHugh Papers. See also Selle, *Donald*, pp. 317–18.

8. Weekly reports, McDonald to Chennault, RKC Papers.

9. Report No. 7-38, 7 June 1938, pp. 4–5, McHugh Papers.

10. Donald to Chennault, 4 June 1938, RKC Papers.

11. Report No. 7-38, 7 June 1938, pp. 4–5; Report No. 8-38, 15 June 1938, p. 1, McHugh Papers.

12. Chennault, reports to adjutant general, 21 May and 1 June 1938, 248.501-65 and 248.211-24, AFSHRC.

13. Smith, diary and author interview.

14. Frillmann, *China*, p. 19.

15. Report No. 8-38, 15 June 1938, p. 1, McHugh Papers.

16. Orange notebook kept by Chennault, RKC Papers.

17. Chennault to Rosemary, 24 August 1938.

18. Ibid.; orange notebook, RKC Papers.

19. McHugh to Marquart, 20 August 1938, McHugh Papers; Ralph Royce, Observations in China, 17 July 1939, 248.211-24, AFSHRC.

20. Chennault family interviews.

21. McHugh, Report No. 7-38, 7 June 1938, McHugh Papers; McDonald to Chennault, 14 March 1939, RKC Papers; Chennault interview, 6 November 1939, 170.2276-1, AFSHRC.

22. Madame to Chennault, 11 April 1938, RKC Papers.

23. Report No. 1-39, 10 April 1939, p. 3, McHugh Papers.

24. Ibid., pp. 3ff.; author interview, Smith; McHugh to Skipper [Overesch], 2 October 1938, McHugh Papers.

25. Chennault to Wright, 13 December 1938, supp. B to Report No. 1-39, 10 April 1939, McHugh Papers.

26. Report 1-39, 10 April 1939, p. 13, McHugh Papers.

27. Ibid., pp. 11, 13, 21.

28. Ibid., pp. 4–5.

29. Ibid., pp. 13–14.

30. Ibid., supps. B, C, and D: Chennault to Wright, 13 December 1938; Chennault to Commission on Aeronautical Affairs, 13 December 1938; Pawley to Chennault, 31 January 1939.

31. Chennault, *Way*, pp. 85–86, incorrectly places the meeting in the winter of 1939 rather than 1938, which his diary (quoted) shows and which is correct.

32. Young to Taylor, 5 January 1965, K239.04365, AFSHRC.

33. Chennault to McHugh, 4 August 1939; Report 1-39, 10 April 1939, pp. 13, 20, McHugh Papers.

34. In McHugh Papers: Report 1-39, 10 April 1939, pp. 14–22; McHugh to Tom, 18 July 1939; McHugh to Paul [Meyer], 26 July 1939; Report 1-38, supp. plus handwritten notes, undated.

35. Chennault to McHugh, 4 August 1939; McHugh Papers.

36. Ibid. (first quotation); McHugh to Paul [Meyer], 5 August 1939, Mc-Hugh Papers.

37. Chennault to Paxton, 15 January 1945, CLC Papers.

38. Chennault to Harmon, 28 July 1939 (first quotation), 168.604-11A, AFSHRC; memo on Chennault's request for active duty, 17 October 1940, and Chennault to Young, 12 April 1939 (second quotation), Young Papers.

39. Chennault, Aircraft Practices of the Japanese and Chinese Forces in the Present Operations in China, 4 March 1938, 248.211-24, AFSHRC; Madame to Chennault, 11 April 1938, RKC Papers; McHugh to Paul [Meyer], 5 August 1939, McHugh Papers.

40. Chennault, Air Warfare in China, 29 August 1952, K239.716252-17, AFSHRC.

41. Chennault to Max, 13 April 1939.

42. Chennault to Harmon, 28 July 1939, 168.604-11A, AFSHRC.

43. Chennault family interviews as well as Chennault's diary; Chennault to Noe, 6 December 1954, Noe Papers.

44. *FRUS 1939*, III, pp. 773–74; report to the naval attaché, Peiping, 27 September 1939, McHugh Papers.

45. Chennault interviews, 6 November 1939 (quoted), (170.2276-1 AFSHRC) and 16 April 1948 (105.5-11 AFSHRC).

46. Williams, oral history and accompanying manuscript, plus letters to the author. See also Leonard, *I Flew*, pp. 183–84; Bruce K. Holloway, "China As I Knew It," *Air Force Magazine 62* (September 1979):112–19.

47. Author interview, Lucy Smith.

48. Chennault to Max, 13 April 1939.

49. Chennault to R. M. Smith, March and April 1958, printed in Robert M. Smith, *With Chennault in China*, p. vii.

Chapter 7

1. Chennault to Noe, 6 December 1954, Noe Papers; Chennault to Harmon, 28 July 1939, 168.604-11A, AFSHRC; Chennault to Gibbon, 22 July 1938, Elwyn Gibbon Collection, San Diego Aero-Space Museum; Chennault diary and family interviews; Chennault to Max, 25 July 1940.

2. Chennault to Max, 25 July 1940.

3. White, *In Search of History*, pp. 76–77.

4. Soong to Chiang, 27 September 1940, Young Papers. See also material in T. V. Soong Mission File, Young Papers; Chennault, interview, 16 April 1948, 105.5-11, AFSHRC.

5. Smith, oral history, p. 89 plus interviews; Chennault to Gibbon, 6 December 1938 (first three quotations), Elwyn Gibbon Collection, San Diego Aero-Space Museum; Edward L. Leiser, "Memoirs of Pilot Elwyn H. Gibbon,

the Mad Irishman," *Journal of the American Aviation Historical Society* 23 (Spring 1978):2–18 (fourth quotation, p. 14).

6. Pawley to Romanus and Sunderland, 6 July 1950, in Background Material to Romanus and Sunderland, NA; Pawley, *Americans Valiant*, p. 6.

7. John King Fairbank memorandum, Air Program, undated [1942], p. 3. This lengthy account of the origins of the AVG was written for Dr. Lauchlin Currie, who furnished a copy to Dr. William M. Leary of the University of Georgia, who in turn made it available to me.

8. Chennault, Air Warfare in China, K239.716252-17, AFSHRC.

9. Ibid.

10. *FRUS 1940*, IV, pp. 428, 672–77.

11. After 23 October 1940, when he was in Hong Kong, the only entry in Chennault's diary until 3 July 1941 is for Thanksgiving, when he had a duck and capon dinner with his family. Memo, 11 November 1940, Young Papers, notes that he was expected in Washington 13 November 1940. Young, *China and the Helping Hand*, pp. 140–41.

12. Romanus and Sunderland, *Mission*, pp. 10–11; report, Chennault to Young, 27 March 1941, Young Papers.

13. Chennault, *Way*, pp. 91, 95–97, 101.

14. Cablegram, 7 October 1940 (quoted), Young Papers; Langer and Gleason, *The Undeclared War*, p. 297.

15. Morgenthau, diaries, vol. 342A, pp. 4–7; the document quoted is also in The History and Status of the First American Volunteer Group, 19 October 1941, pp. 9–10, McHugh Papers.

16. Morgenthau, diaries, vol. 342A, p. 16.

17. For published accounts, see Langer and Gleason, *The Challenge to Isolation* and *The Undeclared War* (pp. 300ff.), and Blum's *From the Morgenthau Diaries: Years of Urgency* (pp. 365ff.). The primary source is the Morgenthau diaries in FDRL, esp. vol. 342-A. The proposal for the Special Air Unit is in the Hull Papers, reel 33, with a note indicating that it was given to Hull by Soong on 28 November 1940.

18. Morgenthau, diaries, vol. 342A, pp. 18 (first quotation), 24.

19. Morgenthau diaries, vol. 342A, notes on conference 19 December 1940, pp. 24–26.

20. Chennault, *Way*, p. 99; Pawley to Romanus and Sunderland, 6 July 1950, in Background Material for Romanus and Sunderland History, NA; *FRUS 1940*, IV, p. 671; Chennault to Paxton, 15 January 1945, CLC Papers.

21. Memo of conference with Secretary Hull, 13 December 1940 (quoted), Stimson Papers; Stimson, diary, 13 December 1940; *FRUS 1940*, IV, p. 711; Young, *China and the Helping Hand*, p. 140.

22. Stimson, diary, 22 December 1940.

23. Morgenthau, diaries, vol. 342, pp. 47–49 and vol. 372, p. 297; *The War Reports*, pp. 99–100; conference, 2 January 1941, Morgenthau, diaries, vol. 344, pp. 46–66. Chennault's role in Chennault to Paxton, 15 January 1945, CLC Papers; interview, Chennault, 15 March 1958, Coronado Cooper Papers.

24. Morgenthau, diaries, vol. 344, pp. 12–13, 258–59 (quoted); interview, P. T. Mow, 28 April 1948, 105.5-10, AFSHRC. (Mao's name was often anglicized as Peter T. Mow.) Mao eventually fell from grace. While stationed in Washington after the war he reportedly absconded with several million dollars in Nationalist government funds and ended up in a Mexican jail. The loyal Chennault tried to help him straighten out his affairs with the Nationalist government. See Smith, oral history, p. 148; Charles Wertenbaker, "The China Lobby," *Reporter* 6 (15 April 1952):24 and (29 April 1952):9; *New York Times*, 22 August 1951 and subsequent articles listed in the *Times Index* under "Mao"; Noe to Chennault, 3 February 1955, Chennault to Noe, 10 February 1955, and W. Woods to Chennault, 24 February 1955, Noe Papers.

25. Currie's report, 15 March 1941, in *FRUS 1941*, IV, pp. 81–95 (quote p. 86).

26. Ibid.; Fairbank memo cited in n. 7 above, pp. 6–7.

27. Corcoran, manuscript, chap. Y; Corcoran to Anna Chennault, printed in A. Chennault, *Chennault and the Flying Tigers*, pp. 78–80 (quoted).

28. Corcoran to Anna Chennault, cited in n. 27 above, p. 80.

29. Report, Chennault to Young, 27 March 1941 (quoted), Young Papers; Romanus and Sunderland, *Mission*, p. 12.

30. Memo, 17 October 1940 (quoted) and telegram draft, 25 November 1940, Young Papers; handwritten notes with unpublished manuscript, McHugh Papers.

31. Plan I, Employment of American Pilots, 27 November 1940 (first, second quotations), and memo, 11 November 1940, Young Papers; Langer and Gleason, *The Undeclared War*, pp. 302 (third quotation), 491.

32. Romanus and Sunderland, *Mission*, pp. 11, 17–18; Notes on CAMCO, 3 November 1941, and Chennault to Paxton, 15 January 1945, CLC Papers.

33. Pawley to Soong, 11 June 1942, courtesy Edna Pawley; Young to McHugh, 13 February 1941 (quoted), Young Papers.

34. Corcoran, manuscript, chap. Y; statement on letterhead of Loftin, Anderson, Scott, McCarthy & Preston, 21 December 1944, Morgenthau Papers; Fairbank memo cited in n. 7 above, p. 18.

35. Currie to McHugh, 14 February 1942, McHugh Papers; letter of introduction from Brett, 18 April 1941, courtesy Edna Pawley; Arnold to Marshall, 29 March 1941, cited in Pickler, *United States Aid*, p. 105; Morgenthau, diaries, vol. 342-A, p. 25 (quoted); Flying Tigers, oral history, Hill interview, p. 9.

36. Holloway and Rector, in author interviews, were certain that they had been approached prior to 1 January 1941. Courtesy Edna Pawley: memo on procedure, 24 April 1941; Aldworth to Pawley, 9 May and 14 May 1941; Claiborne to Chennault, 16 May 1941. The bulk of Pawley's papers pertaining to the AVG were given to the Chinese Air Force in Taiwan in 1961. Also Currie to McHugh, 14 February 1942, McHugh Papers; memo, 7 May 1941, Young Papers.

37. Oral histories of Kuter, McConnell, and Partridge; Pickler, *United States Aid*, pp. 106–107; Romanus and Sunderland, *Mission*, p. 18, n. 46;

Chennault interview, 16 April 1948, 105.5-13, AFSHRC; author interviews, AVG personnel; Fairbank memo cited in n. 7 above, p. 20.

38. Notes on meeting held in Intercontinent office in Rangoon, 3 December 1941, CLC Papers; Joe Y. Chennault to author, 10 November 1980 and 14 February 1981; Chennault to Shu, 26 March 1941, RKC Papers.

39. Frillmann, *China*, pp. 50–55; Frillmann, oral history, pp. 105, 114.

40. Chennault to Young, 27 March 1941 (quoted), Young Papers; R. Taylor, *Claire Lee Chennault*, p. 57.

41. Memos, Philip Young to Morgenthau, 10, 13, and 27 January 1941, in Morgenthau, diaries, vol. 346, pp. 382–83; vol. 351, pp. 300–301 (quoted). Statement on letterhead of Chadbourne, Wallace, Packe, and Whiteside, 3 January 1945, Morgenthau Papers; Chennault to Paxton, 15 January 1945, CLC Papers; notes on 21 April 1941 meeting, Morgenthau, diaries, vol. 390, pp. 121–42.

42. Agreement, 15 April 1941, between CAMCO and the Chinese government (quoted), Young Papers; statement submitted by Commander Leighton to Captain Beatty, 2 August 1941, courtesy Edna Pawley.

43. Trumble to Taylor, 7 April 1965 (quoted), K239.04365, AFSHRC; Chennault interview with E. Lockett, 4, 5 February 1958, Coronado Cooper Papers.

44. *FRUS 1941*, V, pp. 597–98; Kirby, *The War against Japan*, pp. 10–11; Romanus and Sunderland, *Mission*, pp. 18–19.

45. Chennault to Young, 27 March 1941 (first quotation), Young Papers; Chennault to Madame, 27 December 1941, CLC Papers.

46. The Joint Board Paper 355, quoted, is given in part in Romanus and Sunderland, *Mission*, p. 23. Fairbank memo cited in n. 7 above, pp. 30–49; *FRUS 1941*, V, p. 683; *Pearl Harbor Attack*, pt. 19, pp. 3489–92; pt. 20, pp. 4539–44; Leighton to Beatty, 2 August 1941, courtesy Edna Pawley. For a strong reaction to the Joint Board Paper and related policy, see Michael Schaller, "American Air Strategy in China, 1939–1941: The Origins of Clandestine Air Warfare," *American Quarterly* 28 (Spring 1976):3–19. See also Chennault to Madame, 8 August 1941 and Chennault to Soong, 23 September 1941, with accompanying memos, CLC Papers; memos dated 12 July, 6 September, and 30 September 1941 with additional papers, bk. 3, China Pre-Pearl Harbor file, Hopkins Papers; Roosevelt to Currie, 15 May 1941, FDR Papers.

47. Chennault, *Way*, p. 104.

48. Chennault's 1941 passport, RKC Papers.

Chapter 8

1. This account draws primarily on the unpublished diaries of participants, on author interviews and correspondence with AVG personnel, on Chennault's diary, on papers provided by Edna Pawley, and on material in the CLC Papers. A number of books have told the story of the Flying Tigers, including Hotz, *With General Chennault: The Story of the Flying Tigers*.

2. Currie to FDR, 21 June 1941, PSF, FDR Papers; *FRUS, Japan 1931-41*, II, pp. 516-20; Ike, *Japan's Decision for War*, pp. 95, 153; Joe Y. Chennault to author, 14 February 1981.

3. Exhibit A with agreement, 15 April 1941, between CAMCO and the Chinese government, Young Papers.

4. Williams, oral history, p. 31; Flying Tigers, oral history, Hill interview, p. 5; Frillmann, *China*, pp. 62-63 (quoted). Although a few individuals in the AVG found themselves in personal conflict with Chennault, the overwhelming reaction was positive. See Boyington, *Baa Baa Black Sheep*, for a negative picture. Others in the AVG believed the conflict between Boyington and Chennault was caused primarily by Boyington's heavy drinking.

5. Quotation from Chennault's diary, 22 August 1941. The History and Status of the First American Volunteer Group, 19 October 1941, McHugh Papers; B. A. Glover, "Assembling and Testing P-40s in Burma," *Aviation* 41 (December 1942):96-101; Walter E. Pentecost and James J. Sloan, "The Advance of the Flying Tigers," *American Aviation Historical Society Journal* 15 (Summer 1970):137-44; Chennault to Madame, 26 August 1941, CLC Papers.

6. Schaper, diary, 22 August 1941.

7. Order, Generalissimo to Chennault, 1 August 1941, CLC Papers; Frillmann interview, 29 July 1942, 863.549-1, AFSHRC.

8. Paxton interview, 863.549, AFSHRC.

9. *Time*, 20 July 1942, p. 25; Frillmann, *China*, pp. 83-86; interviews and manuscripts in 863.306-1, AFSHRC; diaries and author interviews, AVG personnel.

10. Schaper, diary, 3 November 1941.

11. Diaries and author interviews, AVG personnel; Flying Tigers, oral history, esp. Trumble interview, p. 60 (quoted); Greenlaw, *The Lady and the Tigers*, pp. 94-97.

12. In McHugh Papers: Madame to McHugh, 27 August 1941 (second quotation); McHugh to Madame, 29 August 1941 (first quotation); McHugh to Currie, 14 September 1941; Currie to McHugh, 22 September 1941.

13. Memo in CLC Papers shows the navy released Alsop on 10 October 1941; telephone interview, Alsop, 31 January 1986; author interviews, AVG personnel.

14. Bond, *A Flying Tiger's Diary*, pp. 50, 68-69; Mott, diary, 28 August 1941 (quoted).

15. Flying Tigers, oral history, Schaper interview, p. 36 (first quotation); Donovan, diary, 25 November 1941.

16. Donovan, diary, 25 November 1941 (quoted). Sheean, *Between the Thunder and the Sun*, pp. 365-67; McHugh to Currie, 5 October 1941, McHugh Papers; author interview, Rodewald; Chennault, Military Rules and Regulations, 31 December 1941, CLC Papers; Flying Tigers, oral history, McAllister interview, p. 5.

17. Chennault, *Way*, pp. 131-32; Hunter to Chennault, 23 October 1941 (quoted), CLC Papers.

18. Chennault to Paxton, 15 January 1945, CLC Papers; Hunter to Nason (China Defense Supplies), 13 November 1942, courtesy Edna Pawley. The Fairbank memo cited in n. 7, chap. 7, pp. 8 and 23, confirms that the first P-40s were shipped on 19 February 1941 and reached Rangoon 23 May 1941; it appears impossible for one to have been assembled by 28 May. See the articles by Glover and Pentecost cited in n. 5 above.

19. Chennault to Pawley, 15 December 1941, CLC Papers; letter to Pawley, unsigned, 24 June 1942, courtesy Edna Pawley.

20. Chennault to Aldworth, 5 November 1941 (quoted), and Aldworth to Soong, 15 January 1942, CLC Papers. Additional items in the CLC Papers describe the Chennault-Pawley conflict.

21. Chennault, *Way*, pp. 117–18; Chennault to Soong, 25 November 1941, CLC Papers, indicates that Chennault suspected Pawley of having had private business reasons for wanting to see MacArthur. Alsop, in a telephone interview, offered no insight into the misunderstanding.

22. Currie to Chennault, 22 November 1941, CLC Papers.

23. Chennault to Madame, 16 November 1941, CLC Papers; Thorne, *Allies of a Kind*, pp. 69–70.

24. Fairbank memo cited in n. 7, chap. 7, pp. 11–13; Romanus and Sunderland, *Mission*, pp. 27ff., 41.

25. McHugh to Skipper [Overesch], 2 June 1939, with report of same date, McHugh Papers; Madame to Chennault, 20 November and 1 December 1941 (second quotation), and Chennault to Madame, 27 November 1941 (first quotation), CLC Papers.

26. In CLC Papers: Soong to Chennault, 10 September 1941; Chennault to Soong, undated but apparently 12 September 1941; Chennault to Currie, 22 October 1941 (quoted).

27. AVG diary, 2 December 1941, and notes on meeting, 3 December 1941, CLC Papers; Pawley to Soong, 11 June 1942 (quoted), courtesy Edna Pawley. Pawley and Chennault never settled their AVG differences. When Pawley offered in 1945 to put up a substantial sum of money to help the veterans of the AVG form an organization, Chennault refused to have anything to do with the organization if Pawley took part. (See Chennault to Paxton, 15 January 1945, CLC Papers.) When Pawley closed his Burma operation at the end of 1941, China Defense Supplies took over the business functions for the AVG while the Chinese took over operation of the Loiwing plant and serviced AVG planes. Pawley moved to India, set up another aircraft plant, and sought to service planes for the U.S. Tenth Air Force during 1942–43. After complaints about cost and efficiency, he sold the plant to the United States. See Craven and Cate, *Matterhorn to Nagasaki*, p. 182.

28. Chennault to Nell, 25 October 1941, RKC Papers.

29. Ibid.

30. Eddie Rector/Eddie Lockett interview, 16 April 1958, Coronado Cooper Papers.

31. In CLC Papers: Chennault to Madame, 8 December 1941 (first quota-

tion); Madame to Chennault, 8 December 1941; Chiang to Chennault, 11 December 1941 (second quotation); Chennault to Chiang, 11 December 1941 (third quotation); Chennault to Chou, 11 December 1941 (fourth quotation).

32. Chou to Chennault, 15 December 1941, CLC Papers; Romanus and Sunderland, *Mission*, p. 53.

33. AVG diary, CLC Papers; AVG combat reports, 863.306-1, AFSHRC.

34. *CAT Bulletin* 2 (1 April 1949); Willauer transcript, Willauer Papers, p. 10.

Chapter 9

1. Currie to Roosevelt, 8 December 1941, FDR Papers.

2. *FRUS 1941*, IV, pp. 744–45; RAD 99, 13 December 1941, Magruder to War Department, Hopkins Papers; Romanus and Sunderland, *Mission*, p. 91; Craven and Cate, *Plans*, p. 489. The American Volunteer Group, History CBI, sec. 3, II, Stilwell Papers, pp. 4–16, is a carefully documented account of the AVG induction.

3. Chennault to Madame, 24 January 1942, CLC Papers.

4. Chennault to Soong (12 January 1942), to Magruder (20 January 1942), to Madame (24 January 1942), to McHugh (30 March 1942), to Currie (3 July 1942), all in CLC Papers.

5. Interviews, letters and January entries in diaries, esp. Neale, Burgard, Rodewald.

6. Chennault to Madame, 27 December 1941 (first quotation), with Trumble note attached, CLC Papers; Chennault to Magruder, 26 December 1941 (second quotation), CLC Papers.

7. Chennault to Currie, 29 January 1942 (first quotation), FDR Papers; McHugh to Currie, 10 and 13 January 1942 (second quotation), McHugh Papers.

8. For background history, see Romanus and Sunderland, *Mission*, Matloff and Snell, *Strategic Planning for Coalition Warfare, 1941–1942*, and Morton, *Strategy and Command: The First Two Years*.

9. American troop strength in CBI at the end of December 1942 was 17,091 (about the size of one division), of whom 10,476 were air, 394 ground, and the remaining 6,221 involved in supply operations. Romanus and Sunderland, *Mission*, p. 267. See Tuchman, *Stilwell* (Stilwell quoted on p. 243); White, *The Stilwell Papers*; and the three-volume Romanus and Sunderland official army history of the war in CBI.

10. AVG history cited in n. 2 above, p. 4; Currie to Roosevelt, 8 December 1941, FDR Papers.

11. Chennault to Madame and Chennault to Magruder, 20 January 1942, CLC Papers; Magruder to Adjutant General for AMMISCA, 29 January 1942 (quoted), RG 165, NA.

12. Madame to Soong, 27 January 1942, 864.311, AFSHRC; Stimson to Soong, 23 and 29 January 1942, Stilwell Papers; Soong to Stimson, 30 January 1942, RG 165, WDCSA China, NA; Madame to Chennault, 1 February 1942, CLC Papers.

13. Stilwell, Black and White Book I, 28 January 1942, Stilwell Papers.

14. R. Finney, *History of the Air Corps Tactical School*, does not show Bissell as an instructor at ACTS 1930–31, but the graduation program for 1931 in Barker's history of ACTS (248.1715, AFSHRC) does show him as instructor that year. See Chennault, *Way*, esp. 168. Bissell's views on net and pursuit in Ideas of Maj. Clayton Bissell, 8 September 1936, 248.282-20, AFSHRC.

15. Stilwell, Black and White Book II, 9 February 1942, Stilwell Papers.

16. Currie to Chennault, 4 February 1942, CLC Papers.

17. Chennault to Currie, 6 February 1942, FDR Papers.

18. Stilwell, Black and White Book II, 9 February 1942 (first quotation), Stilwell Papers; Currie to SEGAC [Madame], February 1942 (second quotation), FDR Papers.

19. Cable SEGAC [Madame] to Currie, 23 February 1942, FDR Papers.

20. Stilwell, diary, 29 January and 9 February 1942, Stilwell Papers.

21. Kirby, *The War against Japan*, pp. 24–26, 81, 84–85; Stevenson, *Air Operations*, esp. paras. 79, 80, 85, 232; Wavell, *Operations in Burma*, esp. pp. 1669, 1673–74. See also the AVG diary and operations reports, CLC Papers; Flying Tigers, oral history, Neale interview, esp. pp. 39, 42, 47–48; Rossi to author, 12 November 1980; author interviews, AVG personnel (Rodewald quoted). Interviews, 863.549, AFSHRC, confirm that RAF intelligence in Burma was "very bad"; the AVG sometimes did not learn in advance that certain fields were no longer usable or that the Japanese had occupied certain towns.

22. Some accounts imply that the British pulled out of Mingaladon without notifying the AVG of their intentions (see Paxton interview, 863.549-2 AFSHRC), but squadron leader Neale's account in the Flying Tigers oral history indicates that he was in daily touch with the British, and cooperation was as good as circumstances allowed.

23. Wavell, *Operations in Burma*, p. 1669; Kirby, *The War against Japan*, vol. 2, pp. 84–85.

24. In CLC Papers: Chennault to Chou, 12 and 13 January 1942; Chou to Chennault, 16 and 28 January 1942; Madame to Chennault, 17 January 1942 and Chennault to Madame, 18 January 1942. Churchill-Roosevelt exchanges in SAFE 2 China file, FDR Papers.

25. Tuchman, *Stilwell*, p. 260 (first quotation); Stilwell, diary, 3, 4 March 1942 (second quotation), Stilwell Papers.

26. Madame to Currie, 2 and 26 March 1942 (quoted) and Currie to Madame, 31 March 1942, FDR Papers.

27. Davies, *Dragon by the Tail*, pp. 226 (first quotation), 232; Chennault to Madame, 21 March 1942, CLC Papers; Stilwell, diary, 1 April 1942 (second quotation), Stilwell Papers; Stilwell to Adjutant General, 31 March 1942, RG

165, 311.2, NA; Stilwell to War Department, 2 April 1942, 145.95 WP IV C-1, AFSHRC; SEGAC [Madame] to Currie, 2 April 1942 (third quotation), FDR Papers.

28. Letters, interviews and diaries of AVG personnel; Olson, diary, 21 April 1942 (first quotation); Hotz, *With General Chennault*, pp. 215–16 (second quotation).

29. Keeton, diary, 18 April 1942. See also Romanus and Sunderland, *Mission*, pp. 112–13; Flying Tigers, oral history, esp. interviews with Older, pp. 29–33, Neale, pp. 51–52, Hill, pp. 14–17; G. Bright statement in manuscript filed with Williams, oral history; Bond, *A Flying Tiger's Diary*, pp. 141–42; Frillmann, *China*, p. 140; Hotz, *With General Chennault*, pp. 215–16.

30. Chennault to Currie, 3 July 1942, CLC Papers.

31. Craven and Cate, *Plans*, pp. 438–42. In *Way*, p. 168, Chennault said he knew nothing of the raid in advance; he said the same in a personal letter written shortly before his death in 1958 (printed in R. M. Smith, *With Chennault*, p. vii). Glines, *The Compact History of the United States Air Force*, p. 88, says Chennault was briefed on 29 March. In Chennault to Bissell, 14 April 1942 (CLC Papers), Chennault says he will "maintain a discreet silence" about operations in central and southeast China but wonders how he is going to keep the Chinese quiet. This comment may refer to work on planning and selecting sites for airfields on which to base U.S. bombers, for Chennault had been asked to help in this. Doolittle's statement on why Chennault was not told appears in R. M. Smith, *With Chennault*, p. 106. General Doolittle to author, 26 February 1982, said Chennault showed no resentment or animosity when Doolittle saw him in Kunming shortly after the raid.

32. Craven and Cate, *Plans*, pp. 505–506, 512; Frillmann, oral history, pp. 288–89. Much material on supply of the AVG is in the China Pre–Pearl Harbor file, bk. 3, Hopkins Papers; see also files in CLC Papers.

33. Frillmann interview, 863.549-1, AFSHRC; Greenlaw, *The Lady and the Tigers*, pp. 310–11; author interview, Rodewald.

34. Frillmann, oral history, p. 229.

35. Diaries, letters, author interviews with AVG personnel; Keeton, diary, 21 May 1942; Paxton, interview (quoted), 863.549-2, AFSHRC; interview, TGC [Corcoran], General Allison, Eddie Lockett, 29 March 1958, Coronado Cooper Papers; author interview, Rodewald.

36. Chennault to Bissell, 14 April, 12 May 1942, and Bissell to Chennault, 17 April 1942, CLC Papers; telephone interview and letter, Doolittle to author, 17 February 1982. Chennault's rank as brigadier general, temporary, dated 22 April 1942, RKC Papers.

37. Stilwell, miscellaneous papers, 20 April 1942, cited in Romanus and Sunderland, *Mission*, p. 132.

38. In CLC Papers: AVG intelligence report, 7 May 1942 (first quotation); group field orders, 7 May 1942 (second quotation); group war diary report, 7 May 1942 (third quotation).

39. In CLC Papers: AVG intelligence reports, 8 May 1942 (quoted) and 10 May 1942; group war diary, 8 May 1942.

40. Chennault to Madame, 11 May 1942 (first quotation) and 12 May 1942 (second quotation), CLC Papers; Neale, diary, 2–9 May; telephone interview, Hill. For the Salween battles see also Romanus and Sunderland, *Mission*, pp. 113, 132–33, 143, 147–48; Hotz, *With General Chennault*, pp. 217–33; Madame, interview, 105.5, AFSHRC.

41. Peck, *Two Kinds of Time*, pp. 383–85.

42. AVG History cited in n. 2 above, pp. 12–17; Paxton, interview, 863.549.2, and Bacon, interview, 863.549-5, AFSHRC; "The End of the AVG," *Time*, 13 July 1942, p. 25; Frillmann, *China*, pp. 158–59.

43. USSBS, *Air Operations in China, Burma, India*, p. 64, using Burma claims as cited in Stevenson's dispatch, China claims as reported by the warning net; list of victories given by name in 863.375, AFSHRC; Hotz, *With General Chennault*, p. 260; Young, *China and the Helping Hand*, p. 256; Stettinius, *Lend-Lease: Weapon for Victory*, p. 117; Chennault to Madame, 12 July 1942, CLC Papers. Chennault's discharge (quoted) is among the RKC Papers.

Chapter 10

1. Author interviews, Holloway, Rector, Stewart; Neumann to author, 23 February 1981. For the basic account of the CATF, see Craven and Cate, *Guadalcanal to Saipan*.

2. Ibid., pp. 424ff.

3. Haynes to Chennault, 24 July 1942, 864.306A, AFSHRC.

4. Craven and Cate, *Guadalcanal to Saipan*, p. 428; *The War Reports*, p. 317; Barnum, *Dear Dad*, p. 65 (quoted).

5. Chennault to Stilwell, 16 July 1942, with enclosures, 145.95 WP IV C-1, AFSHRC; Romanus and Sunderland, *Mission*, p. 188.

6. Bissell to Chennault, 2 November 1942, 864.311, AFSHRC; Bissell to Chennault, September 1942, 864.07, AFSHRC; The Administrative History of the Army Air Forces in India, 12 February 1942–15 December 1943, chap. 5, pp. 54a, 54b, 825.01, AFSHRC.

7. Romanus and Sunderland, *Mission*, pp. 172–73.

8. Ibid., pp. 177–79; Tuchman, *Stilwell*, pp. 304–307; Leighton and Coakley, *Global Logistics and Strategy, 1940–1943*, pp. 532–41.

9. Liu, *A Military History*, pp. 126–45; White, *In Search of History*, pp. 132–43. Fairbank, *The United States and China*, pp. 46–53, discusses the Chinese military tradition.

10. Chennault, interview, 5 April 1948, 105.5-11, AFSHRC.

11. Tuchman, *Stilwell*, p. 339 (chaps. 12 and 13 for evolution of Stilwell's conviction); Romanus and Sunderland, *Mission*, pp. 189–90; Pogue, *Organizer of Victory*, pp. 360–61; Pogue to author, 22 October 1980.

12. Craven and Cate, *Guadalcanal to Saipan*, pp. 411–22, 443–49, and *Services around the World*, pp. 114–27; Romanus and Sunderland, *Mission*, pp. 267–68, 288–92, 341–44. William D. Pawley, *Wings over Asia*, vol. 1 (China

National Aviation Association Foundation, 1971), p. 15, gives Bissell's view, as did Chennault in interview, 5 April 1948, 105.5-11, AFSHRC.

13. Leary, *The Dragon's Wings*, pp. 135ff., for CNAC's pioneering of Hump route.

14. USSBS, *Air Operations in China, Burma, India*, p. 64.

15. Author interview, Holloway; Heiferman, *Flying Tigers*, p. 81; Alison, oral history, pp. 57–58. See also Bruce Holloway, "China As I Knew It," *Air Force Magazine* 62 (September 1979):112–19; Bruce Holloway, "The Incredible Tale of the Flying Tigers," *Airman* 12 (January 1968):8–13; Theodore White, "The China Air Task Force," *Life*, 12 April 1943, pp. 76–78. See also White, *In Search of History*, and White and Jacoby, *Thunder Out of China*.

16. Barnum, *Dear Dad*, p. 105.

17. *Brief History of Twenty-third Fighter Group*, p. 6. This was the lieutenant who was "hungry as hell."

18. Bissell to Chennault, 22 November 1942 (quoted), CLC Papers and 864.311, AFSHRC; Bissell to Stilwell, 2 December 1942, *SPF* I, p. 457; Chennault to Bissell, 6 December 1942, 864.311, AFSHRC.

19. Alison, oral history, pp. 98–103. The incident took place shortly after the CATF became the Fourteenth Air Force.

20. Author interviews, Holloway (quoted), Rector; Scott to author, 20 March 1981. For additional descriptions of Chennault's command style: James L. Peragallo, "Chennault: Guerrilla of the Air," *Aerospace Historian* 20 (March 1973):1–6; Holloway interview, 16 November 1943, CLC Papers; Scott interview, 29 January 1943, 105.5, AFSHRC; Cooper interviews, 16 January 1943, Arnold Papers, and 22 December 1942, 142.052, AFSHRC.

21. Certificate from *PM Daily*, CLC Papers; Cooper interview, 22 December 1942 (quoted), 142.052, AFSHRC.

22. Scott, *God Is My Co-Pilot*, p. 193.

23. Craven and Cate, *Guadalcanal to Saipan*, p. 430; Chennault to Chiang, 24 October 1942, 864.1621, AFSHRC.

24. Craven and Cate, *Guadalcanal to Saipan*, p. 431; Cooper interview, 16 January 1943, Arnold Papers; Barnum, *Dear Dad*, p. 91; *New York Herald Tribune*, 4 December 1942 (quoted).

25. Chennault, *Pursuit Aviation*, p. 45.

26. Author interviews, Holloway, Rector; Frillmann, *China*, p. 134.

27. Nowak to author, 2 January 1985.

28. Jack Belden, "Chennault Fights to Hold the China Front," *Life*, 10 August 1942, pp. 70–77.

29. Theodore White, "The China Air Task Force," *Life*, 12 April 1943 (quoted), pp. 76–78. See also *Time*, 8 June 1942, p. 30.

30. Alsop to Hopkins, 10 December 1942, Hopkins Papers; Chivers, *The Flying Tigers*, p. 20; White and Jacoby, *Thunder Out of China*, p. 216.

31. Stilwell to Chennault, 23 August 1942, 864.311, AFSHRC.

32. McClure, *Fire and Fall Back*, p. 54.

33. Brady report, 22 December 1942 (quoted) and CATF notes on report of

Brig. Gen. Francis M. Brady, 22 December 1942, 864.311, AFSHRC. See also excerpts in Bissell to Chennault, 15 January 1942, 864.311, AFSHRC.

34. Chennault, comments on General Brady's memo, 5 January 1943, 864.311, AFSHRC (also in Brady Papers). Exchanges about winter clothing in 864.07, AFSHRC.

35. See additional correspondence about the inspection in the Brady Papers. The Bissell-Chennault correspondence is detailed in the administrative history cited in n. 6 above.

36. Davidson, oral history 2, p. 537; Sevareid, *Not So Wild a Dream*, p. 307; Scott to author, 20 March 1981.

37. Breitweiser to author, March 1984; Holloway, author interview (quoted) and oral history, pp. 86ff.

38. Flying Tigers, oral history, Davis interview, p. 45.

39. Noe to Chennault, August 1942, CLC Papers; files on bomber campaign in Noe Papers.

40. Chennault family interviews; Chennault to Max, 8 August 1942 and another, undated but approximately August 1942.

41. Williams to author, 20 May 1983; author interview, Holloway.

42. Flying Tigers, oral history, Trumble interview, pp. 59–67; Trumble to Taylor, 1, 3 January 1965, K239.04365, AFSHRC; Trumble to author, 19, 23 July 1985.

43. Author interview, Holloway.

44. Ibid. Scott to author, 20 March 1981, reads: "I felt like a son to him—and he treated me that way."

45. In Arnold Papers: Bissell to Stilwell, 22 December 1942; Stilwell to Arnold, 15 January 1943; Stratemeyer to Adjutant General, 3 April 1943. Flying Tigers, oral history, Davis interview.

46. Author interview, Holloway; Brereton, *The Brereton Diaries*, entry 14 June 1942; Frillmann, oral history, p. 99; Sevareid, *Not So Wild a Dream*, p. 332; Chennault family interviews; Williams, oral history, p. 35.

47. Chennault to Currie, 3 July 1942, CLC Papers; Chennault family interviews.

48. Author interview, Hansell.

49. Telephone interview, Williams; "When a Hawk Smiles: Chennault and China," *Time*, 6 December 1943; author interview, Joe Y. Chennault.

50. Miles, *A Different Kind of War*, p. 75 (quoted); McHugh to Currie, 13 July 1942, and McHugh to Knox, 13 October 1942, McHugh Papers; Willauer, diary, 3 November 1942, and journal entry, 15 January 1943, Willauer Papers; Alsop to Hopkins, 10, 22 December 1942, Hopkins Papers.

51. Chennault to Bissell, 29 July, 2 November (quoted), 28 November 1942, 864.311, AFSHRC.

52. Brady to Wheeler, 6 February 1943, Brady Papers; Trumble to Taylor, 3 January 1965 (quoted), K239.04365, AFSHRC.

53. Administrative history cited in n. 6 above, pp. 51, 57–61; local newspaper articles on Carney case and Noe to Chennault, 18 May 1943, Noe Pa-

pers; Peck, *Two Kinds of Time*, pp. 473–75; Chennault to Noe, 21 August 1943, CLC Papers.

54. Cooper interview, 16 January 1943 and Cooper to Arnold, 12 September 1942, Arnold Papers; Bissell to Chennault, 5 October 1942, CLC Papers; Chennault to Bissell, 6 December 1942, CLC Papers; Chennault to Bissell, 8 November 1942, 864.311, AFSHRC; author interview, Holloway; Hager, *Wings for the Dragon*, p. 163; Craven and Cate, *Guadalcanal to Saipan*, p. 429.

55. Chennault to Bissell, 28 November 1942 (first quotation), 864.311, AFSHRC; Bissell to Chennault, 29 January 1943 (second quotation), CLC Papers.

56. Chennault interview, 5 April 1948, 105.5-11, AFSHRC.

57. Ibid.; Davies, *Dragon by the Tail*, p. 257; Vincent to Brady, 17 January 1943, Brady Papers; McHugh, unpublished manuscript, McHugh Papers; author interviews, Joe Y. Chennault, Holloway.

Chapter 11

1. Stilwell, diary, 7 October, and entries on 5, 7 October (quoted), Black and White Book II, Stilwell Papers.

2. Willkie, *One World*, pp. 104ff., quotations from pp. 141–43. See also Barnard, *Wendell Willkie*, pp. 353–67, 375.

3. Stilwell, Black and White Book II, 7 October, p. 126, Stilwell Papers.

4. Barnard, *Wendell Willkie*, p. 375.

5. Willauer to Soong, 1 January 1944, Willauer Papers.

6. Chennault to Willkie, 8 October 1942, appendix A to ONI Report No. 10/42 from Naval Attache, Chungking, dated 11 October 1942, McHugh Papers; printed without attachments in Chennault, *Way*, pp. 212–16.

7. Ibid.

8. Ibid. In the Davis interview of the Flying Tigers oral history (p. 24), Chennault's secretary stated that she took Cooper's dictation and Cooper did a lot of work "about getting the General an air force of his own." Chennault, in *Way* (p. 212), said he stayed up much of the night with Cooper to compose the letter.

9. Chennault to Arnold, 17 September 1942, Arnold Papers; report to ONI 5 October with amendment and enclosures dated 11 October 1942, McHugh Papers. See also Chennault to Magruder, 26 December 1941, CLC Papers; Chennault to Stilwell, 13 August 1942, 864.311, AFSHRC.

10. McHugh to Holcomb, 13 October 1942, McHugh Papers.

11. In his ONI Report of 5 October, McHugh said that Chennault needed 150 pursuits; in the 11 October report he said that Chennault had apparently decreased the number. Willauer (journal, 15 January 1943, Willauer Papers), said Alsop shared Chennault's belief in what he could do with an operating force of 150 pursuits.

12. Author interviews, Holloway, Rector; Scott to author, 20 March 1981;

Chennault to Cooper, 9 November 1953 and text of telegram, Chennault to Twining, approximately same date, Coronado Cooper Papers.

13. McHugh to Currie, Holcomb, Knox, and Pihl, 13 October 1942; ONI Report No. 10/42, 11 October 1942, McHugh Papers.

14. McHugh to Chennault, 11 March 1943, McHugh Papers; Stilwell, diary, 16 December 1942, Stilwell Papers; Romanus and Sunderland, *Mission*, p. 248; Marshall to Stimson, 14 December 1942, OPD Case 107 381 CTO, NA.

15. McHugh to Knox, 1 August 1942, McHugh Papers; memorandum for Mr. Cheston, 26 January 1945, McHugh Papers.

16. Romanus and Sunderland, *Mission*, p. 248; McHugh to Knox, 17 December 1942, McHugh Papers; Marshall interviews, 6 and 13 July 1949, Background Material for Romanus and Sunderland History, NA; Stilwell, diary, 16 December 1942, Stilwell Papers. See also Tuchman, *Stilwell*, p. 338; Davies, *Dragon by the Tail*, pp. 256–57.

17. Chennault to Magruder, 26 December 1941 (quoted), CLC Papers; Chennault to Stilwell, 13 August 1942, 864.311, AFSHRC. Willkie's pilot said the figures he heard quoted while in China were 100 bombers and 400 pursuits (debriefing of Maj. R. T. Kight, 23 October 1942, PSF, FDR Papers.)

18. Willauer, journal, 8 December (quoted) and 11 December 1942, Willauer Papers; *The Tenth Air Force*, pp. 72, 79–80; Romanus and Sunderland, *Mission*, p. 264. In CLC Papers: Chennault to Madame, 5 May 1942; Chow to Chennault, 7 June 1943. Chennault to Chiang Kai-shek, 1 December 1942, 864.6319, AFSHRC.

19. Romanus and Sunderland, *Mission*, pp. 239–40, 256–58.

20. *FRUS 1942, China*, pp. 139–40, 155–56; Feis, *The China Tangle*, p. 52n; Kirby, *The War against Japan*, p. 297.

21. Davies, *Dragon by the Tail*, p. 257; Liang, *General Stilwell in China*, p. 104; Miles, *A Different Kind of War*, pp. 75 (quoted), 308; Scott interview, 29 January 1943, 105.5, AFSHRC; Schaller, *The U.S. Crusade in China*, p. 134.

22. Romanus and Sunderland, *Mission*, pp. 186, 186n.

23. Alsop to Roosevelt, 5 November 1942, and Roosevelt to Alsop, 9 November 1942, FDR Papers; Craven and Cate, *Guadalcanal to Saipan*, p. 439; CBI theater history, vol. 3, sec. 2, chap. 2, pp. 17–18, 825.01C, AFSHRC.

24. Alsop to Hopkins, 10, 22 December 1942, Hopkins Papers.

25. Ibid.

26. CBI theater history, vol. 3, sec. 2, chap. 2, pp. 21–22, 825.01C, AFSHRC; memorandum for General Marshall, 30 December 1942, Arnold Papers.

27. Romanus and Sunderland, *Mission*, p. 258.

28. Chi, *Nationalist China at War*, pp. 107–109; Davies, *Dragon by the Tail*, pp. 242–43, 258.

29. Romanus and Sunderland, *Mission*, p. 251; *The Fourteenth Air Force*, p. 3; author interviews, Anna Chennault, Holloway; Corcoran, manuscript, chap. Y; Hegenberger, oral history, p. 62; Bauer, *General Claire Lee Chennault*, pp. 90–91, citing interview with Wedemeyer; Brereton and Young to Taylor, K239.04365, AFSHRC; author interview, Holloway.

30. Stilwell, Black and White Book II, 8 January 1943, Stilwell Papers.

31. Romanus and Sunderland, *Mission*, pp. 269-72, 277 (first quotation); Leighton and Coakley, *Global Logistics and Strategy, 1940-1943*, p. 543 (second quotation); Churchill, *The Hinge of Fate*, p. 693; Sherwood, *Roosevelt and Hopkins*, pp. 681-82; Pogue, *Organizer of Victory*, p. 24.

32. Arnold's Journal, Trip to North Africa, 9 January 1943-17 February 1943, entry 4 February, Arnold Papers; author interview, Holloway.

33. Marshall to Stilwell, 16 October 1942 and Stilwell to Marshall, 18 October 1942, with attached routing slip, Arnold Papers.

34. Memo to General Arnold, delivered orally, 16 December 1942, Tenth Air Force Situation (quoted), Arnold Papers; memo, Arnold to Marshall, 6 January 1943, Establishment and Assignment of Mission to Separate Air Force in China, Arnold Papers; Air Transportation Plan for the Supply of Increased Aerial Combat Operations in China, 12 December 1942, Arnold Papers.

35. Arnold to Marshall, 5 February 1943, handwritten draft in Stilwell Papers.

36. Arnold's journal, entries 5, 6, 7 February 1943; Arnold, *Global Mission*, pp. 412ff.

37. Craven and Cate, *Guadalcanal to Saipan*, p. 439. For additional information on Arnold's trip, see: staff note on Chennault to Arnold, 17 September 1942, Arnold Papers; Romanus and Sunderland, *Mission*, pp. 272ff.; Coffey, *HAP*, pp. 290-95; Matloff, *Strategic Planning for Coalition Warfare, 1943-1944*, pp. 82-83.

38. CBI theater history, vol. 3, sec. 2, chap. 2, p. 29, 825.01C, AFSHRC; Marshall to Stilwell, 19 February 1943, *SPF*, p. 586; Stilwell to Marshall, 2 January 1943, *SPF*, p. 429; Marshall to Stilwell, 5 January 1943, *SPF*, p. 433.

39. Chennault to Trumble, 12 February 1943, and Trumble to Taylor, 21 January 1965, K239.04365, AFSHRC.

Chapter 12

1. "On the Yangtze," *Time*, 15 February 1943, pp. 64-66.

2. McClure, *Fire and Fall Back*, p. 69; Chennault to Trumble, 8 March 1943 (first quotation), K239.04365, AFSHRC; Romanus and Sunderland, *Mission*, p. 285 (second quotation).

3. Romanus and Sunderland, *Mission*, pp. 189-90, 251, 176. Chennault's intent that the War Department receive his plan is indicated in Air Transportation Plan for the Supply of Increased Aerial Combat Operations in China, 12 December 1942, Arnold Papers.

4. 100 Octane Received and Expended, 1 February 1943, 864.07, AFSHRC; McClure, *Fire and Fall Back*, p. 64; Willauer, diary, 3 February 1943, Willauer Papers; Chennault to Stilwell, Estimate China Situation, 22 February 1943, 864.609 and 864.311, AFSHRC; CM-OUT 10546, 27 March 1943 and CM-IN 16733, 31 March 1943, NA; Romanus and Sunderland, *Mission*, p. 285; Matloff, *Strategic Planning*, 1943-44, pp. 84-86.

5. Alsop to Hopkins, 3, 5 March 1943, Hopkins Papers.

6. Romanus and Sunderland, *Mission*, gives the documents quoted on pp. 278–81. See also Marshall interviews, 6 and 13 July 1949, filed with Background Material for Romanus and Sunderland History, NA.

7. Romanus and Sunderland, *Mission*, p. 284; Craven and Cate, *Guadalcanal to Saipan*, p. 440; Arnold to Chennault, 3 March 1943, CLC Papers.

8. Craven and Cate, *Services around the World*, citing gross tonnage, p. 123. Figures vary, depending on whether gross or net tonnage is quoted and whether the lift of CNAC is added to that of ATC. Net tonnage ran 400–650 tons less than gross because of the weight of the fuel for transport.

9. Romanus and Sunderland, *Mission*, p. 285; CBI theater history, vol. 3, sec. 2, chap. 3, pp. 39–40, 825.01-C, AFSHRC; copy of Glenn to Stilwell, 31 March 1943, 864.311, AFSHRC.

10. Romanus and Sunderland, *Mission*, pp. 289–92.

11. Soong to Hopkins, 25 March 1943, Hopkins Papers; Romanus and Sunderland, *Mission*, p. 317; Marshall to Roosevelt, 10 April, and Roosevelt to Marshall, 12 April 1943, with Chiang's 10 April message to Roosevelt, FDR Papers.

12. Stilwell, diary, April entries, and Black and White Book II, 18 April 1943, Stilwell Papers.

13. McClure, *Fire and Fall Back*, pp. 85–86 (quoted); Romanus and Sunderland, *Mission*, p. 317.

14. Author interview, Holloway; Chennault, *Way*, p. 218; Merrill interview, 4 May 1948, 105.5-13, AFSHRC; CBI theater history, vol. 3, sec. 2, chap. 3, p. 45, 825.01C, AFSHRC; Romanus and Sunderland, *Mission*, pp. 319–20; Soong to Hopkins, 29 April 1943, Hopkins Papers.

15. Chennault, "A Plan for Operation of Air Force in China," 1 May 1943, CLC Papers; Plan of Operations in China, 30 April 1943 (quoted), 862.317, AFSHRC; also in CBI theater history, vol. 3, sec. 2, chap. 3, pp. 45–53, 825.01C, AFSHRC.

16. Plan of Operations in China, 30 April 1943, 862.317, AFSHRC.

17. Minutes of 30 April meeting (quoted), Item 27, Msg bk. 9, OPD Exec. 8, NA; CBI theater history, vol. 3, sec. 2, chap. 3, pp. 53–55, 825.01C, AFSHRC; Romanus and Sunderland, *Mission*, p. 322.

18. Ibid.

19. Romanus and Sunderland, *Mission*, pp. 318–20.

20. Appointment memo, PPF. 9074, Chennault, FDR Papers; Tape No. 6 CLC-EBL, Coronado Cooper Papers; Chennault, *Way*, pp. 224–26 (quoted).

21. Chennault family interviews; Urbanowicz to author, 9 December 1980.

22. Alsop to Hopkins, 26 April 1943, Hopkins Papers.

23. Stilwell, Black and White Book II, 18 April 1943, Stilwell Papers.

24. Alsop to Hopkins, 5 and 26 April, 7 and 29 May, 2 July 1943 (in the 26 April letter Alsop asked for Hopkins's advice so that he could best advise Chennault), Hopkins Papers; Hopkins's telephone memoranda, March–June 1943. Telephone interview, Alsop, 31 January 1986; Shaughnessy memo, 4 June 1943, Alsop Papers.

25. Romanus and Sunderland, *Mission*, pp. 323–24.

26. Stimson, diaries, entries for 30 April–3 May 1943 (first quotation 1 May, second quotation 2 May), and Notes by the Secretary of War after Conference at Woodley with General Chennault, 2 May 1943, Stimson Papers.

27. *FRUS, Conferences in Washington and Quebec, 1943*, has minutes of the meetings and related documents. Roosevelt's comment, ibid., p. 67; example of British attitude, pp. 61–62, 71. See also Leahy, *I Was There*, pp. 187–89; Romanus and Sunderland, *Mission*, pp. 327–33.

28. Alsop to Hopkins, 7 May 1943, Hopkins Papers; Service, *Lost Chance in China*, pp. 9–19; Peck, *Two Kinds of Time*, pp. 22–24, 393–94; White, *In Search of History*, pp. 144–56.

29. Romanus and Sunderland, *Mission*, p. 326; CBI theater history, vol. 3, sec. 2, chap. 3, pp. 56–57, 825.01C, AFSHRC. The Hopkins Papers reflect almost constant agitation.

30. Thorne, *Allies of a Kind*, pp. 22, 25, 42; Romanus and Sunderland, *Mission*, p. 23; FBI Report on Soong Family, 12 May 1943, Hopkins Papers.

31. Romanus and Sunderland, *Mission*, pp. 325–27.

32. Stimson's diary entry for 22 May 1943, also printed in *FRUS, Conferences*, p. 173.

33. Marshall interviews, 6 and 13 July 1949, filed with Background Material for Romanus and Sunderland History, NA; Pogue, *Ordeal and Hope*, pp. 354–55, 366–69; Hull to Marshall, 20 May 1943 (quoted), RG 165, box 108, entry 13, CSA China, NA.

34. Nell Chennault to Noe, 25 May 1943 (first quotation), and Chennault to Noe, 8 August 1943, Noe Papers; Barnum, *Dear Dad*, p. 22 (second quotation).

35. Urbanowicz to author, 9 December 1980; the minutes of the Trident conferences indicate that Chennault seldom spoke. See Chennault, *Way*, pp. 218–20, 227.

36. Smith to author, 14 April 1983.

37. Military aspects of China's internal situation, Chennault to Marshall through Stilwell, 12 May 1943, 862.317, AFSHRC.

38. Alsop to Hopkins, 29 May 1943, Hopkins Papers.

39. Chennault to Arnold, 26 May 1943, Arnold Papers.

40. Copies in CATF notes, 864.311, AFSHRC.

41. Brereton to Chennault, Air Force Combat Operations in China, 24 June 1942, 864.311, AFSHRC; Bissell to Chennault, 25 September 1942 (quoted), 864.311, AFSHRC; Stilwell to Chennault, 11 June 1943, *SPF*, p. 710.

42. Theodore White, "The China Air Task Force," *Life*, 12 April 1943, pp. 76–78; File 864.07-4, AFSHRC; author interviews, AVG, CATF, and Fourteenth Air Force personnel.

43. Hospital Communications File, CLC Papers; Corcoran, manuscript, chap. Y; Trumble to author, 9 September 1985; Peck, *Two Kinds of Time*, p. 472.

44. Stilwell, diaries, entries 24 June (first quotation) through 2 July 1943,

and "Chennault's Whore-House" in Black Book, undated papers, p. 18 (second quotation), Stilwell Papers; Stilwell to Marshall, 25 June 1943, *SPF*, p. 734; Dorn to Stilwell, 28 June 1943, *SPF*, p. 742.

45. Author interviews; Kissick, *Guerrilla One*, p. 27; Lamp, *Gentle Tigress*, p. 200; Sevareid, *Not So Wild a Dream*, pp. 234–35.

46. White, *In Search of History*, pp. 139–40; Tuchman, *Stilwell*, pp. 377–78; Somervell to Marshall, 24 October 1943 (quoted), FDR Papers.

47. Stilwell to Chennault, 11 June 1943, *SPF*, p. 710.

48. Trumble to Taylor, 3 January 1965, K239.04365, AFSHRC; Corcoran, manuscript, chap. Y; author interviews with family, AVG, CATF, Fourteenth Air Force and CAT personnel (Rector quoted).

49. In CLC Papers: Chennault to Madame, 28 October 1941; Vincent to Chennault, 29 July 1943 (first quotation); Chennault to Vincent, 4 August 1943 (second quotation).

50. "When a Hawk Smiles: Chennault and China," *Time*, 6 December 1943; Justin Atkinson, "Chennault of the Dragons," *New York Times Magazine*, 2 April 1944; Sevareid, *Not So Wild a Dream*, p. 307; Brereton, Wedemeyer, and Young to Taylor (three letters), K239.04365, AFSHRC.

51. Rogers, *Descendants*, p. 123.

52. Chennault to Max, 25 July 1940; Chennault to Alsop, February 1946, Alsop Papers; author interviews with family, Holloway, Rodewald, Rosbert, Shu, and Smith; Smith to author, 14 April 1983; Willauer to wife, 3 April 1946, Willauer Papers.

53. Author interview, Holloway.

54. Chennault to Trumble, 7 July 1943, K239.04365, AFSHRC.

55. In Hopkins Papers: Chiang to Roosevelt, 13 July 1943; Roosevelt to Chiang, 16 July 1943; memo, 15 July 1943.

56. Memo, 15 July 1943, Hopkins Papers; Romanus and Sunderland, *Mission*, pp. 345–46; Craven and Cate, *Guadalcanal to Saipan*, pp. 450–51; Sherwood, *Roosevelt and Hopkins*, pp. 739–40, 405; Pogue to author, 22 October 1980.

57. Author interviews, Holloway, Stewart. The forward echelon has been vividly portrayed by Holloway in his oral history and in "The Incredible Tale of the Flying Tigers" (*Airman* 12 [January 1968]), "China As I Knew It" (*Air Force Magazine* 62 [September 1979]), and "Keep Them Guessing" (*Air Force Magazine*, January 1944). See also Samuel Lubell, "Vinegar Joe and the Reluctant Dragon," *Saturday Evening Post*, 25 February 1945; Kissick, *Guerrilla One*; McClure, *Fire and Fall Back*.

58. McClure, *Fire and Fall Back*, pp. 84, 110; Madame to Roosevelt, 30 July 1943, FDR Papers; Chennault to Stratemeyer, 25 August 1943, 862.317, AFSHRC.

59. Craven and Cate, *Guadalcanal to Saipan*, pp. 522–24; Romanus and Sunderland, *Mission*, pp. 337–39; Stilwell, diary, 28 July (first and third quotations), 31 July 1943 (second quotation), Stilwell Papers; Stilwell to Marshall, 29 and 31 July 1943, *SPF*, pp. 801, 803.

60. Craven and Cate, *Guadalcanal to Saipan*, pp. 524–34.

61. Craven and Cate, *Services around the World*, pp. 117, 126, give net tonnage for ATC eastbound as 2,916 and gross tonnage as 3,451. Leighton, *Global Logistics and Strategy, 1943–1945*, pp. 504–505, gives 4,338 as combined ATC and CNAC tonnage.

62. Chennault to Roosevelt, Chennault to Hopkins, 5 September 1943, Hopkins Papers.

63. Alsop to Hopkins, 1 September 1943, Hopkins Papers.

64. Chennault to Noe, 21 August 1943, CLC Papers; Willauer, diary, 9 September 1943, Willauer Papers.

65. In Hopkins Papers: Alsop to Soong, 25 September 1943 (quoted); Soong to Hopkins, 25 September, with enclosure Alsop to Soong, 12 July 1943; Hopkins to Roosevelt, 27 September 1943. Soong to Roosevelt, 27 September 1943, RG 165, WDCSA China, NA; Romanus and Sunderland, *Mission*, pp. 375–79.

66. Roosevelt to Marshall, 27 September 1943, Hopkins Papers; Roosevelt to Marshall, 15 October 1943, quoted as it appears in Romanus and Sunderland, *Mission*, p. 382.

67. Romanus and Sunderland, *Mission*, p. 374; Matloff, *Strategic Planning, 1943–1944*, pp. 323–24.

68. Chennault to Roosevelt, 28 October 1943, Hopkins Papers; Romanus and Sunderland, *Mission*, pp. 374, 376–79, and *Command Problems*, pp. 18–19; Matloff, *Strategic Planning, 1943–1944*, pp. 323–24; Craven and Cate, *Guadalcanal to Saipan*, pp. 528–37; McClure, *Fire and Fall Back*, p. 132; White, *In Search of History*, p. 217.

69. Craven and Cate, *Services around the World*, p. 128.

70. Chennault to Giles, 26 September 1943, Arnold Papers.

Chapter 13

The title of this chapter quotes Willauer, diary, 21 September 1943, Willauer Papers.

1. Leighton and Coakley, *Global Logistics and Strategy, 1943–1945*, pp. 506ff., esp. p. 513.

2. Ibid., p. 514. See also Craven and Cate, *Guadalcanal to Saipan*, pp. 453–56, and *Matterhorn to Nagasaki*, pp. 17ff.; Matloff, *Strategic Planning, 1943–1944*, pp. 230–43, 327–31; Romanus and Sunderland, *Mission*, pp. 355–67, and *Command Problems*, pp. 15–17.

3. Plan of Air Operations in China, 1 July–December 1944, 17 October 1943, quoted in Romanus and Sunderland, *Command Problems*, pp. 22–25; with note indicating that the plan was revised by Chennault in November 1943, CLC Papers, and Romanus and Sunderland, *Command Problems*, pp. 110–11.

4. Romanus and Sunderland, *Mission*, pp. 384–85; Urbanowicz to author, 9 December 1980 (quoted).

5. Romanus and Sunderland, *Command Problems*, pp. 22–25, 112; Craven

and Cate, *Guadalcanal to Saipan*, pp. 536–37; Stratemeyer to Chennault, 16 November 1943, enclosure with Chennault to Wedemeyer, 6 July 1945, WDCSA 091 China, NA.

6. The Cairo and Teheran conferences are thoroughly covered in *FRUS, Cairo*. See also Matloff, *Strategic Planning, 1943–1944*, pp. 307–83; King, *Fleet Admiral King*, pp. 505–25; Feis, *The China Tangle*, pp. 103–25.

7. Romanus and Sunderland, *Command Problems*, pp. 68–72.

8. Ibid., p. 74.

9. Sevareid, *Not So Wild a Dream*, pp. 225–28, 351–52; Tuchman, *Stilwell*, pp. 386–87, 455; Roosevelt, *As He Saw It*, p. 152.

10. Romanus and Sunderland, *Command Problems*, p. 79.

11. Chennault to Beebe, 10 January 1944, CLC Papers; Chennault to Arnold, 26 January 1944, Hopkins Papers; Craven and Cate, *Matterhorn to Nagasaki*, p. 65; Romanus and Sunderland, *Command Problems*, p. 113; Estimate of Enemy Situation, *FRUS, Cairo*, p. 233; Chennault to Hearn, 7 April 1944, 862.3221-2, AFSHRC.

12. Craven and Cate, *Matterhorn to Nagasaki*, pp. 44ff. See also n. 2 above. Personalities were a major problem, and Arnold dared not risk letting either MacArthur or Chiang obtain control.

13. Chennault to Beebe, 10 January 1944, CLC Papers.

14. Chennault to Roosevelt, Hopkins, and Arnold, 26 January 1944, Hopkins Papers. Vincent's diary (McClure, *Fire and Fall Back*, p. 146) shows that the preceding were written by Alsop. Roosevelt to Chennault, 15 March 1944, FDR Papers. Romanus and Sunderland, *Command Problems*, p. 111, incorrectly conclude that Roosevelt did not reply to Chennault's letter.

15. Chennault to Hopkins, 26 January 1944 (first quotation), Hopkins Papers; Craven and Cate, *Matterhorn to Nagasaki*, p. 46 (second quotation); Romanus and Sunderland, *Command Problems*, p. 110; Alsop to Hopkins, 14 January 1944 (third quotation), Hopkins Papers; Chennault to Arnold, 8 February and 30 March 1944, and Arnold to Chennault, 25 February 1944, CLC Papers; Chennault to Hearn, 6 March 1944, *SPF*, p. 1982.

16. Williams, oral history, p. 76 (first quotation); Harold Isaacs, "Surprising the Japs," *Newsweek*, 21 August 1944 (third quotation); Justin B. Atkinson, "Chennault of the Dragons," *New York Times*, 2 April 1944 (second and fourth quotations).

17. Chennault to Hopkins, 8 February 1944, Hopkins Papers; Stilwell-Arnold messages, November 1943, *SPF*, pp. 1113–14; Hill, quoted in manuscript, Haynes Collection; J. Taylor, *Air Interdiction in China*, pp. 5–7; Craven and Cate, *Matterhorn to Nagasaki*, p. 538; USSBS, *The War against Japanese Transportation, 1941–45*, p. 37.

18. Chennault to Hopkins, 8 February 1944, Hopkins Papers. Claims versus established losses are difficult to assess with accuracy. Taylor (cited in n. 17 above) concluded that the figure was 52 percent.

19. Report to Stilwell on the capabilities of VLR, 16 February 1944, 862-3221-2, AFSHRC.

20. Chennault to Beebe, 10 January 1944 (first quotation), and to Vincent,

24 January 1944, CLC Papers; Chennault to Hopkins and Roosevelt, 26 January 1944 (second quotation), Hopkins Papers; Alsop to Hopkins, 28 December 1943 (third quotation), 14 January 1944, Hopkins Papers. The 28 December letter is incorrectly identified in the files as having been written in 1942 rather than in 1943.

21. Romanus and Sunderland, *Command Problems*, p. 111.

22. Chennault to Arnold, 15 March 1944, CLC Papers. In a telephone interview with the author, 31 January 1986, Alsop told of writing, at Chennault's request, a telegram to Arnold on the B-29s that caused Arnold trouble among the Joint Chiefs. After his retirement Arnold sent for Alsop and said that he knew Alsop must have been the one to write the telegram and that he, Arnold, just wanted to see what Alsop looked like. Alsop told Arnold he had warned Chennault that Arnold would have his job for it, but to this statement Arnold did not reply.

23. In Hopkins Papers: Chennault to Hopkins and Chennault to Roosevelt, 27 December 1943; Alsop to Hopkins, 28 December 1943; Chennault to Arnold, 16 December 1943; Arnold to Chennault, 20 December 1943. In CLC Papers: Chennault to Arnold, 28 December 1943 (first quotation) and 8 February 1944; Arnold to Chennault, 25 February 1944; Merrill to Chennault, 11 December 1943 and Chennault to Merrill, 17 December 1943. In Willauer Papers: Willauer to Alsop, 12 February 1944 (second quotation). In Roosevelt Papers: Tully to Mrs. Alsop, 28 February 1944; Alsop to Roosevelt, 6 April 1944. Author interview, Hansell.

24. USSBS, *Effects of Strategic Bombing on Japan's War Economy*, p. 76; Romanus and Sunderland, *Command Problems*, p. 16; Craven and Cate, *Matterhorn to Nagasaki*, p. 28.

25. USSBS, *Effects of Strategic Bombing on Japan's War Economy*, pp. 44–46, 109; USSBS, *The War against Japanese Transportation*, pp. 4–5, 21; J. Taylor, *Air Interdiction*, pp. 1–2.

26. Chennault, Air Warfare in China, 29 August 1952, K239.716252-17, AFSHRC; Welch, *The Life of John Birch*, pp. 12–14, 50; author interviews, Holloway, Rosholt; intelligence report, Birch, 1 April 1943, 862.311, AFSHRC.

27. Chennault, Air Warfare in China, 29 August 1952, K239.716252-17, AFSHRC; Frillmann, *China*, p. 176; Suggestions for Amplifying Intelligence Activity in This Theater, Chennault to Stilwell, 28 December 1942, Arnold Papers; Lewin, *Ultra Goes to War*, p. 256.

28. Gayn and Caldwell, *American Agent*, pp. 96, 103.

29. For Donovan and the evolution of OSS, see Dunlop, *Donovan*, and B. Smith, *The Shadow Warriors*.

30. Dunlop, *Donovan*, p. 413; Hayden to Donovan, 6 October 1942, McHugh Papers; B. Smith, *The Shadow Warriors*, pp. 196–97.

31. Cline, *Secrets, Spies, and Scholars*, p. 74; Davies, *Dragon by the Tail*, pp. 285–87, 302–303; Dunlop, *Donovan*, pp. 425–27; Patti, *Why Viet Nam?* p. 26; B. Smith, *The Shadow Warriors*, pp. 258–60; AGFRTS memo, 20 May 1944,

enclosure with Chennault to Wedemeyer, 6 July 1945, WDCSA 091, NA; Chennault to McHugh, 28 May 1944 (quoted), McHugh Papers.

32. Frillmann, oral history, pp. 106, 118, 141–42, 186; author interview, Lee.

33. Smith, interview, and Smith to author, 14 April 1983; Keeton, diary, 5–6 March 1942; "The Old Man," *Jing bao Journal*, August–September 1983 (quoted).

34. 1958 interview quoted in manuscript, Haynes Collection.

35. Romanus and Sunderland, *Mission*, pp. 353–54.

36. Romanus and Sunderland, *Command Problems*, pp. 316–18.

37. Ibid., pp. 406–407; USSBS, *Air Campaigns of the Pacific War*, p. 33.

38. Romanus and Sunderland, *Mission*, pp. 367–68; Davies, *Dragon by the Tail*, p. 326. See also Chi, *Nationalist China*, pp. 70–74; Romanus and Sunderland, *Command Problems*, pp. 20–21, 102–106, and *Mission*, pp. 384–85.

39. Craven and Cate, *Guadalcanal to Saipan*, pp. 494ff.; Romanus and Sunderland, *Command Problems*, pp. 102–106 on air supply.

Chapter 14

The title of this chapter quotes Willauer to wife, 31 May 1944, Willauer Papers.

1. Chennault to Roosevelt, 19 April 1944, *FRUS 1944*, VI, pp. 57–59.

2. In his 30 April 1943 plan (862.317, AFSHRC), Chennault expressed his belief that, if Japan launched an offensive against the eastern bases, it would need to draw forces from other fronts to reinforce the Japanese Army in China. Also see Chennault to Roosevelt, 26 May 1944, FDR Papers; Craven and Cate, *Guadalcanal to Saipan*, pp. 538–39; Breitweiser, oral history, p. 32.

3. Chennault to Roosevelt, 18 June 1943, Hopkins Papers.

4. Chennault to Hopkins, 2 July 1943, Hopkins Papers; Chennault to Marshall, 12 May 1943, 862.317, AFSHRC. See also Soong to McNarney, 20 May 1943, RG 165, WDCSA China A45-466 NA; Romanus and Sunderland, *Mission*, pp. 301, 335–37; Tuchman, *Stilwell*, pp. 366, 373; Craven and Cate, *Guadalcanal to Saipan*, pp. 521–22.

5. Craven and Cate, *Guadalcanal to Saipan*, pp. 534–35; Chennault, *Way*, p. 256; Chennault to Hopkins, 27 December 1943, Hopkins Papers.

6. Chennault, interview, 5 April 1948, 105.5-11, AFSHRC; Chennault to Wedemeyer, 6 July 1945, enclosure 1, 14b, Alsop Papers; Detwiler and Burdick, *War in Asia*, vol. 13, pp. 262–64; Frillmann, *China*, pp. 181–82, 191–92; Romanus and Sunderland, *Command Problems*, pp. 21–22; Rosholt to Frillmann, 26 October 1966, Frillmann Papers.

7. Chennault to Kuter, 15 May 1944, Kuter Papers.

8. Chennault to Stilwell, 12 February 1944, enclosure with Chennault's letter to Wedemeyer, 6 July 1945, WDCSA 091 China, NA; Craven and Cate, *Matterhorn to Nagasaki*, p. 220.

9. Chennault to Stilwell, 6 April 1944, Stilwell to Chennault, 9 April 1944, *SPF*, pp. 2171–73; Romanus and Sunderland, *Command Problems*, pp. 311–12.

10. McClure, *Fire and Fall Back*, p. 153; Chennault to Stilwell, 8 April 1944, Stilwell Papers.

11. Chennault to Stilwell, 8 April 1944, Stilwell Papers.

12. Ibid.; Romanus and Sunderland, *Command Problems*, p. 312. As early as 12 October 1942, Chennault wrote Bissell predicting a Japanese double envelopment of China (864.1621, AFSHRC). See also Stilwell to Chennault, 12 April 1944, Stilwell Papers; April messages in *SPF*, esp. pp. 2171–72, 2184; excerpts from Chennault's April and May messages to Stilwell, plus analyses, in AAF Evaluation Report 9, 15 June 1945, 138.7-9, AFSHRC; Chennault, *Way*, pp. 280–85.

13. Roosevelt to Chennault, 15 March 1944, FDR Papers; Chennault to Roosevelt, 19 April 1944, *FRUS 1944*, VI, pp. 57–59.

14. Craven and Cate, *Matterhorn to Nagasaki*, p. 220; The Military Supply Route to Eastern China, Summary, 3 March 1944, Willauer Papers.

15. Romanus and Sunderland, *Command Problems*, pp. 264, 288–89; Taylor to Chennault, 15 April 1944, CLC Papers; Notes on the Requirements for a China Air Offensive, 3 March 1943, Hopkins Papers.

16. Chennault, diary, quoted from entries for 3, 27, and 28 October 1938.

17. The Chinese Internal Transport Problem and Special Memorandum on the Management of the Kutsing-Kweiyang-Tushan Highway, CLC Papers; Chennault to Stilwell, 28 December 1943, CLC Papers.

18. Chennault to Hopkins, 28 October 1943, Hopkins Papers; Willauer, diary entries, esp. 31 January and 21 September 1943, Willauer Papers.

19. Land Transport to Advanced Air Bases in China, Willauer to Chennault, 28 October 1943, Willauer Papers; Chennault to Chiang, 23 March 1944, CLC Papers; Chiang to Chennault, 30 March 1944, CLC Papers. See also Romanus and Sunderland, *Mission*, pp. 264, 288–89; *Command Problems*, pp. 288–93.

20. Chennault to Magruder, 7 May 1942, CLC Papers.

21. Romanus and Sunderland, *Command Problems*, pp. 201–202, 362–64; Matloff, *Strategic Planning, 1943–1944*, pp. 310–11, 441–42.

22. Kuter, oral history, pp. 363–64; Kuter to Chennault, 15 April 1944, Kuter Papers; Ethel Kuter to author, 14 January 1981.

23. Report on Fourteenth Air Force by Giles, 16 April 1944, Arnold Papers; CBI history, vol. 4, sec. 3, pp. 7–8; Kuter to Wedemeyer, 21 May 1944, Kuter Papers; Stimson, diaries, 1 June 1944, Stimson Papers.

24. Kuter to Taylor, 24 November 1964, K239.04365, AFSHRC; Kuter, oral history, p. 362.

25. The history of MATTERHORN is given in Craven and Cate, *Matterhorn to Nagasaki*, pt. 1; Stilwell to Arnold, 5 April 1944, quoted in Leighton, *Global Logistics and Strategy, 1943–1945*, p. 519.

26. Stratemeyer to Chennault, 20 April 1944, Stilwell Papers; quotation

from Chennault to Stilwell and Stratemeyer, 16 April 1944, enclosure with Chennault to Wedemeyer, 6 July 1945, WDCSA 091, NA; Romanus and Sunderland, *Command Problems*, pp. 315–16, 322.

27. Chennault to Chiang, 15 April 1944, Stilwell Papers; Romanus and Sunderland, *Command Problems*, pp. 314–15.

28. Craven and Cate, *Guadalcanal to Saipan*, p. 541.

29. History of CACW, 1 October–31 December 1943, 865.01, AFSHRC; Craven and Cate, *Guadalcanal to Saipan*, pp. 529ff.

30. Estimate of Japanese Capabilities on the China Front, 26 May 1944, attached to Chennault to Roosevelt, 26 May 1944, FDR Papers; Romanus and Sunderland, *Command Problems*, p. 327.

31. Service, *Lost Chance in China*, p. 19; Peck, *Two Kinds of Time*, p. 576; White, *In Search of History*, p. 153; Clubb, *Twentieth Century China*, p. 239.

32. Stratemeyer to Chennault, 20 April 1944, Stilwell Papers; Romanus and Sunderland, *Command Problems*, p. 322.

33. Chennault to Stilwell, 26 April 1944, Stilwell Papers.

34. Stilwell to Stratemeyer, 13 May 1944; handwritten memo, Stilwell Papers.

35. Stilwell to Chennault, 30 April 1944, *SPF*, p. 2186.

36. Stilwell to Chennault, 12 April 1944, Stilwell Papers.

37. Romanus and Sunderland, *Command Problems*, pp. 314–15.

38. Quotation from handwritten memo, undated, Stilwell Papers; Romanus and Sunderland, *Command Problems*, p. 326.

39. Chennault to Stilwell, 14 May 1944, Stilwell Papers.

40. Stilwell to Marshall, 27, 30 May 1944, Stilwell Papers.

41. Chennault to Stilwell, 18 May 1944, Stilwell Papers; Romanus and Sunderland, *Command Problems*, p. 326.

42. Chennault to Arnold, 15 May, and Arnold to Chennault, 29 May 1944, CLC Papers; Matloff, *Strategic Planning, 1943–1944*, p. 476.

43. Quotation from letter, 30 June 1944, theater observer to combined and joint staff division, given in CBI history, vol. 4, sec. 3, pp. 4–5, 825.01C, AFSHRC; Ferris to Stilwell, 11 May 1944, *SPF*, p. 2205; Romanus and Sunderland, *Command Problems*, pp. 365–66.

44. Alsop to Grace [Tully], undated but approximately 26 May 1944 (first quotation), FDR Papers; Willauer to wife, 31 May (second and third quotations) and 5 June 1944, Willauer Papers; Chennault to Roosevelt, 26 May 1944 (fourth quotation), FDR Papers.

45. Radio, Chennault to Stilwell, 29 May 1944, Stilwell Papers.

46. Chennault to Stilwell, 29 May 1944, with Stilwell's notes, Stilwell Papers; Stilwell quoted in Romanus and Sunderland, *Command Problems*, p. 367.

47. Romanus and Sunderland, *Command Problems*, pp. 362–64 (first quotation); Willauer to Alsop, 8 June 1944 (second quotation), Willauer Papers.

48. First quotation from Stilwell to Ferris, 30 May 1944 (RAD 1124), Stil-

well Papers; Chennault to Stilwell, 2 June 1944 (second quotation), Stilwell Papers; Craven and Cate, *Matterhorn to Nagasaki*, p. 220, quote Stilwell's 4 June memo.

49. Barnett interview, 11 May 1949 (first quotation), 105.5-13, AFSHRC; transcript of 6 June 1944 meeting (second quotation), enclosure with Chennault's letter to Wedemeyer, 6 July 1945, WDCSA 091 China, NA; Romanus and Sunderland, *Command Problems*, p. 368 (third quotation).

50. Marshall to Stilwell (7 June), Stilwell to Chennault (8 June), Chennault to Stilwell (9 June 1944), Stilwell Papers. Stilwell quoted in Romanus and Sunderland, *Command Problems*, p. 369.

51. McNarney to Stilwell, 8 June 1944 (quoted), Stilwell Papers; Stilwell, diary, 9 June 1944, Stilwell Papers; Romanus and Sunderland, *Command Problems*, pp. 364–65.

Chapter 15

The title of this chapter quotes Vincent to Chennault, 3 June 1944, CLC Papers.

1. Romanus and Sunderland, *Command Problems*, pp. 312–13, 329ff.; Craven and Cate, *Guadalcanal to Saipan*, pp. 540ff., *Matterhorn to Nagasaki*, pp. 207ff.

2. Craven and Cate, *Matterhorn to Nagasaki*, p. 220.

3. Vincent to Chennault, 3 June 1944, CLC Papers; McClure, *Fire and Fall Back*, p. 165.

4. Vincent to Chennault, 3 June 1944, CLC Papers.

5. Chennault to Vincent, 18 March and 5 June 1944, CLC Papers.

6. Flying Tigers, oral history, Davis interview, p. 15.

7. Craven and Cate, *Matterhorn to Nagasaki*, pp. 221–23; Romanus and Sunderland, *Command Problems*, pp. 371–74.

8. Chennault to R. M. Smith, April 1958, printed in R. M. Smith, *With Chennault in China*, p. vii; *Brief History of the Twenty-third Fighter Group*, p. 24.

9. Hager, *Wings for the Dragon*, pp. 215–16.

10. Chennault to Vincent, 26 June 1944, CLC Papers.

11. Kebric, *Dragon Tigers*, pp. 78, 82, 123.

12. "He Came Down to Meet Us," in Rosholt, *A Tribute*.

13. Personal diary, Wayne G. Johnson, paras. 612–13, January 1945.

14. Author interview, Brannon.

15. Kebric, *Dragon Tigers*, p. 123 (first quotation); Urbanowicz to author, 9 December 1980 (second quotation); Chennault to Holloway, 8 September 1943, CLC Papers.

16. Cooper Manuscript, quoting taped interview made in 1958, Coronado Cooper Papers.

17. Romanus and Sunderland, *Command Problems*, pp. 372–73.

18. Service, *Lost Chance in China*, p. 91.

19. Ibid., pp. 78–86, 91–93. See the works by Bianco, Chi, Schurman, and Sheridan for thorough studies of China's decay. For specific incidents, see McClure, *Fire and Fall Back*, pp. 190, 203; Peck, *Two Kinds of Time*, pp. 476–79, 556–57; Romanus and Sunderland, *Command Problems*, p. 373; Langdon report in *FRUS 1944*, VI, pp. 193–96; *New York Times*, 30 November, 11 December 1944; White, *In Search of History*, chap. 4.

20. *Hearings*, p. 1463; The Political-Military Situation in China, 26 October 1944, Alsop Papers; Chennault articles in *New York World Telegram*, 22 March (quoted) and 23 March 1948 (these and additional articles reprinted in *Congressional Record*, 80th Cong., 2d sess., vol. 94, pt. 12, pp. A4490–98).

21. Chennault to Roosevelt, 27 June 1944, FDR Papers.

22. Ibid. (quoted); draft of letter, "Dear Tom," from Chennault and memo, Glenn to Chennault, 862.311-1, AFSHRC.

23. U.S. Department of State, *United States Relations with China, 1944–49*, commonly called the White Paper, p. 553.

24. Ibid., p. 559.

25. *Hearings*, p. 1368.

26. Davies, *Dragon by the Tail*, pp. 308–309; Ferris to Stilwell, 10–21, Stilwell Papers; Romanus and Sunderland, *Command Problems*, p. 375.

27. Statement by Wallace before closed session, McCarran committee hearings, 9 October 1951, Alsop Papers.

28. White Paper, p. 559 (first quotation); telephone interview, Alsop, 31 January 1986 (second quotation); Craven and Cate, *Matterhorn to Nagasaki*, pp. 226–27 (third quotation). For Wallace's visit, see also *FRUS 1944*, VI, pp. 234–37; Joseph Alsop, "The Strange Case of Louis Budenz," *Atlantic Monthly*, April 1952, pp. 29–33; Blum, *The Price of Vision*, pp. 349ff.; Service, *Lost Chance in China*, p. 100.

29. Tuchman, *Stilwell*, p. 465 (first quotation); Stilwell's memo quoted from Romanus and Sunderland, *Command Problems*, pp. 380–81.

30. Romanus and Sunderland, *Command Problems*, pp. 379–83, including text of memo quoted.

31. Ibid., pp. 383–84.

32. Chennault to Roosevelt, 27 June 1944, FDR Papers.

33. Chennault, interview, 5 April 1948, 105.5-11, AFSHRC.

34. Craven and Cate, *Matterhorn to Nagasaki*, pp. 218–23; Japanese reports quoted from Romanus and Sunderland, *Command Problems*, pp. 399, 401; *Fourteenth*, pp. 420–56.

35. Chi, *Nationalist China*, pp. 99, 103.

36. *Hearings*, pp. 1417, 1462; Sih, *Nationalist China*, pp. 65–67; Davies, *Dragon by the Tail*, pp. 289–90; Stilwell, Black and White Book II, 3 August 1942, Stilwell Papers; Chi, *Nationalist China*, pp. 74–75.

37. Romanus and Sunderland, *Command Problems*, pp. 371–72.

38. Ibid., p. 401; Clubb, *Twentieth Century China*, pp. 204–205; Abend, *My*

Life in China, pp. 196–97, 222–23; Tuchman, *Stilwell*, pp. 94, 167, 183, 186, 266.

39. Romanus and Sunderland, *Command Problems*, p. 402.

40. Ibid., p. 368 (my thanks to Elena S. Danielson, who twice searched the Stilwell Papers at my request for the 5 June memo but was unable to find it).

41. Stilwell to Hearn, 22 July 1944, *SPF*, p. 2291. See also Riley Sunderland, "The Secret Embargo," *Pacific Historical Review* 29 (February 1960), pp. 75–80.

42. Romanus and Sunderland, *Command Problems*, p. 403.

43. Chennault to Vincent, 25 July 1944, CLC Papers; Vincent to Chennault, 24 July 1944, CLC Papers; Romanus and Sunderland, *Command Problems*, pp. 404–405.

44. Romanus and Sunderland, *Command Problems*, p. 408.

45. Ibid., pp. 409–10.

46. Chennault to Hearn, 17 August 1944, *SPF*, p. 2328.

47. Chennault to Stilwell, 9 September 1944, CLC Papers.

48. Rosholt to Chennault, 2, 5 September 1944, CLC Papers.

49. Wedemeyer, *Wedemeyer Reports*, pp. 275 (quoted), 308; Chennault, interview, 5 April 1948, 105.5-11, AFSHRC.

50. Stilwell to Hearn, 21 August 1944, *SPF*, p. 2433. See also Romanus and Sunderland, *Command Problems*, p. 413; Craven and Cate, *Matterhorn to Nagasaki*, p. 228; Hearn to Stilwell, 19 August 1944, *SPF*, pp. 2429–30.

51. The original as sent is Hearn to Chennault, RAD CFB 21565, item 2763, bk. 7, SPF, NA, or the facsimile edition, *SPF*, p. 2438. They show "face lifting," as does Romanus and Sunderland, *Command Problems*, p. 413. The message as transcribed, with "face lossing," is an enclosure in Chennault to Wedemeyer, 6 July 1945, WDCSA 091 China TS (Chennault Report), NA. Alsop verified the spelling as it was received in *Hearings*, p. 1430, and in a telephone interview, 31 January 1986. See also Chennault, *Way*, p. 301.

52. Brown to Chennault, 18 April 1943, CLC Papers. Trumble, with Chennault from 1941 to 1944, "never heard [Chennault's] voice raised in anger at anyone" (Trumble to Taylor, 2 January 1965, K239.04365, AFSHRC); Scott, close to Chennault during 1942, said, "He never lost his temper—but cowards and interference . . . could almost make him lose his cool" (Scott to author, 20 March 1981). Hager, *Wings for the Dragon*, p. 221, reported watching Chennault at a press conference and remarked, "I have never seen greater patience shown by a man so quick in action." Romanus and Sunderland, *Command Problems*, p. 24, quote Chennault's observations on support for the Chinese ground forces in his 17 October 1943 statement of plans.

53. Hegenberger, oral history, p. 74; Flying Tigers, oral history, Hill interview, pp. 20–21 (quoted); McClure, *Fire and Fall Back*, pp. 188, 202.

54. Ibid., p. 203; Frillmann, *China*, p. 208.

55. Craven and Cate, *Services around the World*, pp. 137ff.

56. Tunner, *Over the Hump*, pp. 116–24, 130.

57. Flying Tigers, oral history, Davis interview, pp. 41, 43, 46; *New York Times*, 14 October 1944, 7:7.

58. First quotations from Frank, diaries, 1 April and 2 March 1944; third quotation from Breitweiser, oral history, p. 21.

59. Chennault to Max, 26 May 1944; *New York Times*, 16 January 1944, 19:8.

60. Tennien, *Chungking Listening Post*, pp. 144, 180, 185.

61. In Kuter Papers: Wedemeyer to Kuter, 9 June 1944; Kuter to Chennault, 12 July 1944; Chennault to Kuter, 3 August 1944 (quoted). Chennault to Roosevelt, 14 July 1944, FDR Papers.

62. Romanus and Sunderland, *Time Runs Out*, pp. 170–71; Haughland, *The AAF against Japan*, pp. 301ff.

63. Romanus and Sunderland, *Command Problems*, pp. 399, 408; Craven and Cate, *Guadalcanal to Saipan*, p. 267.

64. Romanus and Sunderland, *Command Problems*, pp. 460–63; Madame, interview, 105.5, AFSHRC.

65. Caldwell, *South of Tokyo*, p. 30; Crozier, *The Man Who Lost China*, p. 262; Williams, oral history, p. 62; author interview, Shu; Chennault, interview, 5 April 1948, 105.5-11, AFSHRC. Even Li Tsung-jen had trouble understanding Chiang's accent (see *The Memoirs of Li Tsung-jen*, p. 429). In a telephone interview, Alsop expressed the firm conviction that Ho, not Chiang, was responsible for denying supplies to Hsueh.

66. Romanus and Sunderland, *Time Runs Out*, pp. 8–9; Background Material for Romanus and Sunderland History, NA.

67. Chennault to Roosevelt, 21 September 1944, FDR Papers; Willauer to Currie, The Effect of the North Burma Campaign on the Loss of Our Bases in Southeast China, Willauer Papers; Chennault articles in *New York World Telegram*, 5, 6, and 7 April 1948, reprinted in *Congressional Record*, 80th Cong., 2d sess., vol. 94, pt. 12, A4490–98; *Hearings*, p. 1444; enclosure 1 of Chennault to Wedemeyer, 6 July 1945, Alsop Papers; Farnsworth to Lonsberg, 17 October 1947, 105.5-13, AFSHRC. Stratemeyer agreed with Chennault that he could have defeated the Japanese in the summer of 1944 if he had had supplies (interview, 11 January 1949, 105.5-13, AFSHRC).

Chapter 16

The title of this chapter quotes Roosevelt to Chennault, 2 October 1944, FDR Papers.

1. Stilwell, diary, 13 August 1944, Stilwell Papers.

2. MacArthur to Chennault, 13 August 1944, Stilwell Papers.

3. Stilwell to Sultan, pencil copy, Stilwell Papers.

4. MacArthur to Sultan, 15 August 1944, quoting Chennault's message of 11 August, Stilwell Papers.

5. Chennault to McHugh, 28 May 1944, McHugh Papers; the navy Distinguished Service Medal, awarded in December 1947, was reportedly delayed because Marshall objected to his receiving it (pertinent material in CLC Papers and *CAT Bulletin* 1 [15 December 1947] and 6 [August 1953]).

6. Chennault to Stilwell and Sultan, 16 August 1944; Stilwell to Sultan and Sultan to Chennault (pencil copies), Stilwell Papers.

7. Chennault to Sultan, 19 August 1944, Stilwell Papers.

8. Stilwell to Sultan, 21 August 1944; Stilwell, diary, 1, 2, 3, 4 October 1944, Stilwell Papers.

9. Stilwell, diary, 11, 13, 16 October 1944, Stilwell Papers; administrative admonition, 30 October 1944, 333.9 Chennault, RG 159 IG, General Correspondence, NA. See also Romanus and Sunderland, *Command Problems*, p. 465.

10. Scott to author, 20 March 1981.

11. Chennault to Sultan, 6 August 1944 (first quotation), Stilwell Papers; Chennault to War Department, 26 September 1944, CM IN 24702, NA; Chennault to Stilwell, 23 October 1944, CLC Papers.

12. Stilwell to Chennault, 13 October 1944 (quoted), CLC Papers; Romanus and Sunderland, *Command Problems*, p. 466; Chennault to Arnold, 10 October 1944, 142.041-34, AFSHRC.

13. Chennault to Stilwell, 14 October 1944 (first quotation), CLC Papers, and *SPF*, p. 2508; Stilwell to Chennault, 17 October 1944, *SPF*, p. 2510; Chennault to Stilwell, 19 October 1944, *SPF*, p. 2515; Stilwell to Chennault, 20 October 1944, *SPF*, p. 2517; Romanus and Sunderland, *Command Problems*, p. 466n; Chennault to Stilwell, 23 October 1944 (second quotation), CLC Papers.

14. Stilwell's recall is thoroughly covered in Romanus and Sunderland, *Command Problems*, esp. pp. 435, 439–59, and 468–69 and in Tuchman, *Stilwell*, pp. 483–509.

15. *Hearings*, p. 1812.

16. Roosevelt to Chennault, 2 October 1944, FDR Papers; Romanus and Sunderland, *Command Problems*, p. 468; Stilwell to Marshall, 5 October 1944, *SPF*, p. 2500; Stilwell, diary, 4 October 1944. Liang, *General Stilwell in China*, p. 264, cites Kung's cable to Chiang in the Tachi Archives.

17. Stilwell to Marshall, 5 October 1944, *SPF*, p. 2500; Stimson, diaries, 3 and 4 October 1944; Stimson and Bundy, *On Active Service in Peace and War*, pp. 537–39; Romanus and Sunderland, *Command Problems*, pp. 415–16, 421, 454, 468–69; Marshall interviews, 6 and 13 July 1949, Background Material for Romanus and Sunderland History, NA; author interview, Hansell.

18. Chennault's reactions as later expressed to Wedemeyer and reported in Wedemeyer to Marshall, 1 August 1945, ABC Files 336, China sec. 1-B-4, NA; memo, Davies and Hopkins conversation, 4 September 1944, Stilwell Papers.

19. Wedemeyer to Kuter, 20 November 1944, 145.81-171, AFSHRC, and in Kuter Papers.

20. Chennault to Roosevelt, 27 June 1944, FDR Papers; Chennault to Roose-

velt, 27 October 1944 (quoted), Hopkins Papers; Chennault to Kuter, 11 November 1944, 145.81-171, AFSHRC.

21. Romanus and Sunderland, *Time Runs Out*, p. 22; Wedemeyer, *Wedemeyer Reports*, p. 276 (quoted).

22. Wedemeyer to author, 8 January 1984.

23. Ibid.; Wedemeyer to Kuter, 10 November 1944, Kuter Papers; Mansfield report, 3 January 1945, FDR Papers. Wedemeyer replaced one of Stilwell's staff officers for making derogatory comments about the Chinese. See Breitweiser to Chennault, 9 January 1945, CLC Papers.

24. Mansfield report, 3 January 1945 (first quotation), FDR Papers; Chennault quoted from interview, 16 April 1948, 105.5-11, AFSHRC; Romanus and Sunderland, *Time Runs Out*, pp. 54–55.

25. Craven and Cate, *Matterhorn to Nagasaki*, pp. 111–15, 137, 142–44; Romanus and Sunderland, *Time Runs Out*, pp. 173–75; Chennault to Arnold, 26 January 1944, Hopkins Papers; Chennault, Air Warfare in China, 29 August 1952, K239.716252-17, AFSHRC; Caraway, oral history, sec. 7 (quoted); Wedemeyer to Chennault, 2 January 1945; 862.311, AFSHRC.

26. Minutes of meetings, Generalissimo with Wedemeyer, 30 November 1944 and 18 January 1945, box 7, RG 331, headquarters USF CT, NA; Wedemeyer to Chennault, 11 December 1944, quoted in Romanus and Sunderland, *Time Runs Out*, p. 72.

27. Wedemeyer to Hull, 5 July 1945, quoted in Romanus and Sunderland, *Time Runs Out*, p. 254; Wedemeyer to author, 8 January 1984; Chennault to Wedemeyer, 21 February 1945, box 14, RG 331, headquarters, USF CT, NA; Romanus and Sunderland, *Time Runs Out*, p. 178; memo of notes on staff talk, 17 January 1945, CLC Papers; Wedemeyer to Chennault, 21 January 1945, 862.311, AFSHRC; Chennault, *Way*, p. 334.

28. Caraway, oral history, sec. 7; Romanus and Sunderland, *Time Runs Out*, p. 173; "Aerial Warfare Tactician," *Air Force Magazine*, 68 (September 1985):51.

29. Craven and Cate, *Services around the World*, pp. 150–51, report a grand total of 650,000 tons carried to China; they conclude that Chiang might have collapsed without Chennault and what the lift enabled him to do, but perhaps most important was the development of strategic airlift.

30. Chennault, Fourteenth Air Force Operations from China Bases, United States at War (quoted), 862.311, AFSHRC; Chennault, Air Warfare in China, 29 August 1952, K239.716252-17, AFSHRC.

31. Chennault, Mission Assuming the Japanese Offensive is Held, CLC Papers.

32. Japanese Studies quoted in Romanus and Sunderland, *Time Runs Out*, p. 179; see ibid., p. 47n.

33. Ibid., pp. 52, 64–65, 165.

34. Elsey, *Roosevelt and China*, p. 55.

35. Leighton, *Global Logistics and Strategy*, 1943–45, pp. 528, 621; Romanus and Sunderland, *Time Runs Out*, pp. 15, 336–37. See also Davies,

Dragon by the Tail; Feis, *The China Tangle*; U.S. Department of State, White Paper.

36. Author interview, Holloway; Chennault quoted from Chennault to Wedemeyer, 6 July 1945, as given in Alsop, "Why We Lost China," pt. 2, *Saturday Evening Post*, 14 January 1950, p. 90.

37. Chennault to Alsop, February 1946, Alsop Papers; telephone interview, Noe, 8 February 1984.

38. Willauer, notes in box 2, 10A, Willauer Papers.

39. Urbanowicz to author, 9 December 1980.

40. Chennault, Air Warfare in China, 29 August 1952, K239.716252-17, AFSHRC; Mansfield, report, 3 January 1945, FDR Papers; Chennault, *Way*, pp. 41, 61, 241, 257, 317.

41. Koen, *The China Lobby*, pp. 114–15; Chennault to Wedemeyer, 6 July 1945, enclosure 1, 2d, Alsop Papers; Stilwell quoted from minutes, conference, 30 April 1943, item 27, Msg bk. 9, OPD Exec. 8, NA.

42. Betts, oral history, pp. 11–12.

43. Chennault to Wedemeyer, 6 July 1945, enclosure 1, p. 21, Alsop Papers. See also Chennault articles in *New York World Telegram*, 22 March–8 April 1948, reprinted in *Congressional Record*, 80th Cong., 2d sess., vol. 94, pt. 12, pp. A4490–98.

44. Chennault to Roosevelt, 19 April 1944, *FRUS 1944*, VI, p. 57.

45. Chennault to Roosevelt, 21 September 1944, FDR Papers.

46. Ibid.

47. Ibid.

48. Davies quoted in Romanus and Sunderland, *Command Problems*, p. 302.

49. See Feis, *The China Tangle*, pp. 214ff.

50. Chennault quoted from Chennault to Wedemeyer, 6 July 1945, enclosure 1, p. 22, Alsop Papers; Barnett interview, 11 May 1949, 105.5-13, AFSHRC.

51. Chennault to Roosevelt, 21 September 1944, FDR Papers.

52. Chennault to Mrs. Roosevelt, 29 May 1945, Coronado Cooper Papers.

53. Eleanor Roosevelt to Chennault, 13 June 1945, Coronado Cooper Papers.

Chapter 17

The title of this chapter quotes Chennault according to Trumble in Trumble to Taylor, 7 April 1965, K239.04365, AFSHRC. Trumble recalled that Chennault had made the remark on at least two different occasions.

1. Craven and Cate, *Matterhorn to Nagasaki*, pp. 267–69; Romanus and Sunderland, *Time Runs Out*, pp. 333–36; Chennault to Wedemeyer, 18 November 1944 and Wedemeyer to Chennault, 28 November 1944, 862.311-1, AFSHRC.

2. Minutes of conferences, 19 April 1945, Wedemeyer files, RG 331, headquarters USF CT, NA; Romanus and Sunderland, *Time Runs Out*, p. 343.

3. Wedemeyer to Marshall, 13 April 1945, case 45, OPD 319.1 sec. 1, NA.

4. Ibid.

5. Ibid. Wedemeyer's conclusions were restated in Wedemeyer to author, 8 January 1984.

6. Craven and Cate, *Matterhorn to Nagasaki*, p. 269; Romanus and Sunderland, *Time Runs Out*, pp. 344–46.

7. Chennault to Sultan, 11 February 1945, CLC Papers; Sultan to Chennault, 20 February 1945, CLC Papers.

8. Transcripts of interrogations, CID, Sutter case, CLC Papers; Judge Advocate's Office to Chennault, 22 January 1945, CLC Papers.

9. Chennault to Sultan, 11 February 1945 (quoted), CLC Papers; Chennault to Neyland, July 1945, CLC Papers. Chennault had given dishonorable discharges to AVG members caught in black market dealing in January 1942. See Bond, *A Flying Tiger's Diary*, p. 77.

10. Transcripts cited in n. 8 above; draft of letter, Chennault to Wedemeyer, CLC Papers; Stimson, diary, 8 February 1945; Wedemeyer to author, 8 January 1984; Caraway, oral history, p. 90.

11. Wedemeyer to author, 8 January 1984; Eaker, oral history, sec. 1; Eaker's letter to Wedemeyer in CBI history, vol. 4, sec. 3, pp. 215–16, 825.01C, AFSHRC.

12. Willauer, draft "To be used with MacArthur's Command," Willauer Papers.

13. *Hearings*, pp. 1024–25, 1086. See also Alsop, "The Strange Case of Louis Budenz," *Atlantic Monthly*, April 1952, pp. 29–33.

14. Romanus and Sunderland, *Time Runs Out*, pp. 357–58; Wedemeyer to Taylor, 15 December 1964, K239.04365, AFSHRC; Wedemeyer to author, 8 January 1984. See also n. 15 below.

15. Arnold's letter of 17 June 1945, with attached memo, Cobb to Wedemeyer, 22 July 1948, and note in reply were found in 105.5-13, AFSHRC, although that location appears to be a misfiling. The letter is quoted elsewhere (CBI history, vol. 4, sec. 3, pp. 218–19), but the memo and note further support the conclusion that Wedemeyer made every effort to treat Chennault with consideration. In a letter to the author, 8 January 1984, Wedemeyer said that any respect or consideration he gave Chennault was "fully merited."

16. Wedemeyer to Marshall, 20 June 1945, RG 331, headquarters USF CT, NA. See also Craven and Cate, *Matterhorn to Nagasaki*, p. 271; Romanus and Sunderland, *Time Runs Out*, pp. 357–58.

17. Chennault to Wedemeyer, 26 June 1945, and reply 27 June 1945, RG 331, headquarters USF CT, NA.

18. The letter is on file with the Alsop Papers, available by special request. Enclosure 1 (22 pages) is also in the Alsop Papers. A long paragraph from the letter is quoted in Alsop, "Why We Lost China," pt. 2, *Saturday Evening Post*, 14 January 1950, p. 90. The letter and enclosure 2, consisting of copies

of pertinent papers, most of which are also available elsewhere, is in WDCSA 091 China TS (Chennault Report), NA. Alsop's statement that he drafted the letter is in *Hearings*, p. 1434. Alsop confirmed his authorship to me and explained his reasoning in a telephone interview, 31 January 1986.

19. Wedemeyer to Marshall, 1 August 1945, ABC Files 336 China sec. 1-B-4, NA; see n. 18 above.

20. Wedemeyer to Marshall, cited in n. 19 above.

21. Page 1 of letter plus enclosure 1, Chennault to Wedemeyer, 6 July 1945, Alsop Papers; portions of letter summarized in CBI history, vol. 4, sec. 3, p. 221.

22. Enclosure 1, 15a, Chennault to Wedemeyer, 6 July 1945, Alsop Papers.

23. Chennault to Wedemeyer, 6 July 1945, quoted in Alsop article cited in n. 18 above.

24. Telephone interview, Alsop, 31 January 1986; Trumble to Taylor, 7 April 1965, K239.04365, AFSHRC.

25. Chennault to Stratemeyer, 8 July 1945, quoted in CBI history, vol. 4, sec. 3, p. 222, 825.01C, AFSHRC.

26. U.S. Office of War Information, Kunming Branch, Translation Service, No. 579, 17 July 1945, p. 3, RG 332, CBI box 2, NA.

27. *New York Times*, 15, 17, 20, 25 July, 3, 25 August 1945.

28. Excerpts from Chinese newspapers, CLC Papers. In addition to material in CLC Papers, see press releases, transcripts of news conferences, citations, speeches, and related information in 862.3091, AFSHRC.

29. Award, copy in 862.3091, AFSHRC; Chiang Kai-shek, "My Good Friend Chennault," *Chennault's Flying Tigers, 1941–45*, p. 46.

30. Wavell to Chennault, 17 July 1945, and Chow to Chennault, 12 July 1945, CLC Papers.

31. Hsueh to Chennault, 6 August 1945, CLC Papers; Rosholt, *Days of the Ching Pao*, p. 35.

32. Chennault to Chiang, 17 July 1945, quoted in A. Chennault, *A Thousand Springs*, pp. 113–14; Chiang to Chennault, 29 July 1945, RKC Papers.

33. Chennault to Bond, 13 July 1945, K239.04365, AFSHRC.

Chapter 18

1. Chennault interview with E. Lockett, 4, 5 February 1958, Coronado Cooper Papers.

2. Author interviews, Joe Y. Chennault, Lee; memorial by K. C. Yeh, *CAT Bulletin* 11 (August 1958):12.

3. Transcript of news conference, 14 July 1945, 862.3091, AFSHRC.

4. Ibid.

5. Outline for talk, 1945, CLC Papers; Corcoran, manuscript, chap. Y; Chennault to Alsop, 4 September 1945, Alsop Papers.

6. Chennault family interviews; Chennault to Noe, 26 May 1944

(quoted), CLC Papers; Chennault to Paxton, 4 October 1945, and Paxton to Chennault, 7 November 1945, CLC Papers.

7. *New York Times*, 28, 29 November 1945. For Hurley's resignation, see Feis, *The China Tangle*, pp. 405ff.

8. *New York Times*, 11 October 1945; handwritten speech draft, 10 October 1945, CLC Papers.

9. Speech draft, for lecture tour 1945, CLC Papers.

10. *New York Mirror*, 31 October 1945; Corcoran, manuscript, chap. Y; author interviews, Anna Chennault, Lee.

11. Lecture tour schedules, reports, and speech drafts in CLC Papers.

12. Author interviews, Joe Y. Chennault and Anna Chennault; telephone interviews, Hotz, Noe; memos and letters in CLC Papers.

13. Pickler, *United States Aid*, pp. 288ff.; Hager, *Wings for the Dragon*, p. 279; Chennault press conference, 7 July 1945, 862.3091, AFSHRC; Wedemeyer to War Department, 3 September 1945, RG 165, Decimal Files sec. 1-B-3, NA; *Baltimore Sun*, 23 October 1945; *New York Times*, 23 October, 2 November 1945; Chiang to Chennault, 29 July 1945, RKC Papers.

14. Chennault, transcript of news conference, 7 July 1945, 862.3091, AFSHRC; Leary, *Perilous Missions*, p. 6; Lung Yun statement in U.S. Office of War Information, Kunming Branch, Translation Service, No. 579, 17 July 1945, RG 332, CBI box 2, NA.

15. In Willauer Papers: Willauer to wife, 18 March 1946; Pennsylvania Central Airlines to Willauer, 10 December 1945; transcript, 1 December 1960, pp. 3–5. Corcoran, manuscript, chap. Y; Leary, *Perilous Missions*, pp. 9–10.

16. Transcript, 1 December 1960, p. 4, Willauer Papers.

17. Illegible name on OSS letterhead, to Chennault, 26 September 1945, Noe Papers; *New York Times*, 3, 13 January 1946; John Hersey, "Letter from Shanghai," *New Yorker*, 9 February 1946, pp. 82–90.

18. Willauer to wife, 23 and 28 January 1946, Willauer Papers.

19. Price, *UNRRA in China, 1945–1947*, pp. 2, 3, 42–43, 119, 149.

20. Transcript, 1 December 1960, pp. 5–6, Willauer Papers; Olmstead to Leary, 17 May 1967, in Leary, *Perilous Missions*, p. 227, 37n; ibid., p. 12.

21. Willauer to wife, 26 February 1946, Willauer Papers; Price, *UNRRA in China, 1945–1947*, pp. 324–25.

22. Willauer to wife, 11 April and 13 May 1946, Willauer Papers; William M. Leary, Jr., "Portrait of a Cold Warrior: Whiting Willauer and Civil Air Transport," *Modern Asian Studies* 5 (1971):377–78. See also Promise and Fulfillment, *CAT Bulletin*, anniversary supp., October 1947, pp. 2–4.

23. Chennault to Trumble, 17 July 1946, K239.04365, AFSHRC; Willauer to wife, 10 July 1947, Willauer Papers; Trumble to author, 23 July 1985.

24. "The China Lobby," *Reporter* 6 (15 April 1952):9; Leary, *Perilous Missions*, p. 14; Corcoran, manuscript, chap. Y.

25. Transcript, 1 December 1960, p. 6; Willauer to wife, 26 February, 15 March, 11 April (quoted), 15 April 1946, Willauer Papers.

26. *New York Times*, 12 June 1946; Chennault to Trumble, 17 July 1946,

K239.04365, AFSHRC; Williams to author, 15 May 1981; author interview, Rosbert; Corcoran, manuscript, chap. Y; Leary, *Perilous Missions*, pp. 16–19.

27. Transcript, 1 December 1960, p. 7, Willauer Papers; William M. Leary, Jr., "Portrait of a Cold Warrior: Whiting Willauer and Civil Air Transport," *Modern Asian Studies* 5 (1971):380.

28. Chennault to Max, 29 December 1944; Chennault family interviews.

29. Chennault to Alsop, 12 February 1946 and Alsop to Chennault, 25 February 1946, Alsop Papers.

30. Author interview, Joe Y. Chennault; Chennault to Wedemeyer, 6 July 1945, Alsop Papers; telephone interviews, Alsop, Hotz; Abell, *Drew Pearson Diaries*, pp. 59–60, 467.

31. Trumble to author, 31 July 1985.

32. Handwritten draft for press conference, 11 September 1946, K239.04365, AFSHRC.

33. Ibid.

34. Telephone interview, Noe; Chennault to Alsop, February 1946, Alsop Papers.

35. Chennault to Trumble, 6 August 1946, K239.04365, AFSHRC.

36. Author interviews, Brannon, Lewis, Rector, Rosbert, and Rousselot.

37. Willauer to wife, 15 April 1946, Willauer Papers; Williams, oral history, p. 78; *CAT Bulletin* 9 (October 1956), p. 5; *New York Times*, 22 December 1947, 3:3.

38. Norman Sklarewitz, "CAT," *United Aircraft Quarterly Bee-Hive*, January 1962; Corey Ford, "The Flying Tigers Carry On," *Saturday Evening Post*, 5 and 12 February 1955; Robbins, *Air America*, pp. 46–49. *CAT Bulletins* are a valuable source.

39. Rossi to author, 28 March 1985; Cameron, *Hungry Tiger*, p. 48.

40. *CAT Bulletin* 1 (15 March 1948), (15 June 1948), (1 July 1948).

41. Author interviews, Arnold, Fogg, Lewis, Rosbert, and Rousselot.

42. Author interviews, family and friends.

43. Willauer to wife, 29 June, 10 July, 3 August 1947, Willauer Papers; Jackson to author, 26 December 1984, 9 March 1985.

44. Willauer to wife, 29 June, 10 July, 3 August 1947, Willauer Papers.

45. Author interviews, Anna Chennault, Larson, Rosbert.

46. Frillmann, oral history, p. 400; *CAT Bulletin* 11 (August 1958); *New York Times*, 22 December 1947, 3:3; Chennault interview with E. Lockett, 4, 5 February 1958, Coronado Cooper Papers.

47. Author interviews, Larson, Lewis.

48. Author interview, Rousselot.

49. Transcript, 1 December 1960, pp. 9–11, Willauer Papers.

50. Chennault interview with E. Lockett, 4, 5 February 1958, Coronado Cooper Papers.

51. *CAT Bulletin* 4 (December 1951).

52. *CAT Bulletins*, social notes, 1948 (various issues).

53. Cohen, *America's Response to China*, pp. 185–91.

54. Chennault interview with E. Lockett, 4, 5 February 1958, Coronado Cooper Papers; Chennault to Trumble, 6 August 1946 (quoted), K239.04365, AFSHRC; Trumble to author, 31 July 1985.

55. Cohen, *America's Response to China*, pp. 191–92.

56. Leary, *Perilous Missions*, pp. 38ff.

57. Tape No. 6 CLC-EBL, Coronado Cooper Papers.

58. Transcript, 1 December 1960, pp. 11–16, Willauer Papers.

59. Leary, *Perilous Missions*, pp. 33–37.

60. *CAT Bulletin* 2 (15 September 1948).

Chapter 19

1. Scripps-Howard newspapers such as the *Washington Daily News*, 2 February 1948; also in *Congressional Record*, 80th Cong., 2d sess., vol. 94, pt. 1, pp. 1071–72, or pt. 9, p. A639; condensed in *Reader's Digest* 52 (April 1948).

2. The correspondence is not mentioned in the published Vandenberg papers, but two letters (Vandenberg to Chennault, 28 January 1947, and Chennault's reply of 15 February 1947) are in the Vandenberg Papers at Bentley Historical Library at the University of Michigan. Chennault's letter of 17 January 1947 is not now in the collection, nor is it listed in the original inventory made when the papers were deposited by Vandenberg's son. There is no doubt that the 17 January letter existed, for Vandenberg refers to it in his reply. My thanks to Mark A. Greene, assistant archivist for reference, who searched the files for me. See also Stueck, *The Road to Confrontation*, p. 42.

3. Vandenberg to Chennault, 28 January 1947, and Chennault to Vandenberg, 15 February 1947, Vandenberg Papers.

4. Vandenberg, *Private Papers*, p. 522ff.

5. U.S. Department of State, White Paper, pp. 764ff.

6. For views of postwar foreign policy, see Acheson, *Present at the Creation*; Borg and Heinrichs, eds., *Uncertain Years*; Cohen, *America's Response to China*; Schaller, *The United States and China*; Stueck, *The Road to Confrontation*; Vandenberg, *Private Papers*; Westerfield, *Foreign Policy*.

7. Seagrave, *The Soong Dynasty*, gives a detailed portrait of the Soong family and U.S. reaction to exploitation. Price, *UNRRA in China*, p. 2; Peck, *Two Kinds of Time*, p. 720.

8. Westerfield, *Foreign Policy*, pp. 240ff.

9. Chennault to Vandenberg, 15 February 1947, Vandenberg Papers.

10. Ibid.

11. Corcoran, manuscript, chap. Y; Willauer to wife, 28 June 1949, Willauer Papers.

12. Chennault to Max, 31 October 1947; Willauer to wife, 11 July 1949 and 28 June 1949, Willauer Papers.

13. Chennault testimony, 30 June 1949, cited in n. 72 below, pp. 319–20. See Leary, *Perilous Missions*, for detail on CAT operations. The airline actually

moved four times: from Shanghai to Canton, then to Kunming, to Hainan Island, and finally to Taiwan.

14. Chennault to Trumble, 15 May 1948 and 15 October 1948, K239.04365, AFSHRC; Chennault to Max, 31 October 1947.

15. Eaton to Chennault, 2 March 1948, CLC Papers.

16. Testimony, 10 March 1948, U.S. Foreign Policy for a Post-War Recovery Program, House Committee on Foreign Affairs, CLC Papers.

17. Chennault family interviews; Noe to author, 13 August 1984, and telephone interview; Cain to author, 24 June 1985; entries on 6 and 11 April 1948 in journal of James R. Cain; text of speech in CLC Papers.

18. See n. 1 above.

19. Chennault to Roosevelt, 21 September 1944, FDR Papers.

20. Marshall interviews, 6 and 13 July 1949, Background Material for Romanus and Sunderland History, NA; author interviews, Chennault family and friends; Miles, *A Different Kind of War*, p. 259.

21. Chennault to Alsop, 12 February and a second letter (quoted), date torn away but approximately February 1946, Alsop Papers.

22. *New York World Telegram* starting 22 March 1948 or reprint, "General Chennault on American Military Policy in China during World War II," *Congressional Record*, 80th Cong., 2d sess., vol. 94, pt. 12, pp. A4490ff.

23. "General Chennault on American Military Policy," p. A4493.

24. Chennault to Giles, 10 February 1945, Arnold Papers.

25. Review, *New York Times*, 30 January 1949.

26. Chennault to Trumble, 26 August 1948, K239.04365, AFSHRC.

27. Author interviews, Anna Chennault and Joe Y. Chennault; telephone interview, Hotz; incidental correspondence and memos in CLC Papers.

28. Review, *New Republic*, 7 March 1949, p. 23 (quoted); review, *Nation*, 26 February 1949, p. 244; review, *New York Times*, 31 January 1949; review, *Saturday Review of Literature*, 5 March 1949, p. 16.

29. Chennault to Voorhes, 7 June 1948, CLC Papers.

30. Chennault's testimony, 3 May 1949, printed (with minimal omissions) in *Vital Speeches*, 15 May 1949; also in *CAT Bulletin* 2 (15 May 1949), and the *Congressional Record*, 81st Cong., 1st sess., 1949, pp. 5480–84.

31. Leary, *Perilous Missions*, pp. 48–49; Cohen, *America's Response*, p. 197.

32. Gillin, *Warlord*, esp. pp. 285–88; Borg and Heinrichs, *Uncertain Years*, p. 155; Leary, *The Dragon's Wings*, p. 214.

33. Chennault to Voorhes, 7 June 1948, CLC Papers; *Life*, 22 November 1948, pp. 38–41.

34. *Time*, 15 November 1948, pp. 33–34.

35. "Raising of 100,000 International or Japanese Volunteers to Prevent the Spread of Communism in China by Using American Military Aids," undated, CLC Papers; Chennault to Pai, 25 December 1945, CLC Papers.

36. *FRUS 1948*, VIII, pp. 289–90.

37. Ibid.; *FRUS 1948*, VII, pp. 577, 603, 606; *CAT Bulletin* 1 (1 June 1948).

38. Chennault to Arther, 15 February 1949, and Arther to Chennault, 2

February, 7 April 1949, CLC Papers; Stueck, *Road to Confrontation*, pp. 126–27.

39. Millis, *The Forrestal Diaries*, pp. 532–34; Pickler, *United States Aid*, pp. 407–408; *Hearings*, pp. 1125–26.

40. *FRUS 1948*, VIII, pp. 294–96.

41. John Denson and Charlotte Knight, "World's Most Shot-at Air Line," *Collier's*, 11 August 1951, pp. 35ff.; Leary, *Perilous Missions*, pp. 57ff.

42. Willauer to General, 20 February 1949, Willauer Papers.

43. Leary, *Perilous Missions*, pp. 58–59.

44. Gillin, *Warlord*, pp. 288–91.

45. Chennault to Willauer, 23 April 1949, Willauer Papers.

46. Willauer to Tom and Bill, 5 June 1948, Willauer Papers; Yeh's memoir in *CAT Bulletin* 11 (August 1958):12; author interview, Anna Chennault; Willauer to Taylor gives Chennault's quip, Willauer Papers.

47. Willauer to General, 20 February 1949, and to wife, 21 January 1949, Willauer Papers; Leary, *Perilous Missions*, pp. 73ff.

48. Willauer noted that "adventurous people who had moved behind Red lines were useful to us" and that CAT's survey of the northwest was later "of importance in intelligence circles" (report and annotation, Willauer Papers). Chennault told a congressional committee that in Tientsin and Peiping he left Americans behind "by design" when the Communists advanced (30 June 1949 testimony cited in n. 72 below).

49. Willauer to wife, 21 January 1949, Willauer Papers.

50. *CAT Bulletin* 2 (15 February 1949).

51. Willauer's brief, Willauer Papers; *CAT Bulletin* 2 (15 April 1949).

52. *CAT Bulletin* 2 (15 April 1949); Time, 27 June 1949.

53. Testimony cited in n. 72 below, p. 311; Chennault to Noe, 26 May 1944, CLC Papers.

54. Chennault, Plan for Aid to Non-Communist China, 25 June 1949, Hull Papers, Reel 33, China General File.

55. Stueck, *Road to Confrontation*, pp. 116–17.

56. See n. 30 above. Transcript of executive session testimony and copies of prepared statements and plans are in the CLC Papers.

57. Ibid.

58. Ibid.

59. Ibid.

60. Chennault to Alsop, 22 February 1950, Alsop Papers.

61. See n. 30 above.

62. Chapter 20.

63. Cohen, in Borg and Heinrichs, *Uncertain Years*, pp. 16ff.

64. United States Aid to the Nationalist Government of China, undated, CLC Papers.

65. Summary of Present Communist Crisis in Asia, 10 May 1949, CLC Papers; memo, conversation with Rusk, 11 May 1949, CLC Papers; *FRUS 1949*, IX, pp. 517–23.

66. Chennault quoted from *FRUS 1949*, IX, p. 523.

67. Vandenberg, *Private Papers*, pp. 531 (quoted), 536; Cohen, in Borg and Heinrichs, *Uncertain Years*, pp. 22–25.

68. Chennault statement on domino theory, *CAT Bulletin* 2 (15 May 1949).

69. Chennault to Snyder, 3 June 1949, with enclosures, CLC Papers.

70. Chennault, "Last Call for China," *Life*, 11 July 1949, pp. 36–37; Chennault, "Hold 'Em! Harass 'Em! Hamstring 'Em! The Chennault Plan," *Reader's Digest*, October 1949, pp. 25–28; Chennault to Hearst, 24 June 1949, plus letters of introduction for Sentner, CLC Papers.

71. Kennedy to Chennault, 20 June 1949, plus other correspondence and memos, CLC Papers.

72. Chennault, "Red Cloud over China," *America* 80 (19 March 1949):649–50; testimony, 30 June 1949, to House Committee on Foreign Affairs: U.S. Congress, House, Committee on International Relations, *United States Policy in the Far East*, vol. 8, pt. 2, pp. 283–326 (p. 313 quoted), with Chennault's Plan for Aid printed on pp. 397–99.

73. *FRUS 1949*, IX, pp. 524–27.

Chapter 20

1. "History of the Central Intelligence Agency," in U.S. Congress, Senate, *Select Committee to Study Governmental Operations with Respect to Intelligence Activities*, Senate Report 94-755, 94th Cong., 2d sess., 1976. See also Borosage and Marks, eds., *The CIA File*, p. 8.

2. Corcoran to A. Chennault, printed in A. Chennault, *Chennault*, pp. 78–80.

3. Colby, *Honorable Men*, p. 73.

4. Ibid., p. 75.

5. We are indebted to William M. Leary of the University of Georgia for *Perilous Missions*, his detailed history of CAT. In the course of his research, Leary tracked down a condensed version of an official secret history of Air America and from this document found out how Chennault, Willauer, CAT, and the CIA formed their business relationship. See Leary, *Perilous Missions*, p. 216, for an explanation of the history; pp. 70, 72–73, for initial contacts.

6. Ibid., pp. 72–73.

7. Cohen, in Borg and Heinrichs, *Uncertain Years*, pp. 32–37, 50–51.

8. *FRUS 1949*, IX, pp. 540–41.

9. Leary, *Perilous Missions*, pp. 79–80; Li Tsung-jen, *Memoirs*, p. 547.

10. Willauer to wife, 29 August, 18 September 1949, Willauer Papers.

11. Leary, *Perilous Missions*, pp. 81–82.

12. Ibid., p. 82.

13. Chennault to Symington, Johnson, Vinson, Butterworth, 2 October 1949, CLC Papers.

14. Hsueh Yueh to Chennault, 19 November 1949, CLC Papers.

15. Leary, *Perilous Missions*, pp. 52–53, 90–91.

16. Ibid., pp. 86, 88–89, 98–99.

17. Statement of Facts Regarding Hong Kong Airplane Case, 29 May 1951 and supp., 1 January 1952, CLC Papers; memo, Defection of Air Line in Hong Kong, 16 November 1949, CIA.

18. Rousselot quoted from author interview; transcript, 1 December 1960, pp. 21–22; Willauer Papers; Leary, *Perilous Missions*, pp. 91–92.

19. Chennault to Alsop, 14 January 1950, Alsop Papers.

20. Transcript, 1 December 1960, pp. 23–24, Willauer Papers.

21. Leary, *Perilous Missions*, pp. 93–94.

22. Ibid., p. 94; Corcoran, manuscript, chap. Y. Although the extent of the U.S. government involvement was not public knowledge at the time, thoughtful observers suspected that it was great; see William M. Leary, Jr., "Aircraft and Anti-Communists: CAT in Action, 1949–1952," in *China Quarterly* 52 (1972):654–69.

23. Leary, *Perilous Missions*, pp. 94–96.

24. Transcript, 1 December 1960, p. 22, Willauer Papers.

25. Dunlop, *Donovan*, pp. 487, 495; Leary, *Perilous Missions*, p. 97.

26. Leary, *The Dragon's Wings*, pp. 220–22; Leary, *Perilous Missions*, pp. 95–96.

27. Supplement, 1 January 1952, to Statement of Facts Regarding Hong Kong Airplane Case, 29 May 1951, CLC Papers; Leary, *Perilous Missions*, p. 98.

28. Leary, *Perilous Missions*, pp. 96, 103.

29. For U.S. foreign policy during these months, see Schaller, *United States and China*, pp. 126ff.; Acheson, *Present at the Creation*, pp. 303ff.; Cohen, in Borg and Heinrichs, *Uncertain Years*, pp. 29ff.

30. Transcript, 1 December 1960, pp. 25–26, Willauer Papers; annotation of letter, 10 July 1950, Willauer Papers; Leary, *Perilous Missions*, pp. 103–106.

31. Willauer to wife, 1 April 1950, Willauer Papers.

32. Author interviews, Anna Chennault, Rosbert, Rousselot.

33. Working Paper—CAT—15 March to 15 June [1950], Willauer Papers; Leary, *Perilous Missions*, pp. 109–12.

34. Ibid., p. 112.

35. Author interviews, Fogg, Lewis, Rosbert, Rousselot.

36. Author interviews, Arnold, Rosbert, Rousselot; working paper, 9 April 1950 (quoted), Willauer Papers; Proposal for Use of the CAT Airline, 1951, Willauer Papers; Leary, *Perilous Missions*, pp. 113, 137.

37. Leary, *Perilous Missions*, pp. 113, 137, 211.

38. Notes, 1951, Willauer Papers; Willauer to wife, 7 January 1951 (quoted), Willauer Papers.

39. Corcoran to Chennault, 10 July 1950, Willauer Papers.

40. Stratemeyer to Chennault, 8 October 1950, CLC Papers; CAT's role in the Korean War is covered in the History of the 315th Air Division, K-DIV-315-HI, AFSHRC. "Korean Airlift," *CAT Bulletin* 7 (June, July 1954).

41. Statement by Willauer, *CAT Bulletin* 3 (December 1950):1–2; *CAT Bulletin* 3 (1 January 1950):11.

42. Chennault to Knowland, 27 June 1950, CLC Papers.

43. Memo, Report of Meeting between Generals MacArthur and Chennault, CIA; *FRUS 1949*, IX, p. 545; Chennault to Knowland, 22 February 1950, CLC Papers; Chennault to Bridges, 8 April 1951, CLC Papers; press interview reported in *CAT Bulletin* 5 (August 1952):4–5; Cooper to son, 5 October 1958, Cooper Papers; Wedemeyer to author, 8 January 1984.

44. Patti, *Why Viet Nam?* pp. 56–57; Romanus and Sunderland, *Time Runs Out*, p. 259. See also Thorne, *Allies of a Kind*, pp. 217–18, 347–50, 463–69, 621–33.

45. Chennault, *Way*, p. 342; Patti, *Why Viet Nam?* p. 64 (quoted).

46. Patti, *Why Viet Nam?* pp. 57–59.

47. Chennault, "If Red China Strikes," *Collier's*, 18 November 1950. In a letter to his brother William, 12 October 1954, Chennault said he thought the conquest of Indochina remained the Communists' principal objective.

48. Leary, *Perilous Missions*, chaps. 11 and 13, esp. p. 164; reports in *CAT Bulletin* 7 (April, May 1954); Norman Sklarewitz, "CAT," *United Aircraft Quarterly Bee-Hive*, January 1962, pp. 15–20. See also articles cited in chap. 18, n. 38.

49. Chennault to My Dear Fellow American, CLC Papers.

50. *New York Times*, 21, 28 July 1952; Dunlop, *Donovan*, p. 498.

51. Chennault to Noe, 27 November 1952, Noe Papers; Corcoran, manuscript, chap. Y; letters and memos in CLC Papers.

52. Chennault to Noe, 25 October 1952, Noe Papers.

53. Leary, *Perilous Missions*, pp. 111, 144–45, 171–72, 177.

54. Ibid., pp. 178–79.

55. Chennault to Noe, 4 January 1954, Noe Papers.

56. Leary, *Perilous Missions*, pp. 199–206.

57. Chennault to Willauer, 16 April, 8 June, 12, 18 October 1954, Willauer Papers.

58. Chennault to Corcoran, 2 November 1954, quoted in Leary, *Perilous Missions*, p. 206.

59. Chennault's New Year message, *CAT Bulletin* 7 (January 1954).

60. Leary, *Perilous Missions*, p. 211; author interviews, Arnold, Fogg, Larson, Lewis, Rosbert, Rousselot; individual quoted anonymous by request.

Chapter 21

1. Peck, *Two Kinds of Time*, pp. 62–63.

2. Author interview, Lee; Chennault, Air Warfare in China, 29 August 1952 (first quotation), K239.716252-17, AFSHRC; Chennault to Noe, 6 and 27 November 1952 (second and third quotations), Noe Papers.

3. Merchant memo, *FRUS 1951*, VII, pp. 1760–62.

4. Chennault to Noe, 27 November 1952, Noe Papers.

5. Chennault to Trumble, 11 June 1957, K239.04365, AFSHRC; *New York Times*, 17 July 1945, 2:7, quoting a Chinese editorial.

6. Chennault, "Can Asia Be Saved?" originally in *N.S.A.*, reprinted in *Congressional Record*, 82d Cong., 2d sess., vol. 98, pt. 11, pp. A4320-22.

7. Ibid.; lengthy exposition by Chennault, June 1951 (quoted), sent to Senators Johnson, Bridges, and Brewster, CLC Papers.

8. Chennault, Air Warfare in China, p. 40, K239.716252-17, AFSHRC.

9. *FRUS 1951*, VII, pp. 1760–62; Chennault, "If Red China Strikes," *Collier's*, 18 November 1950, p. 68; Chennault, "Can Asia Be Saved," cited in n. 6 (first quotation); second quotation from Chennault, "My Plan to Fight Red China," originally in *See*, reprinted in *Congressional Record*, 82d Cong., 1st sess., vol. 97, pt. 2, pp. 2567–68.

10. Chennault, "My Plan to Fight Red China"; see also a series in the *New York Herald Tribune*, 26, 27, 28, 29, 30 March, 1 April 1951. Chennault at times had the writing assistance of Edward Lockett. The CLC Papers contain notes on television interviews, manuscripts of articles, and extensive correspondence relating to Chennault's China lobbying. See also interviews and articles in various issues of the *CAT Bulletin* (esp. vol. 6, February 1953, p. 9); interview reported by Tom McClary, "Voice of the Tiger," *Flying*, October 1954.

11. Text of speech for 1950 lecture tour, CLC Papers.

12. Chennault to Noe, 13 December 1954, Noe Papers.

13. *FRUS 1949*, VIII, p. 455; Corcoran to Chennault, 10 July 1950, Willauer Papers.

14. Claire to William Chennault, 8 April 1951, courtesy W. S. Chennault.

15. A. Chennault, *A Thousand Springs*, pp. 261–66; A. Chennault in *CAT Bulletin* 6 (December–January 1952–53), (February 1953), (March 1953); Chennault to Max, 4 April 1953.

16. Chennault as told to Edward B. Lockett, "The Flying Tigers Can Do It Again," *Look*, 7 September 1954, and *Reader's Digest*, September 1954; "How to Hit the Reds," Chennault interview in *Newsweek*, 26 April 1954.

17. Applications and responses in CLC Papers.

18. *FRUS 1952–54*, XII, pp. 456–57.

19. *FRUS 1951*, VI, p. 287.

20. Tape No. 6 CLC-EBL, Coronado Cooper Papers.

21. Interviews with family and friends. In a letter to the author in June 1985, Walter Judd wrote that Chennault "was consistently *so right* in his analyses and recommendations—and frequently got such a raw deal from American 'leaders' who were so wrong. There was none greater in our whole war effort."

22. *CAT Bulletin* 1 (15 March 1948); correspondence between Chennault and C. R. Mooney, courtesy Gordon Pickler.

23. Rosholt, *A Tribute*, p. 15.

24. Data supplied by the Supreme Council, Ancient and Accepted Scottish

Rite of Freemasonry, in February 1982; Chennault family interviews; Harris to Chennault, 23 June, and Chennault to Harris, 13 July 1945, CLC Papers.

25. *CAT Bulletin*; author interviews, Chennault family and friends; Chennault to Noe, 12 March 1956, Noe Papers; Kuter, oral history, p. 365.

26. *CAT Bulletin* 5 and 6 (December–January 1952–53):20.

27. Frillmann, oral history, pp. 405–407; *New York Times*, 29 April 1952, 2:2, 26:3; correspondence in Noe Papers.

28. Frillmann, *China*, pp. 288ff.; Frillmann, oral history, pp. 407–11; author interview, Rosholt.

29. Bachrack, *The Committee of One Million*, pp. 3–6, 55, 60, 68; Koen, *China Lobby*, pp. 27–30; Tucker, in Borg and Heinrichs, *Uncertain Years*, p. 133; Max Ascoli, Philip Horton, and Charles Wertenbaker, "The China Lobby," *Reporter* 6 (15, 29 April 1952); Malcolm Hobbs, "Chiang's Washington Front," *Nation*, 24 December 1949, pp. 619–20.

30. *Hearings*, pp. 4763–75.

31. Chennault to Trumble, 11 June 1957 (quoted), K239.04365, AFSHRC; Chennault, *Way*, p. xxi.

32. Jackson to author, 9 March 1985; author interviews, Chennault family and friends.

33. Chennault to Mrs. Noe, 24 February 1954, Noe Papers.

34. Chennault to Noe, 24 November, 13 December 1954, Noe Papers.

35. Trumble to Taylor, 3 January 1965, K239.04365, AFSHRC; author interviews, Joe Y. Chennault, Rosbert; telephone interview, Noe.

36. Chennault family interviews; journal kept by James R. Cain; author interviews, Cain, Noe; Joe Y. Chennault to author, 15 December 1983; William to Claire Chennault, RKC Papers; A. Chennault, p. xviii; Noe to author, 13 August 1984. In a letter to Max, 26 December 1957, Chennault wrote that he had decided to sell the camp because it seemed impossible to ensure observance of the game laws and none of his sons was in position to look after it. It was sold in January 1958.

37. Chennault to Alsop, 27 June 1953, Alsop Papers; Chennault to Noe, 25 August 1956, Noe Papers.

38. Tunner, *Over the Hump*, p. 124.

39. Chennault to Max, 15 March [probably 1955].

40. Chennault family interviews; letters, Chennault to Max and Rosemary; Memo from Dad, Educational Assistance for My Grandchildren, 20 August 1955, courtesy Simrall; Simrall to author, 1 August 1981; Chennault to Max, 10 September 1955.

41. Author interview, Joe Y. Chennault.

42. Claire to Anna Chennault, 28 August 1956 and 19 November 1957, made available through the courtesy of Anna Chennault. At his death Chennault left an estate of $406,500, of which $362,000 was in securities and was divided equally between Nell's and Anna's interests (*New York Times*, 2 October 1958, *State Times*, 3 October 1958).

43. Chennault to Max, 8 December 1952, 12 December 1956; Christmas letters to Rosemary, esp. 14 December 1955.

44. Author interviews, Anna Chennault and Joe Y. Chennault, Rosbert.

45. Chennault's diary, 1958, made available through the courtesy of Anna Chennault; author interview, Anna Chennault.

46. Yeh's memorial address, *CAT Bulletin* 11 (August 1958):12.

47. *Jing bao Journal*, August–September 1983, pp. 25–26.

48. Chennault, diary; Anna Chennault to Sue, 17 July 1958, Louisiana State Museum, New Orleans.

49. Author interview, Ruth Chennault.

50. Vertical file at Louisiana State Museum.

51. Author interview, Holloway; *Skyway Times*, Lake Charles AFB, 14 November 1958.

52. Chennault to Max, 25 March 1958 (quoted); author interview, Lee.

53. Anna Chennault to family, 17 July 1958, Louisiana State Museum; Leary, *Perilous Missions*, p. 211, citing interview with Anna Chennault.

Bibliography

Books and Articles

Abell, Tyler, ed. *Drew Pearson Diaries*. New York: Holt, Rinehart and Winston, 1974.

Abend, Hallett. *My Life in China, 1926–41*. New York: Harcourt, 1943.

Acheson, Dean. *Present at the Creation*. New York: Norton, 1969.

Adamson, Hans Christian. *Eddie Rickenbacker*. New York: Macmillan, 1946.

Angell, Joseph W., et al. *USAF Tactical Operations; World War II and Korean War*. USAF Historical Division Liaison Office, May 1962.

Army Air Forces in the War against Japan, 1941–42. Washington, D.C.: USAF Historical Office, 1945.

Arnold, Henry H. *Global Mission*. New York: Harper, 1949.

———. *Winged Warfare*. New York: Harper, 1941.

Assistant Chief of Air Staff, Intelligence, Historical Division. *The Development of Tactical Doctrines at AAFSAT and AAFTAC*. Army Air Forces Historical Studies No. 13. 1944.

———. *Organization of Military Aeronautics, 1907–1935*. USAF Historical Studies No. 25. 1944.

Ayling, Keith. *Old Leatherface of the Flying Tigers*. New York: Bobbs-Merrill, 1945.

Bachrack, Stanley. *The Committee of One Million: China Lobby Politics, 1953–1971*. New York: Columbia University Press, 1976.

Barnard, Ellsworth. *Wendell Willkie*. Marquette: Northern Michigan University Press, 1966.

Barnum, Burrall. *Dear Dad*. New York: Richard R. Smith, 1944.

Bauer, Boyd Heber. "General Claire Lee Chennault and China, 1937–1958: A Study of Chennault, His Relationship with China, and Selected Issues in Sino-American Relations." Ph.D. diss., American University, 1973.

Belden, Jack. *China Shakes the World*. New York: Harper, 1949.

Bianco, Lucien. *Origins of the Chinese Revolution, 1915–1949*. Stanford: Stanford University Press, 1971.

Blum, John Morton. *From the Morgenthau Diaries: Years of Urgency, 1938–1941*. Boston: Houghton Mifflin, 1959.

———. *The Price of Vision: The Diary of Henry A. Wallace, 1942–1946*. Boston: Houghton Mifflin, 1973.

Bond, Charles R., Jr. *A Flying Tiger's Diary*. College Station, Tex.: Texas A&M University Press, 1984.

Borg, Dorothy, and Waldo Heinrichs, eds. *Uncertain Years: Chinese-American Relations, 1947–50*. New York: Columbia University Press, 1980.

Borosage, Robert L., and John Marks, eds. *The CIA File*. New York: Grossman, 1976.

Boyington, Gregory. *Baa Baa Black Sheep*. New York: Putnam's, 1958.

Boylan, Bernard. *Development of the Long-Range Escort Fighter*. Maxwell Air Force Base: USAF Historical Division, Research Studies Institute, Air University, 1955.

Brereton, Lewis H. *The Brereton Diaries*. New York: William Morrow, 1946.

Brief History of the First Fighter Group, 1918–1955. Maxwell Air Force Base: USAF Historical Division, Research Studies Institute, Air University, 1956.

Brief History of the Twenty-third Fighter Group, 1941–1955. Maxwell Air Force Base: USAF Historical Division, Research Studies Institute, Air University, 1956.

Brodie, Bernard. "The Heritage of Douhet." *Air University Quarterly Review*, vol. 6, no. 2 (Summer 1953):64–69, 121–27.

———. "Some Notes on the Evolution of Air Doctrine." *World Politics*, vol. 7, no. 3 (April 1955):349–70.

Brooke-Popham, Air Marshall Sir Robert. "Operations in the Far East, from 17 October 1940 to 27 December 1941." Supp. *London Gazette*, 22 January 1948.

Caidin, Martin. *The Ragged, Rugged Warriors.* New York: Elsevier-Dutton, 1966.

Caldwell, John C. *South of Tokyo.* Chicago: Henry Regnery, 1957.

Caldwell, Oliver J. *A Secret War: Americans in China, 1944–45.* Carbondale: Southern Illinois University Press, 1972.

Cameron, Frank J. *Hungry Tiger: The Story of the Flying Tiger Line.* New York: McGraw-Hill, 1964.

Canella, Charles J. "A Study in Combined Command." *Military Review*, vol. 45 (July 1965):55–71.

Carlson, Evans F. *The Chinese Army.* New York: International Secretariat, Institute of Pacific Relations, 1940.

Chennault, Anna. *A Thousand Springs.* New York: Paul Eriksson, 1962.

———. *Chennault and the Flying Tigers.* New York: Paul Eriksson, 1963.

Chennault, Claire Lee. "Fighting for Observation." *Infantry Journal*, vol. 43 (May–June 1936):195–99. (Also in *Coast Artillery Journal*, vol. 79 [May–June 1936].)

———. *Pursuit Aviation.* Maxwell Field, Ala.: Air Corps Tactical School, 1933.

———. "Pursuit in Cooperation with Antiaircraft Artillery." *Coast Artillery Journal*, vol. 78 (November–December 1935):419–23.

———. "Pursuit versus Bombardment and Attack." *U.S. Air Services*, vol. 19, no. 4 (May 1934):15–18.

———. "The Role of Defensive Pursuit." *Coast Artillery Journal*, pt. 1: vol. 76 (November–December 1933):411–17; pt. 2, vol. 77 (January–February 1934):7–11; pt. 3: vol. 77 (March–April 1934):87–93. (Also published in pamphlet form by the Air Corps Tactical School; the Library of Congress copy bears the penciled date 1933. The pamphlet version differs slightly from the *Journal* version in paragraphing; some unnecessary phrases have also been deleted, as was detail about the British net system.)

———. "Some Facts about Bombardment Aviation." *Infantry Journal*, vol. 42 (September–October 1935):323–29. (Also in *Coast Artillery Journal*, vol. 78 [September–October 1935].)

———. "Special Support for Bombardment." *U.S. Air Services*, vol. 19, no. 1 (January 1934):18–21.

————. *Way of a Fighter*. Edited by Robert Hotz. New York: Putnam's, 1949.

Chennault's Flying Tigers, 1941–45: A Commemorative History. Silver Bay, Minn.: Flying Tigers of the Fourteenth Air Force Association, 1982.

Chi, Hsi-sheng. *Nationalist China at War: Military Defeats and Political Collapse, 1937–45*. Ann Arbor: University of Michigan Press, 1982.

Chiang Kai-shek. *The Collected Wartime Messages of Generalissimo Chiang Kai-shek, 1937–1945*. Millwood, N.Y.: Kraus Reprint, 1969.

Chiang Monlin. *Tides from the West: A Chinese Autobiography*. New Haven: Yale University Press, 1947.

China After Five Years of War. New York: Chinese News Service, 1942. (Prepared under the Auspices of the Ministry of Information of the Republic of China.)

Chinese Ministry of Information, comp. *China Handbook 1937–45.* New York: Macmillan, 1947.

Chivers, Sydney P. *The Flying Tigers: A Pictorial History of the American Volunteer Group*. Canoga Park, Calif.: Challenge, 1965.

Churchill, Winston S. *The Second World War*. Vol. 1: *The Gathering Storm*. Vol. 2: *Their Finest Hour*. Vol. 3: *The Grand Alliance*. Vol. 4: *The Hinge of Fate*. Vol. 5: *Closing the Ring*. Vol. 6: *Triumph and Tragedy*. Boston: Houghton Mifflin, 1948–53.

Cline, Ray S. *Secrets, Spies, and Scholars*. Washington, D.C.: Acropolis, 1976.

Clubb, O. Edmund. *Twentieth Century China*. New York: Columbia University Press, 1972.

Coffey, Thomas M. *HAP: The Story of the U.S. Air Force and the Man Who Built It, General Henry "Hap" Arnold*. New York: Viking, 1982.

Cohen, Warren I. *America's Response to China*. New York: Wiley, 1971.

Colby, William. *Honorable Men: My Life in the CIA*. New York: Simon and Schuster, 1978.

Copp, DeWitt S. *A Few Great Captains*. Garden City, N.Y.: Doubleday, 1980.

Cornelius, Wanda, and Thayne Short. *Ding Hao: America's Air War in China, 1937–1945*. Gretna, La.: Pelican, 1980.

Council of International Affairs, Chungking. *The Chinese Year Book, 1938–39*. Millwood, N.Y.: Kraus Reprint, 1968.

Craven, Wesley F., and James L. Cate. *The Army Air Forces in World War II*. Vol. 1: *Plans and Early Operations*. Vol. 4: *The Pacific: Guadalcanal to Saipan*. Vol. 5: *The Pacific: Matterhorn to Nagasaki*. Vol. 7: *Services around the World*. Chicago: University of Chicago Press, 1948–58.

Crozier, Brian. *The Man Who Lost China*. New York: Scribner's, 1976.

Davies, John Paton. *Dragon by the Tail*. New York: Norton, 1972.

Detwiler, Donald S., and Charles B. Burdick, eds. *War in Asia and the Pacific, 1937–1949*. Vol. 13. New York: Garland, 1980. (Translation prepared under auspices of Office of Military History, MAAG, of *History of the Sino-Japanese War*, vol. 1.)

Dickson, Maj. Thomas P. "Guidance from Chennault for the International Officer." Thesis No. 0565-67, Maxwell Air Force Base, June 1967.

Donald, W. H. to H. J. Timperley. 30 December 1938. On file in New York Public Library.

Dorn, Frank. *The Sino-Japanese War, 1937–41*. New York: Macmillan, 1974.

———. *Walkout with Stilwell in Burma*. New York: Thomas Crowell, 1971.

DuBuque, Jean. *The Development of the Heavy Bomber, 1918–1944*. USAF Historical Study No. 6. Maxwell Air Force Base: Air University, 1951.

Dunlop, Richard. *Donovan: America's Master Spy*. New York: Rand Mc-Nally, 1982.

Eastman, Lloyd E. *The Abortive Revolution*. Cambridge, Mass: Harvard University Press, 1974.

Eliot, George Fielding. *Bombs Bursting in Air*. New York: Reynal and Hitchcock, 1939.

Elsey, George M. *Roosevelt and China: The White House Story*. Wilmington, Del.: Michael Glazier, 1979.

Emme, Eugene M., ed. *The Impact of Air Power*. Princeton, N.J.: Van Nostrand, 1959.

Fairbank, John K. *Next Step in Asia*. Cambridge, Mass.: Harvard University Press, 1949.

———. *The United States and China*. 3d ed. Cambridge, Mass: Harvard University Press, 1971.

F.D.R.: His Personal Letters, 1928–1945. Vol. 2. New York: Duell, Sloan and Pearce, 1950.

Feis, Herbert. *The China Tangle*. Princeton, N.J.: Princeton University Press, 1953.

Finney, Charles G. *The Old China Hands*. Garden City, N.Y.: Doubleday, 1961.

Finney, Robert, Albert Hoxie, and F. S. Erickson. *The Fourteenth Air Force to 1 October 1943*. AAF RH-9. AAF Historical Office, Headquarters, Army Air Forces, July 1945.

Finney, Robert T. *History of the Air Corps Tactical School, 1920–1940*. USAF Historical Studies No. 100. Maxwell Air Force Base: Research Studies Institute, Air University, 1955.

Foulois, Benjamin D. *From the Wright Brothers to the Astronauts*. New York: McGraw-Hill, 1968.

Frillmann, Paul, and Graham Peck. *China: The Remembered Life*. Boston: Houghton Mifflin, 1968.

Futrell, Robert Frank. *Ideas, Concepts, Doctrine: A History of Basic Thinking in the United States Air Force, 1907–1964*. 2 vols. Maxwell Air Force Base: Aerospace Studies Institute, Air University, 1971.

Gayn, Mark, and John C. Caldwell. *American Agent*. New York: Henry Holt, 1947.

Generals of the Army and the Air Force. Washington, D.C.: Dunleavy, 1954.

Gillin, Donald G. *Warlord: Yen Hsi-shan in Shansi Province, 1911–1949*. Princeton, N.J.: Princeton University Press, 1967.

Glines, Carroll V., Jr. *The Compact History of the United States Air Force*. Rev. ed. New York: Hawthorn, 1973.

Gorrell, Edgar S. *Early History of the Strategical Section, Air Service*. Maxwell Air Force Base: USAF Historical Division, Research Studies Institute, Air University.

———. *The Measure of America's World War Aeronautical Effort*. Northfield, Vt.: Norwich University, 1940.

Green, William. *Famous Fighters of the Second World War*. 2d ed. rev. New York: Doubleday, 1975.

Green, William, and Gordon Swanborough. *U.S. Army Air Force Fighters, Part 1*. New York: Arco, 1977.

Greenlaw, Olga S. *The Lady and the Tigers*. New York: Dutton, 1943.

Greer, Thomas H. *The Development of Air Doctrine in the Army Air Arm, 1917–41*. USAF Historical Study No. 89. Maxwell Air Force Base: USAF Historical Division, Research Studies Institute, Air University, 1955.

Gurney, Gene. *Five Down and Glory*. New York: Putnam's, 1958.

Hager, Alice Rogers. *Wings for the Dragon*. New York: Dodd, Mead, 1945.

Hahn, Emily. *The Soong Sisters*. New York: Doubleday, 1941.

Handbook for Personnel. CAT Personnel Dept., January 1959.

Hansell, Haywood S., Jr. *The Air Plan That Defeated Hitler*. Atlanta: Higgins-McArthur, 1972.

Haughland, Vern. *The AAF against Japan*. New York: Harper's, 1948.

Hearings of the Subcommittee of the Senate Committee of the Judiciary on the Institute of Pacific Relations. 82d Cong., 1st sess., 1951.

Heiferman, Ronald. *Flying Tigers: Chennault in China*. New York: Ballantine Books, 1971.

Hennessy, Juliette. *The United States Army Air Arm, April 1861 to April 1917*. Maxwell Air Force Base, USAF Historical Division, Research Studies Institute, Air University, 1958.

Hess, William N. *Pacific Sweep: The Fifth and Thirteenth Fighter Commands in World War II*. Garden City, N.Y.: Doubleday, 1974.

Hessen, Robert, ed. *General Claire Lee Chennault: A Guide to His Papers in the Hoover Institution Archives*. Hoover Institution Bibliography Series No. 65. Stanford: Hoover Institution Press, 1983.

Hinton, Harold B. *Air Victory: The Men and the Machines*. New York: Harper's, 1948.

"History of the Central Intelligence Agency." In *U.S. Congress, Senate, Select Committee to Study Governmental Operations with Respect to Intelligence Activities*. Senate Report 94-755. 94th Cong., 2d sess., 1976.

"A History of the United States Air Force, 1907–1957." *Air Force*, vol. 40, no. 8 (August 1957). (Same material and additional in ATC Pamphlet 190-1, *History of the United States Air Force* [Randolph AFB, Texas, 1961].)

Hotz, Robert B. *With General Chennault: The Story of the Flying Tigers*. New York: Coward-McCann, 1943.

Hoyt, Edwin P. *Airborne*. New York: Stein and Day, 1979.

Ho Yungchi. *The Big Circle: China's Role in the Burma Campaigns*. New York: Exposition, 1948.

Huie, William Bradford. *The Fight for Air Power*. New York: Fischer, 1942.

Hull, Cordell. *Memoirs*. 2 vols. New York: Macmillan, 1948.

Hurley, Alfred F. *Billy Mitchell: Crusader for Air Power*. New York: Franklin Watts, 1964.

Hurley, Alfred F., and Robert C. Ehrhart, eds. *Air Power and Warfare: The Proceedings of the Eighth Military History Symposium, United States Air Force Academy, 18–20 Oct. 1978*. Washington, D.C.: Office of Air Force History and U.S. Air Force Academy, 1979.

Ike, Nobutaka. *Japan's Decision for War*. Stanford: Stanford University Press, 1967.

Isaacs, Harold R. *No Peace for Asia*. Cambridge, Mass.: M.I.T. Press, 1947 and 1967.

Jones, F. C. *Japan's New Order in East Asia*. London: Oxford University Press, 1954.

Kebric, Harry L. *Dragon Tigers*. New York: Vantage, 1971.

King, Ernest J., and Walter Muir Whitehill. *Fleet Admiral King*. New York: Norton, 1952.

Kirby, S. Woodburn. *The War against Japan*. History of the Second World War, vol. 2. London: HMSO, 1958.

Kissick, Luther C., Jr. *Guerrilla One*. Manhattan, Kan.: Sunflower University Press, 1983.

Koen, Ross Y. *The China Lobby in American Politics*. New York: Octagon, 1974. (Reprint of 1960 Macmillan edition.)

Kubek, Anthony. *How the Far East Was Lost: American Policy and the Creation of Communist China, 1941–1949*. Chicago: University of Chicago Press, 1963.

Lamp, C. O. *Gentle Tigress*. New York: Leisure Books, 1980.

Langer, William L., and S. Everett Gleason. *The Challenge to Isolation, 1937–1940*. New York: Harper, 1952.

———. *The Undeclared War, 1940–1941*. New York: Harper, 1953.

Larson, Col. Gerald D. "Chennault, the Leader," USAF Maxwell Air Force Base, April 1973.

Leahy, William D. *I Was There*. London: Victor Gollancz, 1950.

Leary, William M., Jr. *The Dragon's Wings*. Athens: University of Georgia Press, 1976.

———. *Perilous Missions*. University, Ala.: University of Alabama Press, 1984.

Lee, Asher. *Air Power*. New York: Praeger, 1955.

Leighton, Richard M., and Robert W. Coakley. Vol. 1: *Global Logistics and Strategy, 1940–1943*. Vol. 2: *Global Logistics and Strategy, 1943–1945*. Washington, D.C.: Office of the Chief of Military History, Department of the Army, 1955 and 1968.

Leonard, Royal. *I Flew for China*. Garden City, N.Y.: Doubleday, 1942.

Levine, Isaac Don. *Mitchell: Pioneer of Air Power*. New York: Duell, Sloan and Pearce, 1943.

Lewin, Ronald. *Ultra Goes to War: The First Account of World War II's Great-est Secret*. New York: McGraw Hill, 1978.

Liang, Chin-tung. *General Stilwell in China, 1942–1944: The Full Story*. New York: St. John's University Press, 1972.

Li Tsung-jen and Te-Kong Tong. *The Memoirs of Li Tsung-jen*. Boulder, Colo.: Westview Press, 1979.

Liu, F. F. *A Military History of Modern China, 1924–1949*. Princeton, N.J.: Princeton University Press, 1956.

Loening, Grover. *Our Wings Grow Faster*. Garden City, N.Y.: Doubleday, 1935.

Lu, David J. *From the Marco Polo Bridge to Pearl Harbor*. Washington, D.C.: Public Affairs Press, 1961.

McClendon, R. Earl. *Autonomy of the Air Arm*. 2d ed. Maxwell Air Force Base: Research Studies Institute, Air University, 1954.

McClure, Glenn E. *Fire and Fall Back*. Universal City, Tex.: Barnes Press, 1975.

McCoy, Alfred W. *The Politics of Heroin in Southeast Asia*. New York: Harper and Row, 1972.

Marchetti, Victor, and John D. Marks. *The CIA and the Cult of Intelligence*. New York: Knopf, 1974.

Matloff, Maurice, and Edwin Snell. *Strategic Planning for Coalition War-fare, 1941–1942*. Washington, D.C.: Department of the Army, 1953.

————. *Strategic Planning for Coalition Warfare, 1943–1944*. Washington, D.C.: Department of the Army, 1959.

Maurer, Maurer. *The U.S. Air Service in World War I*. 4 vols. Washington, D.C.: Office of Air Force History, 1978.

Miksche, F. O. *Paratroops*. New York: Random House, 1943.

Miles, Milton E. *A Different Kind of War*. Garden City, N.Y.: Doubleday, 1967.

Millis, Walter, ed. *The Forrestal Diaries*. New York: Viking, 1951.

Mims, Sam. *Chennault of the Flying Tigers*. Philadelphia: Macrae-Smith, 1943.

Mitchell, William. *Memoirs of World War I*. New York: Random House, 1960.

Mooney, Chase C. *The Organization of the Army Air Arm, 1935–1945*. U.S. Air Force, July 1956.

Morgenthau, Henry, Jr. *Morgenthau Diary, China*. 2 vols. U.S. Senate, 89th Cong., 1st sess., Committee on the Judiciary, Subcommittee to Investigate the Administration of the Internal Security Laws, 1965.

Morley, James William, ed. *The China Quagmire: Japan's Expansion on the Asian Continent, 1933–1941*. New York: Columbia University Press, 1983.

Morton, Louis. *Strategy and Command: The First Two Years*. Washington, D.C.: Department of the Army, 1962.

Moser, Don. *China, Burma, India*. Alexandria, Va.: Time-Life, 1978.

Mountbatten, Lord Louis. *South East Asia, 1943–1945: Report to the Com-

bined Chiefs of Staff by the Supreme Allied Commander. London: HMSO, 1951.

Nalty, Bernard C. *Tigers over Asia.* New York: Elsevier-Dutton, 1978.

Okumiya, Masatake, and Jiro Horikoshi, with Martin Caidin. *Zero!* New York: Ballantine Books, 1956.

Oshinsky, David M. *A Conspiracy So Immense: The World of Joe McCarthy.* New York: Free Press, 1983.

Patrick, Mason M. *The United States in the Air.* Garden City, N.Y.: Doubleday, Doran, 1928.

Patti, Archimedes L. A. *Why Viet Nam?* Berkeley: University of California Press, 1980.

Pawley, William D. *Americans Valiant and Glorious.* New York: Caleb Printing, 1945.

Pearl Harbor Attack, Hearings before the Joint Committee on the Investigation of the Pearl Harbor Attack, Congress of the United States. Pt. 3. Washington, D.C.: GPO, 1946.

Peck, Graham. *Two Kinds of Time.* Boston: Houghton Mifflin, 1950.

Peoples, Morgan. "A Mississippian Moves to Franklin Parish: The Journal of Dr. William Wallace Lee, 1867." *North Louisiana Historical Association Journal,* vol. 6, no. 4 (1975):154–63.

Pershing, John J. *My Experiences in the World War.* 2 vols. New York: Frederick A. Stokes, 1931.

Pickler, Gordon K. *United States Aid to the Chinese Nationalist Air Force, 1931–1949.* Ph.D. diss., Florida State University, 1971.

Pistole, Larry M. *The Pictorial History of the Flying Tigers.* Orange, Va.: Moss, 1981.

Pogue, Forrest C. *George C. Marshall.* Vol. 1: *Education of a General.* Vol. 2: *Ordeal and Hope.* Vol. 3: *Organizer of Victory.* New York: Viking, 1963, 1968, 1973.

Price, Alfred. *World War II Fighter Conflict.* London: Macdonald and Janes, 1975.

Price, Harry B. *The United Nations Relief and Rehabilitation Administration in China, 1945–1947.* Operational Analysis Papers No. 53. Washington, D.C.: UNRRA, 1948.

Pursuit: Course Text, 1924–25. Langley Field, Va.: Air Service Tactical School, 1924.

Purtee, Edward O. *History of the Army Air Service, 1907–1926.* Wright Patterson Air Force Base, Ohio: Historical Office, Air Materiel Command, 1948.

Quisenberry, Anderson Chenault. *Genealogical Memoranda of the Quisenberry Family and Other Families.* Frankfurt, Ky.: Kentucky Historical Society, 1965.

Reynolds, Quentin. *They Fought for the Sky.* New York: Rinehart, 1957.

Rickenbacker, Edward V. *Rickenbacker.* Englewood Cliffs, N.J.: Prentice-Hall, 1967.

Robbins, Christopher. *Air America*. New York: Putnam's, 1979.

Robertson, Minns Sledge. *Public Education in Louisiana after 1898*. Baton Rouge, La.: Louisiana State University Press, 1952.

Rogers, Charlton B., Jr. *Descendants of Estienne Chenault*. Richmond, Mo.: Beck Printing, 1978.

Romanus, Charles F., and Riley Sunderland. Vol. 1: *Stilwell's Mission to China* (1953). Vol. 2: *Stilwell's Command Problems* (1954). Vol. 3: *Time Runs Out in CBI* (1959). Washington, D.C.: Department of the Army, 1953–59.

Roosevelt and Churchill: Their Secret Wartime Correspondence. Edited by Francis Loewenheim, Harold Langley, and Manfred Jonas. New York: Saturday Review Press, 1975.

Roosevelt, Elliott. *As He Saw It*. New York: Duell, Sloan and Pearce, 1946.

Rosholt, Malcolm L. *Claire L. Chennault, A Tribute*. Spec. ed. Pictorial. Rosholt, Wis.: Fourteenth Air Force Association, 1983.

———. *Days of the Ching Pao: A Photographic Record*. Rosholt, Wis.: Rosholt House, 1978.

Rosinger, Lawrence K. *China's Wartime Politics, 1937–1944*. Princeton, N.J.: Princeton University Press, 1944.

Rossi, John R., and Charles Older, comps. *Flying Tigers: A Brief History with Recollections and Comments by General Claire Lee Chennault*. Privately printed.

Schaller, Michael. *The United States and China in the Twentieth Century*. New York: Oxford University Press, 1979.

———. *The U.S. Crusade in China, 1938–1945*. New York: Columbia University Press, 1979.

Schurmann, Franz, and Orville Schell, eds. *Republican China*. New York: Random House, 1967.

Scott, Robert L., Jr. *God Is My Co-Pilot*. New York: Scribner's, 1944.

———. *Flying Tiger: Chennault of China*. Garden City, N.Y.: Doubleday, 1959.

Seagrave, Sterling. *The Soong Dynasty*. New York: Harper and Row, 1985.

Selle, Earl Albert. *Donald of China*. New York: Harper, 1948.

Service, John S. *Lost Chance in China: The World War II Despatches of John S. Service*. Edited by Joseph W. Esherick. New York: Random House, 1974.

Sevareid, Eric. *Not So Wild a Dream*. New York: Atheneum, 1946, 1978.

Sheean, Vincent. *Between the Thunder and the Sun*. New York: Random House, 1943.

Sheridan, James E. *China in Disintegration: The Republican Era in Chinese History, 1912–1949*. New York: Free Press, 1975.

Sherwood, Robert E. *Roosevelt and Hopkins*. New York: Harper, 1948.

Sih, Paul K. T., ed. *Nationalist China during the Sino-Japanese War, 1937–1945*. Hicksville, N.Y.: Exposition, 1977.

Sims, Edward H. *Fighter Tactics and Strategy, 1914–1970*. New York: Harper, 1972.

Slessor, Sir John. *The Great Deterrent*. New York: Praeger, 1957.

Smedley, Agnes. *Battle Hymn of China*. New York: Knopf, 1943.

Smith, Bradley F. *The Shadow Warriors: O.S.S. and the Origins of the C.I.A..* New York: Basic Books, 1982.

Smith, Dale O. *U.S. Military Doctrine: A Study and Appraisal*. New York and Boston: Duell, Sloan and Pearce, and Little, Brown, 1955.

Smith, Myron J., Jr. *Air War Bibliography, 1939–1945*. 3 vols. Manhattan, Kan.: Kansas State University, 1977.

Smith, Robert M. *With Chennault in China: A Flying Tiger's Diary*. Blue Ridge Summit, Pa.: Tab Books, 1984.

Snow, Edgar. *Red Star over China*. New York: Random House, 1938.

Spence, Jonathan. *To Change China: Western Advisors in China, 1620–1960*. Boston: Little, Brown, 1969.

Stettinius, Edward R. *Lend-Lease: Weapon for Victory*. New York: Macmillan, 1944.

Stevenson, D. F. *Air Operations in Burma and the Bay of Bengal, January 1st to May 22, 1942*. Special supp. 38229. *London Gazette*, 11 March 1948.

Stilwell's Personal File: China, Burma, India, 1942–1944. Edited by Riley Sunderland and Charles F. Romanus. facs. ed. Wilmington, Del.: Scholarly Resources, 1976.

Stimson, Henry L., and McGeorge Bundy. *On Active Service in Peace and War*. New York: Harper, 1947.

Stuart, Gilbert. *Kind-Hearted Tiger*. Boston: Little, Brown, 1964.

Stuart, John Leighton. *Fifty Years in China*. New York: Random House, 1954.

Stueck, William Whitney, Jr. *The Road to Confrontation*. Chapel Hill: University of North Carolina Press, 1981.

Sweetser, Arthur. *The American Air Service*. New York: D. Appleton, 1919.

Taylor, Joe G. *Air Interdiction in China in World War II*. USAF Historical Division Study No. 132. Maxwell Air Force Base: Research Studies Institute, Air University, 1956.

———. *Louisiana*. New York: Norton, 1976.

Taylor, John W. R. *Combat Aircraft of the World*. New York: Putnam's, 1969.

Taylor, John W. R., Michael J. H. Taylor, and David Mondey, eds. *Air Facts and Feats*. New York: Two Continents, 1973.

Taylor, Robert C. "Claire Lee Chennault." Thesis no. 1422-65. Maxwell Air Force Base, Military Studies Program, April 1965.

Tennien, Mark. *Chungking Listening Post*. New York: Creative Age Press, 1945.

The Tenth Air Force, 1 January–10 March 1943. U.S. Army Air Forces Historical Division, 1944.

Thomas, Lowell, and Edward Jablonski. *Doolittle*. Garden City, N.Y.: Doubleday, 1976.

Thorne, Christopher. *Allies of a Kind*. New York: Oxford University Press, 1978.

Toland, John. *The Flying Tigers*. New York: Random House, 1963.

Tsou, Tang. *America's Failure in China, 1941–50.* Chicago: University of Chicago Press, 1963.

Tuchman, Barbara W. *Stilwell and the American Experience in China, 1911–45.* New York: Macmillan, 1970.

Tunner, William H. *Over the Hump.* New York: Duell, Sloan and Pearce, 1964.

U.S. Department of State. *Foreign Relations of the United States.* Annual. Washington, D.C.: GPO.

————. *United States Relations with China, 1944–49.* White paper. Washington, D.C.: GPO, 1949. (Reissued as *The China White Paper* [Stanford, Calif.: Stanford University Press, 1967].)

The United States Strategic Bombing Survey. Air Campaigns of the Pacific War (1947). *Air Operations in China, Burma, India in World War II* (1947). *Effects of Strategic Bombing on Japan's War Economy* (1946). *Japanese Air Power* (1946). *Japanese Air Weapons and Tactics* (1947). *The War against Japanese Transportation, 1941–45* (1947). Washington, D.C.: GPO, 1946–47.

Utley, Freda. *Lost Chance in China.* Indianapolis: Bobbs-Merrill, 1947.

Vandenberg, Arthur H., Jr., ed. *The Private Papers of Senator Vandenberg.* Boston: Houghton Mifflin, 1952.

Varg, Paul A. *Missionaries, Chinese, and Diplomats: The American Protestant Missionary Movement in China, 1890–1952.* Princeton: Princeton University Press, 1958.

The War Reports of General of the Army George C. Marshall, General of the Army H. H. Arnold, Fleet Admiral Ernest J. King. Philadelphia: Lippincott, 1947.

Warner, Edward. "Douhet, Mitchell, Seversky: Theories of Air Warfare." In Edward Mead Earle, ed., *Makers of Modern Strategy.* Princeton, N.J.: Princeton University Press, 1943.

Watson, Mark Skinner. *Chief of Staff: Prewar Plans and Preparations.* Washington, D.C.: Department of the Army, 1950.

Watts, Barry D. *A Comparison of "Team" and "Single-Ship" Approaches to Aerial Combat.* Colorado Springs: U.S. Air Force Academy, 1976.

Wavell, General Sir Archibald P. *Operations in Burma from 15th December 1941 to 20th May 1942.* Special supp. No. 38228. *London Gazette,* 5 March 1948.

Wedemeyer, Albert C. *Wedemeyer Reports.* New York: Henry Holt, 1958.

Weeks, John. *Airborne Equipment.* New York: Hippocrene, 1976.

Weigley, Russell F. *History of the United States Army.* New York and London: Macmillan, 1967.

Welch, Robert H. W. *The Life of John Birch.* New York: Henry Regnery, 1954.

Westerfield, H. Bradford. *Foreign Policy and Party Politics, Pearl Harbor to Korea.* New Haven: Yale University Press, 1955.

Whelan, Russell. *The Flying Tigers: The Story of An American Volunteer Group.* New York: Viking, 1942.

White, Theodore H. *In Search of History*. New York: Harper, 1978.
——, ed. *The Stilwell Papers*. New York: William Sloane, 1948.
White, Theodore H., and Annalee Jacoby. *Thunder Out of China*. New York: William Sloane, 1946.
Willkie, Wendell L. *One World*. New York: Simon and Schuster, 1943.
Wilson, Dick. *When Tigers Fight: The Story of the Sino-Japanese War, 1937–1945*. New York: Viking, 1982.
Winfield, Gerald F. *China: The Land and the People*. New York: William Sloane, 1948.
Wings of the Phoenix, The Official Story of the Air War in Burma. London: HMSO, 1949.
Wise, David, and Thomas B. Ross. *The Invisible Government*. New York: Random House, 1964.
Woodhead, H. G. W., ed. *The China Year Book*. Millwood, N.Y.: Kraus Reprint, 1969.
Yoshino, Ronald W. *A Doctrine Destroyed: The American Fighter Offensive, 1917–1939*. Ph.D. diss., Claremont Graduate School, 1985.
Young, Arthur N. *China and the Helping Hand*. Cambridge, Mass: Harvard University Press, 1963.

Personal Interviews and Correspondence

Alsop, Joseph W., Jr., Washington, D.C. 4 January 1984, 31 January 1986.
Arnold, William B., Denver, Colo. 6 June 1981.
Brannon, C. A., Colorado Springs, Colo. 14 April 1981.
Breitweiser, R. A., New Bern, N.C.
Cain, James R., Monroe, La.
Chase, Dan, Baton Rouge, La.
Chennault, Anna C., Washington, D.C. 5 January 1984.
Chennault, C. Patterson, Ferriday, La. June 1981.
Chennault, E. Nelson, and Freeda Chennault, Gilbert, La. June 1981, August 1985.
Chennault, Joe Y., Decatur, Ga. 9 April 1982, 12 August 1985.
Chennault, Mary, Monroe, La. June 1981.
Chennault, Max T., College Park, Ga. 10 April 1982.
Chennault, Robert K., and Ruth Chennault, Ferriday, La. June 1981.
Chennault, W. S., Monroe, La. June 1981, August 1985.
Cooper, Dorothy, Coronado, Calif.
Doolittle, James H., Monterey, Calif.
Fiser, Jack, Baton Rouge, La.
Fixott, Richard S., Colorado Springs, Colo. 15 June 1981.
Fogg, John, USAFA, Colo. 8 June 1981.
Hansell, Haywood S., Hilton Head, S.C. 3 October 1980, 27 February 1982.

Haynes, C. Vance, Jr., Tucson, Ariz.
Hill, David L., San Antonio, Tex.
Holland, John, and Martha Holland, Bronwood, Ga.
Holloway, Bruce K., Orlando, Fla. 5 March 1982.
Hotz, Robert B., Middletown, Md.
Howard, James H., Belleair Bluffs, Fla.
Hurley, Alfred F., Denton, Tex. June 1981.
Jackson, Louise Willauer, Nantucket, Mass.
Jernstedt, Kenneth A., Hood River, Oreg.
Judd, Walter H., Washington, D.C.
Kuter, Ethel, Naples, Fla. 2 March 1982.
Larson, Sigvard O., Denver, Colo. 6 June 1981.
Laughlin, C. H., Coral Gables, Fla.
Leary, William, Athens, Ga.
Lee, Peggy Chennault, North Hollywood, Calif. 11 September 1985.
Lewis, Ronald E., Pueblo, Colo. 13 May 1981.
Lopez, Donald S., Alexandria, Va.
McAfee, William, Washington, D.C.
McDonald, Peggy, Birmingham, Ala.
Matsis, Ted, San Luis Obispo, Calif.
May, Aimee, Cucamonga, Calif.
Neumann, Gerhard, Swampscott, Mass.
Noe, James A., Jr., Monroe and New Orleans, La.
Nowak, A. C., Vero Beach, Fla.
Pawley, Mrs. William D., Miami Beach, Fla.
Peoples, Morgan, Ruston, La.
Pierce, Jerry, Natchitoches, La.
Pogue, Forrest C., Arlington, Va.
Randall, Russell, Pasadena, Calif.
Rector, Edward F., Arlington, Va. Interviewed in Colorado Springs, Colo.
    2 May 1981.
Reynolds, Doreen, Arlington, Va.
Richard, Oscar, Baton Rouge, La.
Rodewald, Donald L., Lake City, Colo. February 1981.
Rosbert, C. Joe, Franklin, N.C. 10 August 1983.
Rosholt, Malcolm L., Rosholt, Wis.
Rossi, John R., Fallbrook, Calif.
Rousselot, Robert E., Wagoner, Okla. 21 June 1981.
Rusk, Dean, Athens, Ga.
Scott, Robert L., Jr., Sun City, Ariz.
Shah, Konsin C., Washington, D.C.
Shilling, E. E., Alta Loma, Calif.
Shu, P. Y., interviewed in Palo Alto, Calif. 14 March 1981.
Simrall, Rosemary Chennault, Monroe, La. June 1981, August 1985.

Smith, Sebie B., and Lucy Smith, Montgomery, Ala. September 1982, November 1984.
Stewart, John L., Monument, Colo. November 1981.
Thompson, Benjamin R., Charlotte, N.C.
Trumble, Thomas, Lakewood, Colo.
Urbanowicz, Witold A., Glendale, N.Y.
Watson, Ivaloo, interviewed in Montgomery, Ala.
Wedemeyer, Albert C., Boyds, Md.
Williams, John M., San Diego, Calif.

Unpublished Diaries

I am indebted to Lawrence Pistole, Kennesaw, Georgia, for giving me access to a number of diaries, incidental papers, and memorabilia, especially pertaining to the AVG, that are in his possession.
Burgard, George T. Personal diary, 24 September 1941–4 July 1942. Pistole Collection.
Chennault, Claire Lee. Personal diaries, 1937–1941, 1958. Collection of Mrs. Anna Chennault.
Corcoran, Thomas G. Incomplete manuscript. Collection of Mrs. Anna Chennault.
Donovan, John T. Personal diary and letters. Pistole Collection.
First American Volunteer Group Diary CBI, 1941–1942. (A portion of this diary is on file at the Albert F. Simpson Memorial Library, Maxwell Air Force Base; the complete manuscript is with the Chennault Papers, Hoover Institution.)
Frank, James C. Personal diary, 1943–44. U.S. Army Historical Research Center, Carlisle Barracks, Pa.
Holland, John M. Excerpts from personal diary, 1937. Bronwood, Georgia.
Johnson, Wayne G. Excerpts from personal diary. Silver Bay, Minn.
Keeton, Robert B. Personal diary, 9 September 1941–23 August 1942. Pistole Collection.
May, Jack, and Aimee May. Excerpts from personal diaries, 1937. Cucamonga, Calif.
Mott, Charles D. Personal diary, 9 July 1941–24 December 1941. Pistole Collection.
Neale, Robert H. Personal diary, 1942. Camano Island, Wash.
Olson, Arvid E., Jr. [Leader, AVG.] Diary of the Third Pursuit Squadron, 24 August 1941–19 June 1942. Pistole Collection.
Rodewald, Donald L. Personal diary, 1941–1942. Lake City, Colo.
Schaper, William E. Personal diary, 1941–42. Mission Hills, Calif.
Smith, Sebie B. Personal diary, July 1936–June 1938. Montgomery, Ala.

Watson, Rolfe. Personal diary, 1937–1940. Collection of Mrs. Ivaloo Watson and Malcolm Rosholt.

Manuscript and Archive Collections

Alsop, Joseph W., Jr., Papers. Library of Congress, Washington, D.C.

Arnold, Henry H., Papers. Library of Congress, Washington, D.C.

Brady, Francis M., Papers. Library, Special Collections, U.S. Air Force Academy, Colo.

Caraway, Paul W., Papers. U.S. Army Historical Research Center, Carlisle Barracks, Pa.

Chennault, Claire Lee, Papers, 1941–1959. Hoover Institution, Stanford University, Stanford, Calif. (Microfilm copy at the Library of Congress.)

Chennault, Claire Lee, Papers. Collection of Robert K. Chennault, Ferriday, La. (Primarily prior to 1941.)

Cooper, Merian C., Papers. Hoover Institution, Stanford University, Stanford, Calif., plus additional papers in possession of Mrs. Cooper, Coronado, Calif.

Frillmann, Paul William, Papers. Hoover Institution, Stanford University, Stanford, Calif.

Hansell, Haywood S., Jr., Papers. Library, Special Collections, U.S. Air Force Academy, Colo.

Haynes, Caleb V., Papers. Collection of C. Vance Haynes, Jr., Tucson, Ariz.

Hopkins, Harry, Papers. Franklin D. Roosevelt Library, Hyde Park, N.Y.

Hull, Cordell, Papers. Library of Congress, Washington, D.C.

Kuter, Laurence S., Papers. Library, Special Collections, U.S. Air Force Academy, Colo.

McHugh, James Marshall, Papers, #2770. Department of Manuscripts and University Archives, Cornell University Libraries, Ithaca, N.Y.

Morgenthau, Henry, Jr., Papers and Diaries. Franklin D. Roosevelt Library, Hyde Park, N.Y.

National Archives, Washington, D.C.

Noe, James A., Papers. Collection of James A. Noe, Jr., Monroe, La.

Roosevelt, Franklin D., Papers. Franklin D. Roosevelt Library, Hyde Park, N.Y.

Stilwell, Joseph W., Papers. Hoover Institution, Stanford University, Stanford, Calif.

Stimson, Henry L., Papers and Diaries. Yale University Library, New Haven, Conn.

U.S. Air Force Albert F. Simpson Historical Research Center. Maxwell Air Force Base, Montgomery, Ala.

Vandenberg, Arthur H., Papers. Bentley Historical Library, University of Michigan, Ann Arbor, Mich.

Willauer, Whiting, Papers. Firestone Library, Princeton University, Princeton, N.J.
Young, Arthur N., Papers. Hoover Institution, Stanford University, Stanford, Calif.

Oral Histories

Alison, John R., Col. USAF (Ret.). Interviewed by Kenneth Leish, July 1960. Columbia University Oral History Research Office and USAFA Library, Special Collections.
Betts, Lt. Gen. Austin W. Interviewed by Cols. Henck and Wehle, 11 and 12 March 1971. U.S. Army Historical Research Center.
Breitweiser, Robert A., Lt. Gen. USAF (Ret.). Interviewed by Dr. James C. Hasdorff, 3–4 December 1975. AFSHRC.
Caraway, Lt. Gen. Paul W. Interviewed by Col. Ray. U.S. Army Historical Research Center.
Davidson, Howard C., Maj. Gen. USAF (Ret.) Interview 1, 3 June 1969, USAFA Special Collections; 2, interviewed by Hugh N. Ahmann and Tom Sturm, 5–8 December 1974. AFSHRC and USAFA Library, Special Collections.
Eaker, Gen. Ira C. Interviewed by Capt. Green. U.S. Army Historical Research Center.
Flying Tigers. Various interviews taped in 1962. Columbia University Oral History Research Office.
Frillmann, Paul. Interviewed by Frank Rounds, Jr. 14 February 1962 and 19–20 June 1962. Columbia University Oral History Research Office.
Hegenberger, Albert F., Maj. Gen. USAF (Ret.). Interviewed by Dr. James C. Hasdorff, 11–12 February 1976. AFSHRC and USAFA Library, Special Collections.
Holloway, Bruce K., Gen. USAF (Ret.). Interviewed by Vaughn H. Gallacher, 16–18 August 1977. AFSHRC and USAFA Library, Special Collections.
Julian, Thomas A., Col. USAF (Ret.). Interviewed by R. L. Bowers, 8 June 1971. AFSHRC.
Kuter, Laurence S., Gen. USAF (Ret.). Interviewed by Hugh N. Ahmann and Tom Sturm, 30 September–3 October 1974. AFSHRC and USAFA Library, Special Collections.
McConnell, John P. Interviewed 24 September 1971, USAFA Library, Special Collections.
Partridge, Earle E., Gen. USAF (Ret.). Interviewed by Hugh N. Ahmann, 23 April 1974. AFSHRC and USAFA Library, Special Collections.
Peabody, Hume, Brig. Gen. USAF (Ret.). Interviewed by Hugh N. Ahmann, 13–16 September 1975. AFSHRC and USAFA Library, Special Collections.

Pricer, Donald, Col. USAF (Ret.). Interviewed by Bowers, 20 October 1970.
AFSHRC.
Quesada, Lt. Gen. Elwood R. Interviewed by Lt. Cols. Long and Stephenson.
U.S. Army Historical Research Center.
Smith, Sebie Biggs, Col. USAF (Ret.). Tapes recorded in answer to author's
questions submitted in writing, February 1981. Columbia University Oral
History Research Office.
Williams, John M., Col. USAF (Ret.). Interviewed by Phillip S. Meilinger, 25
July 1979. USAFA Library, Special Collections.

Index

mother), 9, 13, 14
Chennault, Nell Thompson, 15, 16, 17,
  19, 22 (photo), 23, 26, 35, 58, 61, 63,
  64, 104, 134, 194, 293, 299
Chennault, William S. (Claire's
  brother), 7, 8 (photo), 9, 62, 63, 64,
  76, 355, 362
Chennault Plan (1949), 321, 323–24, 325,
  326, 327, 328, 332
Chennault's aerial offensive, 109–11,
  154, 155, 156–57, 173–75, 190–91, 192–
  93, 194, 201, 202–4, 205–6, 208, 212–13;
  endorsed by Chiang, 180, 181, 186, 188;
  effects on Japan, 215. See also Fourteenth Air Force; ICHIGO
Chiang Kai-shek, 2, 66, 94, 101, 102, 148,
  160, 226, 228, 274, 287, 326, 361; and
  CAF, 67, 77, 90, 180; and Chinese Civil
  War, 72, 73–74, 304, 317; described, 74,
  105; relationship with Chennault, 74,
  77, 82, 100, 142, 173, 196, 246, 263, 270,
  282, 283, 292, 293, 300, 342, 345, 365;
  defense plans, 83, 100; seeks U.S. help
  (1940), 105–7, 108, 109, 110; and AVG,
  121, 125, 132, 139, 145, 146, 147; and
  British, 134–35; supreme commander
  China theater, 140, 225; and Stilwell,
  145, 178, 179, 187, 205, 234, 236, 245,
  247, 263; and three demands, 155–56,
  157, 176, 177, 183; endorses Chennault's strategy, 180, 181, 186, 188;
  and campaign to retake Burma, 181,
  201, 228, 230, 239, 281; assures defense
  of airfields, 191, 222; and Arnold, 182–
  83; in Cairo, 209–11; and MATTER-
  HORN, 208, 229; and ICHIGO, 233; revolt against, 210, 231, 243–44, 249, 250,
  251; and Stilwell's command of
  Chinese troops, 246, 247; and Hsueh
  Yueh, 248–49, 256–57, 266; blames U.S.
  for defeat, 256; Roosevelt's assessment
  of, 269; and unification, 273; postwar
  criticism, 285, 286, 309; Chennault
  supports, 314, 324, 326, 327, 352, 361;
  on Taiwan, 325, 340; and planes case,
  335; and CAT, 348
Chiang Kai-shek, Mme., xi, 94, 101, 182,
  198; and CAF, 67, 71, 72, 73, 74, 80, 82,
  85, 91, 177; relationship with Chen-

nault, 68, 81, 82, 84, 87, 92, 95, 100,
  143, 151, 226, 293, 300, 324, 365, 366;
  and AVG, 128, 133, 134, 140, 141, 146,
  152, 199, 287; and Stilwell, 145; in
  Washington, 178, 193, 194; accusations against, 194, 243; and CAT, 292,
  349
Chien Ta-chun, 91, 101
Chihkiang, China, 256, 268
China, Nationalist, 1, 82, 90, 97, 109,
  111, 112, 115, 143, 146, 165, 178, 259,
  351; in 1937, 66, 67; U.S. relations
  with, 79, 105, 120, 124, 177, 244, 258,
  263, 312; requests U.S. aid in 1940, 102,
  105–8; U.S. policy toward, 105, 113,
  120, 121, 132, 139–40, 268–69, 305, 310,
  313, 319, 325, 326, 332; as Allied base,
  139, 181, 190, 207–8, 209, 224, 232, 275;
  U.S. forces in, 140, 141, 148, 188, 194;
  condition in 1942, 155, 158, 163; condition in 1943, 193, 207; 1943 coup, 210;
  and ICHIGO, 221; separate theater,
  264; condition in 1945–46, 268, 272,
  285, 288, 290, 292, 298; postwar support by Chennault, 295, 307, 312, 314–
  15, 316, 317, 324, 325, 326, 327, 328,
  353, 354; backed by U.S. bloc, 308, 310,
  328, 339; support of Truman administration, 311, 331; in 1949, 319–20, 321,
  334; and planes case, 335, 338, 347; on
  Taiwan, 340, 342, 354. See also Chiang
  Kai-shek; Chinese Civil War; Chinese
  Nationalists (Kuomintang); Sino-Japanese War
China Aid Act, 311, 312
China Air Task Force (CATF), 174, 196,
  216, 245, 299, 357; composition, 153;
  July 1942 record, 154; conditions in,
  158, 159; supply, 158, 168, 169, 171,
  186; missions, fall 1942, 160; image,
  161, 162
China Air Transport Company (CATC),
  291, 305; defects, 334–35, 337, 338
China-Burma-India theater (CBI), 139,
  143, 155, 193, 201, 208, 227, 228, 234,
  235, 236, 238, 267, 314
China Defense Supplies, 113, 120, 121,
  132, 136, 173, 177, 178, 187, 192, 226,
  289, 337, 385 (n. 27)

About the Author

Martha Byrd is historian, writer, and communications consultant in Davidson, North Carolina. She is the author of *A World in Flames: A History of World War II* (1970).